Explorers & Exploration

The Travels of
Francisco de Coronado

By Deborah Crisfield
Illustrated by Patrick O'Brien

STECK-VAUGHN
ELEMENTARY · SECONDARY · ADULT · LIBRARY

A Harcourt Company

www.steck-vaughn.com

Produced by By George Productions, Inc.

3.2530 605 438470

Printed and bound in the United States of America
10 9 8 7 6 5 4 3 2 1 W 04 03 02 01 00

J 910.9
e RIS

Illustration Acknowledgments:
p 4, Collection of the Roswell Museum and Art Center, Gift of the Artist; pp 6, 8, 11, 19, 23, 25, 32, North Wind Picture Archives; pp14-15, The New York Public Library; p 17, 34, The Kansas State Historical Society. All other artwork is by Patrick O'Brien.

Contents

Settling in the New World

At the start of the sixteenth century, Spain had claimed more land than any other country in the world.

Christopher Columbus had reached the Americas in 1492. Other Spaniards came to the Americas soon afterward. Hernán Cortés reached Mexico in 1519. Francisco Pizarro arrived in Peru in 1531.

These men who came to the Americas during this time were called conquistadors, the Spanish word for "conqueror." The land they claimed for Spain, and the gold and other treasures they brought back, made Spain the most powerful and wealthy nation in the world.

Francisco de Coronado

It wasn't easy for a king to govern these huge lands from across an ocean. The conquistadors were men who did not take orders from anyone. Although they still reported to the King of Spain, they really just went ahead and followed their own rules.

The king needed people who would be loyal to him. So he started to appoint men he trusted as governors, or rulers, in the Americas. One of these men was named Antonio de Mendoza. The king made him the governor of New Spain, the country that is today Mexico. Mendoza brought with him a young man named Francisco Vásquez de Coronado.

Coronado was born in 1510, in Salamanca, Spain. His father was a nobleman. Francisco was not the oldest son in the family. This meant that he would not get his father's lands when his father died. He had to find another way to make money. Therefore, when Mendoza asked Coronado to go to the Americas with him in 1535, he eagerly accepted.

Francisco Pizarro was a conquistador who came to the Americas before Coronado.

Mendoza liked Coronado very much, and Francisco quickly became one of his most trusted men, even though he was quite young. By making peace with the native peoples in the area, he soon made a name for himself. He became a member of the council, or group, that helped govern Mexico City. He also became the governor's right-hand man.

Francisco married a young lady named Beatriz de Estrada. Beatriz was very rich. When Coronado married her, he also became very rich. This wealth increased his power. At the age of 28, Francisco Coronado was appointed governor of an area in Mexico called New Galicia. He had youth, good looks, money, and a beautiful woman by his side.

Coronado was born in Salamanca, Spain.

The Seven Cities of Cibola

A well-known Spanish legend tells of seven rich bishops who left Spain in the eighth century. These bishops supposedly set up seven new cities filled with riches in a place called Cíbola. Spaniards always wondered where those cities might be.

When early explorers returned with news of the Americas, people began to think that the seven cities might really exist. Every explorer was on the lookout for them.

Shortly before Coronado was appointed governor of New Galicia, a tired group of men found their way into New Spain. Among the members of the group were three Spaniards.

Spanish explorers such as this one were always on the lookout for the seven cities.

The Spaniards were Álvar Núñez Cabeza de Vaca, Alonso del Castillo, and Andres Dorantes. With them was a black man named Esteban. The men had been on an expedition, or trip, to Florida with Hernando de Soto.

As far as they knew, they were the only survivors of the expedition. They had spent years traveling westward, and almost died many times. Eventually some native people helped them. In turn, the lost Spaniards helped the natives. They helped natives who were sick by using the little medical knowledge they had. Their fame spread. As the Spaniards moved across the land, the native people welcomed them as important doctors. Finally the natives helped them return to other Spaniards.

Mendoza questioned these travelers about the lands they had crossed. None of them had seen anything like the seven cities, but the natives had told them similar stories. Mendoza was thrilled. He sent Esteban north on a scouting trip. Some native scouts and a priest named Fray Marcos traveled with him. The priest was sent on the trip to help keep peace with the natives.

Some explorers found their way to New Spain.

It didn't work. Esteban traveled about a day in front of the others. He came to a settlement of native people. He was killed there before Fray Marcos arrived. Fray Marcos went on a bit farther, but then turned back. When he arrived in New Spain, he told Mendoza that he did not see much of the settlement. He also said that he was pretty sure it was one of the rich cities for which they were searching.

This was all Mendoza needed to hear. He sent another man, Melchior Diaz, out to see if Fray Marcos's report was correct. However, Mendoza did not wait for Diaz's report. He formed an expedition to explore the territory to the north. Mendoza appointed 29-year-old Coronado to be the leader. Over two thousand people were part of this expedition northward. Soldiers made up most of the party. But there were also hundreds of

native people, and even a few women. The
expedition brought a large number of livestock
for food. Wagons and horses carried supplies.
Coronado himself brought along 23 horses,
several sets of armor for the horses, and a golden
suit of armor.

The group left the city of Compostela on
February 23, 1540. Several days later, Melchior
Diaz returned with his report.

**Coronado's expedition carried
many supplies.**

Off for Cíbola

The expedition began in high spirits. The Spaniards had visions of great wealth. They had heard stories of the Spanish conquistadors who had found more gold than they could ever use. Now it was their turn.

However, right from the beginning things went badly. First the expedition met some native people who were not happy to see them. Lope de Samaniego, Coronado's second in command, was killed. It was a terrible loss for Coronado and upset everyone in the expedition. A soldier named Garcia Lopez de Cardenas took over Samaniego's job.

Shortly after that, they met up with Melchior Diaz. He was returning to Compostela. His report was not good. He had found Cíbola, he said. But it was just a group of simple stone dwellings called pueblos. Although Coronado was troubled by Diaz's report, he decided not to tell anyone and to keep going. But Coronado's silence told the people what they needed to know. If it had been good news, Coronado would have shared it.

By now the people were uneasy. One of their leaders had been killed. Now they were wondering whether there were riches out there for them to find. On top of that, the land was very hilly. This made traveling difficult and slow.

Part of Coronado's army on the trail

In order to move faster, Coronado left most of the people and supplies in a town called Culiacan. He and a smaller group pushed on toward Cíbola. They traveled through what today is northern Mexico and on into Arizona. Very little food could be found, and the men were close to starving. Many horses were lost on the rugged trails. The group was becoming depressed.

Then in midsummer, the men reached the Zuni River. Across it was the land they thought was Cíbola. But it was home to the many pueblos of a group of native people called the Zuni. Today it is part of New Mexico.

Cíbola was not what the Spaniards had imagined. Instead of seeing a great city glittering with gold and jewels, they saw a pueblo village called Hawikuh. The houses sat on top of each other and were made of roughly cut stone blocks. There were no jewels, no gold.

Coronado was disappointed, but he still had a job to do. He stepped forward to tell the native people that they were now under Spain's rule. In response, the natives attacked. They shot arrows out the windows of their houses every time Coronado tried to come closer. He finally gave the signal for his men to shoot back.

A Zuni pueblo village

The battle that followed was a fierce one. The Spaniards were hungry, angry, and disappointed. They took all this out on the natives. The natives fought bravely, but they were outmatched. They turned their attention to Coronado. In his golden armor, he was clearly the leader of the army. They threw rocks at him, and knocked him unconscious. Coronado most likely would have been killed if Cardenas and another man named Hernando de Alvarado had not dragged him to safety.

When Coronado awoke, he learned that his army had won. The natives had fled their town. The Spaniards were feasting on all the food they could find. The fight had lasted an hour.

Exploring More Places

Coronado and his men settled into the town of Hawikuh. They made peace with the Zuni, and many of these natives returned to live in the city with the Spaniards.

Now it was time for some more explorations. This time, Coronado sent out small groups rather than the whole army. The first thing he did was to send a few men, including Fray Marcos, back to Mexico City to tell Mendoza that Hawikuh was not one of the seven cities of gold. Then he sent Melchior Diaz back to the rest of the army to tell them to join him in Hawikuh. Diaz was also told to explore the lands to the west. He became the first European to set foot in California.

It was late July when the first scouting mission set off. They were under the command of a soldier named Pedro de Tovar. They headed to the northwest, into what we call Arizona.

Tovar's group came across a tribe of native people called the Hopi. Like the Zuni, the Hopi didn't have any riches. They welcomed the Spaniards into their city. Later, when the Spaniards refused to leave the city, a fight broke out. It didn't last long. As soon as the Hopi saw the Spaniards' swords, they surrendered.

The Hopi were unable to tell the Spaniards about a city of gold, but they did tell them about a great canyon to the west, with a huge river running through it.

Tovar decided that this information was worth passing on to Coronado. He sent word back, and soon Coronado organized a second group of men. The leader of this expedition was Cardenas, Coronado's second in command and one of the men who had saved his life during the battle at Hawikuh.

Cardenas knew he was searching for a great river that cut through a deep canyon. However, he wasn't prepared for the spectacular sight he and his party saw. They were the first Europeans to set eyes on the Grand Canyon.

A distant view of a Hopi city

Even after they saw this huge natural wonder, they didn't believe that the canyon was as deep as their native guides said it was. And the river could not be a great river. They could barely see it. How could it be huge?

Cardenas sent a few men down into the canyon. After climbing for most of the day, the men weren't even halfway down. Cardenas called them back. At that point he had to admit to the natives that the canyon was much bigger than it appeared. In fact, the men spent three days trying to get down to the river but never made it.

While Cardenas and Tovar were away on their expeditions in Arizona, some native people from a tribe to the east came to visit the strange new men who had come to their land. They came in peace.

The chief had a big mustache. The explorers called him Bigotes, which means "whiskers" in Spanish. Bigotes told Coronado that he and his men were welcome, as long as they came in peace. Bigotes said they came from a village in the east called Cicuye. It was on the banks of a great river, which was later called the Rio Grande.

The Grand Canyon—Cardenas and his men were the first Europeans to see it.

Bigotes said he would help the Spaniards make peace with the many other native peoples who lived along the river.

Coronado appreciated the help that Bigotes gave him. He also liked and respected the chief, and treated him as a friend.

Bigotes described fertile lands to the east that were covered by huge herds of buffalo. Cabeza de Vaca, one of the men who had wandered into New Spain shortly before Coronado's expedition began, had talked of these strange animals, too.

Because Coronado trusted Bigotes, he decided to send a third scouting party to the east. Coronado felt that if there was any hope of finding the golden cities, it was probably in that direction. Coronado appointed Alvarado, the other man who had saved his life, as leader of this third party.

Again, the search proved to be disappointing. Alvarado did find buffalo and very fertile land, but no gold. He sent word back to Coronado, suggesting that the army move eastward for the winter. He also suggested that they settle in the villages of a group of native people called the Tiguex, who lived along the Rio Grande.

Each time a scouting party went out, Coronado was hopeful for reports of gold. On the other hand, he was not surprised when there weren't any. In a letter he wrote to Mendoza, he said that the mission to find the lost cities was unlikely to succeed. But he hadn't given up completely, and would still explore the territory for Spain. At this point, Coronado had to choose. He was fascinated by the description of the Grand Canyon in the west. However, he felt that the fertile land to the east was a better choice.

Bigotes spoke of herds of buffalo, which Coronado and his men had never seen before.

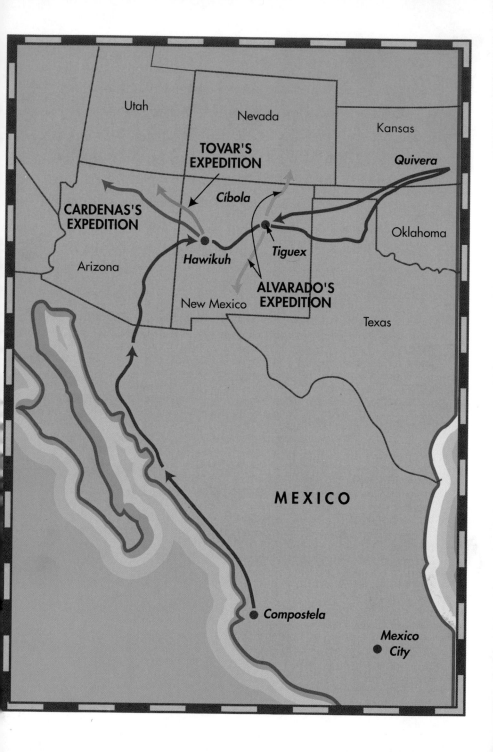

Utah

Nevada

Kansas

Quivera

TOVAR'S EXPEDITION

Cíbola

CARDENAS'S EXPEDITION

Oklahoma

Arizona

Hawikuh

Tiguex

ALVARADO'S EXPEDITION

New Mexico

Texas

MEXICO

Compostela

Mexico City

The End of Peace

Most of Coronado's army reached Hawikuh in November. They were cold, hungry, and tired. Because of this, Coronado didn't leave for Tiguex immediately. Instead, he sent Cardenas ahead with a smaller group to set up camp. Cardenas decided that the army would take over the southernmost village, and he ordered the natives living there to move out.

Meanwhile, Alvarado had taken his group to Bigotes's land of Cicuye. He and his men were welcomed, as the native chief had said they would be. Alvarado tried to convince Bigotes to join their expedition even further eastward, but Bigotes felt that he could not be away from his people for such a long time. In his place he sent two captured members of another tribe to act as guides. One was named Sopete. The Spaniards called the other one El Turco (The Turk) because he wore a turban on his head.

The Turk had no loyalty either to Bigotes or to the Spaniards. He decided to use the Spaniards to help him get back to his people. He told them that the cities for which they were searching lay in the east, in a place called Quivera. He said that in Quivera, gold was everywhere. Even the pots and pans were made of gold.

The Spaniards were excited. Finally they were getting close to the riches they had hoped for. The Turk's tales became more elaborate. He said he would have had proof but Bigotes had stolen his golden bracelets when he was captured.

Instead of going on to Quivera, Alvarado and his group went back to Bigotes to get proof. They demanded to see the bracelets. Bigotes laughed at them and told them that the Turk was a liar. He never had any gold bracelets and there was no gold in Quivera. The place only had a lot of grass huts.

Even though they didn't get the proof they were looking for, the Spaniards believed the Turk's stories. And they ignored the words of their trusted friend. They were that eager for gold.

The Spaniards trusted the Turk, but he always led them astray.

The Spaniards put chains on Bigotes and took him back to Tiguex with them to discuss the situation with Coronado.

In Tiguex, things were not going well. Coronado had arrived with the entire army. It was cold and there was not enough room or supplies for all of them. The soldiers were stealing blankets, food, and clothing from the villages. In turn, the native people killed some of the Spaniards' horses. Cardenas was furious, and Coronado gave him permission to punish the natives.

But Coronado did not know what Cardenas had in mind. Cardenas and his men killed at least 30 of the native people. When Coronado found out about this, he was horrified. But he did not punish

A battle between the Spaniards and the native people.

Cardenas. Besides, now peace with the natives was at an end. The two groups hated each other.

Shortly after that, Alvarado arrived with Bigotes in chains. Seeing a chief being treated in such a way angered the Tiguex even more. To show the natives that he was right to have chained Bigotes, Coronado wanted to prove that the chief was a liar. He tried to force Bigotes to "tell the truth." But Bigotes stuck to his story.

Now the Tiguex rebelled. Fighting began. When they realized they were outnumbered, the natives retreated to their best-protected village, the Moho pueblo. Coronado decided to starve them out. After a winter with little food, the Tiguex surrendered. The Spanish killed many of them.

Coronado's army heads to Quivera.

Following the Turk

In spring 1541 Coronado and his army headed east to the city of Quivera. Coronado's army numbered about 1,500 at this point. As they neared Cicuye, Coronado set Bigotes free.

The Turk led the way. While the men did come upon huge herds of buffalo, they found little else. The other guide, Sopete, kept telling the Spaniards not to trust the Turk. He told them that the Turk was leading them south, away from Quivera. He was right. The Spaniards had just been wandering all around what is now called Texas, while Quivera is in present-day Kansas.

Finally Coronado believed Sopete and put the Turk in chains. The native admitted that he had been trying to get them lost. At this point, Coronado realized that the Turk had been lying to them all along. He sent most of his army back to Tiguex. He continued forward with a small group. Sopete was now in the lead.

When they came to Quivera, they saw that it was nothing like the place that the Turk had described. In fact, Bigotes had told the truth. Quivera only had a lot of grass huts. Quivera did have rich land for farming, however, and Coronado claimed it for Spain. Today we call it Kansas, and it still has rich farmland.

The scouting party stayed in Quivera for about a month. At first the native people were friendly, but that soon changed because the Turk had been spreading lies about the Spaniards. Coronado decided that it was time to leave.

Many of the men with Coronado wanted to stay in Quivera. It had the richest farmland they'd ever seen, and they hoped to become rich landowners. Coronado promised them that the expedition would come back, but first he wanted them to rejoin the rest of the army in Tiguex. So they all headed westward, settling in for the winter in Tiguex once again.

Then, in December of 1541, Coronado had a terrible accident. While he was horse racing for fun, a strap broke and his saddle slipped off the horse. As Coronado fell to the ground, the horse kicked him in the head. The explorer hung between life and death for days.

Although Coronado recovered, he wasn't the same man. Before the accident, the explorer was a great and respected leader. Now Coronado was a weak, injured man who just wanted to go home to see his wife.

Coronado's Return

Coronado told the army of his change in plans. They were all going back to Mexico instead of back to Quivera. Many of the men were furious. They had come to the Americas to find gold and land. There was no gold, but there was plenty of land. Yet Coronado was forcing them to stay in the army and return to Mexico City. It was an angry army that followed their injured leader southward in 1542.

It was a difficult trip back over the rough ground. Three months and 900 miles (1,448 km) later, they entered Culiacan, the northernmost city in New Spain.

Most of the army were discharged, or released from service, at this point. Lying on a stretcher, Coronado continued on to Mexico City with fewer than 100 men. It was not the successful return he had imagined.

Coronado before he became a sickly man.

Coronado returned to Mexico City on a stretcher.

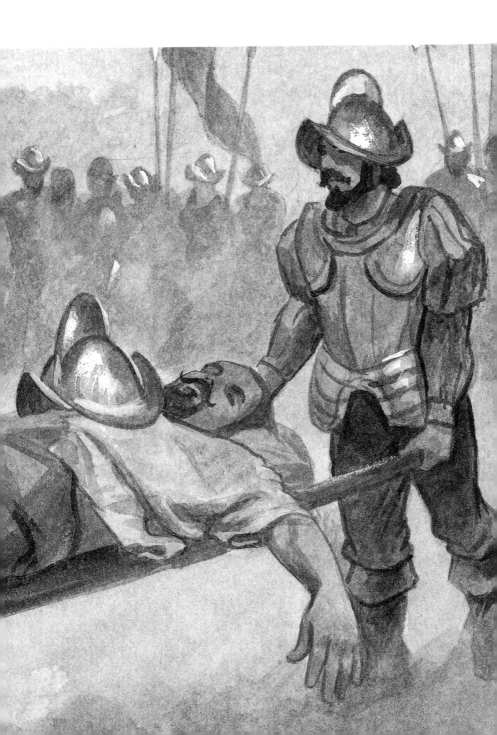

Coronado's misery didn't end there. He was put on trial for the crimes he had committed against the native peoples. Mendoza supported Coronado, and the judge eventually decided he was innocent. However, Cardenas was sentenced to seven years in jail for killing the 30 Tiguex.

Coronado lived the rest of his life fairly quietly. He took a position on the city council, but he was mostly a private man. He never again set out on an expedition. He died 12 years later, in 1544, at the age of 44.

Coronado always thought that his expedition was a failure. And for centuries, so did other people. But he had reached more places than almost everyone else before him. He explored the present-day states of California, Arizona, New Mexico, Texas, Oklahoma, and Kansas. His soldiers were the first Europeans to see the Grand Canyon, the Colorado River, and the Rio Grande. Today he is known as the first European to reach the southwestern part of the United States.

Other Events of the 16th Century
(1501 – 1600)

During the century that Coronado was exploring, events were happening in other parts of the world. Some of these were:

1502   Portuguese navigator Vasco da Gama makes his second voyage to India in order to expand trade.

1521   Hernán Cortés, a Spanish conquistador, conquers the Aztec Empire in Mexico.

1524   Giovanni da Verrazano, an Italian sailor, explores the coast of North America from North Carolina to Maine.

1534   Francisco Pizarro of Spain conquers the Inca Empire in Peru.

1571   Portuguese create colony of Angola, Africa.

1578   Moroccans destroy Portuguese power in northwest Africa.

Time Line

1510	Coronado is born in Salamanca, Spain.
1535	Coronado goes to the Americas with Mendoza.
1536	Cabeza de Vaca comes to New Spain and tells of his trip across the continent.
1538	Coronado is appointed governor of New Galicia.
1539	Esteban and Fray Marcos begin a scouting mission to Cíbola.
1539	Fray Marcos returns with stories of riches; Diaz is sent out to confirm this.
1540	Coronado is appointed leader of the expedition, which departs February 23.
March 1540	Melchior Diaz gives Coronado his discouraging report.
July 1540	Coronado reaches Cíbola and the battle of Hawikuh follows.
July 1540	Tovar is sent out with a scouting party and comes upon the Hopi tribe.
August 1540	Cardenas sets out and later reaches the Grand Canyon.
August 1540	Bigotes arrives in camp.
August 1540	Alvarado and Bigotes head east to the Rio Grande.

September 1540	The Turk and Sopete join the expedition.
November 1540	The rest of the army reaches Cíbola.
November 1540	Cardenas sets up camp in Tiguex.
December 1540	Coronado and the rest of the army arrive in Tiguex.
December 1540	Bigotes arrives in chains.
December 1540	The battle of Moho begins.
spring 1541	The natives at Moho surrender.
spring 1541	The Turk leads the Spaniards all over present-day Texas.
summer 1541	Coronado sends most of his army back to Tiguex and goes on to Quivera.
fall 1541	Coronado returns to Tiguex.
December 1541	Coronado falls from his horse and is kicked in the head.
spring 1542	The army begins the journey back to New Spain.
1544	Coronado and Cardenas are put on trial for their actions at Tiguex. Coronado is freed, but Cardenas is sentenced to seven years in prison.
1554	Coronado dies.

Glossary

canyon (KAN-yun) A deep and narrow valley with high sides

Cíbola (SEE-bow-luh) The area in present-day New Mexico where early Spanish explorers thought the legendary seven golden cities were located. Instead they found the pueblo villages of the Zuni.

conquistador (kon-KEES-tuh-dor) The Spanish word for "conqueror," or leader in the Spanish conquest of the Americas in the 1500s

expedition (ek-spuh-DISH-un) A journey for a special purpose, such as to explore or take over lands

fray (FRAY) The Spanish word for a priest

governor (GUV-ur-nur) The name given to the ruler or leader of an area or a group of people

Grand Canyon A gigantic valley that cuts through present-day Arizona. It was formed by the Colorado River and the shifting of the earth's crust.

Hawikuh (HUH-wi-kuh) One of the Zuni pueblos in Cíbola and site of a battle between the Zuni and Coronado's army.

Hopi (HO-peeh) A tribe of Native Americans from present-day Arizona

Moho (MOW-hoh) The best-protected village of the Tiguex tribe during Coronado's time

New Galicia (guh-LEE-syuh) The Spanish name for an area in western Mexico during Coronado's time

pueblo (poo-EB-low) A village of Native Americans of the American southwest. The dwellings are made of mud and bricks, and are stacked on top of one another

Quiverans (KEEVEE-runs) A tribe of Native Americans from present-day Kansas

Rio Grande (REE-oh GRAND-ee) A long river that flows from a mountain in Colorado to the Gulf of Mexico

Tiguex (TIG-oh) A tribe of Native Americans from present-day Texas

Zuni (ZOO-nee) A tribe of Native Americans from present-day New Mexico

Index

THIS IS REGGAE MUSIC

The Story of Jamaica's Music

LLOYD BRADLEY

GROVE PRESS

New York

First published in 2000 in Great Britain by Penguin Books Ltd.,
Harmondsworth, Middlesex, England

Printed in the United States of America

FIRST AMERICAN EDITION

Library of Congress Cataloging-in-Publication Data

Bradley, Lloyd, 1955–
   [Bass culture]
   This is reggae music : the story of Jamaica's music / Lloyd Bradley.
     p. cm.
   Includes bibliographical references and indexes.
   ISBN 0-8021-3828-4
   1. Reggae music—History and criticism. 2. Reggae music—Jamaica—
History and criticism. 3. Jamaicans—Great Britain. I. Title.

ML3532 .B73 2001
781.646—dc21   2001033462

Grove Press
841 Broadway
New York, NY 10003

01 02 03 04   10 9 8 7 6 5 4 3 2 1

Praise for *This Is Reggae Music:*

"Should you want to know how Island Records founder and champion of reggae Chris Blackwell arrived at ghetto music via being stranded on a reef and passing out before Rasta fishermen rescued him; why Peter Tosh always referred to Blackwell as Whiteworst; why Bob Marley was shot in the name of politics; or why the experimental producer and errant genius Lee 'Scratch' Perry was found walking backwards, striking the ground with a hammer after burning his studio down as reggae disintegrated into computer-led, bass-free rhythms; Bradley nails them all. For anyone who has ever shaken a stick at a skank."   —*The Herald* (Glasgow)

"There are as many versions of Jamaica's music history as there are remixes of this month's hot tune; reggae books have tended either to perpetuate the old myths or get it completely wrong. But Bradley has untangled the tall stories and written a compelling social and musical history . . . filled to the brim with anecdotes to keep the most hardened music-head happy."   —*The Face* (London)

"The most thorough attempt yet to tell [reggae's] whole story. Although the author, the British music journalist Lloyd Bradley, wasn't around to witness at first hand most of the developments he describes, he has spent six years talking at length to many of the people who made them happen—and his whole life, by the sound of it, loving every last detail of the music and memorizing its gloriously rich and expressive slang. . . . He is as attentive to the island's shifting social and political scene as he is to the gradual evolution of the music."   —*The Sunday Times* (London)

"An in-depth and comprehensive study of reggae and its origins . . . that will appeal to the casual reader as well as to aficionados. From the pioneering sound systems of the 1950s through to the 'digital present' via ska and dub, Bradley's reverential awe of the music, and of its practitioners, is apparent. . . . This is a book many musicians would benefit from reading. . . . The technological and production aspects of Jamaican music, with its history of tireless innovation, are also discussed in depth and at length in the book, with the debt owed by other genres of music well acknowledged. . . . Dizzying in its scope, yet at the same time meticulous in its attention to detail."
—*The Independent on Sunday* (London)

"Despite its impact on pop in general reggae has been . . . poorly served by historians. . . . Then again, fashioning a single comprehensive history, one that delves not only into music but its relationship with the island that nurtured it, is a mammoth task. *Guardian* and *Mojo* contributor Bradley has knitted together the key themes of both Jamaica's chaotic record industry and even more wayward history, with barely a visible join. In essence, he tells the story of how an island that lost 250,000 people—one-tenth of its entire population—to emigration, still managed to become an international pop cultural force. . . . Reggae's complex network of labels, producers and artists is negotiated by focusing on a tremendous cast of central characters [who] are brought to life via priceless anecdotes gleaned from the likes of Prince Buster, Bunny Lee and Jimmy Cliff. ****"   —*Q Magazine* (London)

"[*This Is Reggae Music*] attempts—and succeeds—to chart the history of reggae; Jah, guns, politics an' all. With rare suss, a sharp critical acuity and an informed sense of where the music came from and where it's going to, this welcome study is as positive as it is lively, and as refreshing as it is definitive."   —*Time Out* (London)

"Lloyd Bradley's meticulous book traces not only the growth of an art form, but also explores Jamaica's struggle to define its own culture. Bradley's anecdotal sources are excellent, and his love of the music and the culture that inspired it is evident at every turn."
—*The Latest* (UK)

"Every contemporary music form owes reggae money, or at least a debt of influence. Lloyd Bradley plots the course of the sounds that have pulsed from the island; from the days when Jamaican performers copied the look and sound of US R&B artists, up to modern dancehall, taking in roots, dub and rocksteady along the way. Bradley illustrates superbly how the music of the dispossessed, the 'sufferers,' became a global force, and how Jamaica forged its identity through drums and bass. Crucial." —*The Big Issue* (London)

For Diana, George and Elissa

'The people that reggae was being made for never separate it into *this* style and *that* style. No. This is music that's come down from slavery, through colonialism, so it's more than just a style. If you're coming from the potato walk or the banana walk or the hillside, people sing. To get rid of their frustrations and lift the spirits, people sing. It was also your form of entertainment at the weekend, whether in church or at a nine night or just outside a your house, you was going to sing. If you're cutting down a bush you're gonna sing, if you're digging some ground you're gonna sing. The music is vibrant. It's a way of life, the whole thing is not just a music being made, it's a people . . . a culture . . . it's an attitude, it's a way of life coming out of a people.' / Rupie Edwards

Contents

Acknowledgements

Writing *Bass Culture: When Reggae Was King* has been an adventure. It's taken me to Jamaica, New York, Miami, parts of London I'd forgotten existed and the most distant recesses of my record collection. For all this I am enormously grateful. But far more so than that, it's got me into – and, quite thankfully in a couple of cases, out of – situations that have hugely expanded my life-experience, given me a great feeling of privilege or quite simply made me laugh. I've helped Leroy Sibbles move house; I've felt Prince Buster's head; I've sat on a wall with Big Youth eating windfall custard apple; I've talked to Lee Perry for an hour and got secondarily red; I've quaffed fine wine with Dennis Bovell; broken bread at a dreadlocks camp; been stopped, with Bunny Lee, at 3 a.m. by an eradication squad; got roped in as navigator on the Wailers' tour bus; been abandoned on a particularly twitchy Trench Town street corner for forty minutes while the guy that was carrying me round went off and did God knows what; had the piss taken out of me royally by Bobby Digital and Luciano; interviewed Burning Spear when, for no reason I could see, he had no trousers on; taken tea in the very room in which Dennis Brown was born; taken my life in my hands with Junior Delgado's driving on thankfully empty Kingston streets; and, most of all, during the six years it's taken to put the book together I've been treated with massive courtesy, hospitality, helpfulness and respect by almost everybody I've come into contact with.

It's no accident that the handshake you pick up within hours of touching down in Jamaica involves the right clenched fists being alternately struck top against bottom, then the knuckles pressed together. It signifies strength and unity, and sums up how I felt whenever I had to spend time on the island. Therefore, the biggest shout has to go out to the entire population of Jamaica. It was their creativity, spirituality, warmth, wit and resilience in the face of appalling outside manipulation that gave me something to write about in the first place. I hope I've done them justice. But on a more immediate level, very rarely was I treated with anything other than hospitality by anybody I met on my many visits to Jamaica – not just in the music business, but in the bars, in the cafés, in the streets, in the shops and in the hotels. London taxi drivers could do worse than take customer-relations advice from their Kingston counterparts.

Specifically on the island – and its diaspora – I have to thank those who gave up their time to invite a complete stranger into their homes or places of business and show him kindness beyond the call of duty as they told their tales. These were guys who had no product to push but were still willing to share knowledge, history, anecdotes and opinions on a range of subjects way beyond the music itself. Their reward, as several most flatteringly explained, was that somebody finally wanted to write that stuff down. In alphabetical order, a big five on the black-hand side goes to Dennis Alcapone, Monty Alexander, Horace Andy, Buju Banton, Dave Barker, Aston 'Family Man' Barrett, Big Youth, Pauline Black, Dennis Bovell, Burning Spear, Fatis Burrell, Gussie Clarke, Jimmy Cliff, Junior Delgado, Bobby Digital, Brent Dowe, Sly Dunbar, Rupie Edwards, Derrick Harriott, Cecil Heron, Junior Cat, Bunny Lee, Byron Lee, Lepke, Little Ninja, Luciano, DJ Pebbles, Lee 'Scratch' Perry, Ernest Ranglin, Michael Rose, Leroy Sibbles, Danny Sims, Spragga Benz, Jah Vego and Drummie Zeb. The inspiration was all yours, the mistakes are all mine.

Special thanks, however, have to be given to Linton Kwesi Johnson for the loan of the title and to Prince Buster for the Foreword, also to both him and his wife Mola for all the kindnesses they've shown me in Miami and London.

In New York, the reggae archivist, tireless soldier for the cause and all-round excellent fellow Tom Tyrell couldn't have been more helpful. The same goes for Lisa Cortez, who shared some fantastic information; and irrepressible Murray 'Jah Fish' Elias, whose Big Apple anecdotes are matched only by the sheer brilliance of the *Big Blunts* compilation albums he puts together.

At home in the UK are people who deserve as much credit for *Bass Culture: When Reggae Was King* as I do: Allister Harry read every word and passed a series of detailed comments as amusing as they were instructive; Rae Cheddie was the man who, thirty years ago, turned this dyed-in-the-wool soulboy on to reggae, and more recently answered even the most inane queries quicker than you might have thought possible; Eddi Fiegel, whose advice, conversation and friendship did so much to keep me focused; Keith Stone of London's premier reggae retailer Daddy Kool Records (020 7437 3535), who'd not only answer questions but let me listen to virtually any tune I didn't have from the last thirty-five years; Patricia Cumper of the Jamaica High Commission Information Service, who entered into the spirit of things with great gusto; and Margaret Duvall, Deborah Ballard and Gaylene Martin, whose casual reggae knowledge and perpetual helpfulness never ceased to astonish. And of course my family, Diana, George and Elissa, who shared their house, their lives and their holidays with a man who became somewhat possessed, and John Bradley (my dad), of whom I haven't seen nearly enough recently.

Vital to the whole process were Mat Snow, Paul Trynka, Jim Irvin, Paddy and everybody at *MOJO* for sending me to Jamaica several times on the flimsiest pretexts, for their excellent reggae coverage, general services to the vanishing art of music journalism and for putting up with me dropping into the office for extended football/magazine/music reasoning sessions every time the cabin fever got too much. Dennis Morris, Neil Spencer, Penny Reel, Steve Barrow, Chris Morrow, Don Letts and Rick Elgood have all added enormously to my enjoyment of and fascination with reggae over the years, while Rob and Tina Partridge, Liz Greader and Peady have been the definition of cooperation and good humour during this book's research process. And of course Kester, Stanley, Ron Shillingford and Wayne; the JBs FC and Arsenal FC; and all at Parnell's, Upstairs at Ronnies, Bluesville, the Q Club, the Railway in Harrow, Spinners, Columbos and the Birds' Nests Waterloo, West Hampstead, West Ken and Paddington.

Then there are the people who without whom, quite literally, *Bass Culture: When Reggae Was King* couldn't have been possible. Jon Riley, late of Penguin Books, had the good taste to instigate the project; Tony Lacey, currently of Penguin Books, must be in line for some sort of medal for listening to nearly six years of increasingly unlikely excuses and having the good grace to pretend he believed them; and of course his pa Janet for sounding concerned whenever I phoned in with the latest and most blatant lie, which, of course, had the character-building effect of making me feel terrible; John Hamilton, the man responsible for the spookily spot-on cover and overall appearance of the book; and Trevor Horwood, whose patient and painstaking copy-editing of the final draft brought some semblance of order to the proceedings.

But finally, the biggest thanks goes to the late John Bauldie whose advice, instruction and encouragement taught me how to write.

Lloyd Bradley, London,
July 1999

Foreword

I told Norrie Drummond in an interview in the 1960s that my music is protest music, music protesting against slavery, class prejudice, racism, inequality, economic discrimination, denial of opportunity and the injustice we were suffering under colonialism in Jamaica. We were taken from Africa where our fore-parents were kings and queens and brought to Jamaica on ships as slaves, where we were stripped of our names, our language, our culture, our God and our religion. But music is the soul of Africa – its spirit, its DNA, its heredity – and this they were unable to conquer, enabling the birth in Jamaica of the cultural revolution we call *ska*: the mother, the womb that gave birth to rocksteady and reggae, our way of life.

The minds of the Jamaican people were colonized by America's rhythm and blues. Its influence penetrated deep into the fabric of society and had a devastating effect on our folk music, our dialect, even our dress code. America's twang had taken over from our Jamaican patois, mento, Burru and Poco, which were exiled from the city to the hills in the country, and instead of Jamaican songs like 'Slide Mongoose' and 'Linstead Market' the radio station and the sound systems bellowed the music of Duke Ellington, Sarah Vaughan, Fats Domino, Louis Jordan, Wynonie Harris, Willis Jackson and Patti Page, while the great Louis Bennett, Ranny Williams, Bim and Bam – patriots of our culture – were cast aside. Now don't get me wrong, I love rhythm and blues, I love Louis Jordan, but I also have an intrinsic love for things Jamaican; its musical expressions and art forms that are of Africa's heritage.

In 1957, in Kingston, I built my sound system at age nineteen, naming it the Voice of the People. It was the first sound system to have a name that did more than just talk about the operator or about music and dance. Sound men such as Tom the Great Sebastian, Duke Reid the Trojan or Sir Coxsone Downbeat were at ease with the status quo; unlike them, I grew up a disciple of the Right Honourable Marcus Garvey, as did my parents. His words 'You are a man like any other' never left my head. My sound system was to be the people's radio station by way of the dancehalls, where their points of view would be heard, for they were not being heard on the major radio stations. To me it was important to name my sound system so, because the music of the ghettos and the countryside was being created for the people by the people. The ska was the first modern Jamaican music that didn't simply copy the American styles, and hence it meant so much more to the ordinary Jamaican people than the R&B and jazz that was coming out of Miami and New Orleans.

When I started recording this music I had to talk the musicians into playing it. At first, the radio stations wouldn't play it and the other sound-system owners laughed at it. But the people loved it. I can remember when I first played 'They Got to Go', the first ska record, on my sound system at Salt Lane and the people came running! Other dances fell flat because mine was a big system and could be heard from far away in places like the Coronation Market, Back-A-Wall, Smith Village, Hannah Town, Foreshore Road and the Parade, and the people knew they were hearing their own music for the first time. That was the music of the people, and the sound system that brought it to them was the Voice of the People: the means to allow their expression to be heard.

Since then Jamaican music – call it ska, call it rocksteady, call it roots, call it reggae – has always been the people's music. Their statements, their rhythms, their good times, their sufferation, their love songs. And every time the outside world catches up with it the beat changes again, so what's being played on the sound systems remains truly representative of the people who are making it.

Although the roots music of the 1970s, alongside the love songs, is commonly viewed as Jamaican music's first expression of the people's feeling about their lives, it had, in fact, been doing that since the beginning of the ska. There was 'African Blood', 'Shanty Town', 'Black Head Chince Man', 'Taxation', 'Too Hot', 'They Got to Come My Way' (the first unofficial Jamaican national anthem), while the drums in 'Oh Carolina' reminded the people that Africa was not dead. And modern dancehall reggae music does the same thing, with records like 'Black Man', 'Pharaoh House Crash', 'Police Trim Rasta', 'Hard Man Fe Dead' and 'Send Us a Deliverer'. Every twist and turn of Jamaican music for the last forty years has reflected what has been happening to the people, either politically or socially, and often it's the other way around, with the music and sound systems influencing the country's politics.

The government angered the people when it charged me with possessing prohibited literature – a book titled *Message to the Black Man*, written by a black man and upholding the dignity of the black man – declaring my quest in the island at the time to be undesirable. This resulted in mass demonstrations with the support of the intellectuals at the university. There I dubbed Prime Minister Shearer 'Pharaoh', driven by the colonial mentality; after all, he was the one who told his police to shoot first and ask questions afterwards. He lost the election that followed and Michael Manley became Prime Minister. Manley learned from Pharaoh's mistakes and lifted the ban on *Message to the Black Man* and other literature written by people of colour.

Jamaican music has always been genuine folk music, but when its story has been told, it is seldom presented as the story of a whole people, describing how those with the ability and the talent were influenced by it to go into the studio or pick up a microphone at a dance. Too often only half the story is told, and the background, the upheavals and changes the island of Jamaica went through just before and since independence, gets forgotten in the face of so much music. *Bass Culture: When Reggae Was King*, however, omits nothing of what went into making the music from the small island of Jamaica such a force throughout the world. The rude-boy era, the banning of Walter

Rodney, the IMF crisis, mass emigration to the UK, the bloody general elections, post-independence prosperity and the big let-down that was to follow, the British police, the Bob Marley effect, bauxite mining and mass tourism, technology's influence on the music . . . it's all here.

It takes a man like Lloyd Bradley to tell this complete story. I met him after he had telephoned to ask if he could come to Miami and talk to me in connection with a book he was writing. After hearing some of the topics he was interested in I gave him the OK. He arrived an hour and a half early. I'd been in the studio all night and was resting, so he sat and waited. When I got up an hour and a half later, I saw him sitting in my living room and asked him why he was so early. He replied that he was afraid of being late. I burst into laughter and that set the mood for the interview, which was originally scheduled for one hour and lasted for over three. Lloyd Bradley sees beyond the music to how real life in Jamaica made the music happen, and how it in turn affected the people, and he lets those people tell the story. He has worked hard to capture the pride, the passion, the struggle and the humour, but most of all the love that he heard in the music and saw in the people. He has understood the story and tells it with honesty, style and appreciation.

It's been a long wait for a book like *Bass Culture: When Reggae Was King*, but it has been worth it. This is a book that takes folk music from that little island in the Caribbean and treats it as seriously and as intellectually as any other musical form, but never loses sight of the spirit, the strength and the joy that went into making it. A book that knows reggae is serious business, but never forgets you have to dance to it.

Jamaican music at last has the book it deserves.

Prince Buster, Miami,
February 2000

First Session

'It was always a downtown thing, only among a certain sort of people. But more than just hearing the music, the equipment was so powerful and the vibe so strong that we *feel* it. Like when we were dancing you were actually part of it. It was *ours*, and so many of us wanted to do something to contribute to it.' / Derrick Harriott

1

Boogie in My Bones

'Being part of the crowd at a big lawn, like at Forresters' Hall down on North Street, when a big sound system was playing was probably the greatest feeling in the world to any Jamaican kid. But if you had aspirations to make music then it was magical. It was . . . It was *awe-inspiring*.'

Derrick Harriott is now a prosperous music-business entrepreneur, with a family-run record store in Kingston's Constant Spring area and an international CD reissue operation specializing in his own reggae and rocksteady recordings and productions. But from the late 1950s through the next two decades, he was among Jamaica's most consistently successful artists, one of the very few to progress through R&B, ska, rocksteady, reggae and dub producing international hits for himself and others with total conviction. While this dapper-looking fifty-something won't need much coaxing to get up on stage to rock a crowd, if you really want to get his attention ask him about his downtown teenage years. His face creases into a misty-eyed smile.

'The sound system dances were where the ghetto people came to enjoy themselves. No airs nor graces, just be among your own people. This was a big attraction. Sometimes there was trouble, but, back then, more often there wasn't. It seem like to be a teenager in Jamaica during that era was the best thing on earth. The people would have on their best clothes –

when it come to dressing up nobody can look fine like the ghetto people – and you would have a drink or whatever and hear the very best music. It made us feel real good about ourselves. Like we could do anything.'

This was back in the first half of the 1950s, and even then a sound system was more than just a cliff face of speaker boxes, each big enough to raise a family in, powered by amplification of apparently intercontinental capabilities. It was, quite literally, the community's heartbeat, which meant that the dance was always going to be more than simply somewhere to be. In fact, to introduce the sound system as 'a mobile disco', or even 'a mobile disco with attitude', would be to do it, its operators and this new wave of post-war Jamaican youth an enormous disservice.

A reasonable UK comparison to what the sound systems meant to Harriott's and subsequent generations would be Britain's football teams, because in downtown Kingston practically every youngster followed, or *ran wid*, a sound. Home and away, because when your guys played out in an area other than your own, your presence and your vocal support would be counted on. And if it was a sound clash, with two rival outfits slugging it out by playing alternate records and the victors being whoever won over the bigger, noisier part of the crowd, then to stand up for your sound system was a matter of honour. You were standing up for your area, your friends, your good name.

And by that time it had become second nature.

The idea of blasting music from the radio or a record player – the best in American R&B or hot jazz – through a configuration of open-air loudspeaker cabinets became popular in the mid-1940s as a way of enticing passing trade into bars and shops. Indeed, the reason the first sound-system rigs and, later, established dances were called 'sets' was simply because the equipment evolved from large radio and gramophone sets. And as a marketing device these rambunctious methods worked; to such a degree that by the end of that decade the music often became the main reason to visit whatever establishment. After all, with transistor radios not yet part of life and cabinet model wirelesses being beyond most pockets, it was the only way for so many Jamaicans to hear any professionally produced music.

Within ten years or so, the sound system had become a social phenomenon in its own right, and its operator, the sound man, one of the biggest men in his area. Outdoor dances kept by the extravagantly named likes of Tom the Great Sebastian, V Rocket, Count Smith the Blues Blaster, Sir Nick the Champ, King Edwards or Lord Koos of the Universe evolved from merely one more form of urban entertainment into the hub around which Kingston's various inner cities turned. For the crowds that flocked to wherever the big beat boomed out, it was a lively dating agency, a fashion show, an information exchange, a street status parade ground, a political forum, a centre for commerce, and, once the deejays began to chat on the mic about more than their sound systems, their records, their women or their selves, it was the ghetto's newspaper.

Absolutely vital, though, was the economic effect. Dances put on by ghetto men brought new money into the immediate and wider community as people came from out of town or other parts of the city, with money to spend. While this wasn't an enormous amount per head, the numbers involved made a worthwhile total; and besides, proportionately speaking, anything extra was a big improvement. Nor was it just the promoters and operators who were earning: a whole satellite system of ancillary trading occurred, making sure a percentage of that cash ended up in wider local circulation. The streets surrounding any major venue would be lined with hot-food tables offering jerk pork and chicken, patties or fried fish, and push-cart men arrived loaded up with fresh coconuts, sugar cane, bananas and mangoes. It was a rare thing for these vendors not to sell out. Likewise the flatbed drinks trucks, which would lurch up bearing teetering stacks of Red Stripe or Heineken beer and soda crates, supplying the bars inside and outside the arenas. Then, at the far end of this musical food chain, schoolchildren with any degree of nous would be up before sunrise, collecting discarded bottles to return them to the factories for the penny deposit on each.

It's been said that sound-system dances existed only to sell beer. That was never ever true and, with great dismissiveness, it removes any notion of passion and inventiveness from the sound men to imply that the shifting, culturally cutting-edge sound-system phenomenon was driven by outside-the-ghetto big businesses. Of course there were the mutual benefits enjoyed by the sound systems and the drinks trade. Jamaica's Red Stripe brewery built itself up and kept going thanks to the business it did in the dancehalls back then. And, later, Red Stripe, Guinness, Heineken and the larger rum distillers became actively involved in promoting sound-system events – as they still are today. Also, it's no coincidence that the two men who did most to elevate and sustain the situation as the next era's front runners both had liquor-sales connections before they got into music. Coxsone Dodd's family owned liquor stores, as did Duke Reid himself – in fact the first advertisements for Duke Reid's services read, 'For the best in sound and liquors see Reid's Sound System and Liquor Store for Clubs, Bars, Parties and Home.' It was an additional dancehall-related income that allowed them to survive and expand beyond what was achieved by the original operators.

But we're getting ahead of ourselves.

Critically, while these communal and personal fiscal advantages meant that sound systems were there to stay, the defining aspect of them as the crux of ghetto life was that they were *cultural*, as opposed to being merely a culture.

In an environment where any emerging indigenous – i.e., black – artistic or social expression was either discouraged to the point of being stillborn, drastically diluted in the name of artistic sophistication or blanded out to appeal to white tourists, the sound system had been created by and for Jamaica's dispossessed. Thus it would always thrive so long as it remained their exclusive property. To reiterate Derrick Harriott's point, there was a huge sense of self-worth involved here: a warm night inside a big lawn's bamboo fence (clubs were so named because most of the action happened on the grassed-over area outside the actual hall), under the starry Caribbean skies, was about as good as life – anybody's life – could get. When the sweet smells of jerk chicken, bougainvillaea and collie weed swirled around your head, you could feel the hottest R&B jump-up vibrate through a cold bottle of beer, and cut some crisp steps with a big-eyed daughter . . . it was enough to overwhelm anybody. To the point at which it didn't really matter what you didn't have for the rest of the time, because right there, right then, at the sound-system dance, you had it all.

Different areas had different systems, an idea of turf that was taken entirely seriously as far as sound clashes were concerned. However, lively as these cutting contests might have been, they were largely good-natured affairs with audiences out to enjoy themselves. Serious crowd violence was rare (it came later, and then at the instigation and orchestration not of the audience but of some of the more colourful sound men). Of the first generation of significant systems, Tom the Great Sebastian set up camp at Luke Lane and Charles Street, King Edwards controlled the Maxfield Avenue/Waltham Park area and Count Smith was in Greenwich Town. All this was happening in an area which was no bigger than a small London borough, but which accommodated an extraordinary number of venues. Forresters' Hall, where lodge meetings were held, and Kings Lawn on North Street were separated only by Love Lane; both had huge outside areas and would take crowds of four figures. Liberty Hall and Jubilee were both on King Street, yet each could pull in several hundred people on the same night. Dancehalls such as Pioneer in Jones Town, Carnival on North Street, the Red Rooster on Tower Street, The Success Club on Wildman Street and Bar-B-Que on Fleet Street in East Kingston had three-hundred-plus capacities. Cho Co Mo on Wellington Street, though, with its huge lawn out front, was the biggest, easily accommodating a couple of thousand, with a good deal more just outside the fence grooving on the music.

Dances were on most nights of the week, with weekend functions lasting through to the next morning. Many of the smaller places held afternoon sessions – it wasn't unusual for kids to be coming from school, get kinda sidetracked by the music, sneak in, lose track of time and expect a beating when they eventually did get home. Then there were the Sunday outings to the Palm Beach, Gold Coast or Hellshire Beach to the west of Kingston or, more popularly, to the beaches along St Thomas Road to the east of the city. This is the road that runs to Bull Bay (if you turn right when you come from the airport road, that's St Thomas Road), and on the beach side were a series of purpose-built 'clubs'. These were fenced-off open-air areas, with large concrete floors on which the sound system would be set up, and there would be a purpose-built bar area. This way the equipment would stay well away from the sand, but as the dance floor went down to the beach itself the patrons could take full advantage. By far the best along that stretch was the Palm Beach Club, which had trees and shrubs planted around the dance floor with tables placed among them, and little huts woven out of palm leaves to create secluded chill-out spaces. Sound men would organize coaches to pick up from pre-arranged ghetto corners from quite early in the morning, and whole families would come out with picnics, with the serious ravers arriving much later to keep the dance going until Monday morning. And to imagine that British teenagers in the late 1980s thought they invented all-night open-air raving!

But more than just being a lot of fun, or even culturally correct, these sound-system sessions changed Jamaica and its relationship with the rest of the world for ever. It was the continuous stream of exciting, imported American R&B records they generated that gave birth to Jamaica's highest profile, most valuable and as yet inexhaustible export: music. Because, in the mid-1950s, entirely due to the sound systems, the country began to go music mad and something serious had to happen. Quickly.

Eyes shining now, and slapping an index finger on the shop counter to force his point across, Derrick Harriott takes up the story.

'What happened was the musical thing was real widespread,

but only among a certain sort of people. It was always a downtown thing. But more than just hearing the music, the equipment was so powerful and the vibe so strong that we *feel* it. Like when we were dancing you were actually part of it. It was *ours*, and so many of us wanted to do something to contribute to it. Check and you'll see that of the wave of Jamaican musicians that started making original music the majority of them would have been at sound systems back then, soaking it up and *feeling* how the people would love a good song.

'It's easy to see how they were inspired. Which is why, once the sound systems started making a big impression back in the fifties, five years later there was such an enormous amount of youngsters wanting to make music. There was much more music coming out of Kingston in the early sixties than should be expected from a city that size.'

Tom the Great Sebastian's was the most important sound system in the first half of the 1950s. Most veterans agree that his was the original Big Rig, with the most powerful amplifiers and the biggest number of speaker cabinets – or 'houses of joy' as they were called, in reference to their unit size. Close behind in terms of power and prestige were V Rocket, King Edwards, Sir Nick, Nation, Admiral Cosmic, Lord Koos, Kelly's and Buckles. And the rhythms that carried the swing at their dances were very different from the well-mannered tunes wafting across the local airwaves courtesy of Radio Jamaica Rediffusion.

To appeal to as many people as possible, radio played it safe by leaning towards the insipid. A ghetto crowd, however, out to enjoy themselves on Saturday night, wanted to dance until they dropped. Any sound man worth his title couldn't be doing with the conventional Jamaican airplay hits and only the most soulful would do: the fieriest R&B, merengue or Latin jazz; the bawdiest mento; the deepest ballads. Naturally, Jamaican radio wouldn't touch the sound-system specials, no matter how popular they proved with the people, because the airwaves at that time were controlled by middle-class types who aspired to 'dignity' and looked upon anything too wild – too black – as bordering on the savage. Most crucially, though, if the sound systems played the hits then they'd all have the same records, and where would be the sport in that? In the pressure-cooker competition of the dancehall, what gave an operator the edge over his rivals were records that nobody else even knew the name of, let alone owned. This was the rare-groove scene in its purest and most original form, where you'd go beyond the beat to a place in which exclusivity and obscurity were the only yardsticks.

And audience appreciation, of course, which would be instant and unreserved. One of the major attractions of going to a sound-system dance was the chance to participate with some mad noise. Records unique to a particular operation – which assumed a kind of trophy status – or old favourites would be greeted with a big cheer as the dancers settled down to bust their moves. New records that made the place really come alive would end with a barrage of shouts to *Lick it back*, or *Wheel and come again* – an occurrence that could be repeated dozens of times, as long that tune continued to move the crowd. If a record was wrong, though, and the crowd didn't like it, they'd make themselves felt just as lustily – you'd hardly be able to hear the music for the booing and the operator had to change it. Double quick! A feat in itself, because those guys only ever used one turntable, therefore cross-fading was out of the question. It was done like this: one hand would hold the next record between the third and little fingers and the palm; the other hand would lift the needle from the offending disc; the first hand could then be moved over to pluck that record from the turntable using the thumb and index/middle fingers, and drop the other one on to the centre-dome all in the same move-ment. A flick of the wrist. Snap! Then the other hand would replace the needle.

There was always much more of a connection between a Jamaican deejay and his crowd than the idea of a disco or night-club might imply. A good dance would be a group experience; a mutual-appreciation society between deejay and disciples. The crowds would join in singing favourite or exclusive-to-that-set cuts and the operator would kill the volume on choruses to let them do so. It was proof of a system's popularity in a manner that could be heard all over the area, thus vital for the sound man's standing. In return for such a boost the sound man *had* to live up to his hype. Hence the spectacular stage names, the flamboyant behaviour, the sense of showmanship that went beyond simply spinning tunes and a continual supply of the best, the most exclusive and therefore the most prestigious music. It was out of these self-contained cycles of give and take that the sound-system scene's inherent partisanship evolved.

This immediate response to music kept the deejays close to the people and meant that the records offered on sound systems were always popular choices. When a record really kicked, the average sound man would work it to death while he set out to find more just like it for future use, but all that this would achieve was to keep him running on the spot. Essentially, this was a short-term proposition. Although it was absolutely vital to let a hot tune run its course, an audience expecting to hear it several times a night, the real challenge came in anticipating what that same crowd would want *next*, and advancing the music on offer to just such a point. To keep moving on was the only way to maintain continued audience interest, and so build a lasting career. Thus, the dances became testing grounds for new styles of music as well as new records, and the people were always closely involved with how things developed.

In this respect, everything that is Jamaican music today can be traced back to those first sound-system operations – it's important to recognize it was a status quo in place even before there was anything that could be called Jamaican music. Today, more than forty years later, the sound system remains the mainstay of the Jamaican music industry, since nearly all the island's top producers have their own systems, or exclusive links to one. Thus musical evolution remains, quite literally, by popular request.

Such proximity to the people and the need constantly to reinvent itself at this pace meant that Jamaican music, although then based on an American form, would find its own personality sooner rather than later. As it was, less than ten years after sound systems became big news, Jamaican music had forged an identity so strong as to be completely unrecognizable from its original form. It was, however, instantly identifiable all over the planet, and so culturally distinct that it couldn't be made – with any credibility – by anyone with no Jamaican blood in them, or who hadn't been totally immersed in the culture.

But to get from a Denham Town yard dance to a vibrant international recording industry, you must, as so often in Jamaica, take the scenic route.

During the first half of the 1950s, the Jamaican economy was undergoing yet another series of extraordinary upheavals. In fact, it was as near to booming as it ever had been, with a 10 per cent year-on-year Gross National Product growth up until 1957, which for the rest of the decade only slowed to 7 per cent. Sugar and bananas were premium exports, but what was making the difference was the long-haul holiday market opening up as a fashionable upper-bracket pursuit for both Europeans and Americans. This meant the international aluminium industry was in overdrive, as the commercial airline business took off and passenger planes had to be built, while exotic destinations for travellers had to be found. Jamaica was well equipped to service both these demands.

Bauxite, the chief mineral source of aluminium, was present in abundance in Jamaica's red soil, and between 1950 and 1957 the island was the world's largest supplier of said mineral as such companies as Alcan, Reynolds and Alcoa staked claims on the country's interior. During the same period, vast stretches of the north coast were turned into building sites in a concerted bid to meet the need for luxury hotel rooms. Subsequently, there was rapid job creation in mining, construction and the tourist trade. Also, because most of the money behind these operations came from US-owned multinational corporations, the Jamaican Treasury got a boost when the buoyant yankee dollar replaced the weaker pound sterling as its crutch of choice.

Emigration played a big part, too, there being what amounted to an exodus of skilled and unskilled labour. During the 1950s, immigration to the UK, Canada and North America was virtually unchecked – because Jamaica was then a British colony, her citizens were actively encouraged to go to the UK. They had no problem entering Canada, either, as it was also a British colony, and even after the USA introduced immigration controls in 1952, Jamaicans could get into the States on the British immigration quota, which was always undersubscribed. Over a quarter of a million people, or, astonishingly, about one-tenth of Jamaica's population, left for those three destinations during the decade. To this must be added the enormous number of seasonal, short-term agricultural labour contracts – cane cutting a speciality – taken up by Jamaicans in the American South. So, as long as Jamaican jobs were being quit for a chance in one of a choice of Promised Lands, there was less competition for the new vacancies at home.

A significant knock-on effect of this mass emigration was the regular sending home of cash by relatives working abroad, producing new incomes out of, quite literally, nothing. Although this factor has never been taken too seriously – perhaps because there are no official figures – in the tenement yards and the rural cabins, a few pounds arriving from London every month could mean the difference between eating or not, sending children to school or otherwise, and must be counted as a significant contributor to those boom years.

Politically, things were upbeat as well. In 1955, Norman Manley's PNP had come to power on an increasingly appealing independence ticket, and proceeded to push hard in that direction. By 1958 Jamaica's bauxite wealth was such that, in competition with oil-rich Trinidad, it was confident enough to undermine the solidarity of the West Indies Federation (an economic cartel of Caribbean islands plus Guyana and what was then British Honduras) with an escalating gung-ho bullishness. All of which produced a widespread sense of national optimism; a factor which, if you were sitting on the dirt floor of a cardboard shack in Jones Town, was probably of far greater significance than your actual fiscal improvement.

It is true that there was a certain amount of economic-boom moolah trickling down the hill to a certain amount of ghetto people, which, probably for the first time, allowed them disposable income. And yes, some conditions had improved after the hurricane of 1951 left many homeless, resulting in a programme of municipal housing which provided for the building of small, modular, cement dwellings with kitchens and inside plumbing – the 'government yards' or the 'concrete jungle' that Bob Marley would write about in years to come. But the downsides of all these improvements were ominous.

As would be expected, working people with the means to upward mobility quit the slums as soon as possible, taking up residence in the new breezeblock bungalow developments sprouting to the north towards Half Way Tree, so hardly any new money stuck to the ghetto. On a wider scale, it must be remembered that the hotel construction sites were miles away from the capital, so the jobs they created had little direct fiscal effect on West Kingston. Then, perhaps most significantly, the apparently wealth-generating bauxite mines (again not in the capital) did more harm than good to the general population; the farms that were bought up and shut down to accommodate the vast open-cast tracts displaced far more country folk than they employed. Around 300,000 people were forced to move in order to create 10,000 new jobs. Unsurprisingly, a massive percentage of those left without homes or work gravitated to Kingston. The already overcrowded slums downtown mushroomed into a maze of squatter camps around the concrete ditches, gullies and open sewers that gave Trench Town its name.

The bottom line was that, while the economy was expanding for the country as a whole, in much of West Kingston poverty still meant 'desperately poor'. It was at this time that the middle-class/land-owner flight began in earnest, as those with real money relocated to the Blue Mountain foothills and white-washed, landscaped, luxury villas, with high walls and secure gates. Two nations within the one country, defined by geographical as much as social altitude. Old-timers who remember those days talk of the sense of isolation among the ghetto sufferahs, which intensified the sense of ownership and pride as regards anything exclusively theirs. Such as the sound systems. Thus, as the 1950s progressed, the speaker boxes were booming, numerically as well as literally.

As well as the better-known outfits, there were a host of others whose reputations may never have travelled much beyond their particular Kingston corner but which were still contributing to the sprawling cacophony that had turned music into a national obsession. And this music was guaranteed to lift the most down-pressured spirit. Becoming dominant above the Latin and mento was a raw, 'cross-the-tracks funk, fresh off the boat from the dark sides of Miami, New Orleans and New York. Louis Jordan was a perennial favourite, and prolific enough to meet demand; the big blues shouter Wynonie Harris always went down well – his US hit 'Blood Shot Eyes' was virtually stuck to Jamaican sound men's turntables between 1951 and 1953. Jimmy Reed had a number of sound-system hits, the biggest being 'Baby What You Want Me to Do'. Bill 'Mr Honky Tonk' Doggett's records would regularly rock the crowds, as would Professor Longhair's. Fats Domino and Lloyd Price took them to the roots of rock 'n' roll. Jazz would be present and entirely correct courtesy of Dizzy Gillespie, Sarah Vaughan or Earl Hines; while the honey-dripping likes of Nat King Cole, Billy Eckstine, Jesse Belvin or the Moonglows were the lurrrve gods of their time. Although the artists' names had changed since the big-band dominated 1940s, music for getting down in a house party or lawn session in Jamaica was still largely about extremes – the buck wild or the silky smooth.

Only the very biggest operators could afford to travel to the USA to shop for records, so the majority of sound-system music arrived courtesy of merchant seamen and returning migrant workers looking to supplement their income. (True, there were official importers and one or two licensing companies, but if a record was available in the shops that stocked US records it would be far too accessible to be of high priority to any self-respecting sound man.) A proportion of that informal import trade would be pre-arranged, with the secondary level of sound men having made deals with seamen whose judgement they respected, asking them to shop for certain types of record by certain artists or producers, occasionally allowing the voyager to surprise them. But the majority of business was with the little sound men and strictly freelance, resulting in spirited bartering, or 'higgling', being carried out on the quayside between entrepreneurial arrivals and their prospective clients. Kotchels of American singles were negotiated against such desirable domestically produced resaleables as rum, fine cigars, coffee and ganja, or women – time spent with, that is, as some of the liveliest sound-system sets took place in Kingston's most renowned brothels.

But to be a sound man you had to be a showman, so hot new tunes were hyped to a point just past sizzling as soon as they changed hands. The major deejays would be far too grand to meet the boat themselves, so they'd have young runners waiting out on the docks, seeking what shelter they could from the sun and looking for particular ships to tie up. These youths would then get the designated deals over with and proceed to make an enormous performance of whisking the records – by bicycle – straight to their employers, leaving as many observers as possible in no doubt as to how fresh that particular sound system's dance would be that night.

By the time tunes came into Jamaica their original US release date was pretty much irrelevant. Their exclusivity was what was valuable, thus the most important piece of equipment for a sound man bringing in American records was a coin. Any coin, the edge of it being used to remove any information printed on the records' labels. This needed to be done quickly, too, because industrial espionage, employee bribery and all manner of coercion would be brought into play to discover a disc's identity, so the fewer people who knew a killer tune's actual name the lower the likelihood of a rival getting hold of a copy. After all the label copy had been erased, it wasn't uncommon for a newly anonymous tune to be renamed, usually with a title glorifying the sound man or sound system that was playing it – 'Count Smith Shuffle', 'Goodies' Boogie', 'On Beat Street', and so on. Interestingly, the original cool operator Tom the Great Sebastian never scratched the names off his records. While this had much to do with his obsession with keeping his things neat, that he never felt the need for such subterfuge is a mark of by how much sound-system competition had escalated in the 1950s.

This unorthodox importation carried on until the second half of the decade, when, as styles changed in America and R&B was smoothing itself out and jump jive omosed into rock 'n' roll, the supply lines of the big beat started to run dry. Jamaican radio, continuing to model itself on the powerful Southern American stations that could be picked up in the island, followed the US trend by playlisting the Memphis Sound, interspersed with Jim Reeves, Bing Crosby and Frank Sinatra. In what proved to be a split between the establishment radio stations and the preferences of the people that lasted for twenty years, the sound systems opted to, as they saw it, stay black and keep the tempo hot – although, curiously, Elvis's 'Now or Never' was a huge hit in the dancehalls.

It's been much reported that Jamaican dancehall crowds failed to identify with rock 'n' roll because (a) the artists were mostly white and (b) they couldn't come to grips with the new style's dance steps. In truth, it's highly unlikely that radio listeners or sound-system patrons would have known what colour a singer was – for years in the States black artists didn't have their pictures on record sleeves so as not to put off white buyers. And as for the dances being too difficult . . . these are people who could throw each other around with that rare combination of abandon and precision while tearing it up to Louis Jordan and the Tympani Five. Ask anybody who was on the scene at that time and they'll tell you that the real reason for the rejection of rock 'n' roll was, pure and simple, that Buddy Holly, Jerry Lee Lewis and Co. just weren't exciting enough.

For a couple of years the sound-system operators managed to keep the funk flowing simply by digging up existing stocks of old US records from second-hand emporiums, warehouses and (increasingly) out-of-the-way shops. But that was never going to last for ever. Eventually, Jamaican buyers were going to have to look elsewhere. And as things turned out, this would be no further than their own back yard.

By the mid-1950s it seemed as if every Kingstonian youth was a singer. While the sound men had been concentrating on bringing music in from *a foreign*, in the city's theatres Amateur Hour had been flourishing as regular talent contests took place at the Ambassador, the Palace, the Ward and the Majestic. These venues were enormous stuccoed wedding cakes of buildings, hangovers from the glory days of colonialism, and were built gin-palace splendid inside, recreating the gilt and plush of vintage Shaftsbury Avenue for the plantation owners and their wives. Yet by this stage in Kingston's history shifting demographics had left them in the heart of the ghetto.

These talent-show events were the knock-on effect of the sound systems' bringing of music to the masses, the tangible manifestations of 'wanting to do something to contribute to it' as Derrick Harriott stated earlier. Thanks to this generation consumed by music and sufficiently inspired to try and better themselves through it, there was a continuous supply of starry-eyed young hopefuls for the amateur bills. Most were still at school, and some were so small that any stage manager worth his job kept a stout wooden crate on hand to place before the microphone. In theory, these shows were variety events open to the spectrum of performing talent, but in reality they were strictly singing affairs, as not only was that the most glamorous thing to do, but in practical terms it was the skill every ghetto boy could afford to develop and thus visualize a career in. The contest's promoter would organize a band, so all the contestant had to do was turn up and sing. To a man (well brought-up Jamaican girls were unlikely to enter anything as unladylike as a talent contest) they would imitate the cooler US R&B that dominated the airwaves. And, equally unanimously, they wanted to get on the Vere Johns Opportunity Hour.

Of the dozens of amateur talent contests, theatre concerts and radio shows that took place in Kingston every week, Vere Johns' were the top. He was the Don Dada of this arena. No two ways about it: he was, even when compared with the big sound-system operators, the most influential man in Jamaican music in the second half of the 1950s. He wrote a weekly column in Jamaica's *Star* newspaper, articles that discussed music more than anything else, and thus could do a great deal for a singer's career. His shows were the ones the winners of the lesser events aspired to – in fact Vere Johns' Boxing Day and New Year concerts at the Carib theatre were probably the biggest shows in Kingston. Later he began broadcasting amateur showcase events on JBC as *The Vere Johns Radio Show Opportunity Knocks*, an event which was guaranteed to get you noticed. The only way for an act to get on was to have made a favourable impression in one of his theatre shows, which wasn't, perhaps, as straightforward as it might seem. No matter how much talent you may have possessed.

Vere Johns' Wednesday night shows were seriously downtown affairs, the highlight of many a ghetto-dweller's week, and with the price of admission being under a shilling very few were excluded. Which meant that the audience regarded the shows as participatory sport. A blood sport. They were keen to get stuck in, too. The concerts started at eight o'clock but the doors would open prompt at six, to let in guys that had been queuing up since four or five that afternoon. While these contestant-eating, confidence-destroying spectators didn't actually come with a government health warning, to give some idea of what an already almost pants-wettingly nervous, twelve-year-old Sam Cooke wannabe had to face – or should that be 'face down' – think of Christians and particularly pissed-off lions. A general rule of thumb was that if a singer wasn't cutting it by the end of the first verse, the collective kissing of teeth could drown out the chorus. A moment or so later, the deeply personal heckling would begin.

There were ten acts on each Vere Johns bill – singers, dancers, comedians, trick cyclists . . . everything together with no separate categories – and winning was judged purely on the audience response to each contestant as they came out to take a bow at the end of the show. But this is Jamaica, where resourcefulness goes with the territory, so success had its price. Quite literally. Competitors would round up as many of their friends as possible, paying all admission costs on the understanding that they would act as cheerleaders when it came to voting for them (and would roundly boo everybody else, of course). Supplementary to this were the rent-a-crowds who hung about outside prior to showtime offering their services as freelance supporters, for a cash payment up front. Unsurprisingly, their evening's earnings would be maximized by flogging this 'unswerving loyalty' to every performer on the bill. It was not unusual for winning acts to leave the theatre to find themselves surrounded by young toughs who claimed to have cheered them on to victory, and were thus demanding a percentage of the prize. Derrick Harriott remembers how the first time he got in the money at a Vere Johns contest he had to pay out almost half of his two pounds second prize to people he was sure he'd never seen before.

Coming first or second also meant that you were invited back to compete in the next round, probably the following week, then on through the quarter- and semi-finals to a grand final. And the ride wasn't about to get any smoother as an act progressed. Indeed, it was a general rule of thumb that the higher the round the more demanding the audience. To the naturally hard-to-impress Kingstonians successful acts were seen as would-be stars, who probably *t'ink how dey sweet*, and who thus became escalatingly deserving targets. Also, it was more or less *de rigueur* for beaten contestants to turn up at later rounds to boo with gusto in a bid to extract revenge on whoever it was did get through. The competition was never softer than stiff, either, as the Vere Johns Opportunity Hour standards were astonishingly high. This was simply the law of averages, since the number of entrants from the overcrowded music-crazy local community was always enormous; then, once the radio spread the word beyond the capital, these figures multiplied as kids made the trek in from the country to try their luck. And only the very best got past the weekly auditions.

To come back round after round and win a final was truly a mark not only of talent but of perseverance and self-confidence. As well as Derrick Harriott, such giants of Jamaican music as Bob Andy, Desmond Dekker, the Wailers, Alton Ellis, Lascelles Perkins, Jackie Edwards (when he was still Wilfred Edwards), Dobby Dobson, John Holt, Laurel Aitken and Boris Gardiner can all claim the Vere Johns Opportunity Hour as their *alma mater*. Talk to anybody who remembers those shows and they'll paraphrase Frank Sinatra to tell you, 'If you made it on Vere Johns you could make it anywhere. You'd really made it.'

Although everybody who so much as stepped up to a mic had a dream of singing their way out of the poverty trap, under such circumstances it was still pretty much that – a dream. There could be no realistic plan or route to riches, as any prospects beyond the few pounds prize money were virtually non-existent. There was nothing resembling a record business in Jamaica in the mid-1950s, so the most a successful act could aim for was a spot singing at a local club such as the Shady Grove Club, Johnson's Drive-In or the Glass Bucket – venues which, if they paid at all, didn't pay very much.

However, some pretty major changes were about to take place.

2

Music Is My Occupation

Recording facilities capable of cutting an acetate disc, or 'soft wax', direct from a single-track input had existed in Kingston since the middle of the 1940s. These were studios which, in the technological sophistication stakes, were rivalled only by those old make-your-own-record booths that used to be found on the platforms of larger British railway stations. Indeed, to call them 'studios' is flattering to deceive – disc recorders were operated from front rooms, side rooms of shops, nightclubs . . . anywhere the entrepreneur had a bit of space. Artists would perform into one monaural mic, while the engineer/owner's job was to wind the equipment up by hand or, if it was electrically powered, switch it on. He'd then place the needle (or 'drop the biscuit' as it was known back then) on to the blank spinning acetate disc, nod to the performers to begin, watch the needle cut its spiral groove, then nod again just before it hit the centre of the disc and the performers had to finish. The engineer would then stop the turntable and remove the disc. Sometimes, before he handed over the finished article, he'd put it in a cardboard sleeve. Most of the time, though, he wouldn't.

The Kingston radio stations had such studios specifically to record local bands for their own broadcast use, and the two most important commercial operators were Stanley Motta, a true original sound-system owner and electrical goods store proprietor, who was down on Harbour Street, and Ken Khouri, who had a set-up that changed locations almost as often as it changed names. In the beginning only vocalizing was recorded, but by the end of the decade music – particularly calypso or the mento that Motta specialized in – was just as popular.

Neither was the idea of manufacturing records for sale a complete non-starter. Not quite, anyway, as there was the smallest amount of local demand. The tourist trade was growing, and calypso or mento platters had become an almost regulation souvenir of a holiday spent on the island, with spoken-word recordings of Jamaican history or folk tales proving a popular alternative. Plus there were domestic orders for both calypso and homegrown jazz, as a supplement to the American records on the island's juke boxes. But at this point any record business – as opposed to *recording* business – was little more than a cottage industry, because in every case the numbers of copies of each record needed were tiny. There were never more than a couple of hundred per issue, because there simply weren't enough phonographs on the island to warrant any kind of mass production. And so many of what there were would be found in upper-class homes where imported culture held sway over the indigenous variety. Anyway, even if the demand had been there, no mastering facilities (cutting of the metal stamper necessary to press large quantities of any disc) existed on the island. Production of locally originated material was limited to 78 rpm shellacs knocked out on primitive disc-to-disc copying equipment or by one of the island's few hand-operated record presses that utilized none-too-durable resin-based stampers formed from the original disc.

By the beginning of the 1950s, however, the industry was beginning to modernize, relatively speaking. In the post-war years, as pretty much every area of the American economy grew, the large US record companies looked to expand into the Caribbean and began striking licensing deals with existing Jamaican record companies for the release of their product. Companies such as Records Limited, the operation Ken Khouri set up with his brother Richard, that secured a contract with Mercury Records. When Ken originally bought his second-hand recording equipment in 1949 he installed it at his house, but he soon became fed up with people turning up at all hours to sing songs, and moved it to a nightclub in St Andrew. That, however, took him away from many potential customers, so he relocated once more to his furniture store on King Street and launched the Times record label (his store was Times Furniture). By 1954, already fully appreciative of the money to be made from manufacturing and selling records, he had imported two record presses from America, upgraded his recording equipment and all but closed the furniture side of things to go into partnership with his brother.

At this time, however, owing to the continuing lack of mastering facilities, this was a situation geared more towards selling larger quantities of American records as the licensors would provide a metal master for the licensees' presses. Domestic recordings would have to be sent to Miami, New York or London for mastering, a lengthy, costly and risky procedure – acetates or finished masters were frequently damaged in transit, while nearly as many were lost at sea. Stanley Motta took this one stage further. He had switched to electric recording equipment at the start of the decade and his MRS (Motta Recording Studio) label had become a market leader in mento recordings, which he would have pressed in London, then shipped back to Jamaica.

Although Kingston's vibrant dancehall scene was virtually on their doorsteps in the mid-1950s, it's no surprise there were no dealings between the studio owners and sound-system operators. The guys who ran these recording set-ups were businessmen first and foremost, never happier than when turning a guaranteed profit; thus, experimentation or taking risks in order to advance the music and expand the industry couldn't be further from their game plan. It was unusual for them to offer any form of creative input; in fact, their notion of 'producing records' took the term more or less literally, concerning itself with manufacturing discs as commodities to be traded. In spite of the Khouris proving sympathetic to and supportive of the ghetto guys' efforts and Motta devoting time and effort to the marketing of mento abroad, men like them were never going to be part of the shifting cultural development of an indigenous black Jamaican music. Simply because, unlike the sound-system barons, they were uptown men and it wouldn't have made sense. Motta even operated a door policy to restrict usage of his studios.

At this point, you can be sure the studio-owners' take on ghetto music was that it was worthless – both literally and figuratively. They felt they were getting the best end of a deal by hiring their facilities to practically anybody who would pay a pound or so to record a two-and-a-half-minute side.

Actually this was a situation that suited the more enterprising of Kingston's talent-show stars just fine. They flocked to studios such as Motta's and the Khouris'; the prices they paid included a piano-player, or perhaps even a trio, as backing, and were per-acetate cut, finished product which then became the property of whoever put their hand in their pocket to pay the studio owner. In short, it left the artists in charge of their own work. And actually being *part* of the ghetto scene, these slick kids knew exactly the potential profit in these 'slates' or 'plates'. They were lawn-dance patrons, and were therefore well aware of the sound men's constant quest for original music. They knew exactly how their proven crowd-pleasing abilities could be used to maximize both status and profit.

Successful talent-show singers would invest some of their winnings in recording their finest material, then hawk the acetate around the small sound systems in their area looking for the best price. Any bartering would normally take place at a dance so the disc on offer could be road-tested on the spot. If it moved the crowd, the artist could expect five pounds or so for it; if it didn't, he'd be wise to go home and hide until people in his area forgot the shaming experience. Once the sale had been made, the dancers' continued reaction to the tune would set the price for that artist's next disc. And you could guarantee there'd be a next one, as a large proportion of any money made would be reinvested in studio time. Just as soon as this new star had finished telling anyone who'd listen, '*Is mi dat, pon de hi-fi!*'

It's vital to remember that only as an absolute last resort

would any sound man – however small his set – buy records from a regular retail outlet. Because the entire town could do exactly the same, it was as good as wearing a hat with 'Loser' written on it, therefore these transactions were possibly more important to those sound men than they were to the singers. Until the talent-show winners started recording themselves, the small sound systems would be left to buy the imported records that the big ones didn't want. Now, because each of these DIY cuts was a one-off, this slates-for-sale circuit was of enormous value to the small-timers as it represented the only way the second- and third-division systems could spin some unique music. Which they had to if they were ever to harbour thoughts of promotion to the Premiership.

It's one more of Jamaica's class-orientated ironies that this sole chance the small systems had of getting any sort of drop on the major players was because of the latter's innate snobbery. Even though the sound systems were exclusive to the ghetto, within it there was a clear-cut pecking order and, in keeping with the national lack of respect for anything homegrown, the successful operators were obliged to look down their noses at these entirely original Kingston cuts. Down in the dancehalls the hierarchy dictated that once an operator had gone large he became far too important to bother with local boys and must buy his tunes abroad. So, even though this potentially limitless, already proven popular – Vere Johns winners always became local celebrities – source of crisp recorded material was so obviously on their doorsteps the big boys were never going to bother looking for it.

In spite of this, teenage singers touting their wares became a vital part of the grassroots sound-system industry. It was also the last time for many years that performers themselves would be in sole control of their own work, from an artistic or a business point of view. And things might even have continued along those lines indefinitely, but as the 1950s came to an end the sound-system scene stepped up a gear. The next generation of operators was falling into place.

*

The second wave of sound men were mostly young guys, still in or barely out of their teens, who had grown up with the notion that dances held by these bone-shaking musical set-ups were an essential part of Kingston's social scene. Which meant, unlike their predecessors, instead of having to work to establish the concept among the public, or even work out how to use it to their best advantage, they could concentrate their efforts on refining and maximizing the considerable potential of the sound system as both a social and commercial event.

Three men who came up as part of this new wave were Duke Reid, Clement Dodd and Prince Buster, a trio who didn't so much flip the script as put a match to it and watch it burn. Almost immediately Reid's and Dodd's became the only operations that counted for anything, with Buster hot on their heels both chronologically and status-wise. Collectively and individually, these three men were more responsible than anybody else for plotting the path of Jamaican popular music.

Clement Dodd's fascination with sound systems had been longstanding. He was an avid jazz fan and his ambition since he was a boy was to run his own set. He'd bring his collection of Charlie Parker, Coleman Hawkins, Fats Navarro and Dizzy Gillespie records down to his mother's liquor store on the corner of Beston Street and Love Lane, where he'd play them for patrons on a standard phonograph with a big extension speaker. (In the West Indies, liquor stores are far closer to British pubs or American bars than they are to off-licences – many sell food, come complete with seating arrangements and much of the booze that is bought is consumed on or just outside the premises.) It was then, as far back as the early 1950s when he entertained his mother's customers, that Dodd began building his reputation for knowing music, and although his mother made him learn a trade – carpentry – a professional involvement in music was only a matter of time.

Almost perversely, it was the 'proper jobs' his mum made him get that became his passport to what many would assume to be a misspent youth. While checking out the larger local dances as an enthusiastic punter his carpentry skills put him in demand building speaker cabinets. Then, like so many young Jamaican men of his generation, regardless of their having a skilled trade, he took the more lucrative option of short-term cane-cutting jobs in the USA. It was on these sojourns that sound men would have him bring back pieces of equipment, with several sufficiently trusting his ears to let him shop for records for them. Naturally it didn't take Clement Dodd too long to figure out that he really ought to be doing this for himself. After a few more trips to buy what he needed, Dodd set about building Sir Coxsone's Downbeat – Coxsone was a celebrated post-war Yorkshire cricketer, and Dodd had earned his nickname in his younger days thanks to his prowess on the oval field.

Initially, he played more jazz than anything else, but he made an immediate impact as his innate sense of showmanship and shrewd marketing brain saw him present new records as a visual as well as an aural experience. Dodd's partner in the sound was his best friend, Blackie, a talented hoofer who would conceive a flashy new dance step to go with each new disc, and which he and Dodd would perform in perfect tandem the first few times the tune was spun. With the relationship between a sound-system deejay and his crowd being the proactive bond it was, this was guaranteed to please – if there was a chance for an audience to be shown how to drop some stylish new foot, it gave them one over other systems' crowds. Downbeat followers looked forward to doing the dances as much as they did to hearing the cuts and it quickly made Dodd's name.

This was, of course, only half the story. Though the sound of his system made sure he stayed clear of the pack – according to his followers of the day it was the undisputed boss when it came to tonal range and sheer power – it was his often daring choice of tunes that made the real difference. So natural was his feel for music, his record box was always the most interestingly stocked and he could step outside the expected R&B/jump-jive boundaries to deliver a kicking bebop jazz cut or deep blues number without his crowd missing so much as a beat.

Arthur 'Duke' Reid was an entirely different matter. Older

than Dodd and Buster – he was a friend of Coxsone's parents – he was a former West Kingston policeman whose wife had won a large enough sum on Jamaica's national lottery to afford him a career with a longer life-expectancy, and in the early 1950s the couple opened the Treasure Isle liquor store in the same tough downtown area he had patrolled for ten years. An astute businessman, Reid promoted the store by sponsoring the R&B radio show *Treasure Isle Time* (by now, as a result of public pressure, RJR was acknowledging a wider audience), but as an unabashed music fan and a charismatic natural performer he fronted the programme himself. From his theme song of Tab Smith's 'My Mother's Eyes' through the show's entire playlist, the Duke proved himself not only to 'have ears' but also to be in touch with what it was the ghetto people wanted. Thus, *Treasure Isle Time* was an instant and huge success, a position from which it was a very short step to the sound system Duke Reid the Trojan (apparently named after the model of Bedford truck he used to haul his gear around, although those who knew him at the time admit the handle was selected as much for its allusion to invincibility: quite literally a physical invincibility).

Reid set up on the corner of Pink Lane and Beeston Street, soon moving to Bond Street and Charles Street. His days on the beat had left him with as many underworld contacts as the highest-ranking villain, and from among them he put together a gang of both men and women. They were there, he main-tained, for his protection as he claimed he'd made so many enemies as a policeman that his life was permanently under threat, but really it was anybody else's set who needed protec-tion from this crew. Their main function was one of aggression, storming rivals' lawns punching, stabbing and kicking indis-criminately, frightening off the crowd and aiming to get to the rig and cut wires, smash amplifiers, hack at speaker boxes and upend turntables. Maybe even snatch the box of records.

Forty years after the event, Prince Buster will show you exactly how far Trojan and Downbeat took their rivalry by removing his hat, taking one of your hands and rubbing it along the half-inch ridge on top of his skull. It's a souvenir of his days working for Coxsone, where the plates never quite knitted together properly after one of Duke Reid's bad men laid him out with a rock at a Downbeat dance. In the face of such organized aggression, even the far milder-mannered Dodd was forced to go armed, while Buster and Lee Perry, another Downbeat employee of the day but strictly on the creative side, frequently found themselves the last line of defence between Reid's gang and Coxsone's gear.

By then – the mid- to late 1950s – the sound-system scene was no longer just a bunch of guys exploring a new way of doing things, and therefore essentially all on the same side. At this point nobody was in any doubt of their earning or status potential and competition was increasingly intense, with none taking it more seriously than Duke Reid. The accepted term was to 'flop' a rival's dance, by pulling such a crowd on the same night that the other sound-system lawn was empty, and at sound clash you'd *mash up*, *batter* or straight up *murrrdah* the other system with wicked music or devastating volume. When Trojan came on the scene, however, rivalries escalated as the Duke was determined to give such colloquialisms altogether more sinister, dictionary-definition-type meanings. Indeed, Buster is remarkably generous in his description of his then-boss's arch rival: 'Basically, he was an OK guy – a very talented man – he just got carried away with what was going on at the time.'

Carried away to such a degree, it's safe to say, that any culture of violence associated with Kingston's downtown dancehalls can be traced back to those days and pretty much to Duke Reid himself. A large, physically intimidating man, he had not survived a decade as a ghetto cop without a pretty heavy reputation – it was accepted that the only way to keep order downtown was to be badder than the baddest the ghetto had to offer. It was how he kept his liquor store safe from robbery and burglary, and he was now bringing all this to bear on his new way of life. As Trojan's reputation grew, Reid took to turning up at the dance resplendent in an enormous fake-jewelled coronet and 'ermine'-trimmed red cape, while at bigger events he'd have his crew carry him in shoulder-high, sitting up proud on a huge thronelike chair. This was the sort of showboating that was in any good sound man's repertoire. And it was fun. Less amusing, though, was the brace of flashy nickel-plated revolvers he wore in Western-style belt holsters, which would be fetchingly accessorized by cross bandoliers of bullets. Frequently there'd be a rifle or a shotgun tucked nonchalantly under one arm. He'd be firing into the air to announce his arrival, and, according to more than one of his former crowd, there were times when he'd be toying casually with a live hand-grenade.

Whether he ever shot anybody is not a matter of record, but nobody can ever recall seeing Duke Reid without at least two guns close to hand and, having won sharpshooting medals as a policeman, he was never afraid to loose off a few well-placed rounds to emphasize points. At sound clashes he was much given to firing into rivals' equipment as a way of disrupting their performance. Then, if all else failed, there were always the terrifying men and women that were the Duke's 'security'.

It was precisely this climate of intimidation that had brought the teenage Cecil Campbell, aka Prince Buster, into the sound-system world in the first place. He was a handy amateur boxer – taught by such Jamaican greats as Speedy Baker and Kid Chocolate – and never one to shirk a confrontational challenge despite his lack of both years and inches. His introduction to Coxsone happened when Buster, knife in hand, was in hot pursuit of one of Duke Reid's more notorious henchmen through the streets to settle a gambling dispute: the sound man, walking with his deejay Count Machuki, saw the chase, exclaimed Buster was exactly the sort of man he needed and asked for an introduction. For the next few years Buster, or 'Wild Bill' as Machuki called him, became an integral part of the Downbeat operation. He tells it thus:

'At that time Duke Reid control these people from Salt Lane and Back-A-Wall and have them defending him – they were criminals who he knew from their criminal activities when he was a policeman. He used to send them to go round and break up Coxsone's sound system. They'd already used force to run

Tom the Great Sebastian out of Beat Street, and Coxsone was dreading them.

'I grew up with those same people who was mashing up the sound systems because, as a yout', I was always in Back-A-Wall and Dungle following the sounds and [Count] Ossie's things. So I wasn't afraid of them – I was one of a smaller-age gang who were always defiant to them. We had regular conflicts. I knew what was happening at the dances, but because I and Coxsone wasn't really no friends, it didn't interest me. Until Count Machuki, who I knew from my corner of Luke Lane and Charles Street, came to me, and after that I made sure those men left Coxsone alone. At that time I had access to weapons, so they dread me even more. Me and my spars we bar people from the dances, the trouble makers and those that t'ief him, and we make sure all the gate money got back to Coxsone. And people start to come because they knew there was going to be no more trouble wherever Coxsone was playing.

'Coxsone and I became a pair, because anywhere he wanted to go I took him. Although he could front his sound system in the early days, in reality he is a timid person – he'll admit that. I did a lot for Coxsone, a whole lot.'

What he did extended past this role as a minder, to playing a large part in keeping Downbeat at the top. After years of immersing himself in the music being played in West Kingston, Buster had developed such an acute ear for American R&B that he and Dodd would join the crowd outside other sounds' dances, and purely by listening, Buster would identify the tunes being played:

'Duke Reid's liquor business was big, he have trucks and everything, he have much more money than Coxsone to go to America and buy records, so when he come back with a new batch we would go outside his dance so we could listen. Because I'd studied the artistry of the rhythm and blues players so much, as Duke play a tune I could tell Coxsone who it was, who produce it and therefore what label it was on. By listening to the lyric it wasn't hard to work out the title, and then he could get his contacts in America to send it to him.

'I was supposed to get five pounds for each tune he finds, because he was rapid bootlegging, making a record popular then get it press up to sell to other sound men – everybody who brought record in to Jamaica did that. But he'd only give me a little bit of money and tell me this not happen or that not happen. It was very frustrating.'

So stifling that Buster opted to go it alone. His likeable personality and eagerness for what he proposed to do proved infectious, and with a combination of a loan from his mother and 'pay me when you can'-type credit, he built a sound system of monumental proportions. In keeping with his populist approach to life, Buster named his sound the Voice of the People and, immediately, the equally dissatisfied Count Machuki defected from Downbeat to join him.

'Before I open on my first night I have to go and play down Salt Lane in Dungle, where Count Ossie and the Rasta camps were. A new sound have to be passed by them, a kind of respect thing, then you know they're going to be on your side. As a little boy it stunned the people as to how the hell I coulda had all this equipment *and the best deejay.* You had other sounds like Count Boysie and Count John, but they were afraid to challenge Duke Reid, so they come with a halfway sound, but I was going to war.

'After that first session, the news of the Voice of the People spread around and Duke Reid's men are telling say "'im shake up Salt Lane". They knew that if I could shake up Salt Lane I would demolish Beat Street.'

And so, at some time during 1958, the Big Two became the Big Three.

The reason that the intimidatory behaviour persisted as part of the sound-system world was because it appeared to be getting results. Thanks to Dodd's superior equipment and innovative record selection, it was commonly accepted that Downbeat was the ranking Kingston sound system, while Buster's ghetto status and infectious sense of fun meant that the Voice of the People was, genuinely, the people's choice. Yet, although Reid's way with his record box cannot be underestimated, it was down to his thuggish tactics that, for the last four years of the decade, he took the title King of Sounds & Blues by winning the biggest annual knockout sound-clash competition.

Unsurprisingly, such organized violence led to a reciprocal situation among the crowds, as supporters would react ferociously to anything they perceived as being either an attack on or merely disrespect to their system of choice. Sometimes even cheering a rival system could be taken as such. And while sound clashes became escalatingly unpleasant, matters in general were made worse by the police using dances – whether they erupted into violence or not – as an excuse to harass ghetto folk. Kingston's Finest would enthusiastically break events up, often trashing or confiscating equipment, on the grounds that such gatherings represented a threat to public order, but their actions were little more than straightforward politically motivated intimidation. It was a clampdown that came in the wake of the minor industrial unrest that occurred in 1956, and was designed to keep the sufferahs under the heel of authorities determined to avoid any repetition of the events of 1938. Then, in the midst of a nationwide economic depression, Jamaica teetered on the brink of a civil war as strikes and demonstrations escalated into widespread rioting and disturbances and pitched battles between the people and the authorities, leaving many fatalities.

To the uninitiated it must appear remarkable that grown men could get so worked up that they'd go to war for what is, after all, no more than playing records, even in the light of the sound systems' earning potential. Or it probably seems downright unbelievable that other grown-ups, with no fiscal involvement in any set, took what deejay they listened to so seriously as to do or suffer physical harm for them. But it shouldn't be forgotten that during this period, in the almost paralysing poverty of the ghettos, there was so very little to get excited about, and certainly nothing that genuinely belonged to the people in the way the sound-system dances did. Indeed, even though the actual music at the heart of this phenomenon was shipped in from abroad, the unique presentation was strictly homegrown.

In modern Jamaican history, it was the first widespread – almost formalized – mainstream cultural occurrence among what had become the indigenous population. Such is the effect of prolonged marginalization – and it didn't come much more prolonged or marginalized than three hundred years of slavery and a century more of colonization – that anything created outside the boundaries of regular society will always be cleaved to with the tightest embrace by those responsible. In this case, the sufferahs of Kingston's gullies.

By engendering both a popular sense of style and a measure of economic independence, the sound men assumed positions of unrivalled glamour to become the ghettos' first overground heroes. Like the big-time pimps and dope barons who became the unofficial mayors of so many US black communities, the sound men were godfathers of their ghettos – financial aid, legal assistance, advice in general, keepers of order. They were superstars elevated out of the squalor of the shanties, psychologically if not literally. So it's not hard to understand why so many were prepared to go to such extremes to maintain their status, while the youth, at last having something highly accessible to believe in, to aspire to and participate in, were liable to be swept along. In many ways it isn't too surprising that rational behaviour occasionally took a back seat.

All of which proved far too much for many of the old-timers: Tom the Great Sebastian, for example. Maybe this original bigshot operator felt that under this new set of circumstances he would never be judged better than the number two sound man ever again, or perhaps it was after one more visit by Reid's team, but around this time he packed up from his longtime base at the corner of Luke Lane and Charles Street. Tom moved to the comparatively suburban Cross Roads and a residence at the Silver Slipper Club, where he found he was able to make a much better living in this far more uptown environment. Which isn't all that remarkable either: a result of the continued 1950s exodus from the worst ghettos, with those who left taking their newly established culture with them. This is also a vivid illustration of how roughness was never more than a sidebar to

Jamaican music – a result of unfortunate circumstances and not, as so many outsiders have found it easy to imagine, a vital ingredient. The fact that Tom the Great Sebastian was now attracting the biggest, most free-spending crowds of his career at his new no-trouble locale points to there being an enormous amount of people who just wanted to get happy at a dance.

The simple, often-overlooked truth was that the real spirit of mad competition concerned itself with the rigs and the records, and once men like Reid, Coxsone and Buster were at the controls dances became bigger. In every way.

By this point, the scope and quality of equipment seemed to advance on a weekly basis. Wonards Radio Engineering on Church Street was the only place for a sound man to shop. It was run by the Wongs, a Chinese–Jamaican husband-and-wife team, who had effectively taken over from Headley Jones, an RAF-trained radio engineer who, upon returning home after the war, turned his skills to fitting-out recording studios for the radio station and building sound-system equipment for such originals as Tom the Great Sebastian and Sir Nick. It is Jones who is credited with putting together Jamaica's first portable amplifiers that could split the high and low frequencies by means of rudimentary tone controls. But it was now the Wongs, who were importing ready-built units as well as components from the USA and the UK, who became first choice as this cut down the cost while offering a mix of up-to-the-minute technology and reliable old favourites. Goodmans 18-inchers were the bass speakers of choice, married to 15-inch Vitavoxes, Warriors and Eagle tweeters. But for those with a real sense of occasion the only amplifiers worth bothering with were made by a Mr Morrison. Morrison amps were custom built and would be used in tandem or triplicate so as to achieve the required volume without ever putting the valves under strain. A three-decker Morrison amplifier, such as Prince Buster used, was an object of almost iconic proportions.

Although tone controls at this time were still pretty basic, how you manipulated them counted a great deal. An operator had to be inventive and resourceful as far as added SFX went, and anything that gave a sound man the drop on his rivals would be seized upon. There's a well-worn story of an unnamed sound man going into a marine equipment dealership in Miami and trying to buy the type of loudspeaker that ocean-going liners would use to herald their approach in foggy conditions. When the astounded salesman had come to terms with the idea that this decidedly un-nautical customer wanted to use it to play records, the nonplussed Jamaican had but one question: '*It tek two t'ousand watts?*'

Yet still sound-system supremacy was first and foremost about the records, and the falling supply of bottom-kicking American R&B was becoming woefully inadequate in terms of Kingston's spiralling demands. The stakes had been raised to a point at which a particular sound's killer tune and its continued exclusivity was now a matter of paranoiac proportions. The tale of 'Later for 'Gator', a US R&B single by the Miami-based tenor sax honker Willis 'Gatortail' Jackson, illustrates perfectly this obsession with musical uniqueness.

Originally released in 1950, it was unearthed by Coxsone some half a dozen years later on one of his Stateside quests for the obscure. As raucous as you like, the instrumental was a natural choice for a theme tune, so after Dodd had obliterated the title and artist details from the label he renamed it 'Coxsone Hop' and would drop the record at his dances when he wanted to raise the temperature by a couple of notches. Knowing this tune to be theirs and theirs alone, the crowd would respond in an appropriately boisterous manner. To spin it at a sound clash was to get up in any other operator's face and, at the very least, question his abilities. This was a situation that persisted for several years, with Duke Reid seething as the unassailability of 'Coxsone Hop' guaranteed a Downbeat victory in practically any contest. To break this stranglehold understandably became something of an obsession, but the only way to do anything about it was to get hold of a copy. Prince Buster, working for Downbeat at the time, was party to the drama's climax.

'Coxsone hold "Coxsone Hop" exclusively for seven years, but Duke Reid was a relentless man and finally found it. It was likely that one of Coxsone's men who knew what the record was really called had told him, and after several trips to America he bought a copy. When Duke came back from that successful trip he put the word out that he had that and several other Downbeat specials – tunes unique to Coxsone. He planned a special dance, at which he said he would bury Coxsone because he was going to play all these tunes, but before he did, to lead up to the big event, he set up his sound system on the street outside his Treasure Isle liquor store and for about a week he played music day in day out. Right through the night, until that Monday night when the dance was going to be. By this time word had spread all over Jamaica that Duke Reid get "Coxsone Hop"! People come in from all over the country and pitch tent, waiting there until Monday night happen. Coxsone was very very worried.

'I told Coxsone I would go to where Duke Reid was to find out if he really have it – only me and Machuki coulda passed there, any other of Coxsone's guys woulda got licks and had to run. But he said "No", like he don't really want to find out. But I went anyway. I went straight to him and ask "Duke, you 'ave it?"

'Duke was sitting there, carrying a big gun, and he hold up his hand full of rings and laugh real deep. He say "Him sen' yuh, eh? Him sen' yuh?" It was very tense, as all of Duke Reid's men were there. And they still dread me inna sense. So I ask Duke to put the tune on the sound that was playing out there and he just laugh again.

'So I ask him straight out what is the name of the tune. And Duke Reid said "Later", kinda like he was saying "See you later". By this time, Coxsone wasn't aware that I knew the name of "Coxsone Hop", so I ask Duke again. Once more him say "Later, Buhk" – my nickname was Buhk. "Tell him, 'later'". Then I know, so when I get back all I can say is "Duke have it. The man have the tune." Coxsone said "What him say?" I said "The Duke said 'Later'", and I watch Coxsone rock back.

'After he close the liquor shop I say we have to go to the

dance. Him say "*What?*" and his mother and father tell him that I was mad and that if he went there they'd kill him. I told him if he didn't go he was finished. We went up there – Jubilee Hall Gardens – at about seven o'clock.

'We walk up King Street *tough*. The dance is packed from early and they have a lot of green bush, cut off tree limbs, leaning up at the side of the gate for when Duke plays the tune and people will run up and down waving them. All of Duke Reid's top men were at the gate, and they just let us in – they don't want no problem there because they're sure they're going to destroy Coxsone tonight. When we come in, somebody get on the mic and say "Guess who's here? Buhk and Coxsone!" We just went to the bar with Phantom, one of Duke's right-hand men, Coxsone buy us all some stout and we wait. After a while Coxsone wanted to go, but I wouldn't let him. We had to wait until they play the tune because any time they play it and we're there the effect will die right away there, but if we'd gone it would go wide.

'So we wait. Then as the clock struck midnight we hear "*Baaap . . . bap da dap da dap, daaaa da daap!*" And we see a bunch of them down from the dancehall coming up with the green bush. I was at the counter with Coxsone, he have a glass in him hand, he drop it and just collapse, sliding down the bar. I had to brace him against the bar, then get Phantom to give me a hand. The psychological impact had knocked him out. Nobody never hit him.

'We hold him up against the bar and try to shut out the noise. Not only they play "Coxsone Hop", but they play seven of Coxsone's top tunes straight. When that happen, you know that tomorrow morning those tune'll be selling in every fried-fish shop. All we could do was wait it out until they stop playing his exclusive tunes, then we went up to where Tom was playing for the rest of the night.'

As competition among the new order of sound men intensified, even the most innate cultural snob couldn't ignore the locally produced music for much longer. The economic aspect was important – after all, how much was ego worth in fiscal terms when rivals could rock their houses just as wildly with equally singular tunes for a fraction of importers' outlay? But the key was the feelgood factor: at last faced with performers they had a real empathy with, crowds embraced records made by local artists with added vigour. After seeing such reactions, the top-ranking sound systems started checking for Jamaican-recorded R&B. But, as if still either slightly suspicious or wanting to keep themselves at arm's length, rather than record it them-selves they'd use the smaller sound systems as an *ad hoc* A&R department. Derrick Harriott remembers how this worked, and in doing so provides a further insight into the spirit of competition between Dodd and Reid.

'I was half of a duo with Claudie Sang – Sang & Harriott – and we went to Stanley Motta's to cut a disc of our original R&B song "Lollipop Girl". This was some time in 1956. We sold the slate to Thunderbird Disco, a sound from the Maxfield Avenue area, and although it was only Claudie playing piano and me singing it mash the place up on a Friday afternoon after-work kinda session. It became such a hit on that sound that frequently the operator would have to lick it back ten times in a row before the people let him take it off. There was a time when it was that one record alone could draw a crowd!

'And so the big guys got to hear about it. One way they'd try to stay ahead of their opposition was to send their scouts round to all the little sound systems – and there were *a lot* in Kingston at that time – to check out what tunes were going down best then buying them up. And the only original tunes the little guys would have were the tunes made by Jamaican guys like Claudie and me. They'd make offers no small operator could afford to turn down. All the big systems used to do it.

'One time Coxsone himself came down, said he'd heard how "Lollipop Girl" was going great and he swapped one of his big exclusive American hits for it – a record the Thunderbird operator could never have got hold of otherwise. For a good little while Coxsone was mashing up the place with our tune. Then he played a sound clash with Duke Reid down on East

Queen Street and "Lollipop Girl" was keeping him on top, until halfway through the night Duke Reid played the tune too. *Coxsone was vexed!* I was told he wanted to know *so bad* how Duke got the record that he pulled a gun on him right there, and Duke pull one back. There was a big fuss that night, which might have got out of hand if the dance hadn't been situated next to the police station. I was told later that one of Coxsone's men had been bribed to take the record and lend it to Duke Reid to make a dub plate from it.'

Once this hoovering up of original Jamaican-recorded music turned the major operators on to the indigenous scene they were quick to latch on to its potential. As if determined to make up for lost time, they hurled themselves into sponsoring their own recording sessions.

Duke Reid was the first big sound man to dip a toe into recording when he began producing his own sessions, in 1957, at the Khouris' recently opened facilities, Federal Record Manufacturing Co. Ltd on Marcus Garvey Drive. Although he wasn't being recorded himself, he went about things in much the same way as the system had always worked: he paid the bills for studio hire and musicians' fees (such as they were), left the players to sort out the musical technicalities then, as the sessions' financier, kept the acetate once it was done. Following on from the purely business-orientated system set in place by the likes of Motta and the Khouris, creative types like Duke Reid established a structure that remained at the core of the Jamaican music industry for years to come. The 'producer' would be the man who sponsored the recording rather than the man who twiddled the knobs – not that there were too many knobs to be twiddled back then – and, as regards copyright, the producer would retain all rights on the finished acetate to do with as he liked. Importantly, it was ownership of that particular recording that counted, not ownership of the material it featured. Once Jamaican music went international in the 1960s and before the country's copyright laws were applied to music in the 1990s, this system was a music publisher's nightmare, as so many songs were versioned (re-recorded) any number of times, and in each case any royalty claims rested with whoever had charge, physically, of a certain set of master tapes. A lot of lawyers are still getting very fat.

The Duke rounded up local musicians from Jamaica's huge pool of big-band jazzers, named them the Duke Reid Group and cut a number of wild instrumental R&B sides. At that time he also re-recorded Sang & Harriott's sound-system smash "Lollipop Girl", because after that East Queen Street sound clash Coxsone abandoned the tune and Reid turned it into his own, spinning the disc so much that he had literally worn his copy out. Now, two years later, he wanted to cut it again, this time with a more sophisticated instrumentation, and would mash up the crowd once more with this new version of an old favourite. Yet another example of exclusivity being more important than up-to-the-minuteness.

Clement Dodd and Prince Buster had followed Reid into the studio. By the end of that same year Coxsone was in the studio kicking jazz, R&B and a fusion of the two with local artists such as Cluett J and his Blues Blasters – possibly the most storming dance band in Jamaica at the time – Alton Ellis and Basil Gabbidon. Buster's sessions were lower key, but, as time was soon to tell, they were by far the most experimental.

Originally, the Big Three and the many other sound-men-turned-record-producers were cutting discs exclusively for their own sound systems. Such was the introversion of their world that it simply didn't occur to them that anyone except another sound man would be interested in these recordings. There were examples of a commercial record trade growing out of this music mania as early as 1958, but, typically, it was uptown types with no connection to the sound systems who were exploiting this distinctly sufferah state of affairs.

The two most noteworthy were also the first two non-sound-owning producers. One was a white, planter-class-wealthy, Jamaican-born Old Harrovian named Chris Blackwell, whose year-old label, R&B, snapped up Laurel Aitken as its first Jamaican signing. The other was Edward Seaga, a Harvard-educated anthropologist and aspiring politician who recorded

Owen Gray, Joe Higgs, Manny Wilson, Slim Smith and Jackie Edwards on his W.I.R.L. (West Indies Records Limited) label.

Blackwell had arrived at ghetto music after getting stranded on a reef, falling unconscious and being rescued by a group of Rasta fishermen, who tended to his sunburn and dehydration. This was a time when white people's apprehension at the sight of dreadlocks would be almost a given – it wasn't unusual for upper- and middle-class Jamaican parents of all races to scare their children with talk of Rasta as the bogey man – but the incident convinced the twenty-year-old Blackwell that they were nothing to be afraid of. He vowed to promote sufferah culture to the rest of the world, so that as many people as possible might come to terms with ghetto people the way he had. Although for his first recordings he used a white Canadian band to back Laurel Aitken, who sounded as American as possible, that is exactly the sort of US-wannabe style which was doing so well on the sound systems.

Edward Seaga, who was of Syrian descent, had a genuine interest in black Jamaican culture through his post-graduate study of the barely-evolved-from-the-original African religion Pocomania and its music, which was known as Kuminia. In 1956 he recorded an album of historically indigenous black Jamaican music. For several years this up-and-coming politico wanted to present the ghetto folk with the opportunity to make music, and as his agenda changed this CV did him no harm at all, as the crowded downtown constituencies held a lot of votes and so were proving increasingly important come election time. It was taken as read that the best way to reach the people was with the right beat, but as a record producer with his office and record label based at Cho Co Mo Lawn he was right in there with the artists, the studio owners and the sound-system operators. That, in turn, would put him in with just about anybody else who counted.

Edward Seaga had little obvious involvement with music after the mid-1960s when he sold W.I.R.L. to Byron Lee, but by then his political career had taken off. Seaga had built a strong powerbase for himself in the Jamaican Labour Party as he gained an enormous reputation by holding the constituency of West Kingston since 1959 – it was an area so volatile that candidates weren't expected to last, and few wanted to because of its manifest social problems. Seaga's clout, as he became entrenched in the impenetrable ghetto neighbourhood, was such that he became leader of the JLP in 1970 and Prime Minister in 1980.

Whatever their underlying motivations, it's unlikely that such big shots would have come near ghetto music unless they were certain that a payday was involved. But in spite of the evidence that music could earn on a grand scale, the black Jamaican psyche is such that it's understandable that Coxsone burst out laughing when, in 1959, somebody casually mentioned to him that his recordings had a value way beyond the Downbeat sound system. To his enormous credit, he was open-minded enough to allow himself to be talked into having a couple of hundred copies of whatever was his current hot property pressed up to pass on to this apparent entrepreneur.

They sold out in a matter of days. No mean feat considering that, at the time, there were very few dedicated record shops and even fewer that would have bothered with indigenous product. Sales were made door to door, at commercial establishments and people's houses with the vendor talking up the record as Downbeat's latest killer tune – *Yuh know, the one 'im mash up the dance wid last night* – and the punters taking this on trust as there was no information printed on the label. The off-loading of product in this way immediately set a method for Jamaican record sales that endured long after every producer who'd had so much as a minor hit established his own shop – it still survives, in fact – in which a sales force armed with stout shoes, suitcase or a holdall and boundless enthusiasm was as vital as your bass-line. Otherwise, in those early days, producers sold their records at the lawn dances, offering up 'limited' numbers of whatever discs were seriously moving the crowd. The notion of limited should be taken with a pinch of salt here, as although that was how the records for sale would be introduced, pressings were usually only ever limited to how many the sound man could sell.

And sell they did: to nightclub owners, to other sound men, to jukebox companies and lastly, but by no means leastly, to the general public. Such was the relative prosperity of a significant number of the Jamaican working classes by the end of the 1950s that imported electrical consumer goods had crept into a considerable percentage of homes. The centrepiece of appropriate status in any made-it-out-of-Jones-Town family's front room was a substantial, freestanding polished hardwood Philips radiogram. This was a top-shelf imported item, but less-expensive mass-produced record players were making inroads downtown. And all gramophone owners were equally eager for something to play.

A solid gold commercial opportunity. Immediately, Coxsone started the All Stars and Worldisc record labels, and began block-booking recording sessions to meet the public demand for product. Likewise Prince Buster who, in 1960, formed the Voice of the People record label to complement his sound system, and Duke Reid with the Treasure Isle imprint. Curiously, after a few months and such storming releases as 'Duke's Cookies', 'What Makes Honey' and 'Joker', Reid got out of the business of selling records. It was remarkable that such a usually shrewd operator, with an enormous inbuilt audience, elected to miss out on the lucrative first couple of years of this record-sales boom. Maybe he was earning enough from dances and his liquor retail business; or maybe he couldn't see further than how things had been up until then and didn't view selling records as being in any way beneficial to his existing business; or perhaps he just didn't think it would catch on. Back then nobody seemed to be able to explain why the Duke refused to take it seriously, but while he didn't, tiny record labels sprang up all over town.

One of the much misrepresented characters in this initial record business boom is recording-studio/record-factory owner Ken Khouri. He is frequently painted as a sort of uptown robber baron exploiting an underclass who just wanted to make music, but if it hadn't been for Khouri, his brother Richard and Federal, which was now a music factory with everything from recording to label printing to high-capacity presses (except mastering, which he could organize for you) in the same building, this new industry would probably have been stillborn. Ken Khouri was always going to be a central figure: anyone who had a tune in his head could come to Ken to record it on acetate, then either come back with a master or wait for Federal to get one, and get pressed up whatever he thought he could sell. But more than this, he was the one vital ingredient in the record business's passage of power from types like Seaga and Blackwell to Buster and Dodd.

Unlike his initial rivals, he actively courted the sound men, going to find them at the lawns, cutting affordable deals with them and allowing initial pressings on to the streets to be paid for out of the ensuing revenue. Even the less creditworthy customers – the artists taking a gamble on recording themselves or one-man operations – were given a chance, as payment would be made after discs were cut, and if they couldn't pay for all their slates or the entire consignment of records, Khouri would hold back safely what they couldn't afford until they could.

What seems to have been misread was his no-nonsense manner of collecting money: he sat at a desk in the doorway to his premises wearing a kind of bib with deep pockets around his neck; he'd brusquely demand the agreed rate, slap his ring'd hand down on the surface to signify a done deal and stuff the cash into his bib. He didn't see the need to barter because he knew his prices were the most reasonable and he gave short shrift to singers or producers attempting to pull a fast one. While this may have ruffled a few self-inflated artistic feathers, Khouri was a businessman, not a charity – just like the singers who then hoped to sell their records – and the only way to do business in the ghetto was to be as tough as the toughest. But a few bruised egos were a small price to pay for Ken Khouri's making so much music possible, as more than one veteran producer has testified.

Mastering discs was the real key to record manufacture, though. While Khouri made regular trips to Miami to get mastering done for his clients – at a charge – usually friends or migrants would carry them to New York, New Orleans, Florida or the UK, which meant that, although the actual transit cost nothing, they were at the mercy of the overseas facilities who saw no reason to charge the Jamaicans anything less than premium rate. Plus there was the real possibility of loss or damage: Coxsone maintains that his first-ever commercially minded session, with a band led by saxophone colossus Roland Alphonso, disappeared somewhere between the mastering rooms in New York and Kingston harbour.

In late 1959, though, Caribbean Records started up, owned by the Tawari family, who also owned the Regal theatre. The Tawaris understood the embryonic Jamaican music scene through the talent shows held there and, more than that, they weren't operating a recording studio but offering specialist mastering and pressing facilities. They knew what was required and how the volume of sales was there to make it pay provided they struck the right deals. Suddenly the price of manufacturing records fell by nearly three-quarters, and sound men from all over town tucked their latest killer tune under their arms and queued up outside Caribbean Records, hoping to cash in.

And so the Jamaican music business as we know it today was in place. Very profitably too, meaning that, for the first time since being brought over on the slave ships, Jamaica's black population was really contributing to their own country. All that was needed to complete the picture was some Jamaican music. Music the vast majority of its population could call its own. Music that reflected the creeping national euphoria as the island prospered and all talk was of independence within the next few years. Music that acknowledged the myriad influences stamped on Jamaican culture. But, most of all, music that beat with the very soul of downtown Kingston. Sufferahs' music. A true expression of Jamaican blackness.

It was bound to happen, too. Because although the players of instruments, the singers of songs and the men who ran t'ings had set out with little other purpose than to carry on making American R&B, once you get black Jamaicans doing things for themselves, you can be certain it's not going to go in a straight line.

3

We Are Rolling

It's pretty much impossible to say who first coined the term 'ska'. The black Jamaican tradition is oral, thus scientific precision will be noticeable only by its absence. The telling will always be as important as the tale itself, and so it would be going against the general spirit of things to let such a minor detail as factual accuracy stand in the way of a good yarn.

Talk to any number of the major players from the Jamaican music scene of four decades ago and you'll come away with the same number of entirely independent accounts of how the word came about. One school of thought has it as an abbreviation of 'Skavoovie!', bassman and band leader Cluett Johnson's explosive expression of greeting or enthusiasm. Pianist Theophilus Beckford is on record as saying that same 'Skavoovie!' is what the gathered crowds used to shout in appreciation of ska-type riffs he knocked out on the piano on his front porch, so he adapted the term to describe his 1959 hit 'Easy Snappin''. The Coxsone Conjecture, which perhaps holds the most water, is that Dodd himself came up with it while thus instructing guitarist Ernie Ranglin to stress the off-beat 'Play it *ska . . . ska . . . ska . . .*'. Then there's another group of 'eyewitnesses' who'll swear that the original phonetic description bandied round West Kingston's studios was '*staya . . . staya . . . staya . . .*', and that it was the altogether uptown Byron Lee who dreamed up the term 'ska' as an apparently more genteel way of summing the sound up.

It's the same with the music itself. At least a dozen of the prominent players and producers of the time lay claim to 'inventing' it, while the list of songs claiming to be the first ska tune would make the Gettysburg Address read like a note to the milkman. And it would be unnecessarily harsh to accuse anybody of lying. Anyway, such exactness would be nigh impossible to prove, as such was the nature of the 1950s Kingston music scene that as soon as three people had heard something at least two of them would have copied it. Within as many days.

But to attach much importance to the exact identification of whoever it was thought up either ska or its name is rather to miss the significance of what happened back then. As Bruce Lee said in *Enter the Dragon*, it would be like staring so intently at the finger, you miss the glory of whatever it's pointing at. What matters is that so many people felt so involved that they honestly believe they can assume responsibility. This was a cultural movement. A wave of players, producers and performers between them created enough momentum to bring about change for a number of reasons, only some of which were strictly musical. Ska was simply inevitable. And how it happened, could only have happened in Jamaica.

At this point in time – 1958 or so – the music industry was genuinely a village, as in spite of the well-publicized competition between producers and session-sponsors, their apparently exclusive, sound-shaping studio bands were unique in name only. Among the top two or three dozen musicians – i.e., the ones who were getting the work – everybody played with everybody else on just about everybody's sessions. It is only with enormous irony that you can cast an eye down the recording session personnel rosters of such arch rivals as Duke Reid, Coxsone and Prince Buster, because you'll find essentially the same band – Val Bennett, Roland Alphonso, Don Drummond, Stanley 'Ribs' Notice, Rico Rodriguez, Oswald 'Ba Ba' Brooks (brass), Ernie Ranglin or Jerome 'Jah Jerry' Hines (guitar), Theophilus Beckford (piano), Cluett Johnson (bass), and Arkland 'Drumbago' Parkes (drums) – calling themselves, depending on where they were, the Duke Reid Group, the Blues Blasters or the All Stars.

There could be no secrets, because they all had a hand in how everything was done, making contributions, jointly thrashing out ideas or helping to interpret a colleague's innovation. It generated a considerable sense of oneness among this pool of players, and, as so many were steeped in jazz traditions that perpetually seek to push forward, a very real crusade was gathering momentum. This was a hotbed of ghetto creativity seeking to come up with a form they could claim ownership of – both geographically and generationally – and virtually everybody who was singing, producing or playing music in West Kingston at the end of the fifties was involved. What finally emerged was a new rhythm to match the new mood of a very upbeat Jamaica. As a final step towards completely cutting its colonial ties the island had become fully self-governing in 1959, and now cultural independence from the USA was every bit as important as political independence from the UK. A change had to come.

But in spite of ska being a bona-fide collective effort, and the whole process having something of a karmic quality, it would be very wrong to assume it happened by accident. You couldn't travel from, say, 'Muriel' by Alton & Eddy to the Skatalites' 'Guns of Navarone' without passing a few landmarks. Y'know, positive and entirely deliberate contributions by exceptionally gifted individuals. Like late in 1959, when the notion of a widely desired swing away from straight-up US-style R&B was heralded by Joe Higgs & Roy Wilson's 'Manny Oh', a tune which was followed up early in the next year first by Theophilus Beckford's 'Easy Snappin'' and then the Folkes Brothers' 'Oh Carolina'.

Although cut within the same few months, all three records displayed a noticeably different approach to contemporary cultural correctness, each one appearing to up the stakes as regards the definition of 'Jamaicanness'. And after this, as the new decade dawned, there really was no looking back.

Edward Seaga had, for the last few years, been recording and managing local acts with a far more commercial outlook; notably Byron Lee and the Dragonnaires, a slick, self-contained showband who specialized in R&B and US pop, but who could perform, to order, whatever style was required in whatever upmarket nightclub or hotel bar they were booked into. Seaga was also in a unique position as far as Jamaica's music industry went. Much of W.I.R.L.'s business involved licensing and distributing American records all over the island, so Seaga was well aware of sales potential. Plus he was based in the heart of the ghetto, where he promoted dances and concerts, hired his acts out and supplied slates to sound systems, and so had to know what made the sufferahs tick. And, as displayed in his post-graduate anthropology studies, he had a yen for genuine Jamaican art. Seaga knew the runnings from a commercial, popular and cultural point of view – it was only a matter of time before all of this came together in the recording studio.

The song to do it was Higgs & Wilson's 'Manny Oh'. Essentially an R&B-type JA boogie with the popular New Orleans-ish beat, it could easily have slipped by unnoticed. But what the producer had done to it was to apply a mento element in changing the emphasis of the piano's shuffle by gently marking out the off-beat with a guitar chord, in much the same way as the banjo would supply that stress in mento. True, it was an entirely subtle customizing, but shifting the accent in this manner was enough to make the music stand out in a way that nearly all Jamaicans could identify as theirs. The island's record-pressing plants went into overdrive as the tune exploded, going on to sell over 25,000 copies. Clearly there was a demand for a more indigenous and original sound.

Clement Dodd seemed to think so, too. In fact, he'd been having such thoughts for quite a while as he was well aware that the records that got the best reception at his dances were the ones by singers who sounded Jamaican, as opposed to the wannabe-Yankees. In the studio he'd sought to encourage any such vocalizing, but at this point he wanted to take things further by putting greater distance between homegrown and imported music. He called a meeting with Ernie Ranglin, the acclaimed guitarist and musical arranger for the majority of Coxsone productions, and bass player Cluett Johnson. It was a surprisingly formal summons, on a Sunday morning in the back room of the Dodd family's liquor store on the corner of Beeston Street and Love Lane. Ranglin remembers it as the culmination of the ideas the sound man had been playing around with for several months.

'Coxsone didn't set out to deliberately corrupt the R&B that was being played. He wanted to stick with that sound, but to do it with our Jamaican feeling. His philosophy was that there's the same four beats in the bar and it just depends on what we do with them. He was well aware, at that time, that was what the ghetto people wanted, and while of course he was looking for new music to keep his sound system on top, his own sense of national pride played a part in what he was trying to do then.

'The change had been starting to happen with him in previous sessions, because he was a man who'd let the players play, stopping them to tell them to redo bits or telling them "Let's have a bit more of that." This time, the idea was to do it how we *really* want it done, not just imitating.

'Usually in the studio Coxsone would decide on the beat, and now was no exception. He deliberately wanted to keep the R&B shuffle beat, but he moved the stress to the afterbeat – the second and fourth beats – to such a degree that it turned the arrangement around. Instead of the *Chinnk*-ka . . . *Chinnk*-ka . . . *Chinnk*-ka . . . *Chinnk*-ka style we ended up with Ka-*chinnk* . . . Ka-*chinnk* . . . Ka-*chinnk* . . . Ka-*chinnk*. People used to call the very early ska "upside down R&B". Then the guitar came in to stress it even more, and this off-beat became the focus of all Jamaican music that followed on after it.'

Both of Ernie's points come correct: this rearrangement of the music's accents did indeed form a more identifiable foundation for Jamaican popular music for decades to come than Edward Seaga's mento-ish experiments; but, most telling, is the idea that Dodd had no intention of coming up with anything too radical. Check out Memphis R&B man Roscoe Gordon's thumping piano riffs; for years he'd been coming down heavy on the second and fourth beats, so earning his style the title 'back to front boogie'. As well as being a sound-system favourite, Gordon was a frequent performer on the Kingston concert circuit and it's most unlikely the producer would have been unaware of either his popularity or his apparent uniqueness.

A Wailers reissue CD that came out in mid-1999 – *Destiny: Rare Ska Side From Studio One*, it's called – is the most lucid illustration imaginable of where Coxsone was at even as late as 1963. In fact, as it's genuinely sound-system stuff, as opposed to so many retrospectives that are put together with a contemporary view of what ska ought to be, it's a pretty good example of how the majority of Jamaican records presented themselves. While several tunes are conventionally ska, many are pure R&B, with a lead singer and back-up approach as opposed to the later alternating leads. The tracks are also awash with jazz references, figures and ideas that would have come not only from the keen jazz fan Coxsone, but also from the players themselves, as many grew up playing jazz and looked upon recording as another chance to show off. Although the tunes are manifestly hybrids of various American forms, they are also very obviously Jamaican and moving in a certain direction – in fact the title *Destiny* could be applied to the music in general.

This is because, regardless of actual originality, such an atypical rhythm being played by Jamaicans with the Jamaican feel that Dodd was encouraging *was* a genuine first. Ernie Ranglin vividly remembers the effect this change of direction had on him and the other musicians.

'Up until then, when we'd been playing for Coxsone, he might have been pushing us toward a more original sound, but it wasn't something we were getting excited about. We just felt like we were doing a job. Back then if a man ask you to come down the studio and here's two shilling fi play a song, you did it. We were musicians and we just wanted to play the next chorus right, play the next phrase, to make the singers and the producers happy. Then they'll use you again. The real excitement for us, as working musicians, was that a man was going to *pay* us.

'But this time, because of the way Mr Dodd called us to that meeting, we *knew* we were doing something different. That

Sunday, we were dying to get to the studio and get it down. I remember us all feeling frustrated that we couldn't cut it there and then because the studios weren't open. As although I've said we were working musicians, we were *musicians* and we were always wanting to create something new. It wasn't as if we felt we were making history, but right then, we felt kinda like scientists carrying out an experiment and we couldn't wait to test it out.'

The next day, Ranglin took Johnson, Drumbago, Rico Rodriguez and Theophilus Beckford to the JBC studio at Half Way Tree. Following the arrangements the guitarist had worked out in this altered style, they cut a number of soft waxes for exclusive use on the Downbeat sound system, the best received of which became the seminal 'Easy Snappin''. Ironically, the version of the song that was released was recorded at Federal several weeks later with a chap called Ken Richards on guitar (there was a different drummer involved too, Ian Pearson), meaning Ernest Ranglin's name was nowhere near the groundbreaking song he not only co-conceptualized but supplied all the arrangements for.

He'll start chuckling when you ask him about this, because, at the time, such anonymity suited him fine.

'I didn't want to front it. It was ghetto music and in Jamaica they used to put that music down. This is why I didn't object to them putting Cluett Johnson name in front of it. This music was a rebel music even then, the way society looked at it and at themselves, they treated it like it was against the idea of society. It was like we were the outcasts who played that music. When the ska music had properly established itself there were so many tunes I was responsible for but I didn't go in front of them because I also had to be playing up at the society functions and the hotel dances, and there they would be looking down on me. Maybe I wouldn't get enough work. You had to walk the line.'

The guitarist speaks volumes about Jamaica's innate sense of snobbery and to what lengths uptown folk would go to rubbish – deliberately or otherwise – both the sufferahs' endeavours and the notion of a genuine native art form. It's this state of affairs as much as perceived commercial viability that would have been at the back of Dodd's not wanting to 'deliberately corrupt' the R&B sound. Let's face it, regardless of the story behind the 'Easy Snappin'' session, like 'Manny Oh' before it, it was never a drastic departure from such standard R&B/JA boogie as Laurel Aitken's 'Boogie in My Bones' or the Duke Reid Group's 'Pink Lane Shuffle'. It's a clear mark of the island's cultural status quo that aspirational types like Dodd or Seaga were never going to do anything too far out. While they may have physically lived among or done their business with the ghetto dwellers they most definitely saw themselves as a cut above, therefore anything that bore their name was going to be similarly inclined.

Prince Buster, however, had few such hang-ups. Even back then, when social sectarianism was rampant, he prided himself on staying close to his West Kingston roots. Figuratively as well as literally. And, as much as his infectious sense of good humour and all-consuming love of music, it was Buster's synergy with his crowds that was keeping his relatively new sound system on top. While he was just as aware that records with any kind of Jamaicanness would rock a dance that little bit harder, he remained deeply sceptical as to whether the still very US-orientated, essentially upwardly mobile music being made *really* related to the people who packed the sound-system lawns. He believed that to so many black Jamaicans life outside the ghettos remained little more than an abstract notion, and what was required was a music that celebrated its blackness through its African roots and reflected what downtown folk actually took seriously. Only, he felt, by ignoring as far as possible what he saw as American cultural imperialism could anybody create an authentic Jamaican sound.

Less than a year into building his own set, the man who'd dubbed himself the Voice of the People was on a mission – to represent sufferah culture on wax.

When Buster left Coxsone in 1959, he was determined to mount a serious challenge to both his former employer and to Duke

Reid. He was well aware that even a set that could, quite literally, shake up Orange Street would be useless without some killer tunes. But the usual lines of supply were closed off as, unlike his main rivals, Buster was denied initial access to unique R&B records as he was unable to travel to the USA as an itinerant sugar-cane cutter. Back then, after the initial forms had been filled, the dozens of prospective field hands would be lined up at the docks, where a soldier would inspect their hands – Buster's palms were deemed too soft to suffer the rigours of cane-cutting and so he was denied the necessary work permit. While he was devastated at the time, he'll chuckle about it forty years later – 'It isn't as if I even wanted to cut cane!' – because it was exactly that setback that forced him into the studio almost immediately. Because he couldn't cut cane he had to cut some innovative rhythms of his own or flush his investment and, most crucially, his reputation down the toilet.

'When I couldn't get the visa to run up and down to America like Duke Reid and Coxsone, it knock me back. I had already demolished the other two in a street clash, I have the number one set, the number one disc jockey in Count Machuki, but I know I couldn't keep up any challenge if I had to rely on rhythm and blues. I have to have my own music. So I know I have to design a different musical sound, but something that was nothing to do with America. Radio stations in Jamaica – our stations that were supposed to represent us the Jamaican people – were dominated by American rhythm and blues, and even though I loved it so much I knew it had to go. So when I started making records, the chief idea was to start making *Jamaican* records and push out that American thing. What I looked toward was the sound of the marching drum . . . boom . . . boom . . . boom! [Buster is slapping out a quick march-type four/four tempo on his thigh.]

'When I was young I would love the march – lodge processions, funerals, military parades, anything with that marching drum – any time I hear the drum I, and many other children, would follow that sound even if we don't know where it's going. One day when the soldiers march past I follow them all the way to camp – I didn't get home for hours, then I got a beating! But I knew that it wasn't just me that appreciated that beat because plenty people follow the parades. Also, I am a man who love mento and this was the same time pattern, so it has a root in real Jamaican music. I came with the same beat from the hand drum to the foot drum and tell Drumbago to play it like that. Then the guitarist, Jerry, I show him how to strum *chnnk! . . . chnnk! . . . chnnk!* and have Ribs on tenor sax playing *bap! . . . bap! . . . bap!* so it's all still going with the march.

'And although I didn't know it then, this was ska. The belly of the ska sound is that marching drum.'

From his first sessions at Federal, Buster came with tunes such as 'Little Honey', 'Humpty Dumpty', 'African Blood', 'Time Longer than Rope'. He used singers such as Derrick Morgan, Eric Morris or Bobby Aitken (Laurel's kid brother), or cut instrumentals with his All Stars. This alternative to the straightforward shuffle of the JA boogie cranked the sound system rivalry up a notch or two.

'Coxsone . . . Duke Reid . . . They didn't think it was good music at all. After those tunes were big hits on my sound system, they used to talk about how people were following "Buster's little boop boop beat". They *scorned* it. They were jazz men at heart and here I was, a likkle youth, coming what they thought to be simple music. The only big man who support me was Edward Seaga, he want to see a *Jamaican* music develop and he always give support to those who were moving that way. At that time he had no interest in politics, he was talked into going into it by others and then it drag him down. In those days we in the musical fraternity know him as *Ska*-aga, such was his energies in promoting the ska.

'But the people were behind what I was doing. Coxsone couldn't play nowhere because nobody wanted to go to his dance. The others start to keep open dance, when they don't charge at the gate – *free dance* – and still nobody don't come. It go so far as to force Coxsone, Duke Reid and King Edwards into an alliance, which amaze me because although Duke and Edwards are friends, I used to have to defend Coxsone against

Duke! They have money, so they pay Jerry [Hines] to copy that sound for them. But because they couldn't understand what was happening in my tunes – they thought it was all the guitar and didn't know about the drum – they couldn't get it right. I made the records "Three Against One" and "The King, the Duke and the Sir", which tell everybody exactly what was going on. Soon though, they returned to R&B.'

It was in the face of such opposition that Buster opted to move forward once more and, looking to increase the cultural element in his recordings, he dreamed up a scheme to bring the Rasta master drummer Count Ossie and his troupe into the recording studio. Buster had loved Ossie's drums since childhood, when, in pre-sound-system days, dancehalls featured big bands, with Ossie's group often performing during the intervals, and the young Buster would climb trees outside just to sneak a peek. Now their re-involvement in the dances made good sense: Ossie had an enormous standing in the ghetto community as Rastafari became increasingly established; Rasta was black Jamaica's strongest remaining bond to its African roots, and, on a purely practical level, his drummers would provide a completely different sound. But it was never going to be the easiest session to make happen.

Buster's regular musicians were singularly uncooperative, objecting to the use of 'outsiders' on the grounds of why change a winning formula. The movers and shakers of the Kingston music community in general thought anything involving Rastafari was a retrograde step. Ossie himself refused to entertain the idea that anything as outright Babylonian as the sound-system subculture could honestly be interested in what he had to offer. Then, even after Buster had spent several days up at the Rasta camp in the Wareika Hills, convincing the master drummer that there was no hidden agenda, Duke Reid bribed his way into JBC Studios (it was to have been Buster's first time recording there) to take the studio time Buster had booked. As a result of such subterfuge, it was in an upstairs room no bigger than a large, mic'ed-up cupboard that Buster, pianist Owen Gray, back-up vocalist Skitter, Ossie and his four drummers coaxed, coached and encouraged the three Folkes Brothers, John, Eric and Mike, through 'Oh Carolina'.

What he remembers most of all about those sessions is a feeling of frustration. Tempers were already fraying at the discovery of Duke Reid in their studio and threatened to unravel all the way when Reid emerged for no reason other than to laugh at the far from slick looking Rastas. The teenage Folkes Brothers weren't helping matters much, either. Buster had used them because his regular singers found it impossible not to sing in an American style and these novices still sounded Jamaican, yet with this refreshing lack of experience came a supreme nervousness. At one time Ossie almost walked as they appeared to be getting nowhere. It was broad daylight when they finally emerged with an acceptable take of 'Oh Carolina', the spiritual song 'I Make a Man' and a tune called 'Chubby', sung by Skitter. Not, by 1960s Jamaican standards, a great deal for over eight hours of hard work, but Buster was ecstatic.

'When we first get and find Duke Reid there I was furious. I want to do something serious I was so mad – I come with tune, I come with band, I know this sound will be different and I'm anxious to get it down. Then I have to tell Ossie not to be frustrated with John Folkes – "I Make a Man" never hit because on the take we had to go with Folkes sounds too nervous. But I know I've got something special, something that hasn't been done before. As soon as I take the dub of "Oh Carolina" to Machuki him know it, him tell me Coxsone, Reid and Edwards will be buried now.

'The reaction to it even surprise me. I was playing at Cho Co Mo Lawn, and Duke had an open dance just down the street which was filled up with people because it was free. Machuki was playing my set when I got there. I tell him play "Oh Carolina" and don't stop playing it. When he put it on and that drum *pu-do-do-dum* went up in the air for the first time ever it was the sound of Rasta searching for some kind of identity. This was the sound of the poor black Jamaicans. Duke Reid's dance went flat in about fifteen minutes because people were running to those drums.

'Of course the radio wouldn't play it, because society was so terrible against Rastas. First they said they couldn't play it because they didn't think it was a record, because it wasn't constructed the way the American music was constructed. Then they admit they were afraid it would mess up their advertising because the Rasta involvement would cause people to back out. But because my sound was so popular and I was playing this music – constant play – they were forced to. I too use my influence to get it on the air, I was starting to make a lot of trouble, but after they play it a couple of times many people – the people of Jamaica – began to request the record.

'How Coxsone react was to run to Ossie and use his money to get them to come down and make records. Ossie and his men made a whole heap of records for Down Beat but not even one of them came close to "Oh Carolina". Harry Mudie in Spanish Town too – he made a ton of records with Ossie and his men, but none of them hit. It's because the efforts that made "Oh Carolina" was defiance at society and that came out in the music. Ossie knew that. He didn't play like he would play in his camp at Salt Lane because he know in him heart that I am the one brought Rasta out of the woods. I know Ossie was a good artist, and otherwise he'd be up in the huts in the Wareika Hills, smoking ganja and it would end there.'

It is difficult to gauge the importance of Prince Buster's 'Oh Carolina'. While in terms of actual musical construction it probably wasn't that influential, as a piece of cultural legislation it was enormous. For the first time in the nation's history one of the few surviving African-based artforms – a true articulation of black Jamaicanness – had become involved with a commercially viable mainstream expression. It was a bond between Rastafari and the Jamaican music business that is still in place to this day, with each side doing as much for the other – while reggae gives Rasta access to the world stage, Rasta's depth of spirituality means reggae will always have something to say.

Not that this gave it an easy ride. When Buster was flirting with the idea of calling in Ossie, unsurprisingly the only real endorsement he got was from Edward Seaga, who saw it as one more aspect of exploring the island's indigenous culture and was convinced it would be doing the world a favour. The hostility to Rastafari from the middle (or aspiringly middle) classes was widespread and thrown into sharp relief with the broadcasters' reaction to 'Oh Carolina' – bear in mind that this was after the advent of JBC (Jamaican Broadcasting Corporation) in 1959, a state-owned nationwide station with a brief to support all things Jamaican. This is why Buster talks about what is, essentially, a silly love song as being a simmering cauldron of rebel music. To cut such a sound displayed sheer brass neck, when you consider Ernie Ranglin didn't even want his name on a piece of music that stressed a different beat. And perhaps most worryingly of all, it makes perfect sense as to why he didn't.

Of course, 'Oh Carolina' was a huge hit. The Voice of the People had given a voice *to* the people, and it's at this point that reggae or ska, or whatever, became the bona-fide folk music it remains.

4

Message from the King

In an ideal world, when Prince Buster involved Count Ossie and his drummers on the 'Oh Carolina' sessions, the only surprise would have been that anybody was surprised. During the 1950s, as colonialism played itself out to increasingly diminishing returns, Rastafari had blown up in working-class black Jamaica to become a hugely influential spiritual, socio-political and cultural force. Despite perpetual and coordinated harassment from the authorities, by 1958, the year before 'Oh Carolina', an estimated 5,000 people attended the first open Nyabingi – celebratory gathering of Rasta brethren – that was held in Kingston's Charles Square. In May 1959, a large-scale riot broke out in Coronation Market when market traders – non-Rastas themselves – came to the aid of a Rastaman being beaten by policemen. The officers were stoned and had their vehicles set on fire. By this time, a self-sufficient Rasta 'state' of roughly 1,600 settlers had been set up at Pinnacle, in the hills of St Catherine. At least a dozen well-subscribed Rasta organizations existed in Jamaica. And an estimated 100,000 Jamaicans – roughly one in twenty-five of the population – were Rastafarian, with many more openly sympathetic. Although Rasta was originally of a rural bent, thanks to the forced migration from the country to the city the majority of these believers were now concentrated in the ghettos of West Kingston, with large camps established in areas such as Dungle and Back-A-Wall.

It's therefore almost impossible to imagine there had been so little obvious interaction between the Rastafari community and the sound system/music business culture that had exploded in the same area at more or less the same time. Music was an essential part of the Rasta environment, and Kingston is not *that* big. That this was in fact the case, and that it had taken a man such as Prince Buster to make that first move, is a vivid indication of how uptown folk perceived dreadlock society. Rastafari was the underclass's underclass, positioned so far down Jamaica's rigidly structured pecking order that for many people they simply didn't count.

Yet from 1959 onwards, once Buster opened the door, Rastafari became an integral part of the development and popularization of Jamaican music. In spite of the best efforts of several record producers and most key music-industry figures to ignore the mushrooming Rasta influences, the doctrine and philosophy became a popular lyrical theme. Although the dominant memories of the ska and rocksteady eras are the happy-feet-celebratory nature of the former and the uptight belligerence of the latter, there were plenty of tunes such as 'Beardman Ska' (the Skatalites), 'Another Moses' (the Mellowcats) or 'The Whip' (the Ethiopians). It's just that most of them didn't make it beyond the music's core audience. By the time the 1960s turned over into the next decade natty dread had usurped reggae to transform it – lyrically, melodically and production-wise – into a single-minded hymn to Jah Rastafari. Then, by the end of that decade, the most famous Jamaican of all time was a vociferously devout Rastafarian who set up camp (exactly that) in a big colonial-style house in Kingston's Hope Road, just down the street from King's House, former residence of Jamaica's Governor General. Dread inna Babylon, literally as well as figuratively.

While Bob Marley's address was always an appropriately symbolic tribute to the indomitable spirit of Jamaica's dispossessed, most importantly this escalating identification between reggae and Rastafari demonstrates how the music refused to stray more than a few yards from its downtown Kingston roots. It's a connection continuing right up to the present day, and as Rastafari remains solely concerned with the sufferah and his plight, it will ensure that any given manifestation of Jamaican music will remain a genuine people's – i.e., folk – music.

Indeed, from Rastafari's beginnings among the poor to its cutting across the classes in later decades, it has been an absolutely fundamental part of the last sixty years of black life in Jamaica. So much so it is practically impossible to get any kind of grip on the evolution of the domestic music scene without first understanding the hows and the whys of this so-called cult.

If the genesis of Rastafari were to be traced back to one moment in time, that instant would be 2 November 1930, the crowning of Ras Tafari as Emperor Haile Selassie I of Ethiopia. Named Lij Makonnen – *Ras* and *Tafari* were titles translated from Amharic to mean, respectively, 'prince' or 'nobleman' and 'creator' – he was thirty-eight years old and part of an Abyssinian dynasty that declared itself a line of direct descent from the union of King Solomon and Queen Makeba of Sheba. Ras Tafari was reckoned to be the 225th succession. The coronation attracted high-level representation from seventy-two nations and global media coverage, a surprising turnout for what was in economic terms – the only ones that mattered to the Western world – an insignificant African country. But this incoming emperor was proving himself singularly confident on the world stage; during the six months before the death of Ethiopia's previous ruler, Empress Zauditu, he had fiercely promoted himself around the globe. He'd gone on the road to make sure there was total awareness that the only black man to sit upon the throne of a free African nation expected to be treated with due respect by his fellow international leaders.

But whatever splash Ras Tafari had been making among the world powers, for the children of the African diaspora his coronation as Haile Selassie was the single most important event of the twentieth century thus far. Remember, this was in a world not yet a hundred years out of slavery, and where colonialism remained so rampant that Ethiopia represented a lone island of independence in an Africa otherwise governed entirely from Europe. Yet here was a new black king who wasn't simply a figurehead or the white man's puppet, but would actually be running things. To the forcibly dispossessed – 'involuntary pilgrims' as Rastas would call transported slaves – this was a matter of genuine black pride and huge optimism. Because this new sovereign appeared to command the respect of the crowned heads of Europe he came over as, quite literally, living proof of potential black power. It was real hope, no matter how geographically detached the actualities might be. And once the event was written up to the absolute max in the numerous free black news-sheets around the world, the Emperor Haile Selassie became a universal black role model.

In Jamaica, this chord was struck with an even greater resonance. What established the roots of Rastafari as unique to that island was that, by an odd geographical quirk, Jamaican Ethiopian Christians had always taken the notion of Ethiopia to be more actual than simply spiritual. Therefore, to large numbers of Jamaicans the crowning of this new emperor was accepted as a divine realization of writings contained within the Book of Revelation and Jeremiah. As told by three radical and highly influential preachers – of whom more later – the coronation was seen as giving substance to predictions found in the scriptures that one day the Mighty Redeemer would come to deliver the children of Israel out of Egypt, and, most crucially, that this new Messiah would be a black man. Further evidence that this emperor of Ethiopia was indeed Christ reincarnate came in the form of the title he assumed when he took the throne – Haile Selassie translated as 'The Power of the Trinity'. Likewise his other appellations carried a certain biblical sway: Negus Neghest (King of Kings); Lord of Lords; Conquering Lion of the Tribe of Judah; and Elect of God. These were rankings dating back to biblical days, several being brought out of centuries-long retirement to consolidate Haile Selassie's sovereignty. To a faith geared up to the physical notion of Ethiopia, such sanctification was based on an undeniable locational logic, too. The territory that by then went under that name was formerly Abyssinia; it had been Christian since the middle of the fourth century, splitting from Rome one hundred years later to establish the Coptic Church of Ethiopia, the most orthodox and, some say, purest form of Christianity. In 1930, the nation remained officially and essentially Christian, the one such state in the pretty much wholly Muslim North Africa. Obviously the country was some sort of promised land.

By the time of Ras Tafari's succession, Ethiopia itself had been an entirely familiar, if somewhat abstract, notion to black Christians all over the Americas and the Caribbean for well over a century. Ethiopia was how the King James Bible, published in 1611, referred to the whole continent of Africa; thus, after slaves were allowed Christianity in the middle of the eighteenth century, black preachers would adopt the prefix Ethiopian to differentiate clearly between their approach and their *massas'* to the faith. Ethiopian Baptist, Methodist and Episcopalian churches had first appeared in the USA roughly two hundred years before Haile Selassie took the throne.

Such a distinction was most important within the slave system. The constant turnover of manpower meant a continual influx from the motherland, which kept Africa's religions alive on the plantations as the strongest link with everything the displaced masses once were. (In spite of African religions being banned as part of the planters' destabilization programme, they were kept up surreptitiously as one of the mainstays of the slave quarters' internal hierarchy which placed recently arrived Africans at the top of the pecking order.) For this reason, once it was decided to baptize the Africans they actively resisted any such Christianization – slave revolts, especially in Jamaica, were a far more regular feature of life in the colonies than history books have ever cared to reflect. Indeed, Christianity was eventually accepted for no other reason than it was the only route to literacy, as the Bible was the only book slaves were allowed, and in order to read it they had to be taught to read.

However, the first black preachers immediately adapted the scriptures to acknowledge both their people's sufferation and their resolution to remain independent. And as for manner of worship, it was going to be as gloriously, vibrantly African as possible.

The impact of these Ethiopian churches was large. In spite of Christianity among the slave populations opening the doors to the wholesale supplanting of their native culture, accepting the religion was actually an oblique step forward. Quite apart from the imposition of Christianity being the single act that led the slave contingents into large-scale literacy, baptism marked an apparent acceptance of displaced Africans' humanity. For the first two hundred years of the slave trade white people's justifications for their barbarism hinged on their denial of the fact that black Africans were human, and were therefore in no need of 'conventional' (i.e., European) religion as they were without human souls. To allow Christianity, even superficially, overturned such theories.

However, it was culturally that the Ethiopian churches *really* made a difference, as once a slave was able to subscribe to the ideas of biblical Ethiopia he or she immediately became capable of plugging-in to black history as an important chapter in the birth of mankind. A knowledge that provided instant self-awareness and a premise of self-worth, both put into contexts apparently defined by the oppressor. Which meant Ethiopianism as a political theory came about as soon as the religious aspect was established. The moment the slaves themselves set up this separate, black-orientated religion by means of a deliberate and self-defined deed, their uniquely adapted approach to Christianity became the first embryonic act of black nationalism to have made the crossing from Africa. And as would be expected of such, from the beginning the Ethiopian churches were where discontent could be aired and aspirations discussed.

They soon became more than simply the hub of the community. By the mid-eighteenth century the wickedness of the slave trade was never going to be reversed; transported Africans were across the ocean to stay and knew they had to do the best they could in those circumstances. The churches had become new, entirely legal slave organizations that were born both in and out of the New World, and as such took into account the people's resignation to look forward rather than dream of repatriation. It was a change of direction that resulted in far more constructive and focused black insurrection, and meant the black church was never far removed from outright revolt. Quite an irony really, given the apparent 'civilizing' effect Bible studies were supposed to have on the slaves. Baptist missionaries were only able to convince the plantation owners to allow Bible classes among their workforces by arguing that Christianity involved a work ethic that would ultimately increase production, and that the God-fearing Christian concept of humility would make even the surliest African easier to subjugate.

In 1896 the whole idea of Ethiopianism took a further turn towards the political when news crossed the Atlantic of the Battle of Adowa in which the Ethiopian armies, led by Emperor Menelik (Haile Selassie's great uncle), had repelled an attack by an Italian invasion force. The raid's purpose was colonization, and what made the achievement so remarkable was that the African soldiers possessed only an array of crude weaponry, while the Italian army was kitted out with the latest in sophisticated gear. The victory was taken on two levels on the plantations: after hundreds of years of pillage the black nation was fighting back, and, as was written in the Book of Psalms, God was at last delivering his first children from suffering. Either way, the triumph was taken as a sign that redemption was at hand. And Ethiopia, once again, was at its root.

As the twentieth century dawned, a world-wide black political platform began to institute itself. Ethiopianism was morphing into something called Pan-Africanism, a drive for Africans on both sides of the Atlantic to take charge of redressing the imbalances of colonialism for themselves. Black society had changed enormously during the previous fifty years and responsibility for the socio-political agenda had been taken beyond the churches.

Thanks to a partial, post-emancipation redistribution of

wealth, at the turn of the century roughly 5,000 black Jamaicans each owned over 10 acres of land, while at least six times that number claimed title to smaller holdings. This was creating a new social stratum, as virtually all of these new landlords spent any profits on educating their children. Gradually a black professional class evolved in Jamaica, resulting in a surge of black intellectualism which was eager to divorce itself from the church as the sole means of expression. A similar situation had already occurred in the USA. And, as in America, it was this new class which sought to destabilize colonialist values by spreading the Pan-African doctrine of black self-help and self-respect.

By now, for black people to travel between the USA, the Caribbean and the motherland was far from unheard of, and the idea of a World Black Nation was becoming more than simply theoretical. Or even theological. Educated black Jamaicans such as Dr Robert Love and Henry Williams were closely involved with the American W. E. B. DuBois in setting up the first Pan-African Congress in London in 1900 under the slogan 'Africa for the Africans'. A catchphrase that spoke volumes, of both their intention and level of sophistication – it was never ever a straightforward repatriation rallying cry (Pan-Africanists were ideologically opposed to a physical return to the motherland); it assumed Africa to be a post-diaspora nation and called on each of its citizens to take up the cause of every African who needed help. It was a progressive take on Paul Bogle's war cry of 'Cleave to the black, colour for colour'. A kind of nationalistic 'All for one and one for all'.

While there can be no complaints as to what the Pan-Africanist movement achieved in terms of initiating global black consciousness, it could be argued that – in Jamaica especially – it rather hijacked the emerging politicism on behalf of this new, middle-class(ish) intelligentsia. That in by-passing the churches to move political action into the realms of worthy debate and wordy magazine articles, the working classes became increasingly detached from the mechanics of change. In 1901, however, a fourteen-year-old named Marcus Mosiah Garvey arrived in Kingston from his birthplace of St Anns Bay to apprentice as a master printer.

Jamaica's proletariat was about to re-enter its country's political arena, with something of a bang. As was Ethiopia.

Never mind the Bible, nowhere is the basis of Rasta philosophy writ clearer than in what would become known as Garveyism, principles that were little more than Pan-Africanism taken to its logical or practical conclusion. Although Marcus Garvey's name crops up frequently in Rastafari reasonings, his importance stems from his apparent prophecy made just before Haile Selassie's coronation, that once a black man was crowned king redemption was at hand. But he was far more vital to the faith than merely the dreadlocks' John the Baptist.

Central to his theories was the rallying call 'One God! One aim! One destiny!' It was a means of promoting the idea of One Black Nation and of advocating self-sufficiency through self-awareness within the 'host' territories. But it did so on an entirely pragmatic level. A level that enabled ordinary working black people to participate in his vision of black pride. A level that fully understood the basic everyday frustrations of the man in the street and therefore never ruled out the possibility of direct action as an acute form of self-defence. And one that ultimately swept up Africans the whole world over on a tide of resolute black nationalism, to arrive at the point at which Garveyism and Pan-Africanism parted company. Repatriation.

Marcus Garvey's commitment to the working people began with his involvement in print union labour disputes in Kingston when, not yet twenty years old, he was organizing fellow workers and writing and producing radical pamphlets. His international perspective was achieved in similarly hands-on fashion: during the following years he joined the Caribbean labour migration, travelling first to Central America then to the UK, maintaining his level of worker representation among whatever workforce he found himself. After returning to Jamaica in 1916, where he led an ineffective print workers' strike and became frustrated by colonial laws proscribing any sort of black self-help organization, Garvey relocated to Harlem, New York. By this time he had connected with black people of all classes from all over the diaspora, and was well aware that the problems were essentially the same everywhere, but he was equally certain that the only place in which he could put his ideas into practice was America.

He was not wrong. By the early 1920s his Universal Negro Improvement Association was an organization of thousands of members in hundreds of active branches across the USA, Central America and Africa and with a strong presence in any European or South American country with a sizeable black population. UNIA congresses were enormous affairs, with all the pomp of Britain's state opening of Parliament and the circumstance of a full session of the United Nations. His newspapers, first *Negro World* then the daily *Black Man*, were required reading on a global scale and never less than harshly critical of the white world's racial politics or the racist leanings of so many of the popular arts. He'd given the black nation its own national anthem – *Ethiopia, Thou Land of Our Fathers*; and devised its red, black and green flag ('red for the blood that will be spilled in the struggle, black for the colour of our skin and green for the land that one day shall be ours'), colours still very visible across America today as a badge of black pride. On the fiscal side, the UNIA's Negro Factories Corporation owned a string of businesses including restaurants, removal firms and printers. It was on hand to help potential black entrepreneurs get going and a central plank of its platform was to promote support of black businesses wherever possible, to the point that black people would actually feel embarrassed to use anything else. As the results of this black self-help stacked up in commercial terms, the only place for it to go was back to Africa.

Marcus Garvey's Black Star Line shipping company was financed entirely through shares and subscriptions by ordinary black folk, looking to emigrate to his vision of an Independent Negro Nation. It was an unprecedented show of black solidarity, raising enough capital to purchase outright four ocean liners in 1922, and displaying enough global diplomatic clout to have negotiated a vast tract of Africa from the Liberian government. It sent a shockwave through the white establishment the whole world over. Here was a man who'd not only worked out that economic strength was the only way to achieve political power, but who had utilized each to an astonishing degree. On top of what he'd already achieved, the fact that he had got as far as making the Black Star Line a reality gave notice of exactly what a unified black nation was capable of under a strong, resourceful leader.

However, flexing the kind of muscle that can launch four ships and establish its own republic was something of a step too far. There has always been an unwritten rule – unwritten by the establishment, that is – which states that black people can be given so much rope, but if they take any more than what is deemed their allocation, it will be tied into a noose. At this point, quite simply, Marcus Garvey had to be stopped. Which was never going to be that difficult, either, for with the Black Star Line, his most audacious project to date, he was attempting to function purely ideologically within a capitalist system and as such was always going to be open to attack. A combination of the federal authorities, jealous rival black leaders and corruptibles within his own organization conspired to stitch him up on a charge of mail fraud, while at the same time diplomatic pressure was put on the Liberian government to sell his promised land to a multinational rubber company. Marcus Garvey was discredited, jailed and then deported back to Jamaica.

Unfortunately, while this astonishing attempt at repatriation was only part of what he achieved and the subsequent charges were so obviously trumped-up, these are the aspects of the man that tend to be remembered. Which is to do him an enormous injustice. In real terms there was never before, nor has there been since, a black leader of greater international significance or effect. What he did was to unite the black populations of the entire world – the only time it has ever happened. A brilliant, fiery speaker, he was as comfortable among working men and women as he was with professors. He understood the importance of the black church while recognizing the new roles of the schools and colleges. He could take on board the emerging socialist doctrines without allowing the growing labour movement to co-opt his organization. He knew that to stimulate interest, black pride needed tangibility, and in 1920 the UNIA organized a parade of several thousand uniformed black people through Harlem. Direct action was enshrined in his organization's constitution as it called on black people to be ready 'to fight fire with fire'. In more than one country the mere possession of a copy of *Negro World* was an imprisonable offence. And when he visited Jamaica in 1921, the British government was so alarmed at the possible effect on the population that it ordered Royal Navy frigates to be anchored just outside Kingston harbour.

When the deported Marcus Garvey came home to Jamaica it was to a hero's reception. True to form he headed straight back to the dispossessed, but now there was a certain universality to his playing the positive nuisance. While he took his words to both the rural parishes and the gullies and ghettos of Kingston, such was his status that he now attracted the educated as well. Then, thanks to his Jamaican country-boy Christian upbringing and his understanding of the need to incorporate the church and the Bible in what he was doing, he brought religion more to the fore. At the end of the 1920s, Marcus Garvey was telling his enormous Jamaican following, 'Look to Africa when a black king shall be crowned, for the day of deliverance is near'. Hence, events in Ethiopia in 1930 were going to be taken very seriously indeed.

By the time Rastafari had acquired its name – some time during 1931 – perpetual persecution and frequent imprisonment had hounded Marcus Garvey out of Jamaica to London, where he was to die in poverty and virtual obscurity in 1940. So, while his methods and socio-religious principles provided its ideological linchpin, he had no actual involvement with Rastafari. The movement emerged solely in Jamaica, out of an Ethiopianist revival that was sweeping the Western world's black population immediately following Haile Selassie's coronation. Its swift and sudden dissemination was due almost entirely to the individual and occasionally collective efforts of Leonard P. Howell, Archibald Dunkley and Joseph Hibbert, who each preached a slightly different version of a faith that shouldered the discarded mantle of Garveyism (black pride, separatism, direct contact with the masses, self-help and repatriation). However, all three advanced the idea of Haile Selassie as the Messiah – a cornerstone of the notion that separated Jamaica from New Ethiopianism elsewhere – meaning his ascendancy became more than a sharp focus for the rampant anti-colonialism of the day.

Of Rastafari's three apostles Dunkley and Hibbert were primarily left-field Christian clergymen. The former based himself in Kingston with a doctrine rooted in – and rarely deviating from – an Afro-centric interpretation of the conventional scriptures; the latter opted for orthodox Christianity with his newly founded Ethiopian Coptic Church, which went so far as to use a translation of the ancient Ethiopic Bible of St Sosimas (Ethiopic was the ancient language of Abyssinia, part of the Semitic language group from which the comparatively modern Amharic evolved roughly two thousand years ago). Howell was by far the most important player, he was something of a megalomaniac and – rather ironically – the most self-serving of the trio, but he was an enormously charismatic speaker. In 1933, on returning from working in the USA, he picked up where Marcus Garvey had left off to preach a gospel of blatant black nationalism, but delivered it in an overtly biblical context and style, promoting Haile Selassie as the embodiment of God. He went so far as to suggest that he enjoyed some nebulous African mystical powers and claimed to speak an obscure African language. Of enormous importance though, and once again just like Marcus Garvey before him, was the fact that Howell made sure to take the faith beyond the capital into the rural parishes.

Which was perhaps the most fundamental element to the shaping of Rastafari, as inside black Jamaica were two essentially separate nations – countryfolk and townspeople. In spite of the rural population suffering a reputation among the city dwellers for apparent *soon come* slow-wittedness, they were far more insurrectionist and actively nationalistic than their urban counterparts, with strikes and acts of revolt being commonplace among the mining-industry and plantation workers. Also, within the small isolated communities, the church had remained much more central to life in general. Thus, out of town, this new, proudly anti-establishment faith appeared tailor-made to become the latest stage in a line stretching back to the Ethiopian churches' politicization over a century earlier. It's probably no coincidence that Howell concentrated his efforts in the parish of St Thomas, which had a history of bloody rebellion from the earliest days of slavery to Paul Bogle's Morant Bay uprising of 1865.

In spite of the emphasis always being placed on the Rastafari's spiritual considerations, originally it was never less than committed to the very worldly business of social advancement. In fact, insofar as black politics could exist in a British colony in 1932, this was an aggressive black political organization, always intent on offering a very practical take on what had previously been largely abstract concepts. It should be remembered that, with the notable exception of Marcus Garvey's apparent prophecy, in so many of Rastafari's defining instances any enigmatic biblical interpretations were usually arrived at after the event.

And the spirituality itself was securely rooted in the temporal. Rastafari was so called in identification with the person whom Haile Selassie was *before* he took the throne, to make the point that everybody has the potential for divinity. 'Jah' means God (it's believed to be a corruption of the Hebrew word *Yahweh*, the personal covenant name of God), and while it will be applied to Haile Selassie as Jah Rastafari, it's also a common suffix for any Rastaman, stressing the importance of self. Indeed, as you'd expect from a movement devoted to self-esteem, the whole theoretical foundation of Rastafari is oneself as the focus of life on earth. Hence the roman numeral one that suffixes Haile Selassie is pronounced as the letter I, signifying every Rasta's closeness to his god. There is no Rasta expression for 'we' or 'you' (either in the singular or the plural), instead 'I and I' is favoured as it respects each individual's own connotation of oneness. Likewise, the notion of a living God and heaven here on earth (Ethiopia): in this altogether worldly situation believers each became the embodiment of their god, thus Rastafari could offer a personal redemption. Which, after four hundred dehumanizing years of slavery and colonization, was a very attractive proposition.

Howell's, Dunkley's and Hibbert's slightly conflicting approaches to what Rastafari actually was played a part in shaping the faith, too, as, handily given that it was a strictly subversive state of affairs, Rasta became impossible to explain in the terms of a conventional religion. Its doctrine was a shifting, perpetually adaptable – some would say vague – set of principles, which afforded very effective self-defence. Pinning down the dread philosophy was not quite as easy as nailing jelly to a wall, a state of affairs that enhanced its hazy, usefully spooky aura of Dark Continent mysticism. There are no Rasta churches, no hierarchy other than age, few rules beyond diet and hygiene, and to a Rastaman, there is no such thing as a definite statement. All ideas and theories are open-ended, subject to constant evolution and individual interpretation, making it impossible for anybody's views not to count. In these circumstances, the nearest Rastafari comes to a formal sermon would be a reasoning session, an elliptical, rambling discussion to which everybody present is expected to contribute.

While it has been tempting for so many to sideline Rastafari as a conventional religion – just one a bit crankier than most – this couldn't really be further from the truth. The single most important factor here is race – it's Rastafari's true defining statement. If there hadn't been any black people there couldn't have been any need for Rasta. Or, more to the point, if there hadn't been any oppressed black people.

Rastafari was able to establish itself so securely as the natural standard bearer for the Ethiopian Christian churches, Pan-Africanism and Garveyism because its whole point, as a way of life, was for the advancement of Jamaica's black population.

It sought to achieve this by restoring the self-awareness and self-confidence that had been all but bred out through the destruction wrought by transportation, the brutalization of slavery and the subservience that was necessary to maintain the colonial system. Furthermore, it had vast intellectual appeal, as it was an exercise in black pride that acknowledged the idea of a post-diasporal global black nation and drew inspiration from Emperor Haile Selassie's coronation, Mau Mau, King Ja Ja of Opomo, black American Christianity and Nyabingi. But in its arcane, appealingly woozy delvings into African mysticism, Rastafari's presentation of the idea of Africa as a state of mind as well as a geographical location was as attractive as it was understandable. Rasta teachings that every black man and woman – everywhere – shared a cultural legacy, and thus the responsibility for keeping same alive, was a powerful unifying force.

If this in itself wasn't sending shivers of panic down plantocracy spines, Rastafari's social precepts were diametrically opposed to the apparent 'character' of the colonized Jamaican working population. As a defence mechanism in the face of authority and to avoid actively contributing to the system, black Jamaicans – and slaves everywhere – acted the part of docile, stupid, respectful, if potentially wayward children, inherently lazy enough to be in need of constant supervision. While away from the overseer the idea was to be as shrewd or as tricky as possible to get one over on anybody you could – it was a respect thing. These were behaviour patterns established during slavery, as enshrined, respectively, in the Jamaican folk legends of Quashie and Anancy, each of which have West African origins. And of course, such conduct was encouraged by the rulers as absolutely crucial to maintaining such a subservient status quo beyond abolition.

Rastafari, though, held no truck with a submissive demeanour, with black on black hucksterism or with any son or daughter of Africa presenting themselves in a way that was anything other than 100 per cent true. In a world where steppin' 'n' fetchin' it was the norm, the Rastaman walked proud, would look anybody in the eye and was forever ready to assert his rights as a man. Most dangerously, though, he remained convinced that every other black man, woman and child was born to behave in exactly the same way. This, of course, meant Rastafari sought to station itself outside the conventional patterns of Jamaica's class system, an idea that consolidated the movement's place among the so-called lower orders. In a revealing example of how the plantocracy perceived this sort of philosophy, at the end of the 1930s the authorities had no problem getting Leonard Howell certified insane and forcibly committed to a lunatic asylum for two years.

In other words, it wasn't taking long for any uptown lack of comprehension to manifest itself as fear. Fear that swiftly closed a vicious circle of intolerance: the middle classes called for police crackdowns and the resultant high profile, media-justified confrontations only intensified their apprehension, which in turn increased pressure on authorities to 'do something about the problem'. As far back as the early 1930s, persecution of Rastafari by the police and justice system was always systematic and severe – the vagrancy and possession of marijuana laws were particular favourites, and were used apparently at random against individuals or to justify the organized, wholly destructive raids on Rasta camps. Attendant publicity left anybody of any substance with a perception of followers of the movement as workshy, escapist, dirty, insurgent, criminal, violent and borderline insane.

On a state level, the sense of dread at the prospect of Rastafari would appear to have had far more concrete foundation, as throughout the decade the movement adopted an increasingly radical stance. In 1934, Rastafarians began referring to themselves as 'Nyahmen' to acknowledge a bond between themselves and the politically astute and violently anti-colonial Ugandan rebel force Nyabingi. Back in the UK, questions were asked in the House of Commons as to how best to deal with this ominous alliance. In 1935, when Italy attacked Ethiopia again, Haile Selassie declared the conflict racial rather than merely territorial and appealed for the world's black population to help his country in their fight. Several thousand Jamaicans attempted to enlist, only to be refused permission under British law. (In the USA the traditional, often lethal, hostility between New York's black and Italian communities dates back to the fighting between the groups that followed the Emperor's call to arms.)

But at the back of the state's inability to 'deal with' Rastafari as it mushroomed was a total lack of comprehension of the racial pride business. Whereas Marcus Garvey had ultimately failed because he took on capitalism armed with little more than ideology, here things were the other way round. While it was hard enough for hidebound British tradition to come to terms with a philosophical movement that wasn't a religion, vociferously gave capitalism the swerve yet had no political manifesto in any accepted sense, what was quite beyond imagination was an ideology based entirely on race arrived at from *a black point of view*. And even more problems were caused by this contemporary thinking perpetually readjusting its stance to cope with whatever presented itself – remember, in Rasta philosophy there's no such thing as an absolute.

Howell and Robert Hinds (his second-in-command) were arrested in 1934 and imprisoned for two years on charges of sedition. Howell was selling postcard-sized photos of Haile Selassie and proclaiming the Ethiopian emperor as the only sovereign to hold sway over black people; thus taxes need no longer be paid to the British Crown. Although he actually unloaded 3,000 – at the altogether royal sum of a shilling each – the authorities' over-reaction was far more effective: a show trial was presided over by no less than the Lord Chief Justice of Jamaica, Sir Robert Grant, ensuring an outraged, spluttering attendant publicity that made much of Howell's 'devilish' anti-government pro-racial stance. And when Howell was pronounced insane the logic was designed to make the population as a whole think carefully about where their loyalties lay. Why would a 'good darkie' want to carry on this way if he wasn't a total lunatic? When the leader was incarcerated in a mental hospital in a blaze of publicity, the whole sorry affair became an astonishingly effective Rastafari recruitment campaign.

There was a further irony in the ruling classes and career politicians being scared silly of Leonard Howell's rewriting of the political rulebook, too – Rastafari simply wasn't interested in such Babylonian goings-on (Babylon being anything outside Rastafari's righteous environment – a mental more than a strictly physical state). As far as being political in the conventional sense of the word, Rastafari loftily dismissed such matters, renaming them 'poli*tricks*'. However, a credo that involved equal distribution of wealth, sought to empower the dispossessed and embraced revolution on a world scale, would always be viewed with great suspicion by any country's political establishment.

While Rastafari may have stayed away from what it saw as the dirty business of Babylonian politics, its indirect effect was becoming crucial to Jamaica's emerging social agenda. Witness the events of 1938, which were to redefine completely the country's social landscape.

Throughout the 1930s, evidence was mounting that Jamaican colonialism wasn't working – the rich were certainly getting richer while the poor were getting considerably poorer. The agricultural-based economies of the Caribbean, Central America and the American South were in severe recession, forcing overseas workers to return to Jamaica, where not only were there no jobs, but wages had been falling for nearly five years. In January 1938 (coincidentally, the 100th anniversary of Jamaican emancipation) workers took over a plantation in Serge Island, St Thomas, to kick off an unprecedented wave of strikes, protest marches, revolts, workforce takeovers and sufferah uprisings that rocked the island. Whole areas were sealed off by workers; the docks shut down, effectively cutting off the country; cross-island communications were destroyed and roads closed; crops were razed and property looted. The police soon lost control and the army had to be deployed. Such direct action seemed to work, as – at a cost of several protesters' lives, scores of injuries and hundreds of arrests – more equitable social and labour legislation was won, trade unions were officially recognized and the roots of Jamaica's two-party political system were put down.

Although Rastafari had no overt involvement in the civil unrest, it has always been accepted, by just about everybody, that had it not been for Rastafari's teachings giving the sufferah classes the self-confidence and proud sense of purpose to take matters into their own hands the revolt would have been neither so widespread nor so determined. It's no coincidence that the rebellion started in St Thomas, Leonard Howell's parish, where Rastafari had its strongest powerbase.

In 1940, Howell was let out of the asylum and, in the name of his Ethiopian Salvation Society, bought an abandoned sugar plantation at Pinnacle in the hills of St Catherine parish to set up an independent Rasta 'state'. Modelled on the Maroon encampments of the eighteenth century, and the free villages in Sligoville set up at the fag-end of slavery, this settlement was an audacious rejection of colonial values. It was entirely self-sufficient, enjoyed communal property and cooperative labour, conformed to the Rasta creed rather than state legislation, swiftly attracted around 1,600 residents and succeeded for fourteen years. Fourteen years of escalatingly brutal police and military attention, as the idea of a viable alternative lifestyle for Jamaica's labour force posed a considerable threat to the already precarious status quo.

As a consolidation of everything Rastafari meant so far, and in providing an environment for its development, Pinnacle was crucial. Until then, the mainly rural Rastafarian movement was spread all over Jamaica with no focus and no prolonged coming together to exchange ideas and put theories into practice. At the settlement, meditation, spiritual reflection and reasoning sessions sharpened the sense of spirituality. And the Rasta language rapidly evolved into its unique take on English that was both as Jamaican as possible and shot through with the blackest of humour as it absorbed the most arid of puns – the late Peter Tosh would perpetually refer to Island Records' then-owner Chris Blackwell as *Chris Whiteworst*. Pinnacle was also where Rasta culture, in the artistic sense, came together as the people of Pinnacle looked towards the motherland determined to express their purity of spirit in arts uncontaminated by four hundred years in Babylon. Using natural – or *ital* – materials, wood carving, painting and sketching followed distinctive, simplistic lines and were groundbreaking in their depiction of black people as very obviously Africans. This art was equally innovative in that it was never afraid to confront the wrongs of the past and present. For the first time since black people had arrived in Jamaica, there was a large-scale creation of art that accurately reflected their reality, as images of slavery or sufferation were preserved in hardwood, on paper or canvas or tree bark. Also, imaginative 'promised landscapes' became a revelation in aspiration, as they showed the children of the diaspora as happy, productive and running things for them-selves on green and fertile land under the bluest skies.

Music, of course, was a huge part of life within Pinnacle. And once again it drew inspiration from Africa, meaning it was entirely natural for the drum to form the basis of Rasta music. During slavery, the drum had been perceived as a vital tool of the African religions and thus it had been banned. Now it lived on in two distinct but almost underground forms: Kumina and Burru, each of which could trace a line of heritage direct from the motherland. Kumina was the musical aspect of Pocomania, a religion that originated in Ghana and survived slavery in Jamaica. The Burru people, descended from a West African tribe, had kept their identity to an astonishing degree, and had been displaced from Clarendon to the Kingston ghettos about twenty years previously.

Burru drumming provided the biggest influence, the classic arrangements involving three drums working in concert to a startlingly tuneful effect. The bass drum carried the rhythm, the repeater took up a melody, while the fundeh harmonized, counterpointing where required. All were double-headed instruments, the bass up to three feet in diameter, with skins loose enough to generate sub-frequencies, and struck with pad-ded sticks as the player sat astride his instrument. The others were much smaller, usually played with the hands, using palms, heels and fingertips to coax a vast spectrum of musical effects and notes from the finely tuned skins. Burru drumming would be performed at its spectacular best to welcome released prisoners home to the community, an act of pure African defiance which seriously impressed the Rastas who lived side by side with Burrus in the Dungle. It was no surprise that many Rasta brethren, Count Ossie among them, studied Burru drum technique under the tutelage of master drummer Brother Job. The subtle difference between Burru style and what formed the basis of Rasta music was a change in the roles as the fundeh kept the beat while the bass emphasized it, enabling a variation of tempos within a single less-complicated rhythm, while the repeater by itself handled the melodies.

Kumina drumming was a far more intense, frantic affair, opting for only two drums, the kbandu and the cast, each being single-headed and big enough for the drummer to sit astride. It was the larger kbandu that held the rhythm, while supplementary patterns would be set up by a secondary player beating either drum's open end with short sticks. The original Rasta music combined the two styles in groups of varying sizes, supplementing it with a variety of African-based or modern percussion instruments and bamboo and bottle saxes. (These were bamboo tubes or bottles with the bottom cut off, that had a strip of Cellophane or paper stretched across one end and were played by humming against it through pursed lips.) Lyrics began as little more than chanting, hymns to Jah Rastafari or passages from the Bible, but soon expanded to include poetry and original lyrics. The early Rasta drumming was far more sophisticated than may be supposed, and quickly served to attract Rasta-sympathizing conventional musicians, playing hookey from the hotel orchestras, which resulted in the additions of guitar and brass lines to create a uniquely Jamaican jazz form.

It was at the Pinnacle camp during the early 1950s that Rastas began growing dreadlocks, after pictures of the Mau Mau, Jomo Kenyatta's anti-colonialist Land and Freedom Army in Kenya, made their way across the Atlantic. That these totally righteous race warriors wore their hair in ferocious-looking uncombed tendrils was appreciated by Howell's community on a number of levels. To the uninitiated it was just plain scary – the sight of a Rasta spectacularly flashing his locks struck an appropriate sense of dread into the belly of the beast that is Babylon. It was a hairstyle calculated to fly in the face of the then fashionable hair processing and straightening, something that Rastas equated with an abandonment of African-ness. It was a singularly black style – try as they might, white people can't grow proper dreadlocks. But the most important aspect was that dreadlocks guaranteed a Rastaman was true to himself at all times; it was impossible to deny you were a Rastaman with foot-long dreadlocks peeping out from under your tam.

Dreadlocks provided a clear target for the authorities – arrested Rastamen would have their heads shaved in police custody for no reason other than degradation. The growing of locks has never been compulsory, indeed many of the original Rastas who took up the faith before the 1950s have never seen the need, and the notion of false dreads (growers of locks with no interest in the Rasta way) has been a constant cause of disquiet among committed brethren. Criminals have locksed up to blend in with Rasta communities, so inviting police attention into the camp and apparently confirming the popular notion that Rastas were inherently villainous. And the idea that what was a considered, meaningful action could be taken so lightly as to become a fashion has always been viewed as seriously disrespectful.

The regular, highly organized and wantonly destructive police raids on the Pinnacle settlement were carried out under the pretext of searching for drugs. They were the direct result of legislation brought in after the 1938 uprising, which criminalized the possession of ganja in order to crack down on the more rebellious elements of Jamaica's lower orders. Of which Rastafari was close to the top of the list. Marijuana arrived in Jamaica courtesy of indentured Indian labourers who came from the subcontinent to work on the plantations during the second half of the nineteenth century, and spread to the black working class as pretty much a cure for whatever ails you –

Peter Tosh was only ever summing up popular opinion of the herb superb's properties with his 'Legalize It' lyrics. In Jamaica's climate ganja was particularly easy to grow; it was smoked, brewed into tea or applied as a poultice, depending on your desired effect, and usage was more or less universal among the sufferahs as either an inexpensive medicine or as a filter with which to blur the edges of life's harsh realities.

As part of Rastafarian life ganja assumed mystical proportions. The ritualistic smoking of pure marijuana in spliffs the size of ice cream cones or communal water-cooled chalices was seen as a vital part of a Rasta's daily business, as it became an invaluable aid to meditation and contemplation, putting the body in closer communication with the soul. It's unlikely that reasoning sessions would be nearly as interesting without unlimited quantities of what was regarded as the holy herb. And, somewhat unsurprisingly, the faithful will point to several references in the Bible that appear to condone such use of the herb.

But whatever genuine spiritual aspect there was to Rastafari's ganja consumption, once the law was changed this was unrestricted drug abuse and became a stick with which Rastafari has been beaten ever since. Originally, the British authorities had officially imported and dealt the weed, levelling duty in the same was as they would on alcohol – thinking that it kept the masses happy and pacified. Following the 1938 revolt, though, the plantocracy demanded draconian and instantaneous laws to control the people, and expanding the Dangerous Drugs Act to include marijuana for the first time was by far the most convenient. Use, possession or cultivation became imprisonable offences, meaning that just about every Rasta on the island could be banged up at more or less any time. And for the entire fourteen years of Pinnacle's existence they were, as 'drugs raid' followed 'drugs raid'. Each operation was planned with military precision, involved hundreds of policemen, was luridly reported in the press, destroyed huts and property and resulted in hundreds of arrests. The end of Pinnacle as an audacious social (or *anti*-social, depending what side you were on) experiment came in 1954 when, during a 'drugs raid', sixty dwellings were trashed, Howell was once more committed to Bellvue mental home and the Rastafari commune dwellers dispersed.

Which was a significant contribution to what became a concentration of Rastafari in and around Kingston, as most evicted Pinnacle people ended up in the city's already overcrowded shanty towns. They found themselves living alongside Rastas evicted from their smallholdings as the bauxite mines moved in. Large camps established at Rockforth, or in the Wareika Hills above the city, or in downtown areas such as Back-A-Wall, Slip Dock Road and Salt Lane.

Where the Prince went looking for the Count.

It was among these ghetto slums that Rastafari exploded into the cultural and social force it has been ever since. The new breed of urban Rastaman was perhaps more militant and worldly than his predecessor, as without the option to drop out – to somewhere like Pinnacle or the smaller encampments – he concerned himself with justice on a grander scale. Thus he needed to be on his mettle, ready to confront the forces of Babylon.

The connection Buster made when he invited Count Ossie to participate in his sessions was always far more important than simply changing the beat. He'd plugged Jamaican popular culture into a genuinely indigenous expression – well left of centre it certainly was, and light years away from cloned Americana. For the first time, the developing commercial power of the sufferahs had been balanced with an idiom entirely of their own making. Of course the records were enormously successful, which meant a superficial softening by the music business of the previous attitudes towards both Rasta and homegrown creative ideas.

And from this point onwards there would be no turning back for Rastafari. It would never be so much as one step removed from the heart and soul of Kingston's studios.

5

Train
to
Skaville

In 1959, the number of Jamaican radio stations was doubled when, to RJR, the government added the Jamaican Broadcasting Corporation. Numerically, this might not seem like much, but in social terms it was hugely significant as Jamaica steered a path towards independence: RJR was a British-owned franchise, while the newcomer would be state-owned. The cornerstone of the new station's brief was to promote the indigenous arts and to reflect local taste accurately. A kind of populist positive discrimination. Or the promotion of the notion that what went over the airwaves ought to stretch beyond previous narrow definitions of culture.

If you bear in mind that just ten years previously the only radio-as-entertainment broadcaster on the island was ZQ1 (ZQ and a suffixed numeral was the call sign of any broadcaster operating in Jamaica), a transmitter set up in the 1930s and run by civil servants from four in the afternoon until nine at night, then you get some idea of what progress had been made. ZQ1 put out a very BBC Radio 2-style schedule of American and British popular hits and easily digestible classics; when RJR was franchised in 1950, it was allowed longer hours to broadcast essentially the same, only with a slightly increased US bias, since so many Jamaicans were opting for the powerful Miami, Nashville and New Orleans stations. With absolutely no sense of irony, the station's much-trumpeted first Jamaican Top 30 was made up entirely of American records.

Things might have stayed like that, if it hadn't been for two programmes put together for JBC by musicians and band leader Sonny Bradshaw, shows which actively sought out a younger, sharper audience. *Teenage Dance Party* would travel the country, broadcasting live each week from a different location, in front of a crowd of that area's youthful dancers. It featured singers and played records, but what set it apart was the unprecedented 'Hit or Miss' section, during which the audience was given the chance to endorse or condemn new records by cheering or heckling – a democracy that, just as the sound men had been observing, showed a distinct bias towards local product. Bradshaw's other show was *Jamaican Hit Parade*, a two-hour session going out on Fridays from the Regal theatre at Cross Roads. As the name would suggest, it ran down the records in that newly instigated Jamaican Top 30, but with the added *frisson* of the Top 10 being performed live, if not by the respective artists then by an available stand-in. Within two months the Top 30 had gone from being uniquely American to strictly Jamaican – even if it was largely Jamaicans doing their best to sound American, it was definitely a step in the right direction.

For Sonny Bradshaw to get it so right was hardly a Herculean task. His 'day job' playing jazz and R&B in the dances meant he knew exactly how the hipper audiences were arriving at their music. Thus, any similarities between *Teenage Dance Party* and a sound-system lawn – from its mobile nature to the vociferous audience participation – were far from coincidental. Likewise *Jamaican Hit Parade*'s enormous debt to the Vere Johns Opportunity Hour, although now the participants were already stars rather than hopefuls looking for a break. Admittedly, Bradshaw's particular musical background gave his shows an initial bias towards R&B, but by drawing inspiration from the tried and tested ghetto rave-ups the sounds of modern Jamaica's musical development were never far behind. In bringing such a distinct flavour of downtown Kingston to the rest of the country, sufferah music acquired an artistic legitimacy. Coinciding with the green shoots of a domestic record industry, this offered up the means for our men in the dancehalls to challenge the existing power structure on what passed for a level playing field.

In the past, radio access had meant most to those who held licences to distribute American records. The main players were Ken Khouri, who held the franchise for RCA, Edward Seaga, for Columbia, and Byron Lee, for Atlantic, and they would see to it that their records were on heavy rotation before they pressed up copies accordingly. Although reliable rumour has it that payola was so rife it went as far as radio station staff being on record company wages, a more provable point is that the number of US records sent to programme chiefs so vastly outnumbered local product that it was impossible for the likes of Coxsone, Reid and Prince Buster to get a look in. Buster explains how the set-up worked (or should that be *failed* to work): 'If people requested your tune then the radio had to play it, but for people to request it, it had to be played; but when a man have fifty or a hundred American tunes to get through, there was no space for you. Then you had to have big money pay the radio station people, so there was no way we could oppose the situation.'

Until then.

By the turn of the decade, the sound systems were so prolific they offered a viable alternative to both radio stations; and as the airwaves began courting the nation's proletariat so the programmers had to look to the sound men for guidance. At first this was a covert operation, with radio deejays or their people going to dances as punters to check out what was moving the crowd; then, as more sound men started making records, it was done in a spirit of cooperation. Not surprisingly, when popular taste swung away from US R&B the smaller operators' clout increased accordingly and the price of airtime (both official and otherwise) fell to a far more affordable level. After all, these guys could deliver guaranteed hits, which in radio-station terms was probably worth more than hard cash. Even if such a hit went against everything they felt they ought to stand for.

At first, the idea of sound men getting records on the radio was geared up to publicizing the sound-system operations, hence the swift evolution from R&B to ska as operators sought to stay ahead of the game. But with this increasing exposure came a definite shift in emphasis in the Big Three's business plans. As the 1960s got under way – when the number of record players in Jamaica increased significantly – the selling of records was elevated from a sideline to a priority. Of course, the sound systems remained central to their business set-ups; it was just that now they had hard evidence there was more to life than Beat Street sound clashes.

Naturally, behind the setting-up of the Jamaican Broadcasting Corporation and its conspicuous Jamaicanness was a self-serving political motivation. The island had been fully self-governing since 1957, and by 1959 independence from colonial rule was inevitable, so both the ruling People's National Party and the opposition Jamaican Labour Party had it at the core of their manifestos. Each sought to bang their nationalistic drum with greater gusto, and a state-owned radio station championing the nation's cultural identity made an ideal stick for the PNP.

More so than ever at this point, because as the fifties rolled into the sixties radio ownership in Jamaica had blown right up. In the previous decade, there were hardly any radios in the country, as most people couldn't afford what was on offer. Then, when technology advanced around the end of the war and inexpensive mass-produced models began to arrive, only 20 per cent of homes had electricity and batteries were in very short supply. If, back then, you had a usable radio and there was a big event on – a championship fight or a Test match – your home wouldn't be your own for the duration: neighbours or passers-by who couldn't get into your front room or on to your porch would be in the front yard or the street outside. During the 1950s, Rediffusion introduced cable-fed wall boxes for their broadcasts, which were rented by the week and required neither electricity nor batteries, and when JBC went on air it was hooked up to this scheme. By 1960, 90 per cent of households in Jamaica had a working radio, a fivefold increase since 1945, a figure greatly assisted as the electrification of rural Jamaica progressed; by the early-1960s about three-quarters of the country was wired to the national grid.

But while the undercurrents of JBC's instigation were pure politics – a high-profile sop to the masses – in view of what it actually achieved as regards sufferah music, such an itinerary was a relatively small price to pay.

At a midnight ceremony on 5 August 1962, nearly three hundred years of colonial rule came to an end as Jamaican independence finally happened. But it wasn't Norman Manley's government that officially raised Jamaica's new black, gold and green flag. In the general elections held four months previously, Sir Alexander Bustamante's more conservative JLP had swept to power on a ticket that drew on the party's trade-union roots to offer a package of worker-friendly proposals, and had tempered its pro-independence stance by overtly cultivating ties with America.

For the vast majority of Jamaicans, independence was far more exciting in theory than in practice. Being free from British rule meant something tangible to the politicians and the disproportionate few who controlled so much of the country's wealth. However, in the gullies of West Kingston or the remote rural hamlets where 70-odd per cent lived below the official poverty line, it had raised expectations to somewhere approaching danger level. During the years leading up to 1962, the idea of independence had been sold to the people as the answer to so many of their problems, with promises of prosperity, justice and, if not an end to, then at least a serious dent in the class divide. An understandably seductive situation, but, come the glorious day, one that did little to underpin an economic and social infrastructure that had been falling apart for years. The practicalities of life remained the same, and thousands of country folk drifted into cities such as Kingston, Montego Bay and Spanish Town looking for jobs that didn't exist and finding living conditions far worse than those they had left behind. Indeed, this influx sorely stretched the native Kingstonians' stock stoicism as they had genuinely believed things wouldn't be any worse now that they were out from under the colonial yoke.

Not that there wasn't a wave of optimism washing across the island in 1962 – there was nobody who didn't genuinely want independence to work. And besides, when you've got no past of your own then your future quite literally is everything. Government policy was to market this mood for all it was worth, but as far as real life went, the idea of happy, smiling darkies, jubilant with their newly acquired lot was strictly for the tourist brochures.

Less than a year after independence, on Easter weekend 1963, Rose Hall in St James saw the bloodiest uprising since Sam Sharp led slaves in revolt in 1831. Soldiers and Rastas fought a pitched battle that left buildings burned, hundreds arrested and eight people dead. Likewise, the music wasn't so two-dimensional as it's often portrayed. While the radio stations keenly promoted the upbeat side of things, the notion that black expression was limited to a carnival-type jolly-up contrived to dance unrestrainedly and unconditionally in on-going celebration is hopelessly romantic.

Of course, the music industry came to the party, with tunes such as 'Independent Jamaica' or 'Forward March' or 'Anniversary Ska', but their collective B-side was an equal number with titles such as 'Babylon Gone', 'Time Longer than Rope' or 'Carry Go Bring Come'.

A couple of years into the 1960s and the music had settled down into what was to become the classic ska sound. There were still R&B and JA boogie tunes being cut – particularly by Duke Reid and Linden Pottinger – but the radio programmes had inadvertently set ska's tone with their constant demand for uptempo records. Naturally, producers and performers alike figured the way to get ahead was to give the stations what they wanted. What pushed the transition through, though, was something that was to become a noticeable feature of every major change in Jamaican music – a new set of musicians came on the scene.

Drumbago's rhythm section now faced increasing competition from a new outfit consisting of Lloyd Knibbs, Tommy McCook, Lloyd Brevette and Jackie Mittoo, hungry young players keen to prove they had chops. It was these guys – in 1963 they would form the backbone of that seminal ska band the Skatalites – who did much to determine the new beat. Rimshots on the downbeat heralded the change of style as a new beat that practically cut itself in half from what had established the style. While it kept that 4/4 time, with the bass drum accenting the second and fourth beats in that marching-drum style, the off-beat emphasis increased by presenting itself as a single stroke. Which was taken up by either the piano or the guitar; instead of waiting for the return to come over as choon-*ka* . . . choon-*ka* . . . choon-*ka* . . . , it quickened its step and made do with just the -*ka* . . . -*ka* . . . -*ka* . . . A punching brass section added to the emphases already going on inside the structure, while a creeping-type bass-line underpinned the whole thing.

It's a situation best illustrated by dropping the Eric Morris single 'Humpty Dumpty', Derrick Morgan's 'Forward March' and the Wailers' 'Simmer Down', one after the other. They were cut in 1961, 1962 and 1963, by Prince Buster, Leslie Kong and Coxsone Dodd, respectively, and the progression is obvious. The first swings rather than jumps, with Ernie Ranglin's guitar going up and down and Drumbago pushing the whole thing along fairly evenly; 'Forward March' was also a Drumbago session, but by now they're chopping it up; and 'Simmer Down' is practically a gallop, putting so much on the upstroke – rhythm, horns, piano – it allows for melodies and a counter rhythm to go on inside.

As national radio took up Jamaican music, a far greater circle of prospective participants emerged. These newcomers – from all over the country, not just the incestuous Kingston scene –

brought with them a variety of ideas, giving the music no option other than to broaden out. Artists and producers could wear their influences with pride, and the sheer number of shades of ska belies the popular perception of it being, thematically and artistically, a one-trick pony.

As so many of these arrivals were singers, when ska first blew up it was as a vocal expression presented across a spectrum of styles. Incidentally, singing swiftly rose in prominence after producers found the radio stations steering away from instrumentals, which they saw as strictly sound-system specials. Groups like the Jiving Juniors, the Techniques (featuring Slim Smith), Alton Ellis & the Flames and the Gaylads modelled themselves on American harmony acts in terms of singing style and presentation, with repertoires dominated by the kind of teenage-melodrama love songs that had been the US pop staple for a decade or more. Particularly active in this field were the vocal duos such as Keith & Enid, Bunny & Skitter, Alton & Eddie, Roy & Millie and Derrick & Patsy, who, in borrowing from country and western's proclivity for cheesy two-handers, were crucial in establishing the always popular smooove ska ballad.

So far so US residual; but, as new acts came through, ska moved to cover all lyrical bases. Most famously, the Wailing Wailers brought an adolescent swagger to the proceedings as they mixed self-penned tales aimed specifically at Kingston's mean streets – 'Simmer Down', 'Holligan' (aka 'Hooligan') and 'Rude Boy' – with what was their staple diet of love songs and such apparently ill-fitting cover versions as 'What's New, Pussycat?' Social comment or protest had been part of the music scene since 1959 and Clancy Eccles's 'Freedom' (a rudimentary R&B adaptation of 'John Brown's Body'). By the early sixties, ska's conscience was busting out all over: Prince Buster was constantly outspoken with records such as 'African Blood' and 'War Paint'; Alton Ellis's 'Dance Crasher' concerned itself with dancehall warfare; Stranger Cole's 'Rough and Tough' was a barbed comment on street violence; 'Money Can't Buy Life', by Monty Morris, and Lord Tamano and the Skatalites' 'Come

Down' are, respectively, dire warnings about the sins of avarice and conceit; Justin Hinds and the Dominoes' 'Teach the Youth' was self-explanatory, like Desmond Dekker's equally obvious 'Honour Your Father and Your Mother'.

Spiritually, ska's lyricists were on the case, too. The Maytals (who also worked as the Vikings and the Royals) came on with all the fervour of a particularly lively revival meeting. Lead singer Toots Hibbert's gospel-based hollering was backed up by equally raucous harmonies and showed a spiritual bent in numbers like 'Victory', 'Never Grow Old' and 'Six and Seven Books of Moses'. This latter track seems to be a veiled reference to the transported black nation as the lost tribe of Israel, which, like Jimmy Cliff's deliberately ambiguous 'King of Kings' (it's ostentatiously about the lion as the king of the beasts), gives some idea of where Rasta stood in Jamaica's social pecking order. In spite of its phenomenal growth across the black population in general, disproportionately higher among the Kingston music community, it was usually sung about only in laughably oblique terms. Which made the blatant dread of Justin Hinds and the Dominoes' 'Mighty Redeemer', 'Botheration', 'King Samuel' and 'Carry Go Bring Come' all the more remarkable.

But it was in the actual music that things were getting really interesting. In 1960 Jimmy Cliff arrived in Kingston as twelve-year-old country boy James Chambers to tout himself round the recording studios, doing his best to disguise his youth by singing in unnaturally gruff tones. Now, comfortably ensconced in London's upmarket media hangout the Groucho Club, he still vividly remembers Jamaica's ska explosion and how the singers supplied a great deal more than the lyrics.

'When I got to Kingston ska was still an option, like a new-fashioned thing not everybody was sure of. The first few tunes I cut were for smaller sound systems, like Sir Cavalier, who didn't want to take any chances, so the records weren't ska, they were R&B. But within about a year ska completely dominated the music scene in Kingston, maybe not yet on the radio but certainly in the dances. And *anybody* who have a tune they want to record would nod to the session band leader and tell him "It ska beat mi want", because it was the only way they would take your tune seriously. The best bands could play any tune, in any style, in any arrangement, in any key, but with a good strong ska beat. It meant that you didn't have to adapt your style of songwriting to suit them – the chord progressions in my songs were always different from other people's. Like Toots and them brought a rawer style to it with the songs they wrote. Or Derrick Morgan – who I used to listen to when I was in school – he had a kind of rhythmic style of singing. Which was different to Stranger Cole, who was much more mellow. All these guys were singing ska, but they all did it in their own way.

'You have to give credit to Prince Buster for this. He was the first singer/producer and he helped singers get more involved in the studio. He showed us how to get what we wanted from the band, so our ideas could make a solid contribution. It used to be that a singer came into the studio with no more than a quarter of a song, he'd sing this raw idea to the band leader and the musicians who would then have to structure it. To put it together and make sure it turns out as a song. But it would always turn out how the band wanted to do it. Buster taught singers to go in with the complete song written, melody and words and everything, then they could express how they wanted it at every stage. The guitarist or pianist would pick up the tune first, then the drummer would establish a basic rhythm and the bass would follow that – this was before the bass-line became so dominant. If there were horn players, they would work out their own arrangements, but they'd do that last of all to take up the lead part of the melody again once the rhythm was properly in place. Things were different with Drumbago, because he was a drummer as well as the arranger. He'd travel with a flute and you'd sing your song to him and he'd take it up on the flute first then pass it on to the keyboard player to do the chords.'

What this meant was that the singers were now doing as much as the musicians themselves to broaden things out, which is why the style went as rapidly wide as it did. Country-blues elements permeated so many of the love songs; Motown-isms were starting to creep into the back of a few of the singing groups' arrangements, and mento was alive and well. Really, it's least surprising that mento, the original Jamaican music form, should come to the fore: Independence Day fallout lingered a long time, and any cultural roots that existed were being keenly explored. Blending it with ska sounded good, too, as tunes like Eric Morris's 'Penny Reel-O' proved (this one also gave an airing to that other Caribbean music staple, the slackness lyrics). Other 'nu school' mentos were the equally lewd 'Rukumbine', by Shenley Duffus, and trumpeter Baba Brooks' reworking of the old mento standard 'River Bank' into 'Bank to Bank'. It's significant that the best mento-style ska tunes were Duke Reid productions. By this time, 1963 or so, the Trojan had not long returned to the recording industry, and he was very much a traditionalist, hence the mento connection. As a truly devoted R&B fan he viewed the ska beat with such contempt that he believed it to be a craze that wouldn't last, and opted to concentrate on running his sound system with US records rather than suffer the continued expense of recording. Perhaps more to the point, though, is that while he had to rely on R&B, his dances of that period, even the open ones, were known as 'bull parties – jus' a few man drinking rum, no gal', which was when the Duke realized he couldn't ignore ska any longer. It must be said that, when he did put his mind to it, Reid produced some of the best ska ever made, courtesy of the Skatalites, Slim Smith, Don Drummond, the Techniques, Justin Hinds, Alton Ellis and Stranger Cole.

Brentford Road isn't what you might call 'the ghetto'. It's much closer to the business district of Cross Roads than it is to Trench Town. On the short walk from New Kingston's luxury hotel complexes you won't pass very much graffiti'd corrugated iron or more than a couple of abandoned cars, and even in today's particularly twitchy times the only uneasiness you'll experience will be caused by the heat. Brentford Road is where uptown meets downtown: it's funky enough to have some Jamaican street soul, but never so spirited as to be intimidating. Perfect for a man like Clement Dodd to do business. There was more space in this part of town, with roomier buildings set back from the street in bigger yards, yet the area was not too far from ska's natural environment. In 1963 Dodd took over 13 Brentford Road, premises that previously housed a nightclub called The End, installed a one-track board and opened the Jamaican Recording & Publishing Studio Ltd, also known as Studio One.

This was a highly significant development: Dodd was then the only black man in Jamaica to own a recording studio, and was the first sound man to take his profits from dances and record sales and invest them in something as long term as a recording facility (Duke Reid didn't open his own studio until two years later, and Prince Buster put his money into juke boxes and setting up mosques). This was serious business. It marked the coming-of-age of this generation of modern Jamaican musicians, proving that what they were doing wasn't going away and, most importantly, wasn't going away from where it all began.

Having his own studio provided time and space that was vital to Coxsone Dodd. While he might have been a businessman in his head, he was a jazzman in his heart, and what he wanted to do was to give his musicians the room to let go. Musicians who were equally unreconstructed, and whose technical expertise was matched only by a sense of adventure that came from growing up listening to Dizzy Gillespie, Charlie Parker and Coleman Hawkins, then distilled in such big bands as Eric Dean's or Jack Brown's. Having removed the constraints of buying studio time, Dodd then took the unprecedented step of putting a nucleus of the island's best musicians on wages, rather than hiring them as 'n' when and paying them per side cut. His reasoning was that this would allow the players the chance to explore and be genuinely creative, and then to make sure they'd got it right. It's an indication of exactly what such an opportunity meant that, in spite of these wages being pitifully low, many of the best bandsmen in Jamaica took him up on his offer. (Of course, Dodd was buying their time, not their exclusivity, so they still supplemented their income by working elsewhere.)

Clement Dodd pretty much let the musicians get on with it, which was exactly the right thing to do, as it turned out, pushing Studio One into genuinely creating rather than essentially *re*-creating. Until then, Coxsone's definition of A&R involved the teenaged Bob Marley sifting through piles of imported US singles to advise on which should be adapted, plagiarized or just plain bootlegged. More than that, though, Studio One set a trend that remains central to reggae's core – for successful artists to open their own studios, operations that remain as vital to reggae's development today as Coxsone's set-up nearly forty years ago. And for exactly the same reasons. The best ska or rocksteady or dub or dancehall or whatever form it was taking that year, has always had enormous spiritual and populist elements evolving in relation to Jamaica's black nation's mood swings. Such a connection can't be spun to order or to the mainstream music business's usual schedule, so to have your own studio allows unlimited time and a distinct lack of pressure to connect with this essence of Jamaicanness. It gives the room to experiment, the luxury of cutting uncommercial but musically/culturally important records, or to make loads of tunes just because you want to. It's a rare reggae record made outside this ambience that has actually moved anything forward. Hence, nowadays, there aren't *quite* as many tiny recording studios as there are jerk chicken shops in Kingston, but you get the general idea.

Back in Brentford Road in 1963, a loose collective of master musicians were about to organize themselves as the Skatalites. Essentially, this crew was Lloyd Brevette (bass), Lloyd Knibbs (drums), Jackie Mittoo (piano/organ), Tommy McCook (lead tenor sax), Roland Alphonso and Lester Sterling (sax), Don Drummond (trombone), Johnny Moore and Ba Ba Brooks (trumpet), Jah Jerry and Harold Moore (guitar) and Lord Tanamo and Tony DaCosta (vocals). Aside from paying the producer's bills by backing an A-list of singers for the Studio One label's string of ska hits, they had plenty of time to do their own thing(s). A by-product of this was to give substance to

Coxsone's dreams of initiating a jazz genre with a genuine Jamaican flavour, by laying bebop-style solos and big-band instrumentation over a solid ska backing.

The shrewdest of moves on Coxsone's part was to give free rein to Don Drummond's skills, vision and discipline as a musical arranger. Trombonist Drummond had learned his trade at Alpha Boys' School, an establishment for wayward youth on South Camp Road that has more than earned its place in Jamaican musical history by numbering among its old boys a generation of horn players that includes Tommy McCook, Vin Gordon, Bobby Ellis, Rico, Leroy Wallace and Joe Harriott. Run by nuns, the only things stricter than the discipline were the music lessons, in which students were taught theory, composition, space and arrangement by learning the classics. And as one of the few ways to get out of such chores as scrubbing toilets or kitchen duties was to attend rehearsals with the school's acclaimed marching band (hence the emphasis on brass), few shirked music.

Don Drummond was such an outstanding student that after he left he was persuaded to return to Alpha to teach music, and his sessions at Studio One had all the rigid discipline and attention to detail of the schoolroom. Each player followed the leader's meticulously drawn charts, belying ska's later reputation as 'happy-go-lucky' – the Skatalites in instrumental mode could be as formal a proposition as, say, the Duke Ellington Orchestra preparing to play Carnegie Hall. But for all his intrinsic correctness the trombonist knew when to go for a head arrangement, and his real strength lay in his ability to observe the music from outside and direct it as a feeling or a mood rather than as a technical exercise. Often that mood was intriguingly dark. Don Drummond was a fierce black nationalist and a devout Rastafarian, who set out to make music that connected with both the soul of Africa and her displaced sons and daughters on a deeply spiritual level. In many ways, ska never meant so much as when Don Drummond and his mournful, soulful 'bone were leading the Skatalites in such tunes as 'Man in the Street', 'Addis Ababa', 'Eastern Standard Time' or 'Don Cosmic'. All minor-key material, music which, with spooky suitability, would be played largely on the piano's black notes.

Of course, the Skatalites went way beyond Don Drummond and Studio One. Just as many of the group's innovative instrumentals were arranged by saxophonists Tommy McCook and Roland Alphonso, or keyboard "man" Jackie Mittoo – who didn't turn sixteen until 1964 – or were cut for Duke Reid or the Yap brothers' Top Deck label. And the group manifested itself in numerous guises – practically anything from that period with a solo Skatalite as the artist credit will involve the rest of the group too. It was this band's rip-roaring instrumentals such as 'Phoenix City', 'Guns of Navarone' and 'Ball o' Fire' that formed the lasting impression of the music – even Prince Buster, ska's most successful singer, remains best known for the practically instrumental 'Al Capone'. But as strong and as talented as the individual Skatalites were, when Don Drummond left in spectacularly tragic circumstances in 1965 it became very easy for the group to fall apart.

To say *pressure reach* the trombonist would be to put it mildly. In post-colonial Jamaica, schizophrenia among the black urban poor was rampant – although it was seldom diagnosed medically, the victim simply being locked up or cast out of the community – and Drummond developed a pathological hatred of white people. It was for all the obvious reasons, but was enormously intensified by the sense of frustration he felt from years of trying to make ends meet in sterile north-coast cabaret bands. Then, when he did do something worthwhile, he felt he was not being taken seriously beyond the ghettos; his Alpha grounding would have left him well aware of exactly what yardsticks ought to be applied to music. There are reports of his walking around Kingston smiling beatifically at black people then spitting at white people, and he would regularly check himself into the sanatorium, emerging slightly more detached on each occasion.

In the early hours of New Year's Day 1965, for reasons that were never made clear but appear to be a particularly unfortunate example of black self-hatred manifesting itself in violence, Drummond stabbed to death his common-law wife, the dancer and singer Margarita. He gave himself up at Rockfort police station the next day and was committed to Bellevue mental asylum, where he died four years later. Besides his fantastic musical legacy, and there are several Don Drummond albums available today, the most fitting epitaph to his greatness is that one of his trombones, lovingly polished and cared for, is now on permanent display in the music hall at Alpha Boys' School.

As soon as it seemed that downtown operators like Coxsone, Buster and Reid were getting fat from ska record sales, there was sudden interest beyond their own community. Before Jamaica had a record industry, the only means to make money from music there was to run a sound system, and there was no way that the likes of Chris Blackwell, Byron Lee and Leslie Kong would or could do that. Now, however, producing and selling records presented opportunities for large-scale profit from Jamaican music. Paradoxically, while it took their involvement to consolidate the 'business' end of the music market, from which everybody would benefit, this came with a price.

Chris Blackwell had enjoyed considerable success producing domestic acts in the imported music forms of R&B and JA boogie, but as ska took over the Kingston music scene, the creative process became far more impenetrable. Blackwell decamped to London in 1962, where he opened up an official ska export market by licensing tunes from his homeland's top producers for UK release. Long before that, though, he set up Kingston's first formal record distribution and wholesale channels. According to Jimmy Cliff, this boosted Jamaica's music industry by providing budding artists with a viable alternative to the sound systems.

'Chris Blackwell was really the one that opened up the selling of records in Jamaica, because up until then there had been no proper wholesaling or anything like a proper distribution set-up. Producers had just supplied to a few shops they knew with somebody on a motorcycle – when they showed it like that in *The Harder They Come*, that was all exactly how it was – and there was no way anybody was going to sell a lot of records that way. Because Blackwell didn't have a sound system like the other producers and by now the radio was playing Jamaican-made stuff, he knew the way he could get the most out of the music business was to get his records to as many shops as possible.

'Maybe through him not being caught up in the sound-system thing he ran his affairs much more like a business and used to pay higher rates to artists and musicians. That's how people got to hear about Chris Blackwell. They'd say "Go to the white man, him pay better money!" It meant there were quite a few artists willing to forgo the instant acclaim they might get if their record hit big on Duke Reid's or Coxsone's sound system. It was because of Chris Blackwell that artists started getting interested in selling records, yuh know, looking beyond the sound systems.'

Likewise Leslie Kong, the first Chinese-Jamaican to come into the business at the creative end, and who made his name as the most immediately effective 'outsider' producer of the ska era. Kong's reason to get into record production in 1963 was to become typical – he owned a record shop and wanted to make sure it would always be stocked with new and exclusive product. Together with his two brothers, Kong owned Beverley's, a combined ice-cream parlour, cosmetics boutique and record shop, into which walked an enterprising Jimmy Cliff.

'I knew of Leslie Kong's establishment, Beverley's, and how he was interested in the music, and I thought that if I wrote a song called Beverley it would make him listen. I wrote a song that night called "Dearest Beverley" and next day, just as they were closing, I went in and asked the three Kong brothers if they were into recording. They said they weren't, so I said, "Well you should. I'm a singer and I can help you get into it." Leslie Kong said, "You're a singer? Go on sing." So I sung "Dearest Beverley". The other two brothers just laughed, but Leslie said he thought I had the best voice he'd ever heard in

Jamaica and that was it; he wanted to know how he could get into making records. I knew all the musicians, I knew the studios, I knew the business, so I could help him.

'I knew Derrick Morgan, who was ahead of me – already a star – and talked him into joining us, because he was experienced and so Leslie Kong could work more easily with him. Also, he need somebody established like Derrick to start off with so people would take notice and know how serious he was. Leslie Kong had lots of ideas and a good feel for the music but no rhythm whatsoever, so when he came into the studios to put his ideas across to the musicians he had difficulty. It could take a while, because he'd say play it like this, and what he'd tell them would make no sense, so they'd have to try and work out what it really was he wanted! They'd play something and he'd say, "No, a bit faster", or, "Put a break in there", and they'd do it over and over until he said, "Yes, that's it". The first session Leslie Kong had was with myself, Derrick Morgan and Monty Morris, in late 1961 or early 1962, and that was the beginning of the Beverley's label. We did ska right from the beginning, and although we didn't get hit records off that first session, during our second session we got a hit record with my song "Hurricane Hattie". That's what established Leslie Kong; then came Derrick's "Forward March", which was massive.'

The established producers were not so accommodating of Leslie Kong's swiftly escalating success; in fact, they deeply resented the idea of a Chinese-Jamaican moving into what had been an exclusively, and importantly, black neighbourhood. None more so than Prince Buster – Morgan was one of the sound man's best friends, one for whom he'd produced a string of hits, and he believes 'Forward March' ripped off one of his tunes. Soon West Kingston was left in no doubt as to where Buster stood on the matter when the Voice of the People sound system started blasting 'Black Head Chinee Man', a single tempering its unambiguous chastisement with dire warnings: *You done stole my belongings and give them to your Chinee man . . . Are you a Chinee man? Are you a black man | It don't need no eyeglass to see that your skin is black.*

The song kicked off a war of words and music, in which Morgan and Kong responded with a tune attacking Buster, who in turn felt obliged to answer. Such seven-inch battles would become a regular feature of the Jamaican music industry, more often than not bitchy digs at rivals or former employers, but in this case Buster's motives were as political as they were personal and professional. Buster genuinely was a man of the people, enjoying a kind of Godfather of the Ghetto status as people came to him with problems or for advice and providing a genuine role model through his artistic and business achievements. But by 1962 he had converted to Islam, meaning that black advancement through self-help had become an imperative instead of merely a priority. While he sought to maintain the cultural thrust of the developing music, he also saw the business side of this unique art form as a means to generate wealth from outside the ghetto and keep the black shilling in community circulation. Now here was a Chinese man, far less musically gifted than the core of ska producers, looking to clean up. Never less than aware of just how deeply the black Caribbean psyche had been scarred by decades of colonialism on top of centuries of slavery, Buster was determined to speak out against the alarming prospect of black artists becoming subordinate to producers/label bosses of other races – scarily, this could be coming about through force of habit as much as anything else. It must be remembered that his stinging musical rebukes to Morgan – titles that followed included 'Thirty Pieces of Silver' and 'Praise without Raise' – always offered counsel to the man who remains his friend to this day.

Jimmy Cliff, however, was aware of another reality of the situation – like Chris Blackwell, Leslie Kong paid better.

'Most of the other Nubian producers were bitter,' he says. 'They'd talk about "How could we let the Chinee man come into the business? How did we let that happen?", but he was doing well and they couldn't stop him. It was because he paid us. He had a reputation for being straight and paying the going rate, which was what we all wanted. I'd had experience with two other producers prior to Leslie Kong –

Nubians – and one of them didn't pay me, so Leslie Kong made a big difference in that respect. Outside of his race, he was a good person.'

The fact that Blackwell and Kong appeared to play straight – or straighter than the black producers – in their direct dealings with the artists is another damning indictment of slavery/colonialism's aftermath. *Having* to show respect to white people meant that the only people most slaves were able to pull fast ones on were each other, and the only chance many had to assert any sort of cleverness was to do just that. Back then, this blatant lack of self-respect was one of the main reasons Prince Buster joined the Nation of Islam in 1961 and worked to spread the word of an alternative racial reality. But such a sorry state of affairs hung over so far past emancipation and colonialization that many would argue it still dogs the reggae industry. Too many black people within it remain far too willing to be 'smart' with each other, yet will practically roll over and wave their legs in the air for anybody else.

'Out of many, one people' was the new Jamaica's motto. Exactly the sort of heartwarming, let's-put-the-past-behind-us sloganeering needed by a nation emerging from centuries of subservience into serious economic problems and a massive inferiority complex. But if you lived on the wrong side of the tracks, as over two-thirds of the country did, it was exactly that – a slogan. With no tangible value whatsoever. It doesn't really matter what was spoken in the speeches given on 6 August 1962, or contained in political manifestos leading up to the event, or was put in to fuel the programmed optimism of the immediate aftermath; one simple truth remained. If there had been any economic reason whatsoever for the British to hang on to the colony of Jamaica, they would have done so. The bauxite deals were already boxed off, the sugar trade was dying on its feet, the banana trade was never going to sustain an economy and the sophisticated hotel chains that were cornering the tourist market were American owned. The spectacular growth in Gross Domestic Product of the 1950s had shrunk both considerably and rapidly, meaning one thing only – Jamaica just wasn't worth it any more.

In fact, more worryingly, it would only be a matter of time before the island and its under-employed islanders started costing its government huge amounts of money. Better that government be those islanders themselves. In the years following independence the gap between the haves and the have-nots in this supposed One People opened up to enormous proportions.

On the music front, ska's popularity was, by now, phenomenal. It had been kicking for the best part of four years; it wasn't unheard of for records to sell over 50,000 copies, and the combination of this and the attendant uptown business interest had given the music a sheen of respectability. The Skatalites had a great deal to do with this, for when musicians of their stature on the north coast and in the up-scale jazz clubs started taking it that seriously, the higher orders of Jamaican society got curious. The group would regularly be invited to play at municipal garden parties in the well-manicured uptown parks.

More critical to this onslaught of respectability, though, was Byron Lee and his touring band the Dragonnaires, who were by now spreading the music further afield both sociologically and geographically. Lee, a Chinese-Jamaican who was probably as successful a businessman, record importer and concert promoter as he was a band-leader, would travel the country playing a live version of ska in villages, tourist resorts and upmarket functions. He was not a ghetto man and enjoyed access to the island's upper echelons of society through a close association with Edward Seaga: the politician produced Lee's first record, 'Dumplin's', in 1959 and it was Seaga who encouraged him to play ska in the early-1960s; later in the decade, Lee bought Seaga's W.I.R.L. studios to rename them Dynamic Sound, and his Lee Enterprises Ltd never had any bureaucratic problems with show promotions or bringing artists or records into the country. After coming down to Seaga's base at Cho Co Mo Lawn to familiarize himself with ska, he set about smoothing the rough edges off it to include as much of it as calypso and

American pop in the band's repertoire. Lee himself maintains it was this and practically this alone that took the music to the furthermost reaches of the island, and by presenting it in an uptown fashion to an uptown crowd he was the catalyst for radio-station interest. While ska had been on the radio for a couple of years before he took it up, it is true that he opened up new arenas to the music, as there were still large parts of Jamaica with no electricity and thus no access to the airwaves.

Although his motives appear wholly altruistic, an astonishing number of musicians seem to view Byron Lee with suspicion. This is a shame. It would seem to have much to do with Lee becoming Jamaican music's first indigenous millionaire (Chris Blackwell was wealthy to start off with), and such paltry, resentful carping – bitching about instead of getting behind their own success stories – is something that continues to dog the reggae business. Talk to people in the industry and very soon you'll learn how everybody (else) ripped off everybody for both ideas and money; no one (else) can be trusted; and nobody (else) who ever made it would have done so if some kept-in-the-background third party (oddly, usually whoever's telling you the tale) hadn't had all the talent and done all the hard work. Maybe such small-mindedness is to do with Jamaica's continuing painful social problems, or perhaps lack of vision is an integral part of an island mentality, but it's always been such perpetual petty squabbling that has held the industry back in the international arena. By the 1970s, 'difficult to deal with' could almost be mainstream record company jargon for 'reggae act'. The fact remains, though; Byron Lee's championing of ska outside its original environment stimulated the sort of widespread interest required to give it legs.

Curiously, the tune that lent its title to this chapter is one of the most seriously mistitled records ever to come out of Jamaica. To call it 'Train *From* Skaville' would have made more sense. Firstly, it was cut at the back end of 1966, by which time ska in the heartlands of the Jamaican music industry – the ghettos – was maybe not buried but very definitely dead. And any notions of Skaville will make even less sense when you listen to the tune – in terms of time signature, arrangement, and general easy-does-it vibe, it's a textbook example of rocksteady. The cooler, more restrained rhythms that, for the second half of that year, had been battering down Trench Town.

And while there were these changes happening on the island, greater things were happening elsewhere too: ska, in its original form, had gone international. Either officially or otherwise, the men and the music were starting to make waves across the sea in both Britain and the United States. And, wouldn't you know it, it was the organic end of things that was doing best.

6

Strange Country

London in the late 1950s could be a cold place in more ways than the obvious. Or so it appeared if you were one of the 90,000 or so newly arrived Jamaicans.

Official figures for the number of Caribbean immigrants in Great Britain back then ran at around 160,000, although these estimates are at best vague because stowing away to get to England was always a viable option. Sneaking aboard a ship in Kingston harbour, especially for the younger, more cavalier *émigré*, was never going to be very difficult, given the amount of comings and goings just before it sailed; if the worst came to the worst, climbing up the anchor chain at night was a possibility. Once at sea, stowaways would emerge, mingle with the regular passengers during the day – it was unlikely they wouldn't know anybody else on board – take turns for meals and upon arrival legitimate passengers would throw their passports back over the fence at the quayside for stowaways to present at immigration. 'All looking alike' would seem to have its advantages. Add to this the seamen who jumped ship in the UK and the visitors who simply never went home, numbers that were growing as Britain acquired a bigger black community for them to disappear into, and the true Commonwealth immigration count was probably 50 per cent higher than the government's reckoning.

Official immigration from the Caribbean to the UK had been running at between 12,000 and 15,000 a year during the mid-fifties, accelerating to as many as 50,000 per annum towards the end of the decade. This sharp upward curve was precipitated by many wanting to get under the wire before the restrictions that had been mooted in Parliament were set in place. By 1962, when Britain's Conservative government passed the Commonwealth Immigration Bill, the official tally of West Indian immigrants ran at a little over 300,000, spread out in different cities across the country, with the proportion of slightly over 50 per cent Jamaicans still being maintained.

As a proportion of Jamaica's available workforce – or even of its population in general (then, approximately 2 million) – these figures are staggering. And it remains practically impossible for anybody who didn't live through that exodus to appreciate what went on, or just plain why such an enormous amount of people should opt to sail half way round the world to make a new life in a country they really knew nothing about. Proof of a widespread unpreparedness can be taken from the sheer number of stories now laughingly told by 1950s West Indian immigrants of how totally freaked out they were when they woke up to their first snowfall. As well as those who carefully planned their emigration and sorted out jobs to go to – London Transport, the National Health Service and the British Hotel and Restaurant Association all ran aggressive personnel recruitment campaigns in the West Indies – there were an astonishing number who literally just decided to go on a whim. A fairly typical scenario would involve a young man – late teens/early twenties, perhaps, though not always, wanted by the police – getting together with a few of his spars on a morning when a ship was in, and opting to go to *Hinglan* because they had nothing else to do. Simple as that. Then working out how to get on board, and worrying about what to do when they got there . . . you get the general idea.

What they all had in common when they arrived in the UK, whatever route they took, was that it wasn't quite like they'd been told it would be. At the end of the 1950s, after ten years of large-scale immigration, it is estimated that over half the West Indian men in full-time employment in London were doing jobs below their abilities, skills or training. And this was a situation with little room for immediate improvement, because the unions were coming under increasing pressure from white workers to prevent black people getting jobs at all. In the summer of 1958, race riots broke out in two areas of high black immigrant population: first St Ann's in Nottingham, then, much more seriously, in west London's Notting Hill Gate. In the second instance, chaos reigned for several days, leaving scores of people injured, extensive damage to property and a devastating impact on race relations. In each case it was local Teddy boys – the volatile, white working-class youth cult *du jour* – who were rallied by racist right-wing political organizations under cries of 'Keep Britain white' and 'Send them back', then egged on into putting theory into practice. It was an irony acknowledged by many of Britain's black population that, while the apparent reason for the Englishmen's rage was fear for their jobs, the huge majority of the native rioters were hardcore un- or under-employed, who had little else to do except cause trouble.

Not that the violence in 1958 should have surprised anybody – there had been a riot in Liverpool in 1948, during which a white mob attacked black people and their dwellings. In the ten years since the *Almanzora* and the *Empire Windrush* docked in the UK carrying, respectively, some 150 and 420 Jamaican immigrants (incidentally, in spite of the *Windrush*'s 1948 voyage being hailed as the starting pistol for mass Commonwealth immigration, the *Almanzora*'s preceded it by six months), the British government's welcome mat, never superfluously substantial to start off with, was starting to look decidedly threadbare. Racist verbal exchanges often spilling into apparently random street skirmishes had become almost inner-city commonplace, and discrimination in all walks of life was perfectly legal. Delinquent youth gangs were usually drawn up along colour lines. The Nottingham and Notting Hill instances had flared up so dramatically because the white yobs had stepped over a line. When the Teddy boys went on the offensive they began attacking black people indiscriminately, thus drawing respectable, hard working, *Don't want no trouble, baas* types into the equation of violence that had previously been confined to rival black toughs. When these righteous men came together they fought back ferociously, and there was always a lot more of them than delinquents of any colour.

The events in Notting Hill that summer showed that the newcomers weren't about to stand for too much crap, and had a unifying effect that produced a ghetto siege mentality. This is in spite of a significant number of UK immigrants of that generation still going to great pains to explain how the majority of white people went out of their way to prove they 'weren't like that'. Indeed, as a result of the Notting Hill riots, nine white Teddy boys were brought to trial and sentenced to four years each in prison, after being roundly condemned by the judge. The following year a black man, Kelso Cochrane, was stabbed to death in the same area by supporters of the fascist parliamentary candidate Oswald Mosley; the local community was horrified and support for Mosley evaporated – he finished up with fewer than 2,000 votes. None the less, such shows of support weren't sufficient to prevent a consolidation of the fast-germinating notions that the Mother Country wasn't as welcoming as it was supposed to be.

And nowhere was this situation more tangibly manifesting itself than in what to do on a Saturday night.

Many clubs, pubs and dancehalls followed the emergent media line that West Indians were 'trouble', with the root of this 'trouble' being the usually untenable notion of black men fraternizing with white women, and they therefore operated racist door policies. Such socializing was a very probable situation, too. Between 1948 and 1958, the ratio of men to women coming over from the West Indies was two to one, as single men are traditionally more mobile. And in established families the idea was that the men came over, obtained a job and home, then sent for their womenfolk. Of those women emigrants, many were pulling shifts in hospitals or hotels, while most well-brought-up daughters of the Caribbean wouldn't be caught dead in an English club, pub or dancehall. (Or dead is what they *would* be if their father caught them there.) But the

English attitude was that immigrant entertainment had to be self-contained. Given that the majority of West Indians in the UK were from Jamaica, that island's ways were bound to emerge as the dominant force in Caribbean Britain. And among the Jamaican communities, sound-system culture had, along with oversize suits and broad-brimmed hats, been imported virtually preserved in aspic.

The sound system had been part of black life in London since 1955, when Duke Vin – formerly a deejay/selector on Tom the Great Sebastian's Beat Street system – put the first big rig, Duke Vin the Tickler's, together a year after he arrived in the UK. Count Suckle soon followed suit with his own system, and as they were both based in Ladbroke Grove, a rivalry was immediately established.

Jah Vego is a genial dreadlock who beams out from under a peaked tam not quite big enough to have its own postcode and owns The People's Record Store, a bustling red, green and gold-painted reggae music emporium that is the only non-gentrified business on Ladbroke Grove's All Saints Road. Forty years ago, that same street was rapidly evolving into one of London's frontlines – the sociological and psychological as much as the geographical heart of the West London ghetto; almost a no-go area for the police, where hanging out was what you did to a backdrop of drug dealing, prostitution and dubious merchandise bought and sold. At that time, Vego was a selector on Duke Vin's original sound system, so he's in no doubt as to how important it was for Jamaicans to be able to party *inna Kingston style.*

'Although the work here might not have been as tough as the work back home – if you even had a job in Jamaica – the life here was hard. *Hard.* Everything was so different, from the climate to how people talk to you if you go in a shop. So come the weekend you have to relax, completely, among your own crowd and be able to carry on like you did back home. Not that there was much choice for us, because so many places in London wouldn't let black men in. So we have to do our own thing, keeping dances in houses, in basements, in the shebeens, or in school dinner halls. There weren't no big clubs, even though the need for them was big. Which is why the sound-system business take off here like it did. I think people that had come to England was more receptive to a Jamaican-style dance than even they had been in Jamaica; at home it was simply a part of their lives – here they look forward to them as one of the only bits of Jamaica they can still partake in. They used to treat the dances as much more special.

'But because there were only two sound systems back in the beginning, in 'fifty-six or 'fifty-seven, they were always in demand. So much that you couldn't book Duke Vin and Count Suckle because they were always booked up. They'd be playing dances in their own community, or across town in Brixton or Hackney, then they'd do outings where they'd book a hall in Birmingham or Reading or somewhere and their crowd would go up in a coach to mix with the local crowd – often their people had relatives from that area. In summer, the outings would go to the seaside, with a day on the beach then a dance in the evening. What these outings meant was that people from, say, Birmingham would get to go to a dance with a genuine sound system, like they remember from home, so they'd soon come down to London to book the sound to play in their city and so the demand got even more. That's why a lot of people used to keep their own little things in their houses with just their gram[ophone] playing the music. If you have a Blue Spot and some tunes you could push back the furniture and have your own little function every Saturday night. [The Blue Spot was the top-shelf radiogram, a large, freestanding polished-wood unit imported from Germany. It was made by Blaupunkt, which translates to 'Blue point'.]

'That's where the shebeens come from. They were what were always called *illegal drinking dens*, and the press would make out that all sorts went on in them, but they were just ordinary working people's houses or their basement – sometimes it would be in an empty building. And it was only illegal because the guy hosting the gathering have no licence to sell the drink. All he was doing though was covering the costs of the beer and the curry goat he's had to buy. They sell it for what it costs, or might make a little to cover their rent; in those days in London, nobody was making any money out of the dances. Sure, you could raise yourself a lickle few shillings. Not much. It was a social thing – many a time the dance would be full but the man would tell you that all the people came in for nothing, or if the drinks all sell out he still tell you he don't have no money to pay you. But I still go back and play next week. The dance was the place where you went to hear some music, have a dance, drink a little liquor and think about home.

'Maybe now it's a money thing, but back then you just did it to keep the spirit alive.'

Curiously, as if to emphasize the empathy between black and Irish immigrants in the fifties and sixties, the word 'shebeen' is Gaelic for dodgy or weak beer – something many might expect to find in an unlicensed bar. And it wasn't unusual to find Irish women in West Indian shebeens, as by the end of the 1950s a considerable *esprit de corps* existed between these two sets of often-despised arrivals – employment adverts frequently featured the words 'No blacks or Irish', while accommodation notices would routinely expand this slogan to read 'No dogs, blacks or Irish.'

Of course, before a prospective sound man had to worry about where to play he'd need a rig, and there were certain logistical problems to getting a yard-style sound system together in West London in the mid-1950s. It wasn't a question of getting into an existing scene and following already accepted guidelines, this was pioneer country, where the indigenous population were, either wilfully or otherwise, of almost no help at all. And if you wanted a dancehall crowd to take you seriously then everything – equipment and music – had to be just so. Vego remembers what went into becoming a migrant sound man.

'When the first sound men came over here, they had to get their own amplifiers built, because what was available wasn't up to the job. True, you could get loudness from the ready-made equipment in London, but pure loudness wasn't what the big sound systems was about . . . that don't get you moving. What the bigtime sound men like Coxsone and Duke Reid wanted was the bass, the beat of the bass to *make* you move up your waist, and Duke Vin and Count Suckle were no different when they came over here. They knew it had to be how it was in Jamaica, because it was the same Jamaican people they were dealing with.

'Rather than bring a sound system in from Jamaica, they get it built here to their exact specifications, because, other than the people, everything about the dance in England is different. In Jamaica it's mostly outdoors – the lawns – but here it's all inside so you need the amplifier and speakers to work in a different way. Then because of how we dance it have to sound different. The English people in the dance, like in the disco, used to shake, shake, shake their heads, shake their heads to certain rhythms that were high up the frequency, but because we dance down there with our waist and hips [Vego jumps to his feet and nimbly win's up his waist] we need the bass. The music have to hit you down there and for that we need the big bass.

'It was kind of funny, because the man who built the amplifiers for the first London sound systems didn't know nothing about sound systems. He was an African man, an electrical engineer who have a shop – I think Vinnie might have picked him because he was a black man – and we just go tell him what we want. We tell him how we want the music to sound and what sort of circumstances we're playing in and he would build amplifiers to those specifications.

'In the beginning, though, he was so surprised. Duke Vin tell him he want a two hundred watt amplifier with *maximum* bass and the African man thought, "My God, where are they going to play that? That will kill people!" Because in them days two hundred watts was a whole lot of wattage, bigger than he'd ever even heard of before. But he finish up building equipments for all the sound systems, because the nex' man would hear Duke Vin's sound playing and have to have an amp built by the same man.

'If I think about it, maybe it was best that Vin went to a black man, because if you went to a manufacturer and ask for that they'd chase you out of the place. They'd think you were a madman. And then the big complaint from the Englishman was always that these Jamaicans, these black people, play their music too loud. And that was just from their grams, which the top ones would only be a maximum of twenty watts. How would that same English electrical engineer react if you ask him to build a *two hundred watt system*? And even that escalate quickly from there, because the nex' sound man would say, "How much wattage Duke Vin's amplifier? . . . Two hundred? . . . All right, make mine two-fifty". And so on.'

Having the right music threw up another set of hurdles. To pull in the people, UK operators needed a regular supply of kicking new tunes. As in Kingston, in these pre-ska days the records that were moving the London house parties and dances were American R&B. In fact, as the British sound system experience was so derivative, in many initial instances these would be the exact same selections, with the idea that they were hot from Jamaica being something of a marketing point. Because so few US R&B records were coming into London record shops, UK sound men had to rely on tunes being sent over from Jamaica, either from friends and other sound men, or ordered direct from Kingstonian importers or licensees for US labels such as Stanley Motta or Federal.

It didn't take very long for them to work out that they too could order R&B records direct from the USA, either; a venture that came with its own unique price tag. If an ex-pat sound man got to hear of certain tunes that were tearing it up back home, often as not it was thanks to 'spotters' at dances – as Buster used to do for Dodd – so they'd know the singer or the producer but would have no idea what the actual song was called. Even if anybody got close enough to clock the record, all information would have been obliterated from the disc and, likely as not, the cut would have been renamed. Thus it became standard practice for the operators in England to contact the US distributor or record company and request everything recent they had by that singer or producer. This used to result in boxes of records turning up, of which eight out of ten would be useless for sound-system purposes, but the remaining two would make such a carry-on more than worth it. Needless to say, all label copy would be instantly scratched off any newly acquired prize.

Pirating wasn't unknown, either. Regardless of any sense of community among sound-system operators – or maybe *because of* – it wasn't a good idea to leave your new tunes with somebody else for too long. According to Vego, 'There was a little man up in Kilburn, in north-west London, Foxley I think his name was, and he have a little cutting machine. I never seen it, but I know it was there because if you leave a tune with him and come back in a couple of hours, he'll have another copy of it for you. Not a proper single with a label and that, just a 45 dub slate. Which was good for a sound man, because it'll sound all right and only they will know what it is. You could either sell a dub slate of one of your tunes to another sound man, or copy one that you borrowed. A lot of tunes over from Jamaica were circulated through Foxley, which is why I wouldn't let *nobody* hang on to one of my records for too long.'

Towards the end of the decade, as the Jamaican record-production business took off, this traffic switched back to the Caribbean, where so many sound-men-turned-producers now owned record shops, putting them at the heart of the transatlantic mail-order business. And pretty soon a secondary trade grew up alongside their regular retail outlets as the UK became a ready-made market for JA specials that had outlived their usefulness – tunes that no longer rocked the dance would get shipped to contacts in England rather than be sold on to lesser Kingston sounds. Curiously, this seemed a more attractive proposition for the Jamaican operators than getting rid of them down the road – maybe because, with so much music coming through, hit records were being displaced more quickly than they might otherwise have been, and if they were still dimly perceived as having some life left in them would be far less of a threat several thousand miles away.

The briskness of this trade had a considerable effect on shaping a unique character for the English sound systems. There were relatively few of them, so the sheer volume of records coming through meant that English operations could have *all* new music every month or so if they wanted. As a result, English crowds expected to be surprised, and the way an English sound man built his reputation was on his ability constantly to break new cuts instead of relying on a few hardy perennial specials. In turn, this evolved into an adventurousness that became an integral part of the UK sound-system scene, which continues to enjoy a reputation for experimentation that can make its Kingston peer group look staid.

Then there were the sound men who didn't want to wait for records that might possibly be over a year old. These shrewder operators started dealing proactively with their record-producing JA counterparts to secure exclusive ownership of tunes that either were made especially for them or were still hot at the lawns – a situation that resulted in one of the most fruitful and high-profile official licensing deals of Jamaican music in the UK; but more of that later.

In order to get any sort of direct arrangement with sound men such as Prince Buster, Duke Reid or Coxsone, however, the prospective client had to know how to find him, which, as the UK sound-system scene grew, became progressively more difficult for the uninitiated. Guys like Vinnie, Suckle and Vego had been with the sound systems before they came to England, so naturally they had all the contacts, but as the men they had to deal with back home were big stars and conducted themselves accordingly, so anybody who wasn't clued in before he left Jamaica would have to be, according to the saying, 'Kingstonian about it'. He had to play it very clever, getting in the know and digging about to make connections. As the UK sound-system scene blew up and the circles of people coming into it widened to a point where they were pretty much divorced from the Kingston source, this became increasingly difficult to do.

And if sound men couldn't manage to get the records they wanted, then how could the general ex-pat public? A public who were relatively wealthy – by the standards they had left behind – who were becoming increasingly consumer orientated and always hungry for a taste of home. Somebody was soon going to have to take the business – literally – of Jamaican records in the UK seriously.

By the late fifties there was already a tradition of working musicians coming to the UK from Jamaica. Since the end of the war, Jamaican players had featured prominently on the burgeoning London jazz scene; indeed, among the eighteen listing their trade as 'musician' on the passenger list for the *Empire Windrush* were trumpeter Alphonso 'Dizzy' Reece and tenor man Sammy Walker. During the next few years, players of the calibre of sax men Joe Harriott and Wilton Gaynair (who, like Reece were Alpha Boys' School alumni) or pianist Wynton Kelly became Soho jazz stalwarts. As this was before ska, these players brought with them no indigenous Jamaican music, so in order to work they slotted neatly into the UK's jazz and R&B scenes. Also, because this preceded a black record business of any scale, the vast majority of jobs on offer in London were live, a scene which catered almost exclusively to an indigenous white audience – perhaps some visiting black American servicemen or seamen, but virtually no West Indian residents. So even when the likes of Rico Rodriguez and Ernest Ranglin came over in the early 1960s, they left hardly a ripple in what should have been their own constituency. Oddly, this situation of very few West Indians at live shows didn't change much as time went on. There is a well-remembered instance in 1967 when the Skatalites played London's Porchester Hall, a sizeable venue on the fringe of the black areas of Notting Hill and Ladbroke Grove. It was a well-promoted show, and on the back of their 'Guns of Navarone' chart hit, yet the 'crowd' barely made it into double figures. Likewise, Prince Buster took his early tours to university campuses, with only two or three club dates at established inner-city black venues like Brixton's Ram Jam Club or the Uppercut in Forest Gate. And Jimmy Cliff, who had lived in the UK since 1964, remembers how the ska band he put together in London could never pull a Jamaican crowd.

Records for sale, of course, were coming into the UK, but initially this was almost entirely without the involvement of the English music business. The first Jamaican music retail operations in the UK were, according to Vego, an exact copy of how things had started back on the island.

'When I first come here there weren't any record shops selling our kind of music. There were a few selling the hot American R&B, but when the Jamaican boogie and eventually the ska pushed that out, there wasn't any shops stocking any of that. A few of us who had the music business contacts back in Jamaica, but didn't have no shop or no sound system, we would get records sent to us in quantity and take them first to the number of sound men that had set up, because we knew where to find them. We'd go to dances with the records and give the tunes to the sound man to play, and when he see the reaction of the people in the dance then he'd have to buy it – he wouldn't have a choice.

'But we knew that it wasn't just sound men alone who wanted the tunes, just like now you have ordinary people who just love the music, hear a record in a dance and want to have it at home. So as well as selling a few records to people as they were leaving dancehalls, we'd go around on the buses, and ring on the doorbells of people and introduce the music. These were frequently people who didn't have anything to play these records on, because it was usual for West Indians to buy records while they're saving up for the gram, just so they're ready when they get it – and buying a record is like buying a little piece of Jamaica that don't cost too much. So it meant you'd have to do a big selling job, because they couldn't hear the tune, we'd tell them "This the *hottest* Studio One selection, *straight* from Sir Coxsone's sound system . . . We 'ave Roland Alphonso – yuh ever hear dem Skatalites? *Wicked* mi a tell you." And they'd look at you, because they know that if a man trying to sell them fish he's going to say it fresh, not how 'im 'ave it since last week. So sometimes we'd have to sing the tune ". . . We 'ave Prince Buster . . . *Chk-a* . . . *Chk-a* . . . *Chk-a* . . . *ba-ba-ba-baaa!*" All on people's doorsteps. But usually it worked. That's how

Peckings got his start. He didn't have no shop or no sound system, but in Kingston he move around with Sir Coxsone sound, so when he came to England he send back to Coxsone for all these records.

'We started going to shops with records, too; it was the same pattern as we had in Jamaica. The way of doing things doesn't really change – even in the reggae industry today, things are still done exactly the same here as they are in Jamaica.'

Peckings is the late George Price (so nicknamed because he used to have a dance style that closely resembled a pecking bird), who built up one of the best-known and best-respected reggae importers, distributors and retailers in London. Today, the business is run by his son Chris and has the licence to press vinyl runs of old Treasure Isle and Studio One albums. It's a fitting tribute to the Peckings' independent spirit and traditionalism – until 1974, when George opened his Shepherd's Bush shop, he did it all out of a spare room in his house – that Chris refuses to allow CDs on the premises.

Sonny Roberts, of Willesden in north-west London, was another who brought over unadulterated Kingston tradition, but he was prepared to go one step beyond Peckings and actually record and manufacture his own releases. A carpenter who came to England in 1953, Roberts was fascinated by the music business, and at the end of that decade, after pooling his resources with those of some Jamaican friends, he set up Planet-one Records in two rooms in his house. He installed a single-track studio in one room – complete with egg boxes on the walls for soundproofing – while he'd cut his own masters on his rudimentary cutting equipment in the other. Initially, he produced mostly gospel records, but when ska came about he figured that the same people – spiritual, mainly Jamaican, black people – that love gospel would also love ska. Thus he reckoned he had a ready market, and instead of leasing masters from back home he'd record locally based Jamaican artists. His primary sales were of acetates alone, and they lay with London's increasing number of sound men, who greatly appreciated the fact there were now some genuine, brand-new, UK specials. Then, in further duplication of how things had worked in Jamaica, the popularity of these tunes led him to get a few dozen pressed up and sold to the crowds at the dances they had been aired at. Next, he opened his own shop, Orbitone, the capital's first black-owned record shop, providing Sonny Roberts with the name every veteran sound man knows him as: Sonny Orbitone. The store specialized in a range of Caribbean-released and imported sounds alongside his own productions, and although the quality of Planetone's recordings was never brilliant, they were successful because they were both unique and exactly right for the situation. The productions rocked with raw Jamaican energy yet were tempered slightly by the players' and producer's years of living in the UK – the mirror image of their prospective market.

Among his regular vocalists were Dandy Livingstone and Tito Simon (often billed as Sugar & Dandy) and the Marvels, while his 'house band' the Planets was led by Rico Rodriguez, who was supremely grateful for the opportunity to play ska once more. But Sonny Roberts' big contribution was to set in place the roots of a British-originated Jamaican music industry that was geared to serving its own community first rather than to compromise by looking for mainstream hits. Which may not have been the best fiscal judgement – indeed the shop far outlasted both Planetone and its sister label Sway – but in cultural terms was vital to the large body of Jamaican immigrants who were looking for integration rather than assimilation.

However informal these early sales of Jamaican records might have been, they added up to a lot of fairly high-profile activity – obviously there are no numbers available, but it would be no exaggeration to say the sales of many records ran into four figures. Importantly, it was action that was increasing all the time, and as more and more prospective customers were asking in their local record shops for Laurel Aitken or Joe Higgs or Prince Buster, it was inevitable that the shop managers would start to make enquiries to their wholesalers. As the record companies' standard excuse for not handling this music had been 'the demand isn't there', this wasn't something that could go unnoticed for very much longer.

And of course it didn't.

UK record companies – particularly EMI – had flirted with calypso from both Jamaica and Trinidad throughout the 1950s, but never taken it too seriously, so when JA boogie began to usurp American R&B in Jamaica it was greeted with an audible shrug by the mainstream London record business. In fact, the first examples anybody can remember of the style getting a British release came in 1960, when the tiny Starlight and Melodisc labels who put out, respectively, Laurel Aitken's smash hit 'Boogie in My Bones' and the same singer's 'Lonesome Lover'. The latter is probably the first Jamaican single recorded in Britain as Aitken cut it just after he emigrated that year, and is significant because of the investment put into it by Melodisc. Instead of simply leasing a tune from a Jamaican label – as Starlight did from Chris Blackwell's Island with 'Boogie in My Bones' – Melodisc had gone so far as to actually cut a tune. It therefore came as no surprise when they were the first British company to jump into Jamaican music with both feet.

Melodisc's owner Emil Shallit, a large, larger-than-life man of uncertain Central European background, was a confirmed nonconformist and, thirty years before the 1990s indie boom, saw the role of the independent record label to champion music the mainstream wouldn't. Shallit, who died in 1982 in his late seventies, prided himself on being 'in touch with the street', spotting and moving into markets with an entrepreneurial pliability unavailable to the corporately hidebound likes of Pye, EMI, Philips and Decca, the day's big players. Since founding the company in 1946, he'd imported and licensed for release jazz, blues, R&B, African high-life and calypso, and thus was well aware of the thriving, if low-profile, black music market in the UK. And, most importantly, he identified the fact that Britain's black record buyers weren't simply one homogeneous market – a mistake that is still made frequently some forty years later – but composed of very different facets with unique and self-contained demands. From his experiences with R&B he knew what was carrying the swing in Jamaican dances and front rooms, and was straight on it when the music's country of origin shifted across the Gulf of Mexico. Hence the Laurel Aitken track, the success of which convinced Shallit and his trusted lieutenant Siggy Jackson, another Central European Jew also with a good handle on black life in London, to launch the Melodisc subsidiary label Blue Beat in August that year to specialize in this new Jamaican sound. Another Laurel Aitken record, 'Boogie Rock' – also recorded in London – was the débutante release, while, curiously enough, catalogue number Blue Beat B2 was a version of 'Dumplin's' by Byron Lee and the Dragonnaires, the band who so many would claim were seriously misrepresentative of modern Jamaican music.

Not that this proved any sort of setback in 1960. The label's name of Blue Beat came about through this shuffling style being known, also, as Jamaican blues, and as Shallit surfed Kingston's musical explosion the label put out over two dozen singles by the end of that year. He would travel to Kingston on a regular basis, cutting deals with practically everybody – Coxsone, Duke Reid, Edward Seaga, Derrick Harriott, Ken Khouri, S. L. Smith and so on – to give his label a hip, varied and apparently shrewdly selected schedule that ran to classics such as the Jiving Juniors' 'Lollipop Girl', Higgs & Wilson's 'Manny Oh', Keith & Enid's 'Worried over You', Theophilus Beckford's 'Easy Snappin'', the Mello Larks' 'Time to Pray', the Duke Reid Group's 'What Makes Honey', 'The Joker' and 'Duke's Cookies'. And that was all before Christmas 1960. Later, as JA boogie grew into ska, Blue Beat boomed. The label put out over 300 singles in the next five years – that's over one a week – and launched a profusion of their own offshoot labels such as Dice, Limbo, Duke, Chek, Rainbow and Fab. Such was the company's status within the UK black music world that the name Blue Beat became synonymous with Jamaican music over several years, from JA boogie to ska to rocksteady – whether it was actually on the label or not, in the same way as Tamla Motown had become the generic title for black pop-soul in the USA.

It is to Shallit's enormous credit, and doubtless why he was able to secure so many sweet deals, that he was in no way intimidated by having to journey into deepest West Kingston to do business. Indeed, he seems to have approached this task with an altogether wry sense of humour – there are confirmed reports of him carrying a briefcase with the words 'Danger High Explosives' stencilled prominently on it, yet it contained nothing more incendiary than contracts or master tapes. But then you could say some of those tunes were pure dynamite.

It's likely that Shallit's safety had been guaranteed by the Kingstonians he was doing business with. After all, he was a heavy-duty paymaster, and he was also, by all accounts, a reasonably honest one, treating the Jamaican producers he dealt with with fairness and respect and making sure they got paid their due. Which was far from compulsory, given that his records were selling into the tens of thousands in the UK, but mostly away from chart-return shops and often through informal distribution channels so that no audits outside of the English record companies' own needed to be kept.

Shallit also knew how to make good his mistakes. Prince Buster tells this story of how he and Blue Beat hooked up:

'It was back in the very early sixties, I had a deal with Count Suckle in London to send him tunes. He'd pay me five pounds for each of them, on the understanding they were exclusive, for him to use on his sound system or in one of the clubs he deejayed at. It was a good arrangement, until one day he contact me and he was *vexed* because he's found one of the tunes I sold him as exclusive was selling in a record shop in London on the Blue Beat label.

'I calm Suckle down, then I get in touch with Emil Shallit for the first time and tell him he has no rights to that tune. He was perfectly honest about it and apologize, because somebody claiming to represent me – might even have said he was me – had sold the tune to Shallit. He could have just ignored me, or gone on bootlegging my stuff, but he tell me he want to deal with me legally, so I did a deal with him to release my stuff exclusively on Blue Beat in England – Derrick Morgan too. And he treat me right and I stayed with that company for years.

He knew how to promote the music properly and did a great deal for early Jamaican music in Britain.'

It was a partnership that was to give the UK such golden ska moments as 'Al Capone', 'Madness', 'Burke's Law' and '10 Commandments of Man', or the UK-recorded likes of 'Wash Wash'. It saw Prince Buster tour the UK regularly, ripping up the TV pop show *Ready Steady Go!* in a manner only equalled by James Brown's supercharged performance on the programme, and brought Buster a Top 20 British pop-chart hit with 'Al Capone' in April 1967.

Naturally, with such success comes rivalry, and after a couple of years of Blue Beat's virtual monopoly, as the 1960s progressed and the recording industry exploded in Jamaica, the market in Great Britain started to look crowded. As well as Planetone, Starlight had continued to license the odd Jamaican tune, but they never took it seriously enough to make much of a difference. Likewise a shortlived label called Carnival. Meanwhile, in Stamford Hill, north London, Jewish couple Rita and Benny King were expanding their business from simply importing records for retail to licensing them for release. They dealt largely with Coxsone, but also recorded their own ska, Laurel Aitken in particular in London and in Kingston, for their R&B (Rita & Benny, geddit?), Ska Beat, Caribou and Port-O-Jam labels. (So many deals were struck with Coxsone because, by 1963, he had his own studio, his output was enormous and his eye for a business deal as sharp as ever.) Then there was Graeme Goodall's initially low-profile Rio label, which at that time was best known for releasing some of Errol Dunkley's earliest material and also cut tunes with Aitken and licensed from Studio One. Goodall was an Australian sound/studio engineer who had worked in Jamaica for years, finishing up with a lengthy stay at Federal where he had worked with all of Jamaica's top JA boogie and ska producers, and had engineered practically all of Coxsone's recording before he opened the Brentford Road studios. Goodall came to England from Jamaica in 1962 and was determined to put his knowledge of Jamaican music to use.

The real contender, though, was Chris Blackwell's Island Records. Encouraged by Blue Beat's success, Blackwell moved to London in 1962 to do with gusto what Starlight had been doing lackadaisically: release his company's records in the UK. This and to license from other Jamaican producers.

His first record came out in July of that year, 'Independant [*sic*] Jamaica Calypso' by Lord Kitchener, timed to ride the wave of independence fever that was every bit as avid among Jamaicans in Great Britain as it was with those at home. Using his music-business contacts, his means to commute between JA and the UK, and the fact that he was white *and* Jamaican – as opposed to Emil Shallit who was simply white – he quickly cut licensing deals. The Island Records catalogue was studded with productions by the likes of Duke Reid, Coxsone, King Edwards, Lindon Pottinger, Vincent Chin, Byron Lee and Derrick Harriott – only Prince Buster remained loyal to Blue Beat – while an exclusive contract with Leslie Kong gave Blackwell access to Jimmy Cliff, Desmond Dekker, Derrick Morgan and, as he was still billed back in those days, Robert Marley. Plus, the honey-throated Jackie Edwards, who had recorded soul and R&B for Blackwell's Jamaican set-up, came over at the same time to continue writing and recording for the new company. Within eighteen months, in terms of sheer volume, Blackwell's was the leading outlet for Jamaican music in Britain, and during 1963 he launched the Black Swan label, specifically to handle the glut of ska that was flowing out of Kingston.

Chris Blackwell also established the first distribution network set up solely for black product – Blue Beat used established independent wholesalers Lugtons, who carried that and Starlight's West Indian stuff as part of their mainstream business. Blackwell poached David Betteridge, the man who had the inside track at Lugtons, and distributed for himself using his car, Betteridge's van and Jackie Edwards on a bus to deliver boxes of singles. Interesting to see what else had come over with no change from Jamaica: Blackwell and Betteridge motored, while Edwards, the biggest locally based star on their roster, took the bus with boxes of records under his arm, and was happy to pose for publicity pictures doing so. In the beginning their corporate set-up was also essentially unchanged from its Kingston template – they'd get a record pressed up, go out and sell it and with the money they earned from that go back to the pressing plant just outside London for some more and sell those.

Perhaps 'distribution network' is gilding the lily somewhat, but the magnitude of what they were doing shouldn't be underestimated. They were dedicated to Jamaican music and could work from instinct and direct contact with the source – Lugtons had actually turned Blackwell down as a distribution customer, believing there was no room for expansion in the market – but having their own transport they could widen the circle to the satellite Jamaican communities that were springing up in towns outside London such as Aylesbury and Reading. All of which helped to stimulate demand for what the Shallits, Greens and Peckingses had to offer. By the end of 1963 many licensed Jamaican tunes were selling well over 10,000 copies and Shallit was bullish enough about Blue Beat's sense of identity to move into brand extension. He pulled a couple of strokes that wouldn't seem out of place in one of London's current indie operations: Siggy Jackson hosted a Blue Beat club night at London's famous jazz/R&B venue the Marquee, and they also launched an extensive range of Blue Beat clothing – hats, skirts, ties, sunglasses and so on.

In what was a heartwarming show of solidarity, given the usual ruthless nature of the record business, back in 1963 Chris Blackwell and Sonny Roberts were to do each other favours when Planetone needed professional distribution and Island Records, too big to go operating out of Blackwell's home, was after bigger premises. Blackwell offered to handle Roberts' wholesaling, while Roberts introduced Blackwell to the landlord of the building he was now using as a base (shop on the ground floor, studio in the basement), and shared with him his insight into London's black recording scene. The building's owner was an Indian-Jamaican accountant named Lee Gopthal, who rented Island the first floor, leading to a situation whereby sound men would visit both operations to buy new tunes only to be quizzed by each firm as to what the other was up to. And, according to more than one of these same sound men, it wasn't unusual to come across people from either operation 'casually' hanging about on the stairs or leaning out of windows attempting to hear what the other might have.

A postscript to this situation was that Gopthal, who in fine Jamaican middle-class style was originally sceptical both about renting to Roberts and about the black music business in the UK in general, became so enamoured with the Jamaican record industry that he set up a distribution company, Beat & Commercial, specifically to handle Jamaican records. Gopthal's first customers were Planetone and Island, who had by then outgrown Blackwell and Betteridge's whacky racing, and Gopthal's involvement in this branch of the music business was to progress until he and Blackwell formed a partnership that would produce UK reggae's most memorable company.

But we're still a few years away from that.

7

What a World

'It was probably a big factor that the Byron Lee band didn't smoke ganja like all the other musicians. This was the *World's Fair*! In *New York*! The government knew they were putting Jamaica on show. They would have wanted to avoid any potential trouble abroad that way.'

As Jimmy Cliff thinks back to the Jamaican authorities' first attempt at officially taking ska to an international stage he allows himself a chuckle. Understandably, too. By the time he is telling this story, the most famous Jamaican of all time, the man credited with stamping the island's music and culture on the world map, was almost as well known for his ganja consumption as he was for his reggae and his Rastafarianism.

What Cliff is talking about, though, happened back in 1964, when ska music, in Jamaica, was just taking its first tentative steps uptown; in the UK it was ploughing its own largely informal furrow; and in America it was being installed in the government-sponsored Jamaica pavilion at the New York World's Fair, the biggest global shop-window of the day. There, as representative of the Caribbean's most recently independent nation, it would come under detailed scrutiny from heads of state, captains of industry and gentlemen of the press, so it isn't too difficult to come to terms with the idea of those responsible for the delegation taking no chances. Presumably they'd figured out that if you could take the men out of the ghetto but couldn't take the ghetto out of the men, then it would be prudent to leave as many of those men as possible back in that self-same ghetto.

Performing a selection of ska favourites in the Jamaica marquee would be Jimmy Cliff, the Blues Busters, Millie Small, Monty Morris and Prince Buster. All certified crowd pleasers. Then somebody thought to use Byron Lee's Dragonnaires as the house band. Jimmy Cliff seems to still be smarting from it:

'They wanted to promote Jamaican music abroad. Good. They had the singers, they had the dancers, the only problem with it was that they didn't have the right band. They picked Byron Lee's Dragonnaires, so instead of the musicians we recorded with there was a band who couldn't communicate the feel of the music.

'And that band wouldn't necessarily had to have been the Skatalites. Most people knew the Skatalites because they had a lot of success together as a set of session musicians and had recognition as having hits, but there were other people who were just as successful as the Skatalites – if not more so. But even if it had been the Skatalites on that trip, it still would have been better. It would have made far more sense. Lee's band were just a calypso band really, playing dance music for people in the hotels, up on the north coast.

'This was because the whole tour was all fixed up by Edward Seaga, who was then head of Social Welfare and Economic Development. He picked the Byron Lee band because those guys were uptown guys – the sort of people he could understand and wasn't afraid to deal with. Also, he was probably thinking that if the ghetto guys could play this music then the uptown musicians could play it better – it looks like even though he saw the music as a valuable export he still wasn't taking a chance on the people who developed it. Didn't take them very seriously because those real guys were just roots guys. We didn't, y'know, have any nice clothes or airs and graces, *but we could play the music*. Those were the people he should have picked, but he picked the uptown guys thinking maybe they would look better and present a better picture of Jamaica – one that other people would feel comfortable with.

'They might have been to college, but they didn't have no feel for the music. The whole tour wasn't a success at all. You see it didn't sound like it was supposed to – natural – the music just didn't get across.'

Cliff's argument underlines the points made earlier about the widespread resentment towards Byron Lee in the ska days, and in this case such rancour might well hold water. Indeed, this line's been a popular one over the years as to what went wrong at that World's Fair, and centres on the notion that the government had belatedly worked out that it had a potentially saleable commodity on its hands but then, owing to its innate snobbery, went and shot itself in the foot with its marketing strategy. Or maybe that should read 'shot itself in the head', as by taking a band with so little natural feel for the music, its natural habitat or how it had evolved, they couldn't hope to get it across in anything close to a favourable light. With a music this gutsy, regardless of how kicking the singers or dancers could be, if the engine driving them was misfiring they were never going to have a chance.

While such a theory is entirely plausible, it rests on the supposition that the primary purpose of the Jamaican World's Fair delegation was to sell ska to the world in general. Which was actually never the case. The most likely reason that ska was there at all was because of Edward Seaga who, in his quest to unearth genuine Jamaican culture, had championed the music since practically day one and wouldn't have overlooked such a chance to give it international props. Fundamentally, the delegation was there to drum up business for the Jamaican Tourist Board, rather than to promote 'ghetto music'. Think about it. Why would anybody in high office – other than Seaga of course – travel abroad to an international festival of commerce to boast about something they themselves hadn't yet fully accepted as part of the Jamaican way of life? Not that the government were above taking advantage of the music when it suited them, and in a nation as small as Jamaica, you can never hope to put much daylight between business, politics and art, or the potential commercialization of that art.

In the case of the World's Fair, it was on a slightly less-exploitative note that the downtown ghetto music was being officially acknowledged. The idea was to use ska as one facet of an overall canvas of 'Jamaicanness', which, along with Dunn's River Falls, inexpensive domestic staff, Royal Jamaica Coronas Grandes, year-round sunshine and Blue Mountain Coffee could be touted to the American tourist trade. Ska the dance was just as important as ska the music here, because to guarantee audience interaction, and therefore a longer-lasting loyalty, alongside the singers were a quartet of dancers, one of whom was Carol Crawford, Jamaica's 1963 Miss World, to provide an easily accessible ska demonstration. This was the time of the twist and the hully gully, when pop-dancing USA was almost formal in its regimented approach to pre-programmed steps and manoeuvres, and the idea was to present ska as being as user-friendly as possible – a notion not far removed from Coxsone's early sound-system days when he and Blackie would cut the steps. If, when they weren't sipping rum punch, visitors could learn a new dance – one which might even become a 'craze' – then so much the better. But ska, music or movement, was never being sold as an entity in itself.

All of which means that the band that had been booked was the perfect choice: they were sufficiently ska-like to make the point that Jamaica wasn't Trinidad, Cuba or South America, yet nothing they were likely to do would frighten the horses. Besides, Byron Lee's Dragonnaires had been making a good living approximating various American and non-American music styles in north coast hotels for years, thus their scrubbed-clean, easy-listening version of ska would always contain other elements. What they played they called, brace yourselves, *ska-lyp-so* and it was exactly what visitors to the island could expect as the easiest of listening at their hotel's weekly Welcome Barbecue.

Also, as you'd anticipate by now, Lee himself puts a rather different spin on things, and maintains his participation was a matter of straightforward economics. He had already booked the band to tour in America's tri-state area at the same time, therefore it wouldn't further tax the delegation's already creaking budget for them to play the World's Fair shows while they were in the vicinity.

It was, however, highly unlikely that the World's Fair band was going to be any outfit other than the Dragonnaires. Five years previously, Seaga had produced Lee's first record, 'Dumplin's'; more recently, Lee had bought Seaga's W.I.R.L. studio and renamed it Dynamic; and at that point the two had strong political ties.

After Seaga had opted to make a feature of the music in the Jamaica pavilion in New York, he invited interested parties from the Jamaican and US music businesses to get involved. There was a meeting held at Ken Khouri's Federal Records to plan the trip, where one of the most influential voices present was Ahmet Ertegun, owner of Atlantic Records in New York. Byron Lee held the licence to press and distribute Atlantic product all over the Caribbean, a flow of music that was about to start travelling in the other direction when, to coincide with the World's Fair, the Dragonnaires released an album in the USA, on Atlantic, entitled *Jamaica Ska*. It featured their instrumentals interspersed with various singers, and, oddly enough, on the album's artwork the group went under the name of the Ska Kings. But to give an idea of just how seriously the American company was taking *Jamaica Ska*, the album's recording was overseen by Tom Dowd, Atlantic's celebrated engineer who fulfilled the producer's role on so many sixties soul classics, including all of Aretha Franklin's greatest singles. Incidentally, around the same time, Dowd recorded the Maytals in Kingston, which sparked reports that they were about to sign for Atlantic but, as far as anybody I've spoken to knows, nothing ever came of it and certainly nothing was ever released.

The Ska Kings' album, though, was supposed to be the first battalion of the main invasion force scheduled to come in behind the World's Fair scouting party. According to Lee, after the live exposure 'there was now an awareness in New York that here was a music out of Jamaica that they could relate to'. Unfortunately, not enough people chose to relate to it and *Jamaica Ska* didn't sell well.

Not that this was much of a deterrent to American record companies. While it may have been the highest profile bid to market Jamaican music in the USA, it wasn't the first, as the last five years had seen sporadic attempts to take it to market: the Jiving Juniors, Higgs & Wilson and Laurel Aitken had all been released there. And it certainly wouldn't be the last attempt. In the wake of the World's Fair, Epic Records put out *The REAL Jamaican Ska*, a compilation album memorable more for the fact it was co-produced by Curtis Mayfield and featured a couple of Jimmy Cliff tracks than for any particular musical splendour. Capitol went with the Blues Busters, presumably attracted by their Jamaican success, but as this was in a pre-ska R&B-wannabe style, their US releases didn't cut much ice – Americans simply seemed to figure they had enough of that sort of thing already. ABC-Paramount released *Starring Steve Alaimo*, a ska-style album by the white American R&B singer of that name, and in spite of backing from the Blues Busters, it was a pretty woeful effort. Numerous other singles were released on Time, MGM and Atlantic, but, outside of Millie Small's 'My Boy Lollipop' (more of which later), as ska was touted as the Sound of Young Jamaica – an optimistic echo of Motown's Sound of Young America – it failed to gain a foothold in the States. It never really would.

Not that there wasn't a potential audience for ska in the USA. The figures for immigration into America from Jamaica in 1969 were just slightly lower than the British headcount – once again accuracy is impossible as so many short-contract workers like Florida's cane cutters or New England's apple pickers didn't go back or vacationers just simply vanished. And arrivals from the Caribbean (once again, by far the largest contingent of Commonwealth immigrants to the USA were Jamaican) were pretty much concentrated on the East Coast, with roughly half settling in New York and the rest spread out mainly in Miami,

Washington, DC, Philadelphia and Baltimore. Thus Jamaican communities existed in much the same way as they did in Britain, and a home crowd, as it were, was certainly there.

It would be easy to say that the way in which the music was introduced in the USA was wrong. After all, the portly, highly unhip-looking, not-even-black Byron Lee wasn't exactly the best ambassador of the afterbeat; ska's first outing was on sanitized government-approved stages *at an international trade fair*; and big shot American producers had been shipped in to put albums together. Easy to say that this exposition was all far too mannerly, too factory farmed in an arena that should be strictly free range. But, although such a showing definitely didn't do ska any favours, to blame that alone would be to oversimplify what went wrong.

Of course, presenting ska exactly how Byron Lee's band used to play it for the uptown folks back home – with its shirt tucked in and its shoes nicely shined – would never have appealed to the ex-pat Jamaican working class, used to the wilder styles of Duke Reid, Buster and Dodd; but then this exercise was never aimed at them. Neither the Jamaican government nor companies the size of Atlantic and Epic would have put time and money into pandering to a virtually unseen immigrant minority. Because they formed such a minuscule percentage of America's potential record buyers it made no fiscal sense. Then – disregarding the JA government's music publishing interests, and even if selling music not tourism had been top of their list – why should anyone imagine that the government was going to worry about working-class Jamaicans living in America, when it didn't seem too bothered about the ones still living in Jamaica? No, all concerned were only ever looking at the American mainstream black music market, a strong core black audience with overspill into white pop buyers. Just like Motown or rock 'n' roll. However, in trying to sell ska in this area, they overlooked two crucial points. The US black music scene was (and still is) a fertile one, quite capable of creating its own styles and thus notoriously resistant to anything it didn't think up itself. Also, the market in the USA has always been savvy enough to know when it's being sold short. It was one more manifestation of Jamaica's innate snobbery that upper-class types such as those in government imagined that ska, if it was going to go to America, had to clean up its act, but it was going to an audience that had been raised on the most evocative jazz, blues and R&B. A crowd that wouldn't appreciate half measures.

All of this combined to wipe out any semblance of primary audience acceptance, and the informal channels didn't fare much better. Just as JA boogie and then ska crept into the UK courtesy of the likes of Vego, Suckle, Duke Vin and Peckings, there was both record importation and sound-system dances in Jamaican areas of American cities. But this cultural influx waned fairly quickly, since the social conditions for a newly arrived Jamaican immigrant in New York were very different from those greeting his counterpart in London.

Black communities were already established in urban America and West Indians naturally ended up in them, so it became a matter of fitting in with the other black people rather than being tolerated by whites. Not that this was quite as smooth as it might have been – in New York and Washington, West Indian immigrants were referred to as 'monkey chasers' or 'black Jews' by the indigenous black population. Then, because there was a ready-made American black culture, assimilating into that pretty much went with the territory, especially among the younger immigrants. This was a situation almost diametrically opposed to that in the UK, where so many English clubs and pubs kept black people out that when they wanted to socialize they had to set up their own environment, which meant inaugurating their own culture (in that case Jamaican) in the host country. In environments like Brooklyn or Wilmington, the pressure to form their own leisure-time citadels was far less: if a group of black Jamaicans fancied a drink or a dance, the chances were there'd be a black (American) owned establishment within walking distance. And it was unlikely that the said venue would be playing much ska.

Class and the times played a big part in the assimilation vs integration issue, too. In pre-civil-rights late-1950s/early-1960s America, when racial politics were coming to the boil, Caribbean immigrants were usually sought out to join Black America and partake in the fight. Notably the Jamaicans, as Marcus Garvey and the legacy he'd left in America naturally meant a great deal to them. They became involved in the host country, rather than, as remained the case in Britain, looking in almost passively from the outside. Although it might be convenient to draw a parallel between Jamaican involvement in the US struggle and Britain's race riots, it's important to remember the latter were precipitated by localized, almost personal attacks as opposed to looking for the greater good. Also, after the middle of the decade, a black American middle class began to put down widespread roots, creating a far more aspirational environment than anything on offer in the UK, where the swelling black population was rapidly becoming the working class's working class.

None of this is to say that anybody abandoned their Jamaican identity – Jamaica's Independence Day was celebrated with magnificent parades and the jumpingest dances; children born in the USA would expect rice and peas and curry goat on a Sunday; and, as there was heavy traffic between America's East Coast and the islands, it was relatively easy to go home for a dose of Jamaicanness. One interesting occurrence happened in 1967, when Philips got round to giving Prince Buster's '10 Commandments of Man' an American release: it went straight into the Cashbox charts at number 35; proof, if indeed proof were needed, that the genuine article – *skarticle?* – would sell. It's just that in this new land there were so many viable options, most of which involved not wearing their Caribbeanness like a badge.

Handily, it was the sound-system scene that threw up a perfect illustration of what was going on. Ex-Jamaican sound man Kool DJ Herc arrived in New York in 1967 and put together a sound system of Kingstonian proportions, the like of which New York had never seen. But finding Jamaican ska and rocksteady cut little ice, he began playing more and more

American music until he ruled the local R&B and soul scene unchallenged with his earthmoving rig. So deep did he immerse himself in the Bronx disco world that he is universally accredited as one of the founding fathers of hip hop, scratch-mixing and rap.

Back across the Atlantic, things were burgeoning. Indeed, to say ska went massive in England during 1963 would be a serious understatement, as by then it had moved up from the shebeens of Ladbroke Grove into London's West End. It had burst out of its initial immigrant market and was occupying a self-assured position as one of the country's most popular underground beats. Across the complete special spectrum, too. According to Vego it happened like this:

'Ska came in like a rush. It wasn't no little drip, drip thing, it was like a whole era came in at once. It was what so many of us over here had been waiting for. I am a jazz man, I love my jazz, but when the ska came it just lick jazz clean out of my head, because I *know* I'm far more attached to the ska than to jazz. Many other people felt the same, because it was something from our own Jamaica, and that meant so much if you was living in England. You could relate to it more. As a deejay on a sound system you could see it, as soon as you start to spin the Jamaican tunes *everybody* would be up dancing, nobody leave standing on the wall.

'One of the reasons it came in so strong was because it took the people back home a while to realize there was such a market over here. Really, they never like to make a big deal about it because as record producers they don't want their artists to know how many records they're selling abroad. So they play it down at first. But what used to happen was when the sound men or producers in Jamaica send you parcels of records, they also send you a list of what else they have so you can know what to order next time. That meant you know there's more, that they were putting out far more records than was initially coming here. And once the English record companies started dealing with the Jamaican producers they have a big backlog already, and because the companies want to take many more tunes than the sound men would be interested in, so they were taking a whole load at once. Which is how so much records could come over here together and why so many of those tunes were a few years old.'

Ska's establishment uptown in London's West End was more an inevitability than an option. With more and more uptown types checking out the Grove's blues parties, word of ska, JA boogie and the kicking sound-system scene began to spread. As Soho, traditionally a melting-pot of immigrant cultures with the jazz clubs giving the area strong black music leanings, was but a short straight road away from Notting Hill Gate, you knew it was going to make the journey sooner rather than later. Rik Gunnell, who ran the Flamingo Club in Wardour Street in the heart of Soho, made the first move. This shouldn't be confused with the very plush Flamingo bar in Coventry Street where Gunnell originally promoted jazz nights, as the Wardour Street venue was little more than a cellar, a bar (no liquor licence but selling Coca-Cola surreptitiously laced with Scotch) and a low stage with, bizarrely, four rows of cinema seats bolted to the floor in front of it. A factor greatly in its favour, though, in its sound-system suitability, was that it genuinely stayed open until 6 a.m., as opposed to other so-called all-nighters that shut between midnight and two in the morning. At the time the Flamingo Club was just moving from pure jazz to R&B, both live and on record, with American acts coming over to supplement the British and West Indian players, and from which it wasn't much of a jump to the R&B and ska of the London sound-system scene. The club's clientele were essentially English jazz buffs, visiting black American servicemen and London West Indians who, according to one of the Flamingo's regular musicians, 'seemed to have all the dope'.

Prior to Siggy Jackson's Blue Beat nights at the nearby Marquee, an acquaintance of Gunnell's who was a sound-system regular recommended Count Suckle as a man who could fill his club for him. Vego, who was by then working with Suckle, takes up the story, to explain the far-reaching events inadvertently set in motion by the Flamingo owner's decision to employ the sound man.

'The men like Count Suckle and Duke Vin had been wanting to move into the West End with what they did, because when they played local it was only to that local crowd. People who lived in north London wouldn't cross town to go to Ladbroke Grove, so it was pure Ladbroke Grove people. Or in Brixton, it was only the Brixton crowd. Because, like back home in Jamaica, you support your area and that area's dances, but they knew that if they could go into the centre of London – kind of like neutral territory – then people from all over would come – north London, Shepherd's Bush, Brixton, Stoke Newington . . .

'The owner of the Flamingo took Count Suckle on because he'd been told that his sound had the biggest following – which it did – and he would bring a *whole load* of people with him. Although it was somebody tell the Flamingo's owner about Count Suckle, it was right that it was Suckle, because he was a very outgoing man and handle all types of people very well. For example, if Suckle come into one of his dances and see maybe thirty people in there he'd announce "Everybody go to the bar and have a drink on me." Or he'd do it at the end of a night when there's not much people left. He was clever in that he'd only do that when there wasn't many people in the place, but Duke Vin, or most other sound men, would never do that. People remember it and love Suckle for it, which give him that edge. Which was important, seeing that at the time there was only really him and Duke Vin who were the big sound men.

'Originally I think he was looking for Count Suckle to play after the acts had finished so he would either keep people in the club or bring more in, but he ended up putting Suckle on on the Sunday night. On his first time in the Flamingo, Wardour Street *blocked*. Police and everything out there because *nothing* could pass up there either way. And it went on like that, but he didn't want Suckle there on other nights because he's still got his own thing going on with American artists coming and everything. But of course this start attracting attention – the Marquee started its Blue Beat nights, and another man saw what was happening, went and found premises in the nearby Carnaby Street and open the Roaring Twenties down there. And he put the Count Suckle sound system on every night. He set up the club specifically to put Count Suckle in it.'

Although the Flamingo was the first West End venue to play Jamaican music, it was the opening of the Roaring Twenties, above a parade of Carnaby Street shops – which had yet to become the epicentre of 'swinging London' – that had by far the biggest impact. It gave Count Suckle a solid base, in much the same way as the sound men back home had their corner of their lawn, but this headquarters was in central London in a venue that was by anybody's standards very comfortable. Vego continues:

'The Roaring Twenties was the first place in the centre of town like that to be playing *real* Jamaican music every night, and the rhythm and blues and ska was played there in the *real* Jamaican way. It was like being at the dance back home in practically every respect. And while black people come from every area in London - the place was soon famous – because of where it was situated it wasn't just black people there, it was white people as well. Firstly, the white people there was mainly tourists who was just looking for a club to go to, and they'd never heard beat like that before – or definitely not played in pure form like that. Some of them couldn't take it and had to leave immediately, but many jus' take a drink, let the music lick them and they *love it*. Then, because Count Suckle there permanent, the next night they can come back for more, so you had some people who was in London for two weeks and they'd come to the Roaring Twenties maybe ten times. Then they'd buy records to take home so they'd be taking the ska back to Germany or Scandinavia or Italy or wherever.

'It's that that have a great deal to do with reggae spreading all over Europe and the rest of the world, because these same tourists weren't going to Jamaica, or if they did they wouldn't go to the dance. But here in London they were being exposed to the real ska and rhythm and blues and they take it back home with them.

'The Flamingo and the Roaring Twenties is also where the British artists that embraced ska got into it – Georgie Fame was probably the best known one who would regularly play at both clubs. All those ska ideas that he have, I'm sure he picked those up there. Because the English musicians would be appearing at clubs or in concert that finished early and we were all night for real, after they would finish playing elsewhere they'd come over to the Twenties. Sometimes they'd just relax, or they'd play there. Visiting Jamaican musicians might be there too, Prince Buster always made a point of coming down there, so there could be like a jam session going on.

'The Beatles came to the Roaring Twenties . . . the Rolling Stones came to the Roaring Twenties. All of them people came to the Roaring Twenties, because the beat was always there. You could never get bored at that club, and it was a nice club inside. Nicer than the Flamingo, nicer than blues dances and the sort of place that black people, now they was living in England, deserved for a night out.'

Prince Buster recorded several tracks in England using local musicians proficient in ska, with whom he hooked up at the Roaring Twenties – notably Georgie Fame, who Buster taught ska and who played on the Blue Beat classic 'Wash Wash'. It's also highly likely that down at the Twenties, grooving on after-hours ska, is how Mick Jagger's well-documented passion for reggae music began. But, as good as the gig was, it couldn't contain Count Suckle's ambition for longer than a few years. Only on a percentage of the door, but entirely responsible for the crowds that continued to flock there, the sound man correctly concluded that people were there for him and not for the club, that if he were to move up the road the people would follow. He did. And they did. He took premises below a cinema in Paddington, still more or less in the West End but much closer to Ladbroke Grove, and launched Count Suckle's Q Club, one of the plushest, altogether nice black clubs ever to open in London. It remained so for nearly two decades, becoming one of the high spots of any black tourist's visit to the British capital.

In spite of his obvious achievements – I can personally vouch for the level of comfort and sense of occasion at the Roaring Twenties and the Q Club – Count Suckle has been all but written out of reggae's British history. Flick through the indexes of any half-dozen books dealing with the subject and you probably won't find mention of him, while one major work chronicling the post-war movement of the masses from Jamaica to the mother country spells Suckle's name wrongly every time it's mentioned. Such under-appreciation probably occurs either (a) because he wasn't the first sound man in the UK or (b) because he didn't produce records, he just played them, but it's still a shameful omission. Through his adventurous, upwardly mobile presentations his was an undeniable influence on the establishment of Jamaican music in London and beyond.

While Suckle was working so hard to take ska uptown, uptown was doing its best to come down to the ghetto looking for it. Or looking for the less-salubrious aspects of the West Indian immigrant lifestyle that were attracting attention from the idle rich. The area's proximity to Bayswater Road and Hyde Park put it on the periphery of London's booming vice trade, both literally and metaphorically – the girls would take their clients into the park – and as a result, the local black-run shebeens and blues dances were mushrooming into a nocturnal network of illegal drinking, gambling, smoking and sex.

While it wasn't exactly a no-go area for the police, Notting Hill Gate/Ladbroke Grove had become something of a safe haven for Caribbean criminals – illegal immigrants, those on the run from the law back home, or who were wrongdoing in the UK – as the dense black population provided natural cover. It all added up to the area's often undeserved high-profile reputation for sleaze, and a powerful draw for the capital's elite. Stars of the film, fashion and music worlds, the wealthy thrill-seekers, youthful nobility and the pre-jet set party people flocked to what they perceived as a murkily decadent after-hours world. In much the same way, they also populated the East End gangsters' nightclubs, but here was the added *frisson* of possibly ending up in bed with, gulp, *a black person*.

These dangerous liaisons couldn't have been more spectacularly illustrated than by the Profumo Affair in 1963. John Profumo, then Secretary of Defence, was enjoying a lengthy involvement with Christine Keeler, a young Notting Hill Gate prostitute who had also had a regular arrangement with a Captain Ivanov, naval attaché to the Russian Embassy in London and, apparently, a spy. When this came out, it was presumed that Keeler could easily be a conduit for pillow-talked secrets from the British to Soviet intelligence. Initially Profumo denied the affair, but after admitting to lying about it did the decent thing and resigned. Adding real spice to the front pages, though, was what brought the whole sordid business out into the open. At a trial for a shooting incident in which Keeler was the intended victim it came out that she was part of another *ménage à trois* involving her 'boyfriend' Johnny Edgecombe and fellow local hustler Lucky Gordon. When Edgecombe went looking for Keeler with a pistol and ended up blasting away at the door of the house she was staying in, the police were called and the whole mess went public. Johnny Edgecombe and Lucky Gordon were both Jamaican, and the more rabid of the UK's popular press had a field day. As did Kingston's musical community: Roland Alphonso cut a tune called 'Christine Keeler', King Edwards put out 'Russian Roulette' and it wasn't just two tunes that had the words 'scandal' – often spelt '*ska*ndal' – or 'Profumo' in their titles.

But while this upscale interest raised the Jamaican profile across the country – albeit often for entirely the wrong reasons – as far as ska itself went it was little more than musical tourism. The greatest boost to the music's British presence happened at the other end of the spectrum. The mods, a widespread, sharp-suited, amphetamine-fuelled, largely working-class white youth cult of the time, adopted ska as a supplement to their soundtrack of imported US soul music. Deadly serious about their music – it made as big a lifestyle statement about them as the correct trouser width or hat angle – increasing numbers of mods were to be found at the Flamingo, the Twenties, or the Marquee. Blue Beat and Island records, plus an impressive number of imported singles, were cropping up at mod clubs and all-nighters, as were a noticeable sprinkling of black mods. Many social commentators of the day pointed out that the physical proximity of the indigenous working-class mods and newly arrived immigrants – on council housing estates and in the workplace – fostered such cultural alliances. And they might even have had a point.

It was actually the mods and their sartorial obsessiveness that Emil Shallit aimed his Blue Beat garment merchandising at, but it was his records that these kids were buying as they fuelled a demand for ska that far exceeded the music's home crowd. Remember, there were probably no more than 250,000 Jamaican immigrants in the UK by this time, but it wasn't unheard of for ska records to sell more than that number of copies. Prince Buster became a mod icon, and on his frequent tours of the UK phalanxes of mods on their trademark motor scooters would escort him from date to date.

Then, somewhere between the high-class slummers and the twitchy, bespoke-tailored lads on their scooters, were the middle classes. Prince Buster was never one to be daunted by hurdles such as West Indian immigrants' apparent reluctance to go to concerts, so he opted to go and find an audience instead. (The theory behind this live gig reluctance goes back to the sound systems in Jamaica, where the removal of all information on the records meant that the deejays would never announce who the artist was – as it was said, 'They only chat their own name on the mic'. Even the tunes would often be renamed, so while people were well aware of records and songs, they had no knowledge of the artists, and therefore failed to get excited about the prospect of their coming to England.) All this conspired to put Buster on the embryonic college circuit, as although clubs such as the Twenties, the Flamingo and the Q would feature Jamaican artists, there weren't enough of those places with sufficient capacity to make the trip over economically sound. Buster figured the markets in obvious towns like London, Bristol, Birmingham and Manchester were getting saturated, and he wanted to go around more of the country and with universities he figured there'd be a large captive audience. A crowd that, in theory anyway, ought to be more open-minded than most.

They still needed a bit of a helping hand, though. Before each show, Buster would take time to talk to the crowd and tell them that what they were about to hear was probably unlike anything else they'd heard before, that this was music with a point to it and much of it had its basis in social history. Then he'd introduce each song by explaining what the lyrics were about. In what must have presented a mildly surreal tableau in those seats of learning, Buster would take a class, standing on stage, in front of the sons and daughters of Middle England, explaining exactly who the Prince, the Duke and the Sir were, what a Blackhead Chinee Man was or why Pharaoh's house should crash. Then he'd go on and sing a song about it. He worked hard to break ska in these environments – like several Jamaican artists he too tailored records for the UK market – and it worked for him. So, like the tourists and the pop stars in the Roaring Twenties, appreciation spread out in concentric circles from this beginning, and to this day, Prince Buster's ska enjoys a special place in nearly every college disco in the country.

Remarkably, this was happening almost invisibly. The music-industry establishment – major labels, the radio and the media – appeared to be completely unaware of this vibrant scene. BBC radio (then the only broadcaster based in Britain) ignored ska – Blue Beat was perpetually petitioning the station with its sales figures. Although customer pressure had greatly increased the number of record shops that stocked the music, these were still a minority of mostly urban-situated establishments. The music press all but scorned it, and promotion of visiting acts – Buster and Derrick Morgan in particular – was left up to the indie record companies or small independent operators who knew the scene personally.

Not for much longer, however.

In 1964, ska broke through. Big time. Or so it seemed. With all this interest and record sales bubbling under something had to erupt, and the most spectacular example came in May of that year when Jamaican Millie Small – whose age at the time ranges between 14 and 22, depending who you believe – scored a massive, world-wide hit (the first by a Jamaican) with the galloping ska-style cover of Barbie Gaye's R&B jolly-up 'My Boy Lollipop'. The record sold over 6 million world-wide, reached number 2 in the UK charts (where it was the seventh biggest-selling single of that year, ahead of Roy Orbison's 'Oh Pretty Woman', the Beatles' 'Hard Day's Night' and the Rolling Stones' 'It's All Over Now'), and was Top 5 in the USA. She didn't have another hit of such magnitude anywhere on the planet, in spite of a couple of follow-up Top 40 entries, maybe because 'Lollipop' was the climax to a purple(ish) period for ska in the UK. In March, British record buyers had bought sufficient quantities of the Migil Five's over-mannered ska version of 'Mockingbird Hill' to get it to number 10, and a couple of weeks prior to that, Ezz Reco and the Launchers, a London-based Jamaican group, covered Jimmy Cliff's 'King of Kings', which peaked at number 40.

What this didn't in any way do was signal a ska invasion of the mainstream, largely because these tunes weren't, strictly speaking, the real deal genuine Jamaican ska. This isn't in any way a criticism, it's a simple statement of fact. All three of these tunes were recorded in London, using largely English or long-time English-based personnel – 'Lollipop' was produced by Chris Blackwell, but arranged by Ernie Ranglin using a local band – so was far more likely to be appreciated by British pop-tuned ears. Ears that would still find it difficult to make the jump from crisply recorded very familiar sounds within those three songs to the often rough 'n' ready Kingston variety. Also, perhaps most importantly, they were all released by major record labels with corresponding promotional muscle who would have no trouble getting their product played on the radio, into the chart return shops or distributed reliably nationwide. It was an open secret that Blue Beat records wouldn't even be listened to when they arrived at the BBC for consideration, and Island doubtless received the same treatment. Blackwell actually made the decision to license 'Lollipop' to the Philips subsidiary Fontana on the grounds that it was a pop record and therefore needed support services way beyond Island's back-of-a-van capabilities. 'King of Kings' and 'Mockingbird Hill' were put out by, respectively, Columbia and Pye.

Because there was no serious follow-up other than Millie's diminishing returns, the British music business looked on ska as a flash in the pan that had now officially had its day and became, ironically, even more resistant to it. The record companies didn't need a great deal of convincing, since even while those hits were happening they'd had ska boxed off as a novelty. At the same time, 'Lollipop' seemed to open Chris Blackwell's eyes and ears to all sorts of pop possibilities. He'd never ignored what was going on beyond Jamaican music with gimmicky albums on his short-lived Surprise label, including a set of rugby songs (bawdy beer-swilling balladeering) or the easy-listening *Music to Make Love By* or *Music to Strip By* (free G-string with each copy bought!). But now, while he continued to license Jamaican tunes – 1965 was probably Island's most prolific year thus far – he set up the Aladdin label where singers such as Jackie Edwards and Owen Gray covered music by the likes of Jim Reeves and Bob Dylan. In spite of a few minor hits, it didn't last. But then it didn't really need to, as by the end of 1966, via soul hits written by Jackie Edwards for the English soul boys the Spencer Davis Group, Island Records was shifting from ska to soul to rock.

In America, almost perversely, the best chance ska had to succeed was scuppered by the Jamaican government. In the mid-1960s, probably around the same time that '10 Commandments' was an American hit, King Records, a label that had been very successful with R&B and soul, wanted the American rights to Buster's whole catalogue. Syd Nathan, the company's no-nonsense owner, was making moves to acquire it on the recommendation of soul legend James Brown, far and away King's star act, who had been turned on to Buster during a visit to Jamaica. As King had good relations with both black and mainstream radio stations they were the most likely candidates to make it happen, and there's a good chance that the sheer effervescence of Buster's music would have opened the door. However, King and United Artists (who were handling things for the Jamaican Social Development Commission) couldn't agree on the publishing. Buster, by then an outspoken minister for Islam and a perpetual thorn in the authorities' side, remains convinced this was no accident.

What both of these situations meant was that in both countries, Jamaican music once again disappeared from mainstream view. While it would be at least twenty years before it resurfaced in the USA, in Great Britain in 1967 two ska singles whose Jamaican shelf-lives had long ago expired suddenly surfaced in the pop charts. Prince Buster's 'Al Capone' and the Skatalites' 'Guns of Navarone' reached the Top 20 and the Top 30, respectively, to become the first Jamaican-produced recognized British hits.

And they really did usher in, if not an invasion, then definitely a Jamaican line of scrimmage.

Part Two

Simmer Down

'They [the people] knew it wasn't independence at all . . .
and as the music started to slow down – like the party
finish – people start observing what was happening . . .
and they figured they'd better start looking out for
themselves . . . That's when the rude-boy era start, and
to many people it was like some sort of Robin Hood
situation . . . When singers were making songs like
[*sings*] *Rudie don't fear no boy / rudie don't fear*, it was
because that rude-boy fearlessness was seen as an
act of defiance . . . But very soon the violence started
getting out of hand, and so much of the community
started living in fear.' / Jimmy Cliff

8

Soul Style

When Byron Lee brought the first electric bass into Jamaica in late 1959 or 1960, he did so for one reason alone: mobility. He wanted to tour the new music – JA boogie and ska – beyond its Kingston confines, but such traditional equipment as an upright bass or a piano didn't do him or the Dragonnaires any favours.

'Nobody was going to carry the stand-up bass on a truck for you. Or the piano,' is how he remembers his predicament. 'And we were the first band in the entire Caribbean to come up with the idea of touring, but we had to get that mobility. So I went to America and got the basic electronic equipment – the first Fender bass and Fender bass amplifier in the whole Caribbean; and an electronic organ.

'We were about eight, nine or ten pieces, and with this equipment my band could stand up and play anywhere, then jump up and run over the whole of Jamaica taking the music wherever we went. And the people took to this immediately. Because in many places they were hearing music they couldn't have heard before, therefore even the most far away villages could feel like they was part of what was going on everywhere else. Elsewhere, most importantly, it was because the electric bass and organ gave what we were doing much more punch and after the power of the sound systems, they didn't want anything subdued. The people wanted to *feel* the music coming off stage. I was in big demand and used to back all the singers: Jimmy Cliff, Bob Marley and the Wailers, Ken Boothe . . .'

Although this list could go on to read like a *Who's Who* of

Jamaican music, it is Lee's line just before it that is, in fact, most significant. The electric bass was always going to be a much more in-your-face proposition than its stand-up cousin, but it was also a much more precise and flexible instrument. Hence, in Jamaica, just like it did everywhere else in the world, Leo Fender's solid-bodied invention rewrote the rules of rhythm, but in no other nation's popular music did it have such a wide-reaching effect as it did on that island.

By the middle of the 1960s the new instrument had become pretty much regulation in the Kingston studios, at which time its players had stopped using it merely to imitate the acoustic model and were starting to experiment. Boldly so, thanks largely to the innovative talents of Lloyd Brevett. This original member of the Skatalites – his double-bass did so much to power so many ska classics – had taken to the electric model with great gusto and was completely rebalancing arrangements, beginning to delve into different strokes as he slowed his playing down. Instead of going along with the drumbeat he marked out a more precise, syncopated rhythm ('having a rest' it was called) to create time and space for other players to insert counter rhythms, which meant they were able to carry the tune's swing and so give the bass player the opportunity to let his musical hair down and show off a bit inside what were essentially his own patterns.

This was the genesis of what would become a cornerstone of Jamaican music for the next twenty or so years – the bass as a lead instrument. It's (yet) another irony that Byron Lee himself got left behind by the stylistic upheaval he unwittingly kicked off, as he was never remotely musically innovative and his band's well-mannered reggae rhythms tended to keep the bass-lines wa-a-a-y back in the mix.

However, such a progressive approach from Lloyd Brevett was unsurprising. This was a man who had been taught not only to play by his father but how to make his own double-basses. Entirely by hand. The experience gave him such an understanding of the instrument that he was always looking to do more. Although he disappeared from the scene after the Skatalites broke up, and his innovations don't seem to have made much of an impression on the group's available back catalogue, it was an awesome legacy he left behind. No small part of which was the next important phase in the island's music: rocksteady.

'The rocksteady dance is probably *the* most relaxed Jamaican dance ever done. How to dance the rocksteady? It's easy!! Just relax the whole body and allow the pulsating rocksteady rhythms to seep into your system. Then under this spell you sway your limp arms and shoulders from side to side accompanied by a one-step foot shuffle going in any direction. Occasionally you may stand in one place and raise your shoulders alternately to the beat. Forget partners, just relax and let your oily body sway in and out and go with the catchy rocksteady beat.'

An extract from the sleeve notes to the Ethiopians' 1967 album *Engine 54: Let's Ska and Rock Steady*, which came complete with a series of step-by-step snapshots of a good-looking couple letting their 'oily' bodies do exactly that. All that's missing are the Arthur Murray School-style foot diagrams.

This LP happened relatively late in rocksteady's brief lifetime, but the fact that, even at that time, it felt the need to put stepping instructions on the jacket illustrates that it was never at all easy to put any distance between rocksteady the music and rocksteady the dance. So, while the queue of players reckoning to have cut the first rocksteady tune was not quite as long and disorderly as the one claiming the credit for originating ska, what is indisputable is that whoever it actually was was only responding to pressure from the dancehall. Rocksteady the dance, or, to be exact, *style of dancing*, would have existed for at least a couple of years before a soundtrack built up enough momentum to go overground – indeed the name 'rocksteady' was applied to that long before it became a musical term. For evidence, take Alton Ellis's 1966 single 'Rock Steady': the song is widely accepted as the style's starting pistol, but this isn't for any better reason than that it was the first big hit to use the name in the title. In fact, far from innovating, it was obviously only reporting on something that already existed; check the opening lyrics: *Better get ready / come do rock steady / you've got to do this new dance / hope you are ready / you've got to do it just like uncle Freddy / If you don't know it just shake your hips, rock your body line / shake your shoulders everything in time . . .*

By the time this record was cut the crowds had wanted things to slow down for quite a while, and the new steadily rocking moves were already fully formed, only to be reacted to by the sound men/producers.

Bunny Lee, who was not yet making records back then but went on to become one of rocksteady and reggae's truly innovative producers, bears this theory out. During the first half of the 1960s he was working as a record promotions man for first Duke Reid then Ken Lack's Caltone label. Hence he used to get around the lawns and dances, and as a former *Teenage Dance Party* dancer – he was several stones lighter back in the 1950s – he noticed what new moves were going down.

'At the beginning of the sixties, with the sound-system dances being so popular with everybody – not just the kids, you have some of the people there was old and fat and they used to start to complain: "In the blues days you did have some slow tunes, you had Shirley & Lee and Johnny Ace, nowdays it jus' don' let up!" They needed a change of pace, so it became common practice for deejays to do something for them and play some slow tunes for about an hour – blues, R&B or slow ska. They'd do this at midnight and it catch on, so deejays would call it the Midnight Hour, which meant a slowdown session.

'There was a guy named Busby in Kingston, he was a famous guy – what you would call a Don nowadays. *And him could dance.* Whole heap of people used to follow him to the dance, but when he was in the dance, a whole heap of girls used to go crazy over him because him so good. When the Midnight Hour start up he used to stan' up and just rock steady. Literally. He used call his dance the rocksteady and it was an announcer at RJR that heard this and pick it up to go with the slower tunes. He used to introduce them by telling listeners, "Now I'm going to play you a brand new rocksteady,'' and other people used to talk about the dance like, ''I see a guy doing the rocksteady the other night.'' The name jus' catch like wildfire in the dancehalls.

'This would have been 'sixty-four or maybe even 'sixty-three. Long time before they start making records called themselves ''rocksteady''.'

Indeed, the initial response from the guys in charge of the record business to this demand for a 'slowdown session' came in an American soul style. About the same time as the dance-floor developments Bunny Lee describes there was a soul explosion on the sound systems. This was new-school soul rather than R&B; it didn't last long and has been little-noticed since except as, given the developments of the previous five years, something of a step back in terms of cultural identity. But it remains a vital stepping-stone between ska and rocksteady. Derrick Harriott describes this soul boom and how it became part of the inherent operator rivalry:

'Not the very start of the sixties, but just after independence, 'sixty-three or 'sixty-four, a lot of the new type of American soul music was coming to Jamaica. That's what really eclipsed ska. It was so popular with the people the sound systems were competing for it like they used to with R&B – records were being imported and exclusives were being guarded just as jealously as they used to be. Not just on the sound systems, either; even I, with my band the Mighty Vikings, had to work to stay one step ahead. Because I had a car and a record shop I could carry the new material fast to the band and we could rehearse them quickly and have them as early as the sound systems.

'This new soul music – with the Motown thing as well – was having such an effect in Jamaica, not just records being played on the radio but tours by the artists were always popular. Perhaps inevitably, the Jamaican singers were starting to sing in that style, Derrick Morgan, Dobby Dobson, Joe White . . . Bob Marley and the Wailers were sounding like Curtis Mayfield and the Impressions, Jimmy Cliff sounded like Otis Redding, Ken Boothe sounded like Clarence Carter. Everybody was doing a lot of cover versions. And it was working. All this was slowdown stuff, a lovers' rock kind of thing, and the crowds were going wild.

'The competition between sound systems meant the producers were trying out this and that all the time and the turnover of songs was very quick – often these were cover versions of American songs, and it was about then that Coxsone used to have Bob Marley play through American songs and tell him which ones to release. The producers record stuff then judge whether they should ditch it, or come with it and release it right away and make a fortune, or if they should hold it back and how long for. But although the producers' actions stimulated the music a lot because they were constantly looking for where they could take things next, it was the people that dictate the way it was to go as they reacted to it so positively.

'And this went on for a while. The change from ska had been happening for some time before the big guys in the music business sit up, take notice and start making something for themselves instead of copying the Americans. A lot of singing groups started around this period and, although some of them and the smaller producers were moving towards a more *obviously* Jamaican sound, nothing didn't really happen until Hopeton Lewis come with a song called "Sound and Pressure", and right after that with another one called "Take Your Time Take it Easy", both originally recorded for the Merritone sound system – a relatively small sound system. Those tunes were so popular for so long, it was then that a wider circle acknowledge the new beat and start trying this Jamaican style for themselves. But that wasn't until 1966.'

It's interesting to note that, although the Big Three sound men – Buster, Dodd and Reid – each ran major recording operations, there were now so many record producers and record companies working independently of the sound systems that Derrick Harriott sees the sound systems and the music business as two separate entities.

Naturally, the slowing down of the beat that he and Bunny Lee talk about in such detail isn't nearly as clear-cut as that – this is, after all, still the Jamaican music business we're discussing. Of course, it came about for a myriad different reasons, only *most* of them dancehall-related.

Importantly, people just fancied a bit of a change. The turn-over of styles in the producer/sound-system-driven world of Jamaican popular music was even more energetic then than it is now, and after three years or more ska was past its sell-by date. Or at least at the cutting edge of Kingston's dances it was.

Then, as Bunny Lee and Derrick Harriott have explained, these same crowds wanted a rest, quite literally. In the aftermath of independence, so much ska had taken on a frenzied, galloping quality as a result of the radio-promoted, government-sponsored optimism. Not only was this wearing audiences out, but it was proving difficult to dance to with a great deal of panache – cutting competitions were turning into endurance contests, and where's the glory in that? Incidentally, it was always a myth that dancing the ska was a completely wanton affair; like American Lindy Hopping in the 1940s it was never less than lively, but participants prided themselves on their complete control of what they were doing. But it was becoming increasingly onerous as the pace picked up. The weather worked against the music, too, in this respect. The summer of 1966 (just before the above-mentioned 'breakthrough' records) was one of the hottest on record, a heatwave that continued until late in the year, and as air-conditioning was unheard of, even in an outdoor sound-system lawn the night temperature was unlikely to have fallen below 90 degrees. But by now, with the lucrative English ska market opened up, many producers were tailoring their tunes with one eye on export figures and chilly north European conditions demanded an extra hi-tempo sound to get the blood flowing and the feet moving in the blues parties and shebeens of Birmingham, London and Bristol.

Another crucial reason for the downshift in tempo, though, was a measurable increase in tension in the dancehalls. This was the case across Kingston in general, in fact, as street gangs grew in size and stature, but their effect was always most tangible in the dance, where crews could assemble without attracting too much police attention, turf could be defined, and orchestrated crowd trouble was superseding any sound-man wars. The situation is best illustrated as early as 1963 by Alton Ellis's hit 'Dance Crasher': . . . *dance crashers please don't break it up / Don't make a fuss / Don't use a knife to take another's life . . . You won't have a chance / And this will be your last dance . . .* This was the beginning of the rude-boy era, the period in Jamaican history when violence was established as a popular profession; the gun, the bomb and the ratchet knife were the tools of the trade; and fear and intimidation its benchmarks. It was then, in the early 1960s, that Jamaica's enduring bad-man culture took root.

Understandably, this created an atmosphere of trepidation in the dancehalls and patrons, whether they were rudie or not, needed to be on their guard. And as for the effect on the music, it meant less fancy footwork, shuffling or jiving as couples, and more remaining rooted to the spot, moving from the hips and shoulders. You know, rocking steady, either by yourself or locked tight to your best girl, but staying strictly in your own space, ever alert to what was going on around or managing to look detachedly menacing.

Musicians had been picking up on all of these new vibes for a while. There always was a less-obviously commercial side to ska that was slower, more melodic – pensive even – but until very recently, little of it survived on compilation albums as it doesn't sit with the easily marketed idea of the style as strictly good-time. It shouldn't be forgotten that so many of the prominent ska players had jazz or big-band swing roots, and every now and then they'd lead sessions that gave such groundings an airing in terms of melody and cool swing. Much of what Roland Alphonso did under his own name tended towards the mellow – 'Guantanamera Ska', 'The Cat', 'Song for My Father' and so on; Tommy McCook, too, followed this trend over at Treasure Isle – the Carib Beats frequently got an easy-action Latin vibe going – and while the Skatalites' Studio One years threw up plenty of downtempo tunes, as might be expected, most of ska's available slow jams involve the frequently doleful-sounding Don Drummond. Two of his tunes in particular – 'Valley Prince' and 'African Beat' – are actually textbook examples of the rocksteady instrumental, yet the trombonist had died some while before the term was officially coined. Then, as far as vocalists go, check out 'You Done Me Wrong' by the Slickers, or 'No Good Rudie' by Justin Hinds and the Dominoes, or Dobby Dobson's 'Seems to Me I'm Losing You'. All from the first half of the sixties, these are not so much 'transitional' records as transparently rocksteady – just too early to have been so named.

When the music did settle down post-'Take it Easy' – coincidentally another tune that drew reference to 'doing the rocksteady' – there was a clearly discernible way of doing things in the studio as well. What brass was used was usually there to provide an in-your-face intro before fading discreetly to the back of (or out of) the mix, coming back only for a pump-up-the-action-type chorus. What was happening was that the horns, which had been so important in defining so much of the best of ska, were now being used merely for emphasis; they were *underlining* rather than making the point, as it was the rhythm section that had now stepped forward to drive the style. The bass player in particular. And it was a responsibility he assumed with great gusto; witness the imposing bottom-end dexterity on 'Ba Ba Boom' by the Jamaicans, or the chugging, foundation melody delivered by the bass guitar on Alton Ellis's 'Girl I've Got a Date'.

But such musical emancipation always requires a sturdy anchor, hence these tricky bass patterns came with solid drums. Although classic rocksteady stayed in 4/4 time and on the off-beat, the way such a notion was expressed had altered enormously. The heartbeat of this new rhythm was a slowed-down tempo dictated by the kick drum, which was now kicking it on the third beat only instead of the second and fourth beats as it would have done in ska. In the day's studio slang, the arranger would ask for this single strike by shouting to his drummer *'Gimme a one drop'*, and thus naming a way of doing things that formed the basis of generations of Jamaican music – indeed, it was still 'felt' by Bob Marley years later in 'Talking Blues'. Meanwhile, the advent of other electrified instrumentation in Kingston's studios greatly assisted in this beefing up of the rhythm section. The electric organ was proving far more versatile than the old piano in underscoring the new arrangements, as by setting the controls right and arching his fingers the player could provide a stabbing, popping hi-octane addition to the percussive collage – witness 'Come on Little Girl' by the Melodians. Most importantly, the electric guitar chopped out upfront chords on the second and fourth, straight down with a crisp *channk!* . . . *channk!*; it wasn't unusual for guitarists to tune their lowest string in with the bass and augment what the bass player was doing.

Given the prominence of the guitar in this new mix, it's hardly surprising that a guitarist, Lynn Taitt, is given the most credit as the man who consolidated the various musical advances and solidified the rocksteady style. Previously of the Skatalites, after the group split up Taitt worked around town as a guitarist and arranger for hire, before becoming a permanent fixture at the studios Duke Reid had built above his liquor store at 33 Bond Street. In spite of Taitt and his group the Jets hiring themselves out to, and having hits with, a host of other rocksteady producers – Joe Gibbs, Derrick Harriott, Sonia Pottinger (that's right, *a woman*), Bunny Lee and Leslie Kong among them – it was at Treasure Isle that he did his most-loved work. Indeed, under Lynn Taitt's direction the Duke became the undisputed King of Rocksteady, thanks, according to those on the scene at the time, to the guitarist's 'different' way of looking at things.

Ernie Ranglin remembers: 'Lynn Taitt was keen to try new things. Everybody wanted something new – the musicians, the crowds, the producers – but it hadn't come together as such until he start to organize the sound. In the studio when he was running a session, first he'd lay down guitar chords that were a real cool-down thing. Because that's what he was, a guitarist, and he could control the whole way the tune went from his guitar chords. It was always much more likely to keep a slower pace. Then he bring in the one drop that would keep the tempo like that, then have the bass follow that beat but improvise with it. It allowed more room for me or the keyboard player or the saxophone or whatever to play a real sweet melody, and of course it was right for singing.

'Everybody loved what Lynn Taitt was doing. It caught on like wildfire.'

Prince Buster offers a likely explanation for *why* change was so high on Lynn Taitt's agenda. 'He wasn't Jamaican, he was born and brought up in Trinidad and had a very different way of looking at things. He had a lot of outside influences – he used to play different things, particularly calypso and American music. He was an excellent player and was never a man who was satisfied with how things were if they stayed the same for too long. Even though he was the person who really bring in rocksteady as we know it today, he was always looking for ways to move it on as soon as it was established.'

It's one (more) of modern Jamaican music's ironies that Taitt had turned down leadership of the Skatalites when it was offered to him a couple of years earlier because he believed a band so dedicated to promoting Jamaican music ought to be fronted by a native son. Now, that exact same off-island quality had put him in charge of the next stage of development.

There were, of course, a number of largely pragmatic reasons why things were changing, too. As a result of the ska boom there was a proliferation of small production outfits and record labels on the scene, many of whom couldn't afford big bands, thus those producers had to be more inventive with what they could get. Also, as established players would be out of their price range, they recruited from a new wave of musicians eager to impress with their own ideas. Since the brass was considered such a vital part of ska – and, coincidentally, the new soul music too – the players knew it, and it was that which cost the money. Even unknowns were trying to charge over the odds. The obvious solution was, rather than build a track around the horns, to leave them at the back of the room, or even out in the yard, and create arrangements with minimal or no horn lines.

Which resulted in a great deal of space centre stage. Suddenly, oozing electric organs, tricksy lead guitars, harmonicas, the odd solo brass instrument and even a violin (spin the Paragons' 'The Tide Is High' for proof of this) were carrying the melodies. Well, what did you expect? This is Jamaica, where necessity isn't just invention's mother, it's its father, grandparents, aunties, uncles, brothers, sisters and cousins all rolled into one.

As a knock-on effect of this, cost figured among the big boys, too. One side of the argument has it that the ska stars had started to overprice themselves and the top producers were forced to look elsewhere and for alternative instrumentations, bringing them to the same new sounds that the smaller guys were creating. Predictably there's an alternative spin, from the musicians themselves, who claim that once a certain set of players had made names for themselves while working for a lower rate, the producers dropped their pay scale accordingly. Take your pick.

Unarguably though, the new way of doing things permeated the entire music business. However, with equal certainty, once rocksteady had established itself, music almost became secondary as the bottom line was that it was all about singing. Singing that had a very specific role model.

As we have seen, Lynn Taitt's playing of American music was highly significant. For a start, Taitt's fondness for US music meant his rocksteady absorbed many Americanisms and smoothly made the transition out of that JA soul boom; but of equal importance was the kind of American music he was listening to at the time. Soul had superseded R&B in the States in a turnabout that married traditional vocal values – the Impressions, Otis Redding, Motown, Solomon Burke, the Drifters (with Ben E. King), the Dells, Brook Benton – to an entirely modern presentation and far more positive black attitude, a stylistic revolution that wouldn't have been lost on a master musician such as Taitt. This new trend also reestablished the idea that singers could be at the forefront of a musical evolution.

In fact, it had been clear for some time that singers might be coming into fashion. As well as the US soul records now being played on Jamaican radio or being picked up on the island from big Southern stations, impresarios such as Byron Lee and Stephen Hill Jr were bringing a succession of American artists into Jamaica for theatre concerts. Hill's father, Stephen Hill Sr, had been the island's biggest post-war concert promoter, putting on jazz, R&B and classical concerts; now his son had such good relations with the younger end of the US entertainment business that he went on to become Marvin Gaye's manager. Whilst solo artists like Solomon Burke, Wilson Pickett, Marvin and Smokey Robinson continued to exert influence, as did the oozing likes of Sam Cooke and Jerry Butler, it was the soul groups that had a much greater impact.

Instead of the larger groups of the R&B era, with a star lead singer and four or five others handling the back-ups – like, for instance, Harriott's Jiving Juniors – new-style soul opted for smaller, more democratic arrangements. Trios became most popular, but instead of a clearly defined lead singer and with the other two in support, all three members would share duties within the same songs, allowing for far greater depth of harmony and more surprises for the listener. It was a situation that found enormous support in Jamaica. It positively encouraged a black gospel heritage to be displayed, and as most would-be singing sensations had church roots it was very natural. Moreover, the apparently equal opportunities these outfits afforded increased the likelihood of stardom for each member and at the same time removed a degree of in-group subordination that was never going to sit too well among black male Jamaicans just out from colonization. It's interesting to note that the favoured album-sleeve image of Jamaican harmony trios was of all three members clustered around the same mic, with no visible hierarchy.

The most influential of the regular visitors to the island's concert halls were the Impressions. Just consider the number of Curtis Mayfield-written cover versions that crop up in the rocksteady songbook: the Techniques' 'Queen Majesty' is an adaptation of 'Queen and Minstrel'; the same group's 'You Don't Care' is the Impressions' 'You'll Want Me Back'; while the Uniques' 'Gypsy Woman' didn't even go so far as to alter the title. And what was to become the classic Jamaican vocal style of three voices in harmony with tenor and alto leads swooping in and out of each other, and acting out a three-minute musical joust, is pure Mayfield, Cash & Gooden. You know, the Impressions. It was a way of doing things that became so entrenched in the island's music business, that, when presented with duos, producers would often rope in a third voice for recording purposes (the Congos' addition Watty Burnett is a classic, if later, instance). Or, again *à la* the Impressions and their occasional addition of Richard and Arthur Brooks, vocal arrangers would call in backing singers to beef up particular productions – the most famous example of which is Coxsone Dodd employing Bunny Wailer and Peter Tosh to add some low-profile extra scope to the Ethiopians' harmonizing during their Studio One days.

Brent Dowe was – and still is – leader of the top-ranking rocksteady trio the Melodians, who cut such classics as 'Come On Little Girl', 'I Will Get Along' and the all-time-genre anthem 'Swing and Dine'. As one who was at the centre of that scene, he adds another, pretty fundamental angle as to why the trios came about:

'Back in the ska days, most groups was four or five – we was four, the Wailers was five. It's because when we started off we used to pattern our music after the American groups like the Drifters or the Platters or the Tams. We used to try and copy their acts. Then later on, around the time the ska started to die away, every group started dropping members to go down to a trio – the Wailers were the first to go down to three. The thing is, five voices is a whole lotta singing and, while you might need all of that in front of a ska band, as it went towards rocksteady you just didn't need so much. Also, when we all started off nobody wasn't doing any serious recording, or at least you didn't really consider that, and although you would need them for live work when you are doing recording, five voices was often too much sound for the small, very basic studios.

'When we started dropping down everybody was keen to keep it that way because it was much easier to arrange three voices. To most people at the time, artists and producers, a trio was quite enough, because it was so much more manageable than five voices, or even four.'

Rocksteady's subject matter nearly always took its cue from the Motown hit factory or the Stax set-up down in Memphis. The songs for these singers became two-and-a-half-minute pop operas; tales of loves lost, found and gone unnoticed, as good and sloppy as any of the Brill Building mini-dramas. This presentation of Jamaican music in a universally acceptable pop package did more towards putting it on the world map than any amount of trying to flog watered-down ska at the 1964 World's Fair. Sentiments to be found in numbers like 'Lovin' Pauper', 'Wear You to the Ball', 'Pretty Looks Isn't All' or 'Everybody Needs Love' talked an international pop language but did so with a pronounced Jamaican accent.

This essential Americanness in rocksteady provides a handy peg upon which to hang Duke Reid's dominance of the style, because the years between 1966 and 1968 really were all about Treasure Isle. Sure, Sonia Pottinger's Gay Feet label did very well with the sweeter side of it – Monty Morris's 'Put on Your Best Dress'; the Melodians' 'Swing and Dine' and 'Little Nut Tree'; the Gaylads' 'I Need Your Loving'; the Ethiopians' 'The Whip', 'Train to Glory' and 'Stay Loose Mama'; and Stranger Cole's 'Tell It to Me'. And Coxsone more than had his rocksteady moments, particularly with the Paragons, the Heptones, Delroy Wilson and Slim Smith. As did Bunny Lee with the Uniques (featuring the self-same Slim Smith), Lester Stirling, the Sensations and Pat Kelly. New boy Joe Gibbs made his mark, too – Roy Shirley's 'Hold Them' – but the Duke was the king. His huge affection and finely tuned ear for American blues and R&B led to a natural affinity with this smoother sound and a very subtle appreciation of how to wring the absolute best out of a smooove love song. These new soul leanings were his territory because he just *knew* how it was meant to work. Duke Reid, gunslinger on the outside, pussycat on the inside? It's unlikely anybody stepped up to ask him, but that didn't matter at all, because rocksteady hits flowed like water from upstairs at 33 Bond Street. Justin Hinds and the Dominoes' second version of 'Carry Go Bring Come'; the Techniques' 'I'm in the Mood for Love', 'Queen Majesty' and 'You Don't Care'; Alton Ellis's 'Rock Steady'; the Jamaicans' 'Ba Ba Boom' and 'Things You Say You Love'; the Paragons' 'My Best Girl'; the Melodians' 'Come on Little Girl' . . . this is just the tip of an iceberg big enough to have sunk the *Titanic*. Two times.

Duke Reid had a couple of other things going for him as well, as Brent Dowe remembers:

'He was there in the studio most of the time, which was unusual for such a big producer as a lot of the others wouldn't come down – they just left it up to their arrangers and picked what records to put out. But Duke was always there because he was a very strict man and he demanded perfection. He was a fantastic man; he could read things in his head. If he just hear the rhythm and he hear the singer sing so he would always come up with something to add to it. He would look for a kind of symphonic sound, and he had the knack of getting that with a lot of horns, a lot of back-up vocals and very *dense* arrangements. He knew it was exactly the soft sound the style needed, nothing sharp or ragged in a Duke Reid song. He was a very smart man.

'But the key to his getting all of that was because he remain very very active as a producer. I remember even if he was downstairs in the liquor store doing some other business, he have a speaker box connected from the studio to the office down there. So whatever recordings is going on, whether it a new tune or a retake or OK or whatever, he could listen to the whole session from downstairs. So whenever a mistake made, it wouldn't matter what he was doing, he *run* up the stairs! He was a big fat man too, but whenever the song is going nice and suddenly he don't hear the right thing going into it he would run up those stairs, *bam, bam, bam, bam,* and shout "No! No! No! *Don't* do it like that!" And he would tell us *exactly* what he want and he would stay up there for the next take.

'Duke Reid made his records longer, too. In the ska days you have tunes that were two minutes twenty seconds or so, because they was so fast the people at the dance couldn't take no more. But then by the time it come around to rocksteady and it slowed down you could do longer. Duke saw this and would start doing his tunes at three or even four minutes. Which was good for us, because if the tune was going sweet – like most of them would – you'd want to just carry on with it. You'd get swept along with it and, especially the musicians, would have the space to try different stuff. Pretty soon everybody was making longer records, but Duke saw it first.

'All of this made those sessions real nice, real exciting, because you feel like you're being pushed further than you thought you could go. All the time. Everybody, even from the musicians' perspective, they used to enjoy themselves in that studio, and when they get into a good original song they used jus' ride up and want to give it something extra. You wanted to be there to sing for Duke Reid, so you'd put that extra bit into it.'

There's a readily available, first-hand example of the Duke's no-nonsense approach to production technique on the Treasure Isle compilation CD *Ska after Ska after Ska*. The track entitled 'Duke Speaks' is a thirteen-second snatch of when the tape was left running between takes. You hear this sleepy-voiced bear of a man berating his musicians with ill-concealed exasperation: '. . . Look 'ere, it look like you forget the bass and the drum . . . I want it *heavy* . . . *plenty* more bass and drum, I don't hear that . . .'

Although the rocksteady singing style undoubtedly had its roots in the USA it had been honed into a local event – the true Jamaican three-part was that much closer than its American relative – as, post-ska, it was now *expected* rather than merely accepted for Jamaican syntax, slang and pronunciation to be used. In terms of instrumentation as well, rocksteady was far closer to the sounds and balances of the rest of the world's guitar, bass 'n' drums pop music than its predecessor had been, but was so with a particularly island flavour. The room for addition and improvisation within the typical rocksteady structure allowed many a nod towards mento, Kumina and Pocomania. In many ways it's hardly surprising that it was this genre, albeit a few years after these events, that gave Jamaican music its lasting international presence, as it was essentially conventional, easily accessible and keenly infectious.

Given all of the above, it's curious that, in later years, analysis manages to focus on rocksteady as being the result of and the soundtrack to the rude-boys' ghetto violence. The apparently widely held notion is of the music's environment being one of perpetual and unanimous armed conflict, with the players and dancers absorbing these outside tensions to translate them into a display of music and movement that was at once both threatened and threatening. And very little else. Check it: two of the hardest-worked adjectives are 'stifling' and 'oppressive', presenting what is a quite ridiculous, horribly condescending set of assumptions.

Firstly, they ignore the fact that the Kingston ghetto population – like that of any 'hood anywhere in the world – was actually made up of far more proper people than it was hooligans. Therefore they ignore, probably wilfully, the fact that, although these swaggering street toughs enjoyed a disproportionately high public profile, theirs was never the dominant culture. The vast majority of dancehall patrons were respectable people looking for a brief respite from the trials and tribulations of everyday life, and to suggest that sound-system lawns, run by businessmen, suddenly turned themselves over to celebration of such antisocial behaviour is ludicrous. So much so it's frighteningly close to the enduring colonial supposition that all black people are (a) the same and (b) savages.

While the need to reevaluate personal space on the dancefloor was undoubtedly a contributing factor to the music's evolution, this is nothing more sinister than basic nightclub manners – you know, that you do your best not to bump into people – merely made slightly more acute by a peculiar social climate. And true, rude-boy lyrics played their part, but they only ever did that – played a part in the vast, mostly joyous tapestry that made up rocksteady's songbook. It would be silly to try to pretend that 'Tougher than Tough' or 'Rude Boy' hadn't been written, and no better than turning the same blind eye to the huge number of records with titles like 'Come on Little Girl' or 'Feel Like Jumping'.

Rocksteady was the lovers' rock of its time. Celebratory, good time, grab-a-gal music, soundtrack-to-seduction pop music. Which isn't to say the rude boys weren't for real.

It's been a popular notion since the Union Flag was lowered on colonial Jamaica that the country was, post-Columbus, colonized twice: once by the British and once by its own inherent and rigid class system. While the former was brought to an end with the stroke of a pen and the exchanging of flags back in 1962, the latter has proved rather more difficult to dislodge. The modern 'industrialized' Jamaica that came into being in the 1950s institutionalized a kind of elitism that hadn't been seen since slavery. Naturally, bauxite and tourism were far more beneficial to the ruling classes, but these recently arrived corporations and the explosion of the economy as a whole – notably the public sector – had added a new stratum to the traditional professional middle classes: that of management or senior workers. Once more guidelines for privilege were determined by the shadism that continues to rule Jamaican society, and, quite understandably, the recipients embraced their newfound status as a leg up the social rankings. It was only a matter of time before this upper tier of the working class came to dominate the trade unions. These organizations, originally fought for by the labouring classes, then began to devote their efforts to this blue-collar elite. And as a side-effect, a large number of Jamaica's growing university-educated intelligentsia came to trade unions believing that industrial relations offered a short cut into politics. Provided they looked on it from the right point of view, that is – intellectuals who sided with the poor were seen as trouble makers and not to be taken seriously. Consequently, many of these disenchanted graduates became drawn to Rastafari.

This newly created *petite bourgeoisie*, who by now carried

considerable economic, social and political weight, were tight with the government, and were afforded far greater attention than the disenfranchised lower orders. After all, to openly acknowledge the country's massive poverty would be to admit to serious civic problems. Which wouldn't have sat too well with the idea of a boom economy and the quest for continuing substantial foreign investment.

By this time, independent Jamaica's two-party system was effectively a joke. Their manifestos might have appeared diametrically opposed: the People's National Party offered idealism in a version of democratic socialism that relied heavily on support from Cuba and took the view that things had to get worse before they get better, while, in spite of its name, the Jamaican Labour Party's pragmatism was definably right wing, with close links to the USA, who saw the island as a strategic bulkhead against that self-same Cuba. But the reality was that each side had to bend over for Uncle Sam for two main reasons. Initially, the two dominant new industries (tourism and bauxite) and the experimental, hi-tech 'factory' farms that were starting to dot the landscape all involved such enormous US investment they had essentially hijacked the country's fiscal infrastructure. Then the huge reduction in arable land in agricultural use further increased this dependency by necessitating vastly increased food imports, nearly half of which came from America. The irony of the foreign-owned production line-type farms was that their high-yield, aesthetically acceptable crops (perfectly formed bananas, tomatoes, cucumbers, pineapples) were for export to the USA and Europe, while the small farmers they'd displaced got by on foreign-grown staples. The trick whichever party was in power had to pull off was to try to maintain this culture of dependency without alarming the elite.

Neither party was keen to put class or racial politics on its agenda, so great were the problems of Jamaica's dispossessed at this point. To even attempt to take them on would be to put you and your party on a hiding to nothing. Unless it was election time, when every vote counted, the sufferahs were treated like the mad old uncle at a family get-together – had to be there but caused so much embarrassment that all the uptown types that mattered did their best to ignore them. Both sides glossed over the issue of massive social inequality, opting instead to pander to any remaining post-independence spirit of optimism with largely empty slogans and promises tailored to take full advantage of the masses' hopes and dreams. Public money was spent outside the ghettos, among the influential upper classes and where it would impress/benefit visitors to the island from '*a foreign*'.

The gulf was perceptibly widening. Within three or four years of independence, the only additional job opportunities for the working people were short-term casual labouring contracts that offered an absolute minimum in the way of wages and even less security. Indeed, the corporate preference for empowering the lighter-skinned Jamaican workers as charge hands was spookily reminiscent of the old pre-emancipation ways with a plantocracy and privileged slaves bought off as overseers.

One People? Two Nations more like.

It is estimated that, over and above the negative effect of physical displacement, the fiscal growth of the 1950s made no difference at all to roughly half of Jamaica's working population. A working population that was shrinking rapidly: during the first five years of the 1960s, national unemployment figures had doubled to 26 per cent, with estimates of roughly twice that proportion in Kingston, young men under twenty being the worst hit. With a lack of political representation and the conventional church holding little sway, Rastafari offered the most viable avenue for self-respect and self-improvement. Rastafari's backbone of black pride and self-reliance fell into step perfectly with what was happening in America, and word of Malcolm X, the Nation of Islam and the embryonic Black Panthers gradually filtered through to Jamaica. Also, with its open-ended 'reasoning' and apparently perpetually shifting tenets, Rastafari is an ideal philosophy for a people who, traditionally, take a keen interest in their country's socio-political matters, have a strong oral convention and far too much free time on their hands.

However, while Rasta's numbers blew up in the first half of the 1960s, another significant section of Kingston youth had run headlong into the realization that an independent Jamaica wasn't about to solve its problems. There was for them, though, an easier, apparently more rewarding route to social advancement.

The rude boys were a Jamaican phenomenon of the 1960s. Young, male, urban. Un- or under-employed. Loudly disaffected with the state of the nation, yet lacking any formal ideology or physical focus, thus appearing totally apolitical. Anti-establishment, anti-authoritarian, antisocial, hell, even anti-each other, they had all manner of frustrations to vent. Without the discipline that comes from the responsibilities of work, commerce or even schooling there was an audacious wildness about this youth that rewrote the rules of street violence. By the middle of the decade, the rudies were sufficiently widespread to create serious civil disorder in certain areas. They may have ended up being brutally exploited by Jamaica's party-political system, but before that happened they laid the foundation stones for one more layer in the island's social *millefeuille*.

A criminal class. No more no less.

9

Dance Crasher

Given Jamaica's history of insurgence and its bloodily confrontational labour relations, it's hardly surprising that by the end of the 1950s, political violence presented an increasingly popular option to either side. Indeed, practically from their inceptions in the 1930s, both political parties had their 'own' trade unions – the Bustamente Industrial Trade Union was allied to the JLP while the Trades Union Congress was down with the PNP. These were organizations that would, right from the start, pitch their workers against each other for control of the docks or cane fields and would now lend their new friends a bit of campaign muscle, in the truest sense of the word. By 1961, street skirmishes became so much a part of election campaigning that before the referendum on West Indies Federation membership marches and parades were banned all over the island. Then once the island got its independence the parliamentary stakes became much higher. In Jamaican politics, never what you might call a gentlemanly institution, the gloves came off.

Nowhere more so than in Kingston, where, with the enormous concentration of the population and all manner of lucrative public works and development opportunities, winning votes in and holding the urban constituencies became a matter of some urgency.

The street gangs had been a part of downtown life in the capital for as long as anybody can remember, but since the end of the Second World War they had started to organize. Four main outfits prevailed. The Vikings, whose turf was the waterfront area of Newport East and who specialized in dynamiting fish and stealing from ships and sailors; Park, who hailed from Denham Town and took pride in their pickpocketing abilities; the Spanglers from Charles Street, who ran with Duke Reid's sound system and, in their sharp clothes and trademark over-sized belt buckles, considered themselves above street crime; and the most dangerous of them all, Salt City (later known as Phoenix City – to be immortalized in the Skatalites' tune of the same name) based on Salt Lane, off Spanish Town Road, who carried knives and machetes as tools of an unsophisticated street robbery trade. There were also dozens of less-significant Kingston street mobs such as Skull, Zulu, Max, Dirty Dozen and Phantom, but all of these allied themselves to one of the big four.

At the beginning of the 1960s, it was rare for these gangs to fight each other. Why should they? A clear demarcation was accepted and everybody was more concerned with making a living. But in the transitional period immediately following independence, several changes occurred to reevaluate the street status quo: politics found a use for these sufferah gangsters, there was a marked shift in law-enforcement values, and the drug trade happened – on an international scale with Jamaica as an important player.

Politically, union organizing in Jamaica had long dictated a show of force to be the most effective bargaining tool, and it was customary for the street gangs to find gainful employment as freelance rabble rousers, breaking heads during labour dis-putes. Thus they made a smooth transition into politics when they were recruited at the turn of the decade to break up opposing party's rallies by heckling, throwing stones or, in an almost surreal enactment of the PNP's 'Sweep them out' slogan, by brandishing household brooms. Intimidation at and disruption of polling stations was standard election-day prac-tice, with such considerations as publicly funded sports equip-ment or a club house on offer as rewards from successful candidates for 'favours' done. None of this was too pleasant, though neither was it particularly life-threatening. But the situation altered radically after the JLP became the party to take the island into its new beginning by winning the general election of summer 1962.

These were the days of Martin Luther King, Malcolm X, the formative Black Panther Party and post-Batista Cuba. Jamaica's sufferahs followed world events keenly – throughout their history poverty has never been confused with an excuse for ignorance – while Washington got decidedly twitchy. Here was a newly independent black-majority nation, in which a great deal of American money was invested, and where until very recently the whole meaning of life had been based on social injustice; it had a history of violent revolution and the current opposition party preached democratic socialism while openly courting Fidel Castro; and *it was closer to Washington DC than nearly all of the fifty US states*. Suddenly, the island of Jamaica had a skyscraper-high profile in American foreign policy.

The US idea was to keep the ruling right-wing Jamaican Labour Party in power by providing whatever the party leaders felt they needed to maintain the status quo at the ballot box. Which translated into a frightening tide of modern weaponry flowing into the Kingston ghettos, or, more specifically, the ghettos' JLP-held areas. Ground-level recruitment of these unofficial armies was never a problem, as labour contracts, public-sector employment and, importantly, housing was the bounty on offer. The PNP camp armed themselves in response, but with never quite the same sophistication. It's said the party leaders had appealed to Castro for Russian-built guns – Kalashnikovs to answer the CIA-sponsored M-15s – but none came through and they were forced to buy on the black market from sailors or entrepreneurial soldiers.

Pretty soon, what had been no more serious than knockabout rabble-rousing became out-and-out armed sectarian terrorism. The territorially precise nature of the gangs and the very specific nature of voting wards meant West, Central and Southside Kingston was divided into what amounted to a series of politically divided garrisons, so clearly defined they make Belfast look like a free-for-all. Housing projects such as those in Tivoli

181 **Dance Crasher**

Gardens or Rema were built as rewards for frontline troops' loyalty, but they also served as barracks, which greatly intensified the parochial nature of the political turf. From the 1960s onwards, the 'success' of Jamaican general elections has been judged by their respective body counts. And the only way to get anything done has been via the barrel of a gun.

At this point, the police hardly counted as a force for law and order. Once the British had decamped, a different, entirely more pragmatic set of standards was set in place. The ruling JLP assumed the police to be just another, albeit better equipped and more successful, division of their own troops; the hierarchy within the force became much less rigid, therefore power disseminated downwards and outwards, meaning all sorts of unlikely figures wielded great influence on the street. Corruption was rife, large numbers of honest officers quit and some serving officers were so disaffected with their lot that they went so far as to sell their weapons to the under-equipped PNP soldiers.

In such an atmosphere of government-sponsored chaos, it's not surprising that the rude boys' unofficial lawlessness flourished.

The third crucial factor in the anarchy that was overtaking the Kingston ghettos was the ganja trade. During the first half of the 1960s it flared up like a rogue seed in a big spliff, and it was mass tourism that put a match to it. The collie weed tourism that exists today was established not long after the first Boeings touched down, as American and European holidaymakers were swiftly seduced by the power and the glory of the Jamaican herb. Up until then, ganja cultivation had been for domestic consumption only, and as users tended to grow their own there was very little trade. Very soon, though, a draw became as regulation a souvenir as a ska record or a hand-carved coconut shell. It didn't take America's East Coast dealers too long to discover that, in 1962, this superior product could be bought on the island for about five dollars per pound and knocked out on the streets of New York, Washington or Philadelphia for twenty times that.

Jamaica had a largely unprotected coastline less than 600 miles from Miami, docks controlled by gangsters, an interior where a light-aircraft landing strip could be built without attracting a great deal of attention, and farmers operating on subsistence levels eager to harvest a high-yield cash crop. Herb heaven. But, like anywhere else in the world, successful drug suppliers needed protection – the street gangs, some of whom were already involved through their influence at the docks, were a ready-made defence force. By the middle of the decade, guns for grass had become a popular, if highly unofficial, America/Jamaica trade agreement.

A section of the Kingston underclass was now armed to such a degree as to assume an awful significance. As well as the guns, home-made pipe bombs, Molotov cocktails and dynamite liberated from the mining operations were a legacy of the political involvement; while the cane-cutting machete (or cutlass as it was somewhat romantically known) and the ratchet (a mass-imported inexpensive knife that could be locked open with a flick of the wrist) were regulation rude-boy accessories. Due as much to high-level corruption as to grassroots disaffection, these ghetto toughs were subject to only cursory interest from the authorities – on both counts it was very much a 'Why bother?' situation – and a scary, self-regulating status quo had evolved. Rankings the equivalent of general, sergeant-at-arms and infantryman evolved in each area, clarifying a street meritocracy that employed ruthlessness, brutality and fear as its benchmarks. These were the rude boys. So-called because *'dem 'ave no manners'*, local parlance for a complete disregard for society's codes and rules.

Fuelled by the seemingly endless loop of cowboy and gangster shoot-'em-ups on offer at the downtown cinemas and, as they perceived it, empowered for the first time ever, these self-styled gunslingers assumed casual violence as their currency. But political strong-arming and drug running were hardly full-time occupations. Which left a lot of swaggering aggression that had to find an outlet.

It didn't take a crystal ball to see that inner-city Kingston was ready to explode.

*

Of course, this was all going off just the other side of the studio door. Although the rude-boy era was, as we've mentioned, never rocksteady's dominant thematic touchstone, the proximity between the recording session and the street meant that it would always have a significant effect on the music industry. And while, much like rocksteady itself, rude-boy music was an essentially short-lived experience, the effect it had on Jamaican music of the future was huge.

Such was the impression the so-called rude-boy wars were leaving in Kingston that lyricizing it on record became entirely acceptable to the industry and public alike – initially it was little more than a continuation of the tradition that vocalized anything that went on in the community. This is when, more significantly than with calypso, the notion of social commentary as a choice of subject matter in modern Jamaican music took root. True, there had been tunes like Laurel Aitken's 'Judgement Day' or the Maytals' 'Study War no More' since the industry began, and artists such as Prince Buster and Justin Hinds usually had a lot to say for themselves, but these examples were few and far between within the staple diet of love 'n' devotion. Also of note in this respect is that the rude-boy era was a socially localized affair in which the poor black was both victim and perpetrator: hardly a ripple thrown out by it reached the uptown communities. Rather than attacking, and so embarrassing, any part of the system, it was so self-contained that nobody who 'mattered' cared what these songs were discussing.

Given the frequently overdeveloped sense of panache the sound-system men had already shot through the Kingston record business, the lairy, strutting toughness of the whole rude-boy character would have seemed the ideal showbiz pose. It is understandable why the rudies should have been assumed to be the definition of rocksteady. For instance, much has been made of Bob Marley's apparent rude-boy days, yet the Wailers' 'take no shit' attitude was little more than *de rigueur* among his age and peer group. Yet the facts paint a very different picture – the vast majority of the song lyrics took a firm anti-violence stance. Indeed, these records so firmly established the idea of the seven-inch single as an act of edification, it's safe to say that without the rude-boy rocksteady tunes it's unlikely that the consciousness lyrics of the next decade would have become so dominant so quickly.

But there is no denying the enormous increase in the ghetto crime rate – robbery, looting, extortion and arson while-u-wait – as these keen-to-flex street thugs picked on the people least likely to put up too much resistance: their fellow ghetto dwellers.

During the mid-1960s, Kingston's black-on-black crime rate was pushed up to a wholly unacceptable level, and a level of community lawlessness grew that, once it became embedded as a tolerated strand of black Jamaican culture, had a lasting effect inasmuch as it became a formidable obstacle to any serious black unity. You're not so likely to go and stand shoulder to shoulder with your neighbour at the barricades if he might slip away and rob your house while you're there. But so prevalent were so many people's fears for the immediate safety of their person or their property, that several prominent recording artists wanted to try and turn the situation round.

With hindsight, Jimmy Cliff believes that in the beginning people saw what quickly became a social problem as an act of rebellion:

'After independence, after the party and the celebration was done, people start to look and say, "Well, what is this independence?" They knew it wasn't independence at all, it was just replacing one master with another, and as the music started to slow down – like the party *finish* – people start observing what was happening, the problems and such, economics no better, no jobs, and they figured they'd better start looking out for themselves otherwise they'd end up even worse off than they were before. That's when the rude-boy era start, and to many people it was like some sort of Robin Hood situation, with the rudies standing up for the oppressed.

'When singers were making songs like the one Derrick Morgan made that went [*sings*] *Rudie don't fear no boy / rudie don't fear*, it was because that rude-boy fearlessness was seen as an act of defiance. Like my character Ivan in *The Harder They Come*. He was based on the Rhygin, the famous Jamaican outlaw and the original rude-boy from the forties, who was very much with the people. But very soon the violence started getting out of hand, and so much of the community started living in fear. Because they were now becoming the victims of crime and violence, the respectable people realized that the rudies weren't on their side. Fighting the police or trying to bring about change with guns wasn't the way to go about things and could only end up one way. Once more, like Ivan in that final gun battle.'

It was not long afterwards, around 1965 and 1966, that the recording industry started to turn against this bad man-ism too, and tunes like the Wailers' 'Rude Boy' and 'Let Him Go', Desmond Dekker's 'Rude Boy Train' and the Pioneers' candidly titled 'Rudies are the Greatest' became fewer and further between. Strangely, or then again maybe not so, Leslie Kong, who was of Chinese descent and whose only interest in the area was financial, was the producer who remained prominently cutting pro-rude-boy records well into 1967. In contrast Duke Reid, who was an ex-downtown policeman, a genuinely tough character and intrinsically ghetto, virtually ignored the whole rude-boy period, and it is he who is rocksteady's most prominent and most fondly remembered producer. This was a man with a fearful reputation for personal mayhem, yet when you think of Duke Reid rocksteady tunes like 'I'll Get along without You', 'Things You Say You Love', 'My Girl' and 'Wear You to the Ball' start playing in your head.

Not that musically objecting to the havoc being wrought on the community was necessarily a new thing. As far back as 1963, in 'Dance Crasher', the hit that lends its name to this chapter, Alton Ellis predated rocksteady but was beseeching the street thugs: *dance crashers please don't break it up / don't make a fuss / don't use a knife to take another's life ... You won't have a chance / And this will be your last dance.* While that same year the Wailers, with their Coxsone-produced single 'Simmer Down', were imploring ghetto youth to *simmer down, 'cause you know you're bound to suffer*. Pleas that might actually have had some effect, as it wasn't until 1966 that the rude-boy disorder took a serious upturn. And then it was all down to politics.

In the spring of that year a wave of industrial disputes swept the island, starting in the agricultural communities and spreading to the Kingston docks, where it was to turn particularly ugly. The Vikings, the street gang who traditionally thought of the waterfront as theirs, had allied themselves to the PNP, only to come under attack from the JLP-supporting Phoenix, who wanted control of the port and its labour force in the name of the governing party. Whereas there had historically been little contention between the two outfits, the last few years of political partisanship had made the current relationship one of naked antagonism, and a major confrontation appeared unavoidable. This conflict was the excuse the political parties had been waiting for to square up to each other well away from their own backyard. As the various afflicted gangs across the city got involved it became a full-scale war.

At one point the situation on the streets became so bad that the police (previously assumed to be in the JLP's pocket) had to throw their weight in against both sides, at once creating an alliance between the two original factions who turned their fury and their firepower against the authorities.

Later that year, events were to take a further downward turn. Out of the rubbish tips and vacant land between the railway tracks and Spanish Town Road – Back-A-Wall, Ackee Walk and Foreshore Road – had sprouted a series of squatter camps and shanty towns, a tangle of lanes and alleys running between shacks made out of anything from hammered tin cans to dismantled tea chests to opened-out cardboard boxes. Densely populated even by West Kingston's standards, there was no sanitation and water came from a communal standpipe. The area was called 'home' by fresh-up-from-the-country folk, the poorest of the poor, and Rastas (it backed on to the Salt Lane camp), and had become both a PNP stronghold and a hotbed of discontent. The shacks themselves came to represent the post-independence collision of sky-high ambition and broken dreams, a stinking, all too tangible manifestation of how the government wasn't working. Then, the proximity to the docks and the inhabitants' need to scavenge and beg from ships had brought them under the Vikings' sway – in fact many gang members lived in these slums. Understandably worried about when a simmering cauldron might boil over, the JLP, under the guidance of Minister for Housing and Development Edward Seaga, did the worst thing possible. Under the grandiose title of 'slum clearance', and with the army in great evidence, demolition crews were sent in to bulldoze the shanties. Without prior warning to the inhabitants.

The razed land was earmarked for the Tivoli Gardens government yard apartments, which would be allocated to those loyal to the government cause, thus flipping a PNP stronghold over to the other side and taking possession of a strategic area close to the docks. To this day that south side of Spanish Town Road remains one of the most fiercely protected JLP strongholds in Kingston.

But, on the government's part, it was to pull a stroke too many. Rastas, (literally) dispossessed sufferahs and a fair proportion of ordinary working people joined the rudies in their rage against the system – the *shitstem*, as the dreads would pithily put it. Using tactics that were half urban guerilla, half street riot, and wholly true to Jamaica's tradition of slave revolts, the 1938 Frome uprising and Paul Bogle, this motley people's army fought the regular army until autumn. They were never going to win, but they didn't give up until the sheer force of numbers of troops occupying the area made continuing to fight suicidal. By which time over two dozen people were officially counted as dead, hundreds of homes and businesses had been destroyed and a state of emergency declared that stayed in place until well into 1967.

The real legacies, however, were missed opportunity and lasting lawlessness. This was the one and only time the rude boys, the Rastas and the regular people had rallied together against a shared injustice. Such an alliance might have precipitated some sort of radical social change, especially when for a moment the gangsters proved themselves to be beyond the manipulations of the political bosses. But as soon as the fighting was quelled the rudies turned their anger in on their own communities, and street crimes, extortion, robberies, and disruption of concerts, film shows and sound-system lawns became commonplace. The people couldn't stand it any more. The recording industry was starting to talk about it. The Voice of the People in particular.

During 1966 and 1967 Prince Buster, with his seminal Judge Dread series, rode a trend for anti-rude-boy rocksteady records – a style that included such gems as Stranger Cole's 'Drop the Ratchet', Bob Andy's 'Crime Don't Pay', Keith McCarthy's 'Everybody Rude Now', Alton Ellis's classic 'Cry Tough' or the Valentines' 'Stop the Violence'. Far more than merely an appeal for peace on the streets, Buster's creation was a masterpiece of satirical theatre addressing the real self-inflicted damage being done to a community not long up from slavery and still being defined in terms of race. It mixed cartoon presentation with deadly serious sentiments on top of a c-o-o-o-o-o-l rocksteady beat, and survived to define an era. Playing the fearsome Ethiopian magistrate of the title (aka 'Judge Hundred Years'), he made no bones about treating black-on-black crime as a much more serious matter than any trans-racial offence and wanted to make sure his audience got the message. Which they clearly did, as Judge Dread was merely acting out the wishes of so many of West Kingston's decent folk when, with the obviously relished claim *I am the rude boy today*, he sentenced four hapless rudies to a total of 1,700 years' imprisonment and 500 lashes. Buster, by now a teacher in the Nation of Islam, claims such records were nothing more than an artist's civic duty.

'The "Judge Dread" record came out of real life. Those four men that were harassing and aggravating the community were the people I'd grown up with, only now I follow a different path, and the good people were fed up with their behaviour. They came to me as the one who could do something as I was not scared. These so-called big men was harassing old people and schoolchildren, but the thing that made me explode against them was when they went into a school in West Kingston, rape a girl, beat up the teacher and almost rape her too. From that came "Judge Dread", a record that would play on my sound system, and others', to shame them. Which was important for the people.

'Because the sound man has a big standing in the community, if they come out in public against the rude boys it give the decent people something to hold on to, to get back at them and show that not everybody was like that. A lot of artists made anti-rude-boy records around that time, which was probably not good business in the beginning but it had to be done. And although it probably wasn't going to *directly* convince any of them to mend their ways, it gave the ordinary people heart and showed the world that not everybody was a rude boy.

'Remember, it was only pure bad people fighting, the majority of the people were good people and they didn't take no part in the violence and the robbery. They didn't want it or support it. I tried to get order, which I felt was my duty, because people were dying in Jamaica for nothing. They jus' *die*! All these people who were doing the killing were somebody's friends or brothers until the guns were introduced into Jamaica's ghettos. Then they turn into people who only seek to destroy people who look like them – *jus' killing other black people*.

'Away from the men who were bringing the guns in, the authorities didn't care, because it didn't affect them at all. The sound men and the recording artists were the only ones who could try to do anything about it.'

The most eloquent response to Prince Buster's approach came from the guy he frequently ended up protecting when he worked for the Downbeat sound system, Lee 'Scratch' Perry. Unlike records such as Derrick Morgan's 'Tougher than Tough', Honey Boy Martin's 'Dreader than Dread' or Dandy Livingstone's 'We Are Rude' (*He will have to give us one thousand years / and even that can't stop us*), which were more musical accolades to rude boy-ism than bona fide replies, Scratch did his best to get below the surface with 'Set Them Free'. Nothing if not straight-to-the-point, this was a continuation of the calls for proletarian equality he'd made when, a few years previously at Coxsone's, he cut such records as 'Help the Weak' and 'Give Me Justice'. This time calling himself the Defenders, he took up the case of Judge Dread's rude boys with lyrics that took his erstwhile spar's attitude very seriously in attempting to answer the charges in some sort of sociological sense by explaining the situation over a rocksteady rhythm: *I don't think it's fair to sentence these men to 500 years . . . they are from a poor generation / Having no education, no qualification they driven to desperation / George Getajob? They have been forced to rob / I'm not suggesting they should, but as you know a hungry man is an angry one / Give them a chance your honour / give them a break to make up their mistake / . . . As you already know it was robbery was from creation / It was robbery that befall the black nation / our ancestors once ruled this world and all its gold / but now they are poor.*

The jury's still out on whether Perry's concerns were misplaced or not, as, astonishingly, there is a vociferous school of thought that still seems to believe that the systematic plundering of the black world's riches might, perhaps, not be justifiable cause to steal your penniless neighbour's few possessions, or terrorize your own equally dispossessed people. But 'Set Them Free' was one of the first high-profile, albeit unsophisticated, examples of a trend that would come to dominate Jamaican songwriting: blatant black-consciousness lyrics. Which becomes that bit more noteworthy if you check the dates. This was mid-1967, almost six months before the Impressions' 'We're a Winner' was banned by the majority of American radio stations in the first notable example of open racial protest in US music, and over a year prior to James Brown's 'Say It Loud – I'm Black and I'm Proud'. At last someone else in the Jamaican music business was leading rather than being led.

That Jamaican lyricism should be leaning in this direction isn't at all surprising, as Rastafari was playing an increasing – and increasingly vocal – part in the sufferah way of life. In fact it was this, almost as much as popular protest and the draconian state of emergency, that saw the rude boys (as a particular manifestation of what would become an endemic bad-man culture) die out in 1967 and 1968.

As the civil rights movement in the USA was being steadily usurped by the more direct action associated with Malcolm X and the Black Power movement, such purely racial politics struck a resonant chord with Jamaica's Rastas, greatly boosting their communal confidence. (Radical in their thinking the Rastas might have been, but this was still Jamaica, where off-island endorsement was usually the deciding factor.) These rumblings from across the sea worried the Jamaican authorities enough to produce a lengthy list of banned books that was almost entirely black radical literature from the USA, while American black leaders – even the milder-mannered civil rights types – were routinely refused Jamaican entry visas. But the Rastafari brethren had received a wholly tangible shot in the arm three months prior to the slum-clearance operation when, on 21 April 1966, Emperor Haile Selassie of Ethiopia had arrived in Jamaica for a three-day state visit, en route to Trinidad and Tobago.

The government extended an official hand of welcome to His Imperial Majesty. Essentially, this was a gesture of appeasement, as the brethren had been growing increasingly active politically, or, as viewed from uptown, rebellious; but, rather slyly, it was also an acknowledgement of the Rastas' growing influence/usefulness in the street and an attempt to win them round. To put the latter point bluntly, if this government was seen to bring the Lord of Lords, in the flesh, to Jamaica, then surely Rastafari wouldn't take much persuasion to do their bidding at the barricades and picket lines. This would be the one gang that crossed geographical divisions.

Selassie's appearance had a massive effect, both spontaneously and enduringly. Over 100,000 Rastas turned out to meet the plane and line the motorcade's route into town, and at the airport the police lost it totally as any form of official welcome was abandoned when the crowd surged over the tarmac to surround the aircraft. Faced with this incredible outpouring of emotion, it was several hours before the Conquering Lion of the Tribe of Judah would venture out and down the steps. The government had to call on one Mortimer Planno, a greatly respected Rasta elder, to mediate between the mass of people on the runway and the Emperor's party. Coming from an establishment loath even to acknowledge Rastafari – beyond possible exploitation of it – this was a previously unimaginable shift in protocol which, as far as the government was concerned, went downhill from there as they had to invite Planno to all civic functions during the visit. In spite of this superficially bringing the government and the House of Dread closer together, in the longer term Rasta reaction was diametrically opposed to what the government had hoped for. The visit assumed divine proportions, giving enormous heart to Haile Selassie's Jamaican followers. Also, and highly significantly, the turnout at Palisadoes Airport was a show of force, which left both the ruling classes and the dreads themselves in no doubt as to the true scale of Rastafari on the island. From this point onwards its insurrection began gaining momentum.

What it needed, though, was a focal point.

For years the authorities' propaganda machine had been geared up to promote Rastafari subtly as a religion – which is how many outsiders still see it – rather than a philosophy, thus defusing any intellectual purpose by palming it off as some sort of 'zany' cult. And the musical community wasn't doing much to help matters, either.

Rasta records had been appearing ever since Prince Buster's 'Oh Carolina', but mostly in an instrumental style. With the notable involvement of Don Drummond and Rico, these were tunes that looked towards Africa as they offered up, as far back as the very beginning of the 1960s, what came to be called the 'East of the River Nile' sound. It was horn led, minor-chord loaded, wistful and spiritually uplifting in its soloing, and possessed of a kind of 'Come with me to the Casbah' waviness. 'Addis Ababa', 'Blues from the Hills', 'Farther East', 'Reburial', 'Tribute to Marcus Garvey', 'Soul of Africa' and 'Cleopatra' are six of the best. Vocals, meanwhile, had been inclined to follow a far more conventionally spiritual approach as singers tended to go with the flow of the Old Testament leanings while following the more raucous revivalist tradition (often necessary to make their presence felt in front of a full-effect ska band). The Maytals' 'Hallelujah' or 'Six and Seven Books of Moses', Justin Hinds and the Dominoes' 'Carry Go Bring Come' or Clancy Eccles' 'River Jordan' spring readily to mind. With the arrival of the mid-sixties and rocksteady, though, that was changing rapidly. First, the new music's less-frantic pace permitted a hymn-like quality to the religious songs which wasn't a million miles removed from Rastafari's chanting. Then the Old Testament stories of suffering and persecution endured by the children of Israel at the hands of the Pharaoh appeared to become tangible as they gave parable to the situation in Kingston's ghettos – this went as far as Prime Minister Hugh Shearer being known as 'Pharaoh'. It wasn't long before the metaphor was replaced with a reportage to go with the comment established in the rude-boy era. This is sufferah rock in embryo, a line that can be traced forward to the so-called 'reality' lyrics of the 1990s.

(The reason these apparent 'reality' lyrics are viewed with genuine scepticism in these pages is because, although such a style undoubtedly had its roots in a ghetto actuality, by the time the term was coined some thirty years later the majority were about as 'real' as the dime-store Western novel. In the same way as gangsta rap would, all but a few of these songs conjure up a fantasy land catering to the supposedly glamorous, exciting, ultimately degraded dreams of the vicarious thrill-seeker. A virtual tourist trade?)

Justin Hinds and the Dominoes, the Heptones, the Ethiopians, the Slickers, Carlton and his Shoes (later the Abyssinians), the Gaylads, Bob Andy, Peter Tosh, Joe Higgs . . . all peppered their catalogues with sufferah poetry. Utilizing the session skills of established producers like Dodd and Reid or newcomers such as Sonia Pottinger, Ken Lack or Joe Gibbs, these records had all the panache and polish of the smooovest rocksteady and displayed some deep, moving and highly intelligent approaches to their subject matter. Unless you're Marvin

Gaye or Curtis Mayfield or Sly Stone you're probably not going to write a cleverer social commentary song than the Slickers' 'Man Is Going to Leave the Earth'. It was this attention to detail and outright sound-system friendliness that meant these tunes were enormously successful in their day, but what gave them – and the genre – such an enduring future was the timeless blend of spirituality and practicality contained in the best of their lyrics.

'Got to Go Back Home', 'Bam Bam', 'The Whip', 'Happy Land' (the blueprint for 'Satta Massa Gana') and 'Save a Bread' – this was folk music at its most potent. It told of both the situation and the state of mind that was dealing with it. And it was a direct result of Rastafari's influence on Kingston's musical community, as the movement had by this time found the sense of purpose it had been previously lacking.

The credit for introducing this more pragmatic philosophy to Rastafari is down to the teachings of Walter Rodney, a Guyana-born graduate of the University of the West Indies in Jamaica. Rodney had studied in London (specialist subject: the slave trade), taught in Africa and returned to his Kingston *alma mater* to lecture in 1966. A committed black nationalist, and young enough in his twenties to be taken seriously by the dispossessed youth, he had long ago recognized the importance of Rastafari as a social force in a predominantly black nation. Now he was taking his word to the streets. And it was a word that solidified so many of Rasta's somewhat insubstantial precepts while managing not to detract from the movement's necessary ethereality. Also, while he was at one with Marcus Garvey's central concept of black internationalism, he refined several aspects of Garveyism into a far more realistic proposition. But most importantly, and again like Marcus Garvey, he championed the idea of economic independence as being the cornerstone of every other kind of freedom.

This astute young man brought his research and communication skills to bear on large portions of the history of the black diaspora and effectively trashed them, entirely restating what had been written by white people to suit a world where slavery and colonization were the norm. He further defined Rasta's sense of black pride by introducing the idea that the only people black people should be working to please are themselves. Cardinal to Rodney's tenets was an underlining of Ethiopia as an actual country as opposed to Ethiopia the promised land, a principle he used to illustrate the need for black self-interest (crucially, *not* self-help). But the cornerstone of his teachings centred on how knowledge should be passed down: while he was adamant that the black oral tradition must be respected, he knew the history that survived – therefore the one that was taken as the truth – was written history. He constantly sought to impress that unless black history, as defined by black people, was written down it would never count for anything.

Walter Rodney was the first homegrown – if not actually Jamaican-born – intellectual to take his knowledge downtown and give it some practical application, yet he was middle-class enough in his life and his position at the university to be able to bring Rastafari into polite society. While American black-power politics existed as a peripheral to Rastafari, acknowledged but not quite absorbed, Rodney made their principles work in the Jamaican environment. In doing so, he rebalanced Rasta philosophy into something far more meaningful and therefore ultimately more popular – in every sense of the word. And he scared the crap out of Prime Minister Shearer, who, with delicious irony, had taken over from Sir Alexander Bustamente in 1967 as Jamaica's first black prime minister.

After Walter Rodney had attended the Black Writers' Conference in Canada at the end of 1968, he was refused permission to re-enter Jamaica. In making out the exclusion order the Minister for Home Affairs wrote: 'I have never come across a man who offers a greater threat to the security of this land than Walter Rodney.'

But, regardless of any sense of purpose Rodney gave to Rasta and Rasta, in turn, bestowed upon so many of Jamaica's lyricists, there never was a lasting marriage between rocksteady and social commentary. This wasn't just because the two styles were so far apart that the notion of crooning tales of despair over a slick, shiny backing track would have been too much for even the most commercially minded producer to bear. It was because there simply wasn't enough time. By the end of 1968 rocksteady was all but finished.

The true rocksteady era lasted for less than three years, from the spring of 1966 until the second half of 1968, by which time, in everything but name, it had become what we know as reggae. The two styles were always much closer than first cousins – listen to Phillis Dillon's 'Perfidia' or 'Feel Like Jumping' by Marcia Griffiths, both cut in 1968, for Duke Reid and Coxsone respectively, both 24-carat examples of early reggae, yet both classified as rocksteady for no other reason than the term 'reggae' didn't then exist.

With the move from rocksteady to reggae came a freedom of expression the former didn't quite allow, so at this juncture Jamaican popular music got the chance to spread out stylistically. Rasta's increasing influence was a big factor in the change, as rocksteady wasn't quite the right vehicle for what it had to say. The downside was the end of one of the most fondly remembered and enduring periods in the island's musical history. Derrick Harriott speaks for many in the Jamaican music industry when he says:

'Those songs never seem to die. Everybody back then could play, proper musicians who had been formally trained, and the songs written were classically structured. This situation can't be beaten, and what is happening today is that the rhythms and the beats and the bass-lines from the rocksteady era are the ones that are still being used. Sometimes the exact music – probably they bring the tempo up just a little bit, but it's the exact rhythm.

'Ask any Jamaican musician and they'll tell you that the rocksteady days were the best days of Jamaican music.'

10

It Up Mix

Listen to Lee Perry's 1968 single 'People Funny Boy' and, essentially, you're listening to Africa. As it was in the sixteenth century.

Tangibly, the record is just a hastily knocked-off seven inches of vinyl, a cut that has a slightly faster tempo than might be expected and which follows the Jamaican music-business standard of using lyrics to insult those who have, or who are perceived to have, wronged the artist. In this case, Perry sticks it to former employer Joe Gibbs for that most heinous crime of going 'big time' and ignoring the people who helped him to do so. However, concentrate a bit harder and you will notice that 'People Funny Boy' has a subtly changed structure that differentiates it completely from the rocksteady of the preceding couple of years. True, it might still emphasize the off-beat, but there's much more going on than that slightly higher tempo – crucially, the electric bass is much more up-front and almost metronomically metered, while several guitars are used rhythmically rather than merely melodically. It's those guitars that produce a speedy strumming pattern not unlike mento's banjoes, while the overall measured percussiveness leaves all sorts of holes that are artfully filled in with Burru- and Kumina-style rhythmic statements. So, a little way beneath the surface lies a Jamaicanness so intrinsic that it doesn't need to worry about the here and the now as it draws a line – a thick black line – straight back to Africa.

In many ways, it's no surprise that Lee Perry should have come up with such a sound – check his very early singles

'Tackoo' and 'Sugar Bag' and you'll find a vivid mento influence; likewise in the later 'Django'-period (1968–70) Upsetters' stuff: the banjo isn't actually there, but such are the structures that you find yourself mentally mixing it in. Plus it was arranged by Clancy Eccles, who was well known for his interest in traditional Jamaican music and had been part of the recording scene since the dawn of ska, and around performers since before then, being a skilled tailor who made stage-suits. What distinguishes 'People Funny Boy' from these other mento-type affairs is where it was pointing. Although perhaps not a textbook example of reggae, its 1968 release date makes it one of the earliest records to sound the part.

If ska was the birth of modern Jamaican popular music and rocksteady its fairly truculent adolescence, then reggae was its coming of age. The first official reggae-as-we-came-to-know-it records emerged in the early months of 1968, and although the most immediate difference between them and rocksteady was the speeding-up of the tempo, the new style really distinguished itself through the freedom it afforded the island's musicians.

Whereas no audience would deny the previous styles were both exciting and entertaining, from a player's point of view they didn't allow much scope for showing off beyond a bit of soloing. Structures and variations were more or less set in stone – even the spontaneity seemed to have its own rigid set of rules. Yet from day one reggae came across as fluid and flexible enough to incorporate a seemingly infinite number of sub-styles, and could thus accommodate the musicians' boredom thresholds as well as the most demanding lawn-dance crowd. Reggae achieved this by presenting itself as unique to the black Jamaican people, the sufferahs, from both a historical as well as a strictly geographical point of view. Then, once the music established its mento phrasings, Burru and Kumina leanings and its nod to Jah Rastafari, it no longer needed to apologize for or justify its own flights of fancy, because, to any Jamaican who heard it, it was so obviously theirs. This new music had such a nationalistic swagger that it could be anything it fancied.

In putting together reggae rhythms and traditional sounds, as so deftly demonstrated by 'People Funny Boy', Prince Buster's near ten-year-old dream of making genuinely Jamaican records was finally coming to pass.

Reggae was the Jamaican style that at last had the confidence to call its own tune. It wasn't following or adapting any American fashion; indeed, it wasn't borrowing from anywhere apart from the island's own rich folk heritage. And for its evolution to include such longstanding and uncluttered-by-the-modern-world art forms meant that, practically from day one, reggae was an organic rather than a factory-farmed state of affairs. It has always been a tribute to the men and women making this music that, in spite of the by then galloping studio technology's influence both on the swift change from rocksteady and on the style's own internal development, such electronic advancements served to make what was created sound more rather than less human. Indeed, the arrival of reggae created an artistic and spiritual framework so deeply rooted that it was strong enough to support virtually any development; yet, because it was so strictly homegrown, whatever emerged from it would always be Jamaican.

'People Funny Boy' wasn't, however, the first example of the changeover from rocksteady to reggae. That distinction would have to be shared between Larry Marshall's 'Nanny Goat' and 'No More Heartaches' by the Beltones, with both records' producers – Coxsone Dodd and Harry J (Johnson), respectively – claiming the credit for entirely different reasons. Dodd has cited his use of a delay echo unit he'd recently imported from the UK, which he hooked up to the guitar to end up with a distinct *skanga . . . skanga . . . skanga* sound on the previously straight-down timekeeping stroke; a state of affairs that naturally served to hurry the music's pace along. Johnson, however, maintains that it was the rhythmic combination he created of arched fingers stabbing an organ chord, a conventional guitar stroke and a far more percussive bass pattern that produced the same effect.

In truth, both men have a point, and you'd expect nothing

less from how this story's shaping up. But, if you listen to the overall feel of each record rather than try to isolate particular elements, each one clearly occupies a different notch on reggae's chronology. Harry J's horn-laden piece of harmony may demonstrate reggae characteristics but it's essentially a rocksteady record dressed up in some flashy new clothes; Dodd's tune, however, utilizes what was then cutting-edge gadgetry – as well as the delay echo he introduced a few more outboard FX to Brentford Road at the same time – and, almost immediately, so many other studios began to adopt and adapt that sound through the same technology. 'Nanny Goat' would seem to be linking forward, while 'No More Heartaches' ties with the past. Thus it could be argued that, while each played a significant part, Johnson's record is, in fact, the primary example.

What they both shared, although 'Nanny Goat' showed it off far more prominently, is what was known as the 'shuffle organ', a bubbling, brisk-paced keyboard style that allowed former pianists to show off on the electric organs that were by now studio staples. The first two real reggae tunes showed up on the Studio One and Harry J labels, and each set-up employed one of the style leaders along this new ivory way: respectively, Jackie Mittoo and Winston Wright. Mittoo, once the Skatalites' keyboardist, was now, at the tender age of twenty, Coxsone's resident musical arranger/talent scout. Wright had become acknowledged as Jamaica's undisputed master of the Hammond when, as one of Tommy McCook's Supersonics, his lush, infectious tones had been a significant factor in Duke Reid's ruling of the rocksteady roost. Wright had now gone freelance, and found regular employment with Harry Johnson. Johnson had no studio of his own at this point, and booked a room at Coxsone's for those sessions, which meant that both songs were recorded at 13 Brentford Road, with one of the best electric organs on the island.

It was this organ shuffle, probably more than anything else, that was responsible for speeding the music up. Indeed, the organ was so prominent in the studio hierarchy of the day that it defined a style which, just before reggae came into being, briefly carried the swing. This was the John Crow Skank, and Bunny Lee knew all about it.

'It was just after rocksteady, when producers and musicians was wondering what to do next to please the crowds. It was faster than rocksteady, but didn't have the solid rhythm of what you would call reggae, and it started at Randy's studio on North Parade, with that creep organ thing, when the organ just try to steal up in the tune – the Wailers' "Duppy Conqueror" and John Holt's "Stick by Me" both have it. We was looking to move from the creep organ to the shuffle effect, but Vincent's [Vincent Chin, the owner of Randy's studio and record store] organ was out of tune – he wouldn't throw the thing out – and when we try and get that shuffle effect on it could put it further out. So whoever was playing it had to be careful.

'What happened was the only way to play it was to bring your hands off it quick, which would draw the sound like it was flying. And we had Glen Adams, who was then just learning to play organ, and he used to flap his hands over the keyboard like wings, so the name John Crow Skank just come up in the studio, you know, when the musicians were just kicking ideas around. It caught on briefly, too, and when the people in a dance hear the tune is a John Crow Skank they have this kind of wheeling dance, with their arms out, like a crow circling.

'But it didn't last long because the shuffle organ quickly changed things.'

It is, however, a good example of how the players' keyboard exhibitionism was escalating. Soon, as the organs became more sophisticated, there was no such thing as a trill too many, and elaborate, almost baroque electric organ parts became early reggae's calling card. Indeed, it seemed entirely appropriate when, in 1969, Boris Gardiner came with 'Elizabethan Reggae', a single remembered largely for its enjoyably over-ornate organ (once more courtesy of the hard-working Winston Wright) and a Top 20 hit in Britain in the following year. But over a year before that, the shuffle organ chivvied up the Jamaican beat to reintroduce some of the upfulness that had been rarely seen since ska.

Once again, however, it was the dancehall crowds who precipitated this change in tempo.

There had always been a tributary of rocksteady that announced itself with the kind of barrelling piano riffs that might have been taken as a hangover from the previous decade's JA boogie – the Wailers' 'Jailhouse' and the Clarendonians' 'Rudie Bam Bam' are among the best examples. And either for nostalgic reasons or simply as one way in which sound-system operators kept the crowds on their toes, it was a branch of the music that deejays and dancers particularly enjoyed. It was this pumping quality that players such as Mittoo (both of the above examples were Studio One releases) adapted to their new electric keyboards. And as Bunny Lee, who was by now one of the new music's pioneering producers, recalls:

'By that time in the development of the music, because so much music was being made to sell, there were a lot of record producers who didn't have sound systems. These producers, like myself, would have to stay around a lot of sound systems to see what the people were doing; which records, or which *bits* of records, the crowds were reacting to. Sometimes we'd see these things better than the sound men, because we were looking to see what was already there, not what we were going to try out.

'We would see that when the organ carry it up a little faster the dancers were going crazy over these more uptempo bits, the organ shuffling. A lot of people used to complain that the rocksteady was dragging them down because the beat was too slow, and we knew that faster was the way to take it. The people were just ready for a new beat.

'That was how reggae developed. From that organ shuffle with the rest of the music falling into place around that. But the people in the dancehalls were dancing to that organ sound quite a long time before the music got recognized. It was the certain dance they were doing – a much more jerky, stepping dance – that would be called the reggae.'

If further evidence about dancers directing the producers is needed, then look no further than the Maytals' 1968 cut 'Do the Reggay'. The tune is taken to be the first to use the word in its title, albeit with an unusual spelling, and provides the same sort of musical proof as its predecessor Alton Ellis's 'Rock Steady'. When Toots and the guys' lyric runs *I want to do the reggay with you / come on to me / do the dance / is this the new dance going round the town / you can move your baby / and do the reggay, reggay reggay reggay*, it could almost be an echo of Alton's words of a couple of years earlier.

The organ soon relieved the bass of some of the melodic duties it had assumed during rocksteady, allowing the bassman to play a snapping, more fundamentally rhythmic sound – the bass, like everything else, had to beef itself up in order not to be drowned by the organ. It was at this point that these newly percussive bass players began a natural and stylistically individual interaction with the drummers, thus setting up the cornerstone upon which twenty years of reggae music would rest, the drum 'n' bass. And, back then, these same drummers stayed with the one-drop – which is why rocksteady and reggae are so closely related, this singular method being at the heart of both – but in order to keep up with the organ they had to double up into a 2/4 rhythm pattern.

After the studied smooove of rocksteady, this new sound was taking on a dominantly rhythmic feel. Guitars, which had been all electric for some time now, were having crisp chords chopped out of them to roundly emphasize the off-beat, but with the creeping advances made by studio electronics like Coxsone's delay echo unit this strumming was becoming increasingly subtle and interesting. Sometimes, as in the Studio One case, the gaps left over the organ lines by these new bass and guitar ventures were filled with tricksy guitar effects, or, as was more common in the early days of reggae, by a couple more guitars working off each other to elongate the downstroke further and create a chugging *eskanga . . . eskanga* vibe. If you compare the two, this isn't far removed from the banjo strumming that formed the basis of mento. It's unlikely that such mentoism was done consciously, the guitar sound having evolved after the defining organ shuffle, but once recognized –

and any reggae veteran will tell you it was – it would have been considered a huge bonus.

Perhaps, it was something locked in the music-makers' collective subconscious that had been waiting for the right, suitably receptive moment to burst out, a notion not too ridiculous when the other aspect of the new music's historic Jamaicanness are taken into account. The holes created naturally by reggae's virtual syncopation were ideal for percussion breaks, and the percussion of choice was of a strictly roots variety: bongos, hand drums, shakers and graters that harked back to the days of slavery and the Kumina and Burru. All of which had survived to the era of mento, which also persevered with traditional rhythmic instruments. Then, from a purely pragmatic position, these traditional sounds seemed tailor-made for the new music as they fell somewhere in between either purely rhythmic or absolutely melodic devices.

Of course, though, this being Jamaica, where very little is what it seems and even less is what it should be, such apparently artistic development had a little help from Government House.

It was now some half a dozen years after independence, and independence clearly wasn't working. The Jamaican Labour Party had retained power for a second term, but by the end of the 1960s it was feeling more than merely 'uneasy' about the black nationalist ideas coming in from the USA. Because such thoughts and concepts were imported, the Jamaican authorities could exert no control over them – they'd already tried banning books. Now the more politically aware sufferahs were taking what they wanted from the philosophies of activists such as Angela Davis, Stokely Carmichael, Julius Lester and the Nation of Islam and applying it to their lives in Jamaica in a more or less random manner. Or so it seemed to the government, which never had any idea what particular part of which specific rallying cry would be taken up next, or how the reaction to unpopular policies would manifest itself.

Perhaps far more worryingly for the Kingston power structure, though, and due in no small part to Walter Rodney's efforts, was the apparent strength and universality with which these radical new doctrines were being taken on board. These adopted dogmas served to galvanize so many black Jamaicans that they had the astonishing effect of cutting across the country's social hierarchy. The working classes, the middle classes, university students, the dispossessed, the gangsters . . . all could latch on to what was being said. And they came together in a big shout for black control of the means of production and popular influence on the economic consequences, comprising a large and apparently volatile section of the population which had to be appeased.

By this time Jamaica had completed its transformation from an essentially agricultural nation to one of diverse industrial and commercial aspects such as mining, tourism, manufacturing and real estate. But the boom of the years immediately before independence had, within half a decade, all but evaporated, creating an economic vacuum and a whole new set of problems. There was now an owner/management elite; unemployment had increased drastically; inflation, though not yet galloping, was breaking into a brisk trot; and the island was no longer producing enough food to feed its own people. Foreign and (less so) local investment slowed dramatically during the second half of the 1960s – understandably so, as there wasn't really much left to invest in – yet overseas capital had to be enticed in and what was already there had to be dissuaded from pulling out. The only way to do this was to present a rosy-hued picture of an island sufficiently safe and stable for you to want to build your resort hotel or factory, so the politicians *had* to keep the lid on things. In an historic show of cooperation, the JLP and the PNP struck an unofficial bargain to keep race and class issues off their usually lively campaign agendas for fear of kicking off a civil war. Each agreed that to attempt to gain political capital by stressing the other's poor records in these areas would serve to remind voters of exactly how badly they were being treated and possibly trigger an outright rebellion.

The way forward, the authorities deemed, was to turn the

black-power tenets from the negatives they had previously been seen as into positives by using them as a springboard to promote Jamaican nationalism: a scheme that would make the most of the fast-fading memory that was Independence Day fever and, for the first time, give the people their own black pride. Or for the first time with any official acknowledgement. The thinking was that this state-sponsored, therefore controllable brand of black consciousness would be much more manageable and far less scary to American tourists than the imported variety. The government set about promoting Jamaican cultural self-awareness on a national scale, and it was out of this directive that Burru and Kumina music resurfaced, to fan the flames already burning in the ghettos' musical communities.

Much of the force behind this strategy came from Edward Seaga, rapidly rising through the ranks of the JLP, whose interest in and love for Jamaica's cultural heritage could never be denied, regardless of the programme's political agenda. A few years back he had been recording albums of original Jamaican music, and Prince Buster stresses that Seaga was one of the very few people to support his recordings with Count Ossie. Now, he instigated the National Festival, an annual cultural extravaganza celebrating independence through shows of Jamaicanness past and present. At the same time he launched the National Song Contest as an incentive for the burgeoning music industry to turn its attention to Jamaican-sounding songs. Then, as the 1960s played themselves out, traditional Jamaican folklore, music and dance were introduced into school curricula for the first time, while as another innovation, beyond the schools the government encouraged pursuit of Jamaican arts to such a degree as to provide government funding for programmes and practitioners.

Not that the country as a whole took too much encouraging to once again rejoice in its heritage. In spite of the previous – and, it should be said, still underlying – air of self-loathing, by this time blackness and its celebration were high on the social agenda, often for the simple reason that, among so much of the population, a notion of heritage was the only thing of any worth they could call their own. Ironically, even this self esteem was one more aspect of Americanization: post-independence, the British influence over the islanders had been supplanted by that of the USA to such an extent that driving on the left was about the only colonialism that hadn't been usurped by Uncle Sam. Then there was Jamaica's coming to realize its status as a bona fide Third World nation. Events in Africa have always been well covered in the Caribbean, so people were beginning to identify closely with the changing map of Africa and see themselves in the same light as such fledgling republics as Namibia and Zambia. Besides, to explore Jamaica's folk tradition at this point was to explore expressions of blackness or generations of underground Africanness which, in many cases, was viewed obliquely as being largely the point of independence.

It is a huge paradox that while the authorities were promoting Jamaican black pride, they were so out of touch with the mood of their own people that they banned Walter Rodney, a man who had done so much for the exact cause they claimed to be boosting, when the Guyanese lecturer was excluded from re-entering Jamaica following a visit to Canada. In the government's view, his preaching of Rastafari across class barriers was seditious. That in itself marks the degree with which the government and the people parted company on their interpretations of nationalistic pride, but this situation was so woefully misread it provoked major civil disturbances. They started on university campuses, among Rodney's students, *then* spread downtown to the working people and the sufferahs who genuinely tore things up. Maybe the authorities didn't think an educated man like Walter Rodney could mean anything to the lower classes. Or maybe they couldn't imagine insurrection spreading *down* the social scale. Or maybe they expected large-scale rioting to break out and simply didn't care – it probably isn't too much of a coincidence that a large number of Canadian soldiers were on training manoeuvres on the island at the time of Rodney's banning. After all, there was, at the time, much Canadian investment in Jamaica.

So while the whole notion of government-sponsored Afrocentricity may have been a sham, it played a large part in introducing blackness as an integral part of reggae – where it would remain and, over the next dozen or so years, be called into service as one of the people's most potent weapons against authority.

The main reason reggae took off commercially so quickly was that the music industry had changed enormously between 1959 and 1969. Essentially, this was to do with the large numbers of records now being sold retail, such a quantity that a great deal of small and not so small specialist stores were opening all over the country, supplementing the still-active bag men and establishments that sold a few tunes as a sideline to their main business – cafés, barbers, electrical stores and so on. To feed this consumer demand, there was a new generation of producers, like Bunny Lee or Harry J, who *didn't* have sound systems or shops but set up operations making records primarily for sale to the formal record wholesalers and distributors, who were now in place in the Jamaican music business alongside the less-conventional pedal-powered outfits. The new record production companies sprang up like weeds – figuratively speaking – after all, it involved far less outlay of either time or money if you didn't have a sound system or a shop, and there were enough studios to be rented by the hour. Which in turn meant that the amount of music increased vastly as new players joined the ranks and the established guys had to work that bit harder to stay ahead.

This isn't to say that the old ways of doing things had been put to one side, an assumption frequently and erroneously arrived at because there was so much reggae music available away from the lawns. But there was now a viable alternative, one which meant that those outside the actual sound-system axis – either punters or providers – no longer had to pay the dancehalls any mind – either physically or mentally. Therefore they didn't. But the core of the music industry remained the dances, and the most reliable way to have a big hit was to have a dancehall hit with it first. The sound systems remained operating in exactly the same way they always had: new tunes were recorded, dub plates cut which would, within hours, be spun at the dance; and crowd reaction was everything. And don't forget there were still drinks to be sold and gate receipts to be counted – in fact, because there was now so much outside competition for the music fans' minds and moolah, the competition between sound systems in the late 1960s was probably even more intense.

Every sound man continued to go into the studio to record the current hot artist or whatever raw kid he had a hunch on, then expose the tunes in sound clashes. All that had changed in this respect was what happened to the cuts once they'd moved the crowd. Of course, exclusive new tunes were still used to keep a sound on top, but whereas in the past the sound man/ producer would once have held it up as unique for a length of time that may have been measured in years, at this point in reggae's evolution if a record tore the place up he'd have to get it into the shops right away. Procrastination could cost him a small fortune.

By 1969, the radio was helping reggae's cause, too, albeit reluctantly. Derrick Harriott remembers how it used to be, and tells it from the point of view of one with a considerable vested interest in radio's promotion of local music – his label, Crystal, was firmly established; he had wholesale and retail record businesses; and he was successfully segueing his tremendous reputation as a producer of rocksteady into the world of reggae.

'The radio people were supporting the music to a point, but I don't think they were supporting it in the way they should. I always used to fight with them, telling them "It's independence; you people should be playing Jamaican music – at least seventy–thirty." Other producers would have the same arguments, and the people at RJR and JBC would tell us they didn't have enough Jamaican music to even play three days of it. Which we all knew was a joke, as at that time there was *plenty* out there.

'We didn't think we were having much effect, but somebody must have been listening because at the end of the sixties there was a big uproar about a payola scandal. It was front page in the news over here in Jamaica and several people got fired from radio stations over it. All along they'd been taking money from the big distributors and those with licences to press American records. After that they played a lot more Jamaican music, but still not as much as they should have done. Maybe something like fifty–fifty. Which although it did quite a lot to help the homegrown music industry, the radio people were just bias against it, because next they come telling us "We don't know if all-reggae would work."

'Of course it would. But they didn't try it until Irie FM launched in the 1990s and prove everybody wrong. It has been so popular that now all the other stations have stepped up their quota of Jamaican music.'

Something else that was undoubtedly working in reggae's favour was its tremendous width. Such was its spread that without even stretching too far it could happily embrace practically any influence or accent its protagonists fancied. By the time the music's fundamental structures had fully established themselves – at the end of the decade or so – what went on top would reinvent itself on a regular basis. It seems that reggae as an art form had become so strong, both physically and culturally, that it could take anything on board and not have to worry about being swamped. And, as the 1960s became the 1970s, it looked like there was room for everything. Reggae's rhythms flexed to form the backbone of a myriad sub-clauses from bouncy pop music, to strictly roots, by way of 'sophisticated' strings 'n' things, dubwise, lovers' rock, Latin swing (memorably the Ethiopians' 'Mi Amore'), harmony singing, deejay toasting and instrumental cuts. All with varying degrees of artistic success, it must be said, but none of it detracting from the fact that this was reggae. First and foremost. And the producers who were making this case so expressively were, in more cases than not, adding a new layer to the existing hierarchy.

Of course, Coxsone and Duke Reid were in effect, with the former far fuller than the latter. Buster was slower to move on from rocksteady glories. Presumably his frequent run-ins with the government, his establishing mosques and teaching Islam and his juke-box-hire business interests were all proving something of a distraction.

At Studio One Clement Dodd had chosen his musical directors shrewdly, and the idea of keeping them on wages did a lot for the idea of keeping them, full stop. His top men were Jackie Mittoo and Leroy Sibbles who, respectively, played organ and bass, then the two most important instruments in the new style – also, by way of an enormous bonus, Sibbles was a wonderful vocalist with the Heptones and a much more than merely 'accomplished' vocal arranger. Between the three of them they thoroughly assimilated the music's change of direction and it was during the first couple of years of the reggae era that, as a record producer, Coxsone went clear. In Studio One Dodd established a brand identity and a reputation unsurpassed by anything in Jamaican music before or since, and in doing so created a stockpile of rhythms and backing tracks that would still be in regular use long after the Brentford Road studios had closed down, Dodd had decamped to New York and reggae itself had shifted through roots, ragga, dancehall and beyond. More than thirty years later, aficionados all over the world continue to look on the Studio One or Coxsone logo as a sort of kite mark and make decisions to buy based on the label alone.

To call Studio One of the late 1960s 'the Jamaican Motown' would probably be flattering Berry Gordy's company. Relatively, it was of much greater significance in its field – Motown operated as a hugely successful *aspect* of soul's overall development, whilst for the first few years of reggae Studio One *was* the music's overall development.

These days, however, there isn't much to see at number 13 Brentford Road. Walk up to the padlocked gates and anybody passing – on foot, on a bike, or by car – will yell 'Studio One!' or 'Coxsone!' or '*Murrr*dah' or words to that effect. The locals are used to tourists of all persuasions making this pilgrimage and feel obliged to play their boisterous part in their very own landmark. Which is a good thing. Not only because it's so sociable but it's good to know that Studio One, as a figurative and literal presence, isn't forgotten, because in fact there's not a great deal of history left there to be looked at. Even if it's the day of the week that one of Mr Dodd's relatives is there to let you in and snoop around, all you're going to gaze upon is shabby 1960s décor and some piles of boxes. Which may or may not have records in them.

It's probably best to stay outside the gates and look in on the dusty yard, where the great mango tree there used to provide the only shade for the hordes of young hopefuls who'd wait patiently for their turn at the Sunday morning auditions. Or stare at the sheets of corrugated that protect the back of the lot and prevent the studio doors being seen from the street, a function that, as we shall see, was absolutely vital to Studio One's domination. And while you're looking, make out that you can hear tunes like 'Skylarking', 'Baby Why', 'I Hold the Handle', 'Yaho' or 'Armagideon Time' floating out into the yard.

Of course you wouldn't always have had to pretend. Especially not when the 1960s were drawing to a close, when, as the music made the transition from rocksteady, the Brentford Road crew crafted classic tune after classic tune.

The Heptones, Alton Ellis, Larry Marshall and Carlton and his Shoes were just four of the established acts that adapted gloriously to the incoming style at Studio One, but it was the new blood, with bright ideas and fresh approaches, who did so much to instigate changes: the Cables' 'Baby Why', 'What Kind of World' and 'Love Is Pleasure' were the highlights of their 1969 spent at Brentford Road; the same time and place as Horace Andy did his best work – 'Skylarking', 'See a Man's Face' and 'Every Tongue Shall Tell', for instance; while John Holt was getting his post-Paragons solo career off the ground there; and it was where Burning Spear started off, cutting prototype versions of many of the almost trance-inducing spirituals recorded for Jack Ruby in the mid-1970s. Continuing in this more reflective mood, the Wailing Souls began recording in their own right at Studio One – incidentally, like the Wailers, they were taught to sing by Joe Higgs and when they worked as session singers for Coxsone they used to stand in whenever

Peter and Bunny didn't turn up for rehearsals. Then there was a series of instrumentals from the house band, led by Mittoo ... or Roland Alphonso ... or Ernest Ranglin ... or, on one memorable occasion, Alpha Boys' School's musical director Lennie Hibbert playing vibraphone. And as this band featured such brass warriors as Headley Bennett, Val Bennett, Cedric Brooks, Vin Gordon and Bobby Ellis, it would be safe to assume that – post-rocksteady – the horn section was coming back in a big way.

Although Dodd had been a major player since the inception of modern Jamaican music, his company had always been up against competition as big as – sometimes even bigger than – itself. In the rocksteady years it's not unfair to say he played second fiddle to Duke Reid's sustained successes. But as that era drew to a close it was Coxsone's turn. While the Duke was reluctant to move with the times, Coxsone relished the notion of a more percussive music, a style that was increasingly modal and less reliant on communication through conventional chord progressions than its immediate predecessor had been. It was far more in tune with his jazz roots, in the same way as Duke Reid's naturally soulful leanings had been right on the money for a smoother style like rocksteady. Also, at the heart of it all, Coxsone was a dance man. He has frequently spoken of how he made 'dancing' music as opposed to 'listening' music – borne out by the boogie-woogie, shuffle and wild style R&B he started off cutting and the tunes introduced to his public by his and Blackie's steps. These latest developments suited him much better.

Importantly, Dodd was trusting his own and his musical directors' judgement more and more. In spite of impressive jazz credentials, he was actually a deeply conservative fellow, seldom given to taking chances. Now, after three years of owning his own studio, he was starting to relax a bit. His increasing confidence in the musical innovations emanating from sessions at Brentford Road fired his release schedule to move ahead of the pack, and his whole approach to auditioning changed. Before he set up at Brentford Road, the Sunday morning auditions used to be open affairs, held at his Waltham Park Road shop, Coxsone's Music Centre. An audience would crowd in off the streets and loudly express their opinions of each prospective act – and Coxsone would decide which to record based purely on this. It was also good business: he used to sell enough on a Sunday morning to cover the shop's weekly overhead. When he first moved to Brentford Road he held auditions in the yard with the same trial-by-jury element, but by this point he was holding the actual auditions inside and relying on either himself or, mostly, Leroy Sibbles or Jackie Mittoo to make the choices.

When the bass began to assume a greater importance than the organ, Leroy Sibbles edged Jackie Mittoo to one side as the man in charge of the music at Studio One. Every tune had to have a bass-line but not all of them needed the organ. This was a clear case of the pupil outstripping the teacher – when both of them were teenagers, Leroy Sibbles had mastered the bass as one-third of Mittoo's jazz trio, a club-gigging group he moonlighted in to supplement his earnings from the Heptones. Mittoo gave him an enormous amount of help and encouragement with the instrument and let Coxsone know that the lead singer in his most promising rocksteady group had musical talents to match his vocal abilities.

In his various capacities as lead singer and songwriter in the Heptones from 1962, then bass player, musical arranger and interpreter, studio singer, talent scout, tunesmith and recording star at Studio One from the middle of that decade, Leroy Sibbles is one of the true giants of Jamaican music. When Coxsone's company was establishing itself as the Jamaican label of genuinely iconic proportions, Leroy Sibbles was responsible for the signing of so many artists and for the sound and feel of so much of that classic catalogue – although nothing would be released without Dodd's say so, by now he wasn't hands-on in the studio. In purely musical terms, Leroy Sibbles is probably *the* most important man in rocksteady/reggae, yet when he quit Coxsone in 1971, you had to know your stuff to even know who he was – understandably, it was lack of recognition as much as lack of payment that led to the resentful parting.

Any bitterness has now largely faded and Leroy Sibbles is happy to talk about the better times at Brentford Road. Willing to give up time even though he was moving house on the day I talked to him – 'It might mean yuh haffi carry two box . . . heh heh heh'. No problem, I'll carry Leroy Sibbles's stuff all day if that's what he wants. As it was, it didn't wear me out, and after he directed the removal crew where to put several cabinets full of Jamaican, British, Canadian and American music awards we sat out on the balcony of his swish apartment in a gated development in Constant Spring. Leroy bought us a couple of big water coconuts from the vendor who, apparently, still tours the estate every evening about this time (well, it does no good to leave the streets *completely* behind), and challenged me to name a Studio One tune from his period there that he had nothing to do with. Anything I come up with was trumped with 'played bass on that' or 'arranged that' or 'wrote the melodies for that' or 'auditioned them' or 'sung on that', until, with his good natured laughter licking me in my head, I took my ball and went home, so to speak. At which point we got down to business and talked about Studio One until it was dark.

'The Heptones come into music in 1962 or '63, just after independence. The mood of the people back then was nice . . . it was beautiful. Everything was beautiful and nobody had no problems for a time – when the rocksteady came in later, it wasn't just the music was changing, people were thinking about the situation differently. Musically at that time there was much more singing, and that was when a group like ours really came into its own. We were listening to American groups like the Impressions and the Temptations, a lot of the new, soulful R&B, and our style was always more mellow, slower than ska. The Heptones were partly responsible for the change; from "Fattie Fattie" onwards we were mellow when most other guys were known for their speed.

'When the group get successful it encourages other singers – it was a trend thing, because Jamaicans will always follow a trend. The rocksteady thing made it much more possible for groups to sing like that because it was expected of them to be sweet, very melodic. Because we did "Fattie Fattie" at Studio One and it was such a big hit, other groups come there looking for the same hit sound. The Heptones had a lot to do with Studio One going massive like it did, because that record did so much to put it on the map.

'When I write it the other guys still had jobs in the day and I wasn't yet full time at Studio One – I would stay at home and write the songs for the others to finish off and rehearse in the evening. "Fattie Fattie" came as I see this woman, Miss B, coming down the road who was short and fat and have a kind of waddle walk. I see her and the whole song fall into place because I start singing how I want a fat girl, which is a compliment in Jamaica because most man like their woman with some flesh on their bones. It wasn't about Miss B, she was a big woman – maybe thirty or forty when I had not yet turned twenty – it was just that seeing her made me think of the line "I need a fat girl". When we sing it, people love it and we have to sing it so much they know it even before we make the record. Then when it come out the radio ban it – they say it too rude and will corrupt the children – but everywhere, in the jukeboxes, in the rum shops, in the dance, *everywhere* playing it. For nearly a year, pure "Fattie Fattie". That's what made the Heptones and did so much for Studio One, because back then everything was *Duke Reid, Duke Reid, Duke Reid.*'

Leroy paused to take a deep draught of coconut water before continuing.

'After the group started to spend more time at Coxsone's Studio One I got involved in the music there as a singer, writer, arranger, bass player. Jackie Mittoo get me involved. I'm responsible for the first hit song Dennis Brown ever did, I played on that. "Queen of the Minstrels", "Stars", "Sata Massa Gana", "Declaration of Rights" and so much works by so many of the new artists like John Holt . . . I'm playing on first Burning Spear album. A lot of the time, especially when we're just voicing tracks, it was just me and the engineer in there.

'Coxsone was around but he wasn't so much in the actual studio part, he didn't get involved too much and he leave me minding the store. Also, a lot of the time he was out on the road doing the business part, so when I'm round the studio I don't usually see too much of him. Most of the time he don't know what is actually going on in the recording, but nothing would leave there to be release without his say so as he would listen to the songs in the evening, and pick releases of what's going to come out. He wasn't just yes or no either, he would bring songs back and say things like, "It a good song and I want to put it out but it need more of something or less of something on it," and then you would get the time to do more work on it.

'How it work was singers would come in with a tune and sing it to me, and I would start thinking about what I was going to do with it. A lot of the time I already had ideas and arrangements I wanted to try out ready in my head – you could do that because nearly all the songs the singers would come in with were structured so similarly that there wouldn't be too many surprises. Like I said, Jamaicans are very trendy people so you always knew what to expect. They would sing each of their tunes two or three times, and because I could play the bass I would start to work out a riddim there and then. The singers would leave after that and I would then work out the arrangements for the rest of the band – sometimes one of them, like Jackie, might have some melody ideas – but mostly it was the musicians just played and the singers just sung. Everything else I worked out.

'The singers coming in with new songs like that would usually happen first thing in the morning, at about nine o'clock or earlier. They'd come back in about two or three days' time, when they'd practised it and by then, most times, I'd already have the backing track done and we just had to voice it. If it was a group I'd go through the vocal arrangements with them then – I'd already have figured them out – and we'd record it. I would maybe run through it a couple of times then do it in one or two takes, straight, all the way through. The engineer couldn't punch in.

'We'd do five or six songs a day like that. Because it was single track or while I was there it soon went two-track – so we could voice the tunes separate from doing the backing – there wasn't any mixing to be done after the recording, that was all done with levels as the musicians played. But it was still real busy in there because those five or six songs would be done with different artists so there was people coming and going all the time. And that helped. That busy atmosphere was exactly right to create good songs, because everybody know they're part of something successful and they drive each other on. Those were good days there, with a fantastic vibe.

'Coxsone knew how to spur people on, too, and when he was there, he could be quite, yunno, sly. If he was in the actual studio and he didn't think a singer was giving the very best he could, jus' not up to scratch for whatever reason, he would say, casual like, to me "Hmmmm, try that without the singing, mi t'ink this would do well as instrumental . . ." He was just playing, the band would know what he was doing, but the singers who wouldn't have known about this trick would suddenly get better on the next take because they didn't want to lose the payment they would get for voicing the tune.

'A lot of that Studio One sound was possible from the way it was engineered. Even when it went two-track the way it was balanced hadn't changed. Coxsone himself had set it up, because in the beginning he used to do all his own engineering and he knew what he was doing. He had bought two six-track mixers in New York, from a firm called Lang, and because he had so many different channels he could balance the instruments by giving them more than one track if he wanted them to be strong. He'd mic'ed up the bass and the drums to sound strong and fat – I think it was three channels for the drums and three for the bass, and only one for the horns – which was the foundation of that whole Studio One sound.

'It could only have been balanced like that in that room, we had to be careful where the musicians were positioned. Because he wouldn't hire his studio out to other producers they tried to build their places like it, but nowhere else could get that balance. When Channel One took over from Studio One, they might have had that different drum pattern, but their sound was almost pure Studio One; they were the ones that came closest to copying it.'

He broke off to exchange a warm greeting with a passing neighbour, home from work. Leroy Sibbles is still very much a man of the people.

'A big part of my job was to go in on Sundays to audition singers. Those sessions would start around midday and go on 'til about five, depending on how many people was come down. It was pure singers, every time there was twenty, sometimes as many as thirty, and they'd have started a queue down the street before I got there. Then when they were let into the yard they'd wait, sometimes for several hours trying to find a bit of shade under the tree or against the wall. They didn't mind, because this was their big chance and at that time everybody wanted to sing for Studio One.

'There was no band there, just me and maybe some of the other musicians and them in the front yard. Sometimes Coxsone would be there, too. The only time we'd need to go inside would be if Coxsone wanted to tape particular singers, and that would be played back to them when they came in to do the tune to remind them of what could be done.

'Each man would have to come with four, five or six of him songs, because if you only had one song I'd think you're just trying something. That you're not really serious about your music and I wouldn't consider you. You'd have to prove that you'd worked hard by having already prepared more than one song. Then I'd be able to pick the best two songs a singer had, it was better for them like that because it gave me the choice of songs that might have potential but perhaps even they didn't see that. I would choose the guys and the songs that I liked, and give them a time – probably a few days later – for them to come back to the studio having worked some more on those songs. That's when we'd run through them with a band. Some-times, you might see a potential in the singer but the songs he had weren't ready yet, so you might tell him to work on them some more or to come in anyway and you'd give him something to sing by somebody else.

'Those audition Sundays were real exciting, because you never know who was going to come in with a song next. Cornell Campbell . . . the Mad Lads . . . Burning Spear . . . the Meditations . . . they all came through auditions I held on a Sunday. Auditions at Studio One and at other studios were taking over from the talent shows like Vere Johns' as the way for producers to find new acts.'

One of the successful new acts at one of those Sunday morning sessions was Horace Andy. At an audition conducted by Dodd himself, no less. Horace, known as 'Sleepy' owing to his ability to fall asleep almost anywhere and in almost any circumstances, got his career off the ground as a teenager at Studio One at the very beginning of the 1970s, when his beautifully lilting falsetto crooned tunes such as 'Skylarking', 'See a Man Face' and 'Every Tongue Shall Tell'. Looking much younger than the almost fifty that he is, he's settled in London and still records and performs in London, New York and Jamaica. Recently, Horace recut some of his classics with Massive Attack, while his involvement with various drum 'n' bass producers is bringing an interesting, traditional element to modern dance music while boosting roots reggae firmly into the present day. It had, at the time of writing, started something of a trend for over-ambient dub.

When I met him, at his management's offices in West London, he was back at Studio One with Leroy Sibbles and, occasionally, Coxsone. Horace puts it from the singer's as opposed to the management's point of view, and significantly, he always refers to the proprietor as Mr Dodd, whereas Leroy calls him Coxsone.

'I was one of those people in that queue out here on a Sunday. Bwoy, it was *hot*! But it was worth it, because I audition for Mr Dodd, when I do "See a Man Face". I just go in and sing it and he say he like it, ask me to come back in a few days and it start from there.

'It was a good scene at Studio One. All the pros were there and it was like a school where I learn to sing. I learned from Alton Ellis, Leroy Sibbles, Sylvan Morris, Cedric Brooks, yunno. It wasn't as if I was taken under anybody's wing – I ask, that's how determined I was. And because they are all professionals and the vibe round there was so good, so communal, they would help the likkle yout' who just wanted to learn. It was like they took pride in coaching me in all aspects of music. I would be around the studio and when they not doing anything, when they get a spare time I would ask questions. I would say, "Can you show me G?" and the next day I would ask something else. I would always be polite because they were men I respected and they appreciated that. If they're in the studio and they sit down from doing a song and they're not doing anything I would ask, I would say, "Leroy, show me blah blah blah on the bass," and he would do it. Then I would fool around on the bass until they ready to go again and I would give him the instrument back. Or I would bang the piano until they're ready.

'To do it to this degree wasn't too usual. It was just the instincts that I have, all I wanted to do was *learn, learn, learn*, and when I could play an instrument, that's when I started arranging my own stuff.

'Studio One was for learning. The people there, like Leroy and Jackie Mittoo, loved their music and what they did so much that they enjoyed helping other people. That was the vibe. *Everybody* who went there to sing came out better than they were when they started. It was like a college. That was down to the musicians and the experienced singers there, not down to Mr Dodd himself – he wasn't there much by then, Leroy was practically running things. There was always plenty of guys hanging out in the yard, at the back and the sides and out front, even if they weren't recording that day they'd jus' be there soaking up the vibe and learning all the time.'

It's easy to say success breeds success, especially in a village like Kingston's music community, and, like the point Leroy made about 'Fattie Fattie', once Studio One had established itself its hit parade mushroomed. Suddenly, it was attracting the cream of Kingston's players and singers, even though it didn't yet enjoy the reputation of, say, Treasure Isle or Beverley's. Why? Coxsone was adventurous in his outlook, but he'd always been that. And it certainly wasn't because he paid better, if many ex-Studio One stars are to be believed. At that point, as rocksteady became reggae, there was a much more straightforward reason why so many people went to Studio One. Horace explains:

'You could smoke weed there. By now, Rasta was getting big in reggae and musicians want to build a spliff while they're working and Studio One was the only place where you could do that. You couldn't do it in Dynamic or Federal or Duke Reid's – skin up in Federal and they're gonna run you right out . . . *physically*. Duke Reid was once a policeman and apart from the legality – though that wouldn't have bothered Duke if it had suited him – he hated anything to do with Rasta and didn't want it in the place. And Dynamic was owned by Byron Lee, who was real uptown, and he *definitely* don' want that business in his studio. Mr Dodd, though, was sympathetic to Rasta people.

'That's why Studio One was number one because you get the spiritual vibes mixed with the herb. The musicians and singers wanted to come there because they knew that, and then once you were there it help the vibe flow. You could feel *relax*, find a little corner and sit down and smoke and when the ideas come, the studio's right there and you just go in. Other studios you can't smoke in the place so you have to go out in the street, so you're no gonna get no vibes because it'll break your flow. Some places even sent you down the street because they don't even want you near their place with a spliff. Mr Dodd didn't like you sitting down in the front smoking because people are passing and you could be seen, so if you wanted to sit outside you sat at the back, on this tree that had been cut down, or round the sides behind the corrugated iron that screen you from the road. It was funny because although Mr Dodd don't mind, he don't want to encourage it either, so he used to make out he didn't know – if you were sitting down with a spliff and he pass, you have to hide it – kinda like a schoolkid. He knew about it, he just didn't want to see it.

'But that was why Studio One was number one, because you could sit down and smoke your spliff in the place. People want to come there because they know that would make the right vibe for the music, and when they get there it means the music they make is even better. It do a lot for the community atmosphere in there too, because everybody share their spliff or their bag of weed.'

Maybe the reason Studio One's dominance waned as the 1970s progressed was because other smaller, more street-vibey operations took passing the chalice to be a prerequisite. Or maybe it was because Coxsone changed the gear to eight-, sixteen- and, later, twenty-four track mixing capabilities and lost that wonderful sound balance he'd been forced to achieve in mono with imaginative mic arrangements. Or maybe it was because by the middle of that decade both Leroy Sibbles and Jackie Mittoo had left. Time just moved on and Coxsone didn't.

Whatever the reason, the fact remains that, although Studio One enjoyed a last, early-1980s hurrah with a dancehall generation that included Johnny Osbourne, Michigan & Smilie, Willie Williams, Freddie McGregor and the Lone Ranger, Dodd's days at the cutting edge of Jamaican music were numbered. In the mid-1980s he shut up shop and moved to New York, where he runs a record shop and administers one of the world's greatest back catalogues in any form of music.

Duke Reid wasn't having nearly so much success. Perhaps the required syncopation and percussive nature of what was happening grated against his naturally oily ideals, but he found it conspicuously difficult to adapt. Not that he didn't have a few hits – Hopeton Lewis's 'Boom Shaka Laka' (a Festival Song Contest winner), the Techniques' 'My Girl' and 'Moonlight Lover' by Joya Landis in particular – but he wasn't to stamp his mark on any post-rocksteady era until he began recording U-Roy in 1970. And dynamic as that was, it was never more than a retread of the Duke's rocksteady days. The same was true of Prince Buster. While he wasn't a complete stranger to success during this period – John Holt's 'Rain from the Skies',

Dennis Brown's 'If I Had the World', the Heptones' 'Our Day Will Come' – he pretty much took a sabbatical until coming back to make deejay music with Big Youth and Dennis Alcapone a couple of years later.

Derrick Harriott and Leslie Kong made the crossing from rocksteady with considerable ease. Harriott had two major advantages: (1) his Crystal label's house band the Crystalites featured Winston Wright on the organ, and wasn't afraid of a bit of rootsman percussion, and (2) his own soul-boy leanings and silky pipes. Right from the off he not only seemed to understand how each aspect of reggae worked individually, but could put them together with stunning effect. The *Undertaker* album of instrumentals is among the very best Western-inspired reggae, while the work he did with the Kingstonians includes 'Sufferer' and 'Singer Man', from that trio at their absolute peak. And there was *still* a great deal more to come from the man they call the Musical Chariot. Kong's work is the most widely known largely because he had the best international deal, but that shouldn't in any way detract from what he was getting on to wax. His roster included the Maytals, the Melodians, the Pioneers and Desmond Dekker: at the turn of the decade on the Beverley's label you had '54-46 That's My Number', 'Pressure Drop', 'Monkey Man', 'Sweet Sensation', 'The Rivers of Babylon', 'Long Shot (Kick de Bucket)', 'Easy Come Easy Go' and 'Israelites'. Leslie Kong also cut reggae with the Wailers, Ken Boothe, Delroy Wilson and the Gaylads. If he hadn't died of a heart attack in 1971, who knows how far he would have taken it?

Then there were the (relatively) new boys. Clancy Eccles hit his purple period about now, with the same band Derrick Harriott used, except they called themselves the Dynamites. He had hits for himself – the bawdy 'Fatty Fatty' and 'Auntie Lulu' being the most notable – while among his productions were 'Holly Holy' (the Fabulous Flames), 'Herbsman' (King Stitt), 'No Good Girl' (the Beltones) and 'Please Stay' (Larry Marshall), plus there were a string of hit instrumentals from the Dynamites. Bunny Lee came into his own at this point: the easy-action very post-rocksteady vibe he wove around Slim Smith, Stranger Cole and the Sensations gave way to his coaxing some serious reggae out of Pat Kelly ('How Long'), Eric Donaldson ('Cherry Oh Baby' – another Festival Song winner), John Holt ('Stick by Me') and Delroy Wilson ('Better Must Come').

Joe Gibbs released some excellent early reggae records on his Amalgamated label, and was pretty much unfazed by Lee Perry's rancorous departure as he took on Winston 'Niney' Holness to fill the little fellow's shoes as engineer and arranger. It allowed the line that had begun so successfully with the Pioneers and the Versatiles to continue with the Soul Mates, the Soul Sisters, the Reggay Boys, the Slickers, the Hippy Boys (an instrumental quartet that were more or less the nucleus of the Upsetters – the Barrett brothers, Glen Adams and Reggie Lewis) and Nicky Thomas. Although Joe Gibbs didn't build careers, the one-offs scored by his acts form a memorable list that runs to 'Them a Laugh and a Kiki', 'Wreck a Buddy', 'Long Shot', 'Never Come Never See', 'People Grudgeful', 'Trust the Book' and 'Love of the Common People'. Harry J, who was there at the beginning with the Beltones, stuck with it to build a sound around the keyboard skills of Winston Wright and Winston Blake (aka Blake Boy) for a string of bubbling instrumentals by Harry J All-Stars or the Jay Boys (essentially the same personnel) of which 'The Liquidator' will be the best remembered, but which included a cut of 'Je t'aime (moi non plus)' that somehow managed to stay on the right side of cheesy. He was also the man who paired Bob Andy with Marcia Griffiths for a cover of Nina Simone's 'Young, Gifted and Black' and 'Pied Piper', although Andy himself produced the latter single. Incidentally, 'The Liquidator' has lived on as the backing in several British TV commercials and is still played at Wolverhampton Wanderers' home games to rouse their fans – those distinctive six beats at the end of certain lines are tailor-made for chanting, '[*clap-clap-clap-clap*] – *The Wolves!*'.

Then there was Lee Perry. Scratch had split with Joe Gibbs and launched his Upsetter record label. He persuaded players to leave Gibbs and come to work with him, and his floating pool settled down from the group pianist Gladstone Anderson used to organize for him – regulars were Winston Wright (organ), Clifton Jackson (bass) and Lloyd Adams (drums) – to what became the Upsetters. The reason Perry could lure musicians of this calibre wasn't the money but the creative freedom he was offering. As a producer who had been experimenting in this new style for some time he more than understood how far it could be stretched. Considering he didn't have his own studio at this point, Perry put out a phenomenal amount of music between 1968 and 1972 that varied from the mentoed to the demented, with songs of love, protest or pure silliness, and instrumentals that were at once mellifluous and downright spiky, thrown in along the way. If a musician had an idea, then Perry would make it work within a reggae format.

Although the Upsetter label included a number of impressive vocal sides – Peter Tosh, Pat Kelly, the Ethiopians, Eric Donaldson, Busty Brown and the Mellotones all recorded for Scratch during this period – it was the instrumentals that really made a difference. On the surface, Upsetters' tracks like 'Prison Sentence', 'Baby Baby', 'Skanky Chicken', 'For a Few Dollars More', 'Dry Acid', 'Live Injection', 'Caught You' and, the big UK hit, 'The Return of Django' are nothing short of barking mad; but look deeper into them – or have a long session spinning Upsetter cuts – and a crystal-clear logic emerges: musically, the whole point of reggae is its inherent pointlessness. To truly plug this new style into the music of the Dark Continent, reggae had to shuck off the very Western notion of melody as the defining clause. It needed to become apparently randomly rhythmic, out of which its own concept of tunefulness would emerge – one that, to an outsider, seems to exist for no other reason than self-celebration. Like it does if you listen to un-Europeanized ensemble drumming – Burru, Kumina etc. Lee Perry's ideas were subtly meshing to point away from rock-steady's soul inflections to a road that could only lead to roots.

It's small wonder that, in 1969, Bob Marley turned up at Lee Perry's door with the other Wailers looking to advance their cause beyond their teenage rudieisms.

The above-mentioned are the notables, but there were dozens of footsoldiers beavering away in tiny studios and, in general, as reggae progressed beyond the end of the 1960s it was wonderfully productive. Producers and artists seemed to feel they could do anything and in most cases they did. Nothing was safe from reggaefication. While an absence of copyright laws on the island might have had something to do with the astonishing number of covers emerging, this trend was then at its height as songwriters were finding out what they could or couldn't do. It was a ludicrously broad sweep of music, too. US soul tunes were standard fare for the one-drop makeover – the multi-volume CD collection *Just My Imagination – Soulful Reggae For Lovers* consists of nothing else. Likewise, a generous selection of UK Top 40 hits of the day would be overhauled from a reggae standpoint as would a smattering of C&W songs – in keeping with the Jamaican mainstream's fondness for that style: 'Rainy Night in Georgia' was something of a one-drop perennial, the Maytals did a rousing version of 'Take Me Home Country Roads', while perhaps the most unlikely was the Wailers' first openly Rasta song, 'Selassie in the Chapel', which retrod that much-loved Elvis weepie 'Crying in the Chapel'.

Film and TV themes remained as popular a choice of material as they had been back in the ska days, with cowboy motifs a clear first choice – before the 1970s when American blaxploitation came to dominate Kingston's vibrant cinema scene, watching cowboy films was how young men tended to live out their badman fantasies, often – too often – joining in the on-screen gunfights with live ammunition. There has been an album of early reggae western numbers, *Magnificent Fourteen – 14 Shots of Western Inspired Reggae*, available for about the last twenty-five years, just as there have been a number of reggae Christmas albums, notably one collection of late-sixties covers of traditional seasonal songs under the title *I'm Dreaming of a Black Christmas*. Taking that joke a little further was *The Black Album*, a Various Artists remake of the Beatles' White Album including such dubious delights as the Rudies covering 'My Sweet Lord' and a Marcia Griffiths version of 'Don't Let Me Down'.

Such diversity in reggae was inevitable, as the sheer weight of numbers of artists, players and producers grew. As with each previous change of style there was a new wave of musicians, writers and producers keen to break ties with the past and prove themselves with a new way of doing things. And by this time wannabe stars were coming to Kingston from all over the island specifically to try their luck. They brought with them all sorts of outside influences, specifically the ones Edward Seaga was so keen on, such as Kumina, Burru and Pocomania, which were always much bigger in rural Jamaica. These newcomers weren't complete chancers, for by now the music business had spread all over the country and the ideas they had were what they'd been trying out at the sound systems and embryonic studio scenes in such burgs as Port Antonio, Ocho Rios and Spanish Town.

Lee Perry firmly believes the country connection is the main reason for reggae's success. And he ought to know, being a *country bwoy* from Hanover, who in 1968, after 'People Funny Boy', set up his own appropriately named Upsetter label. From practically day one it forged a reputation for off-centre but very natural, warm-sounding reggae – look no further than his work with the Wailers in the following year, which is widely acclaimed as the best work the group ever did. In a rare moment of absolute lucidity he offers up the following explanation as to what a big contribution rural Jamaica made:

'Until reggae it was all Kingston . . . *Kingston! Kingston! Kingston!* All the music business was a big-city thing. *Ska . . . rocksteady . . .* they were Kingston things with the same Kingston men doing the same Kingston things. It was when the country people come to town and get involved they bring with them the earth, the trees, the mountains. That's when reggae music go back to the earth. They used to look on country men as madmen, but so what? Sometimes it takes a madman because these madmen can't play the same thing the same way because it don't mean nothing to them, so they bring a different style. The roots! You hear it in the way they play the bass or bang the drum. The roots of reggae never came from Kingston.'

Extreme as you'd expect his point of view to be, few will deny its validity. While Derrick Harriott adds to the theory of dynamic evolution, going some way to explaining reggae's internal diversity:

'The previous generation of producers weren't musicians. Nearly all of them were just guys with some money and, to be perfectly frank, they hear a song and think that it's a good song but they have no ideas on what to do. They depended on the musicians to actually put it all together for them, and because they didn't know what something might culminate in they weren't flexible enough. The producers know they have the money, so they hear so-and-so is playing a good bass-line or playing a good drum, so they carry them to the studio and tell them to do it a certain way.

'Now, with all the little studios springing up all around the place, musicians and artists were turning producer and they truly understood what could be done with a tune. So when singers come in with a tune, but unprepared with the music – like most of them did – first the pianist, then the other musicians start to play it by feel and the song just falls into place. There was a beauty of going impromptu, because things really start to happen as the musicians start to explore all of a song's possibilities. It was loose. We tried things, so reggae took off in all kinds of directions and the musician-producers understood it enough to go with it. But you'd have to be a musician, or a very exceptional producer, to be able to do that.'

At this time, though, many of the producers *were* exceptional. They were about to take Jamaican music on a roller-coaster ride to towering sales figures, huge critical acclaim, jet-set glamour, deep spiritual awareness and global recognition – to such a degree that by the end of the 1970s one of the best-known faces on the planet would be that of a Jamaican reggae musician. And all of this without corrupting what it was all about.

At the height of its international popularity most of the best-acclaimed reggae tunes were still being knocked out in claustrophobic West Kingston studios, by men with holes in their shoes who were on a promise of ten pounds. The aim was still to hear themselves on the local sound system and maybe have enough cash to buy two brew. But thousands of miles away in the blues dances of Stoke Newington, Handsworth or Chapeltown that very excitement, experimentation and naked anticipation would boom out of speaker boxes to put the new generation of black British in touch with their roots. In contact with who they really were.

During the next ten years or so, reggae music and its self-appointed prophets would take over where Marcus Garvey and Walter Rodney were forced to quit, and it would become the force that would unify the first and second waves of the black diaspora.

11

You Can Get It If You Really Want

'I wasn't thinking about no international hit. As far as I know Ansell [Collins] made both riddim tracks, for "Double Barrel" and "Monkey Spanner", long before Winston Riley got hold of them. I heard Ansell sold them to Winston – either to him or his brother, Buster Riley – then both Winston and Buster came to me, and asked me if I could put a talking voice on the "Double Barrel" track. To which I agreed, and the three of us went to Joe Gibbs' recording studio in North Parade – me, Winston Riley and his brother. When Winston asked the engineer to start play the tape, I wasn't too keen on the track because to me it sounded like some kind of Mickey Mouse stuff – you know, sorta lightweight. So the vibes couldn't really come and flow from me as easily as it normally comes, so his brother help to encourage me: "Look, Dave man, *t'ink big* . . . like some big giant man. Like Hercules or James Bond, Double-O-Seven, or somet'ing." So I said OK and went right into it. *I . . . am the magnificent . . . double o – o . . .* and from there we just went straight through.'

To hear Dave Barker toast his famous opening to 'Double Barrel', complete with echoes and accents, from about three feet away is little short of, well, magnificent. It doesn't really matter that we're sitting on some disused speaker boxes in the upstairs stock room of a record shop in London's Harlesden High Street, and it's mid-January. When Dave goes into that line instantly you're somewhere else. From the look in his eyes, he's just touched down at the Norman Manley Airport, but it's almost as special to be taken back thirty years to be sitting on your living-room floor with your dad doing his dance, *Top of the Pops* on the television and Dave whooping out *I . . . am the magnificent . . . double o − o . . .* From the number 1 spot.

We're talking about Dave & Ansell Collins's 'Double Barrel', which, in May 1971, at the top of the UK pop charts, represented a pinnacle of Jamaican music as a force within mainstream British pop. Released in the previous August, it was played just thirty-three times on the radio before it got into the Top 40 in April, when it shifted almost 300,000 copies to hit the top spot in only four weeks. It came as part of a trend which had seen, during the previous couple of years, an increasing number of reggae records cropping up in pop buyers' collections. While the number of copies 'Double Barrel' shifted makes it one of the UK's best-selling reggae singles ever, what really put Dave & Ansell ahead of the pack was when their follow-up, 'Monkey Spanner', spent four weeks in the Top 10 some two months later. Combined sales were enough to see them as the sixth best-selling singles group in the UK that year, tucked in between the Sweet and Curved Air, leaving Atomic Rooster flapping in their wake.

Dave goes on to explain how the duo became part of the British pop business:

'I had no idea that "Double Barrel" would be so big. We did it late 1969, maybe early 1970, and it was a few months after that I went back into Dynamic's, with the same people and voiced "Monkey Spanner", which was the same sort of thing. After that I forget about them both and I was even so surprised after I hear that it was selling quite well. Then, it was in later part of 1970 – almost a full year after I voice the track – that we heard the news it was doing quite well here, in England. Which took me completely by surprise. But while I'm saying "*No, man, how can that be?*" the next thing I know we get a phone call from Trojan, which was run by a guy named Lee Gopthal. The man was telling us that the record gone Top 10 and could go all the way to number 1 if we are there. That we should jump on a plane and come to England, where we would tour for six to eight months, with "Monkey Spanner" coming out while we were there.

'We jus' pick up and gone. We went practically straight from the airport in London to the *Top of the Pops* studio, and the next week there it was . . . "Double Barrel" *the Number One tune in England*. If I hadn't been there and you just telling me about it I wouldn't have believed it.'

Just because the UK's early-1960s flirtation with ska had cooled off, it didn't mean Jamaican music had gone away. At the end of that decade there was a shameful shortage of honest, uncomplicatedly danceable homegrown British pop music: the Beatles, the Who and the Rolling Stones had moved on from cod-R&B to much loftier concerns; the likes of Herman's Hermits, the Hollies or Dave Dee, Dozy, Beaky and so on were sounding increasingly tired; and it wasn't in any way unusual to find the Top 20 clogged up with singers like Tom Jones (this was *waaaay* before he regained his cool), Engelbert Humperdinck, Des O'Connor and Andy Williams. UK dancehalls' hipper Saturday night soundtrack was almost exclusively American – Motown, Stax, Atlantic, James Brown – shaded with ska's hardy perennials and a helping of rocksteady. The first flowerings of reggae, with its jerkily syncopated, almost dance-by-numbers beat was never going to be more than a two-step away.

Reggae was in a strong position to meet, or perhaps create, a demand for danceable music. Yet the irony was that it mushroomed into a big business without initially attracting any attention from the mainstream.

*

Jamaica's record producers had long been aware of the existence of a large, expatriate market and, as it began to put itself on a more formal footing than Vego's and Peckings's door-to-door dubstyle, were realizing its potential. Which was considerable. After all, this was Britain in the 'you've never had it so good' 1960s. Employment was fairly full and Caribbean immigrants were settling into life in the UK with far greater purchasing power than they had had ten years previously.

During the first part of the decade, Sonny Roberts's Orbitone shop was the exception rather than the rule when, just as the record-retail business had got itself going in Jamaica, records were sold as a sideline to another enterprise. Hairdressers, barbers and wig/hair product and cosmetic shops were a favourite, as they had an exclusively black, usefully captive, clientele – Nat's Afro Wigs in Brixton did such a brisk trade in records that Nat actually turned producer at one point, while Dyke & Dryden, who began flogging imported records and black makeup in Dalston, east London, are now the multi-million pound market leaders in black haircare product distribution. General stores, food importers, black-owned Caribbean-specialist travel agents and electrical outlets figured high on the list, some because of an obvious synergy, others because they regularly dealt with, took delivery of goods from, or journeyed to Jamaica, and fellow countrymen would patronize the business without hesitation. Maybe with much cussing or kissing of teeth, but seldom with reluctance.

It was from these beginnings that, in the middle sixties, a new wave of dedicated shops began to establish themselves. Joe Mansano was one of the very earliest retailers, and the first in the Jamaican stronghold of Brixton, South London. He started with a stall-cum-kiosk in the Granville Arcade, the area's famous covered market, and by this time had progressed to a shop, Joe's Record Shack, where his advertisements boasted 'The latest and the best from Jamaica'. Desmond's Hip City, just around the corner in Atlantic Road, was an early competitor; staying in South London, there was Record Corner in Balham Underground station, Beverley's in Lewisham and

Reading's in Clapham Junction. North of the river there was Webster's in Shepherd's Bush Market, Derek's in Turnpike Lane and Paul's in Finsbury Park.

In fact, by this time every black area in the country had its own specialist record shops, and they were becoming *the* place to hang out on a Friday evening or a Saturday afternoon – most shops would take delivery of import tunes around lunchtime on a Friday. Whereas your dad's generation would treat the barber's on a Saturday as some sort of gentleman's club complete with drinking, dominoes and any amount of escalatingly loud 'back home' chat, their youngsters would take root in the record shop. And, just as it didn't matter that your dad didn't have but three grains of hair on his head yet still took his turn in the chair, you didn't actually have to be buying records to be there. First off, you'd always hear some good, straight-from-Jamaica sounds, few of which would even be on pirate radio. Then you'd get to find out about dances and parties and know whose was going to be good as you'd see what the sound men were buying – this was, of course, the local sound systems, the second division, as the big guys would never be caught in a record shop. But most importantly, as the record shops were *the* place in which to finish up on a Saturday afternoon or start off on a Friday evening (the good ones stayed open until about 9 p.m. or so), you could meet your spars and reaffirm your standing in your own community after a week at work, and you'd learn about much more than music-related events and transactions. Most shop owners at least attempted to discourage such hanging out, and signs reading 'No loitering' and 'Please don't lean on the record racks' were commonplace, a particularly grandiose favourite being 'Selling records is our business. If buying records isn't yours then you have no business here.'

There was a noticeable hierarchy that decided, quite literally, your standing in the shop. The sound men and extreme purchasers leaned on the counter and didn't say anything – not even to each other; whoever was staffing the place played records on the shop system and then looked around to see who would almost imperceptibly nod, a copy of that tune going on to their 'pile' held underneath the counter. When somebody had had enough they'd subtly motion towards the counter, the shop-keeper would total it up, say how much and the chap would pay in silence then, with a brief salutation, leave. Such furtive behaviour originated as sound men didn't want each other to know what they were buying, but it quickly evolved into stan-dard reggae-shop etiquette for just about anybody who felt serious enough not to ask for tunes by name. Like the next rank on the floorspace pecking order. If you wanted to buy a particular tune, you came in, walked straight up to the counter and either jostled for space among the sound men or tried to make yourself heard over their heads. This could take some time, and if what you were asking for was considered rubbish you could expect some sort of reaction in the form of rolled eyes or other unspoken indications of contempt. As likely as not from the guy who was serving you. Then, behind these occasional buyers and as far away from the counter as possible, were the idlers who literally just hung about, nipping in and out, greeting new arrivals, busting the odd dance move and generally enjoying life. It's a good thing shop hi-fis were of sound-system proportions, for little else would be audible over the chatter and raucous laughter coming from these loafers.

Again like the barbers, the record shop on a Saturday was a male enclave. Indeed, although it wasn't unusual for women to shout from the doorway or get one of the idlers to attract somebody's attention for them, they'd rarely come in. Under-standably so, as young men pumped up by the best reggae and encouraged by each other to escalating heights of bullshit, can produce an intimidating amount of testosterone. Well brought-up West Indian girls would have been warned by their mothers about record shops and the *types* who could be found in them, and thus would sniffily tell you 'I don't go in *record shops*'. (Oddly though, females always bought more UK-released reggae records, so what they really meant was that they didn't go in *certain* records shops, and definitely not on a Friday or a Saturday.)

That this growing number of specialist record shops could

support themselves, combined with the few big crossover hits of the past few years, was enough to demonstrate the music's much broader potential. But to exploit the UK to the full would need a man who could make sense out of the Jamaican music business's methods, its proliferation of labels and release 'schedules'; then he would have to understand exactly how the reggae scene – ex-pat and otherwise – worked in Great Britain *and* be able to put some real effort into marketing it. Remember, reggae was going to have to come out of the specialist shops and on to BBC radio, where it would compete with the likes of Lulu, the Bee Gees and the 1910 Fruitgum Company as bona-fide pop music. To pull off such a stunt would take a man who fully understood the Jamaican psyche, commanded respect from the island's producers and label bosses, yet was immersed in the British record business to such a degree that he knew how to get his records heard by the public and into the shops. Or maybe it would take two men. Two men such as Lee Gopthal and Chris Blackwell.

Lee Gopthal was originally Chris Blackwell's commercial landlord but had become so enthralled with the black music industry that he'd made it his business, too. With admirable opportunism he'd recognized the need for a certain formalization, and his distribution company, Beat & Commercial – an apt name given his priorities – specialized in Jamaican product. It meant far greater focus than mainstream operators like Lugtons or EMI could give it and the results, almost entirely from the West Indian market, were such that he began opening retail outlets. Starting off with a stall in Portobello Road Market in Notting Hill, by 1967 he had the Musik City chain, a series of specialist reggae (plus a bit of soul and gospel) shops in London's 'black high streets': Ridley Road in Dalston, Goldhawk Road in Shepherd's Bush, Atlantic Road in Brixton . . . All of the Musik City stores were considered the best for both pre- and already-released reggae in the broad sense that you would always have a huge choice there, even if you might miss out on some of the quirkier, small-label imports. Gopthal opened half a dozen such establishments, plus the more mainstream Musicland chain, whose outlets were never situated in quite such black areas and which carried the pop music of the day as well.

In Jamaica it would have been an entirely natural progression for such a successful retailer to start releasing his own records, and Lee Gopthal saw no reason to buck such a tried and tested trend. Entering into partnership with Chris Blackwell, B&C/Island launched a series of record labels by doing things in a very back-a-yard manner and dedicating labels to different producers. Treasure Isle was Duke Reid's, which kicked off with the Techniques' 'You Don't Care'; Studio One and Coxsone were dedicated Dodd; Amalgamated catered for Joe Gibbs; Dandy for Dandy Livingstone's UK productions; High Note handled Sonia Pottinger; while Blue Cat, Big Shot and Duke featured a number of different producers (the latter being originally strictly Duke Reid, but soon branching out).

But the big deal was Trojan, the orange and white record label that was B&C's flagship and came to enjoy iconic status as *the* purveyors of reggae to the Great British Public. Established in 1967, it wasn't B&C/Island's first reggae label but was pretty near the front and originally came about as another Duke Reid imprint, hence the fact that its first ten releases were Duke Reid productions. The first release, TR-001A, even went so far as to give the Duke an artist credit with a label simply reading 'Judge Sympathy by Duke Reid', although a vocal group called the Freedom Singers did the hard work. Significantly, when Gopthal and Blackwell split in the summer of 1968 – an operational separation, as Blackwell was concentrating on his rock music successes yet kept a financial interest in the partnership – and Gopthal was in sole control, he swiftly turned Trojan into a company in its own right, Trojan/B&C, with the other reggae labels as subsidiaries of it. He was determined to centre on this one as his way into the mainstream, and while his other labels could dedicate themselves to specific producers, Trojan was going to cherry-pick the most obviously commercial stuff from either side of the Atlantic.

Lee Gopthal wasn't, of course, alone in wanting to make the

most of the U K's newly established riddim opportunities, and elsewhere were other characters with the same outlook and the same 'exclusive' deals with Jamaican producers. There was Graeme Goodhall's Doctor Bird group, which had been around since the early 1960s and was now moving into rocksteady and reggae with the J J, Doctor Bird, Pyramid and Attack labels. The Palmer brothers, three Jamaican expatriates involved in the property business in Harlesden, promoted local reggae talent as a sideline, owned Club West Indies, a nightclub in the area, and launched the Pama label in 1967. Its initial releases were licensed American soul singles, but the demand for reggae was so obvious that they soon switched Pama's output and opened the company up with a host of reggae-devoted labels: Nu-Beat was the first, starting with their own U K production of the Rudies' 'Train to Vietnam'/'Skaville for Rainbow City', and it was swiftly followed by Unity (mostly Bunny Lee), Gas, Bullet, Escort (largely Harry J), Camel and Success (solely Rupie Edwards).

There were also a number of small companies operating in this big three's wake, some less successful and longer lasting than others, but the only one of significance was Bamboo, a label established in 1969 by Clement Dodd as he was apparently dissatisfied with the way in which his productions were being handled elsewhere. This was the first instance of a Jamaican record man actually setting up his own label for his own productions in Great Britain (Chris Blackwell was never a Jamaican record man in the sense that Dodd was). Coxsone employed U K sound-system operator Junior Lincoln to run things for him, and although it only lasted three years Bamboo did well enough to support two subsidiaries (Banana and Ackee). If for no other reason, the enterprise ought to be remembered for releasing Burning Spear's 'Door Peep' in the U K years before most young British reggae buyers, black or white, had the remotest idea what a dreadlock was.

What set Trojan apart from the pack, though, was Gopthal's determination to woo a mainstream pop crowd. Once he was in charge of the company there was never any confusion as to which market he ought to be servicing with it, although it took him a while to work out how to do it. In fact, it took three tunes to show him exactly the way to go, and while each was a huge pop hit during 1969 the nearest they came to being Trojan records was that one was on an affiliated label. They were Johnny Nash's smooove rocksteady reading of 'You Got Soul' (Top 10 in February); Desmond Dekker's 'Israelites', the first reggae number 1; and Harry J All-Stars' syncopated Winston Wright-organ workout 'The Liquidator' (Top 10 in November), on the Trojan/B&C exclusively Harry Johnson label Harry J. Each proved the value of tailoring releases to fit prospective audiences rather than expecting the crowd to come to you: in other words, while reggae's primary black market expected a genuine Jamaican experience, if a company was looking beyond that then some effort had to be put in, and it wasn't nearly enough just to whack out UK pressings of JA masters. The Johnny Nash song was built on a solid rocksteady core yet was pure pop in its instrumentation and arrangements, thus providing astonishing ease of access for anybody who 'don't like reggae'. Graeme Goodhall at Pyramid had learned about accessibility the hard way when, even after the success of '007 (Shanty Town)' in 1967, the BBC had rejected Desmond Dekker's 'Israelites' on the ground that its poor production quality made airplay impossible. He remixed the song specifically for the radio, but it was a hit only in the clubs until the radio belatedly picked up on it. It shot to the top a mere eight months after it was released. Then, with 'Liquidator', an underground strand of British reggae, skinhead reggae, bubbled to the surface. It had been around for a while, as skinhead clubs and dances took to rocksteady and reggae in the same way in which mod establishments had embraced ska, and had evolved from the smoother sounds of the Techniques and the Paragons into the jerky, quirky quick-stepping rhythms to accompany what's best described as early line-dancing.

Lee Gopthal was far too sharp an individual to miss what was shaping up to become a bona-fide trend. Between them these three records handed him a template – his records needed to be produced/mastered to UK standards; either slickly pop-friendly or of the popping, snapping skinhead variety – and ushered in what would be known as the Trojan explosion; a big bang made official by the British pop chart of 15 November 1969, which featured three Trojan/B&C singles in its Top 20: the Upsetters' 'Return of Django' (number 5), 'Wonderful World, Beautiful People' by Jimmy Cliff (number 7) and 'Liquidator' still hanging in there at number 17. This was the first time reggae had so great a presence in the national listings.

At the end of 1969 Desmond Dekker's total sales had been sufficiently swollen by 'Israelites'' Top 10 follow-up 'It Mek' to have surpassed Cliff Richard's during the year, while Johnny Nash, with 'I Know You Got Soul' and 'Cupid', was also in the ten best-selling male artists' list. The following couple of years were even better, with an enormous proportion of these tunes being on Trojan/B&C labels: Bob & Marcia's 'Young, Gifted and Black' and 'Pied Piper'; Boris Gardiner's 'Elizabethan Reggae'; Nicky Thomas's 'Love of the Common People'; Desmond Dekker's 'You Can Get It If You Really Want'; Jimmy Cliff's 'Wild World'; the Pioneers' 'Long Shot Kick de Bucket' and 'Let Your Yeah Be Yeah'; Greyhound's 'Black and White', 'Moon River' and (as Freddie Notes and the Rudies) 'Montego Bay'; Horace Faith's 'Black Pearl'; Max Romeo's 'Wet Dream' (his own composition, but turned down by John Holt, Derrick Morgan, Roy Shirley and Slim Smith before producer Bunny Lee talked Max into voicing it himself); and Dave & Ansell Collins's 'Double Barrel' and 'Monkey Spanner'. All were Top 20 pop hits, while the more underground skinhead side was throwing up its own lower-profile big sellers, some of which were obvious to the point of being exploitative, others somewhat unexpected: Dandy's 'Reggae in Your Jeggae' and 'Move Your Mule'; Symarip's 'Skinhead Moonstomp'; King Stitt's 'Herbman Shuffle'; Andy Capp's 'Pop-a-Top' and 'The Law'; Derrick Morgan's 'Moon Hop', the Ethiopians' 'The Whip', 'Everything Crash' and 'Reggae Hit the Town'; the Upsetters' 'Clint Eastwood', 'Dry Acid' and 'Live Injection'; the Kingstonians' 'Sufferah'; the Hot Rod

All Stars' 'Skinhead Speaks His Mind'; King Horror's 'Cutting Blade' and 'Loch Ness Monster'; practically anything recorded in Britain by Laurel Aitken; and all of Lloyd Charmers' rude reggae output – often recorded as Lloydie and the Lowbites.

A lot of the skinhead material was UK recorded by relocated Jamaicans: both Laurel Aitken and the Pioneers' Sidney Crooks had settled in London and got busy in the recording studio, while long-term residents Dandy Livingstone, Joe Mansano and Lambert Briscoe all got into record production from different directions – Dandy had been part of the UK Jamaican music business since he was a kid, Mansano ran a record shop and Briscoe operated the Hot Rod sound system. British-based performers included Dandy and Laurel Aitken, Tony Tribe ('Red Red Wine'), the Rudies/Greyhound, Rico Rodriguez, Owen Grey, King Horror, Nicky Thomas, the Mohawks and numerous 'all stars' and one-hit wonders. The vast majority of the chart successes, though, originated in Jamaica, and became thoroughly Anglicized as remixes and strings knocked off the sharp edges and grafted on a radio-friendly melody. Such practice was something Lee Gopthal had learned very quickly since taking over as chairman, when he realized the whole vibe of mainstream reggae had to maintain a certain exoticism while remaining as un-alien as possible – hence the growing obsession with cover versions of existing or recent pop hits. Artists would frequently comment on how their British releases sounded different, but they couldn't do anything about it because in most cases the licensee bought the right to remaster, remix, or practically re-record. Producers soon got wise to this and would send over the vocals with nothing more than basic rhythm tracks so that the British companies could add all the orchestration they wanted.

And it proved a necessity as far as pop success went because Pama, which at this point rarely 'stringsed-up' anything it brought over, had proportionately far less mainstream accomplishment. Of the previous list of reggae chart hits, only one is Pama, the rest are Trojan/B&C. A clear example comes with Harry J's production of Bob & Marcia covering Nina Simone's

'Young, Gifted and Black': Harry J leased the same tune to both Pama and Trojan, Pama put it out as Harry supplied it and Trojan added a full orchestra – the latter was a Top 5 hit and hardly anybody, probably not even Bob & Marcia, are so much as aware of the former. The Palmer brothers seemed to compound their apparently dismissive attitude towards the mainstream with the graphic for their Punch label, depicting a black fist punching through a printed pop chart. Such an uncompromising approach tended to be balanced by a lot of the spikier skinhead stuff doing well for Pama and its subsidiary labels, while at the same time the company enjoyed relatively greater success in the black market. After all, Pama may have flopped with 'Young, Gifted and Black', but we should be thanking them for 'The Horse' by Theo Beckford, Pat Kelly's 'How Long Will It Take' and Lester Sterling's 'Bangarang'. While some say this was a fierce nationalistic pride on the part of the Palmers, an equally forceful argument has it that they were simply too mean to invest in orchestration. And the latter might just hold sway, for when the bottom was dropping out of the white UK reggae market – in 1972 – Pama resorted to stringsing up in a seemingly desperate attempt to boost flagging sales, but by then it was too late to cash in and too wrong for the emerging next phase.

That's a couple of years away yet, though. Between 1968 and 1972, the British reggae scene flourished to the extent that far more of the music was sold in the UK than in Jamaica during that period. During 1970 alone, Trojan/B&C released 500 singles, on over thirty different labels, with total sales of over 2 million, and Pama's dozen or so labels put out 300 selling roughly the same amount. Albums remained strictly collections of singles, with Trojan's now-legendary *Tighten Up* series being the case in point. They did try with a couple of single-artist albums but after they failed to make any impact, the company spent time and money researching what their market might want, and the response was cut-price recent hit compilations. It's a trend that continues to this day as practically the only way to sell long-playing reggae, but back in 1969 the *Tighten Up* albums sparked one of the most memorable facets of the era. Following suit by retailing at 14s 6d or 19s 6d (seventy-three and ninety-eight pence, respectively), *Club Reggae*, *This Is Reggae*, *Reggae Hits*, *Straighten Up* (Pama's answer to *Tighten Up*, with sleeves tacky enough to make Trojan's lewd efforts look classy), *Reggae Jamaica* and *Reggae Chartbusters* all became multi-volume series, cutting across the companies' different labels and producers to deliver the best-value reggae imaginable. Indeed, the first *Tighten Up* releases proved so popular (volume II went Top 5 in the mainstream listings) that they prompted pop-record companies to complain to the chart compilers about an unfair advantage, and as a result budget-priced albums were excluded from the 'proper' LP charts.

Of course, the commercial potential of the British reggae market wasn't going to be ignored in Jamaica for too long, yet it affected the music industry in a number of complicated ways. First, it became yet another bone of contention between the island's musical community and the government. Also, looking *a foreign* separated the ambitious from the not-so-ambitious, because having to address new demands meant making changes.

Derrick Harriott enjoyed a particularly purple patch during this period, with underground UK hits as a performer on Island and as a producer and bandleader on Pama and Trojan, the latter being where he had two labels, Songbird and Explosion, each for some time dedicated to his output. Derrick's spaghetti-western series of Crystalites instrumentals – the *Undertaker* songs – were skinhead favourites along with Lee Perry's cowboy classics 'Django', 'Clint Eastwood', 'Van Cleef' etc. His own naturally soulful alto was also very well received covering Motown songs, and with the Kingstonians' 'Sufferah', 'Singer Man' and 'Good Ambition' he produced some of the very few records that were equally revered by both black and white audiences. But it's from an understandably Jamaican point of view that he looks back on that UK reggae boom:

'There was an *enormous* value in exporting music. We all knew that, and anybody who could do a deal for their productions in

England did. Naturally, the people who travelled there the most – like myself, Prince Buster, Bunny Lee – did best out of it, but it should be said that we, the music people in Jamaica, initiated it. The only reason reggae got anywhere in Britain was because there was a big Jamaican community to give it a start and through little importers and tiny shops the records were getting over there. Even when it started to take off the government never backed the music, which they should've done for such a valuable commodity, but they never came all out and said it was a valuable export. Since Byron Lee at the World's Fair there's been no official backing to get reggae exported. Which meant it was a frustrating time for us because all we could do was hope that something would break big enough to get into the national chart. Quite a few did – Bob & Marcia, Nicky Thomas, particularly – and the way we saw it was that if those few can carry the music out then everybody will benefit from it.

'It was important to us to start selling in England, and this is without thinking it could get such wide success; this is when the only potential we thinking about is the Jamaican community. You see the market became saturated in Jamaica by the end of the 1960s, in other words there was *a lot of* artists recording. People was coming from *everywhere* to get a recording deal, you turn up at the studio or you try to leave your house and here's a queue of guys, "Please Mr Harriott, mi beg you listen to mi tune." It was more than the audience could really stand, because before, in the rocksteady era, it was possible to sell maybe fifty thousand or over of a recording, then jus' a few years later you found that it drop to about ten or fifteen thousand because there was so much more choice.

'This affect the radio play, too. We still wasn't getting all that we should've done, but now there were so many recordings going to the radio stations every week that they didn't know where to start. There was no way they could listen to them all to decide which ones should go on the air, so they just ignore so many of them and a lot of good tunes got lost. As strong as the sound systems was, by that time it was airplay that counted because there was now a lot more radios in Jamaica so that was how you'd reach the people who never went to the dance. Also, they'd announce your record properly on the air so if people wanted to buy it they knew what to ask for – sound-system deejays are very reluctant to announce anything that they hadn't release themselves.

'So naturally people started looking for other places to sell records, and the English market was the biggest. At first it was the same stuff selling over there as was over here, but once it gone wide and we see what the white English people are buying, we can do that for them. We'd push records to companies like Trojan and Pama, which pushed them to getting so big. It opened up the market with all of the labels they had and made sure there is a good supply of releases. It's the way we do it in Jamaica and how we thought that it should be done in England. Otherwise you lose the excitement of new records playing in the dance – everybody loves that. People were either making the more soulful stuff because it would be better accepted there, or the instrumentals that was very popular, or the cover versions of songs that had been English hits could always find another market when they were done as reggae. Then we was sending over tapes for remixing specifically for the English market. Especially for an English release they'd kind of smooth out the bumps from the productions, maybe adjust the tempo a little bit and add strings to give the whole thing an orchestral arrangement. And if you knew that was going to happen, the tapes you sent over were recorded specially to take that in.

'It made a big difference to how a lot of producers survived, if they could sell records in England or not. It didn't mean we was getting very rich, but it meant you could go on recording more artists in Jamaica or you could upgrade your studio or something. It give the whole industry a boost, which filtered right down to the new artists coming up.

'Also, once the music have success abroad you get that spread, where certain people at home who didn't used to recognize it started to recognize it. In that era, what they used to say was the uptown people made out they never paid the music any mind but what they were doing was, when they go home at evenings after work, they would lock up in their room and dance the reggae. *This was factual*, they'd only do it behind lock and key. They figure "Well boy, I wouldn't be seen glorifying *that* type of music." They would want you to know they wanted something more sophisticated, but once the English people like it that made it all right. Also, it was that plush, what they call decent, sorta reggae that was doing well in England that got accepted uptown here – the Boris Gardiner, the Byron Lee, which meant you then had the uptown reggae and the down-town reggae. So the English success help to break down some barriers in that way.'

Deliberately aiming tunes at the UK market was nothing new – Prince Buster and Jimmy Cliff, both of whom spent a lot of time in Britain, had been doing it for years – but a far more obvious example came out around this time. Never mind tampering with tempos, mucking about with mixes or stirring in the strings after the event, Nicky Thomas's Top 10 hit 'Love of the Common People' blatantly began life with one eye on England. Produced by Joe Gibbs, it was written and recorded in Kingston (it's a cover of an original by the Winstons), yet check the lyrics: *trying to keep your hands warm . . . it's a good thing you don't have bus fare* / *it would fall through the hole in your pocket and you'd lose it in the snow on the ground . . .* On a Caribbean island? Noticeably, when the Wailers cut their ver-sion of Irving Berlin's 'White Christmas' for Studio One in the early 1960s with little regard for potential European sales, Peter Tosh altered the lyric to *I'm dreaming of a white Christmas* / Not *like the ones we used to know . . .*

Performers were as keen as producers on the UK connection, too, because a hit over there gave them the chance to tour and do a lot more live work than they might do in Jamaica; which is, after all, what they got into it for – to sing on stage in front of a crowd. Also, the opportunity to earn more money than they were likely to get from just cutting tunes for session rates was never to be sniffed at. And, fairly importantly to guys who had imagined their futures to be confined to Jamaica – or maybe even to Kingston – it was an adventure. Just to go to Britain was to have something to talk about for ages afterwards; it offered the chance to broaden their horizons both musically and socially, and several artists – Desmond Dekker, Nicky Thomas, the Pioneers, Dennis Alcapone among them – were so taken with what they found that they settled in England on the back of their success.

Dave Barker was one who came to live in London, and he remembers his first British tour with none of the seen-it-all, done-it-all of many of his countrymen. While it's fairly standard for old-time reggae artists to tell you that because they were stars at home, playing dates in England was *no big t'ing*, Dave was seriously impressed and somewhat thankful to be playing to crowds other than Kingston's notoriously hard-faced fans. But he's under no illusion about the 'glamour' of being on the road overseas; in fact, his tales of what went on come over as one more way for the producers to take advantage of their artists, and provide a chilling example of how some record men perceived the status quo.

'Winston Riley got us all together, like a general with him troops, draw himself up real important like and told us, "Gentlemen, we are going to England for six to eight months. 'Double Barrel' has hit the number one slot, and you guys don't have to worry about anything . . . food, clothes, lovely place to stay . . . and anywhere money is concerned, every man will be well off." Winston promised us *the world* when we do that tour. Because he badly wants us to do it as it's important to him that the records do well there. When we came here though it was a different matter.

'As far as being on *Top of the Pops* and being the British number 1 single, I could not believe all this was happening to me so quick and so fast. It took me totally by surprise, I was happy. You start to think, well, Winston Riley going to treat me fairly, so I can be able to build my family a home and do what any sensible thinking man would do as far as his family is concerned. We toured all over England, we used to do roughly three shows per night and we had to rush directly from one to the next one. At first we didn't have our own band, it was me, Ansell, Bobby Davis from the Sensations who did harmony vocals, and a bass player, Rod Bryant, who played with Jimmy Cliff's band. The rest of the guys we pick up in the UK, some of the guys were from Grenada, the drummer and guitarist and t'ing. It was a rush to do that first *Top of the Pops*, and as soon as we'd done it Winston went home and brought over Jackie Parris, who was also part of the Sensations' group, as drummer, and also a different bass player, and we became a team because we were here for roughly eight months.

'The crowds on that tour were amazing. Mostly young kids, teenagers who were *wild*. I was really surprised coming off stage and dashing to the changing room that once you got there you weren't allowed to change your clothes in peace, because of kids from the audience trying to get to you in there. Of course we had to move fast to dash out in the cold, because mostly we had to go to another show, and these kids is trying to grab your clothing and your skin and trying to get at you and they're *screaming*.

'It still make me smile today that it was so many white people into reggae like that. [Dave starts chuckling warmly.] I was amazed. And again to see them get so wild where the music is concerned, it made me have to step back and check what is actually happening. I never believed for one minute that the English people could love the music so much. Because as far as I was concerned, before I came here in England, I have somehow maintained that these people would be sitting here and liking the Beatles and Engelbert Humperdinck and Tom Jones, strictly them sort of stuffs. I was really surprised when I came here to see how the halls and clubs dem *packed with so much English people*. Everything and everywhere we go the places was just busting with sheer excitement. These people, they pile up backstage and *they are telling me* about my life. Telling me the producers I recorded for, Harry J, Coxsone, Duke Reid, Lee Scratch Perry, Striker Lee, and I'm saying how come you know so much? It was amazing.

'Even now, even after all these years, I'm still amazed because when I venture on the Continent – I first went to Germany in about 1996 – and when the MC called me out on stage and I came out and said '*This iiiiiis, upsetting . . .*' I couldn't believe it. They went wild. The people them jump on the stage and some of them even start peeling off them clothes . . . Crazy. And when I came off stage I could feel them trying to grab me and all I could hear was More! More! More! More! It gave me a wonderful feeling. And I'm saying, even though you might have been robbed, at times you feel you haven't achieved anything where this music is concerned, it seems like you haven't really done anything. When that is actually happening it shows you have people that appreciate your works.

'It was so much better than the crowds in Jamaica. *Serious.* Down there, the only way you know you've done OK is when they don't actually boo you. Even you get to thinking that the booing by itself isn't too bad, because at times they would boo *and* they would fling bottle and stone and everything. And sometimes it was nothing you'd done, but down to the promoter or some other such t'ing. I remember, when U-Roy, the great U-Roy, was supposed to do a show up in the country, but he wasn't there, either I think he was fully booked up, or the promoter trying to be slick, because that used to happen all the time, promoters advertising artists they weren't putting on – sometimes you have U-Roy being advertised as playing six different shows at the same time. So Lee Perry and his band the Upsetters took that slot, to which I was the vocalist – the featured artist. We went on stage in the country and the MC came out and said to the crowd, "Ladies and gentlemen, all the way from Kingston, Lee Perry and the Upsetter band with the famous Dave Barker." When I came on stage I heard a few o' them country man down in the front kiss dem teeth and seh "Mi don' waan no Dave Barker . . . U-Roy . . . where U-Roy?" and believe me, Carlton, and his brother Family Man, the Upsetters band, had to leave the stage, because so much bricks and bottle started to come our way. We actually had to dive off stage. Carlton had to dive behind his drum set when a brick just miss his face. So the booing wasn't too bad.

'Touring in England then was very exciting, and I enjoyed it very much because it was such an experience to a young man like I was then, who had never left Jamaica. But in the end everything turned out very nasty and sour because I didn't ever think we got what we deserved. Me and Winston Riley even had big arguments because we were touring all over England and it was the same one stage outfit he bought us that we have to keep wearing all over the place in. I can remember one night we were doing our show and I was feeling pretty good so I was putting my utmost into my dancing and singing. There was some one person who followed us from show after show after show and he was in the front and he shout out from in the audience, "Dave be careful now! Don't forget it only the one suit you've got." And that finish me . . . I feel so embarrassed, and when I got backstage me and Winston Riley had one big argument. It almost came to blows, because I had to make him know "Look man, I not going back on stage unless you mek me have some decent garb." Which that is how him give me one thousand pounds – the only reason.

'The producers were all well aware of the English market and looking towards it. Any sensible producer would want to start thinking that way, then them coming here opened their eyes to how vast this thing could be. Sorry to say, they would come back home to Jamaica and put the artist in the studio or take the music off the artist – who has already paid for his own recording, studio fees, musicians, everything – promise the artist a whole heap of crap, come here, and go to various major companies and totally and completely sell out. They would get quite a nice change and then used to come back home and make the artist feel as if nothing really went on here.

'Of course you had relatives and friends who would be telling you that your record is big in England, but there was nothing you could actually do about it. If you tried to do anything about it, most time it ended up in fist-fights . . . knife . . . gun or a whole heapa threats. And we didn't know the runnings, we wasn't used to this copyright thing from back home. I was naïve to performing to Performing Rights, MCPS, and nobody told me about these things. So even if you had a family member here who took your interest at heart and told you about it, there was so much crap you had to go through to attain some sort of recompense. What most of the artist would do at times like this was to go, "Oh eff it", just leave it and go and record somewhere else. Because they still have the way of thinking that said if you want more money you got to record more song. Also, they don't want to fall out too badly with the bigtime producers who are looking to make a lot of records.'

By the second half of the decade, the British attitude towards black immigrants had both softened and hardened. At surface level, things seemed better than they did ten years previously as the outright hostilities that had sparked the race riots were no longer tolerated across much of the white working class. The word 'working' is the key here, because as the country as a whole headed for a boom, black and white guys worked side by side and similarities became at least as apparent as differences. They lived on the same streets, their kids went to the same schools, their wives shopped in the same markets, so a certain camaraderie, and in many cases genuine friendship, was bound to occur. Probably born more out of tolerance than affection, it nonetheless made life a lot more bearable as both sides gained an enormous amount.

Oddly, the skinhead/pop reggae thing is far from a vivid illustration of how this alliance was working. Although, superficially, the fact that large numbers of white kids were into reggae indicates racial harmony, the reality was that the two reggae scenes, though never openly hostile, wouldn't be caught dead in each other's company. While reggae's mainstream success brought some money into West Kingston and increased opportunities both at home and abroad, it also meant more specialist outlets and devoted rack space in regular high-street record shops, allowing a great deal of the music to reach Britain's black population. However, such music didn't overlap with what the white kids would be grooving to nearly as far as might be imagined. Sure, most Jamaicans would show solidarity with the big specifically crafted pop/reggae hits, as they were infinitely more agreeable to them than what was normally on *Top of the Pops*, and gave cause for a certain nationalistic chest-swelling. But what was being played on the sound systems and bought by the black crowd was pretty much the same as what was going down across the Atlantic – the sound systems were saturated with original cuts of the Wailers, Pat Kelly, U-Roy, Justin Hinds and the Dominoes, the Heptones; and crossover, as with acts such as the Pioneers, the Melodians or the Upsetters, regardless of remixing, was usually one-way traffic from the sound systems to the mainstream. Clubs and dances enjoyed a large degree of social separation, too, and although there were a few black kids who hung out with skinheads, it was very rare to see a white guy in a blues dance. There was a joke cracked about the Bluesville dancehall in north London's Wood Green – a white guy would have to know a lot of people to get in, but he'd have to know *everybody* to get out. This was just the way things were – it wasn't a problem for anybody, and it would be doing a great disservice to a lot of white people to imply that the pop reggae boom didn't do its bit for racial harmony.

Yet familiarity had removed a lot of the suspicion and fear that manifested itself as everyday, street-level racism. Also contributing to this more mellow situation was the fact that the *Windrush* generation were, for the most part, still of the mind they were only in the mother country temporarily and would be going home as soon as they'd stuffed their pockets. Hence the British Way of Life was not perceived as being in permanent jeopardy. As a consequence, there was little politicization of black people: trade-union involvement, other than as a member, was rare, there were few black councillors, mayors or prominent political figures – David Pitt, later Lord Pitt of Hampstead being a notable exception – while black organizations tended to be island-based and more social than anything else.

On the parliamentary political side, things were slightly more complicated. Race had been on both main parties' agendas all decade, with the Labour Party in power and seeking both to be perceived as good socialists when it came to Commonwealth immigrants and to appease what it felt were the fears and prejudices of traditionally working-class Labour voters. So while the Rent Act and the Race Relations Act went some way to easing the discomforts of a decade earlier, the same government also passed the Commonwealth Immigrants Act, severely restricting right of entry. Remarkably, the Labour Party's whole approach to race was almost totally misguided, because it was based on the previous Conservative government's attitudes. Pity they never bothered to consult their constituents, when they might have discovered that, at the end of the 1960s, the British working people weren't quite as obsessed by race as the politicians. Enoch Powell's so-called 'Rivers of Blood' speech exemplifies this. Delivered in 1967, he evoked images of a race war as he melodramatically quoted Ovid – 'I seem to see the River Tiber foaming with much blood' – but as a piece of rabble-rousing his words had little effect. Over thirty years later, many politicians (or would-be politicians) still refer to them in some kind of awe, but at the time, while they caused uproar in the House, in the media and in a few TV sitcoms, the biggest examples of 'popular' support were marches by a handful of East End dockers, Smithfield porters and Midlands factory workers. Most ordinary white people were actually a bit embarrassed by the speech.

The real downside of this political obsession with race was a dense residue of institutional racism which pervaded the United Kingdom. It was a ticking time bomb for a generation of black kids born and/or educated in the UK. They were supposed to do better than their mums and dads, and were about to put themselves on the white-collar job market, having been advised at school that they should view themselves as British and at home that once they had an education doors would swing smoothly open. We'll see how that went off later in the book, but the plot continues here with a look at the BBC, arguably the most prominent face of institutionalized racism at the time.

In spite of reggae records selling in their hundreds of thousands, and the music being a clear choice of large numbers of

British citizens, more white than black, the BBC did its best to pretend it didn't exist. Nothing had improved since the Blue Beat era when Siggy Jackson had to take sales figures to the BBC. 'Double Barrel' had received only thirty-three radio airings before it was a hit, but even that represents something approaching airwave saturation compared with the usual treatment for Trojan and Pama records. One of the important reasons both companies launched so many different record labels was because it was standard practice for reggae records delivered to Broadcasting House to be dumped in a box at reception while regular pop and rock stuff was taken straight through to the producers it was addressed to. The idea then was to sneak a few through that weren't on instantly recognizable labels and hope that somebody in a show's office actually liked them. The standard excuse for any blanket dismissal of reggae was that the demand was too low to warrant consideration – something the major distributors and retailers would have argued with. Another 'reason' was that the records were underproduced, or not up to BBC broadcast standard; again this was nonsensical since many of those records were made, or at the least finished off with full orchestration, in the UK. Then there was the 'doesn't fit in with the playlist' argument. More nonsense. Tunes like 'Black Pearl' or 'Moon River' were as swish and as accessible as practically anything on Tamla Motown. Strangely, the lamentable, audibly jarring 'Johnny Reggae' by the Piglets (aka English broadcaster and pop record producer Jonathan King) apparently fitted in just fine.

There are stories of Trojan's in-house plugger – whose job it was to convince radio producers to playlist his employer's records – literally having office doors slammed in his face or being forced to wait in reception, then having to intercept producers as they hurried from the lifts out into Portland Place. Apparently, trying to do business with the BBC was such a frustrating experience that he left Broadcasting House in tears on more than one occasion.

Once reggae records were in the charts and presenters had no choice but to play them it was usually an excuse to abuse them. Tony Blackburn – who years later admitted the error of his ways, but never explained why he did it – was the worst offender: he'd lose no opportunity to denounce reggae as not being real music; he'd take records off half-way through because, as he'd theatrically explain, he'd had enough of them; or, if it was a cover, he'd play the pop cut immediately afterwards and glowingly hold it up against the reggae version. In 1970, Nicky Thomas even wrote and recorded a song called 'BBC', which took as its subject matter the Corporation's shameful treatment of reggae both on and off the airwaves. And no, it didn't get playlisted.

The press was just as bad, seeming perpetually to rubbish reggae – 'you can't understand the words' was standard fare, as were 'primitive' and 'all sounds the same'. Reggae artists on *Top of the Pops* invariably attracted 'Top of the Flops' headlines, while one paper went so far as to describe it as 'a brand of music that made many of us wince'. And the music press were usually less than accommodating. Among its derogatory reviews the *Melody Maker* once went to such lengths as to round up a bunch of progressive rock stars to denounce the music as 'black music being prostituted' (the Edgar Broughton Band) and 'kind of monotonous' (Deep Purple's Ian Gillan). In 1970, just as the reggae boom was about to peak, the same paper also put together a feature which quoted Desmond Dekker, Jimmy Cliff and Horace Faith as saying, respectively, 'I sing reggae because people pay to hear it . . . I want to progress,' 'I won't be doing any more reggae . . . the big reggae boom is over,' and 'If ever I did reggae again it would have to be darned good reggae and there's not much of that round. It's such a blank type of music.'

Eventually, Trojan and Pama got round to petitioning the BBC along more official channels, and reminding them that they too were licence-fee payers, as were the multitudes who bought their records. Just as Blue Beat used to, they presented fat files of evidence of how much product they shifted and what large swathes of the public thought about it. It may have helped their cause that the Beat & Commercial empire now stretched as far as the progressive rock label Charisma, but the results were hardly ideal: the BBC created a dedicated reggae slot on its local Radio London station and did its best to confine the music to this ghetto. This did little to help the record companies – and to be fair the BBC had no particular obligation to do so – but neither did it advance reggae as part of the now multi-cultural UK's pop mainstream. It wasn't available to anybody who lived outside the station's small range, and it prevented reggae's record companies or supporters from complaining that they were being ignored as the Corporation could now draw reference to this special spot.

Not that this was as crucial as it might have been at another time, because by the end of 1971 the pop reggae boom was all but over.

By 1972 glam rock was booming in the UK and the platform-soled likes of Slade, Gary Glitter and T-Rex were danceable enough to provide the white working class with a Saturday-night soundtrack. And, unlike reggae, with its skinhead associations, glam rock had no problem going universal. (Slade began life as a skinhead band, but quickly realized on which side their bread was buttered.) Greyhound had a big hit with 'Moon River' that year, but that was really nothing more than a death rattle. True, Trojan were back at number 1 for four weeks in 1974 with Ken Boothe's 'Everything I Own', a massive sound-system hit from about a year previously, and John Holt's 'Help Me Make It Through the Night' was in the Top 20 in January the next year, but by then the company was in dire straits. Musik City shops had been closing since 1973, and by the time of the John Holt hit B&C was just months away from being sold. Likewise, the Palmer brothers pulled in their horns when it came to releasing music, and by 1974 had evolved the company into what it is today: Jet Star Phonographics, the UK's leading reggae distributor.

Reggae in Britain and Jamaica was literally reinventing itself around this time, and neither Lee Gopthal or the Palmers had what it took to get up to speed. They weren't record men, they were salesmen who sold to a particular market and flapped around like fish out of water when that market moved on. They weren't that interested in reggae as an organic, evolving state of affairs.

Once Gopthal's pop/skinhead audience grew tired of reggae – which they were bound to do as it was a fashion item like their braces and half-mast trousers, not a way of life – he had no Plan B. In spite of Trojan dipping a toe into roots – with 'Screaming Target', 'Beat Down Babylon' and 'Ital Dub', for example – its boss had so little understanding of the music that he didn't really know how to market it. There was a new wave of producers and label owners in Jamaica with whom he'd have to open negotiations, and the channels for selling a large amount of reggae to a black audience that he had helped to put in place, in terms of both record labels and retail operations, meant that the new generation no longer needed Trojan. Furthermore, a couple of the major labels had noticed that reggae was now an attractive proposition – Chris Blackwell's Island among them.

Pama seemed even more confused. Not only had the label started stringsing up much too late, it also didn't seem to want to touch roots reggae with a barge pole. This may seem surprising given Pama's apparent attitude towards pop music and the fact that it seemed to be far more aware of the black market, but it isn't at all unlikely when Jamaican snobbery is taken into account. Three made-good-for-themselves Jamaicans, *inna Hinglan'* no less, dealing with that Jah Jah business? You must be joking.

But whatever the reasons for Pama and Trojan going no further as reggae record companies, they couldn't have stopped at a less-opportune time. They had done all the hard work and set up so much of the UK reggae industry; now they were about to miss out on its most creative, potentially lucrative and exciting phase.

Part Three

Studio Kinda Cloudy

'The people had enough of pure *dibidibidabidooo*, they couldn't take it any more without some sort of alternative that represent how they feel. That's where myself and the new generation of deejays, younger guys, came in because we could really see where it should be coming from. And on the sound systems we are close to the people, much closer than how so many of the big record producers had become by then, so while the whole deejay thing was still *chick-a-bow*, we realize that the music we possess is a music of teaching. It was an urban, spiritual, cultural concept that we come with.' / Big Youth

12

Pressure Drop

There had been an economic boom in Jamaica during the first half a dozen years of independence. The island's bauxite industry was then the most productive in the world, responsible for 21 per cent of the mineral's global total, and the number of tourists wanting to be accommodated on the island was rising on an almost daily basis. But little of this wealth was actually getting downtown. Just as it had been under colonial rule, a few top-ranking civil servants and company directors were doing very well, as were a rapidly increasing number of overseas-based multinational corporations, but other than that, this new money meant nothing except on paper. Back in the real world, so little of it was getting through to the public at large that it remained theoretical.

During the five years following independence, the right-wing Jamaican Labour Party had based their economic strategy on what was going on in Puerto Rico, whereby the tactlessly named Operation Bootstrap encouraged that country's entrepreneurs to seek limited overseas investment to put them back on their feet. A kind of partnership deal that brought in foreign capital, but limited it to no more than was needed to give Puerto Rican business and farming the boost it needed to get started. This arrangement translated to the Jamaican government without the partnership angle, so throwing open the doors for American corporations to come in and get on with it. Which they did, with great gusto. The result was a resource-sapping equation that increased Jamaica's economic reliance whilst cash was sucked up and out across the Gulf of Mexico. More help yourself than self-help.

Although it was to get far worse within ten years, the situation as Jamaica approached the 1970s was grimmer than it had been at any time post-independence. The country had never fully recovered from the food shortages and agricultural devastation brought about by the hurricane that had swept through in 1963; there had been little government aid to replace crops, and since then large amounts of arable land had been sold off for development. The high proportion of food and consumer necessities now being imported left the people very vulnerable to exchange-rate fluctuations, hence a double-figure inflation rate. Jamaica's social-welfare system, once the pride of the Caribbean, was becoming overstretched and underfinanced, with less being spent to cope with more prospective recipients. The effect of so much skilled labour going abroad was also now being felt, as vacancies for Jamaicans existed among the trades while the national unemployment rate stood at just over 20 per cent. This statistic became even bleaker if you were young – in 1969 the Doxey Report, an officially sponsored investigation into the island's social and economic conditions, stated that 'many young persons will pass through the greater part of their lives having never been regularly employed'.

To go with all this, the rank-and-file were being fed the government-approved version of black consciousness. It's hardly surprising that, from an official point of view, a large proportion of it went down the wrong way.

Earlier, we touched on the government's efforts to dictate the flow of revolutionary ideas with their enthusiastic endorsement of Jamaica's black heritage, but by the end of the 1960s it was a plan that was plainly never going to work. What it did, as it spread that particular word more or less universally, wasn't simply to rouse a sleeping giant but to keep poking him with a stick until he was mad as hell and not going to take any more. Giving people a confidence and a contentiousness they hadn't had much of before made those same people begin to ask questions and to demand response. Response that was too slow in coming. Also, the post-colonial intelligentsia – young, open-minded and largely left-wing – that now made up a fully fledged tier of Jamaica's social wedding cake were becoming as dissatisfied as the sufferahs. But they were making themselves heard far more effectively. As the rioting, civil unrest and media protests that followed the banning of Walter Rodney persisted so long after the event, it reached a point at which the exclusion order began to look like an excuse for the population to make felt far deeper feelings. An uptown/downtown alliance of college students and ghetto folk called for an end to foreign investment, for the nationalization of certain key industries and for the black majority to have proportional representation when it came to government and the economy.

As you'd expect, such widespread discontent was reflected in the music of the day. Spin the Ethiopians' 'Everything Crash', which chronicles the strikes of the time and then makes the observation, *What go bad a morning / Can't come good a evening / Everyday carry bucket to the well / One day the bottom must drop out / Everything crash*, and it's easy to get a handle on what was going on in the country. It's a tune most likely written and recorded before the Rodney incident, and it went on to become the third best selling record in Jamaica in 1968. Really, though, it's just the sharp end of a wedge that included Desmond Dekker's 'Israelites', Carlton and his Shoes' 'Happy Land', the Abyssinians' 'Declaration of Rights', the Maytals' 'Pressure Drop', the Joe Higgs-penned 'Steppin' Razor' which became Peter Tosh's theme tune and Prince Buster's 'Doctor Rodney', which, straight and to the point, took the government to task over the exclusion order. These were records which marked the overture to one of the most fertile and widely appreciated phases in Jamaican music's history: roots reggae.

Although social commentary songs had been a part of Jamaican popular music from the very first recordings, with the arrival of the 1970s came a sense of purpose about the music business that manifested itself in both the quantity and intensity of such material. And, in spite of the above-mentioned records all doing very well during 1968 and 1969, not until two or three years after the wave of disgruntlement brought about by the banning of Walter Rodney did musical protest gain any real momentum. This distinct delay wasn't because conditions in Jamaica had suddenly got better – if anything things were turning down even further as the now articulately expressed pro-nationalization mood was being perceived off-island as being anti-foreigner and therefore spreading ripples of alarm abroad. Outside investment was starting to dry up, meaning that subsidized imports were diminishing, which in turn adversely influenced employment opportunities and the prices of consumer goods and food. The effect was largely felt by ghetto folk, to the degree that malnutrition among Kingston's poor – children *and* adults – had reached alarming levels. No, the reason why the new reggae scene was relatively slow in voicing the people's frustration was because it had been doing very nicely, thank you.

By the end of the 1960s, the music business was one of the few industries to buck several of Jamaica's gloomy economic trends. Those huge sales figures for records in England meant reggae was one of the country's very few growth industries; also it was one of an even smaller number of totally homegrown, Jamaican-owned export businesses; and, no doubt, the single example of one that was having a direct positive effect on life in the ghetto, as even though most artists weren't being paid but a fraction of their entitlements – more of which later – the overall effect gave the whole scene a boost. It's one more mark of a government cutting off its nose to spite its face that it didn't get involved, because if officialdom had (a) been able to keep track of the master tapes being sent across the Atlantic or (b) even acknowledged reggae as a Jamaican art form valuable in the world market, the music business could have made quite an impact on the balance of trade for those years. The producers of the day still feel quite justifiably hard done by that, up until then, the only government help the music industry had received was when Byron Lee was taken to the World's Fair in 1964.

Back on the streets of Kingston, the most significant effect of the music's overseas success was that the Jamaican record business was, for the most part, starting to behave like any other international pop-music industry. This wasn't the first time this had happened – Prince Buster had been tailoring singles for British release more than half a decade earlier – but it hadn't happened on this scale before, and as a result reggae's own internal class system had evolved beyond the simple bipolarization of the big influential sound systems and the rest. By the end of the 1960s, music-scene status was defined in terms of overseas associations. The new aristocrats were those with both the JA-respect-due background and the serious UK connections, which in this case meant, naturally, Coxsone Dodd and Duke Reid (although his star was starting to wane as reggae superseded rocksteady), closely followed by Bunny Lee, Joe Gibbs, Harry J, Derrick Harriott, Leslie Kong (until his death in 1971) and Lee Perry. Each of these men had at least one English record label dedicated to their productions and most had already enjoyed a sizeable UK pop hit. Just below them in the pecking order were the comers, young guys – or men new to the control-room side of the studio – who had to rely on innovation instead of reputation, yet were advanced and focused enough to be looking towards the big market *a foreign*: Herman Chin Loy, Harry Mudie, Rupie Edwards and Winston Riley, for instance.

Naturally, the big boys called the shots, and there was no way these top-deck producers were going to so much as peek inside their gift horses' mouths, let alone attempt to reinvent reggae at the turn of the decade, which would have been equivalent to punching the nags' teeth out. Hence they were quite happy to serve up more of the same, so during the late 1960s and for a couple of years into the next decade they stuck with smoooove soul music-type singles, bouncy cover versions of American or British hits, post-rocksteady serious-style grooves and the jerkily uptempo, deceptively simple struts (rude lyrics, or even lyrics, optional). For the most part, a record's appeal began in Jamaica, moved to the Caribbean communities of the UK metropolises and then, just maybe, out to the British mainstream. As this carried on making a (relatively) large amount of money for those responsible, the second-row record men tucked themselves in behind for a piece of the action.

Not much incentive to change. Even less when you consider how uptown these guys were starting to see themselves as: while a few protest tunes were always going to be tolerated – maybe even seen as vital to any producer who wanted to appear at one with the people – to advance songs of sufferation as the way forward wasn't what being an international businessman was all about. Besides, as many admit to having reasoned, 'We ought to be giving the people something to take their minds off things, not bringing their tribulations to meet them at the dance.' They sort of had a point there, and it was at the dances that the lack of need for change genuinely made itself felt. On the sound systems – still hugely important to domestic record promotion – crowds weren't yet asking for any form of fluctuation because reggae as it was being served up hadn't been around long enough to go stale, and there was simply so much of it and of such high quality that operators could cherry-pick. Also, what was on offer was sufficiently varied within the style to stay well outside the Kingston crowds' notoriously low boredom threshold, so that complaints or flopped dances were relatively few.

Cast an ear over what was going on at the time to see that reggae's rhythms were supporting a level of innovation impressive even by Kingston's standards. Among Coxsone's lovers' grooves were, courtesy of Jackie Mittoo and the Soul Vendors house band, any amount of organ- or sax-led bubblingly funky instrumentals that displayed the producer's longtime jazz credentials. Lee Perry persistently pitched to the left of centre with his spiky spaghetti-western cuts and a cascade of borderline bonkers Upsetter tunes. Joe Gibbs dabbled in prototype toasting with Count Machuki; as did Duke Reid, to much greater effect, with U-Roy. While Derrick Harriott introduced melody to the deejay style with Scotty's instant-classic Musical Chariot series and Herman Chin Loy brought the Melodica to the melody with Augustus Pablo's embryonic 'East of the River Nile'-style as far back as 1969.

And so it went on for a while, but by the time 1970 had seen itself out two factors came into play at the same time. First, proletariat dissatisfaction was approaching its acme as campaigning for the 1972 general election got under way, with the opposition PNP eager to emphasize all that was wrong with the country, while the JLP took their policies of doing practically nothing for the sufferahs to new levels of indifference. Second, the reggae-as-a-bona-fide-pop-music marriage of convenience – international commerciality and the Kingston studio system – had become a bit too cosy for its own good. Reggae's primary audience, the Jamaican population, was starting to object. But, rather uniquely, it was to the subject matter more than the beat.

Burning Spear is a Rastaman so longtime righteous that when he began his career in 1969 at Studio One, he sung his deep-roots composition 'Door Peeping' as part of his Sunday-afternoon audition for Dodd's right-hand man Leroy Sibbles. When I caught up with him, he was comfortably holed up in a swish London hotel suite during a 1993 UK tour, but there was fire and passion in his voice when he remembered back to over twenty years earlier:

'What happened at the end of the 1960s and into the 1970s, when the reggae music had just come into fashion and was doing so well both in Jamaica and in England, was that so much pure money men had become involved with it. These were the people who was behind the music scene, and they started thinking that by presenting something thinner, something more commercial, to the public they would make more money. Now they're not looking on the whole thing as music, they're looking on the whole thing as *money*, so therefore they're not thinking about how it was that Jamaican music came about from the ska onwards, and what it has always meant. Nobody take the time out to record the things we usually do before then, because although there was always so much love song there was also the original sufferah songs, in their original presentation.

'It's what the Jamaican people have always expected from their music that some consciousness and culture get mixed in with the nice-up stuff. Not all of it at a dance, but there must be some.

'There was politics involved, too. Some kinda behind-the-scenes carry-on. Because the situation in Jamaica at the time was getting outta hand; it was almost as if there was a barrier created around the Rasta brethren and sisters or people who sympathize with them in the music business, in order to prevent them presenting what they were doing to the public. I think there was a trick to prevent people from becoming conscious, from thinking properly, and the only thing they could do was to lower the standards of things by stop presenting the conscious side of the music. But they were wrong there, because music like that, that carry a lot of strong vibes, is a strong force to uplift the thoughts and the minds of the people, so you would have more consciousness, less violence and people wouldn't be so ignorant, be so stupid towards each other.

'They forget what music was made for, why it was made. They don't know what is the right thing, what is it the people want. To them the right thing is not music any more, it's a big commercial money-making thing and as a result the record companies start to sign *garbage*. They sign the music carrying no form of quality or education within it or around it. They sign people to let the people become stupid, to become ignorant.

'But this is Jamaica and you know things can't remain that way too long. *The people* know what it is they want, so they themselves go about getting it.'

Which is where the third layer of the island's music-business food-chain comes in.

At the bottom of the ladder – though merely from the point of view of status and not for any lack of talent on offer – were the real ghetto boys. Genuinely young, raw, still on the streets, soaking up the sufferah vibe and not yet trying to filter anything out. *The international market?* These artful dodgers of the drum 'n' bass were more concerned with knocking out a few copies on North Parade or checking how the crowd reacted at a Beat Street sound clash. Step forward Keith Hudson, Winston 'Niney' Holness, Glen Brown and Gussie Clarke. Most importantly, these were guys who had grown up in poverty, could see what was happening in the streets around them and had heard tunes that not only dealt with the reality of life – the Melodians' 'Rivers of Babylon' or Jimmy Cliff's 'Hard Road to Travel' – but copped an attitude about it *à la* 'Belly Full' and 'Duppy Conqueror' by the Wailers, or the Maytals '54-46'. They were in touch with the country's ordinary people, they had a point to make and knew that the best way to go about it was through music. And if they were aware of industry protocol, they weren't at all bothered about it, and set about mixing militant beats and revolutionary lyrics with the love songs.

There was no shortage of artists or musicians ready to record for these guys, either. Future megastars Johnnie Clarkie, Gregory Isaacs, Burning Spear himself, Big Youth and Junior Byles shared an agenda with the new wave of producers; they wanted to add their protest to what was already going on. Or acts like the Abyssinians, the Wailing Souls, the Ethiopians, Max Romeo and, of course, the Wailers who'd been around for a while but didn't truly find their niche until they could start recording rebel music. And they could do it, too, as the plethora of small studios and tiny, almost personal record labels that had sprouted not only in the capital but in burgs such as Port Antonio, Ocho Rios and Spanish Town had created an alternative, indie-type record business. Indeed, this combination of people who wanted to change having the means by which to bring that change about was revolutionizing the Jamaican music industry. Or was it just going back to how things used to be?

Burning Spear takes up the story once more.

'Although we was up against the establishment it actually wasn't so hard, because by then you didn't have to go to one of the big studios to get your record made or pressed-up. You had a lot more people dealing with that kind of music, and because they work independent of the big operators it became much easier to get your records made – by people that understood what it should be about, too. It was people just like me who was dealing with the music from the studio side of things, so it wasn't no problem to get across what it was you wanted to say. Or you could start your own label if you wanted to. Plenty people did. But mostly you don't need to because there was always somebody else who was fed up with the way things were and had already started one. Y'know, somebody who wanted to see more conscious things out there, so you could leave all the business up to them and get on with writing and singing good decent songs.

'Of course, the sound systems too was playing roots music – it was the sound systems that give roots music the first big push. Because this is no longer about pure money-making or making records that will go straight into the shops or on to the radio, it was just like it always used to be. The sound systems first would get the record, which is how it get to the people, and only after that would it get release. Which is when the radio would pick up on it because it's what people is requesting. The sound systems took the first step with roots music, pushing it before the radio pick up on it. That's how it get *directly* to the people and that's how the ball started rolling. It didn't matter that the radio or even the very big sound systems didn't pay it no mind at first, because there were small operations on practically every street corner – all over Jamaica – who would play that stuff. And the people *flock to it*, because throughout reggae history they've wanted to hear the music that represents them. Reggae has always been their music.

'If it wasn't the time at which there were so many small set-ups – studios, producers, sound systems and shops – then the roots explosion could never have happened. And when it did the people were there waiting for it. Naturally, the sound men would mix it up with other stuff, because there's still the reason to go to the dance for enjoyment. But the dance in Jamaica has always been about more than that, operating on more than one level . . . something that uplifts the spirit as well is very important to Jamaican people in their music. There was nothing else that represent them back then, so when they hear this stuff they take it to their hearts right away. Then once it take off properly it was like any other style of reggae or ska or whatever you call it, the people were eager to see what was coming next, they wanted to hear the latest *now* tunes.'

Spear's notion of how the commercially minded producers

almost totally failed to come to grips with how the Kingston massive felt reggae should be developing is perfectly illustrated by the Abyssinians' milestone single 'Satta Massa Gana', a Rastafari hymn to sufferation that draws deeply on the Bible and is sung in part in the ancient Ethiopian language of Amharic. It was originally recorded for Coxsone Dodd at Studio One in 1969, but the producer simply didn't 'get' it, refused to believe the song had commercial potential and stuck the tape on a shelf to gather dust. Two years later, after the group had started their own label, Clinch, and saved up the ninety pounds Dodd wanted for the tune, they put it out themselves to enjoy an instant and sustained hit.

It also became something of a blueprint for roots reggae in its beautiful combination of conventional Jamaican musical values and an almost pre-slave-ship spirituality. This was a tune with a rich pedigree: backed by bass player Leroy Sibbles leading the Studio One house band, Sibbles also overseeing vocal arrangements as the trio of Donald and Linford Manning and lead singer Bernard Collins harmonized in classic Jamaican style; the deeply emotive yet defiantly militant lyrics, which quoted the Old Testament and were so devoted to Rastafari they frequently lapsed into Amharic; the musical backing was supplemented by traditional Rasta bass, funde and repeater drums; and minor chords were prevalent. Exactly what the people wanted.

Indeed, Burning Spear himself was subject to precisely the same treatment at Studio One – yes, his forceful condemnation of Jamaica's mainstream record business was based on personal experience. He was signed to Dodd's label for five years and recorded material sufficient for several albums, but with negligible success. In 1974, disillusioned with the music business, he departed Brentford Road to return to his birthplace in the hills of St Ann and the life of a rural farmer. Early the following year Spear hooked up with Lawrence Lindo, fledgling record man and owner/operator of the Ocho Rios-based sound system Jack Ruby Hi-Fi. One fatter, rootsier, slower, horn-drenched production job later and Spear's 1975 albums *Marcus Garvey* and

Man in the Hill (containing several rerecordings of tunes from his Studio One days) are roots statements of iconic structure.

Not only upcoming or woodshedding artists took advantage of this situation. Many established singers and players were equally keen to add some rebel music to their repertoires – the Heptones, Horace Andy, Alton Ellis, for instance – and just as many turned to this righteous, almost anti-industry generation of record men simply on the assumption they'd get a better deal.

International reggae had derived a kind of trickle-down system of exploitation as regards monies from overseas sales – many producers were getting seriously exploited by British record companies, and they proceeded to rip off their artists with similar enthusiasm. If a producer even bothered to tell an artist that his song was going to be or had been released in England, the standard agreement was for the artist to receive the Jamaican earnings, the producer those from the rest of the world. Brent Dowe wrote 'Rivers of Babylon' for his vocal group the Melodians, a best-seller in Jamaica which sold an estimated 80,000 in the UK before being covered by Boney M, when it shifted several million more on its way to becoming a worldwide hit. Yet Dowe lives in a modest cinderblock bungalow in the Kingston sub-suburb of Hughenden and drives the sort of car you wouldn't expect the man who wrote one of the best-selling pop songs of all time to be seen dead in. He explains it like this.

'When Mister Les [Leslie Kong, who produced the Melodians' hits of this period] offer you that deal, *of course* you take it. I was young, and I'd never even been to the airport – guys like us didn't even think about the rest of the world. Of course we knew it was there, but when you sitting inna your yard writing a song, you're not thinking about how people in England or Germany or America are going to be interested in it. All you think about is how it sound in your own environment and you hope to earn a few likkle shilling from that. Getting rich and *the worldwide market* just didn't figure in your plans. Remember, it was almost unbelievable to most of us that we were even getting paid for singing, something you used to just do in the road. In fact it *shocked* us when the music take off worldwide like that, that people would want to buy it in England, Germany or America or elsewhere. We were never looking for people to recognize the music in those places.

'When they wanted Boney M to do it, in England, I was paid a sum of money to have Frank Fabian [Boney M's producer] share the writing credit with me. I wasn't given no big big royalty and I know I shoulda made a lot more money out of that song, but remember, none of us knew anything about the music business. There wasn't even anybody to turn to because even people who were there long before we – Bob Marley, Joe Higgs, John Holt – didn't know nothing. We were recording for survival, and you go in, sing your song and come out with a cash . . . like ten pounds. The only time you would get any more money would be if you go up to their place and ask for a lunch money: "Bwoy, t'ings dem bad, I got to get something to eat." Otherwise they feel they didn't owe you nothing. I'm not saying the Jamaican music industry is any different from music industries all over the world – in America, all those acts like Brook Benton, the Tams or Louis Satchmo all get the same rap. They record records and not get no money or just get a small amount of money. Just like us down here. Elvis Presley and the Beatles probably even get rob until they know the runnings. Maybe Mister Les didn't get as good a deal as if he'd been an Englishman.

'It don't depress me. I have no grievances with those producers because that was the way that it was in them days. Duke Reid and Coxsone, I love both of them because they let us eat food and mind our children and live in a house. Otherwise, what else would I have done? That's how so many artists look at it and the producers know that.'

While this is a crash course in sufferation-style pragmatism, the underlying attitude from Brent and others of that era is that artists had known for a long time before then how they were being taken for a ride; previously, though, it had been within the bounds of acceptability. But when friends and relatives in

England informed them how successful their tunes were over there, it became too much to swallow. And as so little of the money made abroad filtered back to the artist, potential English chart placings weren't much of a consideration for anybody who turned up at Randy's or Treasure Isle or Dynamic Sound with a song to sing. Hence they saw no disadvantage in going with the new boys.

And Rastafari was never going to be too far away from this equation, as Burning Spear goes on to explain:

'This time was the beginning for Rasta on a big scale. Well of course it had been around in Jamaica for years, but having people start looking for culture now meant that Rasta was coming out much more. Now its philosophies were becoming something that made sense to a much larger number of people than were actually dreadlocks, so it began to spread like fire. Rasta was only one light that sprang up at the time, but it was the brightest light as far as black consciousness in Jamaica went. And of course musicians benefited from it, they *drew* from it. This looking for Africa and culture meant the music's rhythm patterns changed and it became faster – nothing like ska, but not like rocksteady either. The whole thought and the feeling of the artists and songwriters seemed to change as we were singing about Africa and culture and that. Not that we weren't singing it before, but it became more prominent.'

Burning Spear's point about Rasta is aptly illustrated by the Abyssinians. When they put out 'Satta Massa Gana' – an Amharic phrase that translates as 'Give thanks and praise' – they weren't a Rasta group *per se*. Only one of the threesome, Donald Manning, who wrote the song, was of the faith, which is a good representation of how things were at the time, both in and out of the music business: Rastafari was by no means the dominant doctrine among the population at large, but it was becoming increasingly attractive to the country's dispossessed as a lifeline of self-respect. While many may not have adopted the outward trappings of Rastafari, indeed remained practising Christians, Rasta's spiritual connection with Ethiopia and the mother continent had played a significant part in the acceptance of a valid strand of Jamaican black nationalism. In echo of Marcus Garvey, Rasta had for years been preaching a way of thinking that may have had much to learn from its US counterpart in terms of intellectual sophistication, but it had its own very relevant agenda. Now they were being listened to far more frequently. While this helped switch people on to Jamaican black power, in turn Rasta fed off the resultant groundswell of black pride as it had for so long been the natural home for such thinking.

Not only among the poor either. Post-Walter Rodney, Rasta's ranks were mushrooming among the educated and middle classes, which of course affected the music industry from a direction other than the studios as there were now sympathizers among people in the record trade and in power at radio stations. All of which sat very well with the newly arrived *yout' men* producers, as what they wanted to do was now much less likely to wither on the vine. They could encourage the players and singers – many of whom were Rasta anyway (probably dispro-portionately so, which gives rise to the common misconception that the majority of Jamaicans are dreads), who in turn embraced the fact that the change in the music lent itself to the cause. As the tendency towards African percussion and traditional rhythms righteously evoked their faith, reggae's easily accessible structures and internal flexibilities allowed greater culturally based elaboration as tempos could be adjusted to accommodate Nyabingi chanting, psalm singing or – again a throwback to mento – revivalist-type call-and-response vocals. And, now that the government's 'Jamaicanness' policies seemed to give it the nod, the use of overtly Jamaican language and lyricism became more or less regulation. Likewise, its subject matter need have no truck whatsoever with rocksteady's ersatz American love songs, or even with the relatively universal pro-test songs favoured by ska. These days the Old Testament, the holy herb, repatriation, giving thanks and praise to Jah, or just plain sufferation were what so many lyricists chose to write about.

Although there has never been a time in Jamaican music's

history when love songs have been outnumbered by consciousness, from 1971 onwards, while the majority of records were still of the boy-meets-girl/boy-loses-girl variety, more and more were starting to look beyond romance into what became known as reality. And to complement these far more serious lyrics, the rhythms started to get slower, deeper, heavier. They were supporting Rasta percussion, horns wailing in an Addis Ababa fashion, vocalizing that ranged from the hymn to the harmonizing, lyrics that realized it was OK to be contemplative and using more minor chords to make its presence felt above the waist.

By the beginning of 1972, as well as the likes of 'My Jamaican Girl', 'Cherry Oh Baby', 'Mule Train', 'Theme from *Shaft*', 'Wear You to the Ball' and 'Satisfaction', among the best-selling singles so far that decade were 'Trench Town Rock', 'Teach the Children', 'Mawga Dog', 'Better Must Come', 'Freedom Street', 'Deliver Us' and 'Let the Power Fall on I'. Roots music was standing on the verge of the artistic and cultural domination that would carry it through the decade. Jamaica's music and social politics were edging closer and closer together. Indeed, right about now, all that was missing was the dreadlocks, and it wouldn't remain that way for very much longer.

In 1969, Jimmy Cliff had just returned to Jamaica after several years living and working abroad, mostly in the UK. He had, however, kept up with events back home, and welcomed the idea of the people fighting back. Especially using reggae music as their weapon of choice. In 1971, when he himself was cutting such tunes as 'Sitting in Limbo' and 'Many Rivers to Cross', he took a long hard look at Jamaica and its situation and remembers seeing it thus:

'Politics affects our lives a lot in Jamaica, because it's such a small country with so few people that whatever gets decided is felt more or less straight away. Moods travel the country so quickly because there's not much ways you can avoid what's going on. Or so it goes for the poor people – it's only the rich that can afford to isolate themselves from politics and not be affected by governmental changes in the country. But as it is the poor people who makes most of the good music, it's they that have a big say.

'The reason the rude-boy era didn't last so long was because very quickly the people realize that sort of violence wasn't going to change anything. Because it was change they wanted, and to feel they was having some effect in their own country. So they started looking for something deeper. They wanted something that meant something, and as they started looking towards our own culture – like the government had been encouraging people to do – that led them to look more towards Africa and some sort of black consciousness. That's what the roots movement was all about; it was people looking to find their voice and finding it in that sort of black consciousness. Since things had been getting bad for quite a few years, they stepped up their fight to be heard and it was the musicians that provide that voice for them.

'People are surprised when I tell them that even as back as far as 1969 that the musical community was militant, but of course the musicians knew what was going on – just like anybody else. Their songs, at the time, might have been saying one thing because that's what the old wave of producers wanted, but in their hearts they knew what was going on. They knew what was happening in politics, in the streets, internationally, and it was only a matter of time before they would start voicing it on record as there was a new generation of producers coming up fast. They were young and wanted to get more involved with what was happening on the streets because there was a big sense of responsibility back then. Everybody knew that soon artists would be singing to give the people heart.

'Roots . . . roots and culture . . . call it whatever you like – was a necessity at the time. The times called for some sort of positive stance by black people in Jamaica because of the way things turned out after independence. We was getting ground down in the dirt and it seemed like we was the only ones not doing anything about it. America had long since had Malcom X, civil rights, the Black Panthers and all their black movements. And while that had an effect on Jamaica insofar as we could see it was possible to do something about it, it also made us think we had to get our own thing going. People would investigate anything to do with black movements in the United States, as people would go backwards and forwards to there and bring back news or publications about what was going on there. There were all sorts of black movements in England too in the 1960s; I used to go to little black-power organizations meeting in basements and in people's back rooms. It was an underground thing, but news of them and their doctrines used to get back to Jamaica. So when the situation worsened in the ghettos it was natural that something like the roots movement would come about.

'Music in the West Indies has always been about the people, communicating how they feel to each other – it's perfectly true what they say that it is the ghetto's newspaper. Calypso and mento was about that; ska and rocksteady highlight the rude-boy era. Reggae was celebrating independence and the optimism of the time, then the Rasta movement and the roots music showed up the general dissatisfaction at what was going on. It's the same today, the dancehall reggae directly reflects the mood of the people. Whether you think that mood is positive or not.'

By the late summer of 1971, politics began to involve itself with music with a hitherto unheard-of enthusiasm. The People's National Party had been in opposition since independence and leader Michael Manley, the charismatic son of former Prime Minister Norman, needed to pull out all the stops for the following year's general election. Unlike the Jamaican Labour Party, which under Hugh Shearer's leadership appeared to be reaching new heights of indolence as regards the country's rank and file, Manley, whose years within trade unions had left him with real knowledge of the working classes, knew their vote held the key to power. With hindsight, the notion has been advanced that the JLP's policies of foreign investment and neglected social infrastructure had run their course and the government were all but throwing in the towel before the serious squeeze was felt. Which may well be true, but the PNP were taking no chances.

Claiming to be 'profoundly' influenced by the new reggae, and no doubt realizing how much that same music meant to the electorate, Manley formed the PNP Musical Bandwagon. Which was literally that: a flatbed truck decked out with party colours and slogans, touring the country to become an impromptu stage for concerts by significant artists such as Bob and Rita Marley, Alton Ellis, the Chosen Few, Dennis Brown, Scotty, the Inner Circle, Tinga Stewart and Judy Mowatt, who had all signed on for the cause. And it set off a full six months before votes had to be cast.

Then there was the Rod of Correction. That's right, as made famous by the Clancy Eccles election-year hit – *Lick them with the Rod of Correction, father / lick them with the Rod of Correction . . .* – it actually existed as a staff given to Manley by Haile Selassie on a recent visit to Ethiopia. He'd brandish it during rallies, on the Bandwagon or during meet-the-people walkabouts, and the roots credibility that came with it is pretty much incalculable. More so as it combined with his self-styled 'Joshua' persona: Manley's rabble-rousing speeches included plenty of rhetoric about leading his people to a better land and walls a'tumbling down, while Shearer had long been personified, in the media and in song, as Pharaoh. Add to that the rumours – so widely circulating and unrepudiated that they had to have come from party HQ – that, once in power, Manley's government would both legalize the herb and sort out assisted passages back to Ethiopia, and it's hardly surprising that the PNP enjoyed enormous ghetto support.

The musical connection didn't stop there, either, as the politicians were just as apt to 'borrow' from the music business. Just as Clancy Eccles enjoyed heartfelt if somewhat opportunistic success by putting PNP slogans to a reggae rhythm – he had another hit with 'Power for the People', which was little more than a musical rendition of a Manley campaign speech – so Delroy Wilson's 1971 classic 'Better Must Come' became the PNP theme song/battle hymn, even though, until the day the singer died in 1995, he denied it had anything to do with politics but was written in protest about the raw deal artists were getting at the hands of the studio owners and producers.

As well as ensuring the middle class, the ghetto and the Rasta vote, the People's National Party's nationalistic, anticolonial (cultural or economic) and apparently democratic socialist approach also attracted political fringe elements – Black Power, Garveyites, Islam, Communists, etc. – so that, unsurprisingly, they won by a landslide. For a while things seemed to be on the up as Manley, secure in office and determined to deliver on his election promises, got stuck into an ambitious programme of social reform, named the People's Projects. During his first year he introduced a basic minimum wage and legislated for improved labour relations; set about renationalizing industries sold off to private ownership by the previous government; launched a nationwide literacy campaign; poured money into the ailing health and education services; laid extensive public-housing plans; and initiated a scheme to encourage small farms and holdings by providing credit facilities for interested parties to buy land from the government or large corporations. Consumer confidence was up, as unemployment that had been rising steadily through the last few years levelled out and started to decline. The number of homes on the island with electricity, telephones and indoor plumbing rose swiftly – from 18 to 35 per cent by the end of 1973 – as did the amount of electricity generated, because people began buying many more household goods. It was a time of great optimism; indeed, these reforms were so well received among the rootsmen that nobody seemed to notice that weed was still illegal. One of the best-selling tunes on the island that year was Ken Lazarus's 'Hail the Man'. Written by Ernie Smith, one of Jamaica's greatest folksong-writing talents, it talked about Michael Manley in glowing terms: *What would you say to the coming of a brand new day / When the shadows are falling away / You'd say Hail the Man . . .*

But just as the country as a whole began to enjoy a better standard of living, this brave new vision was starting to unravel. Quite simply, there wasn't the money to pay for it and, in spite of the regime's egalitarian foundations, it was the sufferahs who bore the brunt of the shortfall. Just as surely, they put their case in song.

*

It was a roots-music explosion that began when the previous JLP's government's policies of neglect were at an all-time low, but as things started going wrong for their successors, it went thermo-nuclear. Derrick Harriott endorses this chronology by citing the Kingstonians' 'Sufferah', a single he produced for them in 1970, and maintains it was around then the people figured they weren't going to take any more.

'*We a sufferah . . . a sufferah . . . a sufferah . . .*', he sings. 'Reality songs. These were sung by guys who just want to proclaim how they feel it so bad . . . We a sufferah, we no got it, we no have it, we *need* some. When people like that come to sing for you they're not just singing a song that tell you something about a sufferah, they're really suffering. They really feel it.

'Being an artist and a producer I kind of know all the feels – you know what's real and what's not. Most of the Jamaican artists you would see them if not every day then every other day looking for money, and it's a frustrating thing when a guy comes to you every second. What you want is when it time for royalties you see him, but you try and explain that. Then when you check it out some of these guys that are checking you consistently are doing it even before the record come out. But then on a different level there were the real sufferahs, they would come and say, "Mr Harriott they just took away mi bed. I need some money just to get it back from the bailiff." This is a true actual thing that happen to the people – they didn't have enough money to buy food for the day or something. Natural sufferation, and you have to try and do something about that.

'There was hard times in Jamaica at that point, of course not for everybody, but that's how it was in the ghetto where so much of the musicians are, and those same musicians and singers just want to make themselves heard. They sick and tired of feeling so helpless while it all falls down around them. That's why you have so much of those records all at the same time, because if one feel it everybody feel it, and that was the only chance anybody had at representation.'

Perhaps the biggest opportunity for 'sufferah representation' happened in 1972, with the release of the feature film *The Harder They Come*, the tale of a picky-head *'country bwoy'* who comes to town to make it as a singer but, more through circumstances than any inherent badness, ends up as an outlaw of Jamaica's Most Wanted proportions. It's half autobiographical of so many who tried their luck in the studios, and the other half is the story of Jamaica's folk-hero outlaw of the 1940s Rhygin (Vincent Martin). Directed by Perry Henzell from the story he co-wrote, it remains the most frank, entertaining and poignant take on any record business, anywhere in the world. At any time. It opened the curtains on a window that offered an unobstructed panorama across the Kingston studios, producers, artists and the business's internal politics of exploitation, plus it revealed the Jamaican public's unique relationship with same. It offered a razor-sharp insight into what ghetto living was *really* all about, and provided an ABC of sufferah ways. The movie was acted, scripted and directed with such smouldering intensity you could smell the rubbish in the street and feel the heat of the sun. Which was exactly how the music should be approached, as a part of a whole – as part of black life in Jamaica – rather than as a separate entity. Only then would it make sense.

The Harder They Come also had a soundtrack that boasted the title track, 'You Can Get It If You Really Want', 'Sitting in Limbo' and 'Many Rivers to Cross' by Jimmy Cliff, the Maytals' 'Pressure Drop' and the rousing 'Sweet and Dandy', Scotty's 'Draw Your Brakes' (a wild toast on Keith & Tex's 'Stop that Train'), the Melodians' groundbreaking 'Rivers of Babylon' and the song that summed up so much of the film that it could be taken as an alternative title song, the Slickers' 'Johnny too Bad'. Until Bob Marley's retrospective *Legend* was released in 1984, this was the best-selling reggae album ever. The movie became an instant hit anywhere with a Jamaican or Jamaican-influenced population and quickly achieved cult status among audiences beyond this core – in London it's still a late-night screening staple.

As the main character, Ivan, kitted out in a trendsetting blue

T-shirt with a yellow six point 'sheriff's' star, or in thankfully less-widely adopted snakeskin boots, *The Harder They Come* starred an awesomely convincing Jimmy Cliff. An equally opportunistic Jimmy Cliff, too:

'That film did a lot for me and the music. I met Perry Henzell at a recording studio, I was recording the album with "Let Your Yeah be Yeah" on it, and he told me he wanted me to write the music for the film. He asked me if I could write music for films and I said, "Yeah, man, of course I can – I can write anything you want!" It was like being back in the Kongs' ice-cream shop all those years ago – you've got to know your opportunities. Six months later, Chris Blackwell gave me a script for the film and tell me that same guy now want me to play the lead part. I said I thought he jus' wanted me to write the music, now he wants me to act and I'd never done anything like that before – but I took it anyway and read it. I liked it and I could identify with both sides of it because I knew about Rhygin, I understood that aspect of Jamaican life, and I knew the music business because I'd been in it since I was fourteen. It didn't seem like anything I couldn't do, so I accept the part. Well, I wasn't going to tell them "No", was I?

'*The Harder They Come* had a great deal to do with the spread of Rasta and the roots music. It was seen all over the world, and more than just play you music it took you right into roots culture and how people lived in Jamaica at the time. It introduced people to the fact there was more to reggae than the happy stuff that had been hits, because it provided the pictures to go with the music – this was before videos. That movie was socio- . . . economic . . . political . . . religious – *all* the elements of Jamaican society. It was all of that. It told the tale with real depth, put it into context, which was probably a surprise to so many people but it was that that helped them understand it and appreciate reggae for what it really is. That film was like, *boom!*, so visual of the music and where it was coming from, it opened up another set of doors and gave an identity in a lot of places and people. It gave it the identity of the outlaw, the rebel, the rude bwoy; the studio people; the ordinary people; the Rastas.

At one time that rude-bwoy identity was put on to me, because I play the part in the film, but it doesn't bother me!

'It was *The Harder They Come* that opened up the international market, as up until then I don't think roots music could have made sense to many people outside of Jamaica. Because it was honest, that is what life is like in Jamaica. The film is based on a real outlaw, Rhygin, the first outlaw in Jamaica. When I was a little boy going to school you would hear about Rhygin – Rhygin is a word in Jamaican that mean hot, mean bad, people would say that man is a Rhygin man, don't mess with him or look at him any way. But Rhygin was very much on the side of the people, he was a kind of Robin Hood, I guess you could call him.

'The music part of it was also very true, because that is how things stay in the Jamaican music industry, or it did back then. That part was actually my life – or the lives of so many of the guys in Kingston who wanted to make it in the music business. The only big difference between me and the film is I never kill anyone – yet! – but when I came to West Kingston and was growing up I saw killings. There are few people grown up in West Kingston haven't seen anybody killed or seen a dead body. And that isn't big talk, that's just life.

'I'm working on *The Harder they Come Part 2*, I have been for several years now. I resurrected my character twenty-five years later, and I thought I could do that because you never actually saw him dead. You saw him shot down but you never actually saw him buried. The new one has all of those reality elements of the previous film, but set in the modern day. No, I don't know how it will go down. One never knows if something going to take off – you just go into anything with a positive frame of mind.'

Although it's often far more convenient for the Wailers' *Catch a Fire* album, with its innovative sleeve, rock-orientated overdubs and remixes, bigtime marketing campaign and white people's values firmly in place, to be celebrated as the pivotal moment in roots reggae's entering the international mainstream, this

Burning Spear, with regular back-up singers Rupert Wellington and Delroy Hines, re-enact 'Slavery Days' in the mid-1970s. (*Dennis Morris*)

A cool Prince Buster in London, 1967. (*Pictorial*)

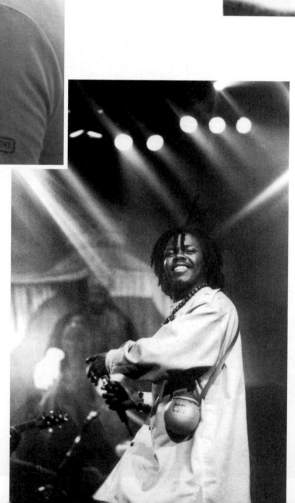

A youthful Big Youth,
an instantly recognizable
ital smile. (*Adrian Boot*)

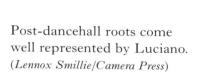

Post-dancehall roots come
well represented by Luciano.
(*Lennox Smillie/Camera Press*)

Kingston, 6 August 1962: Independence Day was, ostensibly, a celebration of indigenous Jamaican culture. (*Reg Davies/Camera Press*)

A 1960s sound system crowd. (*Ebet Roberts/Redferns*)

Bob Marley's state funeral, 21 May 1981, was one of the biggest events in Jamaican history. (*Adrian Boot*)

The Heptones, on tour in
London in the early 1970s: (*left
to right*) Earl Morgan, Barry
Llewellyn and Leroy Sibbles.
(*Adrian Boot*)

Nearly fifty years on, and the street-corner sound system remains the best way to appreciate reggae.
(*Adrian Boot*)

'Modern reggae? ... Boring? ... Never!' Dancehall queens take a breather at Stone Love, Jamaica's biggest late-1990s sound system.
(*Adrian Boot*)

Inside the Black Ark, where Lee Perry displays a singular and personally applied approach to interior decorating.
(*Adrian Boot*)

People too often forget that one of Bob Marley's greatest characteristics was an infectious, uncomplicated sense of fun. (*Dennis Morris*)

'Police and thieves in the street'... There was always a greater sense of purpose to the rioting at the 1976 Notting Hill Carnival.
(*Oliver Waterlow/Camera Press*)

clearly isn't so. Would-be historians should go back in time to *The Harder They Come*, which had attracted an enormous following for months before *Catch a Fire* was, initially, all but ignored by the public (though not by the media). But as well as taking this music to a world-wide audience, equally importantly *The Harder They Come* sold it back to the Jamaican music industry. Or, to be more precise, the Jamaican music industry establishment.

The fact that a 'major motion picture' had been made about the roots reggae industry was impressive enough by itself – many of the bigger record men had peripheral involvement in it – but when *The Harder They Come* became a success, everybody sat up and took notice. More than just interpreting this new musical trend as something glamorous, a little bit dangerous and as meaningful as it was enjoyable, suddenly, to the folks back home, it had an irrefutable legitimacy. 'If it's been made into a film that did hit in *a foreign* then it must be OK. Seen?'

It's now that the guys who had discreetly stayed away from anything too radical as they pumped out what they believed was the international hit sound clambered aboard the roots train. Bunny Lee, Coxsone Dodd, Joe Gibbs and so on all threw themselves into roots music to, as you'd expect from men of this calibre, spectacular effect. The floodgates opened, and as a result many of the records talked about earlier in this chapter were made. But the biggest effect roots and culture had was to elevate, to a height somewhere beyond Venus, a couple of Jamaican music art forms that had been around for ages but had never quite got their props. Toasting and dubwise.

13

Wake the Town, Tell the People

One evening in early 1973, the deejay Big Youth was on stage rocking the house at Kingston's Carib theatre. Midway through his set, during one of his vibrant hymns to Jah Rastafari, the effervescent performer yanked his tam from his head and flashed his dreadlocks. Unlike a later Dillinger tune, there was no lightning clap, and the weakheart might well have stayed standing, but that was about all that didn't happen. The effect on the audience was electrifying. According to one observer:

'When Jah Yout' shake him head and flash him locks, which were quite long even then, there was complete silence for a second or two, then pure pandemonium . . . a noise that, I swear, actually shook the building. Everybody jus' went wild. Any man with dreadlocks follow Jah Yout' and flash 'im locks too, while the other people jus' cheer like they going to burst. I never heard noise like that, *from any audience anywhere*. But it was the first time, ever, the people had seen dreadlocks on stage somewhere like the Carib theatre. The effect was like . . . Joshua at the walls of Jericho.'

It seems remarkable that, given the proliferation of

dreadlocks in 1970s reggae, as late as 1973 this action could produce such a reaction. But the man in the crowd was right – nobody had ever done that before. Although the more dedicated dreads had been growing locks for well over a decade, this was far from universal and yet to make virtually any sort of inroad into the music business. Of the Wailers at this stage, only Bunny had anything that could come close to being flashed – check the *Catch a Fire* sleeve or the family portrait mural on the wall at 56 Hope Road which was copied from a photo taken about 1972 or '73: Bob was only just starting to let his Afro *nat up* at the ends, while Peter had yet to get his locks going at all. There are hardly any dreadlocks on show in *The Harder They Come*, and of the acts that were making the most radical roots music, only the Abyssinians were noticeably locksed.

Even a year into Michael Manley's apparently populist regime – remember this is the man who came to power waving a walking stick given to him by Haile Selassie while riding the roots-reggaefied Musical Bandwagon – dreadlocks were social outcasts. A leper colony would probably have qualified as a holiday resort compared to the sort of purgatory Rastas found themselves condemned to by the forces of law and order, most branches of bureaucracy and the 'respectable' public at large. To wear natty dreads was to set yourself up for pariahty, and the music business establishment went along with this. Promoters weren't likely to book openly dread acts for stage shows; clubs and band leaders were equally disinclined to employ Rasta musicians; Byron Lee was never keen on dreads in his Dynamic Studios, even though he himself was seldom there; Boris Gardiner sacked Earl Sixteen from top live band the Boris Gardiner Happening because he came on stage one night with a couple of stray dreadlocks hanging out from under his hat; while the ex-policeman Duke Reid made no bones about his disliking natty dread – either on record or in person. Of the big guys, only Coxsone seemed to be at all open to Rastafari, and his experiences with Burning Spear and 'Satta Massa Gana' show that he wasn't too sure what to do with them.

Hence many artists who may have been practising Nyahmen

in their own time, Johnnie Clarke, Junior Byles and Max Romeo for instance, hadn't yet grown locks. It's never been compulsory for Rastafari, and anyway, at that point they considered being able to eat food and get their message across to take priority.

Not so Big Youth. But the crucial difference between himself and the above-mentioned artists, who are all from the same 'rebel' generation, was that Big Youth was a deejay, a toaster, not a singer in the conventional sense. He maintains that only a deejay could have pushed roots reggae through to the prominence it came to enjoy. In August 1998 he's sitting on a wall outside what's best described as a mansion, just below the Blue Mountains' cloudline, and we're sharing the windfall custard apples that litter the front lawn. He's dressed in box-fresh brand-name American sportswear, with neatly tied locks hanging all the way down his back, and when he grins – which he seems to do all the time as he tells his tale chanting down Babylon – the red, green and gold inlays in his front teeth are still very much in effect.

'It had to be up to deejays such as we on the sound systems to bring it forward. Back in those days, if you was Rasta even your parents would deny and ignore you, you come like an outcast, so there was many situations in the record business that at that time Rasta was kept out of. But on the sound systems there wasn't that kind of control because there was plenty of sound systems run by people like us. You didn't have to get into no establishment, and as I am a man who, when mi come as Rasta, say if mi have to trim my natty dread then mi no wan' go there. That was my conviction, so I went on the sound systems where we was busting things like togetherness love, instead of boy-girl love. It was on the sound systems long before any deejay made a conscious record.

'Up until that point deejaying was really just about nicing up the dance; none of it wasn't saying nothing – the whole thing was just a *baby baby . . . chick-a-bow . . . bend down low* situation, while people dem was *hungry*. You have Daddy U-Roy before, Dennis Alcapone and all those bredda was there and it wasn't that they weren't working, but it wasn't enough. The people had enough of pure *dibidibidabidoo*, they couldn't take it any more without some sort of alternative that represent how they feel. That's where myself and the new generation of deejays, younger guys, came in, because we could really see where it should be coming from. And on the sound systems we are close to the people, much closer than how so many of the big record producers had become by then, so while the whole deejay thing was still *chick-a-bow* we could see that people need to be looking forward, instead of getting down. It was an urban, spiritual, cultural concept that we come with. We realize that the music we possess is a music of teaching.

'Of course, it wasn't all that way. Ain't nothing wrong with you making jokes and having fun from the music 'cause it's a joy – music has always been a joy – and we don't have to be all that serious every time about the system. We know that people want to go out to enjoy themselves, so sometimes you can just say to hell with the system because the dance is all about the live-ity of the people. But up until then, it was all lovey-dovey t'ing; there wasn't no action; nobody was going out there and dancing and at the same time telling people to do right. Or dealing with everyday talk like the way that the people suffer and the way that the people live, when those were the things that we feel. And even when it was starting to get through on the sound systems, none of that was on record.

'How the people react to that, it show me the *power*; I see what it means to them, and I go on and do a couple of songs for Phil Pratt, like "Tell It Black". In a couple of weeks me and Keith Hudson take a bike in the studio and we did the "S90 Skank", same day we did "Chi Chi Run" for Prince Buster. Both of them was number 1 songs because they were about how the people was living: the Honda S90 was the bike of the day, and you'd see many Rasta ride up and down on one – the song was direct to the people about their real lives. This was Rasta culture.

'In no time I had seven records in both the charts – five in each Top 10 [JBC and RJR each operated independent charts] – and the next week Joe Gibbs came running, Derrick Harriott came running, Sonia Pottinger came running. Everybody want to have a Big Youth track; suddenly they want a conscious deejay record. I wasn't even aware of what was happening.

'This is where it really began, with the deejays. Although Bob [Marley] was studying Rasta at that time, when they come with *Catch a Fire*, Jah Yout' had already done "Natty Dread Inna Babylon'. When Bob Marley was still a soul rebel with "Bend Down Low" and "Simmer Down" and all them things, I'm already telling the people to "Do It Jah" and "Live It Up Jah" and "Jah Wah Wah". I-Roy, too.'

While this may have been the catalyst that ushered in a new era of roots rock reggae and pointed the way to righteous toasting, it was in no way the beginning of deejay styling. As slick and as inventive as Big Youth was, he wasn't the first deejay to rule the record shops; while chatting on the mic went back as far as sound systems themselves.

When the young Prince Buster was about to unleash his first sound system on Kingston's unsuspecting public, he put enormous emphasis on the fact that Count Machuki had defected from Downbeat to join the Voice of the People. This is because who was announcing your records, vibing up your crowd, flogging your beer or advertising your next dance was practically as important as the records you were playing. A boss deejay could cover up the flat bits on a tune or whip up the dancers to even greater heights on the good ones, and, vitally back then, when all you were doing was playing records made by other people, it could give your sound system a character that rivals couldn't approach, no matter if they had the key to your record box.

And like so much that went into working those first sets, the notion of scatting over and in between records (with just the one turntable this latter aspect was pretty much a necessity) was something borrowed from abroad. Jive talking to boost up their shows was standard behaviour for the deejays on the southern US R&B stations that were listened to so avidly in Jamaica. Self-appreciation, nonsense, wild rhyming, whooping and hollering were their stock in trade, and as such were adopted as an almost integral part of presenting the music, with many New Orleans or Miami jocks' catchphrases cropping up on Kingston corners. Not that this in any way stopped them moving the masses.

Count Machuki was the genre's first star, drawing up the blueprint for the verbal and physical showmanship involved in deejaying a sound system years before he helped Prince Buster get to the top. He began in the 1950s as a dancer with Tom the Great Sebastian's Luke Lane set, after his flitter foot shuffling within the audience began drawing its own crowd. From there it didn't take long to earn the job of selector, where his chatting skills began to develop as he continued to cut the spins and steps that gave the crowd something to try out themselves. Interestingly, when Tom moved uptown to his Silver Slipper residency he didn't take Machuki, his proven crowd pleaser, with him. A scatting deejay dropping street-sharp moves was considered far too low rent to make the journey to that high-class joint, where Tom would expect to attract a much more genteel crowd. But Tom's loss was Coxsone's gain, as the Count was snapped up by Downbeat. There he worked hard to extend the role of the toaster, introducing more rhyming and jestering and remarks that were pertinent to that crowd on that particular night. While most Kingston sounds had somebody chatting by now, Machuki was way out in front as he'd quickly become aware of what power the deejay had over the dancers. Which is one of the reasons that he became so frustrated with Coxsone's treatment of him and eagerly went with Buster. The Prince remembers what an asset Machuki was:

'He was the pioneer of all Jamaican deejaying. Right up to what's going on today, it all goes back to Machuki. He worked hard at what he did. Because he was the first to actually go along with the track instead of just talk on top of it, he knew how to do it so you could still appreciate the tune, you're not just listening to him. Machuki devise that technique and so many others who come immediately after him learn from it, because nothing exist like that before.

'Then he not only thought about what he was actually saying, the lines and the lyrics, but he knew he had control over the crowd. He knew the deejay could take them up and, probably more importantly than that, he could calm them down if there was any trouble. So quite apart from him having a superior technique he was the first to really understand the relationship the deejay have with the sound-system crowd. Something you won't find in any other situation.

'And he was funny as hell. If you went to a Machuki dance you know you was going to enjoy yourself. That's why it was so good he join my sound.'

Count Machuki never recorded. Trumpeter Baba Brooks scatted his way through a few singles, notably the mildly obscene 'One Eye Giant', in the mid-1960s, but the first deejays on wax were Sir Lord Comic and King Stitt, both of whom started off as dancers and both of whom admit to drawing inspiration from Count Machuki. The former cut ska tunes around 1965, and the latter, having made his name as a Down-beat deejay, recorded for Clancy Eccles over reggae rhythms starting in 1969. His 'Fire Corner' finished as one of that year's top-selling tunes, and the follow-ups 'Dance Beat', 'Vigorton', 'Herbsman' and 'Van Cleef' (*Harder than hard / You can' believe*) all did well, but neither man did quite enough to remove the stigma of 'novelty record' from deejay cuts – indeed, Sir Lord Comic didn't make a decent record until 'Jack of My Trade' with Joe Gibbs several years later, and Stitt's work with Clancy Eccles would only be fully appreciated in retrospect over a quarter of a century later. Bizarrely, considering the size of the debt they claimed to owe to Machuki, their approach displayed none of the care and thought that the Prince (and others) say the Count put into his work. They were far too US derivative, just interpolating largely disjointed phrases and toasts rather than working to make the track both their own and the originator's. Comic more so than Stitt it must be said, but that's probably because the clipped reggae rhythms lent themselves better to deejaying. However, it wasn't long before somebody came along who forced the world – or at least Jamaica and its cultural colonies – to take toasting seriously.

When Big Youth referred to U-Roy as 'Daddy U-Roy' it wasn't something he did lightly. U-Roy has long been proclaimed as the founding father of modern deejay style, due largely to his ability to ride a rhythm – going with the tune, working inside and around it to embellish spectacularly what was there already – instead of simply throwing stuff on top of it in an apparently haphazard fashion. Maybe it was because he didn't start off as a dancer; although he could always put on a show, he was probably thinking about his vocals more than the others were. U-Roy was the natural successor to Count Machuki, and his records were the first sustained deejay hits. But then U-Roy had had two big advantages in the studio: Duke Reid and an electrical engineer/disc cutter who called himself King Tubby.

U-Roy began his career in his teens at the start of the 1960s, selecting music and occasionally chatting on the Kingston sound system Dickie's Dynamic. The system's owner was Dickie Wong, a Chinese guy, and although not among the biggest, it was serious enough to play at Forresters' Hall. By 1965 he'd moved on to Sir George the Atomic, and after a stint deejaying Coxsone's number-two set, when his key spar Osbourne Ruddock, aka King Tubby, set up Tubby's Home Town HiFi in 1968, U-Roy joined it as number one deejay. This was an ideal partnership, as both men were adventurous, each determined to get the absolute maximum out of what he and the other did, and to do it for the glory of the sound system which was fast becoming one of Kingston's finest. A talented engineer, Tubby's sound was one of the most technically impressive, and while producers such as Lee Perry and Bunny Lee, who didn't have systems, were keen to get their music to him, so were Dodd and Reid, who, it is claimed, liked to see how a new tune stood up on Tubby's rig. Tubby worked for Duke Reid as a disc cutter and thus had access to Treasure Isle master tapes, from which he'd cut discs for his personal use specifically tailored for U-Roy's vocals. He wasn't the first to do this, and we'll go into the broader ramifications of such an exercise in the next chapter, but by dropping the vocals in and out or fiddling around with the instrumentation he'd create one-off specials, then encourage U-Roy to make full use of them by playing his lyrics off the newly acquired spaces and engaging in dialogue with or wryly commenting on the song itself. Of course the deejay would be doing this live on the night and therefore keeping up his spontaneous whoops, yelps, '*yeah-yeahs*', rhyming silliness and scatted exclamations of sheer delight.

When an idea such as this was unleashed on the paying public it was always going to be something of an event, but nothing prepared people for the adrenalin-pumping thrill of being at the particular dance when those slates first hit the turntable and U-Roy took up the mic.

Dennis Alcapone remembers it well. Soon to follow U-Roy into reggae history as the second toaster to enjoy sustained recorded success, at that time he was deejaying his own El Paso sound system in Waltham Park Road and not averse to checking out the local opposition. Dennis, later to settle in London, spoke to me in Kingston, sitting on a terrace in the upmarket Liganea area on a warm June night. The crickets were making a fearsome row and the years were just falling away . . .

'It was in 1969, around the time reggae was starting to hit big, and Tubby's dance was ram. There was a buzz of excitement – like expectation – because word had got round all week that Tubby's was going to do something special that night. Although nobody knew what it was going to be, Tubby's sound was so innovative you knew it was going to be spectacular. He had four dub plates he'd made from Treasure Isle rocksteady tunes, and this is at a time when you never have the rhythm on the record itself – no dub or version yet, A- and B-sides were both straight vocal.

'But Tubby did it quietly. Him and U-Roy start the dance off as normal, and after a while he play "You Don't Care for Me at All" by the Techniques, then when he lift it up to start it back from the beginning again he'd switched it to the dub version, and after a couple of lines of the original all the crowd could hear was pure riddim, then U-Roy come in toasting, *and they went nuts*. He had four dub plates, and for the rest of the night it must have been just them he play.

'That was how it always was on sound systems, you got to give the people something extra – something they can't buy in the shops. Then, rather than just play new tunes, this was putting *extra* vibes on to a song the people already knew. Giving it a bit more. If, for example, a tune's going at fifty miles per hour, when we take up the mic it's going at a hundred. Deejays step up the pace. That was what excite the people more than anything else and why deejays have been there for so long. They jus' make the dance so sweet. Sometimes you hear them talk about gun salute these days, but it's the niceness of the music get to the people in such a way they can't control themselves!

'So you can hardly imagine something that new coming into the dancehall and the excitement it create. It was wild. I believe this moment was the beginning of dancehall reggae; it all start from there.'

Within days, a customized version of the Techniques' 'You Don't Care' with U-Roy chatting on top became Home Town's signature tune. This was genuine deejay style. Whereas it had been previously accepted that Machuki was the ultimate lyricist, that was only relative to what else was going on – this was the real deal as Tubby and U-Roy between them had created a parity between the original material and what was being added. You couldn't listen and say which was the more important as each aspect existed in its own right: the deejay version was now redefining rather than merely supplementing the original. U-Roy's initial string of hits breathed new, contemporary life into many old rocksteady numbers. Although it still was – technically speaking – deejay music, it could no longer justifiably be palmed off as parasitical or with a hyper-dismissive '*yuh talk yuh a talk*', that is to say, 'somebody shouting over the top of a perfectly good record'. And the popular reaction such specials provoked made it, apparently, just a small step to recording. Which indeed it might have been, had anyone other than Duke Reid been involved.

Naturally, Duke knew about these unauthorized soft waxes

and how they could rock a crowd until daybreak. Unsurprisingly, he wanted a piece of it for himself. Using John Holt as a go-between, he sent for U-Roy and his over-enterprising disc cutter. Wary of the Duke's reputation, the deejay, who had never worked the Trojan sound system, dragged his feet as regards any meeting. Only pressure from Tubby, who knew Reid well, convinced him to give it a go – Tubby was well aware of the potential of well-recorded deejay music, was sure the right mixes would allow U-Roy's dancehall exuberance to come through unchecked. Tubby couldn't wait to give it a go.

He wasn't wrong. Once the deejay overcame his apprehensions, he and the producer settled into one of the most productive partnerships in reggae. Throughout 1970, Duke Reid dusted off a series of his classic rocksteady and early reggae rhythms by stars such as the Melodians, the Paragons, Alton Ellis, Hopeton Lewis and the Techniques, all recorded to the highest technical standards, and dubbed U-Roy's dancehall fashion on top of them. 'Wear You to the Ball', 'Version Galore', 'Wake the Town', 'Tom Drunk', 'Words of Wisdom', 'On the Beach' . . . U-Roy's first two Treasure Isle releases, 'Wake the Town' and 'Rule the Nation', both went straight to the top of JBC's and RJR's charts and stayed there long enough for the deejay's third record, 'Wear You to the Ball', to catch them up, giving the music the top three positions in both charts for several weeks. Brent Dowe remembers the first night a deejay record hit the deck:

'The first time U-Roy's "Wear You to the Ball" came out it was a phenomenon. People were in the dance, then all of a sudden comes Duke with these dubs, one of which was "Wear You to the Ball", and the whole place went crazy. It was at the Gold Coast Club, out on the beach by St Thomas Road, on a Sunday night, where they gonna get maximum exposure because that was a place the top promoters would put on shows and all the people from all over the ghetto would be there – you'd even see uptown guys there, they'd even run risk to come there to get some of the beat!

'The way Duke Reid worked, he would cut a dub plate at

twelve o'clock midnight, at one o'clock in the morning he'd be at his sound-system dance playing that dub and trying it out. And *bwoy* he'd make a big fuss coming in through the gates when he had new tunes. Everybody would see him arrive, with the records under his arm or he holding them high in the air just to let everybody know these were straight from the studio. And then when he play them he make sure they get a big build-up – he'd take up the mic and announce *"Right!* A *brand new* recording this! You hearing it for the *very* first time!"* Sometimes this was just hype, but when he dropped the needle on "Wear You to the Ball" and U-Roy start, *"Did you hear what the man said . . ."*, the place jus' erupted. Although everybody knew about live deejaying, nobody had captured that sort of feel on record before; I don't even think people thought it could be done. Now it was part of everybody's lives, not just at the sound system. That, as well as the vibe, is why they get so excited.'

It was certainly part of every producer's life. Hot on U-Roy's heels was Dennis Alcapone. After a few underachieving releases for small labels in 1970, he hooked up with first Duke Reid then Coxsone and Bunny Lee for a lengthy run of success – 'Teach the Children', 'Wake Up Jamaica', 'Number One Station', 'Guns Don't Argue', 'Ripe Cherry', 'My Voice is Insured for Half a Million Dollars' and so on. He also recorded for Lee Perry, Joe Gibbs, Keith Hudson and Phil Pratt. Just behind him, chronologically rather than artistically, came I-Roy, an ex-civil servant who deejayed V-Rocket, Ruddy's Supreme and, for a time, King Tubby's, and who had a penchant for very correct grammar, epic narratives and, in the beginning when he was recording for Harry Mudie, a recognizable U-Roy impersonation in his delivery. Swimming in their wake was Scotty, a former singer with the Chosen Few and the Federals, who took Dennis Alcapone's melodic, almost sing-jay style further with a string of hits for Derrick Harriott ('Sesame Street', 'Musical Chariot' 'Riddle I This', 'Draw Your Brakes') and Harry J ('Breakfast in Bed'); Rupie Edwards was recording Shorty the President and the shamelessly named U-Roy Junior;

Winston Scotland hit big with the marvellous 'Buttercup', a version of an updated take on the Techniques' 'You Don't Care'; Charlie Ace cut records for Lee Perry, Coxsone, Sonia Pottinger and Bunny Lee; and among the lesser lights were Lizzie (occasional partner in rhyme of Dennis Alcapone), Samuel the First and Prince Francis.

Even given the trend-sensitive nature of the Jamaican music business, it came as a surprise to many of the originals that deejay records took off to this degree. Dennis Alcapone explains:

'To us who toast the sounds before the recording started it was dancehall business. You're in the dancehall, it ram and you have a few beers, a few Guinness, a few spliff and t'ing and the riddim is just running and you're just freestyling over it – doing just anything. That's what it was to us. Although you did have a pattern, so that every riddim you've got lyrics for, you still do different things each particular time so when the people come into the dancehall they're hearing something they haven't heard before. You just never thought how it could work on disc the same every time.

'When U-Roy come with "Wake the Town" it's like a new Jamaica was born – he use the appropriate introduction as well: *Wake the town and tell the people / about this musical disc coming your way* . . . It was a new era in the music industry but none of us didn't have no inkling that it could get so wide, because a lot of people didn't want to acknowledge it.

'I personally didn't visualize that it would be so successful or last so long; when we started out as deejays we used to get into a lot of fights because people never used to appreciate it. Singers never used to like it, they'd look down on us because it was so new and they thought it was just talking, not any sort of skill. We would go someplace and people used to say scornfully, "Cha! Yuh talk you a talk", and we'd say "True we a talk, but this is our thing". The radio stations did look down on it, too, and it was only because people like Duke Reid did have certain powers that it got airplay at all. The record companies didn't treat us with no respect, either – even when the records are

'We were *exceptional*. At that time there weren't no singers
at could get a look in. One or two singers even started to
ejay, which was a mark of how the deejay thing started to
ke over the whole scene.'

Both Dennis Alcapone and U-Roy were capable of selling
ound 70,000 copies of a release, and the sheer number of
ejay cuts at the start of the 1970s – Dennis talks of recording
r more than one producer on the same day – meant they were
counting for the larger share of the record business. But even
s was small potatoes compared with the conscious deejay
volution that came next. Every roots sound-system –
ppertone, Black Harmony, Stur-Gav HiFi (owned and oper-
d by U-Roy), Stereo, Channel One and the rest – had its
r deejays, and as the industry rushed to recruit as many as
ssible, any apprehension it might have had about recording
ejays was lost in the sales returns (social/artistic snobbery
ild always be set aside in such cases). As a result, a new wave
microphone masters came forward with recording as their
mary concern.

he slower, rootsier, heavier drum 'n' bass music and mixes
vided a more suitable platform for the deejay's toasting than
es originally designed for harmony singing. Many of the
t wave of deejays maintain that the next bunch usurped them
asily because the music had changed, but in fact there was
ething of a dreadlocks spiral in effect, with the advancement
he Rasta deejays pushing the music's development further
n that path of righteousness. Cultural chatting proved a
arkably versatile state of affairs, too, with the best of the
ch demonstrating a vivid individual approach, embracing a
e range of musical influences. And all of this produced/was
ated by a new stratum of producers who truly understood
t was going on – chiefly Keith Hudson, Gussie Clarke,
an Jackson (aka Yabby You) and Glen Brown.

f course, once this movement established itself, the old
d was keen to get involved. Jah Stitch, who, during the
y years of the seventies, made the transition from singer to
d-system deejay to recording star with toasts like 'Roots

Studio Kinda Cloudy

doing well it's still the singers get all the resp
the studio and do a song and we make a mist;
would say "Leave it man, it a version". Even t'
satisfied. If a singer doing a song, they'd keep
sure it was properly done. With certain produ
studio and you work and you feel you could c
say "That's all right, next tune".

'A lot of deejays couldn't work in the stud
find it actually hard to work in the studio,
make it. You see, in the dance, the vibes wa
you pick up what's going on around you, bec
round the deejay and this man here saying sc
over there saying something else and you
work it into your lyrics. Just answer or col
your own way. Jamaica's a place full up witl
everybody's a superstar, so in the dancehal
with their little stuff so you could pick up
deejay's job to get involved with the crowd,
this dance is theirs – specially for them. Bu
you're on your own with the engineer so yo
own vibes and some couldn't do that. Anc
tricky, too. Some of the songs you go and r
you play in the dancehall regular then you'
it already, so you won't have no problem.
one take and keep the excitement fresh. O1
producer give you a rhythm to work on
before, then you'll have to listen for a li
something out. That's when you have to g
to keep those vibes up and make sure th
sound exciting. Not everybody can do it.'

Prevalent as this first wave of deejays w;
for more than a couple of years before the
roots rockers, began to bubble through.
down.

'They treating us like gods!' is Dennis Alc;
tion of the deejay's status among the ghe1

Natty Roots Natty Congo' and, following his getting shot, 'No Dread Can't Dead', remembers Bunny Lee holding what amounted to an open audition one night at King Tubby's studio.

'It was in 1974; Bunny Lee put the word out that he wanted all deejays who were deejaying sound systems but hadn't yet made a record to go to King Tubby's that night at ten o'clock – Deejay Jamboree Night is what he called it. I had recorded, but I only cut my first record that morning, "Danger Zone" for Channel One, so I went along. There was a big, big turnout and he put you to step up to the mic, then he roll the riddim and have you chat, and if he like it you do it again for a take and he record it. He asked me to go first and I did my *You better set up yourself dreadlocks / natty was down in the valley for a very long time / and now 'im come out . . .* , which he record and it come out as "The Killer".

'It was a mark of how much producers did want deejays that so many deejays got their start that night. Ranking Joe record that night, U-Brown record that night, Tappa Zukie record that night . . . only one man flopped. That was Jah Bull, him get the tune "Guiding Star" and he couldn't manage it, which shock us all because he gwan in the studio and say "*Lion!*" in a voice so big and so gruff he sound so wicked. All of we say "Bwoy, we get flop now, this man gon' kill us", but from when the man say "*Lion!*" he don't say no more. He was good on the sound systems but he just couldn't handle it in the studio. That's when Tappa Zukie jus' step up and come with, *Whether you come by bus or your car / I want you to know Jah is your guiding star . . .* , and he get record.

'Right that night Bunny Lee call up the stampers with the tapes and the tunes were in the shops within days.'

Veterans such as Coxsone, Joe Gibbs and Lee Perry showed admirable adaptability as well, and put out some of the finest cultural deejay tunes. Only Duke Reid was so resistant to the very notion of Jah Rastafari that he refused to play. That decision was so detrimental that it virtually sidelined one of the music's founding fathers until his death in 1974.

By which time Big Youth was, to borrow the title of his LP of that year, a reggae phenomenon. Citing his influences as including John Coltrane, Charlie Parker and the Beatles, his initial chart success mixed talking with singing ('Hit the Road Jack'), blended topical film-flam with righteous advice ('Screaming Target'), a wild sense of fun with praise of Jah Rastafari ('Chi Chi Run'). Neither was he scared to take some-one else's song and rebuild it into his own ('Touch Me in the Morning'). His all-round approach came together most memorably with the 'S90 Skank' single, one of Jamaica's biggest-selling records of 1972, staying at number 1 on the island for weeks on end and being used in a TV commercial for said bike. For five years he ruled, with such sublime deejay albums as *Screaming Target*, *Reggae Phenomenon*, *Natty Cultural Dread*, *Dreadlocks Dread* and *Hit the Road Jack*. In his wake was Dillinger, whose style owed plenty to U-Roy, but who told street-life tales with wit and invention, and produced two of the greatest ever deejay albums, *Ready Natty Dreadie* for Coxsone and *CB 200* for Joe Joe Hookim (which featured the cut 'Cocaine in My Brain'). I-Roy stepped up a gear with yout' man producer Gussie Clarke, and the album *Presenting I-Roy* features the brilliant, hard-rolling 'Black Man Time'. Prince Jazzbo cut the *Ital Corner* album for Lee Perry, a combi-nation which puts Scratch's dense, dripping idiosyncrasies into a lively and accessible but devastatingly cultural setting, and the unforgettable 'Mr Harry Skank' single for Glen Brown. Trinity voiced tunes for Joe Gibbs, Vivian Jackson, Joe Joe Hookim and Winston Riley; his style was Big Youth derivative, but the 'Three Piece Suit' single fully deserves its place in the deejay Hall of Fame. Prince Far-I excelled with Joe Gibbs, and the notion that he sounded as if he'd fallen into a particularly deep well and wasn't too happy about it was half the charm of albums like *Psalms For I*, *Message from the King* and *Under Heavy Manners*. Tappa Zukie's remarkably leaden style found favour riding rhythms from Bunny Lee, Joe Joe Hookim and Vivian Jackson – 'MPLA' and 'She Want a Phensic' being the two most enduring examples. Doctor Alimantado rocked

Kingston long before he became an icon among the UK's punk rockers. And Jah Stitch's deceptively lightweight sound may have been a lover's type of breezy but was as militant as you like with numbers like the above mentioned and 'Original Ragamuffin', 'Zion Gate' and 'Give Jah Glory' for Bunny Lee and 'African Queen' for Vivian Jackson.

Gussie Clarke was barely out of school when, in 1972, he produced two of the style's seminal albums: Big Youth's *Screaming Target* and *Presenting I-Roy*. He applied the same sense of purpose and eye for excellence to his business affairs as he did to crisp productions on the Mighty Diamonds, Gregory Isaacs, Augustus Pablo, Dennis Brown and Leroy Smart. Over the coming years he built the studio that had begun life in rented premises on Slipe Road into the Anchor complex in New Kingston, one of the most desirable recording environments on the island. I found him sitting behind a desk not quite big enough to play football on, in front of a wall covered by American, British and Canadian silver, gold and platinum discs. Unsurprisingly for a man who produced, in *Screaming Target*, one of the very few reggae albums that can be approached as such – as an album, that is, rather than as a collection of singles – the word 'concept' works hard in his vocabulary. And, equally expectedly, he has a lucid, forthright explanation as to why deejay music took off like it did.

'It was like a class situation – like *certain* people with *certain* kind of musical tastes. The wrong people were in the wrong place – I mean in the position to decide what is played on the radio and what is not. The radio stations in Jamaica were just not into Jamaican music – they were run by people who grew up with a calypso or an R&B environment, so what interest or love are they going to show reggae? What interest do they have? They're not part of the music. Once, one of the radio station did break up and t'row away thousands of Jamaican records that they had – because they ran out of space. What sort of message does that give out? It is something you should never see a radio station do. Anything they did play was going to be safe and probably been around for a while, so they were never going to play roots music or that kinda cultural deejay toasting. Because of this, the sound systems get big again. Bigger than they were before in the sixties. People went flocking to the dance to hear *new* records, they go to specifically hear what new records this sound have by what new artists, because that is how the Jamaican music industry's always worked – *the latest* records is what the people want and the sound systems was the only place to hear them. The dances were huge, and there was so many of them. So many sound systems, too – often you'd see two or three dances on the same street, because everybody was interested.

'This definitely had an effect on how the music developed, because as opposed to how the radio would want records to sound, the sound systems needed a different sound entirely. The deejays were representing the people around them with what they talked about, so therefore they talked in the Jamaican style of those same people – street slangs and heavy accents – and once that style came into fashion, the rhythms the producers were making had to adapt to it. You couldn't do the same things you used to do when everybody was singing love songs. And as the rhythms started moving in one direction, like with the roots thing, because the sound systems have such a competitive mentality – they were trying to pull the biggest crowds – they each wanted to take it a bit further. Outdo each other. Remember, the sound systems were the only source we producers had to guarantee us to get our records to the public – we had to make what we think they would want to play, so producers took it down that route. That definitely never woulda happened if we'd had to go for radio play.

'It keep the music as a downtown thing for a long time because people was unaware of there being a world market for it beyond their own immediate environment. At that point, the people who were making the music, who had the creativity and the artistic point of view, were not so much aware of how great the market was beyond Jamaica. They hadn't travelled, like some who had gone before them, so they wasn't making no compromise for anybody other than themselves – they thinking,

"What can I do for Jamaica?", for the people that they *know* will make a hit. And because they live down there, they also got to think, "What will work for me the man as well as me the artist?" Which is why so much of it seemed personal or concerned itself with the artist's immediate surroundings.

'There were so many records coming out at that time, and people who look at it from a mainstream point of view are surprised that there was so many record labels all surviving. But that wasn't hard, because in Jamaica there was always a place for new records. People usually buy records on the premise of "What *new* do you have to John Holt? . . . or by Dennis Brown? What *new* do you have by the Gussie label . . . or whatever label?" And when the guy in the record store hands him over the tune, he don't play it, the customer buys it straight off because he believes in that situation. Here, there is always a market for new creativity; so as long as people keep putting out new things the market will survive.'

Which is, of course, why it moves on as well.

14

Dubwise Situation

The piano chords at the front of the tune are familiar; then, just as something seems to be taking shape, that bizarre organ flourish comes out of nowhere, just off the beat, and breaks your concentration. But three tracks into *African Dub Chapter Three*, you aren't really hearing right, anyway. Different rules seem to apply. The rockers' drum pattern drives the flute and piano into the biggest horn blast you've ever heard, turning it into a brass-fest for a few seconds. Then, as the bass-line builds up underneath, a crisply chopped guitar takes over to duel with organ snatches that seem to be operating in zero gravity. Suddenly it's all spiralling out of control as echoes spin across the hi-fi speakers, only to be pulled back into relative normality as unnaturally taut bongos dominate, which then pass the baton to a renegade trombone almost immediately.

Then it gets really interesting.

Instruments ease backwards and forwards, in, out and around the mix, completely rebalancing the tune four or five times in the space of a minute. New melodies are shaped out of bits of rhythm that have been stretched and remoulded, whereas melodic sequences have been chopped down so brutally they can be stacked on top of each other to become the rhythm. All the while the echo and phaser units are picking up horn lines and keyboard riffs apparently at random, and the percussion is careening around as if in a pinball machine.

Welcome to 'Tribesman Rockers', one of the many high spots of the 1978 dub album, conceived, created and superbly crafted by the Mighty Two, aka studio owner/producer Joe Gibbs and his engineer Errol 'ET' Thompson. Just as you're coming to terms with what's going on around you, a familiar melody percolates out of the maelstrom. Lord Creator's 'Kingston Town'. Somewhat disconcertingly, as it's not really possible to imagine a song further mutated from what its composer intended it to be – either musically or sociologically – yet still remain recognizable.

But disconcerting is just what it ought to be. To take each element of the tune as separate – the bass, the drums, the horns, the bongos, the keyboards and so on – then set out to refocus the whole piece of work by adjusting, tweaking, bringing forward or pushing back each of them individually until the whole is satisfactorily rebalanced is to reach back to Africa and the practices that came over to Jamaica as obeah. Behind the smoke and mirrors and the waving of chickens are the art's central planks – the far less-photogenic healing ways: homoeopathy, herbalism, that sort of thing. It's an ancient African medicine that splits the body up into seven centres or 'selves' – sexual, digestive, heart, brain, etc. – and by prescribing various herbs and potions would, as practitioners always describe it, 'bring forward or push back' different centres; remixing, as it were, a person's physical or mental state into something very different. In other words, obeah could be used to cure a headache, just as it could make the worst grouch love the whole world or set the meekest of souls up to do battle. In the same way, by adjusting the controls at the mixing desk, a tune as bright and breezy (some might say cheesy) as 'Kingston Town' can be reinvented as something so edgy and surprising as 'Tribesman Rockers'.

It's an odd but suggestive coincidence that the tune pretty much accepted as the first to employ a specially remixed version side – 'Hard Fighter' by Little Roy, in 1971 – was reincarnated as 'Voo-doo'. The connection gets stronger as dub evolves: by the middle of the decade, the crushing bass 'n' drum remixes keep us on our toes with such seemingly arbitrary SFX as explosions, crashes, windows breaking and big dogs barking, while through the judiciously employed echo some frighteningly large spaces open up quite suddenly beneath our feet. Such offerings, vividly evoking the smoky intensity of Rasta drumming, were almost allegoric, designed to inspire a notion of simmering, meditative righteousness and to strike dread, both literally and figuratively, into the heart of Babylon. Just as obeah used to scare the crap out of the white folks down on the plantation, which is why the drum was banned among Jamaica's slaves for decades.

However, appropriate and attractive as such theories are, the big part in the evolution of dub is much closer to the twentieth century and concerns modern Jamaica's inherent resourcefulness. This is a Caribbean island that probably hasn't seen snow since the ice age, yet sent a creditable bobsleigh team to a Winter Olympics, so there's nothing Jamaicans can't do with whatever they happen to have to hand. Take the roadside barbecue pit just off Slipe Road that cooks on half an oil drum, where the customer tables are eight foot electrical-cable spools laid on their sides and the seats are cut from a tree trunk. Or that *Cool Runnings* bobsleigh team, who adapted from racing street vendors' pushcarts, itself a vehicle essentially remade from other things, with a low loading bed knocked up from salvaged planking and with modified car steering gear swivelling the front wheels. (The most interesting reuse I ever came across was an awning over a higgler's patch in Coronation Market which was anchored with a string tied to the centre spline of a car's gearbox. This was in 1993; it's probably still in service.)

Dub is part of this astonishing capacity for recycling. It involves taking either the recent or the ancient past (in reggae terms, six months ago can be prehistoric), and refashioning it to fit the contemporary requirements of the present. Duke Reid and U-Roy did it with a bunch of old rocksteady songs, just as Justin Hinds and the Dominoes re-trod 'Carry Go Bring Come' in both ska and rocksteady (coincidentally, another Duke Reid production); and Bob Marley wasn't above redeploying the Wailers' 1971/72 Lee Perry sessions as late as his 1978 *Kaya* album. You could say it's part of a national tradition dictated by the fact that, when you can't afford to throw too much away, things have to be recyclable.

It swiftly became a virtuosity in itself, with sound systems standing proud or flopping not on whether they had a tune or not, but on how many versions of it there were. Indeed, a crisp dub cut could breathe life into a tune that never quite made it first time out, while reworking a rhythm reached a point at which some provenly popular songs were versioned quite literally several hundred times. While this meant that the original producer or soundman could wring every last drop out of a good bit of work, it also meant that rivals could cash in on the action.

But we're getting in front of ourselves. In order to understand dub properly it's necessary to go back to the mid-1960s, before Duke Reid was recording U-Roy's records on top of King Tubby's rudimentary mixes. What's back there, and just afterwards, is a remarkable mixture of resourcefulness, political intervention, sharp business practice, unique musical artistry and vision, advancing technology, opportunism, dancehall patron power and sheer dumb luck. It could be the whole history of Jamaican popular music in microcosm. And, as you'd expect in such a pertinent summing up, it all kicked off on the sound systems.

Although Treasure Isle's rocksteady ruled the nation, by the end of 1967 Duke Reid's sound system, like Downbeat, was not quite the force it used to be. Comparatively speaking, that is. Partly because there were so many studios and record labels by then that sound men didn't need to make their own music to stay ahead of the game, there were plenty of producers to keep them supplied with exclusive new tunes. Also, the boom in the number of systems had engendered a far more parochial approach, and 'local' sounds such as Tubby's Home Town HiFi (Waterhouse), Lloyd the Matador (Waltham Park) and Stereo and Ruddy's the Supreme Ruler of Sound (both in Spanish Town) were starting to carry the swing. This last system was owned by record-store proprietor Ruddy Redwood and featured a range of specials given to him by his close friend Duke Reid. As a Spanish Town set it wasn't in direct competition, yet Redwood's reports back to Reid on how the tunes went down outside of the hothouse atmosphere of West Kingston were invaluable when the Duke was looking for potential releases. Thanks greatly to Byron Lee's efforts and the spread of radio, the music business was by now nationwide, and record men like Reid had to consider more than their immediate environment. Thus they were doing what would have been unthinkable five years previously: giving unique, unreleased soft waxes to other sound systems.

Towards the end of 1967, Redwood fortuitously happened on something that would revolutionize Jamaican music. His Treasure Isle sound system specials came via a disc cutter called Smith, who one day offered him a cut of the Paragons' 'On the Beach' that he had, quite literally, forgotten to put the vocal track on. As he accepted the tune, Redwood was immediately aware of the possibilities of revisiting what was a proven popular record (it had already been released as a huge hit), and that night played the vocal and instrumental versions back to back. By the time the second record was a few bars in the entire lawn was singing along, and according to those who were there, it was a totally spine-tingling moment when the whole point of the island's music business thus far made perfect sense. Imagine it: it's a warm night; Ruddy Redwood, known as Mr Midnight because he begins spinning tunes at precisely that time, comes on to a nicely loosened crowd, and although that instrumental cut must have surprised everybody, within seconds they have claimed it for their own and are joining in. Music made by the people for the people, unique in this respect to Jamaica's sound systems.

The reaction of the audience had repercussions far beyond this one magical interlude. Reported back to Duke Reid, it was more than enough to show him the way forward, and in the following year he reintroduced a whole raft of his old classics in an instrumental style. However, with his all-round fussiness and his fondness for US R&B, rather than just dropping out the voices, which might work for a sound system, Reid wanted to give the home consumers something more. So he replaced the singing with lead instrumentation, remixing or rerecording as necessary. Cuts featuring Tommy McCook, Winston Wright or Lynn Taitt in particular all had the feel of cool American pre-soul music with a rocksteady beat, a sophisticated arrangement and just a hint of West Coast jazz. And it wouldn't have escaped the Duke's attention that it was standard behaviour from James Brown to put an instrumental 'Part 2' on the B-sides of his singles. It's a sign of how an early operator such as Reid had evolved, that he was now more worrying about the reactions of the consumers than about those of the lawn dancers. This revolutionary new music was making such an impact at his and Redwood's dances by the end of 1968 that practically every producer in Jamaica went instrumental crazy.

This is a good example of how fast the Jamaican music industry can reinvent its value system, as only a few years previously other producers had scoffed at Leslie Kong's penchant for producing instrumentals. Now Coxsone was putting out a series of bubbling instrumental cuts of his early reggae hits, performed by the Studio One house band, the Soul Vendors (led by Jackie Mittoo or Leroy Sibbles); Derrick Harriott was doing the same with the Crystalites; as was Clancy Eccles with his regular backing group the Dynamites; likewise Harry Mudie, Harry J and Joe Gibbs, all of whom named their ensembles their All Stars. Somewhere along the line, 'Part 2' was restyled 'Instrumental Version', sometimes further defined with the name of whatever new lead instrument had been added, then simply 'Version 2' or '3' or whatever. Pretty soon the word had acquired verb status: to version meant to remix or to rerecord in order to re-present another version of the original.

Much of this instrumental aspect is part of the development from rocksteady to reggae, a period discussed in Chapter 10, but there was a parallel movement going on. The *really* clever state of affairs. After all, anybody could record an instrumental take of a song, or simply drop the singing off and get it pressed, but what was going on in Kingston involved redefining the song in the studio and turning the actual remixing into the end rather than merely the means to that end. It wasn't happening

313   **Dubwise Situation**

anywhere else in the world, and while Lynford Anderson and Joe Gibbs may have been the first to start using the mixing desk as another instrument on a par with the drums or the organ, it was King Tubby who went clear from a creative point of view.

As an electrical engineer and disc cutter, King Tubby was a perfectionist. His skill as an engineer led to him doing repair jobs or uprating for several studios and sound systems, while his rig, Tubby's Home Town HiFi – put together in 1968 – was perpetually evolving as a result as much of his natural curiosity and audaciousness as of his vocational training. He was probably the first to use high-frequency horn tweeters, and later made full use of the embryonic transistor technology and custom-built filters to split his frequencies between two different amplifiers: a valve amp for the bass, transistor for the treble ('weight and treble' as it still is known). He introduced echo, reverb and sound effects to the dance by bringing a range of specially built or modified outboard gear to his control tower. But he never forgot that the primary purpose of a sound system was to entertain the crowd with recordings of songs, and so his tone and resonance were always second to none.

Dennis Alcapone remembers King Tubby's dances as almost transcendental experiences.

'King Tubby had a sound system that I never hear nothing like it in my whole life. Sound systems, the big ones, was always exciting, but when Tubby came on the scene it was *extraordinary*. Jammy's was around in those days, it had been there from a long time, but it was like King Tubby's Part Two, it was never up there with Tubby's. Most of these dances we talking about were outdoor things, where you always have the big speaker boxes, but Tubby had him steel horns for the treble and he put them up in the trees so it's like the sound is coming from all over. When the night was warm, the breeze is blowing and the music's playing, it's truly something to behold. King Tubby's sound system was definitely magic.

'They had reverb on that sound system, no other sound system had reverb at the time – Tubby was the one who introduce it. Listen to his bass speakers and it's pure melody coming through. His bass was so round and fat that every singer sound wonderful, every song sound *rich*. Even if something hadn't been record so well it would still sound good on King Tubby's system. And the echo was another thing, nobody else had that, either. When U-Roy used to take up the mic to start his session and say, "Now this commence up the *night . . . night . . . night . . . night . . .*", the people would go wild. I've never heard – even to today – another sound system that sound as nice as King Tubby's.'

As a disc cutter, Tubby's attention to detail meant he'd make several test cuttings of the different aspects of a track, just to make sure everything was set up right – that is he'd cut with the voices only or with the instruments by themselves and listen to how each sounded on the disc. Even accounting for Duke Reid's finicky ways as a producer, Tubby's flawlessness in this area has a great deal to do with Treasure Isle's later rocksteady sound: he would always make sure nothing went on the stamper until it sounded exactly as it should, making full use of the *entire* bandwidth to give that full, almost self-satisfied feel to the records. One of the reasons Duke Reid's rocksteady stands the test of time so well is because the recordings were physically so well made and therefore, prior to all the remastering that's gone on of late, were less likely to sound primitive when listened to years later. And it was in these test cuttings that King Tubby's dub adventures began to take root.

As well as making discs with built-in spaces for U-Roy to toast, after noticing how, just as on Ruddy's sound, the crowd would love the plain instrumental just as much as the originals he started playing around with the mix as best he could on his home-made two-track mixer and tape recorder. Once he'd fitted the reverb and echo units to his sound-system's control tower and applied such effects to his exclusive instrumentals, any competition was annihilated. Tubby's Home Town HiFi instantly became the number one sound in Kingston.

As well as earning him this title, it attracted a lot of outside interest, with sound men wanting King Tubby's specials for their dances and producers after that particular touch on their versioned B-side. While his dub cutting for the sound men was an essentially low-profile exercise, the same couldn't be said for the mixing aspect. Without a multi-track mixing desk, Tubby worked off a set-up that would effectively modify the mix of a tune by passing the signal through a series of filters, blocking out frequencies that corresponded to, say, the singing, the horns or the bass. It's a fairly close cousin of graphic equalization, and is the same arrangement he used on Tubby's Home Town HiFi to give the impression of live mixing in the dancehall. It was impressive enough for him to count Glen Brown, Winston Riley, Lee Perry, Augustus Pablo and Bunny Lee among his earliest remix customers. Bunny Lee became so switched on to the possibilities of hooking up with a talent as great as King Tubby's that he encouraged the engineer to build a decent studio. Lee fairly waxes lyrical as he remembers it thus:

'From when I first met King Tubby and see him work I knew there was a man with a great deal of potential. He could make music outta the mistakes people bring him – like every spoil is a style to King Tubby. He would drop out the bits where a man sing a wrong note and bring up another instrument or drop out everything for pure bass and drum riddim; then he'd bring back in the singing. You would never know there was a mistake there because he drop in and out of tracks like that's what he was always intending to do. He do it all live, too. He don't build it up bit by bit, him jus' leggo the tape and do his thing. You watch him, it like watching a conductor or a maestro at work. And of course every time it would be different. He always want to surprise people – I think he even want to surprise himself sometimes – and if he mix the same tune a dozen times you will have twelve different version.

'I could see what he was capable of, through the ideas he have for everything. So I help him out getting a new mixing board, beca' I knew Byron Lee was uprating his Dynamic Studios and throwing out his old four-track board. I fix it for Tubbs to buy that board. That's how King Tubby's Studio, as a multi-track, was really begun.'

It's pure Bunny Lee to act as middle-man in a deal like that.

He was something of a Godfather of the Ghetto figure, a Mr Fixit who could move uptown with exactly the same ease as he felt among the sufferahs and the sound men. He frequently did favours, gave loans, sorted out problems or mediated trans-actions – it wasn't unusual for people within his community to ask Bunny Lee to bail relatives out of jail – and it's rare to find anybody in West Kingston with a bad word to say about him. So even though there is a self-serving aspect to his wanting Tubby to modernize his kit, he probably would have got involved even if there hadn't been.

But if that was typical of Bunny Lee, what Tubby did next was equally characteristic. He replaced the unit's four sliding control channel faders with new sliders which had increased resistance for more accurate control and were physically easier to operate as they were less worn. As a result of its owner's professorial expertise in electronic theory, his phenomenal effectiveness with a soldering iron and his uncanny ability to see beyond the music on the tape, King Tubby's Studio was in an almost organic state of affairs. The Dromilly Avenue yard – actually his mum's house – was a perpetually evolving state of the art, morphing into whatever the master required as he adapted equipment, added – and bastardized – new outboard gear and tinkered with the circuitry on an almost daily basis.

Mikey Campbell, aka Mikey Dread, aka Dread at the Con-trols was a ghetto hero as Jamaican radio's first genuine roots deejay. In 1977 he brought the vibrancy of the lawn dance to the airwaves with his wildly imaginative and technologically cutting-edge late-night *DATC* show. He was also the man responsible for the innovative series of dub-inspired albums based on that same programme: *Dread at the Controls*; *African Anthem*; *Mikey Dread at the Controls Dubwise*; *World War Three*; *SWALK* . . . He was, inevitably, to cross paths with King Tubby. Although Mikey's own way with the mixing desk is impeccable, he went to Tubby's to mix his original radio jingles, and when he launched his DATC label, specializing in his productions of various roots singers, he involved King Tubby in the mixing of some sizzling B-sides. His recording studio apprenticeship under Tubbs left the deepest impression on the deejay:

'It was Tubby who encourage me to get into recording. He was aware of the *Dread at the Controls* show late night on JBC from when it started, and I would go to him from time to cut my jingles. I went to Tubby's in 1977 to cut one on a riddim that he had called "Psalm of Dub", this is when I was getting in plenty fights at the station about my show and I want to do this likkle thing because mi know the more I play it back on air the more I am putting out a message to the people who are giving me a fight. It went [*toasts*] *The Dread you have to love / The Dread you have to love / The Dread you have to love 'cause 'im the Doctor of the Dub / The Father up above he say rub he say dub* . . . And Tubby hear it and say "Bwoy Mikey. That sound like it longer than a jingle, I feel you're gon' make a record of it. Why you don' jus' go in there and finish it?" So I go back inside the studio and finish it as a full-length track, and Tubbs tell mi, "*All right!* All you need now is to make your own label."

'We were both laughing about it, because I jus' see it as a dub plate, but Tubbs tell me it serious and, from back then he tell me I need to take this business seriously because I have all the right ideas. I start the Dread at the Controls label from there, and that, "Love the Dread", was the first release. *Number seven in the Top 10.* Is after that I release one more for Tubby – "Natty Dread Inna Bull Bay" – and do the Joe Gibbs thing and then everything start to work. [It was Mikey constantly playing his Althea & Donna special, *Mi dolly up a JBC / Mi go check Mikey Dread an t'ing* . . . , to rapturous listener response that convinced producer Joe Gibbs to release 'Uptown Top Ranking', which, up until then, existed only as an all-but-ignored alternative cut to deejay Trinity's 'Three Piece Suit' single.]

'But most of all Tubby is the man who teach me a whole heap about multi-track recording and about *sound*. Tubby would come into the studio every Sunday and bring the riddim, and show me the module, the equalization, this is the gain for mic – the line gain – this is mic or line input and so on . . . show me each likkle module down the line and exactly how he get 'im sound. And mi love that because 'nuff producers wouldn't share their knowledge, they like be so secretive with what they know. But Tubby gave me an open door to come in so I had a chance to see how he worked with different sounds, different producers' tunes and everything about how he did his stuff.

'I have eight O-levels and A-levels in physics, maths and applied maths; my electrical engineering qualification is from the University of Technology and I trained as a technician and operator with the Jamaican Broadcasting Corporation. King Tubby knew I could understand the theories of sound, not on the same level as he, but I would be able to truly appreciate what it was he knew and wanted to pass on to somebody – as I've said, he was a very generous man in that, and every, respect. He was always saying, "Yo, Mikey, mi 'ave a book for you," and he'd reach up and get down from offa his shelf some new book. Techniques of sound recording, audio technique, stuff like that. He get every book there was as soon as it come out, and he show me and let me study from some great books. And he knew them all. The man was one of the most brilliant scholars I have ever met – bar none. I study at A-level and at the university and I never meet nobody who study like King Tubby. If there was something out there that he thought could affect what he did, he wanted to know everything about it. He is one of the most brilliant person I've ever met. *Intellectually* as well as technically. It's because he truly understood sound, inna *scientific* sense, that he was able to do what he did. He knew all the theories of how sound work, as well as understanding how all the circuits worked and what electronics did what. Most recording engineers in Jamaica at that time could tell you what every piece of equipment did and how it would work in your system, but Tubby went far beyond that because he knew what every component in every circuit in every piece of equipment did. The greatest engineer I have ever known in my life.

'The man invent a whole heap of things and don't get no credit. He made his first echo machine with two old tape recorders. He build spring-loaded switches for his sound effects, so it's pressure-sensitive and he can hit it hard or soft or slowly to get a different sound from each effect like a thunder clap or an explosion. He would figure out an effect he wanted, then design and construct the circuit that would give him that. One thing he make, it name a high pass filter, and he use it 'pon the snare drum and the hi-hat so it kinda splashes [Mikey makes a sort of squelching/hissing noise]. He use it all the time on Johnnie Clarke mixes like "No Man Can Escape His Judgement in This Time" or "Jah Jah in Deh in Deh". When Bunny Lee come up with that whole flying cymbal thing – *tiissst . . . tiissst . . . tiissst . . . tiissst . . . tiissst . . . tiissst* – Tubby a-mix it through his high pass filter and it cut certain frequencies and boost certain frequencies, so when it coming from the hi-hat – which is like the highest frequency you're going to hear in any mix – the *whole octave* change in that mix. And every time Tubbs come with that, man just scratch their heads and go "How the *blouse* 'im do that?" But King Tubby's board was the only one that could.

'An' he just play with things that people make, too. He customize his Fisher reverb unit until the factory wouldn't recognize it; in fact, not much of his equipment stayed the way it was when it come out the factory. Such was his knowledge that if the man don't think a sound is like how he want it, he would go into the circuitry there and then and change it to create the particular effect that he want. His whole studio was custom made by King Tubby himself. And it always changing because Tubby was looking for new technology more than anybody else. Because he can make it when other studio people they can't make nothing – they can't even solder two wires together.

'There was so much music in Jamaica at that time, so much remixes, that a man have to come with something special to stay out in front, and that's what kept Tubby there. Plus he worked *hard*. Even when he not actually at the board, he still working beca' 'im thinking about things or trying new things out or reading a book or just practising – like the great musicians practise all the time, so did King Tubby. He knew he had to, and nobody out there could keep up with him.'

According to Mikey Campbell, King Tubby was a warm, giving and humorous man, if a little straitlaced compared with so many of his left-of-centre clientele, and his fussiness extended into all aspects of his life, from his sartorial approach to how he treated his apprentices – there are even entertaining, though probably apocryphal stories of his going to the bank to exchange the used notes in his pocket for crisp, sequential new ones.

'Tubby was a man who was very neat. Everything about him *had* to be in order. His workshop, his studio, you have to have some stuff lying about when you're working, but apart from that, everything was where it should be. The chrome on the valves and the fronts of the amplifiers always highly polished. You couldn't work to the kind of precision he worked to if you couldn't find things or wasn't sure what was what. He knew that. Him dress up good, too. Every day he come to work looking *crisp*, him clothes always well press and t'ing. Sometime him come to work and him take off him shirt, but he always have on a singlet that was clean and fresh – you couldn't take your shirt off in there if you didn't have a T-shirt or a singlet on; the man didn't like no bare chest in his studio. But his shoes . . . *bwoy*, King Tubby's shoes, *well clean and shiny*. Everyday. And it difficult to keep your shoes clean in Jamaica, so much dust. He always stopping if he see something on his shoes – not if he doing a mix, but otherwise, if he look down and see a speck he reach back, pull out him hanky and dust it off. He didn't like you burn spliff on his premises, either.

'He was very critical of his apprentice work: they do well and he seh, "It *all right*", or "It not *that* good". Just to keep them on their toes, because he wanted to see them try harder or try new things, for them to find out how far they could go. He wasn't being rude or anything because he wasn't like that. And they respect him for it. Just to be around him was enough for them.

'It used to go like this: we play the track, balance up the board and we listen to it. Then after a likkle few minutes Tubbs say "All right, we a-record *now*", and, bam, just take a mix. It all come spontaneous, because he know the board and he heard the tune, so he *know* when to echo. He done hear the song already, so him know more or less the transitions that's going to happen down the line. It's like there's certain points that you can anticipate; for instance, when the drummer roll *dgadgadgadgadgadga* he must crash 'pon the cymbal because it the only place he can go, an' Tubbs know so. By the time the boy go *dgadgadgadgadgadga* . . . *crash* Tubbs ready with echo long time and it . . . cra-cra-cra-crash. And the man fast, like he part of his board. While he knows certain things he going to do, he always putting in other things straight as they pop into his head. The man a marvel, he move *rapid* and touch up 'nuff likkle things to go *blee-blee-bleep* and t'ing. That's like his sense of humour and his joyfulness coming out.

'And he's a man like me and we take five mix on the tune and we sit down and listen back and choose one we really want. Then we use that. No two mix would be quite the same, either; every one done spontaneous and straight off, nothing gone back and punched in. Many engineers wanna just do one mix for you, like, "Boom! All are done man, next tune!" Tubby not like that, Tubby perfect the damn thing. *Every* damn thing.'

Of course, it wouldn't have mattered how cutting edge this technology was had Tubby's appreciation of a tune been open to question. His uncanny ability to get inside a song and, as he stripped away the layers, expose its heart produced some of the best roots music to come out of Jamaica. Militant, conscious, righteous, praising Jah Rastafari, lovers' rock . . . it didn't matter; King Tubby would get to grips with everything. Mikey Campbell's remarks about his eagerness to learn are borne out by the clear progression in Tubby's work through the decade.

The early singles are relatively restrained, with the two-track facilities allowing only minimal additional effects as the filters 'phased' the instruments in and out. Then the beginnings of what was to make King Tubby an icon can be heard on the 1973 LP *Blackboard Jungle Dub* – a collaboration between Tubby and Lee Perry that lays claim to being one of the first dub albums. Too often the idiosyncrasies on this set are attributed to

Scratch alone, but it shouldn't be forgotten that by then Tubby had both his modified four-track board and the ability to realize whatever ideas either of them had. In the same way as U-Roy's and Dennis Alcapone's deejay singles of a few years previously had captured the excitement of a lawn dance and put it on wax for people to enjoy in the comfort of their own homes, so Tubby was doing exactly that with the versions. And, also as with the deejay singles, the people loved it.

King Tubby didn't produce anything, he simply worked on master tapes other producers would bring him. This was the genesis of the remix that, years later, would come to dominate certain areas of music. There was no shortage of raw material, either. Other LPs followed, and Tubby's technique became more imaginative by the day. Hence it was inevitable that the new wave of roots producers wore a path to Dromilly Avenue. Vivian 'Yabby You' Jackson, Bertram Brown, Winston 'Niney' Holness, Prince Allah, Jack Ruby and the Morwells all provided rhythms and came away with some incredible sides.

By 1975, such was the added value of one of Tubby's B-sides that he was being credited on singles' labels merely by name, not even as 'mixed by'. The engineer as the artist, and a host of albums followed: *King Tubby Meets the Aggravators at Dub Station*, *King Tubby's Meets the Upsetter at the Grass Roots of Dub*, *Harry Mudie's Meets King Tubby's in Dub Conference*, and so on. Augustus Pablo also followed this sequence for his collaborative LP *King Tubby's Meets Rockers Uptown*, a subtle, strikingly orchestral album, with the shimmering melodic depths of Pablo's production and the cocky, high-stepping, high-end rhythms giving the mixer plenty to work with. Quite rightly, this is reckoned by many to be the greatest dub album of all time. It had a huge and far-reaching impact, too. When Island Records UK released 'Baby I Love You So' by Jacob Miller, the vocal cut of the album's title track, the original plan was to put 'King Tubby's Meets Rockers Uptown' on the flip, but somebody, apparently from Island USA, suggested reversing the running order. Dub as an international entity had arrived.

It was a huge hit, taking the notion of dub and the name of King Tubby to areas no such version had ever reached. It went beyond the core reggae audience into the mainstream and so began an international, pan-racial relationship with King Tubby that influences to this day. This wasn't the engineer as artist, this was the engineer as rock god.

Of course, by then, King Tubby was no longer alone.

If your mum had been driving you to school in 1972 in the Port Antonio area on Jamaica's north-east coast, the chances are that JBC's breakfast show would have been on the car radio, an innocuous diet of country, calypso, R&B and a sprinkling of highly polished reggae. Or it would be until another signal cut in, jamming the frequency to replace such easy listening with Lee Perry's *Cloak & Dagger* album, an abrasively typical Scratch instrumental set. One side would play after the other, with not a word said over the airwaves. If you were a pupil at Tichfield High School, Port Antonio, then you'd be in on the joke, for it was two Tichfield pupils who, most mornings, would retune the school's licensed radio transmitter (Radio Tichfield) to illegally override the larger station within a five-mile radius of the town.

Apart from simply amusing their mates, and royally pissing off a great deal of upwardly mobile parents, this was a comment on the fact that official Jamaican radio (there were by now more than a few small-scale pirate operations) wasn't catering for a younger generation to whom sound systems and representative music had always been a part of their lives. And it wasn't by chance that *Cloak & Dagger* was the soundtrack chosen to make such a protest – the adolescent airwave hijackers had to play an album because it could be left to roll, and that was the most obnoxious, radical LP available on the island. Although this 1972 set cannot accurately be termed a dub album, a full twelve months before Perry's Tubby-mixed *Blackboard Jungle Dub* it was the nearest thing to it. Making its musical statements through clever arrangements, instrumentation and elementary mixing technique, it attempted to create, at the recording stage, the vibe King Tubby would achieve on Scratch's B-sides after the event. It was the most tangible link between the instrumental style we discussed a few pages ago and the truly dubwise occurrences of a year or two later. But, most crucially, it formed a template for Scratch's later efforts, which would be some of the best dub music ever committed to disc.

Remarkably, at that point Lee Perry didn't have his own studio but worked mainly out of Randy's, and must have spent a small fortune there. He was putting out a phenomenal amount of music either under his own name, with the Upsetters or with singers such as Dave Barker, Leo Graham and Junior Byles, plus there were any number of secondary takes, alternative mixes and dubs of his tunes (he even called himself King Chubby for some work). It was during this period, between 1971 and 1974, that what became the Lee Perry sound began to emerge. He slowed down his beat from those earlier instrumentals, but did it without overweighting the overall balance, while the sheer density of what was going in the mix and his apparently chaotic approach to lyrics and lyrical ideas gave his material an intrigue and a multi-dimensionality too seldom even attempted in reggae. It was in 1974, though, when he opened his own studio at the house he had bought at 5 Cardiff Crescent, in the relatively uptown suburb of Washington Gardens, that Lee Perry's creativity ran rampant.

The Black Ark, as it was called, had its circuitry designed by King Tubby (another example of the man's generosity) and cost a fortune to equip, but its four-track Soundcraft board, Teac recorder, Echoplex delay unit and Roland space echo hooked up to a phaser unit were as state of the art as could be bought off the shelf. Unfettered by time or expense, Lee Perry could literally do what he liked, and his almost perpetual rhythm-building, tune deconstructing or extending of an original idea often went way past the point at which logic tells most people to stop, into a place where the instrumentation took on ethereal qualities. Unlike Tubby, Scratch didn't mix other people's tunes but worked with his own material, and as he produced the original music he was already hearing the instruments and (very often) the voices with a version or three in mind. On a single rhythm he would cut singing, toasting and two or three different lead instruments, mixing a number of dubs and even combining more than one version on the same cut. Perry would continually sculpt away at his vast stockpile of rhythms and tunes, adding, chipping bits off, echoing, distorting and stirring in just about anything that took his fancy – his children's toys were always popular, notably the moo-cow box (turn it upside down and it moos), as were snatches of TV dialogue. Although he was particular about not opening up until 10 a.m., because his common-law wife Pauline and their four children lived at that address (he was also very hard on anybody cussing in the yard where they might be overheard by his family), more often than not he'd been at the desk for several hours working by himself.

Although so much of the instrumental work that came out of the Black Ark is credited to the Upsetters, you shouldn't think of this as the same group who cut the Django-era stuff. The drum and bass engine room of those earlier sessions, Aston (aka Family Man) and Carlton Barrett, respectively, were now full-time members of the Wailers' band and thus were unavailable to work elsewhere. Within his new studio set-up Perry used a fluid session crew that comprised most of the best players on the island, but couldn't be pinned down to any regular line-up. Among them, Boris Gardiner and Robbie Shakespeare played bass; Sly Dunbar and Mikey 'Boo' Richards were on drums; the guitarists were Chinna Smith, Geoffrey Chung and Willie Lindo; keyboards were manned by Augustus Pablo, Theophilus Beckford, Winston Wright and Robbie Lynn; percussion came courtesy of Skully Simms; and the brass section included Vin Gordon, Glen DaCosta and Bobby Ellis. While his being able to get the same sound from so varied a group of highly individual players gives an indication of Lee Perry's abilities as a producer, it also shows a man keen on the wider range of alternatives that a flexible session crew such as this could offer. For many of the players it was a chance to flex muscles that other studios might have ignored.

Leroy Sibbles was the leader of Studio One rocksteady champions the Heptones, who enjoyed something of a second coming with Lee Perry in the first half of the 1970s, both just before and after he opened the Black Ark. Sibbles remembers the studio as a place of great opportunity and creativity.

'Nothing not finished when Scratch catch hold of it. He was like an explorer going into the future of the music and he always want to push that little bit further. When you think a tune's done, you hear it play back the next day and there's even more gone into it, yet it still sound like the tune. It still sound good. Scratch could look *deep, deep* into a tune the way other people would just look at the surface, and reach down into it to pull things up that most people hadn't even really noticed. Sometimes he strip so much away you think it too bare, too empty, but once he put the vocal or another instrument on top you know exactly the vibe he was going for. We re-record a lot of our old Studio One hits there, and he could see layers to pull apart and put back together to give a new vibe to something that you've sung a thousand times before.

'It could be difficult sometimes for the singers like us and for the musicians, because he ask you to sing or play things you think can't make any sense. He want you to play a rhythm in a certain way, or hit the cymbal *so*, and once he fully explained what it is he want you still can't see how it going to work. But he's thinking about what he's going to do with it as part of the whole thing, so when you hear it played back you know it make sense. His dubs were done in the tune's first arrangements as much as the final mix. That's what gave him the edge in the music business – his arrangements. Scratch was a truly great arranger.'

All of which afforded a far more musical quality to Lee Perry's remixed output than the primarily rhythmic musings of so many of his dub contemporaries. Whereas King Tubby's style couldn't have been so successful without the mixer's innate musicianship, there can be no doubt that at least a proportion of it was technically led. Not so with Scratch. Although his use of sound effects was as tricksy as anybody else's, his echoes were relatively low key and the reverb was there largely to fatten things out. The playing was then looped into snatches that tended to retain their original melodies rather than become practically percussive devices – he always used genuine percussion instruments for that purpose, sometimes playing them himself. While this musical bent was already making sure there weren't too many sharp edges in a Lee Perry mix, it was his quest to add ever-increasing layers that produced the trademark Black Ark sound. It was only a four-track recording operation, so he was continually having to 'bounce down', combining two tracks on to one in order to free up space for whatever he wanted to add on next. Bouncing down reduces flexibility in the final mix – which accounts for Perry's Black Ark output never being as drop-dead wild as others of the time – and squashing tracks together thus is what led to that luxuriant density characteristic of this later work. But, most significantly, such combination blurs the edges of each original track, as every time a recording is bounced down it loses a little definition, and each track starts to encroach on the others with an organic, woody-sounding fuzziness, bringing a soothing, entirely *ital* naturalness to such words of confrontation as 'War in a Babylon', 'Zion Blood' and 'Chase the Devil', and infusing a glowing warmth to the sparsest of mixes.

Working barefoot, spliff burning and dancing virtually non-stop, Scratch would become one with the music, rather than with the equipment, to create a unique spatial geometry within his mixes. Dubs of all his hits, such as 'Groovy Dub', 'Sufferers' Dub', 'Revelation Dub', 'Party Time Pt 2', 'Corn Fish Dub' and so on were always far more imaginative than their titles suggest, and boosted his reputation to the sky. He put out the *Revolution Dub* album in 1975, and *Upsetter in Dub* is a later compilation of tracks from that era, but all of this was little more than an overture to *Super Ape*, which might just have the edge over *King Tubby's Meets Rockers from Uptown* as the best dub reggae album ever made. Released in 1976, the set was the absolute distillation of Scratch at the Black Ark. Using vocal snatches from himself, Prince Jazzbo, George Faith and Max

Romeo and bits of tunes both well known and unfamiliar, it builds a jungle of a soundscape so thick you need a machete to hack through the undergrowth, while the vines and creepers continually swing back and hit you in the face. Like nothing else at the time, it shows how far roots reggae could have gone, as it explores roots both thematically as well as musically, Rastafari, righteousness and repatriation from a perspective so skewed it comes back into line as the absolutely spiritual. This man is the Salvador Dalí of Dub.

Spiritually closest to Scratch was Augustus Pablo. Away from his King Tubby's Studio mixed material was a later body of work he produced and mixed himself. This was nowhere near as viscous as Perry's, but the tracks always began life as tunes – in the strict rather than the colloquial sense – and never forgot it. Whatever they were put through. This is best illustrated by the East of the River Nile trilogy, three albums which sum up what versioning was supposed to be all about by showing what can be done without being silly. The first chapter is *Let's Get Started* by vocal trio Tetrack, a Pablo-produced album of serviceable though unspectacular music made up for by the group's delicate roots harmonies. Over the page is *East of the River Nile* by Augustus Pablo, the same songs done over as instrumentals but now presented as the most engrossing example of Pablo's Addis-type sound, delicate but punchy with his Melodica, clavinet, harpsichord and xylophone floating just above the mix. Then finally the Rockers International Band's *Eastman Dub*, that same collection of tracks remixed into dubs that strip away enough to bare the powerful pumping Rockers rhythms that are the other sets' soul, yet retain sufficient phased chord progressions, echoed horns and guitar signatures to give the melodies a look in. Laid out like this it was a sound man's dream come true. By juggling between two turntables (UK style) you could spend ten minutes on any one of a number of crisp Pablo tunes *before* you had to lick anything back to the beginning.

Although it is Tubby, Perry and Pablo who have enjoyed by far the highest profile, both at home and abroad, they were by no means the only dub masters. Clive and Vincent Chin's at Randy's Studio had been cutting dubs – as opposed to merely vocal-less versions – since 1972 with the Errol Thompson-engineered Impact All-Stars sessions (Impact was one of the Chin's labels) and *Java Java Java* which, in 1973, was another of the very first dub albums. Likewise Herman Chin Loy, whose *Aquarius Dub* LP appeared at roughly the same time – in 1969 Chin Loy was the first producer to record Horace Swaby, as Augustus Pablo used to be known. And Keith Hudson, the youthful ghetto dentist (no kidding), whose foresight made him one of the first to be seriously interested in recording deejays and who was equally self-assured when it came to dub. His 1972 LP *Furnace* featured dubs of the regular tracks; then, in 1975, he came with *Pick A Dub*, an album of remixes of his earlier hits – plus, rather notably, a take on 'Satta Massa Gana' – that is up there with *King Tubby's Meets Rockers Uptown*, *Super Ape* and *African Dub Chapter Three* as one of the supreme heavyweight champion dub sets.

The refreshing thing about the above-mentioned sets is their lack of effects. This was the remixer's art in its purest form: a minimum of outboard gear and often using buttons, rather than sliders, to drop the tracks in and out; an abundance of imagination; an ear for what a tune could be turned into without smothering it; manual dexterity; and good solid underlying riddims. You're still listening to the track, but your mood is manipulated by the dub as the bass and drums take over or fall away. Derrick Harriott's two classic dub albums *Scrub-a-Dub* and *More Scrubbing the Dub* were built on the firm foundation of his old rocksteady rhythms, as were Coxsone's series of dub albums (which failed to convince owing to surprisingly half-hearted mixes, apparently by the great man himself), while Treasure Isle dubs came courtesy of engineer Errol Brown, the late Duke Reid's nephew, and owe their standing more to the bass-lines of the rocksteady classics they were built on than to any particularly innovative mixing.

Which wasn't the case once Joe Gibbs and Errol Thompson, aka the Mighty Two, hit their stride. Gibbs had been recording at Randy's, where Thompson was the house engineer, practically since it opened in 1968, and after he opened his own two-track studio at the back of his record shop he would return to North Parade to get his dubs mixed. Courtesy of Thompson at the board, he came away with the *Serial Dub* and *African Dub Chapter One* LPs which were, like Thompson's Impact All Stars mixes, comparatively temperate as they eschewed effects to concentrate on cutting instrumentation away from the drum and bass. When Gibbs opened his sixteen-track studio at Retirement Crescent, he took Thompson with him and began the adventures that took them as far as *African Dub Chapter Three*. Thompson had sixteen tracks to weave around each other, and his total deconstruction of rocksteady tunes re-recorded solely to make dub mixes, his use of mad echo and reverb, and his addition of SFX that included roosters crowing, phones ringing and doors slamming earned him the right to be thought of as King Tubby's heir apparent.

Dub hit a creative peak around the middle of the decade – although *Eastman Dub* and *African Dub Chapter Three* didn't happen until 1978, at which point dub records were still incredibly popular. As we've seen, everybody and their *muddah* was either cutting dubs or paying someone else to do so. Dub seemed to be dominating the market place, with some sound systems playing nothing else. In 1974, singer/producer Rupie Edwards put out *Yamaha Skank*, not simply a dub LP, but a dub LP built on just one rhythm: fourteen or so cuts of the Uniques' 'My Conversation'. With hindsight, this presaged the endless versioning of the eighties, but back then it seemed like the reggae industry was taking the piss; that it was trying to see exactly how much the audience would put up with before it started giving dub the swerve. Not a bit of it, or at least that's how Rupie Edwards himself tells the story.

Rupie Edwards cut hits for Joe Higgs, Bob Andy and the Ethiopians, and was the first to record Gregory Isaacs and Johnnie Clarke ('Everyday Wondering' was one of his), and had a big hit in the UK with 'Ire Feeling', the same year as *Yamaha Skank*. These days he records gospel music for his own label and administers the back catalogue of his Success and Cactus imprints from his shop in north London's bustling Ridley Road market. The one-rhythm album, he explains, was never premeditated, and there's another big myth about it he'd like to clear up:

'There was no way it planned. When I bought the rhythm from a guy name Martin Riley of the Uniques, which is the group who actually recorded the song, I had no intention of making that album. And although it's always said that Bunny Lee gave me that rhythm, he didn't, I *purchase* it from Martin Riley. Bunny Lee was the song's original producer, but it wasn't he that sold it to me.

'Martin came to me because, I suppose, he needed some money and wanted to sell the backing track to a song that was a hit for him a long time ago. It was common back then, when everything was *Version this* or *Dub that*, for people who had a good strong rhythm track on tape to sell it on for somebody else to bring it up to date, and producers were buying and selling rhythms all the time. He approach me, I bought it off him and just put it down for a while; didn't start doing any work on it for maybe a few weeks. That situation was different to if you were recording a new song and needed a version side, then you'd do it right away and maybe have one or more idea worked out already, and if you needed another one later then you'd come back to it. But with this you do some work on it when you feel the inspiration – like one day or one night you just think "I got something to say on that tune," so you go in and do it.

'There was no real plan, but as I was doing it and I was having a load of different ideas on that rhythm so I thought to put them all on the same album – just them, nothing else. There had been plenty of all dub albums, but this had never been done before.'

Wasn't he in any way worried that, even given the amount of dub and version records being bought, the public might think this was going too far?

'No, no, no, not at all. This was a record-buying population that would come into your shop and ask "What have you got that's *new?*'', and to them the version was just another new song, it just happen to have the same backing track as one that already release. The Jamaican audiences are quite happy with the same song again, as long as it was good enough. If it kept them entertained then it was all right. Like sound systems will always play a song again and again and again if it is good enough to continue to move the crowd. This was no different than that.

'Just like so much of the old rocksteady that was being versioned during the early part of the seventies, "My Conversation" was a *good* song. When you have the musicians that can play properly and the correct production and sound balance and the recording was done real well, then of course you can version it again and again. As long as it's balanced: drum, bass, guitar . . . everything. With those songs all the ingredients was always there, not like so many modern songs where it isn't cooked properly so it can't last too long.

'Also, in reggae it has never really mattered if something sound familiar. What was actually known as *versions* wasn't exactly a new thing, either, because the duration of songs and the instrumentation had always meant some songs are very similar to each other in patterns and chord changes. You could have song A and song Z, both songwriters have no meeting or knowledge of each other, it just happen their songs fit *identically*, because reggae is two or three, occasionally four chords, so it don't leave you a lot of choice – some of the nicest sounds from that era was two-chord songs. So it's the drum pattern that decides it, and if you have certain patterns that are a hit in the dancehall at the time because of the latest dance craze or something, then you're even more restricted. Of course, the melody can change, but it's the rhythm, as the basis of the real authentic reggae music, will be the same, meaning two completely separate songs – different subject, different lyrics, different melody – will fit like a size-seven shoe fit a size-seven foot.'

Is that why dub and versioning exploded so strongly when it did, because the people wanted it? Or, even, would accept it?

'Not really, because if it hadn't been good they wouldn't have accepted it. There had been versions for a little while at the end of the sixties, but why it blew up when it did was because the government put a restriction on the price a producer can sell a pre-release record for. This was at the end of 1971 or the beginning of 1972, before the elections, and it devastated the music business in Jamaica.

'Before then, we have the white-label business, where if a tune popular in the dancehalls we give it to the shops pre-release and we can charge what we like for it because it in demand. Twelve shillings and sixpence . . . fifteen shillings . . . even seventeen shillings and sixpence for some record. Anything we think we can get. Then overnight the Minister of Trade and Industry, Mr Robert Lightburn, pass a law that say the maximum a record can sell in the shops for is seven shillings and sixpence, which is what release records sell for. Too many shop owners and the wholesalers had been complaining that it was a free for all and they couldn't sell to the public at any sort of regular price, and when we was selling pre-release direct like that the government weren't getting any tax like they would on a release record. So this wiped out pre-release, and it hit the music business *hard*.

'The industry was already suffering because there was so much music being made – you put out a record before and sell a few thousand, but in them days you put it out and sell a few hundred, minor thousands at the most. Now this, and it meant producers like myself and others were laying out vast amounts of money making these records and then we weren't getting the returns. Session fees had just gone up to a minimum of three pounds per side, which was a lot back then if you've got eight or nine musicians, and then you got to pay studio hire. This lasted a few years, and it knocked a lot of producers out because they couldn't get by on the likkle shilling that come in – what had been coming from England had virtually dried up because the reggae boom there had finished.

'It stopped creativity because no money was being put back into making more music and nobody could really afford to experiment too much. That's when the idea of version took off, because it didn't cost you any more session fees to put the same rhythm out again. Everybody started doing versions and the dub thing was just that taken a stage further, whereby it became something new, something just as creative as making new music. Jamaicans can adapt to anything; they adapt to this situation and turn it into an art. It was what got a lot of people through those years when the price of records was fixed – making versions is what kept me going.'

By the mid-1970s though, dub's next generation was already falling into place. Joe Joe and Ernest Hookim's Channel One studio had been up and running since 1973, but it wasn't until 1976 that they employed the house band the Revolutionaries, which hooked Sly Dunbar up with Robbie Shakespeare, the rhythm section who came up with the 'rockers' rhythm pattern.

A rhythm that would not only change the balance of dub, but the sound of roots reggae altogether.

15
Dreadlocks in Moonlight

Meanwhile, in spite of the deejays and dubmeisters assuming such a high profile that for many they were the sole definition of roots reggae, there was always a great deal going on alongside them. A great deal that owed as much to longer-standing Jamaican music traditions as it did to any hard-times style, as for the majority of its patrons the dancehall was exactly that – a hall were you danced. Important as any educational aspect was, to many it was strictly secondary and there was always another facet to roots reggae, one that owed itself to orthodox singing, established musicianship and more straightforward studio skills. In spite of the deejays and dubwise grabbing the high international profiles it was, in fact, this third side to the roots reggae triangle that was its base, with forthright songs of sufferation, of social statement, of Jah love or love and hurt.

As we've established, social comment or protest songs had been a consistent feature of the modern Jamaican musical landscape, yet at the end of the 1960s there wasn't anybody who had gone so far as to try and make a living out of them. It was as if no record producer figured it was worth the bother. This was as much from a commercial as a cultural point of view – even those record men who had sympathy for Rasta and the sufferahs were unconvinced that the record-buying public shared their concerns. Hence the Abyssinians' 'Satta Massa Gana' was still languishing on the shelf; Burning Spear was confined to a lengthy period of woodshedding at Studio One; and Joe Gibbs wasn't to invest in that area until he opened his own recording facility at the back of his shop in 1970. Only Justin Hinds and the Dominoes had been conscientiously conscious in their lyrical outlook, but what they recorded for Duke Reid was, on the surface, forthright biblical morality tales that seemed to owe more to rural folk traditions than to present-day slum sufferation. Which was how they'd have to appear in order to sneak past the Duke's notorious intolerance of all things Rasta.

So it took a maverick to make that first move, and they don't come more maverick than the brainy, volatile combination of the three Wailers, Peter Tosh, Bunny Wailer and Bob Marley, and producer Lee 'Scratch' Perry. Individually, they could each give the world pause for thought; together, they were never going to take anything other than a reliably rebel stance. Scratch and Bob were both around the same height and both in possession of all the pugnacity so often associated with men under five foot six, with an impish, insatiable curiosity to match. All three Wailers had recently brushed with the law – Peter had been arrested with Prince Buster on an anti-Rhodesia demonstration; Bunny had just completed a one-year prison sentence for ganja possession; as had Bob, but his term was merely a month. Bob had also spent most of that year living and working in Wilmington, Delaware, with constant first-hand exposure to black struggle in the USA and, as we'll see later, had learned a lot from his black American manager, Danny Sims. Although their fan base was growing, the Wailers had a reputation among local record businessmen as Trouble – with a capital T. Lee Perry was and is a perpetually positive nuisance of the highest order, and never needed a reason to be contrary – the man would buck trends that weren't even there.

For this alliance to jump straight into roots reggae from the disparate points of view of ghetto injustice and old-school, love-ballad-based, three-part harmonizing was pretty much an inevitability as consciousness and commentary were the two central planks of the Wailers' whole purpose. Their rude-boy dramas are well known, but prior to that among the group's mainstream Studio One output in the early sixties was a single called 'Rasta Put It on' and Peter Tosh's solo ventures, 'Maga Dog' and 'Rasta Shook Them up'. The group had been studying dread since early in the decade, and were now becoming much more overt about it: Bob had started to locks up once before, then reverted to an Afro; and during the 1968 Independence Day Concert at the Regal theatre, when other artists were suited and booted and doing cheerfully optimistic numbers, a solo Bob Marley came out in his Rastaman fatigues and sandals and chanted. He stood his ground and completed the number, apparently regardless of the hoots of laughter that went up from the audience. As a producer, Scratch was far and away the most innovative, risk-taking, witty, intellectual, stylistically articulated, knowledgeable and lucid on the Kingston music scene, and he'd been delving into revivalism, Pocomania and Rasta from a musical and spiritual angle. In 1969 his pockets were fat from the UK successes of his Upsetter instrumentals, and he was eager to spend his money on something a little more artistically gratifying than the new car he'd just had shipped over from England.

It should be no surprise that both Lee Perry and the Wailers were the first to put some long-term consideration and effort into what they did. They thought more deeply about what they were doing than did most of their peers, and were already assuming there had to be more to making music than churning out singles. It was a mark of the increasing regard shown for them by their fellow artists that they started a trend in this area, and the fact that the likes of Joe Gibbs, Coxsone and Bunny Lee also took note shows a sly respect coming from Kingston's producers. But what *was* remarkable about the liaison was that, had it not been for Bob's persistence, it might not have happened. Lee Perry wasn't remotely interested in working with the Wailers.

This was nothing personal – or it was certainly as impersonal as any dealings with Lee Perry could be. After the commercial and creative successes of his late-1960s Upsetter singles, he had little desire to work with singers. He'd decided they were more trouble than they were worth and used vocalists only on the B-sides of his instrumentals. It's a particularly Perryesque piece of perversion that, while the rest of Jamaica was discovering the instrumental flipside, his version excursions involved vocal cuts to his instrumental originals. Of course, it might just have been a sales-friendly insurance policy. It's a matter of record, though, that when Marley walked into Lee Perry's record shop to discuss collaboration – they would have known each other from their Studio One days – the producer got such a strong vibration from him that he retooled his policy on singers on the spot.

Dave Barker performed singing and toasting duties for Perry around this time – it's Dave who comes with '*This i-i-i-s Upsetter . . . Sounds of now . . .*' to introduce late-1960s Upsetter hit 'Shocks of Mighty' – and he regularly sang additional harmonies with the Wailers or substituted for an absentee member. He remembers such impulsiveness as very much part of the Lee Perry method, but also endorses the notion that Scratch's 'spontaneous' approach was tempered with what he calls a 'futurism', a more cerebral, bigger-picture-type view than might be expected from the Klondike mentality that comprised so much of the reggae industry. And, according to Dave, it was this apparent far-sightedness that did most to instate roots singing as an art form to accompany the embryonic toasting and dub schools:

'Scratch and the Wailers working together was a wonderful time. Being amongst Bob and Bunny and Peter and Scratch it was a wonderful rich vibe. There wasn't no ifs and buts; it was just magical. We used to go into the studio and the track dem just lay. All the music, the right vibes, the right information just flowed. From Family Man 'pon the bass to Carlton, his brother, on the drums, the man dem just nice and sweet and have an *understanding*. Not much talking, they jus' *knew*. Then the music *flowed* between them to the Wailers. It was the first time I've been among a set of guys who didn't take two cut of anything. One cut and it done. Them set up round the mic and from when they open their mouths the harmony was always exactly right – sweet and nice and no bad notes, and then it done. A take. And Scratch just let this flow, that was his genius.

'But you have to understand how Scratch operate. It all seem to be done on feel, like it only make sense to him, but when it done you could see how it work. The first time I properly meet him, myself and Glen Brown, who was still singing then, was passing by Randy's recording studio on North Parade and suddenly this big car drove up and the doors flew open and guys just jump out all over the place and everything was pure noise and excitement. It was Scratch, he had just completed a tour of England – I think it was about four weeks for the "Return of Django" – and he came back home with a big Rover car. Everybody run up the narrow stairs to the studio, which was over the record shop, so myself and Glen followed the crowd and upstairs the booze and the spliffs were passing like nobody's business. Glen knew Scratch, but I found the darkest corner in the studio to sit and I had my fill of booze; I'm not a smoker.

'Scratch put a tape on and Busty Brown was there round the mic trying to get a vibe for that particular track, and no matter how he tried he just couldn't get a vibe at all. And Scratch start to get upset, him well peed off and decide to call it a night, but Glen, who was also in the control room with him, said, "No man, try Dave, try Dave." Scratch leave the control room and start to bawl, "Who name *Dave*? . . . Where *Dave*? . . ." I identify mself and he said, "You can sing? . . . Well let me hear what you can come with on this track." With the booze in me and feeling nice, I went behind the mic and Scratch play the track and I just came out with "*You made me a prisoner . . .*" right through. Scratch start to jump up and down in the control room, him *excited*. The tune came out as "Prisoner of Love", and was a hit, and it worked because Scratch gave me the chance to do what I felt. But it all spur of the moment kinda thing.

'Scratch is a spontaneous guy, sometimes you sitting 'round with him somewhere and 'im just jump up and say "Baas, studio", with real urgency because he have an idea. And you follow him there. Once, when he started playing the track that end up as "Shocks of Mighty", I could not feel a vibe at all – it was a nice track, a nice feel, a bit fast, but I just couldn't feel a vibe, Scratch got *upset*. He start to shout and cuss and grab up him tape and storm out of the studio, leaving me saying to myself, "Now this don' feel right. I know this man love music so much, he should have the intelligence to know that one couldn't call upon ideas or vibes any time they feel like. It got to come in its own time." I was surprised at how this man get vex, but that's part of how him thinking so quickly he get frustrated when people don't always keep up. But it never serious; the next day it like it never happened and you try again.

'The Wailers could keep up with him, because they always had that vibe. When it came to music and they know they going to sing about reality, Scratch would tell them seh we have to look 'pon this reality. We would all pile into Scratch's big car and go driving, all over Kingston, into the country sometimes, but mostly in town, jus' driving around, and Bob and Bunny and Scratch would be writing down lyrics same time. We drive everywhere and every time we see an incident and they discuss it, put it down as lyrics and just turn everything into music. Everything they see on the street down deh. Then when they get back to the studio, they put it down on tape. One take. And it still fresh. That had never been done before.

'Scratch see his job as the producer as making sure everything relaxed in his studio. So the musicians can relax and not worry about anything, just come with what they can do. In this case he want the Wailers to be able to come with the songs they've really got inside them, to be able to sing from their hearts. Him and Randy's had an arrangement, so it didn't cost him as much as it might have done, because he would spend a lot of time in there. And Randy's had a very good engineer – Errol Thompson – he was brilliant. He could capture the vibe that the Wailers was bringing into the studio and it was he and Scratch at the board every time who bring them tunes out like they're supposed to have sounded. Errol got to know how all of our voices sound so he was always set up right and could put on all the reverb and delay stuff, which was encouraged by Scratch. Everything was so smooth, which meant the vibe could flow with no worries.

'Scratch and the Wailers started that sound, the roots singing as a serious business. Because Scratch had a long-term view. Even though he did think of the present with all his spontaneity, where each of his songs is concerned he had that sense of *futurism* that make him think it got to last. That's why he came with reality songs so early, because he knew there would be a time when they would be accepted and appreciated. Then when he did them, we drive round looking for what it is the people are feeling because that's what we have to sing about. Bob knew it would come, too. I hear with my own ears, in Randy's recording studio; the Wailers dem in the studio and Bob come outside into the part where the musicians is and I see him say, "Everybody a-laugh at me, everybody don' wan' know me, no one is really interested 'bout me, but a time will come when the whole world shall hear and know the Wailers." So it said, so it done.

'Both Scratch and Wailers grew during that time. He had that spark that Wailers being with him or he being amongst them, gave all of them the chance to grow and see what they could really achieve. The more we went into the studio with the Wailers is the more richful source came out on the records. Which is actual proof now in those sides being the best the group ever did.'

Dave Barker is only wrong in that last respect. The work that Peter, Bob and Bunny did with Lee Perry isn't merely the best work they did as a group, but the best any of them did in any circumstances. And that includes all of Bob's later material. Scratch had seen the potential for a singular rebel sound, and had rebuilt the group's approach to a song to sideline any rocksteady-type wannabe Yankeeisms. He rebalanced the vocals in favour of a lead and harmony situation, but insisted that whoever took lead (usually Bob) opted for a take-no-more-shit attitude with just a hint of menace, elbowing any notion of pleading.

There is a freshness, almost a naïveté, about the material from this time that comes from those afternoons spent driving around Kingston and the thrill of being able to chronicle street drama in song. *On records*. This was genuinely getting involved in what they saw as the struggle. And the ability of Lee Perry and Errol Thompson to remove any filters between the artists and the tape means that the listener loses none of that sense of urgency and expectancy, while the producer's unabashed enthusiasm for what was going on encouraged his artists to the very top of their game.

The songs that came out of those sessions include 'Duppy Conqueror', 'Small Axe', 'Kaya', '400 Years', 'Mr Brown' 'Cross the Nation', 'Rebel Hop', 'African Herbsman' and 'Soul Rebel'. Unadulterated by rock-friendly remixes, reworked time signatures, guitar overdubs or harpsichords, this was the essence of the Wailers and Jamaica's embryonic roots reggae scene in microcosm. It's a shame that in the light of what came next for Bob Marley and the Wailers, this crucially formative period tends to be reduced to a mere introduction.

It was also the last time for a long time that Bob Marley would have any sound-system credibility – the singles rocked the lawns in JA, while the *Soul Rebel* and *African Herbsman* albums gained a big black audience across the Atlantic in Britain. These songs more than re-established the Wailers' ghetto standing, they served notice of what reggae was capable of and how rude-boy anger became far more potent if it had a focus. Dave Barker continues the story:

'Those records did well because by then you had quite a few people in Jamaica who really check for that; quite a few roots people who would check for anything Wailers did at that time. But where it make the biggest impression was with the other musicians, as at that time there was a lot of the musicians and the people in the ghetto who wanted to sing from the heart and soul about what their life was like, but with nobody having done so before it was difficult. Most Jamaican artist have gone through hell, not just in the record business but in their daily lives, and most of them are strongly in touch with the spiritual side of life. They have always wanted to get the chance to do that type of roots music, to identify themselves to the public who they really are, the type of life they've lived, where they're really coming from and would like to go. But in those early days in Jamaica it was not accepted. It was all there, just under the surface, but nobody want to make the first move. It was just a matter of them being given the opportunity and the chance, and the Wailers and Scratch helped *immensely* in opening the doors for other people to do the same thing.

'It help show producers that it would sell, too. Because while most of the people in Jamaica didn't accept the Rastafarian movement, which is pure snobbery – I call them toffee-nose aristo*rats* who if you meet them same way they behave as if the sun shines outta them bum – you also had fear. If you sit down and check the words of the best roots songs – of Spear and of Culture and of Bob – it is like you are checking *you*, you are checking your inner self. Like Bob say in one of him songs, *I throw corn but I don't call no fowl*, he's not pointing a finger at you, but in his telling it like it is he's getting *you* to do that for yourself. Songs that bring that kinda truth make people fear them. It's the truth . . . the truth is an offence, but it's not a sin. But when you got producers that are behaving like robbers, they would fear to hear truth and they would try their best to blank it or fight it in any way they can.

'And some of these producers would tell you the roots music would not sell as much as the everyday stuff. We knew it was down to us to educate the people by hitting them with the facts of their life, then eventually they would look at themselves and know where they were actually coming from and where they would love to go. But with so many producers, it all was just a quick-money thing. They don't check things for the long-term effect they might have and are purely looking in the short term every time. I call them "peanut vendors", and what the Wailers and Scratch achieved together did a lot to change their views.

'Until that period people rarely spoke up. After that, the world really opened to that type of song, and that gave those people the chance to come forward on a higher plane.'

Scratch broke with the Wailers fairly soon after those groundbreaking recordings. Many who were there say it was an acrimonious split over money, which may well be true, but it couldn't have been helped by the fact that neither party remained particularly focused on collaboration. Bob and the boys were looking out internationally, courtesy of Danny Sims and Johnny Nash; while so much of Lee Perry's 'spontaneity' was down to a hyperactivity that would make a three-year-old on orange squash look sluggish. Why do you think the man reinvented his own beat every couple of months? But the pairing had done its job: 'Small Axe' and 'Duppy Conqueror' were Top 5 tunes in Jamaica in 1970 and 1971, respectively, while 'Trench Town Rock', produced by Bob himself at Harry J's studios, set the lawns on fire and became the island's best-selling single of 1971.

The people, already beginning to be turned on to musical roots ideas by the sound-system deejays, had instantly latched on to these records. After all, while representing their inter-action – or not – with society, they were entirely and contempor-arily musical. It wasn't quite enough to open a floodgate, though. Reggae's – or rather *certain* reggae's – move uptown, combined with overseas pop success, had polarized the music into the respectable and the ragamuffin, with the better-established record men, the ones with strictly old-time perspec-tives, unable to embrace the idea of any edges being blurred. Also, they didn't yet see the figures adding up sufficiently to balance out their innate upward mobility. So for a year or more roots music was virtually the sole property of the people at the dancehalls, with only a few of the radical young producers starting to experiment with it – Phil Pratt, Randy's, Herman Chin Loy, Keith Hudson, for instance. And, surprisingly, Coxsone.

'Surprisingly' because at the same time Dodd, one of the most important names in reggae, seemed to have taken his eye off the ball as he squandered 'Satta Massa Gana' and was criminally under-utilizing Burning Spear. Perhaps those two examples were simply too left-field for him to put out – he was now as much a businessman as a sound man or a record man, and Coxsone's musical history was one of refinement, perfection and occasional advancement of what was already there rather than out and out innovation.

What Dodd really wanted was a Rasta singer who could slot in with the Studio One way of doing things, with musical ideas that could carry a conventional structure in terms of rhythm patterns, arrangements and production. And lyrics more archetypical than chanting in praise of Jah or musing in an ancient African language. Somebody who would minimize any potential risk by turning out roots music as *acceptable* as Studio One's more secular offerings. That somebody was Horace Andy. He had been with the label for a year or more, employing his lilting falsetto voice and supernaturally light, pleading delivery to spectacular effect in a series of songs of love lost, stolen and unrequited. Yet he was a committed Rastaman who for several years had been going to the Ethiopian Federation in St Davids Lane, where, incidentally, the Wailers were regulars, and where the Sunday afternoon meetings would be well attended by musicians from Studio One's morning sessions at nearby Brentford Road. Understandably, Horace wanted to sing something with a bit more substance and the producer had confidence in his delivery, while being aware that his songwriting had been shaped at Studio One and was therefore unlikely to rock any stylistic boat. Plus he was a fast-rising local star, which certainly did no harm.

It was practically a repeat of Horace's namesake Bob Andy's Studio One situation when, some five years previously, that singer (also a big star and again a righteous Rastaman) was nominated to carry the label's torch for the protest music of the times by mixing the very conventionally recorded conscious ('Crime Don't Pay', 'I Got to Go Back Home', 'My Time', etc.) into his largely lovers' output. Now, Horace Andy (who had his name changed from Hinds by Coxsone in reference to Bob) seemed the ideal candidate as the foundation stone in Coxsone's House of Dread. Or maybe that should be Annexe of Dread.

It wasn't, however, quite as straightforward as that. As Horace tells it, if you could sing sweet, why waste time with that sufferation nonsense?

'Studio One was a place that respect Rasta. The other established studios didn't have no time for Rasta – Duke Reid, Byron Lee . . . Mr Dodd wasn't Rasta, but he *understood* Rasta and have sympathy with what they were doing. So many of the musicians at the time – whether they had dreadlocks or not – were Rasta and Coxsone respect them in that. I don't know why he never became Rasta, because he was always interested in what it was all about because he spent so much time among them.

'In spite of those of us involved in Rasta being able to tell Rasta reggae was going to get big, because we knew what the mood was, you could see why some producers were reluctant to do it. There wasn't much in the way of protest songs in the sixties, not like the seventies, so there wasn't much proof that it was what the people wanted. There was Bob Marley in the sixties, and at that time he had just had a next set of hits, but that was about it. Producers, including Mr Dodd, were a bit reluctant to try it because they thought it might have involved something too far out. But Mr Dodd really did want to, it just that he have to do it *his* way, the Studio One way. That's why nothing no happen with Burning Spear, because it couldn't fit that pattern. I think he went with me because he already knew my style and knew he could work with it.

'A lot of people were surprised when, with the voice I have, I wanted to start singing the protest songs. They used to say, "What a waste of a voice"; they said that what I'd sing like that wouldn't sound really good. Then after I start recording protest songs and having hits people still saying to me, "What type of foolishness that you a-sing?" *Even my mother* used to call them *fool fool songs*. I get quite a hostile reaction, even though I still sing a lot of love songs: "Rock to Sleep", "Natty Dread a Weh She Want", "Girl I Love You", "You Are My Angel". I wanted to do something that was going to get played in the dance so the guys can take up with a gal, but also it's got sentiments and lyrics that they can relate to. It means something to them as it talks about their day-to-day existence. Early on, though, so much people seemed to think that protest songs and love songs should be kept separate, but they're all part of how life is.

'Anyhow, I always think the light voice can have as much effect, sometimes more, with the protest songs as the very militant voice. Bob's voice was light.'

As a result, during and after Horace's time at Studio One, although his songbook continued to contain its share of superior smoochers, it was laced with the likes of 'Every Tongue Shall Tell', 'Skylarking', 'Conscious Dreadlocks', 'Spying Glass' and 'Money Money'. These tunes were inspirational in bringing to bear a series of falsetto-voiced, mostly forgettable wannabes, who paled in comparison with the 1976 British sound-system classic 'Natty Dread a Weh She Want'. In tandem with Tappa Zukie, Horace impeccably combines, as the title suggests, the notions of Rasta and romance in such an entertaining spirit that any deejay worth his decks would kill the volume on the chorus to have every man in the place, locksed up or otherwise, sing out the title line. Meanwhile, the *young gal dem* looked on with a bemusement bordering on derision.

Coxsone followed up with the Gladiators. Again, this was far from a radical departure as they were a group he already knew and who sang straight-down-the-line Jamaican three-part harmonies. Comprising Albert Griffiths, Clinton Fearon and Donald Webber, the Gladiators had been knocking round Studio One and Treasure Isle during the last years of the previous decade, singing back-ups and occasionally getting their own reasonably popular pop releases; then, during 1970 and 1971, they worked with Clive Chin and Lee Perry and acquired a deep-roots perspective along the way. Hence they were tailor-made for Studio One when Dodd took them back on in 1973: Griffiths was a strong Rasta songwriter, but one who told stories in a more regular verse/chorus manner; theirs was the classic singing style Coxsone felt comfortable with; and they played instruments and worked out their own arrangements – very handy, as Leroy Sibbles was long gone from Brentford Road and Jackie Mittoo was in the departure lounge. All it needed was for the Studio One sheen to be applied and buffed up to brilliance by Dodd himself. He was a hands-on producer with the Gladiators, and they ended up with a catalogue that includes 'Bongo Red', 'A Prayer to Thee', 'Tribulation', 'Jah Jah Go before Us' and 'Roots Natty', and which brought them international acclaim continuing well into the 1980s.

Coming hot on the heels of Horace Andy, the immediate success of these tunes on the Kingston sound systems kept Coxsone on his self-prescribed roots path. Thanks to his uncompromising view of exactly what a song should be, during the rest of the decade Studio One turned out roots music that was as listenable to as it was effective: the Viceroys, Freddie McGregor, Willie Williams, the Wailing Souls, Freddie McKay and Sugar Minott. These were artists whose sufferah music was so smooth, so silky – *so Studio One*, it was perfect for pursuing the pleasures of the flesh while bathing oneself in the glow of righteousness. It's just that Dodd didn't turn out that much of it compared with what was going on around him.

By 1973, post-*The Harder They Come*, producers and artists were fully aware of roots-music sales potential, while to rock their crowds the sound-system operators would take all they could get. Roots riddim fell like rain, with Bunny Lee and Joe Gibbs getting involved to such immediate and copious effect that by the middle of the decade their labels – Striker, Justice, Jackpot and Attack for Lee; Joe Gibbs Record Globe, Belmont, Errol T, Town & Country for Gibbs – had replaced the former Big Two of Studio One and Treasure Isle.

Bunny Lee built his empire around a shifting pool of session players known as the Aggrovators – clearly his interest in the UK skinhead audience followed him home to Jamaica. They were a formidable crew that included, though not all at the same time, the Barrett brothers, Sly Dunbar and Robbie Shakespeare (before they were an item), Lloyd Parkes (bass), Carlton 'Santa' Davis (drums), Tommy McCook, Vin Gordon, Bobby Ellis and Lennox Brown (brass), Winston Wright, Bernard Harvey and Ansell Collins (keyboards), Earl 'Chinna' Smith and Willie

Lindo (guitar), and Scully Simms (percussion). It was the perfect mix of the veteran, the fresh-faced and the in-between to give wings to Lee's notions of rehashing tried and tested Studio One and Treasure Isle rhythms from a roots point of view. Not that this idea in itself was in any way innovative – Jamaica's lack of copyright laws positively encouraged such behaviour, and 'doing over' other producers' tunes had been a factor even before ska. Now toasting and dub's voracious appetite for crisp, well-recorded rhythm tracks meant a growing trend for producers to sell on rhythm tracks. But this time the gusto with which Lee recycled was a far cry from, say, Justin Hinds re-recording 'Carry Go Bring Come' with a new beat. Bunny Lee's refitting of old rhythms was entirely comprehensive: the tunes he took on acquired new arrangements, modern drum patterns, a shift in tempo and different, more relevant lyrics.

A popular theory is that this was precipitated by cost – Lee had to hire studio facilities, usually from Harry J, Randy's or Channel One; and the capping of retail record prices was still in effect – but this is an unlikely explanation. The extent to which these rhythms were done over would have involved about as much time and effort on the musicians' part as starting from scratch. The most probable reason is, in fact, the most straightforward: they were very good rhythms, they were hanging about doing nothing new and Lee was loath to ignore them.

Indeed, Bunny Lee himself takes the Jamaican penchant for recycling to extremes. The inside of his tiny studio looks as if nothing has been thrown away since he acquired it in the 1980s, and the couch couldn't have been new even then. Although he is the very soul of generosity and hospitality, he simply hates waste, both points being illustrated in my first meeting with him. He came to pick me up from my hotel, bought me a chicken dinner on the drive back first to his house then his studio, and in the early hours of the morning dropped me back. The hotel had a big, lushly planted drive where he had waited with his car when he collected me, and on our return Bunny and his engineer/pa Newton got out and spent a good ten minutes combing the ground, finally going to speak, at length, to the night security guards, asking if anybody had handed in the newspaper he'd inadvertently left on a wall out there earlier.

The eventual dancehall trend of excavating ancient Studio One/Treasure Isle hits for a new generation and then versioning them a shameless number of times had its seeds sown here, when Lee and his immediate contemporaries – Joe Gibbs, Clive Chin and Joe Joe Hookim – went down that route. You can hardly blame Coxsone for taking himself out of reggae's frontline during the second half of the 1970s, to devote the large part of his energies to re-releasing his back catalogue: he'd proved he could cut it with numbers like 'No Man Is an Island', 'Skylarking', 'Vanity', 'Yaho' and 'Armagideon Time'. Other producers were advertising what was in his vaults, so why not give the people the real thing? Sonia Pottinger, who owned the Gayfeet, Tip Top and High Note labels, spent most of the late 1970s doing the same thing with the late Duke Reid's back catalogue. Why make new tunes when the old ones seem to be doing just as well?

The important thing about Bunny Lee, though, was how he moved things forward at the same time. It was at his instigation that the Aggrovators developed the 'flying cymbal' sound, a brisk, skimming with a clipped end to it, *tsssst . . . tsssst . . . tsssst . . .* hi-hat led drum pattern, said to be Kingston's answer to American soul producers Gamble & Huff's incredibly popular Sound of Philadelphia – Johnnie Clarke's 'Move Outta Babylon' is classic flying cymbal. For a couple of years after 1974 it was *the* roots reggae style, implying that even at the core of all this nationalistic cultural dread was the yoke of US musical imperialism. Nobody seemed that bothered, though. Least of all Bunny Lee's singers, Horace Andy, Cornell Campbell, John Holt, Linval Thompson, Delroy Wilson and Johnnie Clarke, who rode that sound to full and fantastic effect.

But then Lee's bossing of the roots-singing market was given almost unfair advantage by developments at King Tubby's yard on Dromilly Avenue. Again with a little persuasion from Lee, Tubby had bought another four-track board and the bungalow's bathroom (his mum no longer lived there) had been commandeered as a makeshift vocal booth. Lee took full advantage of Jamaica's greatest sound engineer's facility for singers to 'voice' rhythms recorded elsewhere – the righteous lyrics now had power in more ways than one, while the love songs really felt as if they were wrapping you up. For the second half of the decade, Johnnie Clarke was the ranking roots singer with a string of wonderfully recorded hits for Bunny Lee – 'Live Up Jah Man', 'African People', 'Blood Dunza', 'Move Outta Babylon' and 'None Shall Escape His Judgement' – all cut in King Tubby's toilet. The dub versions are pretty lively, too.

Joe Gibbs always ran Bunny Lee a second so close it was difficult to separate them. His big advantage was that, in 1975, when his own very modern sixteen-track studio was up and running, he poached Errol Thompson from Randy's as his house engineer and thus had the time, the space and the person- nel to experiment to a far greater degree than could Lee. As a result, his roster was bigger; because any new studio opening would immediately attract a crowd of both wannabe singers and established artists looking for a better deal. Once that same studio had a few hits or created its own style, that number would multiply. The late-seventies legacy of Joe Gibbs was possibly the most eclectic of any big-time producer. Jacob Miller, Junior Byles, the Ethiopians, Leo Graham, Dennis Brown, Wayne Wade, Gregory Isaacs, Cornell Campbell, the Morwells, the Mighty Diamonds, Culture, Junior Delgado, Prince Far-I and Althea & Donna all cut tunes at Gibbs's Retirement Crescent premises, and in doing so created some of reggae music's most enduring classics.

Culture's 'Two Sevens Clash' was a Mighty Two (Gibbs' & Thompson) production, a tune that showed off the trio's stark harmonies, their terrifyingly righteous approach to Rastafari – this was *dread* in all senses of the word – and leader Joseph Hill's sense of the dramatic to a stunning, ominous effect. Bluntly portentous, it drew on cabbalistic teachings – an ancient Jewish interpretation of the Old Testament studied by some Rasta sects in which the number seven is an omen of apocalypse.

Against the nerve-jangling wide open spaces of Errol Thompson's backing mix, the lyrics prophesied that the year of its release – 1977, when the two sevens clash – would be the year the world would end. It was a monster hit on the sound systems and in the shops on both sides of the Atlantic, and demonstrates the sheer power of song on the island: on 7 July of that year – when *four* sevens clashed – Jamaica registered record absenteeism from work and school.

Sylford Walker took time out from Glen Brown to cut 'Burn Babylon' at Joe Gibbs', which, contrary to the tone of the title, was one of the breeziest, sunniest, musically optimistic slices of roots reggae without the Mighty Diamonds' name on it. It's an open, chugging beat with guitars (electric and acoustic) and a piano trading off, while Errol Thompson should win an award for Best Use of Echo in a Regular Song – 'Burn Babylon' opens with *It's a long-long-long-long-long-long-long-long / It's a long time-ime-ime I'm burn up the collie weed . . .* , which never failed to raise a cheer from a sound-system crowd. Prince Far-I's 'Heavy Manners' was a thunderous comment on the state of emergency which had been introduced as a measure against organized street violence. As a deejay tune it shouldn't, strictly speaking, be mentioned here, but the enormously subtle musical edifice ET teased out of the backing track never diluted any notions of dread, yet it was still swinging with more than enough to easily nice up any dance. And while Far-I's tones may have been modelled on a bear roused from hibernation a month or so early, they were always melodic. Then there was Althea & Donna's international hit 'Uptown Top Ranking', as promoted by Mikey Dread (see chapter 13). Go back to the 'original', Trinity's 'Three Piece Suit and T'ing', and you'll find another essentially deejay record that did itself no harm at all by rocking a mainstream crowd. ET's expertise is again in evidence as he deftly deconstructs Alton Ellis's 'I'm Still in Love with You', then redefines it by working echoed snatches back into the melody with enough spring to launch Trinity's Big Youth-ish (therefore always tuneful) paean to his own sartorial impressiveness. *Wi' mi diamond socks and t'ing*, indeed.

It was as if the Mighty Two felt they could do anything, and therefore did: from novelty to deeply dread to vocal harmony to toasting to love songs to instrumentals (Joe Gibbs & the Professionals cut several music-only albums). This worked both for and against them. On the plus side, in the second half of the 1970s the Joe Gibbs labels were home to a fantastic variety of reggae music, some of it genuinely mould-breaking, among which were an enormous number of unforgettable songs – 'Money in My Pocket', 'Rockers No Crackers', 'Malcolm X', 'Heart and Soul', and 'African Queen' . . . But such variation precludes any definitive sound. As a result, the Mighty Two tend to be overlooked as major players, as what they did is virtually impossible to pin down or sum up in a single shining example.

The third prong of this new wave comprised the Hookim brothers, Joe Joe and Ernest, who began life as jukebox/fruit machine operators and moved into the music business when the Jamaican government outlawed gaming machines. They started with the Channel One sound system, then in 1973 opened the studio of the same name. Joe Joe Hookim was the hands-on producer, but I-Roy did a lot of the work there, and although only at the top relatively briefly, from 1974 till 1976, Channel One changed the course of the music and left a legacy that has had repercussions far beyond the realms of reggae and is still proving its worth today. It was there that Sly Dunbar and Robbie Shakespeare were put together in what is the pivotal Channel One moment.

The duo had known each other for a while, often playing the same sessions or sitting in club bands together, but Sly's usual partner-in-riddim was Ranchie McLean. These two were the backbone of Skin, Flesh and Bone, a fairly upmarket live band who had a residency at Kingston's Tit for Tat Club, playing as much US soul and disco as they did reggae – and then it was always very well-behaved reggae – while Robbie was the first-choice bass player for Bunny Lee's Aggrovators. They came together as a unit when the Hookims took on Skin, Flesh and Bone as a group to become the backbone of what would be the Revolutionaries – as with any other chapter in Jamaica's musical history, the number of players involved is relatively tiny compared to the musical output.

Once at Channel One, Sly wanted more than simply to play catch-up with Lee's flying cymbal and began to leave his then partner behind as he, with assistance from the Hookims and I-Roy, started to fool around with the beat. First he beefed up the studio's sound by playing a clapping snare-drum beat under certain bass notes, then moved flying cymbal on by doubling up the drumming within the same rhythm with what sound like rim shots. The music was still paying a noticeable debt to US disco, which Sly would have been entirely familiar with from his nightclub cover days, but balanced with the bass and keyboards it was an intrinsically Jamaican roots sound. And the bass player that brought most to the party was the one Sly was being increasingly teamed up with: Robbie Shakespeare.

Junior Delgado didn't work with them until they'd become established, but he remembers clearly the effect of Sly and Robbie's coming together:

'When Ranchie was there with Sly it was good, but it wasn't *wicked*. That come with Robbie. As soon as him hook up with Sly they just click, like they both want to try new things and *develop* their sound. The vibes coming offa them was *terrible* . . . pure terror, the other studios running for cover as Channel One rockers' sound rule the whole scene in Kingston for maybe two years. Until the others learn how to copy it and Joe Gibbs open his place on Retirement Crescent and some of the Channel One musicians go down there to play in his band.'

Sly himself takes a slightly more laid-back view of this historic meeting. Mind you, he takes a more laid-back view of just about everything. He's sitting – or should that read *lounging*? – in one of the studios in the Mixing Labs, the state-of-the-art digital complex he and Robbie built which is now the headquarters of the duo's Taxi production company and record label. In true King Tubby's tradition, it's situated in the middle of a residential street; this Dumbarton Avenue address means you're in an impeccably groomed street in the rather upmarket

Kingston 10, *not* Waterhouse – there isn't a single raised eyebrow when I opt to walk back to my hotel. It's also an establishment that's seen a number of major stars – Gregory Isaacs, Dennis Brown, Junior Delgado, the Tamlins, Black Uhuru, up to Luciano, Beenie Man and Yami Bolo – come through the door hoping for a sprinkle of Sly and Robbie's magic dust, while the twosome have worked both on stage and on record with Bob Dylan, Grace Jones, the Rolling Stones and James Brown.

They're not working today; Sly's come in just to talk and nobody's quite sure where Robbie is.

'When me and Robbie meet we hit it off right away, because we both have the same idea – that we wanted to do more. We had both worked in nightclub bands, and done sessions – sometimes the same sessions – and we already knew each other, but neither of us was interested in just standing still or going with the crowd. It was a natural partnership right from the beginning. We shared the same views and the same ambitions about how we wanted to work – not just musically but we understand each other from the business point of view as well.

'We set up Taxi quite quickly, it just didn't get no kinda high profile until into the eighties, because we decide that instead of recording our songs on all those different labels we should start owning ourselves some tape. The problem was that if the producers on those labels decide not to use our ideas or not to put out songs that we're playing on then nobody would hear our playing. We wanted to start owning our own material, producing our own things and keep our own label, that way we would feel free to release our records any time that we wanted. We decided to make some record for ourselves and a particular set of people. Eventually.

'In Jamaica at that time, that sort of thing was happening more and more. It was because musicians turn producer, and that meant that other musicians get their ideas heard more. Before, producers were usually just the financier, and although they knew what they wanted, they weren't musicians and so couldn't really take on board the musicians' ideas, not the wilder ones. The producer would hear if the song was rocking, the groove was right, he might say let me hear a little more of that. But it is why music spread out so wide in the roots era, in the seventies, because it snowball as more and more musicians were getting their ideas through on to vinyl or starting to produce themselves because they see other musicians doing it.

'This bring about the big change in the music, too, as until then the musicians were playing for the singer in the studio – we play whatever the singers come in to sing. There will be some arrangements and t'ing to be done, but we were there to play for the singer and have to follow their lead. Once the musicians take charge then it start to become more musically led, which means it develop a lot of different styles and much more complicated structures because the musicians could express their ideas and then the singer would have to go with that. Like with what they call the *rockers* sound of my drumming. Already there was the *tssst-tssst-tssst-tssst* on the hi-hat which was based on the American disco style, and we listen to a lot of Philadelphia stuff, Gamble & Huff, and want to take it a bit further, so I double up with the drumming, but keep it in the same tempo. It was taking the idea of the drum pattern from disco, but by keeping it in the reggae tempo it still reggae. That change couldn't happen if it hadn't been musicians who make those decisions.

'And it also mean that the singers then have to adapt and things couldn't stay in the American style that it had been during rocksteady. Which lead to some of the best singing there had been up until then, because now people have to sing sounding like Jamaicans, even if they're still using the soul-type harmonies.'

Sly is accurate in describing the quality of the singing: if ever there was a roots label that left a lasting impression with its vocalizing then it was Channel One. Junior Byles cut the enduring roots classic 'Fade Away' there, likewise Leroy Smart and 'Ballistic Affair', while John Holt's 'Up Park Camp' and Barry Brown's 'Far East' were all Channel One solo protest classics. With harmony groups, however, the studio excelled. It was as if they managed to harness the expression and emotion of the classic Jamaican trios and give them a roots refit without detracting from either. Which is probably less complicated than it sounds, given the calibre of musicians who made up the Revolutionaries, the Maxfield Avenue studio's house band – Robbie Shakespeare and Ranchie McLean (bass), Sly Dunbar (drums), Ossie Hibbert, Ansell Collins and Robbie Lynn (keyboards), Sticky Thompson (percussion), and a brass section featuring Tommy McCook, Vin Gordon, Headley Bennett and Herman Marquis. The end products were the textbook-perfect conscious vocalizing of the Wailing Souls ('Things and Time', 'Joy within Your Heart', 'Very Well' and 'War'), the Meditations ('Woman Is Like a Shadow'), and a pre-Puma Jones Black Uhuru, who cut 'The Sun Is Shining' there, not to mention Channel One's greatest triumph, the Mighty Diamonds. Unlike Culture, Burning Spear and the Abyssinians, who were *dread* rather than just roots and culture, and therefore moved towards the minor keys instead of the traditional Impressions-based upfulness, the Mighty Diamonds reintroduced plaintive, intricate old-time singing but with thoroughly modern sentiments. 'Right Time', 'Country Living', 'I Need a Roof', 'Have Mercy', 'Them Never Love Poor Marcus', 'Africa' and 'Why My Black Brother Why?' . . . it's an impressive list that goes on and on.

While Channel One's tenure as the top Kingston roots set-up may have been brief, it was only the phenomenal standards set by the opposition in the second half of the decade that led to the Hookim brothers getting sidelined. A situation exacerbated by the re-emergence of the man they called Scratch, comfortably ensconced in his own recording studio.

Although the Lee Perry sessions were the best the Wailers ever did, they were nowhere near the top of his own creative tree. This is probably to do with personalities, as all concerned were strong, and therefore would have assumed their right to input. Although the results were marvellous, they were never truly about any one individual. Away from such strong-willed cohorts as Bob, Peter and Bunny, Lee Perry's genius is easier to see. It shouldn't be forgotten that in terms of rhythms and textures – which, after all, is what so much of Jamaican music is about – he was by far the most talented of the quartet.

The Black Ark was not only a laboratory of dub. Scratch also excelled in recording vocals, by individuals and groups, roots songs and love songs or even his own eccentric toasting. Like every other clever producer, Scratch approached singing from a dub point of view; he'd use dub techniques and sounds in backing tracks he created, then he'd put singing on top of an already subtly dubbed-up tune. In less than five years, the Kingston music business had reversed the idea of starting with a 'song' and deconstructing it into a dub. Because Perry's mix techniques resulted in a softer, rosier sound, his backing tracks were always highly suitable for singing over, especially as he leaned towards singers with a more delicate delivery who could float just above it with neither element intruding on the other – the Congos, Junior Murvin, George Faith and so on. Not that the producer wasn't capable of turning out his share of sparse, hard-hitting roots, but even then he used it as a contrast to rather than in contest with his singers.

Once his own studio was set up, his attitude towards singers that nearly stopped him working with the Wailers softened, and he began to take on vocalists immediately. This had much to do with economics on two counts: first, he now had his own overhead to meet and songs sold much better than instrumentals; but less obvious was his propensity for stockpiling and continually playing around with rhythms and backing tracks. He could do that now he was on his own time, and as a result had literally hundreds of reels of tapes and a mental filing system that never forgot anything he had. When a singer came in with an idea Scratch would already have something to fit it, or knew he could bend the lyrics to make sure it did, and it would cost him nothing in session musicians' fees to take a punt.

Working with singers regularly began to shift his working practices. Although essentially still as spontaneous as he had been when working out of Randy's five years previously, he had become far more dictatorial in his manner. This side of the Lee Perry character had always been there: it was at his insistence, and under coaching at his record shop, that the Wailers, especially Bob, dragged their singing style out of the late 1950s. Now, however, he was virtually a control freak. In the most positive sort of way.

Junior Delgado, as part of the band Time Unlimited, recorded for Perry just prior to the Black Ark, then returned as a solo singer later into the decade. Still an active and successful recording artist – he is one of the very few to have survived the changing styles and have hits in roots, ragga, digital and dancehall – Junior is currently working with new lords of the drum 'n' bass such as Smith & Mighty, Jerry Dammers and Stereo MCs, as they offer a modern take on his classic tracks. He has a record shop, a record label and a production company based in London, but he splits his time between there and Kingston. Where we're in his car, and he's driving, it has to be said, in a worryingly cavalier fashion. That it's the Independence Day public holiday and the capital's roads are all but deserted seems to be making things worse – corners are taken wide, caution at junctions is optional and he seems to be paying more attention to the tunes on the stereo than to the road. Excusable, perhaps, as it's a stream of top-quality old-school roots – Fred Locks, Jazzbo, the Twinkle Brothers et al. But later, when he sits down to discuss Scratch and the Black Ark, the man's all business and keen to emphasize the effect that Perry's environment had on not just him but on a whole generation of Jamaican singers.

'The Black Ark was a school. They say that about Studio One, but the Black Ark was just the same – when you get trained by Scratch, and you are coming from the Black Ark, then you are a well-trained man. You have to know *music* inside out, all singers had to know not just the singing but from the chords, the chord changes, the rhythm patterns . . . everything. And if you come with a song he go over it with you so much that when you done it's only fifty per cent of what you started with. He make you have to pay attention to not just the words but each syllable in every word to make sure everything sound right and fit exactly how he want it. Even when you're right and you know it he would say, "No, that's wrong." Him say it to make sure you are one hundred per cent sure of what you are doing. He wanted you to get it *absolutely* right.

'Then Scratch is a man who is going to drill you . . . *drill you, drill you, drill you*, because he know if you're so tight then there can't be no mistake and when you get into the recording studio because this is all automatic then you can put extra feeling into it. You don't have to worry about the basics. Although it seem like a heavy duty regime actually it relax you before you get round the mic. He had his favourite singers he love and he would work with them extra – myself, Bob Marley, the Wailers, Junior Byles, Max, the Congos. He would drill them some more, and tell them all the phrasing and how to sing every little part of a song. When I listen to Bob Marley, 'nuff times I hear him sound like Scratch, with me too, I can still hear some of Scratch in my singing.

'They say Scratch is a genius . . . *believe*. It wasn't just what he heard that made the man a genius, but he could describe it to you. It did make sense. Everything he did say in those times made sense, because if it don't make no sense then he's going to just bring it all down, stop the session and say, "Come again with the riddim," and we start again from the beginning. But most of the time you can understand what he wants, because we all work hard to. We knew what we get from Scratch was more than we could get anywhere else. Another producer might tell you, "That's not the way to pronounce that," but Scratch don't even business, he would be down there in the mic telling you and showing you how to sing it and what to do. Before the rhythm reached that part of the song. He was like a scientist, in him lab.

'This wasn't just with Scratch, although he was fanatical. With most of the other producers there was no room for errors. It's because the work had to be done to the standard that had been set before, back in the ska and rocksteady eras. Like

Bob Marley and the Wailers, Toots and the Maytals, Scratch, they're all ska people, they was around in them days and knew what need to be done. Rocksteady people too – Ken Boothe, John Holt, Phyllis Dillon, Marcia Griffiths, Alton Ellis, all of these people used to make good music coming down in the rocksteady era and brought those ways with them. The producers too, the producers that start making the roots records at the beginning of the seventies – Bunny Lee, Joe Gibbs, Studio One, Scratch, Glen Brown – there was a lot of the original ska and rocksteady people there. They knew the standards they had to reach. It wasn't until later that things start to get sloppy, in the seventies everyone was putting their heads down . . . nice music, good lyrics, good clean lyrics, that's the flow of those times. Not only in Jamaica in the seventies, R&B was good music, good constructive music at that time, too.'

Perry's personal philosophies gave him something of an advantage over his big-time producer peers, too. Unlike operators such as Gibbs and the Hookims, he wasn't establishment, or even establishment wannabe. In fact, although he enjoyed the trappings of his success – the car, the house, the studio, and years later he would marry Swiss nobility – it's hard to imagine anybody less socially ambitious than Lee 'Scratch' Perry. He was worse than middle-class Jamaica's worst nightmare: he wasn't simply another dissatisfied sufferah, he was a man with the means and the brains and the talent to go uptown yet had opted not to. While Bunny Lee and Coxsone were well known for their Rasta empathy, Perry was a true believer: it's far from coincidental that the studio's name was an Old Testament reference (the Jews' most sacred symbol was the Ark of The Covenant, carried on the Israelites' journey from Sinai to Canaan, the Promised Land). Rasta murals and designs decorated the Black Ark both inside and out, and above the doorway was a picture of Haile Selassie that all who entered were expected to acknowledge. Lee Perry was a rebel, walking the walk as well as talking the talk, which gave the roots sentiments in the songs he produced a particular edge. And despite the strong discipline in the studio itself, it was in the semi-communal, largely relaxed atmosphere of the Black Ark yard that Scratch's inherent spirituality came into play.

To the passer-by, 5 Cardiff Crescent must have looked like a dreadlocks camp moved down from the hills to the Kingston suburbs, as there was always a great deal of hanging about going on. It didn't take long for artists to come looking to work with Perry – at one point an African group turned up: not just a group that played African music, but a group from Africa who had travelled to Jamaica simply for Scratch to produce an album for them. There'd be a little oil-stove lit under a pot to which everybody who expected to eat would contribute – a few fish, onions, a bagful of peas, a chopped oxtail, perhaps a plantain, or maybe a couple of shillings towards any additional grocery shopping. Herb and liquor was in abundance, and the ideas flowed just as freely, as singers would contribute to or finish off or take over each other's material. Understandably, the Ark attracted a solidly Rasta contingent; as the potential singers and songwriters brought the sufferah vibe up from the ghetto, Scratch could tune in perfectly to what they wanted to express. Moving around the yard or listening in through a window, the producer was like some sort of consciousness antennae or dread ringmaster, picking up on and orchestrating what was going on around him, often before whoever was verbalizing that particular notion even realized it. And he'd already have a rhythm in his head, which he'd simply have to go in and fetch down from one of the shelves.

This apparently chaotic creative process kept Scratch as spontaneous as he had been back in the Wailers days. It allowed him to stay flexible within the tune-building process and to remain open to all possibilities, but it was the tightly focused sense of purpose which took over once the tape was rolling that made Black Ark music such an event. Junior remembers this translating to the musicians involved as a feeling of empowerment:

'It was massive. It went that way because with Scratch we knew what we could do provided it was of that high standard. We realize the power of the music. It was flowing with the vibes of peace and love and spirituality and Scratch was *totally* aware of that. There was an awareness all over, and it come from doing everything properly and being serious about what you do, in every respect. It was dedication.

'The singers wanted to do a good job, they know they have to: Bob done a good job; Jah Youth done a good job; Peter done a good job. At that time, it didn't matter what you had in your life, none of us wanted no sympathy or nobody feeling sorry for them because they knew they could do a good job for themselves. Like Peter sing *If you feel sorry for maga dog / maga dog will turn round and bite you*. The politicians were doing their thing and now the musicians was doing their thing, too. It was kind of a way of hitting back because every little thing done against the people, the massive, they lick about it in a song.

'Every nigger is a star.'

And Scratch most definitely turned out the stars. Max Romeo truly laid his smutty 'Wet Dream' image to rest with the searing roots anthems 'War Inna Babylon', 'One Step Forward' and 'Chase the Devil'. The Heptones cut the *Party Time* LP with Perry at the Ark, which includes the title track, 'Mr President' and 'Sufferahs' Time' and is among the best work the group ever did. Junior Byles' other landmark tune 'Curly Locks', a masterpiece of lovers' roots, is a Black Ark production. The Meditations, Jimmy Riley and Scratch himself (the tune that titled this chapter, 'Dreadlocks in Moonlight', is one of his best) all made brilliant singles. Jah Lion half-spoke, half-sung through the edgy *Colombian Colly* LP. We all know about Junior Murvin's 'Police and Thieves' which, along with its numerous versions, could only have happened there.

The Congos' majestic *Heart of the Congos* album is really nothing less than the Heart of the Black Ark. Scratch's techniques had been growing in sophistication up to these 1977 sessions and he had the tunes and the ideas to record a classic Jamaican harmony trio (falsetto, tenor and baritone), but bending them to his left-field Rasta ways rather than simply grafting their singing on to a roots riddim. His vision involved the voices as three more instruments to be used in the mix and the arrangements, much like the keyboard or the guitar, rather than the music's *raison d'être*. Of course, to do this he had to add another member to the group – until then the Congos were Cedric Myton (falsetto) and Roy Johnson (tenor), but Perry was so convinced that they were right – in sound, attitude and lyrics – for his vision that he took them on and added Watty Burnett, one of his regular vocalists, as the baritone voice. He pulled it off, too, marrying old-time technique with modern technology and thought process to create Jamaica's equivalent of what Norman Whitfield was doing with the Temptations at Motown. *Heart of the Congos* is one of the most consummate reggae albums ever made, nosing in front of masterpieces like *East of the River Nile* and *Right Time*.

Perhaps the Black Ark's output was never the biggest or most consistent of the roots-reggae era, but it was brilliantly eclectic and totally unafraid yet, thanks to Perry's deep-roots core, always recognizably reggae. Thus it made a far greater impact on the reggae world than practically anything else going on around it, and, as before, that includes all of Bob's later material. Lee 'Scratch' Perry was the decade's one true genius.

Once again closest to Scratch, this time in terms of musical perceptions, was Augustus Pablo, whose Rockers International productions played host to Jacob Miller, Junior Delgado, Tetrack, Hugh Mundell, Earl Sixteen, Paul Blackman, the Immortals and Delroy Williams. Although the catalogue contained such tunes as 'False Rasta', 'Earth Wind and Fire', 'Let's Get Started', 'Blackman's Heart' and 'Africa Must Be Free by 1983', and the delicate, subtly produced sides left nobody in any doubt as to Pablo's commitment to musical roots, you felt this was only the hors-d'oeuvre for his instrumental and dub entrée.

Other serious players were Glen Brown, who turned from singing to producing. His Pantomine and South East Music labels will be better remembered for quality than quantity – Sylford Walker's 'Lamb's Bread' and 'Chant Down Babylon' and the instrumentals 'Dirty Harry' and 'More Music' led by Tommy McCook, Niney, aka The Observer, or, even as his mum knew him, Winston Holness, had hits with Dennis Brown ('Wolves and Leopards'), Johnnie Clarke, Max Romeo ('Rasta Bandwagon'), Junior Delgado, Gregory Isaacs, the Morwells and a pre-Black Uhuru Michael Rose. Central to this canon, though, was that essay in the apocalypse 'Blood and Fire', a dire warning rasped out by Niney himself over the most minimal of backing tracks. The Morwells (Blacka Wellington and Bingy Bunny) produced two excellent albums themselves, *Presenting the Morwells* and *Crab Race*. Bertram Brown's Freedom Sounds label came with Phillip Fraser, Earl Zero, Prince Alla and Brent Dowe, in a remarkably straightforward but correspondingly effective style. Vivian Jackson kept up a stream of heavy-duty dread with his own efforts and occasional contributions from such luminaries as Wayne Wade, Michael Rose, Willie Williams and Michael Prophet. And, of course, Jack Ruby had been going from strength to strength with Burning Spear, while his work with acts like Israel Vibration, the Viceroys, the Twinkle Bros and original Ethiopian Leonard Dillon, who continued to work the group's name by himself, gave us plenty to give thanks and praise for.

By the second half of the 1970s, roots reggae as an expression – the riddims, the instrumentations, the vocal phrasing and the dialect – had become so ubiquitous within the Jamaican music industry that it was no longer possible (or practical) to differentiate between that and lovers' rock. This was one more example of the sound systems and their crowds dictating the direction the industry should take, because it was down to them that the walls quite quickly came down. Rupie Edwards, both as a singer and as a producer, understands why:

'It was never a problem for the people who went to the dancehalls and the sound systems. The people that reggae was being made for never separate it into *this* style and *that* style. No. This is music that's come down from slavery, through colonialism, so it's more than just a style. If you're coming from the potato walk or the banana walk or the hillside, people sing. To get rid of their frustrations and lift the spirits, people sing. It was also your form of entertainment at the weekend, whether in church or at a nine night [a Caribbean wake traditionally lasts for nine nights] or just outside a your house, you was going to sing. If you're cutting down a bush you're gonna sing, if you're digging some ground you're gonna sing. The music is vibrant. It's a way of life, the whole thing is not just a music being made, it's a people . . . a culture . . . it's an attitude, it's a way of life coming out of a people.

'Although the authorities and the people uptown would have liked to see conscious music pushed off to one side – and such was the thinking that those who are looking to put on airs and graces would start to do so – in Jamaica, among the people, all music was played together. Of course you want to hear some stuff that means something to your way of life, but at the same time you just want to forget your troubles and dance. There were some sound systems only play one sort, but the best ones, the ones that draw the crowds, play everything. They had to, because we had old people and young people coming together to socialize – there was no old-people dance and young-people dance and old-people music. There was no separation, when I was a little boy I used to go to the dance with my grandma and you had little kids running up and down in the dance. It's only recently you got what they call "big-people music" and young-people raves.

'Back then it was because everything got played together in the dance that so many of the establishment producers saw what could be done with the music. Then you had the artists want to do *everything*, to express themselves in different moods, so the different styles developed side by side.'

Horace Andy's problems with singing 'foolishness' became non-existent as he and singers like the Tamlins, Barry Biggs, Errol Dunkley, Derrick Harriott, the Chosen Few, the Heptones, George Faith, Earl Sixteen, Freddie McGregor, Jacob Miller, Leroy Sibbles, Freddie McKay, Dennis Brown and Gregory Isaacs mixed it up with feeling in an absolute cascade of music. Producers too were keen to tear down barriers: Lee Perry, Niney, Bunny Lee, Coxsone all welcomed the chance to record more traditional pop material under the freedoms afforded by the new roots styles; after all, the reason they got into the business in the first place was to nice up the dance. Everybody integrated their rosters, while a lot of singers put a foot in each camp and some people did both in the same song. Like Lee Perry's production of Junior Byles' 'Curly Locks'. A poignant tale of two childhood sweethearts who had been split up by the girl's father after the boy had locksed up, the lyric goes, *Curly Locks, now that I'm a dreadlock / your daddy say you shouldn't play with me . . .* , and it ruled the dancehall for years.

The man who epitomized this crossover best was Gregory Isaacs. Dennis Brown and Freddie McGregor (who came later) were longstanding sound-system heroes with a seamlessly blended range of material, among which was 'Here I Come', 'Money in My Pocket', 'Ain't That Loving You', 'Things in Life', 'Cassandra', 'Wolf and Leopard' and 'No Man Is an Island' for the former; 'I Man a Rasta', 'Rastaman Camp', 'Bobby Bobylon', 'Natural Collie', 'Big Ship' and 'Love Ballad' for the latter. But both producers were really just princes in the court of King Gregory.

Also known, for very good reason, as the Cool Ruler, Isaacs had been in the business since the early 1970s and recorded for Rupie Edwards, Niney, Gussie Clarke and GG Ranglin – he's even supposed to have sung back-up vocals at the Black Ark, notably on *Heart of the Congos* – and founded his own African Museum label. Originally nothing more remarkable than an easy-rocking crooner, it wasn't until he developed a distinctive style that he began to count for much. By the middle of the decade he'd evolved a style that was perfect on both sides of the divide as it shot his delivery through with an apparently desperate thread of disaffection. Either in love or in society at large, Gregory's trademark approach to any sort of song was one of loneliness and rejection. Couched in terms clever enough for him to be singing about either the love of Jah or the love of a good woman, he's either posing as an outcast from the community or he's just been dumped; you decide. Women loved this apparent vulnerability, while the guys admired his mix of rude-boy style, dreadlocks attitude and lurrrve god way with the ladies. All of which comes together, plus a sense of the Cool Ruler's charisma, on a live recording of 'Border', a session which also gives insight into his relationship with his fans — apparently unprompted they sing, note perfect, each chorus of *I'm leaving outta Babylon / I'm leaving outta Rome . . . we wan', we wan' go home*, while he ends the song with a triumphant, smirking '*Yuh like it?*'

Astonishingly, he managed to transcend changing styles and a spell in prison with no noticeable drop in quality. Any British blues dance over the past twenty-five years was likely to produce a shout of 'More Gregory!' during the wee small hours. And if the deejay knew what he was doing then that call wouldn't be heard twice.

All this added up to roots reggae enjoying a fantastic run. It had pervaded the music as a whole, it was enjoying unprecedented international success and had a recognizable figurehead in Bob Marley, and it had survived for over ten years with little change other than what was needed to keep it hot – the drumming patterns and contemporary jargon. Technological evolution was raising standards without becoming a burden, and the music had a sense of purpose.

As the 1980s beckoned, it was difficult to see reggae heading anywhere other than to the stratosphere . . .

16

Ah Fi We Dis

'By the time "Caught You in a Lie" was a hit, in 1974 or 1975, I'd personally begun to disregard Jamaica. Because by that time, we'd come so much into our own in the UK, and there was a lot of reggae selling here that could only have been made in Britain. Tunes that couldn't have happened anywhere else. It had got to the point where I thought if Jamaica wants to be in this then they'd better listen to what *I'm doing*. And a few years later, by the time "Silly Games" was a hit, I was cocky enough to try and change the drum beat in reggae.

'We'd had the flying cymbal thing dominating, now there was this steppers rhythm that Sly Dunbar had . . . that go deh steppers style, like horses galloping *chkachak . . . chkachak . . .* well fast. And that was just all over the place – every bloody record that came out had that rhythm on it and I was fed up with it. It had got boring. I wanted to change the beat in the drums, because if the drum beat changed then it was a whole new theme. You had to have a lairy drum pattern back then, or you wouldn't get noticed, so I invented the pattern of "Silly Games", the *chk-pdpdpdpd-pah . . . chk-pdpdpdpd-pah . . . chk-pdpdpdpd-pah . . .* It was sort of remotely African and a bit calypso, with the majority of the beat kept on the hi-hat with just occasionally an off-beat on the snare. But it involved rolling the tip of the stick in the bell of the hi-hat to get that thin, ethereal *tsssss*. Playing across the side was too fat, too thick; I wanted a *featherweight* t'ing. Then *bap* on the snare, well heavy.

'I thought, I'll make loads of tunes with that one drum pattern, flood the market and then it'll take over here and in Jamaica. It won't be one drop, it won't be go deh steppers, this'll be *ticklers*.'

Dennis Bovell roared with laughter at his attempt, over twenty years ago, to appropriate Jamaican music's tiller and shift the force from Kingston to London. But if anybody could have done that it would have been Blackbeard, as he used to be known.

Probably UK reggae's most innovative and celebrated son, Dennis can look back on a three-decade international recording, writing, deejaying, playing and production history that stretches back through Matumbi, the Dub Band, Blackbeard, Sufferer HiFi, 4th Street Orchestra, the Lovers' Rock label, Linton Kwesi Johnson, Alpha Blondy and, more recently, the Tokyo Ska Paradise Orchestra. Matumbi put on one of the best live shows in Britain – dubwise or otherwise; for a long time his groups were the first choice to back visiting Jamaican singers; his projects used to saturate the UK reggae charts and make regular riddim raids into the pop Top 40; while his way with the bass-line was employed by a range of pop acts from Bananarama to Captain Sensible to the Slits. For years, back in the 1970s, Dennis Bovell was the hub at the centre of British reggae's wheel: very little of any worth happened that didn't have his fingerprints on it somewhere.

On a break from an Italian film production of a modern-day version of *Romeo & Juliet*, for which he was commissioned to write the music and ended up with a pretty hefty role (he learned his lines phonetically), and chilling in his comfortable London suburban home with a very good bottle of Chablis, he found it altogether amusing that, back in 1979, he was far too successful to actually manage to change reggae's beat:

'First of all, I tried to get Matumbi's drummer, Jah Bunny, to play it, but he kept going, "Nah man, too different," and he wouldn't play that hi-hat with the tip of his stick, so what he ended up with was always too heavy. Then Janet [Kay, who sang "Silly Games"] suggested Angus, Aswad's drummer.

Great idea. And I'd worked with him before, so I got him in and the minute he heard this new beat he was off on it. Why it clicked like that was because Angus was a kid so it was something new and adventurous, whereas Jah Bunny was an older drummer – and he was a young *British* kid as opposed to an older Jamaican guy, therefore had more influences and was more willing to go forward on stuff. Angus grabbed hold of that beat so much so that when it came to the bit where it goes up high – *play . . . your . . . sill-ly games* – he stopped. Dead. I said I didn't tell you to stop there, but when I listened to the playback it sounded good so I kept it in – the beat should've been strong all the way through, but he stopped there to accent that line, which is like the climax of the song. He read my mind.

'I gave the tune to the London reggae label Arawak to put out, and I was so pleased with it I thought I'd re-release it for the national market, but before that I'd do another vocal take because the main vocal could have been better. Then a few weeks later I heard it on Capital Radio, straight in their chart at number 27, and I thought, "Bloody hell, he's gone and released it and it's in the bloody charts – too late to revoice it." Then it's in the national charts, and it's gone up to number 2 within a couple of weeks. For about a month it's like all you can hear on the radio or in shops or at discos – because this was the height of summer so everybody's got their windows open – and then it was gone. If you'd blinked you'd have missed it. But while it was up there that record had become so successful and so well known that I couldn't make even one more song with that drum pattern. It was pop. The pop market wouldn't have taken another one and if I'd tried to use it again for the reggae market people would have slagged me off. They would've laughed at me, so the whole idea had to be dashed.'

Really, whether Dennis succeeded in changing the beat or not is neither here nor there; what is important is that he *tried*. Or, as he puts it, he was 'cocky enough' to want to try. It's a vivid illustration of how far Jamaican music in Great Britain had come on in the twenty years since it made the crossing. The story further epitomizes what was happening in the UK: Jah

Bunny, an older drummer with much stronger ties to Jamaica and how things were done there, was unwilling to experiment, whereas it was entirely natural for a younger, British-born player such as Angus, who took Dennis's idea and ran with it. This was a teenager who had lived his whole life in London, and thus had defined his blackness – or even his Caribbean-ness – against a broad canvas of musical, cultural and social influences.

Reggae in the UK had been setting its own agenda for a number of years by then, a syllabus that involved adapting to a primary market that was more about black people born or raised in the country than immigrants who imported their culture as part of their baggage allowance. But in many ways this was to be a development far closer to its Jamaican roots than the stringsed-up pop fodder that had given the music such a high profile at the beginning of the decade. Mainly because this time around it wasn't being dictated by a consumership with no (or at most very little) vested social interest, but by the current manifestation of its original core audience – black youth in the ghetto. The way these kids looked at reggae music was through a window very different from the previous generation's; within the first couple of years of the 1970s the whole idea of roots and culture gained enormous currency in Britain's inner cities. After all, if you're one step further removed from Africa, as either a continent or a state of mind, then any form of conduit is going to be attractive. And by then the sound systems and specialist record shops were well enough established to service reggae's audience directly, without having to rely on national radio or the mainstream retail trade. Much as it had been in Jamaica at the beginning of the music business.

Or at least as regards this framework it was. Otherwise, British reggae pretty much played by its own set of rules, which began to be written as the end of the Trojan Explosion coincided with the rise of roots-and-culture UK.

In 1975, Trojan Records' parent organization Beat & Commercial was sold off for £32,000, in what was a swift sequence of events. First of all, Charisma, the rock record company marketed/distributed by B&C, was offered a better deal with one of the majors who apparently had never taken much of an interest in it before. This left B&C with costly, understaffed premises in central London plus a large building in the suburb of Acton into which it had been intended to move the blooming Trojan empire, and the original site in Harlesden. While thus desperately overextended, suppliers and other companies B&C dealt with suddenly reeled in credit lines. Instant insolvency.

Even in the mid-1970s, £32,000 was a distinctly bargain-basement price for a seemingly thriving indie record company with a useful back catalogue, but quickness of sale was very much an issue. Just to rub a bit of salt in, it was the enormous successes Trojan had enjoyed at the turn of the decade that were the core of B&C's undoing. The Trojan-associated labels' track record of several dozen pop hits, many 50,000-plus sellers and the odd tune passing the million mark, all achieved outside the usual channels of radio play, music press, regular distribution and retail lines, stood to prove what could be done by anybody with enthusiasm, ingenuity and an aptitude for hard work. But as the company racked up those pop chart hits it devoted increasing energies to trying to have some more, and took its eye off the ball. Trojan had become its own mainstream; it was the pop market that it had so successfully been poking with a sharp stick, and it was no longer paying close enough attention to those it had been set up to service in the first place – black Caribbean immigrants. And the real danger in such a perceptible shift in values lay in the *mainstream* mainstream not remaining where it had been when 'Double Barrel' was at number 1 and skinheads roamed the land.

To be fair, some evolution on Trojan's part was a necessity, as its core audience had changed – by 1970 it was weighted in favour of black kids born or brought up in the UK rather than the archetypal immigrant. At the beginning of the decade too much of Trojan's contemporary catalogue was trying to per-petuate its past. And it seemed to still be chasing a skinhead audience with a continuing stream of fast-paced, popping, jerking post-rocksteady reggae, or trying for pop hits with the lightly stepping likes of Nicky Thomas and Greyhound. A movement oddly exacerbated by Trojan's dabbling in all things cultural, as the reliable old orange and white label was appearing to be letting the white kids down with all this *Jah Jah business*, as half-hearted as it might have been. A comforting thought perhaps, not necessarily from a racist point of view, but by Rasta's own definition there'd be something uncomfortably askew in the dreadlocks camp if its basic tenets and principles could be readily taken up by a bunch of white guys in England. With shaven heads.

As we saw in Chapter 11, as it was rare for reggae records to cross over from a white audience to black buyers, so it was seldom that tunes aimed at that white market succeeded elsewhere. As their target audience withdrew, the records had nowhere to go. At the same time a number of tiny UK-based reggae labels were springing up with a full appreciation of the new sounds and attitudes coming over from Jamaica – companies like Shelley's (run by London sound-system operator Count Shelley), Ethnic Fight, Ital Records, Burning Sounds and Different began to corner the roots market. But where Trojan really missed a trick was in its handling of UK acts.

Trojan had been building up a roster of domestic talent across its labels, and, as the most visible reggae company in the country, was understandably something of a magnet for homegrown acts. This was an ideal position to be in as there was a new wave of young acts with very British musical sensibilities, righteous aspirations and nowhere to express themselves on vinyl. Trojan could have gone forward with a revolutionary approach to roots reggae that catered specifically for the domestic audience and, who knows, may have crossed the Atlantic the other way. It didn't, though. Instead, it opted to play (what seemed to be) safe and continue the Jamaican reggae tradition of covering soul and pop hits of the day – just doing it on the off-beat.

The Beatles, the Temptations, Roberta Flack, Lou Rawls, Kris Kristofferson, the Chi-Lites, Cat Stevens . . . few escaped the reggae cover version. Dennis Bovell's 1973 dealings with Trojan sum up what was going wrong:

'The first Matumbi record was on Trojan and was a cover of Hot Chocolate's "Brother Louie". It wasn't meant to be like that, I can assure you of that, but by that time Trojan was too cover version-bound. We were a young group, who had been saving the money we were earning from our jobs – I was a contact lens technician, the singer was a bank teller, one of the others was an electrician – and we didn't split money we earned from gigs, we put it in a band bank account, and we'd finally got enough together to get into the studio. We went in with our own money to record our own compositions thinking that we were *quite possibly* going to change the face of reggae from all this parrot fashion, as we used to call it. You know, the situation where it seemed that as soon as there was a pop hit you'd get the reggae version hot on its heels by the next weekend. It seemed to us, that in England anyway, the cover version thing had just gone too far and nobody was writing any original material. We wanted to be the first to do that, because even in Jamaica the covers of R&B songs were plentiful and for a while reggae seemed to have lost its creativity and originality with too many people just waiting for the next pop song to come along and cover it.

'The studio we'd booked was R. G. Jones in Wimbledon, South London, and in it was a Mellotron that had belonged to Brian Jones, the Rolling Stones guy. It was a huge great thing that didn't take to transporting around so it was just left in the studio – Brian Jones was dead by then – and at the end of the session, after we'd recorded all the stuff we'd written for our demo, we had some time left and we had a go on it. Because of the string sounds on it, this was like the first synthesizer, I fancied fooling about with it, and, not being able to afford an orchestra, we just had to try it. We wanted to have a go at sending up all that cover version, stringsy reggae. We made a spoof version of "Brother Louie", that Hot Chocolate song that had just come out. And just to show we couldn't have been serious I sung it and I wasn't the vocalist of the band, we had two other singers. I was guitar player but I'd taken lead vocal on this, just to show how *not serious* we were. But when we were copying the session off on to cassette, this got copied on the end of it.

'Our manager took the tape to Trojan to try and get us a deal. They *hated* all of the original material, but then they homed in on the cover version of that Hot Chocolate tune because it was still on its way up the charts. Somebody at Trojan actually said, "Yeah, this is going to be a big hit for Hot Chocolate, so we should put your version out as well . . . *Now*." The rest of the band were really pissed off, it was like "Bloody 'ell, we only did it as a joke, and they've gone and taken it really seriously." But worse than that, it was the only thing they wanted. *The joke*.

'So, hungry for a record deal as we were, we went along with it. Consequently, that was our first release. No, it didn't sell brilliantly.'

Trojan Records was sold to Marcel Rod, a music-business entrepreneur who had made a fortune from budget-priced classical music albums and who bought the company for its past rather than any notion of the future. Or even the present, as it no longer concerned itself with new music but filled its schedule by repackaging what it already had. This has a route that was followed by whoever owned the label subsequent to Rod – during Trojan's continuing twenty-five years it has only ever repackaged what was in its vaults by 1975. Which is some-how suitable for an organization that seemed to strive to remain conservative in the face of the adventurousness and excitement that had gained momentum among Britain's prevailing reggae culture.

Underneath Trojan's early-1970s decline, a roots reggae scene was thriving in the UK, the most immediate aspect of which was the second wave of British sound systems. They were taking over from the likes of Duke Vin and Count Suckle, and, while they might have had sets built along the same physical lines as their predecessors', these new operations had names like

Sufferer HiFi (Dennis Bovell's sound system), Ray Symbolic, Moa Ambessa, Java and Jah Shaka, and were keen to make a deeper impression than simply nicing up the weekend. Once again, the sound systems were part of a circle that both accurately reflected and was a product of their immediate environment: both the operators and their followers were black youth of varied Caribbean/African origin who, if not British-born, would have spent more than half their lives *inna Inglan* and who were looking for some form of unique cultural touchstone. A blues dance, late at night, in the heart of the black neighbourhood, publicized by word of mouth or flyers in record shops or other blues, was about as far underground as you were going to get in mainland Britain in 1970. Fuelled by the new roots music coming out of Jamaica, before the decade was two years old such part-time dancehalls as Brixton Town Hall, Battersea's Providence House, the Red Lion in east London or Harrow's Railway Hotel were playing host to earth-shaking expressions of righteous dread.

Remarkably, this began to develop *because of* rather than instead of the previous British-based sound men, as they demonstrated a combination of flexibility and closed-mindedness. In their steadfast refusal to play anything made in the UK, they had to rely on whatever came out of Jamaica, and as roots music gradually took over the studios' release schedules so it started to dominate the boxes of specials and pre-releases that were coming to Britain to service the sound systems. Those systems' operators were far more likely to play them than their generational peers back home because they didn't have the same direct influence as JA sound men had, and were therefore limited in choice. And, quite simply, there wasn't enough new music in Britain for them to be choosy. Besides, the young crowd that was starting to turn up at their dances seemed to like it. So rather than cut off at a certain point with a next generation picking up the baton, there was a crossover period in which the future sound men were turned on to roots reggae by hanging out at dances played by the original R&B likes of Vego, Duke Vin and Count Suckle.

And they turned on to it in serious fashion, as DJ Pebbles remembers. So named because his fellow sound men likened his deejaying style to 'a man with a mout'ful of pebbles', after following sound systems all over London during the late 1960s, Pebbles spent most of the next decade toasting Sufferer HiFi, and was, as he's quick to tell you, the first British-born deejay to hold the mic on a major sound system. Because, at that time, Sufferer was the sound system others measured themselves against when they tried and failed in sound clashes at Ladbroke Grove's Metro Youth Club, he had a ringside seat for the coming of consciousness to the UK reggae scene. Which seemed to take off more quickly and more comprehensively than it had in Jamaica.

'This was back at the end of the sixties and the early seventies, when the sound systems played a major role in pushing the music on to the next stage. For the simple reason that the sound system was the main media for the music. If you go back to that time there wasn't no David Rodigan, there wasn't no Tony Williams [British radio presenters who specialized in reggae]; you might hear the odd reggae record on the radio every now and again – maybe a Desmond Dekker, a Millie Small, Nicky Thomas . . . the few records that climbed into the national charts . . . Johnny Nash's "Cupid" or "Hold Me Tight", but that was it. If you wanted to hear the latest reggae hits you had to go to the dance.

'And it was there you got to hear something that seemed to make sense to you. If all you heard was those pop reggae tunes and the cover versions they used to turn out on Trojan, then you probably thought it was selling out. And that was all you'd hear at discos or youth clubs, too, where the deejays couldn't play or wouldn't play or couldn't get hold of the roots stuff. But the sound systems wouldn't play anything that had been released – as soon as a tune came out on the Pama or Trojan label then that was the end of its blues dance life – so you wouldn't get that pop stuff, just the real deal straight from Jamaica. The youth dem latch on to it because it was identifying with black. Roots reggae gave us a lot of guidance, it opened our eyes to *who* we are *where* we are . . . what we're doing here and how we came here.

'It also opened our eyes to the systematical wickedness we were living in. Remember, the black youth in Britain had been taken from where we were to be put somewhere else *not once but twice*. There was a lot of frustration and confusion and people could identify with the messages in it, so they used to soak up roots reggae like a sponge. It opened your eyes and made you be a bit more aware. The music, as played in the dancehalls in England, provided a lot of spiritual uplift. It gave us hope. Without that we would have been totally lost because there was no alternative. A lot of black people who know themselves today, it's only through listening to reggae music.

'I know cultural lyrics didn't start with Burning Spear. Go back to Blue Beat days there was a lot of culture stuff – Prince Buster has been preaching a long time – it was a rebellious music even since then. But this was music that related directly to the situation we were finding ourselves in.'

Once again it's Jamaica being recreated in Britain, but this time from an emotional rather than commercial or social point of view: in exactly the same way as the Kingston sound systems became the single widespread expression of black ghetto culture, so they did in London, Leeds, Birmingham or wherever. Mentioned earlier was 'black youth of *varied Caribbean/African origin*', while Chapter 6 advanced the notion of Jamaica emerging as the 'dominant cultural force in Caribbean Britain', but never had the latter been so relevant as at this time. The children of the *Windrush* generation of black immigrants were far more homogeneous than their parents who had actually grown up abroad. Of course, nationalistic differences existed among the youngsters, but this was seldom more serious than playground-type teasing and insult – kids who had never been outside London knowingly pronouncing how somebody messed up because they were a 'small islander'; or that it was important to 'never trust a Kingstonian', when the Kingstonian in question was born and bred in Finsbury Park. This was all essentially ludicrous, for the real business of the day was the search for a cohesive identity, a particular necessity because of the creeping institutionalized racism in the United Kingdom that was closing doors to a wave of boys and girls who had a British sense of expectation to go with their British standard of education. Indeed, DJ Pebbles' statements only hint at the prevalent dissatisfaction that was smouldering within the black communities. While it wasn't going to flare up for another few years, it was enough to create a siege mentality with the sound systems as a way of temporarily pulling up the drawbridge.

The English dancehall scene differed from Kingston's inasmuch as it was indoors, a state of affairs that particularly lent itself to the inherent portentousness of deep roots music. In an enclosed environment any decent bass response tipped over from weighty into grievous, while the noise from supporters at big sound clashes could turn it positively claustrophobic. It was standard for the joyous racket of whistles, tambourines and compressed-air horns to supplement the cheering, clapping and drinks-tin banging that would accompany the opening bars of unanswerable specials. When a sound as well followed as Fat Man came to the Metro to take on the resident Sufferer, you could hear what was going on almost as soon as you left Westbourne Park tube station, yet the hall was nearly a quarter of a mile away in St Lukes Road. But this was about the only way 1970s UK sound systems varied from their Caribbean counterparts; otherwise, true to their predecessors' way of doing things, operators took all steps necessary to recreate Jamaica in Great Britain. 'Recreate' isn't used lightly, either, as if you were a blues-dance patron in London during that period you could've gone out and rocked to big-time deejays calling themselves King Tubby's, Sir Coxsone's or Duke Reid's with no apparent sense of shame. It was more a matter of *in tribute to* or *hoping for recognition by association with*, but it didn't bother the people, who all knew they weren't the genuine article and accepted it as part of the idea of versioning the same rhythm over and over again. In fact, the London-based Duke Reid went so far as to have a deejay who called himself U-Roy – which sometimes led to problems when those who didn't regularly follow that set and had journeyed in from out of town, expected Ewart Beckford 'pon the mic.

This blatant harking back to Kingston serves best to define the British sound-system scene, as even those who'd put more effort into the name game – King Tropical, Sir Jessus, Fanso, Count Shelley, Neville the Enchanter, Quaker City, Soferno B, Stereograph, Java, Sir Biggs, etc. – would only take music direct from Jamaica. They used a number of different methods, each of which reflected their standing in the sound-man hierarchy. Buying pre-release (import) tunes over the counter in London record shops was far from ideal, because although it would remain unavailable to most of your crowd, there wasn't much to stop rival sounds getting hold of it. On the next level, striking deals direct with Jamaican producers opened up the world of the special, but too often said producer would be supplying more than one British sound or, almost as dodgy, it was an active special on the Kingston scene. Among these big operations, top-shelf status involved obtaining specials *so special* that even Kingston's higher-ranging systems were left gasping for air. Which, with the Jamaican record industry aware of the money to be earned in the UK, happened frequently.

Unfortunately, this insistence that their music had to be as authentically and as obviously Jamaican as possible created an unhealthy climate of apparently irrational prejudice among the movers and shakers of the British reggae business, the sound men. DJ Pebbles is little short of vehemently anti-UK reggae, and this comes from a man who toasted a sound run by Dennis Bovell, whose group Matumbi was dedicated to advancing precisely that cause:

'Back then, you could tell what was made in England and what was made in Jamaica. Even though there was English tunes that played their part, that did their bit on the sound-system circuit, it was only the real Jamaican stuff that was always in demand.'

Why? When, by the middle of the decade, Aswad, Matumbi, Black Slate, Mexicano and so on were cutting highly creditable, very popular tunes.

'It was more authentic. The English stuff was always seen as second best. Today it still is second best in my eyes, but in those days, in the 1970s, nobody would play it – the only big sound I knew that played English records was Sufferer because Dennis was a member of Matumbi; other than that it was all Jamaican stuff. English reggae will never be as good as Jamaican reggae.'

Why not? Sufferer was London's top sound.

'Because the best reggae *always* came from Jamaica. That's how it was to those who know. There was a lot of English stuff that is creditable, and credit should be given to it – there are a lot of good English-made twelve-inchers, but a lot of those UK-made tracks are Jamaican rhythms being done over, perhaps with new lyrics. The best reggae came from Jamaica and I will always see it that way. I could never *ever* say that UK reggae could conquer Jamaican reggae.'

It's paradoxical that somebody who takes such pride in being the first British-born deejay on a big sound system should take such a stance, but then if you ask Pebbles what his Britishness brought to his craft it's nothing he's willing to admit to. And perhaps this whole approach is easier to come to terms with when you compare it to the original sound men's attitudes to music that initially wasn't American; when music that didn't sound like it was 'Buster's little boop boop beat'. It's exactly the same sort of snobbery, this time passed off in the name of authenticity. While it may fall back on the excuse that at least the favoured music is Jamaican, such an excuse is never a reason.

Regardless of any condemnation or justification, the fact remains that for the first few years of the decade Pebbles' attitude was the rule and not the exception. This meant that the other aspect of the UK's burgeoning roots-reggae scene, the groups, received virtually no support from what should have been its strongest allies, the sound systems.

Self-contained reggae bands were the one aspect of the UK development that didn't owe its all to Jamaica. The island had never bred self-contained US/UK-style group acts; not since the Skatalites anyway – and even they came out of a nightclub/hotel dance big band jazz scenario. Even the club bands like Byron Lee's Dragonnaires or Sly Dunbar's Skin, Flesh and Bones behaved more like sessioneers. Jamaican bands enjoyed an essentially passive existence in which, although they would be largely responsible for the musical arrangements, they were rarely there to do anything other than make the singer sound good. This was always going to be a fact of life in such a recordings-biased music industry. Great Britain, on the other hand, had a deep-rooted, post-rock 'n' roll tradition of kids forming a band and then taking it to the stage for a year or two before they even sniffed a record deal, and it was only natural that the new wave of consciousness-seeking black groups should be swept up in it.

At the dawn of the seventies there was a circuit of what were known as 'grown-up reggae clubs', catering for a perhaps older, but definitely more aspiring, upwardly mobile crowd than the dancehalls. This was a nationwide situation that included the Apollo in Willesden (north-west London), the Venn Street Social Club in Huddersfield, the Santa Rosa in Birmingham, the Bamboo Club in Bristol (which, incidentally, was owned by the spectacular round-the-world yachtsman Tony Bullimore), the unconnected International Clubs in Leeds and Manchester . . . anywhere with a sizeable West Indian population had at least one of these sit-down collar-and-tie joints, often with restaurant facilities. A Count Suckle's Q Club meets West Indian social club kinda thing, far removed from the notion of the dancehall. And, in *proper* nightclub fashion, they embraced the idea of live music as the featured attraction. As well as the bigger names in the Trojan posse, bands playing these venues included the Gladiators (not the Jamaican group of the same name), the Undivided and Black Volt (Frank Bruno's brother Michael's group), and each had a repertoire consisting almost entirely of cover versions of reggae hits, reggaefied pop hits and a generous helping of soul standards. This latter inclusion was vital, as a large part of any black British band's income came from bookings at the American airbases that were then dotted around the British Isles, where they'd function as jukebox-type bands (soul Top 40 covers), warm-up acts or backing musicians for touring Americans – bases-only tours were big business for black US acts in the 1960s and 1970s.

This was hardly the sort of circumstance that was going to promote musical or conceptual growth. In fact, it makes the sound men's scorn for domestic reggae seem almost under-standable, and was increasingly at odds with the roots move-ment's expansion of the music's perception of style and content. Then Matumbi were formed, and for a couple of years before they got into the studio to, as Dennis Bovell maintains, 'change the face of reggae', they opted to play nothing else:

'We'd been together as a group since school and we were serious about what we wanted to do – we were budding song-writers and budding young entertainers, and as far as we were concerned we were making a career out of this thing. So we *had* to do it that way. But once we decided to play just reggae, it was considered professional suicide, because at that time the most work black musicians could get was at the bases playing for black servicemen who, while they liked the idea of a black group *from the islands*, wanted to hear Wilson Pickett, Otis Redding. You start playing riddim and it's [*affects cornball American accent*] "Hey, what's that funny beat, man?" The agents definitely would not book a band that played just reggae into an American airbase, you had to be playing soul or blues.

'In fact all we heard was "You're not going to work, lads. You're not going to work", so we went to the clubs that would book groups, the evening wear, middle-class black people's scene. I'd been to clubs like that and seen groups there who were all "Good evening ladies and gentlemen . . .", trying to be on their best behaviour. But for us the roots thing had started, so I'd get on stage and say "*W'aaappen* . . . Right about now, I and I ah bring yuh . . ." and then hit some true reggae. The audience would look and say "What a cheeky little fellow." We were just trying to be rude boys, but without really knowing it we were crossing all sorts of barriers.

'I'm sure none of those people in the audiences in those clubs could come to terms with the kind of English accents we had, because we'd been to school here. It was like you'd be speaking with a cockney accent all day at school or at work and then you'd come out as a musician in the evening. You couldn't talk cockney in front of a bunch of black people, you'd have to switch instantly into some kind of Jamaican tone. But then the audiences at those places were the same ones who were trying to get out of that, who were aspiring to a very English Englishness. Which is why they had their children over here because they wanted their children to grow up with this English tone. And there we were, a bunch of kids who should know better, who were brought up in England, reverting back to this roots Rasta, I and I talk. It made some people – in the crowd and on the stage – look at what was happening in England, and at least think about how things were for us.

'But that wasn't enough, and we didn't think we were reaching the crowd we wanted to reach – our own peer group. So we started targeting reggae clubs that had sound systems but weren't yet hip to live performances. These were places like the Georgian in Croydon, where groups were frowned upon and people would rather go and listen to records than see a group. And they could be *hostile*. In the Four Aces in Stoke Newington they used to have live groups on Sunday night, and some famous groups that had been on TV would go on there and get booed off after the third or fourth tune. Sir Coxsone [the English version] did the sounds there and the crowd would start chanting "*Coxsone . . . Coxsone . . .*" and he would have to start to play because people were so disappointed and making so much noise. Then came the time for Matumbi to play there and I was determined to hold that crowd, so we learned and played all the latest dub plates, all the latest soft wax, all the latest pre-release, and mixed it up with our own songs. We sounded just like the sound system playing records – bass and drum and everything. So every time I'd look in the audience and see they was getting a bit fed up we'd play a popular pre-release; otherwise we'd throw in one of our songs about . . . you know . . . what a bastard

Enoch Powell was. And they'd just go *Hmmm* to the whole of it. There was no actual applause, they never clapped, but equally *they didn't boo us off*, so it was like we'd gone down really well. We played and they stood there and we played and they stood there and when we finished it was like, "Thank you and goodnight", and they stood there completely silent until somebody shouted, "Right, records now." But it was like we'd conquered because there wasn't none of the usual "*Come out! . . . Yah idiot!*"

'That's how we approached these sound-system places, thinking that if we could play as well as the records, we were bound to be given an ear. And it worked. Then as I had a sound system, Sufferer HiFi, our manager Noel Green would book out the sound and the group, so really it was like an all-in package – sound system and group from London. But because it was *our* sound system, it meant that the sound system would stop and let the group play, because usually the promoters would have hell to get the sound system to stop to get the group on stage. In most places, especially out of town, as soon as the sound system stopped and the group introduced themselves people would start to keep up noise: "*What's this . . . What's this . . . Put the records back on . . .*", and then it was normal for the deejay not to be overly cooperative with the group, so the promoter would have to ask the group to stop there and then. But we had it so we could make the changeover completely seamless, getting on stage and ready while the records are still going and then, with no pause or introduction, going into one of the latest pre-release sounds.

'If it worked, then the crowd were into us before they even realized. They still never actually clapped, but we kept it up because we did feel we had broken through a little bit.'

Dennis is being uncharacteristically modest. Matumbi had made an enormous breakthrough: they had successfully accommodated the idea of forming a band, playing self-penned material and getting gigs within the contemporary Jamaican music business's way of doing things. Moreover, they managed to marry contemporary Jamaican music to traditional pop/rock 'n' roll song structures without depreciating the innate feelings of dread. This was *the* most serious matter. Dennis and Matumbi had worked out that it was where you started from rather than where you ended up that was going to determine a song's point of view, and they by-passed Jamaican routine to recreate roots reggae from a Western template. This, far more than Trojan's stringsed-up airiness, was what brought original reggae firmly into the mainstream. And it did it on rootsman's terms, dragging commercially acceptable reggae back from the pop shallows it had drifted into.

'There's a big difference between *popularize* and *pop* . . . Of course we were trying to *popularize* it, because that was what we wanted to do with our lives – nobody wants to go out there and sell ten records – but we didn't want to turn it into *pop* music. So of course we wanted to make it acceptable, but we weren't going to be bending it as far as to try and make it acceptable to that ordinary pop listener's ear without him having to think twice about it. "After Tonight", "The Man in Me", "Empire Road" . . . pure pop, but the drum parts and the bass-lines are *reggae roots*. Also, what was really important to us as musicians was to have people recognize that we could play. We wanted to let people know that our musical ability was more than two chords.

'In trying to popularize the music we knew we had to colour it differently to the Jamaican forerunner and to have lyrical and musical content that would catch the ear of the British born, the next generation-to-be of reggae lovers. The ones who had inherited it. We'd taken our parents' thing, as it were, and mixed it with the things that we were having to go through daily at school, with friends and what was being thrown at us on the radio . . . that kind of feel. Musically there was a way of doing it. We'd get into the catchiness of pop choruses, how simple and repetitive the choruses of pop songs were, and make our own catchy pop repetitive choruses. Like "After Tonight": *Baby after tonight, baby after tonight, baby after tonight, baby after tonight* . . ., that relentless "Baby after tonight", promising her something – after tonight it's going to be cool, just trust me – and what he promises her you have to listen on to the words of the song to find out. That melody was as repetitive as any Beatles chorus, or so we thought.

'But what usually came with a repetitive chorus was the lightening of the rhythm section. And we didn't want that. We wanted to *darken* that rhythm section, make it really heavy and deep. So we put the song together around a bridge. "After Tonight" is one of the first *original* reggae songs with a bridge part in it. It's like verse, bridge, chorus, and that's a very American way of writing. If you look at a lot of Isaac Hayes and Dave Porter compositions and a lot of Holland–Dozier–Holland compositions there's like the verse, then there's a bridge bit where the chords go off somewhere, presumably a platform to the chorus. It meant we could change the chords to give some sense of progression, the song was *going somewhere*.

'That was what we felt was the key to good songwriting, and it enabled us to make the bass-line and drum patterns as dark and as rootsy as possible. Too many reggae records that were potential pop records thought they had to lighten the bass-line – like if a group's first record wasn't a hit and they thought, "too heavy for Radio 1", so they'd ease off on the rhythm section and the next record would just sound limp. We knew we had to accommodate that heavy bass-line, so we wrote songs with a verse, then a bridge to the chorus then the chorus leads back into the verse then a bridge again and then the chorus is out.

'Which is like a formula, the Jamaican counterparts though would just have what we used to call a roundabout – you listen to nearly all reggae songs up until then and they're just going around and around and around and around and around on two chords. On that roundabout they would create a verse-chorus-verse-chorus-verse-chorus thing, but it was not possible to have a bridge with only two chords. I mean, you can have the chorus and the verse with the same chords but different melodies, that seemed to be quite clever to do, but then how're you going to knit one to the other? You've got to change the chord. It's like driving your car and you're off in first gear and you could stay in second gear if you don't mind the whining of the engine or you could go to third gear, or you could, if you had synchromesh, go from first straight to fourth.

'It was like the different gears that we wanted to bring about as a style of writing. "After Tonight", "Man in Me", "Bluebeat and Ska", "Empire Road", "Point Of View" . . . all these songs were verse-bridge-chorus format and it allowed us to not lighten up the rhythm section. Not have some little twee bass-line, but have a really deep, heavy kinda rootsy bass-line that let anybody know they was listening to real reggae but was acceptable in a pop format. It worked; they were all hits, and they all got radio play because they weren't completely alien to the songs that were all around them.'

A great deal of weight is added to this theory by the fact that, years later, London reggae singer Maxi Priest would have big hits with cover versions of pop songs when his original material was all but ignored outside the reggae market. Yet his charismatic star-quality, media-friendly presentation would be the same in every case, as would the emphasis on the heavy-duty drum and bass parts. Likewise Aswad: brilliant musicians with a vibrant, engaging presence, they created a whole slew of fantastic blues-dance tunes from lovers' rock to Rastafari yet only broke through on a big scale with a cover version of 'Don't Turn Around'.

What Dennis had done was to consciously – literally and itally – acknowledge his environment which, after all, was where he knew his music had to go. Such a reggae revolution could only have happened in Britain. Quite apart from the more varied musical surroundings, it makes a difference that the UK black community's heritage was so disparate – in the necessary refusal to dutifully toe the direct-from-Kingston line it can be no coincidence that the man with this vision, Dennis Bovell, isn't Jamaican but came to London from Barbados as a young child.

None of this, however, stopped him having to come to terms

with the sound-system scene in London. Operations other than Sufferer, that is.

Within the first few years of the 1970s, London sound systems had multiplied to the degree that every third person you met *'ave a likkle soun'* – it's no exaggeration to say that builders were driven to distraction as so many of the boards they'd put up on half-finished or derelict houses would be removed and turned into speaker boxes. Underneath the champion sets mentioned earlier there was now a second and third division for whom economic necessity precluded too much artistic snobbery and, in an echo of Derrick Harriott's Kingston youth, they were forced to look closer to home for their original music. Which didn't mean they lacked standards. Although the sound men who were buying British enjoyed having a straight-to-source relationship with somebody like Dennis, it came with its own strict code of ethics. There was a lingering bigotry against being seen to be using too much domestic product, so suppliers had to resort to dub plate subterfuge. But it was as vital as it had been in Jamaica that the producers got the sound systems on their side. Dennis explains:

'Why it was so important to us not to compromise our rhythm section was that was the only way the sound systems would play it. We'd have a cut that was going to be released and a cut that was going to be played for the sound systems and we'd give the sound systems their cut two or three months before any release date – in fact, in the case of "After Tonight" it was two years before it was released.

'It was the strategy, because we'd studied the market and the only way reggae in this country gets really noticed was if black people notice it first, or if the fanatics get in there first. How do the fanatics get in there first? Sound systems. So what did we have to do? Service the sound systems with our record, and the only way to get them to play it was to tell them, "Look, this is new and gonna be new for the next year. You gonna be playing this as an exclusive for the next year. People can't buy it." Just like in Jamaica, the sound systems *loved* that. If they're gonna have a record that the general public's not gonna get their hands on for at least a year they will flog that record *'til it bleeds*. They will boost it up: "New Matumbi, yeah . . . yeah . . . yeah . . . *but yuh cyan't buy one to play at your 'ouse.*" It's really like sticking two fingers up at the audience, but that's the way it's always been and they will go for it all the time.

'Then you had to stick to your word. If you bring a sound man a record one week and then next week it's released, you bring him another record and he's not going to play it in case it release too quick like the last one. Sometimes though it can go on a bit long, like with "After Tonight". We'd left Trojan by that time and wanted to form our own label, so we thought, let's give the tune a run for six months on pre-release and then we'll put it out. Then, when the six months was up, sound-system guys were telling me, "You can't release the record yet, man, we've only been playing it six months," so we let them carry on with it and then they come again with, "Look, no . . . hold back just a little bit more," and we said OK because we wanted it to be as strong as possible. But then we had to put a stop to it on pre-release because we had to earn some money off it at some point.

'While that was one way to get to the sound systems, even the little ones didn't like to imagine they were reliant on English-made music so they wouldn't take a whole heap of tunes from you. They frowned at music that was recorded in England, but I always said it doesn't matter where it's recorded because if the players know what they're doing and the engineers know what they're doing then it's going to come out well. So I thought, "Right, we are going to confuse the general public into not thinking these songs are English recorded," and decided not to give them any information as to who was playing on the record. No information whatsoever – about anything at all – on the label. It was – "Yuh like dis'ya record? Yuh wan' buy it? *Why not?*" We got Steve Gregory and a horn section together and just started making all these tunes and getting them pressed up with a label that was just red, green and gold, sometimes it had Rama on it – our label's name – sometimes it had the name of the tune, sometimes it had nothing at all.

'I even went out and bought a dink machine. A dink machine is the thing that made a bigger hole in the centre of the record, release records have a little small hole in for the spindle, but pre-release – imports – have that big fat hole where you have to have a record dome – you put the record on to the base, pull the handle and *dink* the centre out. We'd get the records pressed up in Wimbledon, then bring them back to the office, sit there with this dinking machine and lick the hole out of the middle, then sell them for a quid each as pre-release.

'We had a Volkswagen van, fitted out with shelves, going round the record shops selling it. Totally like the old days – record a tune, press it up, take it round the shops. We didn't have any major distribution at all. We'd have a van driver, he would stock this Volkswagen van up during the week and drive from London to Leeds and sell records. Do the books over the weekend, then on Monday morning stock up again if we needed to re-press or whatever. Because we didn't have Made in England put on it and with the label being seriously void of other information the buyer had only to decide on the quality of the sound. Sound systems would play them and they were selling reasonably well. We had about a fifteen-strong company earning out of it, a good seller would be a couple of thousand, but there was nobody else to pay except us.

'As well as the singles, and there were a lot of them because we didn't have to worry about release-schedule timing, we made a few albums: *Who Seh Go Deh*, *Ah Fi We Dis*, *Leggo Fi We Dis*, *Higher Ranking Scientific Dubwise* and *Yuh Learn*. The name of the group we did those under was supposed to be the 4th Street Orchestra, but we'd been exposed by then and learned not to do that any more.

'While it was a brilliant plan, we shot ourselves in the leg because I'd let our singer sing on one track. It was entirely our fault, because the whole idea was supposed to be dub things, no vocals whatsoever, but the singers in the band were always complaining – "What we supposed to be doing while you're off having fun making dub plates?" Singing little bits of dub things wasn't enough. So I let one of our singers have a go and we didn't reckon on him having such a distinctive voice, because "Man in Me" came out after that and the *Black Echoes*' [a British black music weekly] columnist Snoopy did a big exclusive – "I know who's behind all this Rama stuff, it's Dennis Bovell and his mates from Matumbi". The band thought I'd told him, because they knew Snoopy was a friend of mine, so I asked him to tell the guys how he knew and he said, "It wasn't too hard, see that record there, that's him singing on it, see that one, it's the same voice and it's got Matumbi written on it." We never imagined we were that popular people could tell it was a Matumbi record only from the voice.'

But by then, 1976, Matumbi *were* that popular. Reports were that 'After Tonight' had sold close on 100,000 while 'Man in Me' was the biggest-selling reggae record in the UK that year. Although they made it on to *Top of the Pops*, very little reggae was sold in the chart returns shops so Matumbi's efforts were vastly underappreciated in the wider scheme of things.

But perhaps such disappointments were made up for by the group's real achievements. It was they who brought together sound-system culture with pop sensibilities in a way that was as logical as it was emotionally sound. And in 1972 and 1973, they were the first act to do it too. Sure, the Cimarons, who had been gigging and recording around the UK since the mid-1960s, made it off Planet Trojan with their credibility intact, but at this point they were still cutting reggaefied pop and soul cover versions: theirs is a catalogue that manages to include a take of Neil Diamond's 'Mammy Blue', while the album that sanctioned their roots perspective, the highly rated *On the Rock*, was recorded during an extended stay in Kingston. And although it would be a couple of years until we saw the wave of groups that gave UK roots its identity, the fact that there was now an example for the next set of hopefuls to aspire to made sure there was a wave at all.

As the middle of the decade passed, acts like Steel Pulse, Misty in Roots, Ijahman Levi, Aswad, Black Slate, Tradition, Reggae Regular and Delroy Washington explicated British roots reggae in spectacular fashion, using the medium to express their disaffection and dissatisfaction in protests every bit as eloquent as anything coming out of Kingston.

17

Trench
Town
Rock

It's impossible to overestimate the significance of Bob Marley as part of this story. The biggest selling, the most toured, the biggest audiences, the most widespread, the most talked about . . . the superlatives are so many they almost become, well, superfluous. The Bob Marley box set, *Songs of Freedom*, that came out in 1992, has sold over a million, at one point was the best-selling box of all time – in any musical genre – and today it is still up in the top five sets. Bob is the only reggae act to consistently interest the mainstream music press and, occasionally, to be risked on their covers. There are a dozen or so biographies and books about him in print at the moment, and it's a brave publisher that will put out a volume about reggae in general without its jacket artwork conspicuously featuring Bob Marley's face. Honoured by the government with the Jamaican Order of Merit – the third highest civilian honour and more or less the equivalent of a British knighthood – he was the Honourable Robert Nesta Marley OM. He was the biggest star in the country's history, and his face has appeared on stamps not just in Jamaica but all over the world.

In the eyes of officialdom, Bob Marley brought a legitimacy to reggae and Rastafari that meant he was, to the Jamaica Tourist Board, a national institution more highly marketable than Dunns River Falls, Ocho Rios rent-a-dreads or Wray & Nephew Rum. Thanks to its continued use in 'Come to Jamaica'

TV commercials around the world, Bob's 'One Love' has become an unofficial national anthem. His former home is now one of the capital's larger and better-attended museums. In the arrivals hall at Norman Manley Airport the piped Muzak is mostly Marley. His image and song quotations beam down from billboards on the twenty-minute drive from there to Kingston proper, and once you get there T-shirts, posters and wood carvings are on sale practically everywhere. All of which is right and proper, as he's the reason so many tourists come to the island in the first place.

For many people, Bob Marley *is* reggae. To them, quite simply, the whole four decades of modern Jamaican popular music starts and ends with the Tuff Gong. And even those considerations will be condensed into the nine years between *Catch a Fire* and his death in 1981, the era during which Bob Marley – first as part of the Wailers then as a solo act with a backing band – became a rock star in every sense of the word.

Astonishingly though, during this period in which his was the best-known name in Jamaican music, he was actually very much removed from it. What was going on around him made hardly any impression on his world, or vice versa, as regards either presentation or content. This isn't any form of judgement, it's a simple statement of fact, and an apparently colossal irony that, during his tenure at the top, reggae's most famous exponent exerted practically no influence over the music's development at grass roots – i.e., Kingston studios – level. To the home crowd, the core audience or whatever you want to call it, anywhere in the world, Bob Marley's puissance was of the spiritual, inspirational, intellectual and socio-political variety. Although the later-seventies Bob Marley swiftly became the rest of the world's metaphor for reggae, if not for the Caribbean and the black race in general, in his own artistic constituency he was greatly respected while all but ignored. In fact, from a purely musical point of view, he wasn't even operating in parallel to reggae's growth lines but marking time somewhere behind the cutting edge.

It's precisely because he took himself out of reggae's mainstream, almost as much as his uniqueness and importance within the big picture of reggae, that Bob Marley has a chapter to himself. It's also why so many Bob Marley biographers find it so easy to ignore the reggae context around their subject without detracting from the story they're telling, because, most pronouncedly in the latter stages of his career, he was off to one side of reggae's main story.

At the time *Catch a Fire* was released, at the very end of 1972, with the sole aim of breaking Bob Marley big around the world, the Wailers were superstars in Jamaica. Tunes from the Lee Perry sessions were still active and a series of self-produced hits in the summer of 1971, culminating in the lawn-shaking 'Trench Town Rock', meant they were more than able to survive long periods spent off island. But, post-*The Harder They Come*, guys like Big Youth, Horace Andy, Prince Jazzbo and Max Romeo were carrying the swing alongside Nicky Thomas, Delroy Wilson and Ken Boothe, so on the surface of things any one of several Jamaican artists would have seemed to be a much more appropriate candidate for international stardom than Bob Marley. For example, Jimmy Cliff already attracted adjectives like 'sophisticated' and 'worldly' because he had lived abroad, toured all over the globe to great acclaim, recorded at Muscle Shoals with an American producer and musicians, wasn't scared to try different styles and was now an international movie star. Then there was Big Youth, with buckets of charisma, exotically yet approachably roots and obviously widely influential. Nicky Thomas, Ken Boothe, Dennis Brown and John Holt were natural pop stars. While the Maytals represented raw Jamaican ghetto culture virtually unfiltered.

All of the above had sold more records abroad than Bob Marley and the Wailers, too. Plus there's that naggingly persistent rumour that Bob wasn't even Chris Blackwell's original option to be the roots lab rat in his bold experiment to elevate a Jamaican reggae act to international rock-star status. The rumour suggests that the Wailers were 'trouble', only taken on because a post-*The Harder They Come* Jimmy Cliff wouldn't return to Island and the Maytals went to Byron Lee at Dynamic after Leslie Kong died. The rumour might not be true, and would signify very little even if it were: Jimmy Cliff had already been groomed for international stardom by Blackwell's company in London to little avail; while the Maytals . . . *grooming?* . . . you get the impression they were never about to play by somebody else's rules.

Jimmy Cliff can lay claim to being the Man Who Discovered Bob Marley, as it was he, working for Leslie Kong, who got the sixteen-year-old his first recording session. Jimmy and Derrick Morgan acted as intermediaries for potential talent in the area by auditioning singers in rum shops – the sort of establishments a man like Kong would see as beneath himself to go in – and taking them down either to Beverley's or to Federal to hook up with Kong. According to Jimmy, Bob had a hunger and intensity about him which combined with an astonishing self-confidence to make him, even back then, an all but unstoppable force. As it was, he'd already been turned down for audition by Kong without singing so much as a note and was therefore doubly determined to show what he could do – ironically, the producer had believed that Bob's Caucasian(ish) features and bright complexion wouldn't do him any favours on the take-no-prisoners Kingston ska scene.

Jimmy remembers the meeting thus:

'This was early in 1962. I was A&R man for Leslie Kong – Derrick Morgan was number one there, senior to me, I was his second in command. Derrick Morgan and I used to hang out in a bar in West Kingston, where the singers knew they could find us and we could listen to them sing. That's how they had to do their audition, on the spot with no instrument – that way you really knew if they could sing or not and whether their song was strong – and if they was good we'd take them down to Leslie Kong.

'Bob came after Desmond Dekker. Desmond came to Beverley's that way, and we tested him and the first song he recorded was called "Honour Your Father and Your Mother" – I tested that and put in a few lines for him. Desmond and Bob used to work in the same place doing welding, so after Desmond get his record he went back to Bob and told him, "Bwoy, I meet up with two bredren who help me get my music recorded. Them 'ave put me on record." And Bob, who had already been rejected by Leslie Kong but he don't know why, said, "Go 'way, Yuh lie!" So Desmond tell him about Derrick and me, and Bob knew the bar where we used to hang out, so he sent somebody down there to talk to Derrick about him. *He sen' someone else*, he wouldn't come himself, like he's a little bit shy. We haven't got nothing to lose, so we tell the guy who brought the message to tell Bob to come to Beverley's at a certain time.

'When Bob arrive at Beverley's Derrick wasn't there, just me sitting down playing the piano, working out a tune. And Bob walk up behind me and say "That sound good y'know." I look round and see this likkle short fellow who I'd never seen before. What strike me about him immediately was how he just walked in – wasn't nervous or anything. So why he send someone else to see me and Derrick must be because he don't want to be told "No!" twice. Then how he say "That sound good" show he picked up what I was doing with the song immediately and could follow the verses and choruses that I was working out. He was very sensitive, naturally, to how music worked and could be put together. I'd say that with him it was completely instinctive; although he had learned a lot about music from Joe Higgs, his understanding was so quick it must've come naturally.

'He tell me he have some songs, he sing them and I start to play, picking up the tune he wanted to give them. I think he had five songs, and I picked three of them – "Judge Not", "One Cup of Coffee" and "Terror" – and Leslie Kong take him to Federal to record them a week or so later. "Judge Not" and "One Cup of Coffee" were released. The first one they call him *Robert* Marley on the label, then because Leslie Kong don't think that soun' so good on the next one he called him Bobby Martell on the records. "Terror" didn't come out – I don't know why, it may be being saved for the next Bob Marley compilation!

'It could've been, too, because it was from back then that you *know* Bob Marley was somebody special. Because it was all there already – from just those three songs you have everything that was Bob's character. They sum him up completely. "Judge Not" was a song that protest about the injustice in all around us, a song that said, "You have your legal right, I have my legal right, so who are you to tell me that because you are more educated than me then you are better than me? So judge yourself before you judge somebody else." "One Cup of Coffee" was a love song, and Bob write some of the best love songs ever written, because he was a man that love woman! I mean *really* love! I think he love love itself, too, because that was the sort of happy, optimistic person he was. And then "Terror" was his revolutionary side. It was about the oppressed people, the sufferahs, something that would give them hope, because even from when he was a yout' he was thinking about the suffering of his black people. That might even be why "Terror" don't come out, because it was perhaps too revolutionary for the time.'

Jimmy talks about Bob being 'a yout' at that time, but it ought to be mentioned that he himself – the man who gave Bob Marley the audition – was two years younger and had yet to turn fifteen!

Ten years later, Bob's elevation to the big league was down to luck. But, crucially, that's as defined by the old West African saying: 'Luck is what happens when preparation meets opportunity.' Of course Bob Marley had an abundance of talent and star quality, just as he had quick wit, an analytical mind, towering ambition and a poet's soul. But none of that would have counted for anything without both preparation and opportunity.

We've talked about the value of the work the Wailers did with Scratch as music in its own right, but in preparing Bob for what he was to become it was perhaps even more important. It taught him – and Peter Tosh and Bunny Wailer for that matter – that you don't have to follow fashion or necessarily do what you're told, and that in many cases the best way to get a result is to poke things with a pointy stick. What they immersed themselves in with Scratch in 1969 was total fearlessness, borderline terrorism in both the musical and lyrical senses. Perry's gift for musical experimentation plus the correspondingly free rein he gave to the group's lyrics epitomized the Wailers as they were to become: seething frustration, harmonic stridency and mellifluous love poems. But, crucially, the group's work forged an almost metaphysical connection from pre-slave ship Africa to post-colonial Kingston.

Almost thirty years later, while on tour with what's called the Wailers Band, Aston 'Family Man' Barrett, bass player in both the Upsetters and the Wailers, offers up a pertinent explanation of why the Lee Perry/Bob Marley connection came together with such deep-seated harmony. In so doing he endorses Scratch's theories of rural reggae pointing the way forward:

'Bob was a country bwoy . . . Scratch was a country bwoy and that's the level they meet on. Scratch know that in Jamaica there is a vibe you get from growing up in the country that is so different from the city. You appreciate things on a more spiritual level and can see more than just making songs to get play at the dance, you appreciate the song and the music for what it is – like you have learnt to appreciate the trees and the beauty all around you, for what it is, not for what it *do*. Mr Rodney . . . yunno, Burning Spear . . . was another country bwoy who had that spiritual vibe.

'Scratch know that Bob have that vibe and that together they can take music to another dimension. Like with myself and Carlie [Fams' brother who played drums in the Upsetters and the Wailers], although we were from Kingston we spent most of our time different from school and Christmas in the country too – by the riverside and up in the mountains – so Scratch knew we could connect with him. We have that spiritual vibe, that mental riff, we *connect*. Music has no limit and Scratch could see that. With Bob, and before that, he was always going to take it to the highest limit it could go and I could feel the inspiration flowing between them – feel it more than just in the head, I could feel it in my stomach. At the time we know that what we had was a special touch and what we were putting out was what nobody else has ever achieved.'

Indeed, the group became so absorbed in this sense of what could be done that they'd never really be satisfied playing by musical rules again. But either side of the Wailers' adventures with Scratch came one of the biggest single influences in Bob's career: Danny Sims. Outside of the actual recording studio, this immensely likeable and equally successful music-business hustler did more than anybody else to put the singer in touch with the big time.

'Broader than Broadway' isn't, you feel, a synopsis that the Mississippi-born, onetime pro-football hopeful Danny Sims would argue with. Never less than knowingly roguish, he has, during his sixty-odd years, been a producer, promoter, song publisher, booking agent, manager and record-label owner in America, Jamaica and Europe. He describes himself as 'a revolutionary', assumes a textbook Garveyite stance and has a long impressive record in the struggle. In the 1950s he opened Sapphire's, a gourmet soul food restaurant in downtown Manhattan – such a thing was unheard of below 110th Street – which became a high-profile hangout for the likes of Melvin Van Peebles, Harry Belafonte, Ossie Davis and Sidney Poitier. He was also one of the first black men to promote and book on an international level, and as a result had a client list that included Curtis Mayfield, Aretha Franklin and Sam Cooke. And as an agent he represented Malcolm X, booking his lecture tours and speeches.

Danny Sims decamped to Jamaica with his business partner, singer Johnny Nash, and their respective families in 1965, because the American climate of the time was hardly encouraging to an ambitious young black entrepreneur.

'We got out because it was crazy in America at that time and it wasn't safe for us to remain there. Or definitely not remain there and do business without interference from the CIA or the FBI. Because we did so much revolutionary stuff – as a booking agent I booked Malcom X – we had a stigma. And we had to do business, because, as Marcus Garvey said, commerce should be the first act of revolution in the African-American community, so we *have* to do business, and we have to do business *together* before we can do anything else. I'm not the kind of revolutionary that wants to go out there and fight or throw a bomb, and Jamaica was our safe haven to operate from because one thing about the CIA is they never shoot an African-American in a foreign country.

'I *was* paranoid back then . . . they were paranoid times. I'm living in Manhattan and I'm operating downtown and I'm seeing nothing but white people – just a few black people, yet we're *ten per cent of the population* so no wonder I'm paranoid. Then I found, going to Jamaica and Trinidad, that I'm doing good business and I saw maybe one or two white people. I said this is incredible, this is great . . . I go to Jamaica and I'm a king. I go to Barbados I can see the Prime Minister . . . I was a friend of Bustamante, I did business with Michael Manley and his father, I put on shows, I was friends with Eddie Seaga, I did the benefit show Nuggets for the Needy. In the Caribbean I felt this was how it was supposed to be so I moved my operation down there.'

Once he did, it was somehow inevitable he would cross paths with Bob Marley. Having met, it was just as likely that the two would 'do business' together as each man had what the other wanted – Danny saw in Bob a potential superstar; Bob, just back from eight months' living with his mother in the USA, felt he'd be best served by a black American manager – and the pair formed an alliance that lasted six years. It was during this time that Bob's approach to what he would have to do was formed. Danny's story, told at the well-appointed London offices of his music-publishing partnership, says a great deal about Bob and no small amount about Jamaica in its treatment of the future Order of Merit recipient.

'I had set up home in a large house in Russell Heights, an upmarket area in the suburbs of Kingston. I was in the record business and I used to entertain buyers, racking jobbers, disc jockey and record pluggers from America and England there –

they used to say, "I'm going to go to Danny's house in Jamaica for a few days R&R!" I knew about the Jamaican music scene, of course, but I wasn't having much to do with it, I was more concerned with promoting American artists in the Caribbean. Then one day in 1966 Neville Willoughby, the radio disc jockey, took Johnny [Nash] to a Rastafari *grounation* – Neville's father was our lawyer, which is how we knew him. Johnny came back very excited and described Bob to me and described Rita to me, and how they sang and the songs they sang. He told me, in complete seriousness, "Danny, the guy's a superstar."

'He had invited them to my house, and the next day Neville brought up Bob Marley, Rita, Peter Tosh and Mortimer Planno, who seemed to be taking care of business on behalf of the Wailers, the nearest they had to a manager – Mortimer was a Rasta elder, there was no Twelve Tribes back then. With just acoustic guitar Bob sang about fifteen songs straight off. He wasn't a great guitar player at that time – he developed that later, Peter was the really good musician – but Bob was a great songwriter and lyricist. His melodies were great, his style was unique, he was a very commercially minded artist and had great commercial potential. That much was obvious. I wanted to sign him, to manage and record him, and Mortimer said he wanted Bob to be with a black American company. They wanted to break into R&B, in the black community in America, and thought that was the only way to do it; plus Bob was a fan of all those artists we'd brought to Jamaica like Curtis Mayfield, Brook Benton and Sam Cooke. So I asked Bob and Mortimer to come to breakfast in the morning so we could talk about a contract.

'They came the next day for breakfast and my servants wouldn't serve them. I really got pissed off, but they wouldn't serve Bob and Mortimer. Point-blank refused because they were Rastas. I got rid of those servants and got some others but they still wouldn't serve him. Bob virtually lived at my house for three years, and when I was on the road with Johnny with "Hold Me Tight", Bob took over the house and the neighbours complained *badly*. They were always complaining when I was there, but when I went away they reported it to the police even though they knew Bob had the right to be there. The police were always being called out to Bob when he was walking in the vicinity of my house and he'd be arrested. The police would grab him and they'd call me up – "Do you know a Bob Marley? . . . Is he coming to your house?" They'd know who he was and where he was going because they'd have pulled him in a few days before, but they'd still go through this charade of making me vouch for him. I used to have a go and get him, and often, by the time I'd get there, they would have beaten him up.

'What I did when the last servants wouldn't serve him, was I got in somebody who wouldn't have that sort of snobbery – Bob brought a guy named Jeff in, and Jeff became my cook. He was a Rasta and would only cook ital-type food, which was strange at first but worked out great for me because it got all of us Americans into a much more healthy regime as we started eating fresh fruit and vegetables and fish instead of so much junk. Today people say I'm health obsessed and it began then with Bob Marley.

'Also, it got me and Bob closer as we began to connect on other levels. Remember, this was my first encounter with Rastas, I'd never seen a Rasta before, but I felt safer among them than in the upper-class circle in Jamaica that I had been in. Being with Ken Khouri and the richer Jamaicans was to me like being with that circle in America who we just didn't trust. We were what I called revolutionaries and that's how we saw Bob and Mortimer. I perceived Rastas to be like the black American revolutionaries, because at that time we were coming out on the street in America fighting to even vote. As African-Americans we never even had the vote until after 1964. Bob and Mortimer wouldn't hurt us because they were on the same trip we were on, we were in the same pathetic situation that they were in. So we embraced them and their way of life and philosophies and we stayed with them.

'I started hanging out in Trench Town with Bob and Mortimer, they'd sit around and Mortimer would read the Bible and they'd talk and stuff. To me that was safe. We had Marcus Garvey in common and I could appreciate what Rasta meant as a faith because any religion that isn't an African religion is to us, as a people – a captive people, using somebody else's religion. Can you imagine me, now, praying to my captors' god? I wonder about that and whether, if I pray to my captors' god will I be brainwashed by my captors through their religion, no matter what it would be? And what is an African religion? How could I get to my ancestors and deal with that? With Bob, when I saw those guys, that's what they were saying and we would talk – reason – for hours about all of that. They said Haile Selassie was their god, and that made just as much sense to me as everything else I'd heard about religion.

'We got a lot of resistance from our friends uptown about what we were doing and who we were associating with, but because we were so popular, people didn't get to us as bad as it could have been.'

Over the next couple of years, while signed to Danny's Cayman Music publishing company for a generous retainer of $50 per man per week, the Wailers wrote and demo'd a vaultful of rocksteady-style songs. Songs that tried more for international commercial potential than revolutionary zeal, it must be said. At some time during 1968 Danny cut an album with them called *Bob, Rita, Peter* – it couldn't be billed as the Wailers because Bunny wasn't on it, he was in jail on a ganja charge at the time – and to say it didn't do well would be dictionary-definition understatement:

'We went into America with this album and the reaction was *total* rejection. Then we literally couldn't give them away in England, which had a proven market for Jamaican music. Our distributor in England, Major Minor, wouldn't take that Bob Marley album for free – and they were having huge hits with Johnny's "I Know You Got Soul" and "Cupid" [Johnny Nash was the tenth best-selling male singer in Britain in 1969]. There wasn't one country in the world that wanted Bob Marley records.

'But Bob was an act who wanted to record. He wanted to record his songs and he wanted to record *every day*. If you didn't record him he wouldn't stay with you, so I let him record with other producers because it was so important to him at that time.'

Which is where Scratch came in. Exactly the right person at exactly the right time, because while Danny was always a shrewd manager and slick publisher, as an American he didn't have a handle on quite how quickly the Jamaican music business was changing in the late 1960s. Thanks largely to people like Lee Perry, the mild-mannered, American-derivative, love-song-saturated rocksteady of *Bob, Rita, Peter* sounded dated in both style and content. Not that this period was at all wasted. Danny's Americanness, which had so adversely affected the album, meant that his house was full of the more modern and openly revolutionary black music – Sly, James Brown, Jimi and so on, as well as the sharp end of jazz and blues. His management strategies as regards internationalism and adapting to suit the market concerned may not have been entirely successful in this instance, but the theories were sound and pretty radical for Jamaica in 1968. And, as he admits, Bob 'soaked all this up like a sponge'. That and the prolonged reasoning sessions with Mortimer, to which Danny Sims would bring a more pragmatic American revolutionary element.

Then he took Bob to Sweden for a year.

Not perhaps an obvious move for a young Jamaican radical, but Sweden had long supported a black arts scene – a significant number of US jazzmen and writers had settled there during the previous twenty years as an alternative to Paris. At this point urban Sweden was proving itself receptive to reggae with Desmond Dekker's 'Israelites' a number 1 hit single and Johnny Nash's rocksteady crooning also proving popular. Indeed, it was Nash who was invited to Sweden in 1970 to star in and write the music for a film (Nash had American TV and movie acting experience), and Bob and Danny simply went with him. The film got a very brief and unsuccessful release exclusive to its country of origin and the soundtrack album never saw the light of day, but for Bob Marley this Swedish sojourn and time spent in London directly afterwards was another growth experience.

Danny goes on:

'We were there for about a year, during which time we couldn't get musicians' licences, so outside of writing material for the movie soundtrack we couldn't work for pay. We had to work for free in Sweden, so we found whatever club that was the hot spot, went down and auditioned and worked it for no pay. They gave us food and we gained popularity. There were some African musicians living and working there who Bob hooked up with, and when they weren't jamming they'd talk about Africa. Bob was fascinated by it, because this was the closest he'd come to first-hand experience of a land that was really just a dream to him. He'd ask endless questions about the continent and its people – he just wanted to talk about it. This gave him an even stronger bonding with Africa than he'd previously got from Rastafari. Two of those African brothers, they played drums and percussion, came to London with us where we stayed for about another year.

'We signed with CBS in London because we liked Clive Davis, we thought he was one of the best record men we had come across and he had a taste for the R&B and black music. I brought Peter and Bunny over, but while Bob and Johnny had signed to CBS, the company wasn't interested in signing Peter or Bunny, and they weren't interested in Bob's band, either. I used them to record backing for some of Johnny's *I Can See Clearly Now* album, which Bob wrote songs for, and on the recording of "Reggae on Broadway", which would go out as a Bob Marley solo single for CBS. But outside of that, there was nothing for them to do – we worked some clubs for free – so the Wailers went back to Jamaica for several months, and Johnny and I stayed to finish Johnny's album.'

By the end of 1972 *I Can See Clearly Now* was breaking in several countries, and the whole band were called back to London for promotional work on that and the 'Reggae on Broadway' single, that CBS had put out in *Clearly*'s slipstream. Not that it worked out quite like that. 'Reggae on Broadway''s promo budget was virtually nil, so there was no tour or appearances to be done around it, and there was no follow-up work taking place because the single only sold a couple of thousand copies – although it did get a fair amount of London sound-system play where its quirky, proto-funk structure and Bob Marley's name gave it a cult status it still enjoys today. The promised tour supporting Johnny Nash didn't happen, either. The reggae on Nash's album, as recorded by the Wailers a few months before, now had all manner of extra instrumentation on top and had been mixed and mixed and mixed some more to come over as vaguely Caribbean pop music, and a group as rude-looking as the Wailers wouldn't have gone over very well with Nash's supper-club-style audience. However, the hits kept coming off it: 'Stir It Up', 'Guava Jelly', 'There Are More Questions Than Answers', 'I Can See Clearly Now'; and as the first two were Bob Marley compositions Danny was keen to get some recognition for the Wailers by piggybacking the group on this success.

'What we did here, because we wanted to promote Bob and Johnny together, was I got CBS and Rondor Music, the publishers I did a deal with, to finance it and we did a tour of high schools. Both Bob and Johnny had clean reputations, there wasn't any such thing as *they were bad guys*, so there wasn't any problem there and we got the national schools system to let us go in. For about a month we did two in the morning and two in the afternoon. The school would call an assembly for an hour, Johnny and Bob would do thirty minutes of question and answer, then they'd sing for fifteen minutes each and Bob backed both sets with an acoustic guitar. Mostly Johnny talked about the music business, while Bob spoke about Rastafari and Africa. The schools system was very happy because they didn't have to pay as we brought all our own equipment in.

'We worked on the London reggae club circuit too, for free. We did a lot for Carl Palmer, now of Jetstar, in his club in north London because it was near where the Wailers were staying. Bob and the Wailers were starting to make big inroads into the black British community, which is where we had to start building their fan base; then Johnny and I had to go to the States to work his album out there.'

It is well documented how the group felt abandoned after

Danny and Johnny left, although people who hung out with them in Harlesden at the time remember all of them except maybe Bunny as starting to get into the area's large black community. Bob, for instance, had several London girlfriends. But what they didn't have was any money or Musicians' Union work permits, and another cold winter was looming. It's at this point, and again a well-trodden story, that Brent Clarke, the young black British guy who had taken over day-to-day management duties from Danny, went in for an historic meeting with Chris Blackwell of Island Records.

Almost karmically, the final aspect of the equation was about to fall into place. Danny had done everything he could for Bob Marley, and what he'd done was enough. The Bob Marley that went into the deal with Island was more or less what the world would latch on to in a few years' time.

When Danny says, 'Musically and lyrically, Bob Marley was a genius. He just needed grooming, which is what we did,' perhaps without realizing it he is being modest. He and Johnny Nash did much more than mere 'grooming'. Without taking anything away from Bob's readiness and ability to absorb and assimilate every experience and environment, it was Danny Sims that put him into those situations and spent hours reasoning with the Wailers and Mortimer Planno from the empathic point of view of a fellow black revolutionary.

They had Garveyism and the struggle against oppression as a meeting point, but Danny's Stateside Civil Rights and Black Power experiences were an education for Bob, expanding his radical consciousness beyond Kingston's ghettos. Just as what Bob had to tell about colonialism and how that worked would be edification for the Americans. The prolonged visits overseas gave far more opportunity to appreciate *a foreign* than the usual touring schedule of travelling within a tight bunch of fellow countrymen – not that Jamaican acts did that much touring anyway. And the duo's dealings elsewhere, not least the stream of music-business types holidaying at the Sims villa, would have reinforced the notion of it genuinely being a big world out there.

All this gave a man like Bob Marley an enormous sense of internationalism, in itself a huge head start but still a long way from making the difference. The most valuable lesson learned was exactly how much went into having large-scale hits. In terms of balanced musical compromise – Johnny Nash's reggae was remixed and sweetened, the Wailers were recorded in a soul style – Bob knew he couldn't remain artistically parochial; it was just a question of what to incorporate and how much of it. And how much sheer, relentless legwork was required. Again according to Danny, Bob never missed anything going on around them as they toured, gigged and tried all manner of skanks and wheezes to make sure the public knew about the Wailers and their music. After years spent in these circumstances, Bob was fully aware that he not only needed to tour as part of a self-contained unit, but that he had to tailor his show to fit his *potential* audience rather than his existing crowds.

Having been exposed to these revolutionary and artistic influences, during the six months Bob spent in Jamaica in 1971 he wrote and recorded songs like 'Midnight Ravers', 'Satisfy My Soul', 'Concrete Jungle' and 'Natural Mystic'. Plus the tune that dominated the lawns all through the summer, became the country's number 1 record that year, named this chapter and perfectly summed up where the band were at that precise moment, 'Trench Town Rock'.

It was a vivid manifestation of the preparation we spoke of earlier. All Bob Marley needed now was the opportunity. Chris Blackwell, come on down.

Reggae international – i.e., in the UK – in the late 1960s was perceived by the punter as a particularly user-friendly pop style; almost anybody could follow the beat, and against the domestic industry's penchant for increasingly progressive concept albums, its three-minute values came as welcome light relief. However, there was a price tag involved: reggae was pitched in with the likes of the Mixtures' 'Pushbike Song', Dawn's 'What Are You Doing Sunday' and New World's 'Tom Tom Turnaround' and had to compete with those tunes *on their own terms.* Consequently, exported rhythm patterns tended to owe more to a straight count than they did to Count Ossie, while wardrobes were worryingly influenced by Peter Wyngarde's Jason King character in the TV series *Department S*. In every respect it was a 100 per cent polyester situation.

So in the serious world of the serious British music critic and his serious tastes in serious music, reggae had nearly as much credibility as the tooth fairy. Plus it had a frighteningly short shelf life that was rapidly approaching its outer limits – reggae sales in the pop world had all but evaporated by 1972. Maybe those dealing with reggae in the UK had no idea that there was any other way – after all, this is how it had always been done in Jamaica and it seemed to work – but Chris Blackwell looked at the British pop world from another angle.

Since virtually getting out of reggae a few years ago his Island Records was doing very nicely selling 'sophisticated' British rock music to the album-buying market – the not quite progressive but a couple of steps removed from centre likes of Nick Drake, Traffic, Roxy Music, Free and Vinegar Joe. When Blackwell signed the Wailers for the *Catch a Fire* album, the plan was for the company to treat it in exactly the same way as it would a mainstream rock release, and the point was to tap it into this market, which had been developing for several years, of music fans who expected a bit more for their money than a clutch of three-minute jolly-ups.

This was hardly original in concept, since the idea of taking reggae to a market on that market's own terms is precisely what Gopthal and Trojan had been doing a few years earlier. What what was without precedent, however, was the amount of money spent on it. Up until *Catch a Fire*, if reggae album artwork didn't look like publicity material put out by the Jamaica Tourist Board, then it featured somebody's girlfriend looking nervous, near naked and not very sexy at all. (OK, the *Tighten Up* covers were high erotica at the time, but take a long look at them tomorrow.) The Wailers' album featured the now legendary – and legendarily useless – sleeve that was fashioned as a giant Zippo lighter, with a top that actually flipped up and the record itself concealed behind a cardboard cutout of a windguard and burning wick. It was completely impractical, of course, because the rivet used to join the top to the bottom was brass, therefore much stronger than the cardboard it was hingeing, which would quickly fall apart as your friends had fun 'flicking' it; then, as you replaced the inner sleeve and record behind the flame it usually caught on the tip of it, squashing it down into a far from infernal looking state. Original Zippo-sleeved *Catch a Fires* in good nick are not quite as common as hen's teeth.

The album duly attracted an appropriate amount of attention for its packaging, which in turn mildly hyped the music. Music that was recorded in Kingston at Harry J's and Randy's studios, but extensively tinkered around with in London – clavinet, guitar and percussion overdubs by rock musicians, quickened tempo, fathomable mixes – until it sounded unlike any other reggae record. Also, another first, it was put together as an album with new tracks written to go with the selection of existing Wailers material, thus forming a centric thread instead of presenting itself as a collection of singles. The whole package was designed to create some form of Anglo-Jamaican hybrid, but was weighted so far to the former that it ignored the whole idea of sound systems and lawn dances to be as rock-audience-friendly as possible.

And it pulled it off. Sort of.

Although *Catch a Fire* is the one everybody goes on about – 'a new dawn for reggae', 'the turning point to the music becoming truly international' and so on and so on – so much of that is with hindsight. At the time it sold poorly, critical acclaim though fairly enthusiastic was largely patronizing, and as for changing the face of reggae as we knew it, it's impossible to name a single tune cut in *Catch a Fire*'s wake that so much as nods towards that album. Also, again something mostly obscured by the rose-tinted mists of time, Britain's black reggae crowds ignored it completely. They simply didn't like it. Significantly, while Bob willingly went along with what was done to his work, it was very much a case of hoping the end would justify the means rather than what you might term 'enthusiasm'. Family Man will chuckle as he recalls the others' reactions when they heard the UK-finished album, but he maintains that their somewhat resentful view was shared by Bob back in Jamaica: 'We jus' laugh. We say to each other "Bwoy, sooner or later those producers gon' sing and play for themselves and won't even need us."'

For whatever reason, the Wailers' pudding had been over-egged. When Chris Blackwell took them on, they were fully formed. Or as near as dammit, and didn't need reinventing. Plus it shows scant respect for the rock market's sense of adventure to assume that the people wouldn't listen to reggae unless it sounded like rock – ask yourself, why did they want to listen to it in the first place? The follow-up album, *Burnin'*, seemed aware of these issues as it opted for a far less adulterated sound and was far more successful. Of course, the promotional groundwork done around *Catch a Fire* had a knock-on effect (*Burnin'* was released within twelve months of its predecessor), but the point remains that the first album tried so hard it ended up selling itself short. It came at what it was doing from a rock rather than a reggae stance, and in doing so took the Wailers too far away from what they were. Although the record isn't without its moments, and underneath everything the songs are first rate, it was always much too much like 'reggae for people who don't really like reggae' to end up with much of a point to it.

Burnin' was much better received both critically and commercially and is the essence of the latter-day Wailers, reflecting as it did three unique characters – Bob the thinker, Peter the fighter, Bunny the spiritualist – all strong, each pulling individually, but all in perfect revolutionary harmony. The result was a whole with true depth and engagingly different facets, so much so that it played an enormous part in shaping what was to become Bob's international career, and between them, the two albums set in motion a world-shaking chain of events. The combination of music that rock critics could get a handle on and lyrics with a bit more to offer than simply rhyming 'all right' with 'all night' meant it took a hefty swipe at the widespread media prejudice against reggae, allowing the genre to be intellectualized. And on a personal level it put Bob Marley on course for global superstardom, alongside Curtis Mayfield, Marvin Gaye, James Brown and Sly Stone as one of the ranking ghetto poets of the time. Or of any time, for that matter.

It's in Bob's next LP, *Natty Dread*, that you can hear the triumvirate Wailers to fullest effect. Of all the albums this is the fattest and the most fulfilled, with a range of songs embracing 'Three O'Clock Road Block', 'No Woman No Cry', 'Dem Belly Full' and 'Talkin' Blues', to show up all aspects of their personalities. This is all the more remarkable since Peter and Bunny had left by then, but clearly there was so much residual influence that Bob couldn't help but put together a Wailers-style album. It was the last time any of his LPs would be so three-dimensional, as without his two creative foils there's little variation on the series of albums that followed. The high spots are still up there – 'Redemption Song', 'Natural Mystic', 'Waiting in Vain' to name the three pinnacles – but the depth of writing doesn't run through and these peaks are relatively few and far between.

Not that that mattered by the end of 1975. Such was Bob Marley's star status that his reggae needed to be more reaffirmative than groundbreaking. He understood how to write songs that could keep a rock crowd skanking without intimidating them, and stuck resolutely to his task. Hence the structures, arrangements and sound of so much of the later work didn't change: take, for instance, 'Exodus' and 'Coming in from the Cold': they sound like they're off the same session but there's four years between them, a lifetime in reggae terms. By this point, though, audiences were buying into Bob the man as much as Bob the musician, and he, always the most charismatic of characters, didn't let anybody down.

Good-looking, glamorous, seldom outside the company of the most fabulous women, exotic, enigmatic, enthusiastic, sought out by other rock stars, supremely street and a herbsman of legendary proportions, he was never less than good copy. But in true Tuff Gong fashion he'd Mau Mau the media in a way that gave no quarter yet still had them gagging for more. On the road or in his Hope Road mansion, he'd either righteously harangue attending journalists on the path of Jah Rastafari or mumble what amounted to quasi-mystic conspicuously stoned gibberish. Either way it sent most interviewers home happy as hamsters – as if they'd been party to some sort of inner ritual – but meant that few came within arm's length of what Bob Marley was all about. Maybe this technique had much to do with his shyness.

Whatever the reason, it never proved possible to capture the essence of Bob Marley in print. Not in the formalized sense of the magazine interview, anyway, or even in a book. So many of the former simply provide evocative editorial snapshots, while the best of the latter fill in the details of his thirty-plus years, but both pull up short. To attempt to get to grips with the shifting layers and the complexities that made up Bob Marley's true character, either in the space of an allotted hour or in reverent retrospect, was always going to be a futile task. Or it would be, without trivializing what the man was about and reducing him to the level of any of pop's more disposable protagonists.

It was impossible in anything as constricted as formal journalism to transcribe, unadulterated, the clarity of spirit, and to get across the complexities and bizarre leaps of logic that comprised Bob Marley. Rasta reasonings have no beginnings and no end and there's nothing so Babylonian as an answer to a question. Of course you could take his picture. Bob's face was an open book in the way the spiritually and emotionally pure have no need to wear a mask, and work by trusted photographers like Dennis Morris and Adrian Boot offers an access to Bob Marley no magazine feature ever did.

Danny Sims sums it up:

'If you knew Bob and you were with him he would never talk. He would only take his guitar and he'd strum and the songs, the lyrics he'd come out with would be how he would talk to you. And the smiles. He would always smile. If you knew Bob Marley you could read his face and know how he felt. He communicated through expressions. Bob wasn't a talker, he had this vibe when you knew when he didn't want to talk, when he didn't want to be bothered, but you could still understand what he wanted to tell you.'

It's been suggested, even in print by a few 'experts', that Bob Marley's success should be attributed to his being half white. That somehow it allowed him to deal with the world at large – i.e., white people – so much better than if he hadn't had the benefit of an almost entirely absentee Caucasian father. Like it was something hereditary, and is somehow borne out by the fact that the obviously black Peter and Bunny couldn't quite 'hack it', which is why they left. True, under many Jamaican circumstances Bob's high colour would have opened a few doors for him, but by the same rules his dreadlocks and seemingly chippy attitude would have slammed them shut again with sufficient force to make his eyes water. Remember the problems he had at Danny's house?

Interestingly, while these speculators like to see Bob as 'half white', that didn't seem to be how he viewed himself. As far back as his dealings with Danny Sims:

'We knew that he had relatives on the white side, that the Marleys were very rich, they were lawyers and engineers, I think. [As a clan they were comfortable, and Norval Marley, Bob's white father, had been a construction supervisor in the Jamaican Army.] I met them through Ken Khouri and I tried to get Bob with his family, but Bob, no matter how much money they had, lived in Trench Town. And that's where he wanted to stay. He embraced poverty, he saw himself as being among the oppressed, and rejected living with his family, who said to me that if he cut his hair and denounced Rastafarianism then they'd take him in. Bob wouldn't even discuss it; he said he wanted to be Rasta . . . that he wouldn't cut his hair *for Jesus Christ* is how he put it. Bob Marley was a black man and wouldn't have it any other way.'

The lengths he went to try to reach black America show his attitude didn't change, either. To his enormous frustration, black radio ignored his music because it didn't fit any existing format and the only US audiences he could attract were white college kids (college radio would programme reggae) and liberal types. At the end of the 1970s, at his insistence, the band were booked in for a week at the Apollo theatre on Harlem's 125th Street, black America's high street. When the curtains went up and Bob kicked into his set he found himself looking out at the same faces that would have been there if the show had been at a club in Greenwich Village. Every night of the engagement, such was the pull of Bob Marley, his downtown crowd had dared to cross 110th Street after dark. Many of them going back on more than one night.

This is still the case, Danny will tell you. 'Bob Marley can't get arrested as far as black radio in the States . . . never could.' By some way of compensation, though, his rebel soul was enormously appreciated – go into many black American households (more than just those of Jamaican descent) and it's not unusual to find a picture of Bob Marley up on the wall with Malcolm, Martin and Marcus. Just don't waste your time looking for any of his music.

I only met Bob Marley once, at the very end of the 1970s, somewhere near the peak of his success. I was working for the security team at the Venue, a huge London nightclub/concert hall of the time, standing at the door between the club and the backstage area checking backstage passes and laminates. It could get a bit lively on that door just after an act came off, as all manner of people tried to blag their way backstage, but there was one simple rule – no pass, no get past. It had been explained to me that to let *anybody* through without a stuck-on pass would be, quite literally, more than my job was worth. And it was a good job.

This particular night – I think it was Al Green who had played – a large posse of what we called Gucci Dreads (locks held back with sunglasses, leather trousers, shiny shirts, too much jewellery, blonde women and a load of attitude) approached the backstage door shouting about being let through. Not a pass between them. Then somewhere, in amongst the *raaas*ing and the *claaat*ing, one of them pipes up didn't I know who I was dealing with. To be perfectly honest, I didn't. I apologized to him, assuming he must be the star of his particular show, and as a bit of a wind-up added that I only recognized 'the famous ones'. They all seemed to stop talking at that point and turned towards the back of their group where, hidden behind them, was Bob Marley, dressed in his denims and chuckling quietly at the exchange that had taken place.

Naturally, I explained, I hadn't seen him there (he was much smaller than I imagined), and then I had the sticky task of telling him that without a pass I couldn't let him through, either. I said we'd have to wait for somebody to come down and get the manager to sort it out. Bob replied that was fine, that he respected I had a job to do. The assembled dreads clearly found this a bit hard to swallow, but as Bob was prepared to wait without any fuss they figured they'd better wait as well. Said passes were soon sorted, and as they filed past with barely disguised petulance and much teeth kissing, Bob gripped my arm, smiled softly and said, 'Easy, mon.'

I never saw Bob Marley again, not even backstage later that night. I didn't really need to; that little exchange had left a profound impression. In a situation in which superstar behaviour was probably more expected than merely excusable – imagine, say, Puff Daddy in the same circumstances, or how Bob's entourage seemed to think it should be played – he behaved like an absolute gentleman.

It's not hard to understand how Bob Marley reached the heights he did, and a last word should be from Danny Sims, who did so much for him as a young man and whose New York house he stayed in after his collapse in Central Park during the final stages of his illness.

'Bob Marley was a messenger, he was a prophet. When he first lived at my house I would look at him and talk about how could a guy like him write these kind of lyrics when he'd never been outside of Jamaica except to Delaware to live with his mother? Where would he get those lyrics from? Where did the vision come from? How could he talk about all the things he talked about from love to politics to the world to life? Bob Marley was a prophet. I think now looking at Bob and looking at where he's gone and where his lyrics have gone, I think Bob Marley will be around here for the next thousand years and he's going to grow and grow and get bigger and bigger. There's no end to how big he's going to get.

'Like our great leaders, like Marcus Garvey, like Malcolm X, like Martin Luther King, Bob Marley was one who, once he knew he had something to get across to the world, he couldn't rest because of his vision. Because he made us record him, then throughout his career he kept recording these same songs over and over; he was searching for acceptance for those visions. And he was willing to record them in any style, from R&B to Country & Western to rock 'n' roll, whatever it would take to get his music and his message to the people. Especially the African-American people – that was his great frustration. But he has become an African-American icon. Even though nobody will buy his records and he can't get played on the black stations, we love him. We love what he stood for and what he still stands for.

'To a generation, Bob Marley was a Malcolm X for the 1970s, a true revolutionary and a man who never left the people he loved and struggled for. During his life Bob Marley never changed. He never changed his outlook . . . he never even changed his wardrobe.'

18

Warrior Charge

'It was Friday 13th, October 1974. The Carib Club was above Burton's in Cricklewood Broadway, and there were three sound systems in the place. Mine, Sufferer, was nearest to the toilets; there's another one, Count Nick's, on the stage; and there's Lord Koos down the other end of the hall. This was a *serious* sound clash.'

A regular end of the week in north-west London, with Dennis Bovell at his secondary occupation, operating Sufferer HiFi and seeing off the opposition. Much like he did in the Metro days. He continues:

'That day Lee Perry has come in from Jamaica, I've met him at the airport and he's brought me some *spanking* dubs. While Bunny Lee, who has been in England for some time, he's in there in Lord Koos' corner. Lord Koos is his bredren from time so he's given him lots and lots of dub plates, but because my group Matumbi has been backing Johnnie Clarke, one of his singers who's on tour here, Bunny Lee's also given them to me. The same tunes. He didn't know I double as a sound man and that me and Koos were bound to meet in competition sometime soon, he just knew me as the leader of the band that's backing Johnnie Clarke. So while the crowd was really hyped up, we've all got lots of support there, there's a kind of stand-off between me and Koos because all the songs he's got I've got. It's just a question of who's going to play first. If I play one first as an exclusive then Koos going to play it back on me; and if he plays it first then I'm going to play it back on him. So we're going through without touching that selection, because I know he's got it and he knows I've got it and the first one to touch it *dead*; it's gonna come straight back in your face. And these are tunes that people will love, "Move Outta Babylon", new versions and now nobody can hear them in the dance.

'But I've got more than that – remember, I met Lee Perry that morning. I reach out and I slam on a tune by the trombone player Vin Gordon called "Vix", which starts off with a kind of easy jazz thing *dum da da da dum . . . da da daa . . .* then it drops, *boom*, into a rub-a-dub style, and when I spin this track the crowd go wild, "*Yaaaaaaah!*" I've won the dance now. Lord Koos can't touch this tune and he knows it and Nick's not in it because Nick's is only the house sound. So I'm playing against two sound systems that night and I'm battering them both. 'Cause even without the Bunny Lee dubs I have music *like dirt*.

'Then at the same time as that big roar goes up from the crowd, the police are coming out of the toilets with a prisoner. And the guy's friends pick that exact moment to free him from the police. Which they do; and after the police lose their prisoner they run. They're shitting themselves, and in their panic they run the wrong way and are trapped in the toilets and there's people hammering on the door to beat the shit out of them – one policeman actually got stabbed down there.

'But I don't know too much about any of this because in the commotion my sound gets broken, a wire got pulled out and something got shorted out. I'm trying to fix my sound system, but Lord Koos and Nick's are still playing because all the commotion's been in my corner of the hall and when I've got dislodged the other two are taking their opportunity. Lord Koos puts on "*I and I a-go beat down Babylon . . .*".

'Eventually, more police arrive and it all seems to be over, with them saying "Right, can you all leave in twos and threes, please; we've got the people who we wanted." *Lies.* They've got a load of other police in from surrounding areas, all wearing coats so you couldn't see their numbers, and there was two on each step all the way down from this top-floor club, and they beat the shit out of the clientele as they were going down. They arrested forty-two people, and all those who didn't have visible bruises they let them go.'

Under the headline 'The Battle of Burtons' and a photo of a thoroughly trashed section of the club, this incident made the front page of a London newspaper. Although Dennis escaped police attention as he stayed to pack up Sufferer HiFi, his involvement was just beginning.

'The next day, all I'm hearing is how the police are looking for me. It's like I'm Most Wanted, to the degree it's like some great big elaborate joke. But I haven't got a clue what it's about so, muggins, I go to the police station and ask, "I hear you're looking for me. Is that true? What have I done?" They take me in the back and tell me they've got information that I was on the microphone last night stirring up this thing, and that I was saying beat the police, get them, kill them and all that.

'I denied it. Told them my amplifier was busted. So they asked me if I'd said *anything* and I told them I'd said "*Babylon 'bout ya, any man who have weed, dash it 'way now.*" Which I did say, when the police first came into the club. They jumped on that, like "Aha! So you did say something on the microphone." But I told them that any sound man would have said that, told man to guard dem ganja because police in the area. The club owner would tell you the police was in the building so you'd make an announcement for the man who smoke weed to pull dem spliff right now. Then two police officers came and said I said "Get the boys in blue." Like a hardcore cockney kind of accent . . . as if I would be speaking like that in the dance. Which black man you know going to refer to the police as the boys in blue? *Never*.

'I was charged with causing an affray. Twelve other people were charged with crimes against policemen and, according to the prosecution, they were my *gang*, of which I was supposed to be the ringleader. I didn't know any of them. I'd never knowingly seen any of them before in my life . . . I didn't even know their names until the trial, when we became friendly, because nine months at the Old Bailey every day, ten 'til four, you get to know the defendant next to you at least. Then at the end of that trial nine people were acquitted. It was obviously a sham, because although some people did beat the police and the police did beat some people nobody knew with any certainty who had actually done what. It was bedlam in there that night. But somebody had to pay and they've attributed it to me.

'When my case was heard, I was so determined to defend myself that I was completely wrong in my handling of giving evidence. In court I was so at pains to make sure they knew I could speak English, that I wasn't some sort of ruffian, that I spoke with a perfect English accent. It was only natural, because that's the way black kids of my generation, whose parents came over from the West Indies, were brought up in this country – when you're dealing with authority, i.e., the white man, it's been drummed into you to speak properly and show him you're not as ignorant as he might assume. At the very least, your parents knew it showed you'd been well brought up. So, unlike my co-defendants, I spoke in perfect English and they attributed those remarks to me because the jury was left thinking, "Well he does speak like that, he's so much more English than all the others." If I'd have spoken pure roots and acted ragga then the jury never would have believed that I'd made those remarks, but, stupidly, I didn't see this was what was happening.

'The trial was a farce at some points. When I was asked about what was said over the speakers about fighting the police, I said that for all I knew that could have been a toasting record. The judge said, "A *toasting record*? What's that?" I explained it was a record where people speak over music or a song. He looked at me with complete contempt and said, "Do you expect me to believe that people *talk* over records?" and completely dismissed the idea.

'There was a hung jury on the first trial, and he ordered a retrial. There were only three others on trial the second time so it only lasted three months, and at the end of it the jury went out and came back with a "Guilty, Dennis Bovell". "Is that the verdict of you all?" the judge asked. And it wasn't, it was ten to two, but they took a majority verdict and the judge sentenced me to three years in prison.

'I was in prison for six months before my case was heard on appeal. I'd appealed against conviction and sentence, because if you appeal against sentence that's like you think you're guilty but you got too long, but if you think you're innocent then you appeal against conviction, and you have the conviction quashed. Within two days the Appeal Court judges are saying it was a shambles, that I shouldn't even have been charged, let alone convicted . . . "Get him out *now*." My conviction was quashed and I was let out of jail, but they carefully worded it so it read that it was nobody's fault that I got sent to prison other than the jury misunderstanding the case – it claimed the judge had actually directed the jury to acquit me, but they hadn't followed his summing up. So I had no case for compensation.

'Up until then, I was sceptical about it when friends had said the police had fitted them up. Really and truly, I thought they must have done *something*. Then it happened to me.'

It happened to an enormous number of young black men from the 1960s onwards. It's prevalent still – the very morning this sentence was written an official report on London's Metropolitan Police (the investigation into the handling of the Stephen Lawrence case) accused the force of pernicious and institutionalized racism – but the maltreatment of black people at the hands of Britain's police reached its apex in the second half of the 1970s. Exempted then from Race Relations legislation, the police forces in the UK's major cities appeared to have taken it upon themselves to declare black youth as undesirables in, usually, the country of their birth, and adopted a policy of attrition. Cases such as Dennis's were by no means isolated, usually arising out of the routine harassment and brutality that was meted out on the inner-city streets – a couple of black kids would be stopped for no reason; any form of objection would count as 'resisting arrest'; *actually* resisting arrest would constitute 'assault on a police officer'; which in itself was enough to earn the 'prisoner' a bit of a kicking under the guise of 'self-defence'. And guilty verdicts in subsequent trials were the norm, as this was long before a string of very high-profile police-corruption cases meant that the judiciary no longer automatically believed the police in a his-word-against-ours scenario.

Arbitrary intimidation ranged from the verbal to the physical to the decidedly irritating stop-and-searches, and such overbearing interaction between the police and the youth was usually accounted for under what were called the Sus Laws. 'Sus' was a feature of the 1824 Vagrancy Act, a piece of Georgian legislation passed in the wake of the Napoleonic Wars, designed to keep beggars and vagrants off the streets of London and rediscovered some 150 years later as a licence to vex. It involved those considered to be 'suspected persons', and it allowed the officer who suspected you – of just about anything he fancied – to stop you, pick you up, take you down the station or even arrest you on no grounds other than his or her utterly intangible suspicions. And even if nothing came of it, which most of the time it didn't, arrest on Sus was officially condoned in the name of crime prevention.

If further proof were needed of the rancorousness of the modern-day application of Sus, consider that it was never a national statute but could only be applied in certain regions, yet at the same time as it was being revived in London, areas where it wasn't valid were finding their own archaic vagrancy laws to implement in much the same way. Then there were the Special Patrol Groups, non-local, deliberately aggressive police units whose sole purpose seemed to be to cruise inner-city streets implementing the Sus Laws – they seemed to fancy themselves as American SWAT squads but, thankfully, nobody gave them guns. As a result of the Sus campaign, it's extremely rare to meet a black man who was a teenager in Britain during the 1970s who has never had a brush with the law – at one point in the 1970s a survey showed that black guys in London were five times more likely to get stopped by the police, yet three times *less* likely to be charged with anything. SPG figures for one London borough in 1975 showed a 35:1 stop:arrest ratio. This is easily understood when the term 'overtly suspicious behaviour' had been stretched to include being out with your girlfriend, carrying a bag, waiting at a bus stop or, to quote Steel Pulse, *'walking along just kicking stones'*. Comedians and pundits have wrung much mileage out of the idea that any black man driving a nice car could expect to be stopped by the police, but for those who were actually getting stopped the reality was that the car didn't need to be nice and you didn't even have to be driving it.

Underneath the obvious issues of rank unfairness or just wanting to get on with your law-abiding life without fear of persecution or prosecution, what many police victims found so shocking about this state of affairs was its absolute pointlessness other than as an act of supreme malice. It was like a sport, but the best one side could hope for was that the match would get called off, as there was no way they were ever going to win. Indeed, the absolute absence of logic had much to do with the situation being allowed to exist for so long unchallenged by wider society: if you didn't live through it, it was difficult to believe that the if-you-want-to-know-the-time-ask-a-policeman police more or less waged war on a large section of the citizens of the country they had pledged to serve. But it happened. In areas like Handsworth, Brixton, Chapel Town, Toxteth and Moss Side the police, cruising the streets in cars and vans, were perceived as an army of occupation, to be avoided at all costs.

Of course, sound-system dances, blues parties, discos and Caribbean-type festivals were easy and frequent targets – the very notion of reggae had become police shorthand for 'dangerous individuals smoking illegal substances' and the busting-up of gatherings was usually done on the pretext of a drugs raid. When, in this chapter's second paragraph, the words 'regular end of the week in north-west London' were used, it wasn't in any way frivolously. The Metro Youth Club in Ladbroke Grove was frequently raided; the black-owned, much-raided Mangrove restaurant in the same area became something of a *cause célèbre* when a demonstration against local policing methods was organized there and the resulting arrests on highly dubious, but very serious, violent disorder charges led to the high-profile Mangrove Nine trial at the Old Bailey; other reggae clubs and regular blues dances in the area accepted having their doors kicked in almost as an overhead. And this went on all over the country.

Understandably, it informed the embryonic British reggae bands, giving the unique voice the music had found something singularly relevant to discuss. Something other than Rastafari, repatriation, ganja, girls and reggae itself.

Surprisingly, it took a few years for other roots acts to follow Matumbi's lead, but by the time they did their dread credentials were formidable and UK reggae assumed its own rebel voice. London's Black Slate were the first major contenders in 1974. Steel Pulse from Birmingham were formed around the same time, and the next year won a local talent show; three members of Matumbi were on the judging panel and the first prize was a studio session produced by Dennis Bovell. Aswad rumbled out of Ladbroke Grove in the same year, and Misty in Roots, another London act, followed soon after. Delroy Washington, who had actually cut a tune called 'Jah Man a Come' very early in the decade, made something of a roots comeback in 1977 backed by the Aswad rhythm section. At about that time Reggae Regular began having local hits, as did the relatively short-lived Brimstone, the harmony trio Black Stones and Wolverhampton's own Capital Letters.

By the middle of the decade, dreadlocks, red, green and gold, combat fatigues and impressive-looking staffs were common-place on Britain's inner-city streets, making tangible the watershed between the pre- and post-Matumbi bands. As discussed earlier with Jimmy Cliff, *The Harder They Come* did a great deal to establish roots culture in the UK, but it was never a dreadlocks harbinger because Jamaica had yet to locks up *en masse*. It's an easily arrived at misconception, but rent *THTC* on video today and you'll be surprised at how few actual locksmen get any screen time. While UK sound systems carried essentially the same music, therefore much the same message, as their JA equivalents, it was released records and their sleeves that played the biggest part in shaping attitudes, beliefs and barbering – British youth had to learn how to locks up. Quite a few records were starting to talk about natty dread, but it was the sleeves of such albums as Big Youth's *Screaming Target* – probably the first big-selling album to have dreadlocks on the cover – and Keith Hudson's *Pick A Dub* that gave the youth something to aim at. The Abyssinians, Prince Jazzbo, Niney, Junior Byles, Johnnie Clarke and Max Romeo did much to advance dread philosophies, the word 'ital' was introduced by Pablo's *Ital Dub* LP to sit alongside such terms as 'skanking', 'welding', 'Babylon' and 'ites' in the UK dread vocabulary, and Burning Spear taught Marcus Garvey For Beginners.

As we've already seen, the Wailers and their Lee Perry recordings were vital back then, assuming an extraordinarily long shelf life on the sound systems and in the shops, particularly 'Duppy Conqueror', 'Small Axe', 'Soul Rebel', 'Trench Town Rock' and '400 Years', as they provided the ideal soundtrack for rebel posing. 'Burnin' made sense in the UK thanks to its unadulterated rhythms, as did 'I Shot The Sheriff' and retreads of several of the Lee Perry-period numbers, while the *Natty Dread* album featured 'Three O'Clock Road Block', 'Talking Blues' and 'No Woman No Cry' which were the last time Marley's records were taken seriously in the nation's dancehalls. Although the album did much to break the idea of dreadlocks to the mainstream, they'd been part and parcel of reggae life for a few years: therefore its ghetto impact was minimal.

To the new young bands roots reggae was a particularly relevant expression of blackness. Although US soul was an equally eloquent voice of protest, it wasn't from the Caribbean. Whereas the older generation of West Indian immigrants used American Civil Rights and Black Power as a revolutionary template – the 1968 Olympics clenched-fist protest had considerable global impact – their children seemed determined to break this connection. To them, America of the 1970s was represented by movies, music and TV detectives, and although those racial reference points included the keenly received John Shaft, James Brown, Marvin Gaye, *Black Moses*, *Superfly*, Huggy Bear, Curtis Mayfield, Richard Pryor and *Roots*, they were never celebrated with the same seriousness as, say, *This Is Augustus Pablo* or Burning Spear's *Social Living*. And compared to a Jah Shaka sound-system dance – as it frequently was – there was never going to be anything righteous about a discotheque. The British kids looked to make the most of their island heritage, as to assume an English identity was becoming increasingly at odds with a welcome mat that was wearing woefully thin, and with Rastafari and roots reggae presenting a 'home-grown' rebel stance they just didn't need the USA. And the bonus was that to absorb the whole dread package was as much about going forward as it was about somewhere to take refuge.

Oddly, Rastafari's notions of displacement actually made greater sense in the UK than they did in Jamaica, as the teenagers in the British bands, like their contemporaries in their audiences, either had first-hand knowledge of moving from the West Indies to a relentlessly adverse landscape or they knew somebody who did. It was easy to brood on the idea that if you were born in England or arrived as a child it wasn't by choice and the Caribbean was where you ought to be. Thus it wasn't a quantum leap to mentally translate the Africa/Jamaica theme to a West Indies/Great Britain enforced exodus.

The more conventional Western pop-music structures that British bands were adhering to helped enormously here, as they lent themselves to songwriting storytelling. Music and lyrics being written together was a great advantage in this area, too, as it made it far easier to start a song with the idea of recounting a tale – as contemporary pop tunes usually did – and fit the music to that rather than arrive with a set of lyrics looking to be assigned a rhythm. As a result, UK roots had a far greater sense of narrative, with lyrics drawing a wealth of imagery from the high-rise estates and grey streets of Birmingham, Bristol or London. The more vivid songwriters poetically expressed the frustrations of a generation being treated as second-class citizens in the land of their birth; they recognized their duty to their peers and refused to allow the spirit to be crushed; and, of course, they frequently indulged in the romanticism and joy that lies at the heart of so much good pop music from a dreadlocks point of view. Steel Pulse particularly wove elaborate stories shot through with weighty philosophizing – 'Handsworth Revolution', 'Tribute to the Martyrs' or 'Soldiers', for instance. Aswad told a good tale, too, and their party/love lyrics – 'Smokey Blues' or 'Bubbling' – were every bit as narrative as their militancy. Likewise Black Slate.

Matumbi frequently found room for satire. Dennis recalls the reasoning behind their hit 'Write Dem':

'You have an awful lot of sitting around to do when you're in a band, and you'd just get to chatting. We'd read somewhere that Queen Victoria had left a load of money to be given to the slaves in British colonies when they were freed, and we got into a conversation that was: "You got yours yet?" . . . "Nope." . . . "Me neither, let's write these bastards a letter and tell them we know all about this money Queen Victoria left for black people, so where is it? We want our share . . . With interest." We were going to send this to the Home Office, asking them to get in touch with Social Services to speed up this money, because it's not come through.

'That was the thing, to *write dem*, because all around the place at that time there were all these tunes called "Fight Dem" and suchlike, so we thought we'd write dem . . . *Long time now, since I man come outta slavery / and until this day they never give me my money / I man a go write dem a letter / Tell 'em seh dey haffi do better / I man a go write dem a letter . . .*'

This is probably the only recorded instance of roots reggae meeting Monty Python. Specifically, though, all UK acts dealt with the police and their relationship with Britain's black community. While unemployment, racial injustice, bad housing, sub-standard schools and prejudice against Rastafari all figured lyrically in a general sense, the fiercest condemnation about life in England was reserved for the police. Every group seemed to agree on this, as if *Babylon*, as the police were known, was what pushed them too far. When Steel Pulse's 'Blues Dance Raid' vividly describes the sheer brutality, callousness and vandalism of a sound-system's destruction it is fact rather than fiction. Aswad's 'Three Babylon' deftly caught the mood with the opening lines: *Three babylon try to make I and I run / They come to have fun with their long truncheons* . . . , going on to tell how righteousness prevails: . . . *The first one come, he tumble down* . . . *Ah weh the third one deh? See him a-run lef' his truncheon* . . . Sound systems did what they could, too: at the 1976 Notting Hill Carnival – the year London's huge annual West Indian street festival exploded into violence – by wandering from set to set it was possible hear Junior Murvin's 'Police and Thieves' virtually non-stop, with 'Beat Down Babylon', 'Blood and Fire', 'War inna Babylon' and 'Legalize It' not far behind. A matter of days later, London sound systems began to spin specials with a *Police and youths in the Grove* . . . lyric on top of the 'Police and Thieves' rhythm.

That the UK reggae industry reacted so categorically to police harassment is an explicit parallel to youthful black life in the UK in general. It was, indeed, *sipple out deh* and only a matter of time before police behaviour tipped people over the edge: when the 1976 Carnival turned from a celebration of Caribbean life, music and culture into a pitched battle between black kids and the police it had been building up for years. Incidentally, this was never the race riot much of the press chose simplistically to describe it as – triggered by over-zealous policing of the event, it was a shamefully treated section of British society hitting back at those they perceived as the oppressors. Likewise the waves of inner-city rioting that swept across the country during the first half of the 1980s – almost every instance was kicked off by an insensitive police action. Although social conditions, black unemployment and youthful frustration were frequently cited as causes of the trouble, the rioting was all about the police. Other black areas in Britain were equally deprived, yet without a local police force acting as a particularly provocative army of occupation disturbances were without focus and blew themselves out relatively quickly – it seems that the prospect of looting shops wasn't enough to spark too much off, which rather worked against the column inches devoted to the notion of the riots being a front for large-scale thieving.

British roots developed rapidly into a musical art-form that, when it wasn't shy about its own sense of identity and purpose, could more than merely stand beside its Jamaican counterpart. Along with the far more conventional songwriting and lyrical approaches, British groups tended towards albums rather than collections of singles – Aswad's *Hulet* and *New Chapter*; Steel Pulse's *Handsworth Revolution*, *Caught You* and *Tribute to the Martyrs*; Matumbi's *Seven Seals* and (as 4th Street Orchestra) *Ah Who Seh? Go Deh*, *Yuh Learn* and *Ah Fe Wi Dis*; Black Slate's eponymous début album; and Tradition's *Moving On* were among the market leaders. These bands embraced the long-playing format, as it allowed them to flex their muscles in a way that meant a satisfying development of their themes, while letting them display the light and shade that was the whole range of their stylistic achievements. Matumbi, Steel Pulse and Aswad particularly have produced some of the most inventive, complex and enjoyable reggae to be made anywhere – just check the intro to Steel Pulse's 'Ku Klux Klan' on the *Handsworth Revolution* LP. This artistic success was a direct result of the UK grassroots music business working so differently from how things were in Jamaica, with acts taking far more responsibility for their own careers instead of leaving it to an almost feudal producer-controlled system. Misty in Roots even released an excellent live album, an event which, in the reggae world, is practically unheard of. And while a few of these albums did *really* big business, the rest sold well enough.

In fact, roots stage shows were always a particularly enjoyable aspect of UK reggae as the live performance conventions were much stronger in Britain than in Jamaica – at that time touring JA acts often seemed to believe that simply turning up and singing their songs was enough. Far more attention was paid to stage presentation in Britain. Steel Pulse shows often bordered on the theatrical as they acted out numbers like 'Blues Dance

Raid' and 'Ku Klux Klan' with great skill and vitality, complete with roadies and group members in appropriate costume. Aswad's live sets presented the group's roots reggae with all the slickness and performance values of a US soul revue, but were always clever enough to ensure that this enhanced the sense of dread rather than detracted from it. Matumbi possessed a vivacity that was almost interactive, and were sufficiently confident to send up what was going on around them: they'd have a section in which – just to prove it could be done – they'd perform a medley of contemporary pop hits by reducing them to the same one or two chords; then there was the ever-entertaining 'white man reggae' spot when the band would subtly get reggae wrong by emphasizing the first and third beats instead of the second and fourth. Dennis still laughs aloud when he remembers it:

'When white bands started getting interested in playing reggae they could never find the timing. It was like, "Where's the one? Where's two? . . . One . . . two . . . oh . . ." It resulted in a lot of them playing on the first beat of the bar and counting off *one* and two and *three* and four, instead of one and *two* and three and *four*, completely the other way around. It came out with more of a ska feel to it than reggae, because they were playing the ska timing with reggae on top of it, not knowing they were marrying two different rhythm forms. So it always sounded a bit funny to us who knew; then when we twigged that's what they're doing we named it English One Drop. We even put a section in our show where we'd go and play white man reggae – *Now dis a white man reggae tune, seen?* – and get our emphasis the wrong way round.

'It was just to amuse the audience and have a bit of fun ourselves.'

Surprisingly, there weren't an enormous amount of British toasting records at that time, which seems remarkable in light of the fact that every sound system had its own deejay and there was never any shortage of volunteers begging to *hol' the mic* in the dance. Nobody is really sure why, but one explanation is that while singing styles could be easily transported from Jamaica to the UK, chatting could not, since (a) it is a far more exposed art form and anything not quite right will be thrown mercilessly into the spotlight and (b) it was purely Jamaican in invention and hard to pull off without self-consciousness. It's a bit like British rap, which never got past the Derek B syndrome – Englishmen sounding mildly ridiculous as they strove to pretend they'd never set foot outside the South Bronx. Like the music itself, toasting needed a complete refit to establish a set of British credentials and so dictate its own pace and direction, which didn't happen to any degree until well into the 1980s. Five years before that, though, Great Britain gave us dub poetry, most prominently an intriguing, engaging hybrid of Dennis Bovell's dub rhythms and the Jamaican dialect verse of Linton Kwesi Johnson, who, as a committed black political activist, used lyrics like a sword.

Linton's poetry was an intrinsically Jamaican medium, dating back to long before roots deejays took it upon themselves to sound genuinely Jamaican. Dialect poetry and plays had been performed by black Jamaicans since the days of slavery as a way to establish some form of cultural identity and send up the planters and their flunkeys back in the slave quarters. Dramatist, actress, orator and dialect poet Louise 'Miss Lou' Bennett is probably roots poetry's most famous exponent, moving seamlessly from folk tales to sly (and not so sly) sideswipes at authority. Her monologues and performances were the highlight of the Jamaican pantomime season at Kingston's Ward theatre from the 1940s onwards. In the 1960s, with numerous books already published, she became a radio star and has been justifiably credited with introducing to Jamaicans the idea of performance in Jamaican English as opposed to the Queen's variety or cod-American. Clapping, stamping her foot or simply swaying to each piece's own rhythm, Miss Lou reads her poems in the unadulterated syntax and slang of the Jamaican working people, and they assume a vitality and connotation that go way deeper than what's written on the page. African anthem meets sugar plantation work song meets revivalist meeting meets dubwise. Which is the point at which Linton took it up and added a riddim and a large helping of black British political awareness.

After having two books of poems published and his readings becoming ever bigger affairs, Linton met Dennis Bovell in his capacity as a journalist – Linton had gone to interview Dennis – and this led to the pair putting a selection of Linton's poems to music for the *Dread Beat and Blood* LP credited to Poet and the Roots. This was like toasting, but approached from completely the opposite direction inasmuch as the music was written to fit the words – some might say this was a very English-pop-song way of going about things. In this way, stories could be told and points made with far more clarity and precision than if the main concern was riding the rhythm. Linton drew inspiration from past and present memberships of such London organizations as the Black Panther Youth League, the Black Parents Movement, the Black Students Movement and the Race Today Collective. He had a journalist's eye for what made a story interesting and belied his slightly prof-essorial, mild-mannered appearance with a wry and thoroughly devilish sense of humour. He never forgot what he was sup-posed to be doing and brought the full power of lyricism to bear on subjects such as bourgeois blacks, third-rate schools, street life, general hard time in England and, of course, the police. That these poems were delivered in an easily understood text-book patois added enormous weight, and titles such as 'Inglan is a Bitch', 'Di Great Insohreckshan', 'All Wi Is Doin Is Defendin', 'It Noh Funny' and 'Reggae Fi Dada' left nobody in any doubt about what was going on.

His later works – *Forces of Victory*, *LKJ in Dub*, *Making History* and the album that would make a wonderful title for a book, *Bass Culture* – remain among the best received and best-selling reggae albums of all time, proving popular all round the world. Linton is still recording and performing, backed by Dennis Bovell. He runs his own record label and has been the inspiration to a whole slew of English and Jamaican dub poets: Mutabaruka, Benjamin Zephaniah, Michael Franti, Michael Smith, Oku Onuora, Sister Farika and Jean Binta Breeze all owe him a debt for his spectacular union of words and music. Jean Binta Breeze, for example, studied at the same Kingston drama school as Michael Smith and Oku Onuora, then ended up in London recording with Dennis Bovell's Dub Band, putting her books out with Linton's publishers, the Race Today Collective, and releasing records on his LKJ Records label. All of which is a mark of how much ground English reggae had made up by the end of the 1970s, and placing dub poetry as one of the rare examples of a reggae art form originating off island but going home, as it were, to have a genuine effect.

Another strictly English invention was the lovers' rock of the 1970s, but whereas dub poetry made the crossing back to the Caribbean, this one stayed in the UK. And unlike dub poetry, which was embraced by the mainstream as being a meaningful, relevant and genuinely roots expression of what it is to be black in Britain in the 1970s, lovers' rock was reviled as sloppy, soppy, generally worthless and somehow not quite black enough to make the grade. Not that this made any difference whatsoever to the thousands of black teenagers – girls *and* boys – who loved it, bought it, supported the many '*pure lovers*'' sound systems and made superstars out of schoolgirls, because for them lovers' rock was the first indigenous black British pop style. Although the way it came about was far more 'authentically' Jamaican than the UK roots bands.

By the mid-1970s, the dreadlocks way so dominated reggae coming into the UK that its appeal was starting to look a little narrow. While it was undoubtedly an uplifting experience to be part of a roots sound-system dance, with the music, the deejays, the crowd and the herb creating the notion of a Stoke Newington (or wherever) Nyabingi, a generation who grew up with *Top of the Pops* and youth club discos wanted Saturday night at the dancehall to present a more traditional alternative – y'know, to grab a gal, or even be grabbed by one. Which is where roots reggae could sometimes let you down. The sound-system sessions were a long way from the English discos, soul clubs or upmarket establishments like Count Suckle's Q

Club; thus, to large numbers of British-raised black kids, that scene simply wasn't upwardly mobile enough. It was, after all, never set up for romancing and strutting about in your finery, and it could get tricky trying to equate the pleasures of the flesh with the path of true righteousness.

It wasn't as if these kids wanted not to be black or even to disclaim their Caribbean roots. Far from it. But while some of the roots ideologies made perfect sense to city-dwelling British youth, others didn't. Some of the tenets weren't particularly practical or just didn't sit comfortably alongside contemporary English society – most notably, Rasta attitudes towards women and consumerism – but largely it was because the music wasn't right. Never mind when Saturday comes, the sounds of sufferation or chanting down Babylon were never going to get a man through the week if he lived his life as an aspirational junior local government clerk, saving for a mortgage and a hotted-up Ford Escort. Although pre-disco soul music like late-model Motown, Philly, funk-lite and so on had the right essentially superficial boy-meets-girl attitude, it wasn't reggae, therefore it was sort of second-hand (this isn't to say artists like James Brown, Curtis, Marvin, Al Green or the Blackbyrds weren't important if you grew up black in 1970s Britain, they just never quite *meant* as much). And if you wanted to do it inna JA style you'd pretty quickly end up with Pat Kelly, Ken Boothe, Eric Donaldson or the Paragons, all top-shelf stuff but a bit like your mum and dad would be playing. There was a huge demand for something credible, Caribbean and easygoing. Enter lovers' rock. Unsurprisingly, given that this want was felt most acutely at the dance, it was a sound man who initiated it. Perhaps it's even less remarkable that the man he turned to to put it all together for him was none other than Dennis Bovell.

Lloydie Coxsone (real name Blackwood but self-styled in recognition of the Kingston giant) was one of London's top reggae deejays, whose Jamaican music connections were the stuff of legend, but he was most unusual in that for a long time he had music – *a whole heap of music* – and no sound system. As a result, he'd played a lot of purpose-built clubs, an environment where the need for a change of pace stood out keenly. Nowhere more so than his residency at Dalston's Four Aces, where he observed it from the other side as he ran the club's weekly talent night – contestants would sing over his instrumental-only dub plates – where the majority of singers were (a) very young, (b) female and (c) not dread at all. Coxsone had his own record label, too; hence as well as being aware of the demand he had the talent and the outlet. In 1975, after one young lady persistently trounced all comers and audibly moved the audience, Coxsone booked a London studio, took her in there and, for his Safari label, recorded what's universally acknowledged as the first lovers' rock record: 'Caught You in a Lie' by Louisa Mark.

This truly was a traditional back-a-yard way of doing things. Like his sound-system namesake, he knew what the audience required and it didn't take him long to put two and two together and come up with the sound of cash tills ringing to a new reggae beat. Coxsone's actual involvement at the session was as peripheral as his JA counterpart's, with somebody else running things on the shop floor, in this case Dennis Bovell. As the studio's resident engineer and the session's band leader – Matumbi were engaged to provide the backing – Dennis ended up running the recording to such a degree that in any other music genre he'd be recognized as the producer. The tune was an enormous hit, and became something of a template for the glut of lovers' rock records that followed: enormous among its target audience but virtually invisible elsewhere; a lilting, sweetly rocking beat featuring a big bass-line underneath an airy arrangement; lyrics that could've been C&W in their wallowing in infidelity and heartbreak; vocalists so close to their crowd they were probably part of it the week before their tune came out and, therefore, were probably not old enough to get into the clubs they'd subsequently perform in – Louisa Mark was fifteen years old and still at school when 'Caught You in a Lie' broke.

The tune's success marked the instigation of a genuinely black British musical style that owed as much to its host country's pop music (itself derivative of the R&B and Motown that came over from America a decade or so previously) as it did to the West Indies. As such this was enormously important in establishing a cultural identity that could take in both aspects of how these kids were living. Then, as well as any purely geographical considerations, the intrinsic shininess of lovers' rock sat well with the notions of self-improvement or upward mobility that was part of so many second-generation immigrants' psyches. And while lovers' rock couldn't be accused of flogging off the family silver, at the same time it was far enough removed from what went before not to owe it any debt. In all of this, lovers' rock and its pop purpose probably expressed far more organically what it meant to be black and British than any amount of roots, which makes it doubly ridiculous that the mainstream media, who were by now skanking like their lives depended on it, chose to rubbish it as not being authentic (i.e., black) enough.

Not that, at the time, anyone involved in playing, producing, selling, buying or grooving to it even noticed, let alone cared. Lovers' rock fell like rain across the UK. Louisa Mark followed up with 'Six Sixth Street', 'Keep It Like It Is' and 'All My Loving'; before that, Marie Pierre rocked houses with 'Walk Away', 'Can't Go Through' and 'Nothing Gained'; Ginger Williams hit with 'Tenderness'; 15-16-17, a trio previously known as the Gorgon Sisters until it was felt more opportune to announce their ages rather than an affiliation to Rasta, cut the genre classics 'Black Skin Boy' and 'If You Love Me Smile'; Two in Love successfully duetted 'You Are Mine', as did Carolyn & Roland with 'You're Having My Baby'; and a year or so after 'Caught You in a Lie', Brown Sugar's début single 'I'm in Love with a Dreadlocks' was the first release on the London-based Lovers' Rock record label, meaning suddenly that the music had a name and, through that label's catalogue, a stylistic yardstick. Although this really was a female affair, the guys got a look in, too, with Victor 'Romero' Evans, the Investigators (featuring Lorenzo Hall and Michael Gordon), Blackstones and Trevor Hartley. As well as the Lovers' Rock

441 **Warrior Charge**

label, there was Morpheus, DIP, Eve, Santic, D-Roy, Third World and Hawkeye, all producing the style as it found favour across the whole spectrum of black dancehalls. As well as the 'lovers only' sound systems (who usually threw in a bit of The Sound Of Philadelphia or soft soul too), the cannier roots operations would, in the wee small hours, drop a lovers' selection to allow the dreads to *rub up the pleat outta their gal skirt*, then even the slickest black soul clubs and sound systems would have a rub-a-dub or roots rocking section two or three times a session.

The records listed above were just the more spectacularly successful tip of the iceberg, and Dennis Bovell was involved in more of them than he wasn't. In fact he was so close to the heart of lovers' rock that he's been credited with inventing it. And it didn't surprise him at all that lovers' rock was so successful; after all, it wasn't as if it came about by accident.

'After I'd done the Louisa Mark stuff and Marie Pierre and I'd done "Black Skin Boy" for 15-16-17 on Castro Brown's Morpheus label, I knew there was something in it. It was black pop music . . . you know, *popular* music. Then I started working with this Jamaican husband-and-wife team, Dennis and Yvonne Harris, who had been licensing tunes to release over here on their DIP and Eve labels – he was a landlord who sold some of his houses and a supermarket he owned in order to get into the reggae business. They'd had a massive hit with Susan Cadogan's "Hurt So Good", which was produced in Jamaica by Scratch at the Black Ark, and they in turn had licensed it to the mainstream Magnet Records over here and it had got to number 4 in the mainstream pop charts. Stayed up there for about a month. So now Dennis wanted to do it for himself, and with the proceeds of that tune he built an eight-track studio in Brockley [south London] and set up the Lovers' Rock label. Incidentally, the guy who *physically* built the studio was Steve Wayley, who used to be the drummer in a group called Los Bravos. He wrote their huge record "Black Is Black (I Want My Baby Back)", but was so disillusioned with how many places the song had been a hit and how little money he'd made out of it he'd got out of that end of it, but he was also a brilliant technician and with a soldering iron and components he could make anything work. He built his first eight-track machine, and DIP had bought it off him and I was the engineer working it in the studio – a home-made eight-track, built by this guy who used to be the drummer in Los Bravos! It was also where I did all the RAMA stuff – the 4th Street Orchestra albums and the singles people thought were Jamaican.

'We knew what we had to do because as well as seeing what was going on in the dancehalls and at the talent shows, we did some market research. We went round record shops on Saturday mornings checking who was buying records and talking to the people in the shops about who their customers were, how many men bought records, how many women bought records, what their ages were, etcetera etcetera. And it came back that, in reggae at that time, *more singles were sold to women than they were to men*. It was roughly sixty/forty women to men buying records, which surprised us first of all but then it fell into place. Young guys would go to a blues dance and listen to records and get off on records, but that was how it worked for them – they wouldn't want to own it, and if you went round their houses not many of them would have a copy of that particular record that they liked so much. Whereas you go round to a girl's house and she's got the record because the lyrics mean something to her and she wants to take it home. But she'd want records by female vocalists because that was who she identified with, and because there was a lack of female vocalists to choose from she'd support the ones that were there – they didn't even need to be any good. Remember we were in that very hardcore reggae period which was *deep* roots . . . *Rastafari* coming in a big way, and you know the views that Rasta, or some of them, had on women – this is a *man*'s world . . . Rasta for *I*, not Rasta for *us*.

'That was the marketing strategy, to elaborate on that selling point and make records with girls singing for the girl buying audience. Or it would make a nice present for a bloke to buy this for a girl. It had to be girls singing, because it was going to be the soppiness of the lyrics coupled with the *e-e-easiness* of the melodies that made it work, and blokes just didn't sing this kind of love song easily. Most male singers considered them a bit wet. Especially in reggae with all the dread and burn down Babylon going on. But in many ways that made it easier for me as a producer, because as reggae started doing better and better male lead singers were becoming increasingly arrogant and big-headed, and you'd get guys who had perhaps had two singles out now had their own opinions and had to be coaxed into seeing your point of view. It was all "I'm a man as well, I've got ideas of my own", regardless of how much they actually knew; then there's got to be a huge debate while somebody's paying for the studio time, which would always end up with me saying, "Look, I'm the bloody producer. Now do that." And the guys were treating the women in the studio like, "Don't overshoot the mark, you're not the star, you lot are only the backing vocalists." So when the girls – for instance Louisa Mark or Marie Pierre or Janet Kaye or even the Slits – who had not been previously given a go, got their chance to come to the centre stage, they were so eager to get let in on the scene they responded accordingly and they'd do as they were told. When they were told "You've got to sing this way, look these are the notes," they would do it to try and please the producer, which is the whole idea of having a producer there in the first place. Every female lovers' rock singer I worked with did it very well. Professionally.

'So we were pretty sure of ourselves, and when we got this studio up and running we decided, "Right, let's just turn stuff out," because to get a catalogue with any clout and have distributors or shops take you seriously, you have to put out six or seven records a week. Not one a month or anything like that; that way nobody'll take any notice. Every Sunday we'd have talent auditions, just like they did it in Jamaica, when people would come down, show us what they could do and we'd decide there and then if we wanted to sign them or not and what it was we wanted to do with them. We knew we'd need a label, something exclusive to this stuff and with an identity people would recognize right away, and we batted ideas around until Dennis Harris came up with Lovers' Rock. Augustus Pablo is actually to be thanked for those two words put together, because he had a song called "Lovers Rock", but when we wanted a title to fit this record label that we were going to be putting all this girlie music on, Lovers' Rock said it all.

'Immediately Dennis came up with a heart with an arrow through it – a pink heart – as a logo. And then John Kpiaye, our guitarist had written this song, [*sings*] *I'm in love with a dreadlocks and I never felt this way before* . . . Brilliant. That's it. Had to be the first record on the Lovers' Rock label, "In Love with a Dreadlocks". But we had nobody to sing it, and this is where it got a bit like the early days of Motown. We had these three girls who had come in separately to the first audition – one of whom was Caron Wheeler, who went on to sing with Soul II Soul – and Dennis said, "Right. You, you and you. You should all be together in a group and we'll call it Brown Sugar." "In Love with a Dreadlocks" by Brown Sugar – it had all the ingredients of soppy lovers, and women being as sentimental as they are . . . and then guys, who obviously wanted to stay in with women, who would normally slag off that kind of soppy rendition, went for it too.

'That's why it didn't surprise me that the lovers' rock thing took off like it did, because we'd actually given the mantle to the females to hold, to shine the light about reggae, and they supported it like we figured they would. For the first time young girls were starring, and wherever you find young girls you're bound to find young boys. But it's not strictly true the other way round. Never mind that so much of what they were singing about was slagging off men and talking about what bastards they were. Men like to hear that kind of thing – "You're a bad boy" . . . "OK then, spank me. I'll do better next time!"'

From 1975 onwards, lovers' rock, both the style and the label, was phenomenally successful. And although for some reason the records didn't cross over to Jamaica – Gussie Clarke licensed 'Caught You in a Lie' for JA release, but it didn't exactly set Kingston on fire – there was quite a flow of contemporary reggae balladeers coming to England to record where the lovers' posse guaranteed them an audience and the industry taught them a few moves. Dennis Brown moved to London, where, with Castro Brown, he set up the record labels Morpheus and then DEB, producing 15-16-17. Gregory Isaacs spent so much time in the UK he might as well have moved there, and recorded for the Browns' labels – it was in their south London offices that he was first dubbed the Cool Ruler. Leroy Smart did an album with Matumbi in the Brockley studio on the spur of the moment and in one night – 'He pulled out this big wad of cash, we looked at it and said "Yes please!"' Producer Leonard Chin came to Britain to produce lovers' rock for his Santic label. And, in pre-Sly & Robbie days, it wasn't unusual to find Sly Dunbar and Lloyd Parkes as the rhythm section on London sessions.

It's easy to see why some dispute exists as to whether the style is in fact English or not, especially in the light of such high-profile Jamaican lovers' singers as Gregory, Dennis Brown, Junior Delgado and Freddie McGregor. English it is, though. Beyond those big names Jamaicans never took to it at all; besides, it's grossly unfair to single out the above mentioned given the sheer volume of sales by the British kids. Records were selling tens of thousands, occasionally crossing into six figures as the branding became so strong that lovers' rock became the most consistently popular style of reggae ever in the UK. The formula was so tightly adhered to – although songs were intrinsically different, they all existed within the same stock parameters – that buyers would ask what new lovers' shops had, and if it was the heart with the arrow label they usually wouldn't even ask to hear it. Had singles like 'Caught You in a Lie' or 'Let Me Be Your Angel' or 'I'm Sorry' sold exclusively in chart return shops there would have been a huge amount of reggae in the Top 40. Even as it was, a hit as big as 'Silly Games', by the end of the decade, was nothing short of inevitable.

While lovers' rock was happening virtually out of sight, roots reggae was being welcomed by the mainstream world with open arms. Things started moving that way in 1974, when guitar god Eric Clapton's cover of Bob Marley's 'I Shot the Sheriff' went Top 10 in the UK and to number 1 in America. It seemed Island Records' marketing spend was finally paying dividends. During the next twelve months, Bob's face smiled from a series of rock-magazine covers on both sides of the Atlantic, just as it did from the T-shirts worn on stage by Keith Richards throughout the Rolling Stones' 1975 US dates. Mick Jagger and Richards, both hardcore long-term reggae fans, had wanted Bob to open for them on those shows, and Bob's American tour of that year was the place to be seen for rock luminaries such as George Harrison, Joni Mitchell and the Grateful Dead. All of which conspired to send white people flocking to his concerts at London's prestigious Lyceum theatre in the summer of 1975 in such droves they made up well over half the audience. The album *Live!*, recorded at those shows, was the first of his albums to crack the British Top 40.

It wasn't just Bob Marley they liked, either. Big Youth's *Natty Cultural Dread* album, Burning Spear's *Man in the Hills*, Culture's *Two Sevens Clash* and Peter Tosh's *Legalize It* shifted enormous quantities to white kids getting off on the beat, the sentiments or both, while Dillinger's *CB 200* album was practically compulsory for anybody at university in Great Britain in the second half of the 1970s. Twenty years later, nobody seems to be able to remember quite why. But none of this was to boost reggae's mainstream acceptability nearly as much as when punk, the nihilistic, petulant, spectacularly non-conformist British youth cult of the second half of the 1970s, adopted the music as a ready-made soundtrack to its rebellion. A defining moment of this somewhat uneasy partnership was when, in summer 1977, Sex Pistols singer Johnny Rotten went on Capital Radio, London's leading station, to discuss his personal top ten tunes. In at number 3, behind two tracks by English miserablist rockers Van Der Graaf Generator, was Doctor Alimantado's 'Reason for Living (Born for a Purpose)' single. Up until then, even most reggae fans were unaware of this distinctly left-field toaster, but following this broadcast his name was spray-painted on walls all over west London and the otherwise unremarkable single sold 50,000 copies. Punks just had to have it. And while they went on to buy a lot more reggae besides, their relationship with the music went back much further than this particular instance.

Punk first cropped up in west London in the first half of the 1970s. The originals were, like the skinheads ten or so years earlier, white kids who had grown up around black families on London's less-salubrious council estates, with reggae as a natural aspect of their lives. These were working-class youngsters who felt at the bottom of the heap – unemployment in the UK was just becoming a fact of life – but by and large weren't about to take it out on the one sector of society they might've looked down on – black immigrants and their children. Dressing down had become a sort of fashion statement, though this was a long time before the artily fashioned bin liners, the ornamental safety pins and the elaborate hairdos of King's Road designer punk. This was more likely to involve dad's trousers, GPO-issue donkey jackets and hair apparently cut by the council. While this sartorial approach was a reaction to the glam rock and heavy metal excesses of the decade so far, the adoption of reggae music came about by a rather more remarkable set of circumstances.

Don Letts, now a respected film and video director (*Dancehall Queen* is one of his, as are Chris Blackwell's *Reggae Archives*) and former vocalist of Big Audio Dynamite, was there at the first flowering of punk and reggae. Running his dad's sound system, in 1975 or so he and his young spars controlled the deejaying, the bar and the door at the Roxy, in Covent Garden's Neal Street.

'The Roxy became the first specifically-opened punk venue in London – anywhere, in fact – not just an existing club that had punk nights. I can't remember how we got to work there, but it worked out well for everybody because punks came there with the idea that black guys always had the best weed and they could always buy a draw over the bar. But the funny thing was that hardly any of these kids knew how to build a spliff, so after we'd sold them a bag of weed they'd come back and we'd charge them another 50p to roll it for them.

'With the music, I played the sound in between the live bands that were on. That was the thing about punk; it was all about forming your own band no matter how good you were, it was about just having a go. Anti-pop music. There was always bands to play, but at that time there was only about ten punk records in existence, and they were all short, so once I'd played them I had to fill in the space with something else. I started playing my own reggae and dub tunes to amuse us as much as anything else, but the crowds loved it. Pretty soon they were telling me to forget the punk and play pure reggae. *They were bringing me reggae records to play*. And although some of the early ones must've been records they already owned, soon they were going out and buying them.'

Roots reggae's revolutionary sentiments and relentless defiance of all things Babylonian were exactly what punk's scattergun-style, rebel-without-a-clue dissension needed as a focus. The rioting at 1976's Notting Hill Carnival left a deep impression, as did Jamaican evergreens like 'Two Sevens Clash', 'War inna Babylon' and 'Police and Thieves' – the latter so much so that the Clash released their own version of it *and* went as far as going to Jamaica to record an album with Lee Perry. (Not a happy experience, but we'll get to that later.) In fact, the whole package of dread, dub and the herb superb were altogether agreeable to punks who wanted to change the world, but maybe not today. On the other side of the coin, Rasta's gentler philosophies appealed enormously to a generation who had just missed out on hippiedom – a state of affairs ritually reviled by punks – and who wanted to get in touch with their caring, tender side without losing street cred.

There were commercial considerations, too. Honest Jon's, a record shop not far from the Roxy and on the fringes of Portobello Road – a favoured punk hangout – became something of a Mecca as it began selling punk and reggae singles side by side.

According to Rae Cheddie who looked after the riddim end

of things, 'I loved it. I'd never taken reggae into an environment like that before, and the punk kids were so into it. They were knowledgeable, too; they'd come in and know exactly what they wanted but then they'd still be keen to hear what I could recommend. They liked their heavy dub, but they'd go for the more unusual stuff, and they were more open minded than a lot of my black customers who just wanted the new Gregory Isaacs. A lot of the punk bands lived round there so they'd come in; Glen Matlock and Johnny Rotten were always in there, and when Elvis Costello changed his name from Declan McManus, the first cheque he ever wrote under his new name he wrote in Honest Jon's. He bought about forty quid's worth of reggae tunes, one of which was "Uptown Top Ranking".'

Local promoters (Honest Jon's included) started putting reggae groups on. It became almost obligatory for punk acts to take a roots group on tour with them – Steel Pulse opened for Billy Idol's Generation X, Matumbi toured with Ian Dury and the Blockheads, Aswad supported Eddie and the Hotrods, the Clash took deejay Mikey Dread to warm up their audiences with his wild lyrics and a dubwise selection. In accordance with this apparently multiracial trend, in 1977 the Anti-Nazi League, a British political organization dedicated to stopping the rise of the far right among the young, launched Rock Against Racism. Under the slogan Black and White Unite, it was a nationwide series of big open-air concerts, carnivals and events, boasting bills topped by Steel Pulse, Misty in Roots, Aswad or Tradition, and propped up by such likely lads as the Police and Elvis Costello. And the value of such involvement for a reggae act, in terms of sheer sales, is sharply illustrated by Dennis Bovell's tale of two bands:

'This was during the Rock Against Racism era when Matumbi and Steel Pulse had the same management company. Because we'd been around longer we'd get first refusal on any gigs – if we couldn't or didn't want to do them we'd pass them to Steel Pulse, and one gig that, with hindsight, we should've done was to open for the Stranglers on a tour. The Stranglers wanted us and the Police – who weren't famous then – as support and we didn't even think about it. Immediately it was "Nah, nah, nah. Can't possibly. Can't possibly have Matumbi on the same bill as the bloody Stranglers, and some white reggae band . . . calling themselves *The Police*, or some kind of foolishness. Give that one to Steel Pulse."

'Which they did, and Steel Pulse took it. Their album of that year, *Handsworth Revolution*, sold over a quarter of a million. We've never done anything near that.'

British radio started taking more notice of reggae now as well. Up until then it had been strictly specialist shows, and they were consigned to London local stations – Steve Barnard's *Reggae Time* on BBC Radio London was the first in the early 1970s, with Tommy Vance's *TV on Reggae* on Capital, then Tony Williams – but as sales of reggae and media attention grew, it began to filter through to the main broadcasters. John Peel, an ageing, ex-hippy but pioneering Radio 1 deejay, had taken up the punk cause with gusto and reggae got swept along with it, and Steel Pulse were one of the few black bands to perform on his legendary *Live* sessions. Elsewhere his eagerness to liven up his abrasively left-of-centre evening show with some heavy-duty riddim alongside the Buzzcocks, Souxsie and the Banshees and the Exploited was enough for the dour-sounding, balding Liverpudlian to get himself called Jah Peel. This was the sharp end of the wedge, whilst daytime radio's producers now began to look beyond the annual novelty reggae hit and would programme Bob Marley, Dennis Brown or Big Youth on the same schedules as Abba, Brotherhood of Man and Smokie.

As importantly, though, Rock Against Racism and the reggae 'n' punk flirtation provided creative fillip. As reggae acts proved themselves popular draws, venues opened up that would never previously have booked them, particularly the university circuit and the small theatres/big clubs that were opening in all Britain's major cities in response to punk being an essentially live experience – places such as the Vortex, the Zig Zag and the Venue in London. This meant not only that more bands got more work, but that those same bands became much better than they otherwise might have, as these almost wholly white audiences had different expectations from the black crowds that used to heckle Matumbi. It meant that songs and arrangements had to be stretched way beyond the one drop of sound systems, and the market leaders opened up Dennis's restructuring of reggae to include all manner of musicianship. It is impossible to imagine the song that gave this chapter its name, Aswad's awesome 'Warrior Charge', being created in any other circumstances.

That record uses the day's technology, a full horn-loaded line-up, arrangement dexterity that goes to the very limit of a reggae riddim, dub ideas that left contemporary Jamaica looking silly, mad musical skills and exactly the sort of joyous spirit and bravery that deserves to be called dread. 'Warrior Charge' is an as-yet-unsurpassed pinnacle of British reggae. It's spiky sense of adventure epitomizes what so much of the music was about and what so much more of it *should have* been about. To use the tune as the theme song and the central dramatic device of the 1980 feature film *Babylon* was an entirely logical choice. The movie, directed by Franco Rosso – who probably isn't of Jamaican descent – was an acutely observed, sensitively scripted and sharply played slice of life on the London sound-system scene, which starred Brinsley Dan, Aswad's lead singer and former child TV star, and featured a Dennis Bovell score. It detailed the racial and social politics of trying to graft such an intrinsically Kingstonian set of values as a sound system on to a London landscape, the family pressures of growing up as a second-generation Jamaican immigrant and how sound-man paranoia is the same on both sides of the ocean – 'Warrior Charge' was the sound's secret weapon, the tune which, entirely believably, was going to annihilate all comers in the dancehall. *Babylon* remains the most enjoyable documentation of British reggae culture.

Unfortunately, though, the other high-profile souvenir of those 1970s was the lamentable Bob Marley single 'Punky Reggae Party'. Cut in England with musical backing by Aswad and production duties courtesy of Lee Perry, the lyric relineated the terms 'trite' and 'vapid' to go something like this: . . . *The Wailers will be there, the Slits, the Feelgoods, the Clash . . . rejected by society, treated with impunity, protected by their dignity . . . It's a punky reggae party, we hope it will be hearty . . .* Remarkably, but probably because it had 'Jamming' on the other side, the single got to number 9 in the UK. It's hard not to blame Island Records for this blatantly exploitative opportunism. True, there were some interesting precepts being bandied about at the time by misty-eyed white musicians and journalists – and, it must be remembered, a few malleable reggae acts – that centred on this rather one-way alliance as being a genuine social coalition of the dispossessed. The thought was that punks and Rasta/black youth were both outcasts, therefore it was natural for them to band together and, thus united, these apparent dregs would shake society to its very core. But it never quite happened like that, as any time they felt like it the punks could wash their faces and return to their real lives.

The British bands really moved up a gear when the bigger record companies started noticing them, something that had a great deal to do with what they did being presented in a reasonably non-threatening – i.e., white – environment. A&R men were far more willing to come to the Zig Zag or the University of East Anglia or the Rock Against Racism Festival in Roundhay Park, Leeds, than to the Four Aces in Dalston or one of the reggae all-nighters at Hammersmith Palais which would mix visiting Jamaican acts with local hopefuls, starting at midnight and turning out at 6 a.m. on Sunday. Island Records signed Steel Pulse and Aswad – the former ending up on WEA, the latter going on to the equally major CBS Records; Virgin and Island each released Linton Kwesi Johnson's dub poetry; EMI flirted with Matumbi and Dennis's later incarnation, the Dub Band; Delroy Washington cut an album on Virgin; the Cimarons went to Polydor; and Black Slate signed to the Phonogram subsidiary label Ensign. By the end of the decade, as the mainstream music media started running sufferah-empathic 'Black New Wave' stories, these groups sold a lot of albums, probably the greater share of which went outside the established reggae market.

Jamaican acts started attracting bigger-time attention too. In Bob Marley's slipstream, Island gave UK release to, among others, Burning Spear, Lee Perry, a righteous Max Romeo, Jimmy Cliff, Toots and the Maytals, Jah Lion and Junior Murvin. Although this relationship undoubtedly increased sales potential, Island UK and Jamaican reggae artists were never the easiest of bedfellows – which might seem remarkable, seeing how the company's owner was himself a Jamaican, but there's many who will tell you it was *because* of this. An almost universal complaint concerned the apparently unapproved remixing indulged in by Island to make the music more access-ible to English ears, while the 'Babylonian conspiracy theory' lobby to this day remain convinced they were only signed to be underpromoted in order to protect Island's positioning of Bob Marley as reggae's sole superstar. Ganja paranoia? . . . *En masse?* you decide.

The most spectacular spat between a Jamaican artist and Island Records involved Lee Perry: dissatisfied with the pro-motional push the company had put behind the *Super Ape* LP and stung by its reluctance to schedule his *Roast Fish, Collie Weed and Cornbread* vocal set, he withdrew *The Heart of the Congos* from the UK company (there are stories, which might not be apocryphal, of his physically stealing back the masters). As a result, the album became practically impossible to obtain until the Blood & Fire reissue label had the good sense to put it out twenty years after it was recorded.

In the second half of the decade, Richard Branson's Virgin Records became the other big player to travel to Jamaica. Initially Virgin was looking for some of the Marley Magic, having wooed and won Peter Tosh, whose classic *Legalize It* became one of the company's first reggae albums. Taking a slightly more adventurous (and unadulterated) tack than Island, hot on Tosh's heels Virgin signed Keith Hudson and U-Roy, and while their releases sold well in the black market they didn't set the mainstream on fire. Not in the UK anyway, but take said records to Africa and you'd have trouble pressing them fast enough. According to a report in the British music industry trade magazine *Music Week*, in 1975 alone Virgin sold £150,000 worth of reggae to Africa, a large amount of money in those days. Nigeria was the main consumer, to the degree that the company even started knocking out eight-track cartridges for the Nigerian market, a format that had long since died a death in the UK. To meet this voracious demand, Richard Branson, A&R man Jumbo Van Hennen and Johnny Rotten (the Sex Pistols were signed to Virgin) flew to Jamaica to sign more reggae. And did so with, quite literally, a suitcase full of American dollars to pay out as advances. It didn't take an awfully long time for the word to get round Kingston's musical community that a bunch of white men down at the Sheraton Hotel were handing out free money to singers. It was only prompt and spirited police action that prevented the people in the soon-formed audition queue, many bearing guitars or hand drums, from getting out of hand. Astonishingly, two weeks and over $100,000 later, the Virgin contingent left Jamaica with a roster that included Prince Far-I, the Gladiators, the Mighty Diamonds, the Twinkle Brothers, Johnnie Clarke and Big Youth.

The theory among musicians is that Africans appreciated the roots reggae sentiments and believed that by buying the records they would be assisting their Caribbean brothers in their struggle. Others believed they went for it just for the beat. It was this African involvement that led directly to Virgin establishing its Frontline label, the most consistently credible mainstream British reggae label. The story goes that a shipment of pressed and packaged albums was in the air en route to Nigeria when the new political regime announced that the country had closed its economy, meaning no money was going to get out. Rather than deliver the records and face the prospect of losing most of the revenue in bribes in order to get any hard currency payment at all, the plane was ordered to turn round and come back to Britain. To get rid of this huge amount of now surplus stock, the specialist Frontline label was launched and took off to the degree that the clenched fist and barbed-wire logo became a hallmark of roots quality.

One footnote to the 1970s reggae-to-Africa trade was the amount that was ending up in the then culturally boycotted South Africa. This isn't, it must be stressed, an issue particular to Virgin. Many artists who signed deals with UK record companies had a clause inserted that precluded sales of their work in South Africa. Yet it remains a fact that when they toured the Republic post-apartheid expecting to find virgin territory, they discovered that they were well enough known to sell out arena-sized venues because so many people had bought their albums years ago!

Reggae in Britain had never looked healthier, from either a creative or a commercial point of view. From the deep roots sound systems through to *Top of the Pops*. From lovers' rock to deejay style. Bob Marley, Dillinger, Steel Pulse, Althea & Donna, Barry Biggs, Big Youth, Matumbi, Janet Kay, Burning Spear . . . they were all having hits. And it seemed that anybody who heard a reggae tune liked it. As the 1980s rolled around, reggae UK looked unstoppable. With or without continued support from the mainstream.

19

Sipple Out Deh

Back in Jamaica, by the middle of the 1970s the People's National Party's economic strategies were in dire trouble. The island had been living beyond its means for two or three years and the higher taxes, both personal and corporate, initially seen as the most straightforward of coffer-fillers, were turning out to be a liability. Increased income tax, company levies and import duties underpinned the party's socialist values – a 'soak the rich' bid to create at least the impression of trying for fiscal parity among Jamaica's class divisions – which, while it raised desperately needed revenue, served to trigger upper-echelon protest. There was a middle/professional-class flight to the USA and Canada, while those of the upper classes who stayed made sure their money didn't – in spite of stringent foreign-exchange controls introduced in 1974, so much currency was being illegally exported that the government went on record as saying how greatly this was contributing to the economic decline. About the same time, in an official statement, the Governor of the Central Bank of Jamaica said of the privileged minority: 'They have done nothing but fight us at every turn and protest loudly at any measure that threatens their creature comforts.' Then, as the right was making its displeasure felt, the left was shouting just as angrily about how these increased revenues were benefiting the middle classes far more than they were the sufferahs: schools, roads, hospitals and municipal services in the suburbs were all being improved, while, as in the pre-independence economic boom, not much money made it downtown.

Import duties meant that materials needed for Jamaican commerce and manufacturing became enormously expensive, and at the same time industry had to cope with the introduction of another foundation stone of the PNP's socialist dream, the minimum wage. Foreign-owned corporations began to cut down on the amount of business done on the island, partly because of these economic considerations and partly because they were getting twitchy about Manley's continual courtship of the Third World's left-wing regimes, which gave the impression that PNP socialism equalled Soviet-style communism.

That hurt, but when applied to the bauxite industry it was a *big* problem. Following the lead of Peru, Guyana and Bolivia, who had all recently nationalized US mining interests or entered into partnership as 51 per cent shareholders, Manley wanted Jamaica to take over an equal share in the extraction and processing of the red rock. When his suggestions were all but laughed at, he slapped greatly increased taxes on the industry. While this raised foreign revenue by approximately 600 per cent for the year 1974, it was all but wiped out by the oil crisis which increased spending by roughly the same proportion. Furthermore, this policy made bauxite so expensive that it forced the US companies to look for alternatives, which led to a worldwide fall in demand for the mineral. The immediate effect in Jamaica was to reduce production, which further unnerved potential (and existing) overseas investors.

The drying up of foreign business meant local manufacturing and trade faltered as there was no more credit for materials and goods. Or no materials and goods, full stop. Which devastated food production and employment levels. And with the balance of trade swinging so heavily towards the import side – oil costs were continuing to soar, going from $65 million in 1973 to $240 million in 1977 – inflation went into double figures. The government's increasingly radical stance was distancing the North Atlantic Alliance's economic magnanimity (albeit a rather self-serving generosity), its new best friends being Third World revolutionaries such as Robert Mugabe and Fidel Castro. Ironically, Manley's chumming down with Castro irritated the Jamaican proletariat as much as it did the American State Department. This was because Cuba didn't actually have any money, so sent over help in the form of engineers and 'advisers', something that didn't go uncommented on by Jamaican workers and trade unionists. Delegations of unemployed Jamaican youngsters were sent on work study to spend time in Cuban factories and fields, learning agricultural and construction techniques – the Soviet Union made sure the island had its manufacturing and farming showcases – and they returned home with all sorts of 'big-time' ideas which left them profoundly dissatisfied with the way things were.

Jamaica resumed full ambassadorial relations with Cuba in 1974 (there had been consular relations between the two countries since independence, but the JLP had always kept Castro at arm's length). The government then blatantly endorsed the deployment of Cuban troops to back up the MPLA in Angola, and established direct flights from Kingston to Havana. While the USA didn't actually take immediate punitive action against Jamaica over the government's verbal support for the Cubans in Angola, Washington wasn't best pleased – Secretary of State Henry Kissinger actually visited Jamaica to appeal to the people not to endorse 'interference' in Africa. The USA seemed convinced that Manley was being used as a stooge for the Cuban communist regime, allowing Cuba to bring in American goods via Jamaica and thus skirting the blockade, and the Cold War blew particularly frosty as America waged a campaign of economic attrition against JA. It's estimated that in 1975 nearly $10 million of US aid was quietly withdrawn as a direct result of Jamaica's full trade relations with Cuba. The virtual collapse of the bauxite industry was accelerated by US conglomerates avoiding doing business with Jamaica if they could.

The American media too lost no opportunity to denounce the island as a hotbed of communism and all things un-American. This took serious toll on the tourist industry as increasing numbers of Americans began to feel uneasy about holidaying in Jamaica, which is very much a double irony. It was Castro's takeover of Cuba that kickstarted US tourism to Jamaica as American holidaymakers sought an alternative destination; while the recently inaugurated air route to Cuba was a genuine sanctions buster as it started bringing American tourism back to Cuba – travellers could visit the island from Jamaica without having their passports stamped, and there remains a huge market in sex and cigar tourism through this back door from the USA.

Forced on to the back foot by a crumbling infrastructure, the PNP began to rely on the politics of ideology and bombast – most of the country's problems, it appears, were a CIA plot. But all of this did nothing to bring in foreign currency, and a five-year decline in the island's balance of payments hit a deficit of almost $300 million during 1975. The island was heading for an economic crisis, and during 1975 Michael Manley was forced to go knocking on the door of that fiscal Last Chance Saloon, the International Monetary Fund.

Naturally enough, this worsening state of affairs was reflected in the music of the times. Lyrics became increasingly focused on specifics instead of the usual sweeping swathe of general injustice. And the perception of the PNP as being sufferah-sympathetic meant there would always be a great deal of mileage in that party's politics. Deejay Tappa Zukie's smash hit 'MPLA' – *MPLA | Natty going on a holiday* – and Pablo Moses's 'We Should Be in Angola' advanced the idea of Rasta joining up with the Cuban troops to go and fight in Africa as being spiritually sound. The Mighty Diamonds' *Stand Up to Your Judgement* LP features a sleeve drawing of paramilitary-styled, machine-gun-totin' Rastamen and such scrawled slogans as 'Death to capitalism', 'Death to Maoism', 'Death to Yankee Imperialism', 'Death to English Colonialism' and just plain 'Death'. Joe Joe Hookim's Channel One house band were called the Revolutionaries and put out instrumentals with titles like 'Angola' and 'Leftist', both of which were off a huge-selling album called *Revolutionaries Sounds* that had a red cover featuring that classic beard 'n' beret portrait of Che Guevara.

Around the same time, singles were surfacing in the UK with version B-sides by the IMF Players, believed to be an amalgamation of Bunny Lee's Aggrovators and Channel One's Revolutionaries. As ironic a statement as the name might have been, it was more the effects of the fiscal constraints the Fund put on the Jamaican treasury rather than the organization itself that was attracting musical interest. In order to meet the Fund's criterion that economic targets must be reached *before* Jamaica's application could be considered, the government had to impose wage restrictions, curb public spending (health and education budgets were slashed in 1975), allow prices to rise and introduce such draconian exchange controls that the holding of foreign currency actually became illegal. Inflation galloped to over 20 per cent per annum, and food prices rose at a greater rate as a result of so many staples being imported. Unemployment reached 31 per cent by the end of the decade; over 40 per cent of wage earners were on less than $20 per week, meaning that three-quarters of the country was living below the official poverty line; and food shortages – particularly of rice, flour and cooking oil – were becoming a fact of life. The sufferation singles of that time threw up some true classics: Horace Andy's 'Skylarking' was about the perils of a hardcore, unemployed sub-working class; the Maytals' 'Time Tough' subtly juxtaposed slavery with the current hardships; Bunny Wailer's 'Arab Oil Weapon' pulled few punches; Bob Andy's 'Fire Burning' warned of a potential class war; Bob Marley's 'Talking Blues' – *Cold ground was my bed last night / Rock stone was my pillow too* . . . – was a hard-times chronicle. The Heptones' Lee Perry-produced 'Mr President' appealed directly, if perhaps gently, to the government on behalf of the sufferahs, but it gained a certain edge when Jah Lion toasted on top of it with lyrics like *Come offa your big chair / I and I need I share* . . . Peter Tosh's 'Arise Black Man', Junior Byles' 'Beat Down Babylon', and the Mighty Diamonds' 'I Need a Roof' are all self-explanatory. Dennis Brown figured he'd be better off in chokey with 'Three

Meals a Day' – . . . *three meals a day | No rent to pay | No wife to obey . . .*; and Jacob Miller's 'Tenement Yard' bewailed the dehumanization of the ghetto's overcrowding, although occasionally from a purely selfish point of view – *Dreadlocks can't smoke his pipe in peace . . .*

Just as the people thought things couldn't get any worse, 1976 brought a general election.

Organized political violence in the densely populated ghettos was now a fact of life, as it became the former rudie street gangs' purpose in life as well as their means of support. Until now it had been pretty one-sided, with the more established JLP gunmen (notably the ranking street gangs Skull and Phoenix who controlled Tivoli Gardens and the area south of Spanish Town Road) firmly in charge. Now, with the JLP having spent a term in opposition for the first time since independence, the PNP-sponsored warlords were living fat and had the resources and weapons to make a fight of it – Tel Aviv and Spanglers were the posses involved, and Red Tony Welch was the Don in Concrete Jungle, north of Spanish Town Road taking in Denham Town and Jones Town.

Far from ridding the city of the partisan gunmen, as he promised to do in 1972, Manley had actually made things worse in more ways than simply arming one side. He led an increasing reliance on rhetoric which served to polarize each party into socialist or anti-socialist, drawing a line in the sand that required no further discussion. Such simply defined, purely ideological differences made it so much easier to get involved on a pretty basic level. Thus freed from any notion of actual politics, the ghetto youth took to the partisanship aspect with such enthusiasm that ordering the wrong beer could be enough to get you shot: Red Stripe was, understandably, the PNP's tipple, while Heineken's green bottle allied it with the JLP's party colour. Added to this, the outlawing of the Yankee dollar meant small planeloads of pistols, shotguns and ammunition had been coming into Jamaica on a regular basis, because the booming ganja trade had to get paid somehow.

A State of Emergency was introduced in June (the election

wasn't until December), along with the Gun Court, a forbidding, barbed-wire-enclosed stockade near the cricket ground on South Camp Road. The mere possession of a gun, a bullet or a spent cartridge was enough to get you 'indefinite detention' in the prison's deeply unpleasant conditions, never mind a trial. This was Prince Buster's Judge Dread come to life. It's difficult to tell if it made any difference or not to gun-crime since there were still over 200 apparently politically motivated murders in Kingston during the lead-up to the election, a period of campaigning that was to become dominated by the shooting of Bob Marley.

For many citizens this situation was all too reminiscent of the rude-boy wars of the previous decade. PNP 'soldiers' might have fashioned themselves as freedom fighters, while the JLP ranks assumed the role of heroic defence against a tide of Communism, but behind the sloganeering was nothing more socially concerned than gangsterism. In many cases these self-styled paladins were above the law – Tony Welch regularly sat down with high-ranking government ministers; Michael Manley himself attended the funeral of Winston Blake, a celebrated gunman. It was widely accepted in Kingston that the local forces of law and order were equally partisan, with the police force acting as Seaga's private army and most of the officers and men of the Jamaican Defence Force lining up behind the PNP. As the gangsters and their followers enjoyed such high-level protection and the authorities had enormous vested interests, crime flourished on all levels. Most of it, of course, was perpetrated in the ghetto against fellow sufferahs – rape and gang rape were among the most frequently committed acts of barbarism, as the gangs sought to terrorize their environments into submission. But this time, unlike the rude-boy era, there was no sense of ambiguity among the music community, and the condemnation of the violence that was tearing the city apart was universal.

This chapter's title is the original Jamaican title of the Max Romeo tune that came out in the UK as 'War inna Babylon', a scathing diatribe against political corruption, ghetto violence and government heavy-handedness. It drew the conclusion that this war's only losers were the sufferahs and its bottom line is a word of caution to Kingston's massive: *it sipple out deh* means it's slippery out there; you know, dangerous. Produced and, arguably, co-conceived by Lee Perry, the record is a work of near genius in tone, tune and what it tells, setting a benchmark for musical denouncement of the ghetto violence. In its wake came some of the most eloquently focused protest songs ever written. Anywhere.

Leroy Smart's 'Ballistic Affair' served up a poignant reminder of the effect the gang wars were having on everyday life for an entire generation of Kingston youth: . . . *We used to lick chalice and cook ital stew together | We used to play football and cricket as one brother . . . Now you go fight against your brother . . . Everyone is living in fear | just through this ballistic affair . . .* Barry Brown's 'Far East' expressed much the same sentiments, and John Holt's 'Up Park Camp' took its title from the Jamaica Defence Force's 200-acre barracks. Junior Murvin's 'Police and Thieves' was in no doubt that this was sheer criminality, and that to call it political would be to flatter it. Johnnie Clarke decried the mercenary aspect of gunmen on the party's payrolls in 'Blood Dunza' ('dunza' being sufferah slang for money), while Burning Spear, Jah Stitch and Culture appealed for peace with, respectively, 'Throw Down Your Arms', 'Cool Down Youthman' and 'Stop Your Fussin' and Fightin''. 'Fire inna Kingston' by Vivian Jackson and the Prophets told, with an effective first-person expression of shock, of coming to the capital from the country and the devastation encountered: . . . *I make a little move and I check Tivoli | people them-a fight, police can't go in there | I make another move to check Trench Town | people a-go run run run them a-run left them house . . . Fire, fire and we have no water . . .* Prince Far-I's roots masterpiece 'Heavy Manners' called for self-control among the ghetto people, and in doing so wrote a question mark against the PNP's anti-crime policies, which clearly weren't working and which were being used by police to harass Rastas. To 'put criminals under heavy manners' was Manley's catchphrase for

coming down hard on crime, and in the overwhelming, fore-
boding toast built on a tune called 'Su Su Pon Rasta' by Nago
Morris, Far-I likened it to how you'd treat a dog, making the
point with terrifying timbre as he told the world natty-dread-
style that self-discipline was the only way forward. With an
Errol Thompson mix perfectly setting up the toaster's deep,
brooding menace against pertinent snatches of lyric from the
original song, it's one of the most portentous deejay records
ever made – the lyrics may read like nonsense (that's why we
won't go into them on the page) but the attitude drips with
dread.

'Heavy Manners' was one of the few records that offered an
earthly solution to the situation. Literally truckloads of tunes
told of Jah's vengeance which would be soon, swift and final,
while many took the stance that – divine retribution or otherwise
– the righteous should simply vacate the area and leave Babylon
to collapse under the weight of its own wickedness. Johnnie
Clarke's 'Move Outta Babylon', the Mighty Diamonds'
'Country Living', Bob Marley's 'Exodus' (although that may
have been more figurative), Big Youth, Pam Hall and Jackie
Parris's 'You Got to Live in the Country', Junior Delgado's
'Natty Want to Go Home' and Vivian Jackson and the Prophets'
'Run Come Rally' were among the very best. The last was a
classy piece of roots rocksteady, with a central theme not simply
imploring the masses to leave Babylon to its own devices but to
join the ranks of Rastafari: . . . *Run come rally rally run come
rally rally round Jahoviah's throne . . . Run away run away run
away from the land called Sodom and Gomorrah . . .* Cut at Lee
Perry's Black Ark (produced by Vivian Jackson but mixed by
Scratch himself) in 1974, it was a recruitment song, and came
at a time when the inadequacies of the new government were
really starting to kick in. It was one of the first of many such
rallying calls – Horace Andy's 'Zion Gate', Hugh Mundell's
'Jah Say the Time Has Now Come' and the Abyssinians' 'Jah
Loves' are just three that immediately spring to mind – and
coincided with the start of a tremendous upsurge in Rasta
consciousness, especially in the city.

This was Burning Spear's prophetic statement from Chapter 12 coming full circle. Whereas the musicians were previously drawing inspiration from a section of the people and their faith, during the last couple of years the music business had so zealously embraced Rasta that it had a disproportionately high profile (even in the second half of the 1970s there were more love songs being released) and was now setting an example for its audience. While previously people were investigating Rasta from a more or less theological point of view, it had now become pretty much a necessity as the masses wanted to put some daylight between themselves and the mayhem on the streets. Rasta was very visible by the middle of the decade as dreadlocks grew across the social strata and its humanitarian principles were difficult to find fault with, whether you believed in the biblical side or not. It was proactively black; had a simple credo of living good, treating people with respect and enjoying a spiritual, unpolluted way of life; and came with a ready-made mythology and ideology that could adapt to its environment. Altogether this was an understandably attractive proposition for people living in a war zone, with a government that, to all intents and purposes, had failed them.

As before, there were still enormous prejudices, so not all those who began thinking righteously grew dreadlocks, but it was now, in the mid-1970s, that for hundreds of thousands of Jamaicans Rasta's philosophies became a spiritual escape hatch from their environment. The records – heavily Jamaican in delivery, often like chants or hymns in structure, with lyrics promising a better life and the deejays incessantly ramming the message home – did a great deal to nudge things along. In an uncanny echo of how Prince Buster saw the people's reaction to the rude-boy gangs of the 1960s, Big Youth tells how it worked:

'Rasta as it present itself to the people on the sound systems had been there for a while. Now as the sound systems are always the most important appeal of reggae music, it soon spread to the records. That's when so many more people got to hear about Rasta and its principles, through those conscious records. At that time so many of the yout' was Rasta or Rasta sympathizer – at the sound system and elsewhere – but this is when the mass of the people start to take up with it. In their daily lives you had oppression and repression, and the political separation was starting so you had yout' killing off yout', and if you know within yourself you're not supposed to be a victim of environment nor of the system, then Rasta was the best choice. Back then most of we yout' is nice thinking people, think educated and want the best out of life – like anybody else – so why discriminate and police brutality and gang warfare and so forth. We didn't want that and we see Rastafari as the way forward.

'Of course you have people follow the wagon because them feel if they can *appear* to be Rasta and sing some songs then they can be a star. You have to be real because Rasta is naturality and love, togetherness. Back then Rasta teach people to share, so instead of teaching about *baby-baby* love they teach about together love, and that was how people could find an alternative road to the violence and the political business. The music is our media, so it became our form of teaching other people about Rasta and how it could help them live good.

'And they listen to it, too. You had a generation of yout' coming up in the 1970s who were born after 1962 and therefore born independent – "I got independence" is what they *knew*. So getting independence, out from colonialism, wasn't what it was all about in their lives, and all they could see was what was wrong. They didn't think this *independence* it was anything to be thankful for. Then the teachers at school telling them about Jerusalem and heaven and those places in the sky when they die, then leaving school you can't even get a job. *But they don't want to rob.* So they come to Rasta, they sit down, smoke some herb as a sacrament and with a steady mind try to find how to plan a way out. Because life in the ghetto – any ghetto anywhere in the world – is just the fittest of the fittest, and if you're strong then you've got to leave. Not necessarily leave in the actual sense, but offer them something spiritual and natural in all that is going on around them.'

*

That the PNP won the 1976 general election wasn't because of any particular track record in office, or because its election promises made a great deal of socio-economic sense, or because its ghetto soldiers were any more effective – the mad irony of the West Kingston political warfare was that the number of parliamentary seats it could deliver was insignificant. Michael Manley's party rolled to an apparent landslide victory – 47 seats to the JLP's 13 – because it managed to convince the electorate that the opposition would be far worse. This had scarcely been a gargantuan task since Edward Seaga, leader of the JLP, had by then acquired the nickname 'Blinds' due not only to his habit of never going out in public without dark glasses, but also as a reference to his apparent inability to see the needs of the ordinary Jamaican.

The PNP embarked on a policy of marking all Jamaica's financial problems down to the legacy left to them by the JLP – even the flight of international capital was attributed to JLP encouragement; while everything else was blamed on American-backed destabilization – Seaga found himself demonized as *CIA-ga* in street graffiti. A series of explosions and high profile shootings during a Commonwealth Prime Ministers' Conference held in Jamaica were held up as proof, but it was widely speculated at the time that the PNP had in fact been behind the incidents in order to state its case on a worldwide stage.

Then there was what, years later, would be called 'the race card'. Manley's manifest support from the reggae music business and his eagerness to assume dread by association – the Rod of Correction was an ace in the hole in this respect – had meant enormous sufferah support at the last election, and he built on this and the climate of black consciousness to portray the PNP as Jamaica's black party. The best way to do this was to snipe at Edward Seaga's Syrian ancestry. It was argued he would disregard the black population in favour of the higher tones uptown, which, given the nation's unshakeable shadism, wasn't entirely unbelievable. As it turned out, Seaga's support at the election was rigidly defined by class and caste. Of the upper classes, four times as many voted JLP as PNP, and of the middle and professional classes it was nearly three times as many.

Yet the margin of victory wasn't quite what it appeared. If you apply proportional representation, the vote came out at 57–43 in the PNP's favour, with the rural parishes being strongly PNP and the densely populated Kingston split almost straight down the middle. Never mind the Musical Bandwagon, too many promises weren't being delivered on by PNP. Quite apart from the periodic food shortages and IMF-imposed spending limits that were now being felt as schools, hospitals and the country's infrastructure ran out of resources, people believed they'd been abandoned in the face of growing ghetto violence. And to a degree they had, as there were now a number of quite clearly defined no-go areas for the police. Then Manley's government further distanced itself from the dispossessed by launching an all-out assault on the country's number one export, marijuana.

Whether the idea of ganja being legalized, or at least decriminalized, was ever anything more than an optimistic yet idle rumour has never been fully ascertained. What nobody was prepared for, though, was Operation Buccaneer, an initiative planned and executed by America's Drug Enforcement Agency designed to stamp out the trade on both an international and a local level. During the years since independence it had become the island's biggest earning cash crop, the whole industry being worth roughly $400 million per annum by the middle of the 1970s. Most of that was the lucrative export market, in which Jamaica was the USA's biggest Caribbean supplier with an estimated two million pounds' weight of herb moving to the States during 1974. The trade was becoming an embarrassment to a government that didn't want to antagonize America any more than it did by simply being there, and, in an unprecedented move, Manley invited a massive US task force to the country to 'disrupt the unabated marijuana cultivation in Jamaica'. Setting up internal bases and bringing in an enormous amount of troops and equipment, jungle warfare tactics – as deployed in Vietnam – were used to locate and burn ganja fields while any weed found on boats or drying in the sun was seized and people held under the new Dangerous Drugs Act.

Once again, marijuana laws were being used to harass dreadlocks – the DEA operatives seemed almost paranoid about Rasta's 'involvement' in the drugs trade; small-time dealers were getting locked up; and destroying the crops wiped out the only means so many small farmers or ex-sugar cane growers had to make a living. All of which hit the unofficial economy hard, and therefore had the greatest negative impact on the poor. It's interesting to imagine what would have happened had Operation Buccaneer succeeded, as the bullish ganja market was playing a not-inconsiderable part in keeping Jamaica afloat. Although an aid package would undoubtedly have been offered in return for cooperation, it's difficult to see how it could have measured up to these nine-figure sums. Not that anybody needed to worry on that account, as it made surprisingly little difference to the island's international drugs trade – seizures by US Coastguards operating in Jamaican waters during the operation were negligible, and as for 'eradicating' anything, by the end of the decade the JA-to-USA traffic was worth an estimated annual $2 *billion*. What it did do was make criminals out of smokers, small-time dealers and growers, who began to stand shoulder to shoulder with the big-time cultivators in opposition to this government-endorsed heavy handedness, and saw the beginning of the political thugs' eventual move into the drugs trade.

Operation Buccaneer was a threefold disaster for the PNP. The PNP's anti-imperialist stance took a serious jolt as Operation Buccaneer was perceived as the party doing business with the same monster that the JLP was all too willing to sit down with. It also provided ample cover for CIA-backed and *CIA-ga*-cooperative forces of destabilization that Manley made so much of – what did he expect if he was going to *invite* large numbers of American Special Forces into his country? And its effect on rural and urban incomes was instrumental in turning the tide of sufferah opinion against him.

Max Romeo's 'No Joshua No' was one of the first anti-Manley records to come out of a constituency he clearly thought of as his own, and remains if not the most eloquent then certainly the most direct: *You took them out of bondage / and they thank you for it . . . but now in the desert / tired, battered and bruised / they think they are forsaken / they think they have been used / Rasta is watching and blaming you . . .* Romeo continued this line of thinking in 'One Step Forward', with the lyric *One step forward two step backward* being a pointed indictment of how things had certainly got no better since the government changed colours. The Heptones weighed in with 'Mr President', a straightforward plea to Government House, and 'Sufferah Time', which gave the idea the massive was running out of patience: *See wi time / It's a sufferah's time / Time fi sufferahs drive big car / Time fi sufferahs live it up . . .* Ernie Smith warned that 'Jah Kingdom Go to Waste', while Peter Tosh's collieman anthem 'Legalize It' came as a direct result of Operation Buccaneer's attempts at curbing the herb.

Big Youth takes up the story again.

'It was getting too much to bear. We can't take it any more so we feel we have to hit back with something. Which is our music.

'Rasta don't need to get involved with politics, there is a higher reckoning than any *Prime Minister*, but we were living in a serious time back then. The system didn't care for us, it was telling us to fight against ourselves, fight against each other, and be covetous and stupid, so instead of trying to get something from the system you had to try and take something from yourself. It prove you should really go to the illiterate place and learn to get civilized because the people there 'ave no reason not to be straight with you. And those people is the same ghetto people who 'ave to teach the yout' around them, because nobody else is gonna do it. It's we the deejay, the singers and the Rastas who tell them you mustn't skylark and all them t'ings because you gonna go to jail where people will take steps with you. We tell the people that they have to live right so there is no reason for them to go to court, and if they don't go to court they can't go to jail. We tell them to try and keep their families together.

'Of course the forces is there, the forces that didn't want that to go on. They don't want people to be anything other than stupid, but we can't let that happen. That's why the music was made that way then, because instead of just to praise Jah it had other work to do. We knew we held the power.'

Never was this power more graphically illustrated than on Saturday 22 April 1978, at the National Stadium in Kingston and the One Love Peace Concert. A 30,000 capacity show, headlined by Bob Marley and the Wailers, supported by, among others, Peter Tosh, Dennis Brown, Leroy Smart, Inner Circle, Trinity and the Mighty Diamonds, brought together both PNP and JLP politicians and gunmen to endorse the ghetto gang treaty that had been signed on 5 January that year. The gunman truce had already been marked in music by tunes like Jacob Miller's 'Peace Treaty Special', Dillinger's 'The War Is Over' and Culture's 'Natty Dread Taking Over' – all best sellers during that year – but the concert was to bring it to the attention of the entire Jamaican people, regardless of class or colour. Remarkably, this whole affair, and the peace movement of which it was a high-profile expression, was the brainchild of two killers from opposing sides of the divide, Bucky Marshall and Claudie Massop. The former was a rising star among the PNP gunmen, the latter a ruthless gangster, a murderous robber and a JLP warlord, and both men were Bob Marley's bredren.

In what was an unplanned side-effect of the Gun Court justice, rankings from both parties found themselves sharing cells. In this way Massop and Marshall discovered they had a great deal in common with each other – namely, or so reports go, that the political warring was interfering with their real business of armed robbery, extortion, drug running and racketeering. They hatched the idea of a gang truce in order to turn down the heat in the ghetto and, in a spirit of criminal cooperation similar to the American Mafia syndicates, leave each other free to felonize. After gaining endorsement from the Rasta organization the Twelve Tribes of Israel, and knowing they needed to make a big statement in order to be taken seriously, Massop and the PNP's top gunman Tony Welch (Marshall was too small-time for such a task) held protracted negotiations with Bob Marley in London – Kingston was deemed unsafe for such a conference – to convince the singer that such a concert was worthwhile. He, in turn, talked Michael Manley and Edward Seaga into attending the concert, sitting near each other in the front rows – a vantage point from which they must have felt the full force of Peter Tosh's molten rage as he opened his set by rebuking both political leaders at great length and with a force that was scary even by his own fearsome standards. Then, once they were in no doubt about the plight of the sufferah and the level of police brutality, the man who called himself the Steppin' Razor pulled out a spliff – or, as he referred to it that night, *one lickle draw of blood claat 'erb* – and fired it up. While the politicians literally squirmed in severe embarrassment, the massed ranks of police officers seethed with fury.

But none of Tosh's haughty histrionics could overshadow the moment that, during the Wailers' band's climactic rendering of 'One Love', Bob invited Michael Manley and Edward Seaga up on stage to shake hands. Sheepish as they might have looked, it was a genuinely historic moment and utterly impossible to imagine being pulled off by anybody other than Bob Marley.

That the peace only lasted a matter of weeks after that night, that Peter Tosh was arrested and beaten into unconsciousness by the police, for, surprise surprise, possession of ganja a few months later, and that it's an open secret that the PA system for that night arrived from Miami packed with guns for the JLP gangs is neither here nor there. That night reggae music flexed muscles that were unique among popular music anywhere in the world.

Boosted from every direction, reggae was bigger than it had ever been. The plight of the sufferah gave the righteous teachings of roots music a market, while the escapism factor involved in a night at the dancehall allowed the lovers' sounds to thrive alongside. Just as in the 1960s, the trickle-down effect of roots reggae's UK success was reaching back to the Kingston ghetto music world. The deals that producers were cutting with UK companies meant they were able to record more music in Jamaica. Not that anybody was pocketing large royalty cheques – talk to Big Youth and he'll tell you he still hasn't been paid for *Screaming Target*'s international success; Rupie Edwards has vowed not to go back to Jamaica to live until he's collected all that's owed him from twenty-five years ago; and Max Romeo reckons he only ever received JA$2,500 (not very much) for the *War inna Babylon* album. Touring possibilities in Britain opened up another avenue of earning, one which would appear to have its own peculiar sidestreet as one well-known reggae singer – who is still alive and therefore shall remain nameless – allegedly held up post offices around the UK as he followed his concert schedule. But as so much of the industry was focused locally, one of the most significant advances in the late 1970s was Jamaican radio's eventual acknowledgement of roots or sound-system style reggae.

The bribery that was previously rife had, during the decade, given way to outright physical threat – there's a well-known example of Skilly Coles, Bob Marley's right-hand man, giving courtroom evidence in which he vividly describes his and Bob's personal involvement in violent intimidation of radio station personnel and vandalism of their property in order to get airplay for Wailers music. But in 1977, a genuine street-centric radio show cut through the foreign-biased programming to recreate the excitement of the dancehall over the airwaves. It was Mikey Campbell's *Dread at the Controls*, broadcast from midnight to 6 a.m. every night except Monday. While he still puffs up quite justifiably proud of it as he recalls how it came about, the reasons why the show was so direly needed are one more indictment of Jamaica's class structure, and how fifteen years of independence and half a decade of so-called socialism had done nothing to change things:

'A lot of the people in Jamaican broadcasting were trained in the United States or in England by the BBC, so when they come back to Jamaica they still have that kind of foreign programming look at life. Either they come back with this very British thing and try to work it on the radio in Jamaica and the radio sound stupid, or the guys who was trained in America or Canada they come back with these great American accents that are so far fetched they don't even sound like it's our people. Which was the problem. Instead of looking at their own country and programming authentic Jamaican music that would appeal to Jamaicans, they were trying to appeal to people who want to listen to Mozart. They play calypso . . . they play American music . . . they play plenty Country & Western, these guys never had any identity – even now I'm not afraid to tell any programme director in Jamaica that you guys don't have no culture. They tried to ruin our culture by imposing on us a foreign culture and foreign programming. The man just don't want to play certain music, they think reggae is for the lower class – *they don't even play Bob Marley.* Them is Jamaican people who act like they not black.

'It's the upper class t'ing. In Jamaica certain people who have money or education, or people who come from a certain hierarchy, was acting like they was better than the average Jamaican – for example the browner [fairer] complexion you are the more you are recognized, the blacker you are the less you are recognized. There is a lot of prejudice in Jamaica right now still: the brown, the white and the black – you go to certain jobs and certain offices and you not going to see no real black girl up front. The people who run the JBC and RJR are like that. Them alienate themselves from real society, they live uptown, they speak real perfect English – not *Hinglish* – and they acting like they forget they used to go to the shop for their mummy and speak patois. Patois is a part of our upbringing and you can't forget it, but if you're going to go and present the news you know you're not going to read it in patois, but you're still going to sound like a Jamaican. You don't have to fake your voice to sound famous. And that's what they were doing.

'So when I start my programme *Dread at the Controls* in 1977, mi just come with the street talk, the street expressions and the street feeling. Mi wan' reflect the street right there on their national radio station, mi looking to address the masses. And when the people hear it they step back and say, "Wah! *This* is what we were waitin for!" They embrace it and they embrace me with it, but within the hierarchy there was a lot of people didn't like what I was doing.

'It wasn't anything to do with the hierarchy that I got the show, because after university I went to become a transmitter engineer with JBC, but they want to give me six months inside to see the operations before they send me out in the field. For some reason they forget me, the six months turned into about a year and I start enjoying it. At that time the radio station was like this – the announcer over there with the mic and the headphones, me as the operator over here with the control board with no mic that can go on air. I seh, "All right, well, mi have the big board, mi have the log, the music, the commercials and cards and everything and I know how to use them," so I spoke to my director, the supervisor of operations, and ask why we don't we go twenty-four hours? Until then the station used to sign off at midnight. Him seh, "Well, if you're suggesting you want to do that shift then you've got to come here every night at eleven o'clock right down to six o'clock in the morning. Or seven. You got to work Monday to Saturday, but you can have Sunday off. Can you handle that?" I said I could because I was from Port Antonio, I've just finished college, so mi nuh really have a whole heap of nocturnal activities. And by then I had all these reggae mi wan' play.

'That's really how I come up with the *Dread at the Controls* thing and it *freak* them out. When mi bus' that on them head-phones . . . a *dread at* the controls . . . It create a certain amount of resistance from the authorities and they took me to a lotta board meetings – I been to board meetings until I'm weak. But that was the same before, if a programme was missing they have to fill it, they give you, as the operator, some *fill* music. We operators, all young guys, used to call it *kill* music and I always carry two dub plate there in mi bag so if something was supposed to go on and the music not there I give them the dub plate to play. So before I had the show they were always trying to chastise me for playing three reggae back to back or doing this or doing that, seen? But mi 'ave mi qualifications so I wasn't frightened of these people if they tell me I'm fired beca' I can get another job. So I tek a whole heap of chances from time.'

Mikey chuckles at the memory.

'With *Dread at the Controls* it was just me, and apart from the jingles everything is live. *Live, live, live . . .* It was taking sound-system technique to the radio, and programming the radio to fit the Jamaican society – *not the other way around.* Giving the people what they want. First of all the people had to pay to go to dances and hear some exclusives and hear some songs they like. If they hear songs like the Heptones' "We're Having a Party Tonight", and they hear it at a party on a Saturday night why can't they hear it on the radio? So mi just give the people what they want. For years, the people in control were ignoring even the fact that people want to listen to the radio after midnight.

'I had to make all the jingles and sound effects myself – I used to go to King Tubby's – and I wanted to use street sayings and slangs so people can hear them, but I didn't want to use my voice every time. So I had different people doing lines for me – I write a line and have them say it for me; I use Hammer, Big Youth, Clint Eastwood . . . The artists loved what I was doing and support it, because mi know all the artists, so if they say, "Bwoy Mikey mi have them tune and mi naw get no airplay," I would tek their tune, tek out the best ones and get the airplay for them. I have people who go studios, too, hang around Scratch studio, Joe Gibbs, Channel One, Coxsone, Aquarius, everywhere, so I know what's going on. Then I'm playing exclusives like rain because the artists wan' get their new tunes to me. Like mi go studio and mi see Sly and Robbie, them doing this Gregory Isaacs tune "Soon Forward" and me seh, "Sly, wicked tune that . . . Come, give me a dub plate or give me a reel to reel let me go cut a dub." And when I make a fuss about it, mi play and mi play and mi play it until, by the time they ready to release it, "Soon Forward" at number 1 already. Just like sound system. Cassette sell in Jamaica more at that time than at any other time period, because every man used to record my show because I play so many exclusives. And people wan' get their tune to me, but beca' I work nights when I leave and go home already there's a crowd – people queuing up at my house from six or seven o'clock. So my day begin.

'It was exciting, because when mi at the controls at JBC it like pure craziness. The place is like upside down. Phone a ring, man from the JDF coming in – police and soldier – bring me food and drinks, telling me keep it up because you're keeping the crime off the streets, keep it up. And them man there they support me. Because crime rate fall. When I was on the radio, no crime because everybody at home – even rude boy put down them gun and dance or run cassette.'

Mikey left the JBC in 1979 to concentrate on his recording and producing careers. He won Radio Personality of the Year (voted for by listeners, *not* the authorities) in 1978, but still didn't win the respect, let alone the approval, of his bosses. The good news was he gave raw roots reggae an enormous boost and his manic radio deejaying style remains available thanks to the 1979 album *Dread at the Controls*, which accurately recreates a Mikey Dread show on disc.

The first significant release of 1980 was Bob Marley's 'Redemption Song'. Possibly the ultimate sufferah statement, it was one of the very few examples of a Jamaican protest song crossing over to genuine world relevance without losing sight of what it was there for, and irrefutable proof that Bob's international adventure hadn't turned his head. The tune, with its clever lyrics and unconventional arrangements, also stands as a valid sign of how far reggae had come during the previous ten years.

The lovers' rock sounds filtering back to Jamaica from Britain courtesy of the likes of Gregory Isaacs, Dennis Brown, Beres Hammond and Jacob Miller (with or without Inner Circle) expanded the strictly roots outlook into an extra dimension. Meanwhile, roots music had diversified as new waves of players and producers came to the fore, and previously established artists gained the confidence or the facilities to try their own thing. Sly & Robbie had gelled into a skintight rhythm section who, through their work at Channel One during the second half of the decade, pulled the swing away from Bunny Lee's flying cymbal to the double drumming of the rockers sound. They developed a 'militant', high-stepping style that upped the roots tempo, rebalanced reggae and is remembered by Sly Dunbar as having a great deal to do with the studio itself:

'The drums was always up the front of any Channel One production, it how Joe Joe Hookim like to hear things – he cut dubs just to make sure the drums was perfect. So when I play out this new rhythm on the rim of the snare drum he like it and encourage that style. It just that likkle device which switch the whole rhythm up a gear. Also, that studio always have a big bass sound, so with the drums up the front like that the bass can really go on and play *strong*. Which in turn means the drums can do even more without overpowering things. That's how me and Robbie used to work at Channel One and how the rockers thing happen.

'You first really hear it on the Mighty Diamonds' "Right Time". When that tune first come out, because of that double tap played on the rim nobody believe it was me playing the drums, they thought it was some sort of sound effect we was using. Then when it go to number 1 and stay there, everybody started trying for that style and it soon become established.'

It was followed with such variations as clappers and steppers, and the one which made the most impact at the dance, Augustus Pablo's trademark Rockers International riddim. So named after his record label, production company and brother Garth's sound system his patterns took things even quicker, to triple or quadruple time, precipitating energetic, ecstatically abandoned dance moves, perfect for praising Jah Rastafari in a truly joyous fashion. Almost uniquely for the Jamaican music business, nobody copied the Rockers International style, but this wasn't out of respect for copyright control and definitely not because they weren't popular, but because nobody needed to. Nobody else played a Melodica, as Junior Delgado, who worked extensively with Pablo at the time, explains:

'His Melodica give that *bidibidip . . . bidibidip* sound so high and quick, and he construct his riddims around that. He too was a very smart man and know he couldn't just take normal riddims and tempo of everyday songs and slot his Melodica into that so him *construct* a style that will carry his instrument. He knew it was the only way to get it to sound good, and because of that his sound was *always* exclusive to Rockers International.'

By the end of the 1970s the Roots Radics had superseded the Revolutionaries, for all the same reasons as the Hot Session Band of the Day has been being superseded since the days of the Skatalites. This crew were built around, respectively, the bass, drums and guitar of Errol 'Flabba' Holt, Val 'Style' Scott and Eric 'Bingi Bunny' Lamont and pulled together players from the Morwells and the Revolutionaries. Once again they changed the beat by slowing it down and injecting a far more syncopated, almost metronomic feel. Check a tune called 'Jumping Master' which, on the surface, is little more than a throwaway workout with the Radics fooling around, jamming, showing off and generally getting as loose as only a unit so inherently tight can be, but it's the nearest you're ever going to come to that band in microcosm. Listen to the slower, sparer rhythm, the precisely clipped guitar and the mesmerizing bass, all sounding as if they'd been looped, and you're listening to roots reggae on nodding terms with the digital age.

Toasting was pretty much as you were, with names such as Michigan & Smilie, General Echo and the Lone Ranger cropping up among the Dillingers, Trinities and Big Youths. Echo and the Lone Ranger were of particular note, as they were the first green shoots of a radical deejay rethink, with the former favouring bawdy humour over righteous teachings and the latter bringing a British style to the art, but for the time being this was more potential than actual and they essentially conformed to a modern roots way. Dubwise, King Tubby's apprentices Scientist, Prince Jammy and Mikey Dread were showing what they could do on their own. Mikey Dread took the lunacy and excitement of his radio show and committed it to wax in the spirit of the mixes and dubs. It built on the way Tubby's and Errol Thompson did things by combining rudimentary electronic trickery with a very human quirkiness, invention and 'needs must' innovation. Likewise Scientist and Jammy, both of whom had engineered for Tubby's and had recently been responsible for more and more of the mixes. Like Junjo Lawes and the Roots Radics, these were guys who had respect for the past but looked to the future.

With the old-school dreads – Spear, Culture, the Mighty Diamonds, Big Youth and Pablo – still commanding a huge audience at home and abroad, an apparent infusion of new life vibing things up in general, and Bob taking Rasta culture to stadium-sized crowds, reggae had never had it so good. Only twenty-odd years in existence, Jamaican music had established itself on a world stage, and roots stood on the verge of being hailed as the new international pop form.

What could possibly go wrong?

Part Four

Fist to Fist Days Gone

'You find a carpenter come in and say 'im is a producer now, or a plumber gwan come in and seh, "Bwoy, dis ya what mi gon' do now." You *must* find it deteriorate, because he don't know the writing or how to start or how to go about it. So 'im just seh, "So?" and jump right into it. It must mislead you and mislead the people dem.' / Bobby Digital

20

Ring the Alarm

On 11 May 1981, Bob Marley died. He'd been ill for quite a while, had been forced to cancel a US tour in September the previous year, had collapsed in New York's Central Park during that October and had been receiving treatment for cancer in Bavaria, New York and Miami. He was thirty-six years old.

His state funeral was attended by Prime Minister Edward Seaga, who had been elected during the previous year, and rankings from both political parties. It was presided over by the Ethiopian Orthodox Church, while his coffin was carried by members of the Twelve Tribes of Israel. More than 40,000 mourners queued for hours to view the body, and over half the island's population lined the fifty-five-mile funeral route from Kingston to Nine Mile in St Ann. Jamaica's farewell to Bob Marley was – second, *maybe*, to independence – the biggest event in the island's history and probably the only time the nation has been irrefutably united.

Which was no less than he deserved.

But Bob's tragic passing had an equally spectacular effect on reggae's newly acquired standing within the international pop industry, and none of it good. In fact, 'catastrophic' is probably a better description. Well before the end of the year there was very little left of reggae's global perspective except a huge Tuff-Gong shaped hole. It was an almost total collapse that paradoxically was more a result of Bob's phenomenal international success than anything else.

This could be observed most acutely in Britain, which at that point still dominated European pop-music styles and trends. So much of that country's recent audience assumed that Bob Marley *was reggae*, their whole concept of Jamaican music beginning and ending with him, pretty much to the exclusion of anybody else within the genre. Although it's always been touted that Bob's music turned a global (i.e., white) audience on to reggae in general, this really doesn't have a great deal of basis in fact. Yes, thanks to Bob's phenomenal efforts, roots reggae had succeeded overseas to a far greater degree than either ska or the early reggae adopted by Britain's white working-class youngsters. In fact, a dreadlock soundtrack appeared compulsory in some European circles, and it had even started to get noticed in America. But it was only ever a comparative few who did dip a toe into reggae as a wider proposition during the second half of the 1970s, and a lot of them probably would have got there anyway. After all, there always was (and still is) a hardcore of a few thousand white British reggae fans, as shown by some of the successes that came about before Bob broke big: Big Youth's *Screaming Target* was 1973; *The Harder They Come* was 1972; the Maytals' *Funky Kingston* was 1974; and as late as 1976, Dillinger's *CB 200* album could be found in a lot more student bedsits than Marley's *Rastaman Vibrations*. Importantly, though, many who did arrive at reggae record collections wider than Bob Marley through Bob Marley, didn't hang about too long when there was no figurehead for them to relate to. In many ways, reggae became pointless to them round about summer 1981.

Over and above his sheer raw talent and extraordinary charisma, the difference between Bob's mainstream success and almost every other reggae act was down to his presentation of both himself and his music as being so user-friendly. However, the downside of this singular success was that, by the second half of the 1970s, the leap from, say, 'Jamming' to the kind of reggae that was holding sway at the average blues dance was quantum. No matter how much the latter got itself tickled up by the UK record companies, the gulf was often too great. Not surprising, really, when you look at the lengths Bob went to.

From turning the plain old Wailers into Bob Marley *and* the Wailers, a self-contained band-and-singer situation, to tailoring the music specifically to fit the world's stadiums, Bob's subject matter may have been roots reggae but his application was mainstream rock. Just as he'd learned how to behave like a rock star off stage too, playing the part to the hilt – the combination of exotic and earthy, the locks, the licks and Rastafari, the women, the weed, the almost otherworldliness . . . Bob Marley could conform to every stereotype of a black man abroad, but at the same time rewrite the book on what that same black man could be. And he fully understood just how vital this was to his crowd's appreciation of his music: people wanted to buy into the whole Bob Marley experience, which he skilfully delivered as a package without ever losing sight of who he was.

Compare him to, say, Peter Tosh. A master musician, maybe a better tunesmith than Bob, his *Legalize It* and *Equal Rights* LPs made a big impact. At six foot seven he cut an imposing figure, and he could attract mixed crowds by virtue of his signing a deal with major labels and being marketed in the mainstream. An obvious candidate for crossover success? You'd think so; but the self-styled Steppin' Razor then spent his time doing his best *not* to win pop friends and influence people. Peter Tosh would be as difficult as possible with record company personnel. A martial arts expert, he'd deliberately physically intimidate journalists and would imperiously harangue audiences from the stage – 'Your tiny minds cannot hope to understand what you are about to witness' was always a favourite. While this example is as extreme as Tosh's life and his brutal demise, it vividly illustrates the point that cooperation with the mainstream was vital if an act were to succeed within it. Unfortunately, too few roots reggae acts followed Bob's realization that it could be achieved with a minimum of personal compromise.

There were quite a few artists poised to make it in the mainstream in Bob's wake, but nobody really pulled it off, and when you look at the names involved, it confirms the notion that crossing over entailed more than just their musical ability.

The Island Records contingent was well in front; acts such as Burning Spear, the Maytals, Lee Perry, Max Romeo and Dillinger were marketed directly to what was Marley's audience, but in spite of healthy (for the genre) sales and critical appreciation they were relatively insignificant compared to Bob. While Virgin Records were responsible for releasing some of the strongest (and strongest-selling) music outside of Jamaica – their roster included Prince Far-I, Peter Tosh, Johnnie Clarke, the Gladiators – they always seemed to succeed more in a roots tradition.

Punk's abandonment of reggae and its subsequent collapse as a viable pop style didn't help matters. A couple of years before Bob died the punks and the Rock Against Racism festivals drastically cut back on the amount of roots reggae on their respective agendas, firstly because it fell out of fashion and secondly because there were now plenty of white bands playing reggae. From 1979 onwards, the Two Tone craze supplied sufficient exoticism into the UK pop mainstream to hasten roots reggae's redundancy. The Two Tone acts were young multiracial ska bands that revived that music as a natural hybrid of punk's speed and the timing that went with English one drop. This all had a significant effect on reggae sales in the UK, removing the more specialist end of the mainstream – punks who bought records by acts like Culture, Prince Far-I, Tappa Zukie and the dubmeisters. So that when Bob was no more, there was very little to cushion the sales of UK reggae.

After Bob's death, record labels panicked, dropping roots reggae acts as fast as they could, often preferring to spend their money on bands like the Police, Madness or the Clash who played what could be called 'reggae', but who were so steeped in all aspects of the English pop/rock idiom that they represented a far better investment for a record company. The consequent shockwave shook the British roots community to its core, with bands having to adapt to survive. Matumbi split, and Dennis re-emerged with Dennis Bovell's Dub Band, working extensively with Linton Kwesi Johnson: 'Linton wanted to do it on stage with a band instead of just backing tapes, and as he'd become far more famous outside England than at home, we'd go on the road for two years at a time – all over Europe, Japan, America – then have to start all over again because there was a new album out.' Steel Pulse, after enjoying success in America on college radio and touring campuses for a few years, virtually moved there – it's said they did well in the USA because they never tried to sound Jamaican and thus were one of the few reggae bands whose lyrics were intelligible to middle America. They continue to make a good living touring the USA for six months a year. Albeit with a few hiccups, Aswad made the tricky shift into pop – a kind of reggaefied pop/soul – by peppering their innovatively evolving roots catalogue with cover-version hit singles. But so many acts like Reggae Regular, Tradition and Black Slate simply melted away. None of this was helped by the fact that the pirate radio boom happening in Britain about then laid waste to so many of the sound systems. People didn't need to go out to hear the best reggae tunes played by roots deejays, and as many sets called it a day the scene lost much of its focus.

It should be said that few British acts made it as easy for themselves as they might have done. Aswad, Dennis Bovell and Steel Pulse survived the crash either by adopting a new approach or developing a style that went beyond what had become, to a great extent, reggae typecasting. Over the preceding years, too many impressionable young reggae acts had done what they felt was required of them to get a deal and conformed to what many mainstream critics defined as reggae – *heavy* bass 'n' drums, dread sentiments, and that's about it. Unfortunately this limited repertoire had pushed them out on a limb. Also, instead of coming up with a sound that was identifiably British, they went out of their way in their quest for 'authenticity' and so took themselves even further from the mainstream. The Sons of Jah were part of the Grove Music posse from west London, but they always recorded in Jamaica; Aswad allegedly tried to recreate Jamaican studio conditions by steaming up the room with industrial hot air blowers playing on tin baths of water; if true, this would have been before they had the budget to cross the ocean to record at Music Works and Channel One with Gussie Clarke and Scientist. Maxi Priest, likewise, recorded in Jamaica with Gussie, but in each case the most successful music was the stuff that sounded unique rather than generically Jamaican.

Really, though, it was Bob's passing that tolled the bell. As Aswad's drummer Drummie Zeb told me at the time: 'Bob had subtly taken militant reggae into the mainstream and was keeping it there. With him gone, reggae lost a lot of credibility – if the collapse of punk took reggae's crutch away, then Bob Marley's death cut off its legs.'

This was only reggae as it was perceived in the UK mainstream. In fact Bob's passing didn't even mark the death of roots reggae.

It was too far behind the beat to do that.

In Jamaica, by the end of the 1970s roots reggae's future was in its past. Not that it hadn't had a good run. Ten years is a stylistic aeon in terms of the island's popular music – ska hung around just half that time; rocksteady had been and gone in a couple of years; but roots had dominated an entire decade, during which time it vitalized, financed and recruited the Jamaican music industry to the point at which it was putting food on a *whole heap* of tables and had brought this little island in the Caribbean respect from all over the world. Men like Lee 'Scratch' Perry, Mikey Dread, Sly & Robbie and Dennis Bovell became in demand from acts as diverse as James Brown, Bananarama, Bob Dylan, Grace Jones, the Clash and Simply Red. Rock acts from Britain and America were booking themselves into Jamaican studios to evoke reggae's vibe. And, relatively, it was selling by the cartload. But at some point or another the dancehalls had simply had enough of it and the music took its last draw.

This is just the way Jamaican music has always behaved, an aspect surprisingly easy to forget under roots' peculiar circumstances. As the music appeared to have become an integral part of the world-wide pop mainstream and began to be discussed in terms of 'units', 'territories', 'album-chart placings' and 'global market forces', it was perceived as playing by a set of rules that had nothing to do with the Kingston studios and sound systems. It therefore becomes easy to forget that, whatever the wide world required of its reggae, the music was still essentially dictated by the folks back home. In spite of a few producers catering for what was going on overseas, there was always going to be more concentration on the immediate, local audience, an audience which, superficially at least, had been moving away from roots for a while even before Bob died.

Interestingly, and probably because the roots scene was so enormous, there was no identifiable moment at which things changed. There was no pivotal point or definitive single, more a series of situations and circumstances that began to unfold just before the end of the seventies and undermined roots reggae's dominance. The style became so enshrined that it evolved its own set of clichés, both musically and lyrically, which in many cases were starting to come across as pretty pointless platitudes. Having been around for almost ten years, roots reggae was now increasingly removed from the circumstances and musical generation that brought it about. Newcomers had far less reason to understand what it was they were actually singing about: the House of Dread might as well be the House of Pancakes as a significant number of artists started to perceive lyrical righteousness merely as what you had to do to get a deal. Max Romeo's 'Rasta Bandwagon' predicted such a situation very early in the eighties, as it ran down a roll call of improbable Rastafarians – from an ethnic point of view – and paid off with the chorus line *Everyone riding Rasta bandwagon . . .*

The cardinal sin, though, was that roots reggae seemed to have become soft and had been standing still in an environment where turnover and freshness make or break reputations. Check out *Dangerous Dub: King Tubby Meets Roots Radics* or Sly & Robbie's *Raiders of the Lost Dub*, as examples. Both albums are crisply produced, eventful and entertaining enough, but they could have been cut at any time during the six or seven years leading up to their 1981 releases. Bass and drum well up front, spin echo, thunderclap SFX, and strike 'n' fade melody snatches, which instead of writing a new chapter in the Book of Dub, seemed to have turned it back a few pages. In fact these LPs coming when they did, around the time of Bob's death, pointed up how very little things had changed since the glory days of *King Tubby's Meets Rockers Uptown* – cut, coincidentally, around the time Bob broke big. Even Scientist, the engineer/mixer standard bearer for dub's new generation, who apprenticed under King Tubby then was promoted as an artist in his own right by Henry 'Junjo' Lawes, wasn't offering too many new ideas other than superior recording thanks to vastly improving technology. Wild as his series of early-1980s albums were, the most truly inventive aspect were the titles and cartoon artwork: *Scientist Meets the Space Invaders*; *Scientist Wins the World Cup*; *Scientist Rids the World of the Evil Curse of the Vampires*.

It was much the same with the singers, too: Freddie McGregor's 'Bobby Bobylon' or Willie Williams' 'Armagideon Time' or the Wailing Souls' 'Jah Jah Give Us Life' . . . or most of Culture's turn-of-the-decade material – it could all have been released five years before it actually was and nobody would have needed to step back in amazement.

One possible explanation is that this stagnation came about because the industry genuinely believed the idiom had been explored to its absolute outer limits, and therefore nothing new could be added and still be called 'reggae'. This is unlikely, given that every time such an *impasse* had been reached in the past, guys like Buster and Coxsone and Lynn Taitt had popped up to take the music in a fundamentally new direction. Such deviations have been Jamaican music's life blood. Also, there were several recent precedents for reggae moving into completely new areas without compromising what it fundamentally was – witness Third World's first three albums; practically anything Steel Pulse did; *Warrior Charge* by Aswad; Black Uhuru with Sly & Robbie; or the jazzy fusions Rico Rodriguez was trying out, most of which can be found on the *Roots to the Bone* album. That these acts were doing most of their business off-island and were all but ignored by Kingston's producers speaks with enormous eloquence about the level of interaction between the studios and the outside world. Even after Black Uhuru tunes like 'Shine Eye Gal', 'Sensimilla' and 'Sponji Reggae' dominated Jamaican dancehalls there was no effort made to follow Sly & Robbie in that direction.

And that was while Bob was all-conquering.

Far more feasible is the notion that such was the value of roots reggae, in relative and real terms, that the usually adventurous reggae industry figured 'If it ain't broke, don't fix it', and decided it wouldn't be financially astute to step outside or attempt to redefine the deceptively rigid stylistic boundaries. On close examination, many of the players and producers who, in previous chapters, appeared to be (a) tirelessly innovative and (b) standing on the verge of exploiting reggae to the absolute max pulled up short of actually taking it to another stage. Therefore, though guys like Joe Gibbs/Errol Thompson, Augustus Pablo, Lee Perry and Keith Hudson had done inspired work, reggae's rhythmic parameters were always going to limit their inventiveness. There is only so much that can be said – and still make sense – inside reggae's structure in the musical language available to the instruments on offer, so guys who, a few years before, appeared to be rewriting rules and were constantly threatening to take things to another stage were by now playing with a pretty straight bat. And the perpetual recycling of existing rhythms, which by the end of the roots era was reaching epidemic proportions, couldn't have helped matters.

Then the so-called new wave of producers – Junjo Lawes, Don Mais, Sugar Minott – weren't exactly living up to their early promise. Sure, they made a lot of excellent and exciting tunes, but their undoubted potential to reinvent reggae never got beyond that. Audiences were getting desperate for a *real* change in the beat, as sound shifts were superficial rather than basic. There was a massive trick missed with the techno-logical advances: wastefully, these producers and engineers were using new-generation studio equipment to imitate or enhance traditional instruments rather than exploring it as an entity in itself. You can hear this as far back as the late 1970s, with what Don Mais was doing on his Roots Tradition label, when what were essentially the Roots Radics backed the likes of Philip Frazer, Peter & Lucky, Little John and Ranking Toyan, and that sparse, almost metallic touch was beginning to develop. By the time Mais left for New York at the start of the next decade and Lawes' Volcano label took over the same band, their jangling, quasi-industrial sound had been refined into something of a trademark. It goes on as late as Michigan & Smilie's *Downpression* album in 1982, when Lawes and the group still weren't exploring what could actually be achieved by the new studio systems: although the sounds themselves are totally contemporary, the music made with them definitely isn't. Incidentally, Mais and Lawes were near neighbours in Waterhouse, and to this day the former maintains that the latter used to ask him to recommend musicians, which could go some way to explaining the lack of progression in this case.

While, with hindsight, you don't need a university degree to identify these changes in sound and arrangement as proto-dancehall, it was only the departure lounge – the first four of a middle eight. The music industry still needed a nudge to tip it over the edge out of the roots and culture lineage. A shove that, atypically, came from the performers rather than the producers.

The other big factor in roots and culture's decline was that it didn't appear to be working. As we saw earlier, the gang truce brought about by the One Love Peace Concert didn't last as long as the show took to put together, but by the end of the seventies there was even less reason for optimism. The economy was shot, unemployment was soaring, Manley's ambitious social policies had largely failed to get out of the starting blocks and the promise of future redemption wasn't cushion enough for the here and now. Then, importantly, the music, regardless of how righteous it was, wasn't having the effect it used to. Throughout modern Jamaican music's history there's been a two-way relationship between the producers and artists and the socio-political establishment, with songs and records enabling the people to get through to the state. But by the end of the 1970s, as the beleaguered PNP government became increasingly detached from the electorate, any communication was strictly one-way. Of course, Bob Marley could wield statesmanlike clout at the very highest level – the One Love Peace Concert, for example – but reggae's lyricists had lost their influence because Manley's parliament couldn't afford to care any more. Survival, in every sense, was the priority as the government fought for its life from about halfway through their second term of office.

In the run-up to the 1980 general election it must have seemed as if Jamaica had gone mad. The country had been urging Manley to go to the ballot box for the best part of a year, as the situation slid into pandemonium thanks in no small part to the opposition's sustained destabilization efforts. Food shortages, particularly of cooking oil, flour and rice, were commonplace. As a result, rioting broke out regularly and the JLP-biased police had little hesitation in opening fire on unarmed sufferahs. The continuous tide of money and the moneyed leaving the country wasn't slowed by JLP-instigated whispering campaigns among Jamaica's smart set. Social services and the country's infrastructure had all but collapsed – reduced revenue from taxes and duty meant that there wasn't the money to support the day-to-day operating of such services – while the long-term effects of the IMF curbs on public spending were kicking in viciously. And the shrinking economy's assault on employment levels was made more brutal by the mystifying but fairly widespread presence of Cuban workers on the island. Something the anti-Castro JLP was never slow to point out.

Another feature of Manley's government was the establishment of the all-inclusive resort hotels as the preferred way for the (reasonably) well-heeled to visit Jamaica. The first of these appeared in the mid-1970s, and their presence mushroomed as Manley's second term played out. Like luxurious walled citadels on the beaches, their guests paid a tidy sum in advance, in their own country, in its own currency for *everything* – accommodation, food, drink, entertainment, sports. There was no need to stray outside into the 'real' Jamaica – in fact guests were encouraged not to, on the notion that to stay within the walls meant tourists could enjoy a totally risk-free corner of the island. Tropical paradise, for true. But it was hugely damaging to an economy that had tourism as one of its biggest contributors: food, furniture, equipment, drinks were all brought into Jamaica in containers, so virtually no local produce or materials were used; most management-level staff were foreigners; tourists had no need to spend any money in the local economy, either in the resort area or in the country in general; and as for the one-off payment for this all-inclusive holiday, well, that never came anywhere near Jamaica. In many cases, all the Jamaican treasury got from these visitors (inmates?) was the departure tax payable at the airport.

Equally destructive was the all-inclusives' effect on how visitors perceived Jamaica and Jamaicans. A siege mentality came with the sea view – otherwise why go there? Reports of mayhem in the streets and crime against tourists actually became a selling point for these vacations, and if you never went to find out what really was *out there* it was easy to perpetuate poolside gossip.

It was no more difficult to leave an all-inclusive with an unbalanced view of the island and its inhabitants than it was with a souvenir t-shirt. And you can only speculate as to why successive governments have allowed the all-inclusives to occupy an increasing percentage of the tourist market.

It's true that an astonishing level of political violence accompanied the 1980 general election – 'astonishing' even to a country of 2.5 million people that saw 200 lives lost during the 1976 campaigns. This time around it was far worse. The death toll during this run-in was over 800, and the overall brutality – intimidation, rape, assault, vandalism – that accompanied those murders was phenomenal. As the PNP forces and their gangster followers attempted to instigate a reign of terror in order to suppress Labourite support, dawn raids, the shooting up of houses, bars and street corners and execution-style killings became standard behaviour. Not surprisingly, this led to fierce retaliation by JLP gunmen, who were always better armed (in many cases better than the army) and had been awaiting their chance for years. Which prompted even harsher action from a government determined to crush the (opposing) gunmen and in doing so – somewhat ludicrously – declare itself the party of law and order.

Urban political rallies frequently degenerated into gun battles, and in one such situation Roy McCann, a PNP candidate, was killed: the first murder of a politician in recent times. Firefights in the street turned sections of Kingston into literal war zones, and with many innocent people getting shot it was a state of affairs that played right into the opposition's hands. To most Jamaicans the horror on their streets represented a complete abandonment of the protection a government ought to be affording its citizens, and they voted for the JLP in droves.

In less than a decade, we'd come a very long way from the PNP Musical Bandwagon and *lick them with the Rod of Correction, father* . . .

On top of all this, cocaine was now entering the country in significant amounts. Never a Jamaican drug of choice, it had been noticeable on the island for most of the 1970s as, concurrent with its boom in the US market, American tourists brought it in for their own recreational use. It's no coincidence that police records for the first part of the decade show arrests for cocaine possession were all around the north coast resorts and never in Kingston or the interior. By 1980, though, the drug was starting to get a grip in the ghettos as the status-obsessed gangsters were using it for all the obvious reasons. Many people attribute the paranoia and wanton violence of that year's election campaign to rampant cocaine usage among the gunmen.

The drug made alarmingly swift inroads into Jamaican society, its diametric opposition to Rasta's woozy ganja-based ital culture appealing greatly to a new generation of youth to whom natty dread was old and obsolete. Of course, it was helped by the South American producers who were both looking for new outlets and a reasonably easy-to-operate staging post close to the USA. Very soon into the new decade, Jamaica had evolved its own sophisticated international drug economy as shipments stopped off to be moved on to New York, Washington and Miami, and the domestic demand was inflated as the local herb controllers turned to dealing white powder. They'd be encouraged by the South American cartels to trade collie weed for coke – weighted heavily in the cocaine dealers' favour – transactions which soon became as popular as guns for ganja.

It was only a matter of time before the crack pipe took over.

All of the above added up to pressure reaching every part of Jamaican society, but the musical community felt it particularly acutely. Exchange rate movement was dramatically affecting revenue from overseas earnings, which in themselves fell off the edge of a cliff after Bob died. The violence had taken its toll on West Kingston's social life at the same time as Seaga's draconian social policies dried up so much of the ghetto's spare cash. Added to all this, the music itself was having to find a whole new direction, after being pushed along a particular path for an unnatural length of time. Technology was changing the way things were done and audience expectations were being rewritten practically on a daily basis.

The pressure showed itself in a number of different ways. Many of the most influential figures just packed up and left: Keith Hudson and Lloyd 'Bullwhackie' Barnes had long since gone to New York, now Horace Andy and Coxsone joined them there; Leroy Sibbles decamped to Canada; Harry Mudie and Joe Gibbs relocated to Miami; and Sugar Minott moved to London. By the middle of the 1980s even Henry 'Junjo' Lawes, one of the most successful of the new breed of producers, had gone – he'd taken advantage of the post-Bob Marley upsurge in appreciation for reggae in America's Jamaican communities and moved his formidable Volcano sound system to New York.

Others were less fortunate. Augustus Pablo started to show the first signs of myasthenia gravis, the rare nervous disorder that would eventually kill him in 1999, and whether or not this was related to Jamaica's high stress factor, it meant he was to become much less active. For Junior Byles, things were even more serious. He had been in and out of Bellevue mental hospital since the middle of the 1970s and now, according to reports, was scaring the crap out of producers when he turned up to collect any monies owing. On several occasions and for no apparent reason he flung a quantity of alarmingly large clean white bones at their feet. But perhaps the most dramatic example of an adverse reaction to his environment came – wouldn't you know it – from Lee Perry. There are reports, which he doesn't deny, of his walking backwards, talking gobbledegook while striking the ground with a hammer, which, given Scratch's day-to-day behaviour, isn't unlikely and doesn't tell you too much you didn't know already – you could never be sure what was contrived eccentricity and what couldn't be helped. Then in 1979, after his wife Pauline had left him, taking their children with her, he flipped. He'd already completely covered the walls of the Black Ark studio with tiny, meticulously written nonsensical graffiti, and a few days later he crossed out the same particular letters in each and every word. Nobody seemed too concerned – in fact people marvelled at Scratch's powers of concentration. Then he trashed the place and burnt it to the ground.

At the time, quite why Scratch did this was a mystery. While some reports had it as an accident, he was held overnight by police on an arson charge which was subsequently dropped. Twenty years after the event, though, he told me quite genially that he'd burnt down his own studio because he believed *everybody* – from his family to his friends to his contemporaries to his protégés to his record company's bosses – was stealing his music and the only way he could stop them was to remove the means to make that music. He also claimed that it was then that he realized he was 'a white man', because 'The way black people was treating me, how could I be one of them?' Bob Marley and Perry's ex-wife Pauline came in for particular criticism in this respect.

Once again this seems to be a moment of lucidity on Perry's part, as back in 1979 the common theory was that, while drinking and smoking more than was good for even a man of his superhuman tolerance levels, he simply gave up the fight in the face of extreme strain. Gangsters – with and without dreadlocks – were perpetually demanding, and often getting, money; he responded to this by ripping off his artists and potential customers and pulling all sorts of studio-hire skanks. The open-yard policy that had so contributed to life at the Ark was backfiring as any number of stoned or mad (or stoned *and* mad) wasters would congregate there, giving the producer the hardest of times. According to people who knew him back then he had been losing control for a while.

But it really was a chilling sign of how bad things had become in Jamaica that a man with Lee Perry's instinct for self-preservation, downright dauntlessness, total immersion in music and love of confrontation couldn't take it any more. The Ark had been everything to him, and no matter how mad he appeared to have become he had known what he was doing in there and had treated his environment with respect.

It was the end of the Ark that really marked the close of the roots reggae era, as Lee Perry had been at the cutting edge of it since it started. Something radical was going to have to develop. But could it change the beat and still keep the faith?

21

Kid's Play

'When computers came in, that's when the amateurs took over. The Japanese got stuck into reggae and they made it so easy that any man could go down the road there and buy an ordinary little synthesizer that's even got one beat already in it called *reggae*. You didn't need a band, you could do it at home on a four-track and release it – just press up a couple of hundred copies and sell it.'

It's one of the few subjects guaranteed to break Dennis Bovell's seemingly perpetual good humour: the rise of dancehall reggae during the 1980s. Although what he's talking about isn't, in spirit, much more than a slightly hi-tech version of what he and Dennis Harris were doing with the Lovers' Rock and Rama labels, as he goes on it becomes easy to understand his total dissatisfaction with what happened to his art form.

'Reggae had slipped into its karaoke phase. The whole thing about groups fell apart, the whole thing about learning your craft fell apart . . . You didn't have to take a group into the studio, or get yourself a riddim track or anything, just buy a Casio, plug it in in the studio and chat what you wanted to chat. There was no *flair*. Everybody used the same programs, you had no group input any more, or they'd just blatantly nick somebody else's tune and say, "I've written these words to it so it's mine now." And they don't even rework it like versioning used to be, building a new track on an existing riddim, because it's so minimalist it's exactly the same.

'Reggae music had always been about the *new*, now there's

fifty, sixty . . . seventy versions of records out and the buying public's spoilt for choice. But the bloke in the record shop's still only got ten quid in his pocket to buy three records, so now instead of having one huge hit by one person there's pockets of hits, which didn't do artists much good because it was all spread too thin.'

As a master musician, Dennis's reaction to reggae's next phase is unsurprising. The idea that, as he puts it, you didn't need a band or a singer any more, 'just a playback, and one microphone and one man to chat some rubbish on it', was always going to be an affront.

But although he has a valid point, it wasn't quite like that.

Or not immediately. And not without reason, either.

Dancehall reggae was the backlash from those apparently left behind by roots's internationalization – Jamaica's sound-systems crowds, operators and deejays and the producers who were servicing them. It was the ghetto's reaction, taking their music forward in a way that seemed to be deliberately rubbing against the roots and culture that had been selling *a foreign* for so long. Although the style is – in every respect and in all of its manifestations – extrovert to the point of being in your face, it was very much a cultural internalization. Indeed, as the name would suggest, it had no particular interest in straying too far from where the music began; exponents deliberately looked inwards instead of to the outside, concentrating on taking reggae back to its original audiences. In its original locations: Jamaica's dancehalls.

It was as if some sort of safety valve had been opened, cutting in because the reggae of the last few years of the 1970s had started straying too far from the crowds it was supposed to be catering for. As if, and this was something underlined by Bob Marley's massive overseas success, it was being defined by influences other than its immediate environment and was in danger of losing control of itself by conforming to somebody else's parameters. This vibrant, life-affirming folk style was in danger of becoming just another pop music, subject to the whims of the global marketplace – in other words, European/ North American daytime radio.

Producers had seen this happening, or at least those that weren't part of the relatively small bunch having the big over- seas successes had, especially those with an active Kingston sound system – Jammy's, Henry 'Junjo' Lawes and Morris 'Black Scorpio' Johnson, for example. It meant there was far more at stake than simply changing the beat to sell their own records or to big up their set, as had so often been the case in the past. This time they felt the Jamaican music industry was on the line, a bona-fide culture they had seen built up, almost entirely by their sufferah efforts, into something as prestigious as it was profitable. It's worth remembering too that the rise of the music business had coincided with independence, and the two were subconsciously linked. So reggae was always taken to be the most vibrant metaphor of the country's self-reliance. Thus it was vital to stay in charge of the music. The best way to do this was to bring the game back to the dancehalls, where the home producers made all the rules.

There was never any committee meeting or Producers' Association of Jamaica memo sent round (indeed, as far as I know, there never was a Producers' Association of Jamaica). The movement just happened, thanks to the village nature of Kingston's music business and the idea that everybody wanted the same thing. Then, because there never was much of a divide between the sound systems and their supporters, the people took it in pretty much the same way. There was an underlying frustration with roots reggae's continuing shelf life: the roots movement had made so little difference to everyday life in the ghetto that for it to go on dominating lyrics in the dance was clearly a nonsense. Remember, Bob the man may have been deified throughout poor black Jamaica, but Bob the musician wasn't taken at all seriously on those same people's sound systems. Also, resentment was growing into rancour at what was perceived to be a shift in reggae's sensibilities, as those sensibilities were no longer considered quite as Jamaican- oriented as they ought to be. Rasta took hold because it was

503 **Kid's Play**

fiercely pro-black, and roots reggae's advancing 'rainbow culture' sentiments didn't sit too well alongside it.

The most blatant reaction to all this was the deejay explosion at the beginning of the decade. It was a retreat into an area the sound men and record producers controlled; quite literally, a retreat into Jamaicanness: toasting can't happen without a deep yard-style accent – or at least it can't happen with any conviction or sense of purpose. In spite of Big Youth's and Dillinger's successes, nothing had really changed since the judge in Dennis Bovell's trial sneered, 'Do you expect me to believe that people *talk* over records?' To the outside world, including an enormous proportion of reggae's recent converts, toasting was never a valid art form in itself; it was either a pointless, almost parasitical abomination or consigned to the drawer marked 'novelty'. This latter aspect wasn't helped by a clutch of opportunistic deejays who believed the best way forward *was* through gimmickry – step forward, Smiley Culture and a host of others who know who they are, which in itself must be penance enough.

The truly significant thing about the rise of the deejay, though, is that it came from the people within their own arena in the most direct way possible. On the mic in the dance. The beauty of deejaying has always been the lack of investment needed for talent to show up: even the smallest sound systems will attract their share of outgoing types who'll beg the operator to let them *hol' the mic, nuh*, and all that is needed is lyrics, an ability to ride a riddim, verbal dexterity and a quick mind. No cash up front for studio time or for backing musicians; or, as would be more likely, no need for a producer's patronage. And as for auditioning, the crowd would soon let you know if you were rubbish. Practically anybody could get up and have a go, and if a newcomer started seriously rocking the set down there on the corner, the bigger operations would soon snap him up. From which, the recording studio was just one (small) step beyond.

It was never only deejays in dancehalls at that time. There were plenty of singers, too. Little John, Philip Frazer, Peter Lucky, Half Pint, Cocoa Tea and Barrington Levy made their names in it, while the more established figures of Dennis Brown, Al Campbell, Gregory Isaacs, John Holt and Bunny Wailer seemed to have been born to it. But it was the toasters who shaped the style. Theirs was a virtually flawless democracy, of the sort that had been in the engine room of Jamaican music's continuing popular development during the preceding twenty-five years. And as the dancehalls were where the vast majority of reggae's core audience consumed its music, it was always gratifyingly insular.

Subject matter addressed audience needs that were of far greater concern than acceptance into the Kingdom of Jah. But more so than the boy-meets-girl love songs that had always punctuated roots and culture, this was all about what went on when boy takes girl home, or at least to somewhere reasonably discreet. It was slackness: the deejay as some sort of loose-lipped Lothario, bragging to the beat in the time-honoured style of bawdy calypsos, R&B and skas, merely updated to fit in with the 1980s' rhythms and moralities. And while it had been around on the sound systems for a few years, by now its premier practitioners were taking it to the studio, where, in the case of General Echo, whole albums of lewdness were cut. His 1979 set was simply titled *The Slackest LP*, and the Gemini and Ray Symbolic sound-system deejay wouldn't have lost any sleep over a possible Trades Descriptions Act prosecution. That and his follow-up album *12 Inches of Pleasure* marked the opening of this particular floodgate.

Coming through in the lead was Lone Ranger, who deejayed on Virgo HiFi, went on to record for Studio One and Channel One, and did a great deal to move toasting on from the portentous and sometimes grandiloquent ways that had gone before. His was a brisk, bouncy style that put humour high on the agenda as he spiced up his breezy delivery with all manner of scatological noises and daft voices – the trend for *rrribbit*, *bim* and *oink* as lyrical punctuation is widely believed to have started with Lone Ranger. It's an approach that could be down to his growing up in England where sounds like Front Line International and Saxon had on their respective mics Clint Eastwood

& General Saint and Papa Levi, Peter King and Tippa Irie, all of whom are credited with rewriting the rules as regards speeding up the chat and upping the entertainment factor. Early Lone Ranger stuff sounds a lot like Eastwood & Saint, while his sense of fun reflected Tippa Irie's irrepressible good humour. However, interesting as it would be to see another example of the UK's vibrant reggae scene influencing JA, there's a valid school of thought that reckons the fast-talk deejay style came to Britain with Ranking Joe, who was part of Kingston's Ray Symbolic sound system's extended and influential English 'tour'.

Riding hard behind Lone Ranger in Jamaica was a varied and varying posse of dancehall deejays, proving the music and lyrics were never as one-dimensional as is often supposed. The likes of Welton Irie, Johnny Ringo and Nigger Kojak might have merely followed fashion, but Ripton Hilton, as out there as his stage name Eek-A-Mouse would suggest, took scatting way beyond any logical conclusion as he *beng beng, biddy beng beng, skiddy beng biddy beng*-ed through tales of love, life and sufferation over Junjo Lawes' increasingly hard and shiny rhythms. Indeed, in the liberating atmosphere of 1980s dancehall it was remembered that the primary purpose of going out was to enjoy yourself, and humour was a huge part of the original style. Not that roots was completely forgotten: Charlie Chaplin, late of Stur Gav HiFi, kept it cultural as did Brigadier Jerry and, mostly, Josey Wales.

Then there was Yellowman.

Yellowman, or King Yellow as his status afforded him, could only have happened in the Jamaican dancehalls, where the selection of heroes is an entirely self-contained process. Nowhere else in the entire world could a six-foot-plus albino black man survive a childhood spent in orphanages and as a virtual outcast (albinos aren't much above lepers and homosexuals in black Jamaica's pecking order of acceptance), start boasting about how attractive he was to women and become a reggae phenomenon. He was a leering, self-celebratory triumph over more than one adversity, who had the sheer brass neck to title an album *Yellow Like Cheese* and became dancehall's first international icon, the original superstar of slackness.

Thanks to his relentless devotion to slackness, significantly offset against a sharp, often self-deprecating wit and several wholly pertinent sufferah anthems – 'Soldier Take Over' and 'Operation Eradication' being the best remembered – he became dancehall's biggest star. A success that, if you remember the enormity of the roadblock he caused when he first played in London in 1984, has yet to be usurped in scale. During that year he gave the dancehall genre a further boost with *Yellowman & Fathead Live at Aces Disco*, on which he was shrewd enough to want to capture on vinyl the adrenalin-pumping excitement of his deejaying a major sound system. As the first-ever live sound-system record it sold massively, both in JA and abroad, allowing access to dancehall reggae in its ideal environment – a raucous West Kingston lawn – to those who could or would never go near such a place. It's in *Live at Aces'* wake that 'yard tapes' – cassettes recorded at Kingston sound-system dances – started to surface and sold to British youth and Jamaicans of all ages in very large quantities, a trade that remains as brisk today.

Naturally, it wasn't long before Yellow's success made a wider impact.

Once the international connection woke up from the daze they'd been in since May 1981 and realized that reports of reggae's death had been somewhat exaggerated, they busied themselves with looking for the Next Bob Marley. Dennis Brown . . . Freddie McGregor . . . John Holt . . . Virtually anybody with an engaging smile, a headful of dreadlocks and a one-drop way with a pop-tinged tune earned such a prefix – even Gregory Isaacs was briefly touted as a suitable candidate, until those concerned had the privilege of attempting to do business with a decidedly un-Cool Ruler. A few of these NBMs had a similar number of hits, but nobody quite made the grade. Which is when Yellowman's impeccable NBM credentials got noticed: huge core following, proven ability, already an international attraction, highly marketable hard-times background. He was a natural. CBS in New York swallowed hard as regards his un-PC peccadilloes and signed their first dancehall deejay in 1984.

The resultant album, *King Yellowman*, wasn't a huge success, not because it wasn't any good – it had its moments – but largely because Yellow and the Junjo Lawes dancehall sound was just past its combined peak. The deejay had ruled the dance for over three years at that point, and the *King Yellowman* LP saw him start to repeat himself, which, such was the devotion of his Jamaican audience, he might have got away with had the album not been the result of his high-profile dealings in New York. And as for the pop world, there was something of a miscalculation as to Yellow's gimmick factor – CBS thought he *was* one, he, by this time, didn't even think he had one. It left a Grand Canyon sized gulf between what he was and how CBS presented him, into which the company's prospective punters fell.

Yellowman made up for it to his home crowd immediately afterwards with two explosive 'in tandem' albums, recorded with fellow toasters Josey Wales and Charlie Chaplin. With the latter he cut the self-explanatory deejay clash set *Slackness vs Pure Culture*, in which both parties delivered some inspired imagery and rhyme around their chosen subject matter, and Slackness won by a knockout. Although the set was more or less Yellow's last hurrah – the doubling up gave him a boost, but his style and sound was starting to come across as tired – it served a much greater secondary purpose. *Slackness vs Pure Culture* became not so much a defining dancehall moment as a stylistic marker buoy. It made palpable what had been happening to reggae music during the last five or six years and, through Yellow's thorough routing of the righteous, pointed the way forward. It was about this time that previously spiritual deejays such as Ranking Toyan and Ranking Joe realized the wind direction had immutably changed and were sharp enough to reinvent themselves. The latter provided a particularly vivid illustration: in the 1970s he'd had a hit with the single 'Natty Don't Make War'; now, a few years later, his songbook included a number called 'Lift Up Yuh Frock'.

*

While dancehall's and the deejay's development was a classic and a culturally very healthy Jamaican music business way of doing things, there was an inevitable downside. To have such readily available stardom was crucial to the regeneration of the scene, as it removed the filters and barriers and any influence other than the dancehall itself, but inevitably it affected standards. Admittedly, the dancehall crowds were always going to be their own boisterous quality control, but grabbing the mic at an already kicking sound system dance is just treading the foothills of knowledge compared with the celestial peaks of Lee Perry's roots academy or Coxsone's double-decker auditions. And as this boom was for deejays, existing rhythm tracks assumed enormous importance, with recycling and reuse taking precedent: they had to toast on top of something, yet only a comparative few had the resources to create their own backing. Naturally enough, this led to old Studio One and Treasure Isle rhythms being retrod on almost a wholesale basis – particularly Studio One's. Coxsone jumped on the trend himself and started recutting tracks, using mostly singers instead of deejays.

None of this was particularly sinister, or even that unusual, but sitting less comfortably was the continued reliance on contemporarily successful rhythm tracks without the benefit of re-recording. Versioning had for years been a valid and vital part of Jamaican music, but now in the dance it was taking on a life of its own as the backing track became as important as who was on top of it. Riding a killer rhythm could make a star out of a mediocre deejay, because having that particular tune was what counted, and simply coming up with a new(ish) version of it would get that particular toaster noticed, albeit briefly. That so many novices and those without access to fresh riddims were coming through did much to spur this situation on, and it became increasingly commonplace for versions of a track to run into the three-figure bracket. Indeed, it became a craze in its own right – the *new version* of an existing hit became more desirable than a new hit *per se*.

Several of the industry's better established figures began to wonder about the level of creativity involved. Gussie Clarke was one, who redraws his sound-system correlation of a previous chapter:

'Like before, the heights of competitiveness between the sound systems contributed to the way the music changed. Most of the sound systems aren't making records, so instead of worrying about making a good song, the sound system mentality is where everybody is trying to make one record to compete against another sound system. So they get somebody else to do a different toast on top of a record that is popular at their rivals' lawns. Because this period was all centred in the dancehall, that whole competitiveness transcend into the spirit of the music and artists become competitive with artists, and all everybody want to do is outdo each other and be the man. Nobody concentrate on making good songs.

'The problem is the nature of our people. I think in our industry we have more followers than leaders. More *re*-producers than producers. There will always be more versions than originals. People will wait until they see somebody try something and it working and then they'll follow the leader. If one person comes up with a good concept then everybody here jumping on the same concept. It's not surprising to look at the whole situation now – if one person makes a rhythm that works then everybody starts to do it over.

'A few years ago when this really start, it was kind of a stagnating thing. It hold up creativity. You might have one great idea for a tune and then ten . . . twenty derivatives of it, so if you add that up a different way and you have twenty-one great ideas then that would have added up to development. But as it was, all those twenty-one ideas end up the same idea. So the whole thing was stagnating or moving at a very slow pace. Rather than work at what they were doing, everybody just wanted to be a producer or an artist so in the end nobody had no standard to which they were following or trying to set for themselves. Naturally things start to slip.

'With all this sort of competitiveness, the only way people could get the better of each other is by being more extreme. They can't try to do it by writing better songs, because this isn't about good songs. The riddims start to get more and more raw, and the lyrics of so many of the new records is just about slackness and gun and that. It turn a lot of people off, and the atmosphere in the dance changing. Before, you went to the dance because everybody's interested which sounds will pull the crowd tonight; you go to hear what *new* records he 'ave by what *new* artists. Then with dancehall it become a different thing, because there aren't so much new records for people to get interested in. People go to the dance just to watch other people in the dance – it *'ave* to lead to trouble. Man jus' stan' up there and dance, women jus' stan' up there so, and they don't dance with each other. And everybody dressed to kill. And tomorrow everybody will dress to kill again even though they don't have enough money to send them kids to school – fancy hairdos and expensive clothing and they broke the other day.

'There was a big change in attitude, this was more a showpiece statement than fun and enjoyment as it was before. Before it was like a way of life. The big difference between now and when this happened before, this time was there wasn't much of an alternative set of values like there was at the beginning of the roots era.'

Technology was by now speeding up change, but the way new recording techniques were being employed wasn't exactly enhancing stylistic growth. A few years previously, to achieve his bass and drum balance Coxsone had to mic his studios up in a particular way, and moving instruments around could have a dramatic effect; Lee Perry bounced things down too many times than was good for his tapes and so ended up with that wonderful warm sound as the inputs literally knocked the sharp edges off each other; King Tubby experimented until he could reproduce exactly what he heard in his head and often arrived at some equally interesting sounds along the way . . . Different rooms, different techniques, different equipment all led to differing sounds right across the music's spectrum, driving people on by encouraging exploration. Bands of musicians exchanged ideas and chipped in on each other's sessions, as the communal vibe at the Black Ark or Studio One thrived. Over-computerization essentially put an end to all that. Quite regardless of producers working increasingly in isolation, hardware and software were now mass-market and for them to use the same computer program of the same piece of identical – and identically functioning – equipment ruled out any pushing of studios beyond their intended limits. Or trial and error. Or surprises in general. And if that wasn't enough, then you just used the same samples as whatever record was a hit. It made reproducing those successful backing tracks so much easier.

To a master drummer like Sly Dunbar, this was yet another eroding of creativity, but, from an expectedly skins-orientated point of view, he explains how it didn't have to be that way:

'When technology a-start, Jamaica start to move forward with it. From time, people in the recording business rely on good technology – good recorder, good EQs, good microphones – because the musicians were listening to all them American records and trying to get that sound. We knew what we wanted and could go for a good bottom end and get it. It's like everybody say that only Studio One and Treasure Isle give you a good bottom end, but they come first, they really catch the bass stuff, everybody admired them. But because we take to the new technology meant it was available elsewhere, too. Everybody down the line use computers as long as they've been available – Bob [Marley] use computers too.

'You have to know what you're doing with the technology, though. Me and Robbie was using technology that other people was ignoring; I was creating riddim with things in it that wasn't there. I was using my drums to play things that other people might play on guitar. Where other people might use an instrument, I could play that phrase on the drums. It wasn't like we were reinventing reggae music, we just shift the drum pattern to play different beat. If you listen to some of those Black Uhuru stuffs you could hear the elements I was playing like soul drums, totally, instead of reggae because what happen is the tempo of the music is the same, it's just the riddim that goes within that tempo that makes *this* obviously reggae, *this* obviously soul. For us growing up playing reggae and R&B like in clubs, we sort of studied the elements and how to switch and interplay both kinds of music. We knew it was easy to just switch it over and turn it around.

'The drum machine should sound good – it *could* sound good – but they overdo it and so much of it don't have the feel of playing live. As the eighties went on, the music took a dip, took a nosedive. No records coming out in Jamaica that showed any progression of musicianship – there were no songs, there was no creativeness in the riddims and all the music was sounding alike. There was no percussion, there was no little thing going on inside the tunes. It was getting tiring playing the same record over and over again, and then it didn't sound much different from the next one.

'That's why it took such a nosedive because people was coming at what they was doing like it was a computer and not an instrument. When the computers come in they think you don't even have to try, like the computer will do it all for you. Me and Robbie, we don't do nothing we can't do live; that way you can *feel* the music you're playing and when you do start to feel something and you can just go for it. That livens up the tunes, and keeps them connecting with the people on a very human level because they are played by men. Mind you, [*rich chuckle*] some of the things I can do live other drummers can't even do on a drum machine.

'But people using the computers without the skills made the music go very simple, then so many people want to get into it because it don't seem too difficult and so they keep it simple once they're in and it stops it progressing. And a lot of those people don't last because they don't pay no attention to what they're doing, because as soon as a better computer come out then somebody else going to be better than you. I'm still playing because I still play the drum machinery and the computers as if it's real, and I can play drums live. The machine makes it easier for production, you can do a lot of post-production work with a drum machine, but that's all. To rely on them too much means the musicianship will get lost.

513   **Kid's Play**

'These days you try to get a band together to go on the road and you can't, not enough people can play live. That sort of explains the rise in deejays to go along with this rise in technology, because the singers can't get the bands to back them. Today, it would make a change to find a drummer that could even hold a tempo . . . like Mikey Boo, Horsemouth, Santa, or Paul Douglas.'

A third factor in what appeared to be a radical shift from reggae's past came from outside the music business. Or at least outside the Jamaican music business. It was the singularly grim combination of changing political attitudes at home and the rise of gangsta rap abroad.

After the bloody mess that was the 1980 general election, Seaga's new JLP government distanced itself from the gunmen who had previously been so useful in controlling the garrison communities. While it seemed to be a belated pandering to the people, who genuinely couldn't take another such bullet-riddled campaign, what had happened was that this government (and subsequent regimes) realized that if it took a firm grip on the army then it didn't need its own private militia, so it ran out the political thugs.

The gangsters and their gangs – the posses – who had been dabbling in the crack cocaine trade for a little while, followed the trail north from Kingston and introduced themselves to the street trade in New York, Washington and Miami with a ferocity and firepower that effectively laid the locals to waste. They brought with them a Trench Town propensity for gunplay that caught both American law enforcement and drug rivals on the back foot, to take over crack wholesaling and retailing with apparent ease – one mob assumed the handle Shower Posse because, apparently, they showered their adversaries with bullets.

Success on this scale in the cocaine business *a foreign* affected life in the areas they'd left behind in two crucial ways. It firmly established the drug among Jamaica's underprivileged, particularly in the form of crack, because it wasn't expensive and was highly smokeable, and therefore far more attractive to the average ganja user. Ironically, while foreign-aided government anti-drug programmes went to war on Jamaica's ganja business, they virtually ignored cocaine's creeping menace and by the middle of the 1980s the crack pipe held a worryingly high number of citizens in its grip, while casual powder abuse among young men and women was becoming a dancehall staple. Secondly, it brought a relative prosperity to these street dons and their entourages, a significant proportion of which found its way back to the Kingston ghettos they'd not long left behind. There was always a theatrical largesse involved in the gifts that would be sent down from the USA to be distributed among the sufferahs of their particular area, but behind this benevolence there was a serious intent. The 'treats', as they are still called, took the form of clothes, consumer electronics, white goods and furniture – stuff more readily available in Wal-Mart than it is in Tivoli Gardens – and their arrival, by the containerload, usually coincided with lavish gang-financed street festivals held on national holidays. There was always a good deal of cocaine cash being spread around the ghettos too, Godfather style, to help individuals out of trouble or get things fixed that the government never quite got round to.

This was a financial investment that bought security. What had previously been political garrisons turned into gangster bastions, bought and paid for by the drugsmen and therefore under their total control. They were somewhere safe to hide out if things got too hot in the USA, as these guys apparently had the powers to slip in and out of North America and the United Kingdom like black ghosts, and once in their Kingston ghetto strongholds they were virtually untouchable – the drugs dons and their devoted followers were usually far better equipped and much more ruthless than the Jamaican military.

Back home in Kingston was also where they could simply chill out, while making the most of their aristocratic status. And with this involvement in the community came involvement in the music business. The way people tell it, record labels, event promotions and nightclub ownership were ideal fronts for money laundering, with the added bonus of further raising their local profiles. Then as all this offered a chance at national (or at least city-wide) stardom, many actually got interested enough in the business to take on sidelines as producers and impresarios – well, Sly did explain how people got into it thinking it was easy, and a background in pitiless and terrifying violence probably worked in your favour in some parts of that particular music industry. They also offered sponsorship and patronage of their local sound systems and deejays, both at the treats and at their favoured lawns, which all added up to a distinct gangster influence on a significant part of the grass roots of dancehall. And this influence didn't take long to translate itself into lyrics, sounds and attitudes, as deejays and producers either sought to impress their bosses or were virtually functioning under orders. When people talk about 'reality lyrics' they ought to ask whose reality are they dealing with: the man trying to make an honest living or some coked-up drug dealer who, as still is the style, has assumed a nickname taken from a character in a violent Hollywood western.

It formed a vicious circle of desensitivity. There was no improvement in law and order; in fact Seaga's open season on gunmen resulted in an almost open warfare that was catching increasing numbers of innocent bystanders in its crossfire. Social conditions under this government meant hard times as crushing as any that had gone before. Large swathes of the city were under the fist of some of the world's most notorious killers – it wasn't unusual for Jamaican newspapers to liken parts of the capital to Beirut, Mogadishu or Kinshasa. Many of the youth were adopting a gangster attitude to each other and their women – once gun-talk and slackness became popular lyrical currency, so the 'reproducers', as Gussie Clarke put it, felt obliged to take up a similar stance.

And the more there is the more there will be.

Further legitimizing of such behaviour came with the rise of gangsta rap in the USA. Nothing had really changed since the ska guys copped licks from R&B or rocksteady borrowed soul statements, and dancehall looked across the water at the latest black American style. Unfortunately, it was a similarly nihilistic, escalatingly dehumanized 'art' form that, with bizarre symmetry, had also followed on from years of conscious protest soul, solid party-time funk and finally the internationalization (and distinct blanding out) of the style that was disco. It had likewise retreated into itself with rap, hip-hop and break dancing, but that had quickly evolved into something far less ethical – the cult of the gangsta. Although taking a cue from records that weave stories of nightmarish ghetto violence with casual degradation of women is nothing to be proud of – the idea of a clever gansta couplet would be to rhyme *pokin' bitches* with *smokin' snitches* – gangsta's effect on dancehall is undeniable. The reggae style might have got under way first, but the fact that the same perspectives were seen to be held in the USA gave them even greater credibility.

If ever there was a point of no return for Reggae As We Know It, it was the 1985 hit single by Wayne Smith 'Under Mi Sleng Teng'. Curiously, the record had nothing to do with guns or slackness – it's a good old-fashioned ode to collie weed – but it was the first to have no bass-line, and is, therefore, dancehall's clearest line in the sand.

22

Johnny Dollar

There was no reason whatsoever why modern reggae – bass-line or not – shouldn't have continued to do the job it had done since the Sir, the Duke and the Prince shook up Orange Street forty years earlier. After all, it had already survived stylistic and cultural twists and turns every bit as radical. But the route it took through most of the 1980s and the 1990s was never so much evolution as *re*volution. In the past, statues had been moved to one side and the new ones put up next to them; this time around those same statues were being determinedly kicked over. With big hobnailed boots.

It would be easy to say that the reuse of old rhythms kept the lines intact, but that's not really the point. What happened post-roots was that attitudes changed. The reasons for making reggae records were no longer what they had been, and so the spirit of one of the world's most powerful folk musics was diluted. This isn't just a matter of moral corruption in face of the guns and slackness that came in around the beginning of the eighties, either – much Caribbean folk music has a bawdy element; and the shootist pantomimes has been around for years. What made the big difference this time round was the globalization of popular music in general, which meant that the fixation with America as an integral part of the island's music business appeared to be vindicated. Which tended to detract from the effort that might have been put into finding an alternative to titles like "Gunderlero" and "Punaany".

Of course, there's nothing wrong with wanting to sell records in the biggest single music-consuming market in the world, but what counts is on whose terms these sales are made. Kingston's producers had kept one eye on the USA since Seaga's World's Fair trip in 1964, yet, as we've discussed before, the idea had always been for them to crack it in their own way – their reliance on their sound-system crowds was so crucial to the whole industry's configuration they couldn't afford to alienate them. It's significant that after Bob Marley made his compromises, he enjoyed huge sales everywhere *except* Jamaica. Once 'Under Mi Sleng Teng' had introduced a sound and a structure that wasn't traditionally Jamaican – that is, Jamaican as perceived by largely uncomprehending black Americans – and computerization allowed usage of the same samples as hip-hop, US airwaves-friendly 'reggae' tunes stopped being a contradiction in terms. Curiously, at about that same time major US record labels started coming down to Jamaica looking to sign deejays for more money than was previously thought possible: the biggest deals meant Supercat went to CBS, Shabba signed with Epic and Buju Banton settled at Phonogram. It was spending power that unbalanced the fragile, unique ecosystem that was the indigenous record business to the degree that, a few years back, this joke was doing the rounds: it's not applause you hear at the end of Sunsplash performances, but the furious flapping of American record company chequebooks.

That none of the above-mentioned deejays fared much better than Yellowman – Shabba did best as he exchanged Grammies for sustained ghetto credibility . . . you do the maths – is neither here nor there; what mattered was that it was only a matter of time before the home audience started to get bypassed and tunes were being made with America in mind. But the standards involved could never be the same as they would be for making a tune whose primary function was to rock a Kingston lawn dance. It was on the recalibrating of these fundamental values that modern reggae deliberately detached itself from its own history, did its best to behave like every other pop music and subsequently lost a great deal of what had previously made it so fascinating.

Such sentiments may seem like innate prejudice against dancehall or modern reggae in general. You know, an 'Everything was better in the old days' vibe. Or that Dennis, Gussie Clarke and Sly – and myself for that matter – are somehow 'too old' to understand what's going on in the dancehalls today. Not a bit of it. Dennis, Gussie and Sly all work in the new idiom as a musical form, each with a staggering degree of success. What doesn't make sense to them – or me – is the new perspective on life in general that is held by a generation of the country's music business, and the widespread disregard for humanity (or human life for that matter).

Every time in the past that reggae stopped and took on a new direction, it did so with no little acknowledgement of its own history, musical and cultural, meaning that lines remained unbroken and values and standards didn't slip. But it's possible to talk about reggae's latter period in terms only of contrast, not of continuation. The comments made in this and the previous chapter merely show the width of the gap between then and now, and serve to emphasize the point that it's impossible to tell the two stories in the same volume from the same perspective. Reggae pre- and post-Bob's death are different tales and it would be confusing not to treat them as such.

That said, it's important to acknowledge the contrast. The fact remains that reggae in the 1990s may have shifted more units than its 1970s counterpart, but how many genuine superstars has it produced? How many acts today even have any shelf life beyond their initial impact? And it seems highly unlikely that, in twenty years' time, we'll be looking forward to reissued ragga albums. The roll call of deejays dead by gunshot became intolerable, as did the ritual violence that became associated with the dancehall – it wasn't during the roots or the rocksteady eras that the Kingston police had to ban gun records because life was too closely imitating art. And watching women take pride in behaving as coarsely as a minority of men is no fun at all.

There is, of course, the argument that this is 'reality', that these songs are only reflecting the way things are in the ghetto and are therefore a valid expression – they even became known in some circles as 'reality records'. This holds about as much water as a fishing net. There has been a tendency for detached observers to romanticize America's gangsta rap records as being the fractured cries of a suffering people, and Jamaica's gun and punaany records are frequently subject to the same patronizing analysis. But you'll find the vast majority of Jamaicans – i.e., those with no vested interest in this music – are well aware that being poor and living in the shadow of violence doesn't mean you have to degrade yourself, and being black doesn't turn it into something cultural. Indeed, most people take such a strong stance that they believe that if you're not obviously part of the solution then you must be part of the problem, and that anybody who writes lyrics about sex and violence without heartily condemning them is somehow glamorizing them. And history shows how the music business doesn't have to succumb to such allure: witness Bob Marley, who survived a shooting, or the hundreds of other artists who lived in Kingston through the 1980 election campaign and still managed to find upful subject matter. During the rude-boy wars twenty years earlier, the vast majority of Kingstonians heartily disapproved of the violence, but that sort of attitude had simply gone out of fashion among the young, vociferous dancehall crowds.

It can't be denied that such behaviour is having an effect on how things are on the island generally, where there has been an escalating spiral of declining respect for fellow sufferahs. Today's ghettos are literally twitchy with fear, intimidation and paranoia – each visit over the six years of writing this book has been increasingly less relaxed. The traffic lights on the long stretch of Spanish Town Road dividing Trench Town and Tivoli Gardens have long since been switched off because nobody would stop at them. In 1997, a spectacularly tooled-up Tivoli Gardens posse took on the Jamaican militia in a firefight that lasted for hours and resulted in an army retreat from the gang's stronghold – only for the army to return later and, apparently, open fire from a helicopter, injuring innocent bystanders. The time before last when I was leaving Jamaica, as I waited at Norman Manley Airport, news reports of a

Denham Town gun battle the previous night came over the radio, with the announcer mentioning that nobody knew how many were dead because the authorities were unable to go in safely and bring out the bodies.

Obviously, you can't blame the music for all of this, but it doesn't come off completely blameless. Or at least one of the creators of that epoch-making record 'Under Mi Sleng Teng' doesn't seem to think so.

Subject matter wasn't 'Sleng Teng''s only traditional aspect. The tune came together at Jammy's studio in a way that would have done Sir Coxsone or Prince Buster proud. Bobby 'Digital' Dixon was the engineer for that recording, and the way he describes it tells a story that is a virtual clone of those very first ska sessions twenty-five years previously.

'It was Noel Davey, a singer and musician, he was the one who had the computer box and he and Wayne Smith was friends. It was the Casio Rhythm Box, and most of them come with built-in drum beats, but they are not reggae beats, they are like rock beats . . . hard rock beats. But because the sounds sound interesting, what was really done was we took down the speeds of what they had in the machines originally to what was closest to a reggae tempo, *then* we could start constructing something from it. We were just playing about with it, looking for something that could be done; I wouldn't say we really knew where we were going with it. But that sorta thing was usual, because Jammy's a man who was always looking to move forward with what he was doing, and he encourage us to try things. Like if we don't have anything to do, then to experiment.

'Wayne Smith heard the beat that we were playing around with and he start to come up with that lyrical idea – *Under mi sleng teng / mi under mi sleng teng / mi under mi* . . . It was something he'd been thinking about for a while for a song, but didn't have the right riddim for it. Then, because he already had it so far figured out, he come up with the keyboard riff and it starting to sound like a song. From that point we knew we was going to do something different.

'Wayne Smith and Noel and Jammy's start talking about how they would like to do a song that was nothing like anything else, but would still get played at the dance. We all knew that reggae was already for a shift as not much had changed for a few years – studios was going digital but there wasn't nothing *radically* new. After they talked, Jammy's say "Come tomorrow" – I think it was a Sunday – "An' we'll see if we can do something."

'Wayne and Noel come back the next day, and he have the lyrics all worked out, but it had been an effort for us because it was so different from all the other things at the time. *It have no conventional bass-line.* "Sleng Teng", I would say, was the first big song not have one. And the beat was a manufactured beat – it was already in the system – and we had to take that beat and add the chords to it to make it what it was. To make sure it would still work in the dance, but was different enough to get noticed. It was like, *Mek we try and do a little thing with that*, then we hear the sound on playback and it was, *Now mek we do a little thing with this*, and so on. That was how it was done.

'Jammy's took it to play on his sound system either that night or in the next day or so, and it *mash the place up*. Once we put it out, all you can hear is "Sleng Teng", or next versions of it done on the same slowed-down Casio Music Box rhythm. And it did surprise us the way it took off.

'When you do something – anything – you must have confidence and hope that it will turn out to the best, that way anything you do you're gonna do it with a clear conscience and know that you are truly going to try and create something. Then all you can do is give it that chance to go out there and prove itself. True, Jammy's was always looking to push forward, but you never know where it's going to go when you try something so new.

'Like me, Jammy's sticks to what he believes in and he wouldn't put out something if he ain't going to put him heart and soul into it. I feel that's why "Sleng Teng" took off like that, because although it was all digital, we put heart and soul into it to try to make it work on a genuine level, because then even if it don't work we can feel good about it. If you ain't going to do that then don't bother. It will just be a waste of time, a waste of money and a waste of effort – what effort you did put into it, that is. It don't make sense.'

Bobby is 'at home', in his state-of-the-art Digital B studios in the almost suburban area of Hughenden. It was from here, post-'Sleng Teng' and once he'd left Jammy's, that he spear-headed reggae's digital revolution by recording backing tracks by Steely & Clevie and voicing the likes of Shabba Ranks, Johnny Osbourne, Garnett Silk, Cocoa Tea, Tony Rebel, Beenie Man, Frankie Paul, Ninjaman and Red Dragon. This morning, though, there's not a lot of commercial activity at Digital B, other than one of his deejays putting down a special for the Heatwave sound system, the set Bobby has owned since the late 1980s and operated for longer than that. The vocal is a freestyle semi-sung/semi-toasted wordplay on the idea that the Heatwave set and Kingston town are both '*Hot!*' and Bobby is working the thirty-two-track desk surrounded by all manner of outboard equipment. As he deftly but gently teases a springy, instantly uplifting tune out of what started off as an essentially flat riddim track, the playback sounds as exciting as practically any hit single.

While this is going on, the producer himself is relaxed enough to play a game that might or might not have been a test. Each of the three or four guys at work in the studio, including the dread voicing the jingle, very straightfacedly introduce themselves to me as Bobby Dixon and convulse with laughter as I look understandably confused. Eventually the real Bobby emerges from a side room laughing just as hard, and I'm not sure which one of us is more relieved that I know who he is.

Bobby 'Digital' Dixon is good humoured, hospitable, informative and very very funny. And why shouldn't he be? Thanks to his involvement in 'Sleng Teng' and his subsequent years of success advancing the digital style, he enjoys a thoroughly deserved place in Jamaica's music hierarchy. But then as the continuation of the line that will see King Tubby's legacy into the new century – Jammy's apprenticed under

Tubby; Bobby learned his trade from Jammy's – he was always assured as much. He is one of the most relaxed and comfortably seated men in Jamaican music. Except when you get him talking about what that same Jamaican music has become in the years since 'Sleng Teng'. Ask Bobby Digital about this period, the one he and Jammy's more or less fired the starting gun for, and his sunny demeanour clouds. He's no less eloquent and his remarks are no less carefully considered, he's just not as happy about things.

Perhaps the notion of no bass-line turned out to be far more ominous than it appeared at the time, as during the decade or so since 'Sleng Teng' dancehall reggae – or digitial, or ragga, or roughneck, or whatever you want to call it – lived up to Gussie Clarke's worst fears. That's when it became that culture of extremes, pushing itself into new areas of musical bleakness and lyrical unpleasantness. The slackness of Yellowman and General Echo seemed gentle compared with the humiliating 'punaany' lyrics that were to come; that all-important MTV-friendly video became an exercise in lewdness; deejay clashes became literal rather than musical situations; and artists boasted about their propensities for violence to such a degree that 'gun records' became an accepted sub-section of the music. Yes, there were some alternatives, much of it from the Digital B studios, but the new style achieved by far the highest profile and became reggae music's most obvious growth area. It got to a point at which the police banned gun records in response to the appalling rise in violence at sound systems.

Bobby takes no blame at all for what happened in the wake of 'Sleng Teng'. In fact, he remains quite horrified at how it affected not just the recording industry but the dancehalls themselves and Jamaican life in general. Tellingly, his summation of this 'new-generation' producer bears out a great deal of what Gussie Clarke had to say:

'It wasn't going digital make it go that way, just a lack of creativity. Like 'Sleng Teng' or 'Boops', people tend to use one riddim too often now when in the earlier days you only find like one song on a riddim or perhaps two or three. *That* was the problem right there, too much songs have been putting on one riddim, it sorta make people less creative and the audience less imaginative. In this age and time people are jus' dancehall fans, they're not *music* fans. They are just buying riddims, not the vocals or the personalities or anything . . . just pure riddim.

'That's why I don't try to use a riddim that is just one straight beat, you have to have riddim with melodies so people can recognize that. Otherwise all riddims are sounding alike. You have to establish certain things with each artist and make the artist have their own sound, then people are looking forward to hearing *this* person sounding *that* way. It gives you certain standards that you try not to go below, or you try to always improve. But when you're just dealing with a riddim that everybody else is using you have your standard there and there's no need to improve.

'But where it goes most wrong is it's not making reggae music for the people, just for the sound systems. It's a sound-system thing, with deejays in competition, which was going on fine until it deteriorated down the line from the real parties and the real dance, and end up as the swearing and the disrespect and the arguments and whatsoever. The tunes they started making were really pure sound-system tunes – specials – but when it get popular response in the dance, that is what they going to put on the record and say that it will sell. Because if it going on so well in the dance then it *must* sell – with the vulgarities and swearing and everything. And it get the things outta line.

'The violence escalated. Sure, parts of Jamaica are violent places, but it was above what it was supposed to be. I don't know if it is something in the atmosphere make people just get violent, or if it's the system or how people are living or what that they get so, but the whole thing just get outta hand and the music don't help matters at all. With those records it's seen that the dance is the centre of those things and people start get scared to go to the dances. Which don't do the whole industry any good. Then the police start to come to the sets and clamp down on any sort of music – any way they hear a little music they go to turn it down. From when the music turned down, it like the people dem are *"Bwoy, mi can't tek them low music,"* and them gone. We lose even more people.

'I don't even attend a dance any more – if I want to go to a dance I have my studio, so I play what I want to play in there. Or to go to a dance where you can really enjoy yourself, the best thing you can do is drive out to the country and stop by one of those neighbourhoods where you hear a little music playing and find the little sound systems like in a village or something. It's there that the vibe will be nice, you can sit down and drink two beer and t'ing and hear some sweet reggae music. That's where you can enjoy yourself.

'The radio don't help it, either. True, Irie FM [Jamaica's first all-reggae radio station, on air from 1990] give a lot of youth the privilege to be heard, because when there was just one radio station they dictated, so if there was one little act out there that needed that thing from the public and it couldn't get play then it wouldn't get heard. Same way as you wouldn't have heard of Garnett Silk and such and such and such artists. But now there is so much radio they start to behave like sound systems – as soon as one station hear a Power FM playing it, or Class FM, or an Irie FM playing it the next one is going to play it – or maybe a next version – because it a popular song now, and they start with that same competitiveness. All radio stations did play their part in boosting the music and giving certain youth an opportunity to be heard, but they let things get out of control.

'The competitiveness situation lead to so many records being made that there wasn't the same vibe of a few big tunes like there was a few years ago, so everything suffer. It spread too thin. And with this number of records is producers who don't know what they are doing. It's like you find musicians who used to play live can't get no work, can't get nowhere to play so they start to produce . . . any little act they can find to really keep bread going on their tables. So this musician tries to produce, but his real thing is not producing, his thing is really creating music, *but that don't stop him*. Like you find a carpenter come in and say 'im is a producer now, or a plumber gwan come in and seh, "Bwoy, dis ya what mi gon' do now." You *must* find it deteriorate, because he don't know the writing or how to start or how to go about it. So 'im just seh, "So?" and jump right into it. It must mislead you and mislead the people dem. Most of these producers right now, they cannot produce a vocal song, they only can produce a deejay song.

'Then there is the producers who choose to produce certain songs. It's like they stop look 'pon it as a *message* and to educate the people, and start look on it as a 'ustling – how much they can make off this, or if they do that how much they can make. *And they are not looking at the damage they are creating along the way.* Is like "All right, make a piece of money offa this one *now*," but don't look at the long term. Like they are just thinking of today and not tomorrow. And they must remember that they have children coming up also. They cannot fill up the place with certain things and have kids coming up and hearing that and believing that's what they got to do when they grow. These producers just trying to reap what they can reap, but we don't want that. We want to try and curb that right now, because with so many 'ustling songs, songs of the moment, you hear about the other songs because they don't fit and they don't get played. It like they weren't done good enough for the public, but really is they get lost in the rush.

'So it's not just the quality of the songs either, the whole music business . . . the whole record industry deteriorate. The dancehall thing was pushin', pushin' at young people and creating a very small scene that wasn't universal like you used to have with old-time tunes or the Studio One sounds.

'Look, a big person not even *looking* to go and buy a dancehall song or wanting to hear them in the dance. They're looking to hear a nice singing song, a nice vocal song, that they can take home and put on their turntable or in their CD and listen to. A person of forty years old going into a shop to buy a deejay song? *To do what?* Go and play that in their house and feed their kids on? That is totally impossible.

'It's created a wider gulf between the young people and the old people, at a time when the young people need guidance.'

Gussie Clarke is no less damning, further castigating recent developments from a strictly business angle. He believes that corporate American involvement in reggae, for so long the industry's Holy Grail, was as damaging as any creative influence, with the big deals with the American companies in the early 1990s curtailing too many Jamaican careers.

'Shabba made a lot of waves, at a time when everybody still sitting down looking for another Bob Marley. Major companies abroad looked at dancehall and saw this as a new music that was happening – after all, it somewhat felt international, now it related to other forms, you know pop and non-traditional. It look like it woulda happened and a lot of record companies came in, signed a lot of artist left, right and centre and are now dropping them left, right and centre. 'Cause when you add the numbers up it just can't happen.

'Most of the reason is because they took the artist out of their environment, and in this country, in my opinion, an artist alone don't make things happen. It's a package, and success depends on a lot of elements going on around the artist – to make it make sense you have to carry them the way they are or leave them alone. And by the time they've taken an artist back up to New York, or wherever, for a year to do an album, by the time they come back to Jamaica they've lost their market here.

'Then many people believe the deal is to get a record deal alone. That's not the deal – the deal is to keep the deal. But because of the way so much of the business works here so many get it wrong. Hypothetically, if a man got ten dollars to make a record he probably try to make a five-dollar record and have five dollar left for himself. In reality, too many artists and producers took the advances, spent off the money and delivered a substandard record; when that get rejected there's no money to do no proper work on it to put it right. So when the record don't work the company don't want the next. Me personally, I woulda made a *fifteen-dollar record*, then I might have five more albums to do. I'm not interested in the immediate though, I'm interested in long term, but that wasn't the way many Jamaican artists saw foreign deals. But then a lot of them inexperienced and got into music too easily.

'Now, if you look at many artists, the companies are dropping them. Managers are trying to shift them round, trying to get a next deal, and three-quarters of them will be dropped within the next two years. Those who isn't dropped by now.'

While it might seem remarkable for two guys who have always had a strong international aspect to their businesses to be as uncomplimentary about the first Jamaican music to have genuine overseas opportunities, the point they're both making is a vivid description of what went wrong. The music's branches strayed too far from the roots and so began to wither. Maybe it was losing the bass-line, but as dancehall has progressed through its various manifestations it hasn't done the music as a whole a great deal of good. Reggae's total volume of sales is apparently up in recent years, but its profile hasn't been this low for a long time.

Thankfully, though, things appear to be turning round. Or at least they are in the music world.

23

Healing of a Nation

Phillip 'Fatis' Burrell is representative of how pre- and post-'Sleng Teng' attitudes to both music and life in general can work together in perfect harmony. Directions to his 'yard', once you've found the street in the Blue Mountain foothills just above the city, involve looking for the house that has the biggest satellite dish. It doesn't disappoint, either: Fatis's receiver is such that you could comfortably raise a family underneath it, and the house is of a similar superiority – he'll proudly tell you a couple of judges and Kingston's police chief live in that very road, a neat avenue of sprawling, whitewashed bungalows nestling in large, beautifully landscaped plots. Once you get inside the gate it operates like a dreadlocks camp – albeit the five-star version, but there's a communal pot on the stove, locksmen wandering about, everybody quiet and courteous, blessings said before eating and the koutchie is passed with regularity. It's the sort of borderline bizarre world within a world within a world you could only expect to find in Jamaica and it gets you thinking . . . would a dread yuppie be a duppie?

Fatis runs the Xterminator record label and sound system in Kingston, and with a history going back only as far as the mid-1980s his grounding is utterly digital – apparently Xterminator was the first big sound system to incorporate a CD player, although they still play mostly off vinyl. But he's astute enough to know how much can be learned from the past, and is of sufficiently wide vision to realize how much the future has to offer. When he produces tunes for the likes of Sizzla or Cocoa Tea he'll create a hard, exciting dancehall sound, but he'll give the rhythms true depth by using seasoned musicians of the calibre of Sly & Robbie, Dean Frazer, Robbie Lynn and Steve 'Cat' Coore. Fatis's global perspective is second to none, as he knows the music has to succeed off-island to advance itself, but he also appreciates it can't lose touch with what it started out as. Only that morning he has flown up from South America where his Spanish-language reggae tunes do very well indeed – a rootsman's vibe is, apparently, the same in any tongue – and he'll create a modern Rasta reggae sound in environments as apparently unlikely as samba and bossa nova. But, importantly, he has long been aware of the need for change within the dancehall, and thus has brought his Rasta ideology to bear on his musical sensibilities when working with his cultural singers and deejays, notably Sizzla, Ras Shiloh, Mikey General and Luciano. The result has been a refreshing, rootsy warmth and openness that – surprise surprise – does very well abroad.

He doesn't let what needs to be done get in the way of what he knows he should be doing, and as a result has gained success and retained integrity. While not too keen on being formally interviewed, he's quite happy to sit and talk about his situation, and what's going on in general. And, for such a mover and shaker, he's surprisingly modest.

'It was inevitable, somebody like me should end up living so. Before, so-called respectable people used to think that Rasta was mad, that the bredren were sick in dem head. But now it's everywhere – Bob [Marley] did a lot to make this happen, because he showed what Rasta can achieve and how much of an asset Rasta can be to Jamaica. In many ways it was only a matter of time, because the youth who were part of the dreadlock explosion of the 1970s have grown up and many are now middle-aged and in respectable employment. People up here might not want a dreadlocks for a neighbour, but then they see you've got the same standards as they have and you want the same for your kids as they do and so their attitude start to change.

'In many ways, it's a mark of how far Rasta has come that it doesn't need to be intimidating any more. It's like in the music, we know the pop style can work, because there's now the idea that it has to connect on a number of levels. And not be afraid to put on a performance, because the people want some entertainment – that's why although all the big sounds have CD players, they mostly play off decks because it's still about putting on a show with the twelve-inch singles on the decks. Juggling.

'The performance element is coming back in many ways, as nothing but the specials on the sound systems got rid of a lot of that, and people need it. Now reggae is working hard to include those values of putting on a show – it's returning to a very old-style way of doing it.'

One of the most spectacular of those performers is Luciano, who I'm here to talk to this evening, and if Fatis is the textbook example of a what can be achieved as a manager/producer, then Luciano is the very model of how an artist can bring consciousness to dancehall. He's the leading light in the Xterminator stable, bringing a much-needed combination of joyousness and piety to the music with cuts like 'It's Me Again Jah', 'Black Survivors', 'Sweep Over My Soul', 'Moving Up' and 'Where There Is Life' frequently topping the Jamaican charts and doing very well in the UK, and getting this over in a stage show that works so hard it leaves the audience in need of a little lie-down.

Born of a strict Adventist family in Manchester, up in the hills of Jamaica's interior, Luciano's approach to his craft has always been one of spirituality – he got into music because, at the age of eleven, the only memento his father left him when he died was his homemade guitar. Now, twelve years later, he's a devout Rastafari and is another who remains convinced that a country upbringing means an understanding and respect for life that is perhaps not so prominent in Kingston.

While words such as 'consciousness', 'humanity' and 'positive' crop up an awful lot in his conversation, Luciano isn't above the odd earthly practical joke. When he drives me back to my hotel, he exhibits a sharp sense of mischief. Hanging from the interior mirror of his car is a generous sheaf of freshly picked herb superb, not the ideal travelling companion for two dreads and a '*Hing*-lishman' in an upscale suburb after dark. When such a consideration registers on my face, he and the dreadlocks in the back hoot with laughter. 'Go on, touch it!' It's very fine latex. Apparently many people, including a few police officers, have fallen for this ital prank.

But that comes later. For now he rather appropriately sits us out on the terrace under a canopy of branches where Jamaica's vociferous nocturnal wildlife occasionally threaten civilized conversation levels as he explains his alternative strategy:

'For a long time I feel there was a need for change. Since when I start get into the music business in the early nineties – when I first come to Kingston I train as an upholsterer. It was as if I felt within myself that I had that extra little thing that people would be willing to hear. I said to myself I've been listening to singers and deejays ever since Bob Marley and I really didn't feel or hear that kind of protesting spirit in the message or in the songs. I knew what I was listening for but I didn't hear it fully until Garnett Silk come, or Tony Rebel. Or Capleton started coming about or Buju Banton turned about. That's when I started to make my own little contribution, because then I *knew* that was what the people wanted.

'I was at least more concerned about expressing myself as I saw it fitting, than becoming like a scholar watching the music. It was more wanting to exist and make myself known – make my presence felt. So I didn't watch much about the other deejays and what they had to say, because I knew within my soul that people out there really want to hear the positive music, and as long as you give it to them they'll appreciate it. These are the elders, people who respect righteousness and have a love for the Almighty and have a love for themselves.

'This is really important part, as we realize that what has really caused the drift, or all the negation in the music, is really wrong teachings and the very sickening environments that the people that had been coming into it had to be growing up with.

They grew up seeing guns and seeing girls dressed X-rated and people being abused and manipulated, so they come and they sing about it – then others who *don't* see it, start sing about it because they think that's what they *should* be singing about. Their consciousness may not have afforded them a better inspiration, and I believe it took a one from a more spiritual environment, like Bob . . . or Garnett Silk . . . or myself from the hills. Growing up with a very Christian kind of family with my father an Adventist, my mother a very strict Adventist also, we grew up with that spiritual awareness and this is what I brought with me in the music. I never left that roots and I know that it's that same righteousness that has brought me to this position in life.

'I've never done anything else . . . I for myself could never express myself in no other way but in a positive way which I consider expedient or useful to help or to uplift humanity at large.'

Why did he think it took so long for consciousness to raise its head again, and why did it happen when it did?

'Based on my observations, it would seem as if everything in life goes according to cycle. Same in which crops may come in which season, banana may come this time, or mango or pear, you realize that consciousness has that same kind of cycle. Especially the consciousness of man. It's like the swinging of the pendulum, we drift from the consciousness of the fold into negation, we suffer and then we acknowledge where we have been wrong and rise again. And then you'll see it.

'People who may not have been as stern and as ardent as Bob Marley is – and as I am – drift constantly, because, as I say, it's a constant struggle for that righteousness . . . even me, many times I feel like I wonder if I'm making any sense or if I'm making any difference. But you still keep doing it because you know it's as if this new consciousness has dawned, and, luckily, you're a recipient of the inspiration that come from above. I just realized that all that was missing was someone who was willing to sing for the cause of humanity, for the uplift of the young generation. Musicians are like Moses, they take messages through music through the oppression, the depression.

535 **Healing of a Nation**

'But people will not appreciate or realize how powerful the music is and how useful it can be to uplift the youth until they've really suffered a lot. There's a saying that the cow will not take care of its tail until the butcher cuts off a piece! I observe carefully and I realize that it's as if our souls were cave in under the pressure and we realize we *had* to find some alternative, 'cause we have teenage pregnancy, we have drop-out from school, we had high-school graduates leaving school have no job, no skill or no trade, we realize the politicians are not really helping fully and it's only when election time is near you see them coming out. We had become spiritually bankrupt and the only way to go was to come back. When I read the holy scriptures, Paul says "The same one who goes to the abyss is the one who will rise again and feel the glory of the Almighty, a taste of his heavens."

'Basically, what I gathered there is that when I listen to certain tunes with certain derogatory lyrics – deejaying about sex or secular things – I realize that no doubt the music had reach its limit in terms of derogatory statements. That was its abyss and this new consciousness no doubt had to reassure itself in temples like myself, Capleton, Garnett Silk and Buju Banton. It's as if people saw the consciousness has dawned upon us and the spiritual initiation gripped us to a higher level of expression as they appreciated how we seek to express ourselves in a positive way.

'It affect the musicians, too, because I realize that the musicians tends to get a natural feed off the singers or the deejays – the singers and the deejays having the word and that thought create the thought form in the minds of musicians. So when I come with reference to the Almighty – "Lord Give Me Strength", "It's Me Again Jah" – these kinda songs kinda trigger off new a thought form in the minds of musicians, and so we all saw fitting to go and do some *fine* sounds that were in agreement with the words.

'Fatis went back to pick older musicians, who didn't come up in this environment, who would understand more and be more open to the vibe we were trying to create. But we could never have done that without love. Music is really an expression of love and it's because of the love – we have respect and natural love for each other in the studio – when we in the groove to play we just have this natural thing. Nobody not uptight, because if you want to send a message of love then it has to sound like love.

'Also that we've actually got musicians make all the difference, something which hadn't been happening for a while, but because that's how Fatis work that's what he did. That's where the hard work is. He *spends time* on his music, and he spends money, he makes sure the quality's good and it's not just about that overall big profit. It's about getting a message out there in a decent package, so people can have something to feed on, psychologically. It will last longer that way, too, because it's not just jumping on whatever bandwagon is come along.'

And the future?

'It have to keep moving. Reggae music always keep moving, never stand still. Life is a constant movement and everything in life moves: this earth moves around the sun and within the sun is lots of movement, movement of gas from the inner to the outer. So I realize that it's the same principle with anyone who come as spiritual; they have to be in that form of moving – searching to find better ways of expressing themselves. Wanting to know more about their existence, this life, their being, about the higher being behind everything and all that. Especially in the city here when you start recording, if you become too complacent and stop moving it's too easy to lose that spiritual essence. So you got to be moving to and fro, going back to the countryside, getting the natural vibes and keeping that inspiration flowing.

'The music has to stay open and relaxed, too, because before when you have the spiritual music it get too deep, it go in on itself and become too 'eavy. I and the others realize that when we sing we sing not for ourselves, but we sing praises unto the Almighty and we sing for the uplift of humanity out there. If you get too deep and too complicated people will not get that message or the essence, so you need to be as natural as the wind that blow. That is what life is really about, and once you start getting too deep and going lower down, anything that goes too deep suffers decay.

'I and I realize that just like the wind, I and I come and go. And if I express my inspiration in a very natural, imaginative way I know I can touch the hearts quicker, because people don't want anything to really burden their souls and they don't want anything too cumbersome. They want something they can meditate upon, or *relax* with . . . something that they can really pull through the day with.

'So I hail my brothers and my heart beats with love and the warmth and the respect. And that's the same thing as you will feel from my songs – my songs are nothing but an extension of my soul.

'It was never easy. There were times when it wasn't usual to do that sorta music and not everybody want to try and make it work, but what really kept me going or gave me the additional impetus was that love for singing and wanting to make a joyful noise. When I started singing – some cover versions and so on – it was just to lift my soul and lift my spirit, because that really is the best way to go through life. So although sometimes it was hard – very hard – even to make an entry into the music fraternity, I realize is that love for music and that humility at all times kept me going.

'Now, as I feel I get to know more about life so my conscious-ness grows, and I expect that growth also in the music. It's really inevitable. I seek to know more about myself and the music, and I'll find better ways to express that love that I feel within. It's a principle that runs right through what I do. How I see it, we have to approach life that way if we're going to be any meaningful role model for the youngsters coming up – the musicians – then we've got to live and express ourselves in the way Jah live and shine his sun. The way in which the sun shines, the way in which the river run, the way in which the wind will pass against us.'

Alongside Luciano is a whole next generation of roots artists, as articulate, as contemplative and as unburdened. Vitally, though, they're dancehall veterans, who understand the blind alley aspect to so much of it and have worked out how to satisfy the music's need to exist in the 1990s without compromising from either a musical or a spiritual point of view. They also understand that by remaining true to its roots it probably stands no *lesser* chance of succeeding on a world stage, but, if it does all go horribly wrong, there will still be an audience for it back home.

The new roots roll call includes, most prominently, Tony Rebel, Junior Reid and Michael Rose, who have been ploughing this furrow longer than most, Sizzla, Everton Blender, Admiral Tibet, the late Garnett Silk, Bushman, Yami Bolo and Capleton – who saw the errors of his ultra-slack ways, as did Buju Banton. The latter became notorious for the anti-homosexual tune 'Boom Bye Bye', then seemed to step back from his own violence and slackness to grow locks and cut the deeply spiritual *Til Shiloh* album in 1995. It was said that a big-money deal with the US giant Mercury Records was at the back of such a conversion, but his next album, *Inna Heights*, saw him back on the Jamaican Penthouse Records with no noticeable drop in righteousness. Added to this register is the lovers' rock brigade: a formidable array of talent including Sugar Minott, Frankie Paul, Cocoa Tea, Beres Hammond, J. C. Lodge, Nadine Sutherland, Chaka Demus & Pliers, Sanchez, Wayne Wonder and a reborn Marcia Griffiths.

It's a mixture of the old, the new and the in-between that is turning what was a wave into a tide, as their combined audience credibility and modern musical achievements entice other acts to test this righteous water. Youngsters coming up on the little sounds are as likely to chat spirituality or love (as opposed to sex) lyrics; nowadays hardcore guys like Beenie Man, Bounty Killer, Simpleton and Ninjaman feel the need to have one or two praises to Jah tucked away in their repertoires; and the compilation album series Conscious Ragga now runs into several volumes.

There is a real dancehall alternative being presented, and knowing how swiftly Jamaican music can change direction total reinvention could come about sooner rather than later. Bobby Digital thinks so, and a man with his skills, history, foresight, intelligence and lyrics deserves to close out, a touch more pragmatically than Luciano:

'It is cleaning up now, it had no choice, the music business was killing itself. Literally. We still need to get more grip on what we are doing, it need a little more help and force behind it, but right now we are organizing. Me and Gussie Clarke and Mikey Bennett and Jammy's and Xterminator, we're trying to clean up the act. We are trying to get things on more of a clean level, and because we are doing it so I don't see why the other people them can't do it same way.

'In the long term I think reggae is heading right back to where it once was. Good tunes, good singers, good messages . . . This is what the people want. I think the people needs it to really take them away from their anger because all what the people dem can trust in all over the world is music. Music lead you. They say that all the badman records were what the people already were, a reflection, but that wasn't true at first. They lead many people into those ways because if that's what the yout' hear on the radio and in the dance then until they know better that's what they're going to think is reality. But it isn't the reality for most Jamaicans. Most Jamaicans want it to stop.

'You have to stop right there and turn over a new page and let the people hear what they need to be educated. Is what you fill people with, that is the way they grow and that is what will be within them. If you feed them with violence they're going to be vile. If you fill them with love they're going to be lovely.'

Further Reading

Over the past twenty-odd years I've read and collected books about Jamaican music and culture. These are the ones that have made the biggest impression on me and my thinking; they are works that have taught me stuff, let me into worlds that would otherwise have remained closed or simply kept me entertained. As such I have no hesitation in acknowledging them as sources of reggae intelligence or direct information and recommending all of them as required reading for anybody who wants to go deeper into either the music or Jamaican life in general.

Hope you get as much out of them as I did.

Kevin O'Brien Chang and Wayne Chen, **Reggae Routes:**
The Story of Jamaican Music (Ian Randle Publishers)
A fine detailed history of Jamaican music from 1960 to 1997 traced through a chronology of crucial singles and interviewettes with key people. The book that succeeds on two distinct levels.

Sebastian Clarke, **Jah Music** (Heinemann Educational)
Working from the point of view of Rastafari as the foundation for reggae music – this book was written *way* before dancehall – Clarke is one of the few writers to draw any form of connection between Jamaican music and Jamaican life. As a result, *Jah Music* is one of the most absorbing narrative histories of the music there is, perpetually surprising with its never obvious interview choices as it goes so far beneath the surface and reintroduces some of the music's almost forgotten heroes. Lively, opinionated and never less than fascinating.

Marc Griffiths, **Boss Sounds: Classic Skinhead Reggae**
(ST Publishing)
Essentially a selective list of reggae singles favoured by skinheads,
released in Great Britain at the end of the 1960s/beginning of the
1970s, and categorized by UK label. But it's not nearly that dull.
Griffiths' entirely personal viewpoint on an aspect of the music now
so deeply unfashionable it's almost been forgotten is most welcome,
and is as entertaining as it is informative. Meanwhile, the pen
portraits of key figures, anecdotes and reproduced memorabilia and
record labels allow a peep into his world that makes *Boss Sounds*
more than merely a reference book.

Colin Larkin (ed.), **The Virgin Encyclopedia of Reggae**
(Virgin); Steve Barrow and Peter Dalton, **The Rough Guide
to Reggae** (Rough Guides)
The only two reggae reference books you'll ever need. *The Virgin
Encyclopedia* runs in alphabetical order from the Abyssinians to
Zukie, Tappa, with potted biographies and detailed discographies,
and in doing so describes Jamaican music from the first ska to the
up-to-the minute dancehall. All in an entirely accessible fashion.
Reggae historians Barrow and Dalton spent several years putting
The Rough Guide to Reggae together, and it shows in the meticulous
detail as they tell a forty-year story record by record. This
indispensable work reviews over a thousand currently available
albums, peps up this parade of music with interviews with artists
and producers and illustrates it with an enormous amount of rare
record sleeves, single labels and exclusive photographs.

Lloyd Bradley, **Reggae on CD** (Kyle Cathie)
While this selective guide to reggae available on CD fancies itself as
being up there with *The Virgin Encyclopedia* and *Rough Guide*, it's
not nearly as pernickety. Instead it's a kind of combination of the
two – potted biographies, record reviews – and what it lacks in
minutiae it more than makes up for in opinions and knockabout
humour. Definitely worth buying, I'd say. (Well, I would, wouldn't
I?)

Chris Morrow, *Stir It Up: Reggae Cover Art* (Thames & Hudson)

To treat reggae sleeve art with the reverence afforded to, say, jazz album sleeves and devoting a large format full colour 'art' book to them is such an obvious thing to do you can't work out why it hasn't been done before. But it probably wouldn't have been done with the love and inspiration Chris Morrow has brought to *Stir It Up*, as he's collected 200 sleeves from four decades to tell the story of Jamaican music/street fashion/social attitudes with a rare and fascinating eloquence. And if this wasn't enough there's an illuminating foreword by Neville Garrick, who for years was Bob Marley's art director.

Brian Jahn and Tom Weber, *Reggae Island: Jamaican Music in the Digital Age* (Kingston Publishers)

A collection of informal interviews with dancehall's stars that suffers slightly from its lack of contextualization and some subjects' rambling remaining unchecked. However, the candid photos of the artists and Jamaican life in general and the fact that you get a collection of apparently unedited quotes from guys like Bunny Wailer, Garnett Silk, Joseph Hill, Super Cat, Yellowman, Buju Banton, Shabba Ranks and Ken Boothe more than make up for any stylistic shortcomings.

Stephen Davis, *Bob Marley: Conquering Lion of Reggae* (Plexus)

The best, most accurately written biography of Bob Marley. Acclaimed author and journalist Stephen Davis keeps himself out of the picture almost completely and lets Bob's amazing life do the talking.

Observer Station, *Bob Marley: The Illustrated Discography* (Omnibus Press)

As detailed a discography as you could hope for, going back to Bob's Studio One days and listing all the recordings, in the UK and Jamaica, by Bob, the Wailers and spin-off entities Peter and Bunny, the I-Threes, Rita, Judy and Marcia as solo performers, the Melody

Makers (Bob's kids' group) and Aston 'Family Man' Barrett. Records are listed with recording details and, where possible, studio personnel and illustrated with album sleeves and single labels. Quite a task.

Ray Hurford (ed,), **More Axe** (Muzic Tree/Black Star)
The collected extracts from that most formidable of reggae fanzines *Small Axe* now runs into several volumes. Always worth the price of admission – either as a 'zine or like this – as the subjects are often unexpected and the interviews unfiltered and conducted with no angle other than love and respect. One of the few places, these days, where a range of reggae stars express themselves with very few constraints.

Don Taylor, **So Much Things to Say: My Life as Bob Marley's Manager** (Blake)
Enormously entertaining account of Don Taylor's association with Bob, a relationship with so many ups and downs I'm sure some readers will get seasick. Apparently, Taylor received scant cooperation from Bob's family or other associates, therefore this is likely to be the nearest thing we'll ever get to a warts-and-all portrayal. Throws a chilling light on the shooting – it was Taylor who bore the brunt of the assault – and its alleged 'ghetto justice' aftermath.

Dennis Morris, **Bob Marley: A Rebel Life** (Plexus)
Remember Dennis Morris's large-format photography 1980s books *Bob Marley: Rebel With a Cause* and *Reggae Rebels*? This latest work takes what Morris excels in – candid, emotive photography of reggae stars – and marries it to his own commentary on the background to each shot. And in so doing, because Morris and Bob were so close, adds a dimension perhaps unavailable anywhere else as to what Bob Marley was all about. *A Rebel Life* also stands out against other photobooks as Morris's associations with Bob go back further to 1973 (when the photographer was still at school) therefore the story is more complete. Features a reasonably interesting introduction by Lloyd Bradley.

Adrian Boot and Chris Salewicz, **Bob Marley: Songs of Freedom** (Bloomsbury)
Second only to Dennis Morris's, Adrian Boot's Bob Marley portfolio is outstanding and the design and overall quality of this large format 288-page book does it justice. While Salewicz's essays on Bob's life do much to give the work a solid context, Boot's secondary photos of Jamaica's people, situations and scenes presents Bob's world in a perfect setting.

Horace Campbell, **Rasta & Resistance** (Hansib Publications)
The most approachable in-depth examination of Rastafari on the market. Campbell, a Jamaican intellectual and political activist, examines the faith from sociological, historical and revolutionary stances. With an easily approachable style, he tells more than just the story of Rasta, but explains why and how it makes sense to so many Jamaicans, what it means to the rest of the Caribbean and the black world in general, and where it must go to maintain any momentum as a revolutionary force into the new millennium.

Chris Potash (ed.), **Reggae, Rasta Revolution** (Shirmer Books)
A carefully put together American collection of essays, book extracts and articles from newspapers, magazines, books and websites around the world that traces reggae from its musical and cultural roots to dancehall, third-generation ska and bona-fide world music status. A superbly dippable anthology that builds into a multifaceted viewpoint of the music's structure, politics, religion, sociology, internationalization and practitioners.

Laurie Gunst, **Born Fi Dead** (Payback Press)
Subtitled *A Journey Through the Jamaican Posse Underworld*, this is a brilliant and chilling account of Kingston's gunmen's transformation from political thuggery to international drug barons. Gunst, a mild-mannered, middle-aged white American academic, has got inside the yards of the Kingston ghettos and followed the trail from the 1980 general election to dancefloor shootouts in Brooklyn over a decade later. Along the way she uncovers the

destruction cocaine and its derivatives have wrought on Jamaican life and the callousness of the authorities' lack of concern. An extraordinary book, recommended for anybody genuinely wishing to study modern Jamaica's social history.

Ronald Segal, **The Black Diaspora** (Faber & Faber)
Don't let the somewhat textbook tone put you off; *The Black Diaspora* is an engrossing work that follows, quite literally, the black diaspora from Africa to the Caribbean and the Americas and then on to Europe. An invaluable primer for anybody remotely interested in any form of black art as it traces every situation back to pre-slavery Africa along both physical and cultural routes.

Mike Phillips and Trevor Phillips, **Windrush: The Irresistible Rise of Multiracial Britain** (HarperCollins)
The book of the TV series, that perhaps does an even better job as it allows the reader time to appreciate, at his or her own pace, the wealth of information, personal tales and cultural analysis the Phillips brothers have put into this book. Meticulously researched, then driven along by a series of wonderful interviews with original Caribbean immigrants and their descendants, *Windrush* tells the true story of 'How we came to be here'. The link between then and now, between this home and back home.

Christopher Baker, **Jamaica: A Lonely Planet Travel Survival Kit** (Lonely Planet)
If you're going to Jamaica – and I sincerely hope you will be – either on a musical pilgrimage or not, you'll need a trustworthy guide. This is it. From where to stay to how to get laid to what drugs to avoid and how to dress for the dancehall.

Index